LET'S GO

New Zealand

■ Let's Go writers travel on your budget.

"Guides that penetrate the veneer of the holiday brochures and mine the grit of real life."
—*The Economist*

"The writers seem to have experienced every rooster-packed bus and lunar-surfaced mattress about which they write."
—*The New York Times*

"All the dirt, dirt cheap."
—*People*

■ Great for independent travelers.

"The guides are aimed not only at young budget travelers but at the independent traveler, a sort of streetwise cookbook for traveling alone."
—*The New York Times*

"Flush with candor and irreverence, chock full of budget travel advice."
—*The Des Moines Register*

"An indispensable resource. *Let's Go*'s practical information can be used by every traveler."
—*The Chattanooga Free Press*

■ Let's Go is completely revised each year.

"Only *Let's Go* has the zeal to annually update every title on its list."
—*The Boston Globe*

"Unbeatable: good sight-seeing advice; up-to-date info on restaurants, hotels, and inns; a commitment to money-saving travel; and a wry style that brightens nearly every page."
—*The Washington Post*

■ All the important information you need.

"*Let's Go* authors provide a comedic element while still providing concise information and thorough coverage of the country. Anything you need to know about budget traveling is detailed in this book."
—*The Chicago Sun-Times*

"Value-packed, unbeatable, accurate, and comprehensive."
—*Los Angeles Times*

Let's Go Publications

Let's Go: Alaska & the Pacific Northwest 1999
Let's Go: Australia 1999
Let's Go: Austria & Switzerland 1999
Let's Go: Britain & Ireland 1999
Let's Go: California 1999
Let's Go: Central America 1999
Let's Go: Eastern Europe 1999
Let's Go: Ecuador & the Galápagos Islands 1999
Let's Go: Europe 1999
Let's Go: France 1999
Let's Go: Germany 1999
Let's Go: Greece 1999 **New title!**
Let's Go: India & Nepal 1999
Let's Go: Ireland 1999
Let's Go: Israel & Egypt 1999
Let's Go: Italy 1999
Let's Go: London 1999
Let's Go: Mexico 1999
Let's Go: New York City 1999
Let's Go: New Zealand 1999
Let's Go: Paris 1999
Let's Go: Rome 1999
Let's Go: South Africa 1999 **New title!**
Let's Go: Southeast Asia 1999
Let's Go: Spain & Portugal 1999
Let's Go: Turkey 1999 **New title!**
Let's Go: USA 1999
Let's Go: Washington, D.C. 1999

Let's Go Map Guides

Amsterdam	Madrid
Berlin	New Orleans
Boston	New York City
Chicago	Paris
Florence	Rome
London	San Francisco
Los Angeles	Washington, D.C.

Coming Soon: Prague, Seattle

**Let's Go
Publications**

Let's Go
New
Zealand
1999

Jennifer L. Burns
Editor

Eli Ceryak
Associate Editor

Researcher-Writers:
**Lily Childress
Nick Grossman
Matt Heid
Ron Rosenman
Nick Weiss**

St. Martin's Press ❈ New York

HELPING LET'S GO

If you want to share your discoveries, suggestions, or corrections, please drop us a line. We read every piece of correspondence, whether a postcard, a 10-page email, or a coconut. Please note that mail received after May 1999 may be too late for the 2000 book, but will be kept for future editions. **Address mail to:**

Let's Go: New Zealand
67 Mount Auburn Street
Cambridge, MA 02138
USA

Visit Let's Go at **http://www.letsgo.com**, or send email to:

feedback@letsgo.com
Subject: "Let's Go: New Zealand"

In addition to the invaluable travel advice our readers share with us, many are kind enough to offer their services as researchers or editors. Unfortunately, our charter enables us to employ only currently enrolled Harvard-Radcliffe students.

Maps by David Lindroth copyright © 1999, 1998, 1997, 1996, 1995, 1994, 1993, 1992, 1991, 1990, 1989, 1988 by St. Martin's Press, Inc.

Distributed outside the USA and Canada by Macmillan.

ISBN: 0-312-19492-7

First edition
10 9 8 7 6 5 4 3 2 1

Let's Go: New Zealand is written by Let's Go Publications, 67 Mount Auburn Street, Cambridge, MA 02138, USA.

Let's Go® and the thumb logo are trademarks of Let's Go, Inc. Printed in the USA on recycled paper with biodegradable soy ink.

About Let's Go

THIRTY-NINE YEARS OF WISDOM

Back in 1960, a few students at Harvard University banded together to produce a 20-page pamphlet offering a collection of tips on budget travel in Europe. This modest, mimeographed packet, offered as an extra to passengers on student charter flights to Europe, met with instant popularity. The following year, students traveling to Europe researched the first, full-fledged edition of *Let's Go: Europe*, a pocket-sized book featuring honest, irreverent writing and a decidedly youthful outlook on the world. Throughout the 60s, our guides reflected the times; the 1969 guide to America led off by inviting travelers to "dig the scene" at San Francisco's Haight-Ashbury. During the 70s and 80s, we gradually added regional guides and expanded coverage into the Middle East and Central America. With the addition of our in-depth city guides, handy map guides, and extensive coverage of Asia and Australia, the 90s are also proving to be a time of explosive growth for Let's Go, and there's certainly no end in sight. The maiden edition of *Let's Go: South Africa,* our pioneer guide to sub-Saharan Africa, hits the shelves this year, along with the first editions of *Let's Go: Greece* and *Let's Go: Turkey.*

We've seen a lot in 39 years. *Let's Go: Europe* is now the world's bestselling international guide, translated into seven languages. And our new guides bring Let's Go's total number of titles, with their spirit of adventure and their reputation for honesty, accuracy, and editorial integrity, to 44. But some things never change: our guides are still researched, written, and produced entirely by students who know first-hand how to see the world on the cheap.

HOW WE DO IT

Each guide is completely revised and thoroughly updated every year by a well-traveled set of over 200 students. Every winter, we recruit over 160 researchers and 70 editors to write the books anew. After several months of training, researcher-writers hit the road for seven weeks of exploration, from Anchorage to Adelaide, Estonia to El Salvador, Iceland to Indonesia. Hired for their rare combination of budget travel sense, writing ability, stamina, and courage, these adventurous travelers know that train strikes, stolen luggage, food poisoning, and marriage proposals are all part of a day's work. Back at our offices, editors work from spring to fall, massaging copy written on Himalayan bus rides into witty yet informative prose. A student staff of typesetters, cartographers, publicists, and managers keeps our lively team together. In September, the collected efforts of the summer are delivered to our printer, who turns them into books in record time, so that you have the most up-to-date information available for your vacation. Even as you read this, work on next year's editions is well underway.

WHY WE DO IT

We don't think of budget travel as the last recourse of the destitute; we believe that it's the only way to travel. Living cheaply and simply brings you closer to the people and places you've been saving up to visit. Our books will ease your anxieties and answer your questions about the basics—so you can get off the beaten track and explore. Once you learn the ropes, we encourage you to put *Let's Go* down now and then to strike out on your own. You know as well as we that the best discoveries are often those you make yourself. When you find something worth sharing, please drop us a line. We're Let's Go Publications, 67 Mount Auburn St., Cambridge, MA 02138, USA (email: feedback@letsgo.com). For more info, visit our website, http://www.letsgo.com.

HAPPY TRAVELS!

Table of Contents

Maps

How to Use This Book

The best way to use this book is to put it down from time to time. Chances are, by the end of your trip it will be worn, dirty, scribbled with notes and addresses, and literally falling apart. That's OK, because by then it will probably be spending more time buried in your backpack than clutched safely to your chest. Traveling is about taking your adventures global, and the best memories come when you wander off your itinerary into the unexpected.

A few practicalities are in order. The beginning section of the book, **Essentials** (p. 1), has a host of information that will help you plan your trip. It lists organizations that cater to budget travelers, important facts about New Zealand, and rules and regulations you may encounter along the way. This is probably a good section to read before you go, as it could save you quite a bit of money. Also, the tramping section discusses the amazing outdoor resources New Zealand offers, and provides a ranking of the country's **Great Walks.**

Which brings us to **rankings.** *Let's Go* researchers list accommodations, restaurants, and nightlife from best to worst. This year, we've identified the researchers' favorite business establishments in large towns with a 🖐, in addition to listing the spots they liked most in the beginning of the book (p. xii). Within cities and towns, the most popular sights and outdoor activities are usually listed first. While *Let's Go* strives to be a discriminating travel companion, we also want to provide a wide range of options, especially in accommodations. Thus you will occasionally find backpackers and hotels that may offer a less than perfect stay, but are included because they are well placed or are the only choice in town. Read between the lines. Another addition to the guide is a **Highlights of the Region** box in each chapter, which lists some noteworthy activities and sights. If you have no idea where to start, checking them out might be a good idea.

Please use the summer/winter rates and dates and opening/closing times we list as guides, not law. Don't look for regimented, come-hell-or-high-water schedules for transportation or anything else—you're in Kiwi land now. On any night, a restaurant's owners might decide to close early and head home if no customers are in sight. On the other hand, if you come by after closing time and look hungry enough, they just might open up their doors again. In New Zealand, hospitality is a flexible thing.

This chapters of this book are divided according to regions. While New Zealand has no political regional distinctions like states, the chapters match generally recognized regions on the two islands. In addition to standard coverage, chapter two is a mini-essay about New Zealand's people, culture, history, and attractions. It makes for good plane reading, but you'll pick up a lot more of the Kiwi vibe by just being in the country. If some of the language you hear confuses you at first, check out our Kiwi-English and Maori-English glossaries in the back.

The rest is fairly self-explanatory. Have fun, be safe, and don't forget to write home. **Cheers!**

A NOTE TO OUR READERS

The information for this book was gathered by *Let's Go*'s researchers from May through August. Each listing is derived from the assigned researcher's opinion based upon his or her visit at a particular time. The opinions are expressed in a candid and forthright manner. Other travelers might disagree. Those traveling at a different time may have different experiences since prices, dates, hours, and conditions are always subject to change. You are urged to check beforehand to avoid inconvenience and surprises. Travel always involves a certain degree of risk, especially in low-cost areas. When traveling, especially on a budget, always take particular care to ensure your safety.

Let's Go Picks

IN THE GARDEN OF CULINARY DELIGHTS: FOOD Even those warriors with the most violent of appetites will find their hunger defeated at a traditional **Maori hangi** (see Rotorua, p. 185). At **Tull** in Dunedin, the desserts are so decadent they oughta be illegal (p. 337). If papa did preach, he'd undoubtedly deify **Musical Knives** in Auckland, a place so good it feels like the very first time (p. 72). Picture-perfect and almost too pretty to eat, the treats at the **Saltwater Cafe** in Paihia nourish all the senses (p. 98). The kebabs at Wellington's **Ali Baba** are, well, a Turkish delight (p. 228).

GET YOUR LIQUID FIX: CAFES AND BARS Why are kids getting jealous of **Brazil**? Because it's f-r-e-s-h...That's fresh, as in fresh roasted beans from this Auckland cafe, and fresh beats—never recycled—by the DJs upstairs (p. 73). Heading south, it gets worldwide at Christchurch's **Caffe Roma** (p. 248) and Hokitika's **Cafe de Paris** (p. 299). A caffeine fix at the **Percolater** (p. 338) in Dunedin is perfect fuel for an all-nighter, and there's good energy aplenty at New Plymouth's **X Bar and Cafe** (p. 148). On the bar scene, the party crowd gets loaded at Gisborne's **Smash Palace** (p. 204), gets smashed at Christchurch's **Loaded Hog** (p. 249), pounds puppies at Auckland's **The Dog's Bollix** (p. 74), and clicks those ruby slippers together at Ponsonby's **Surrender Dorothy** (p. 76).

SWEET DREAMS ARE MADE OF THESE: ACCOMMODATIONS Fit for royalty, **The Palace** in Nelson left us feeling properly pampered (p. 277). We wanted to shack up in the **Opoutere YHA** (p. 144) and simply not deal for a few weeks. At the female-only **Frauenreisehaus** in Christchurch we (or at least one of us) lived the oh-so-easy life (p. 246). We strayed into the **Stray Possum** on Great Barrier Island (p. 89), got stuck in the **Mousetrap** at Paihia in the Bay of Islands (p. 97), and then took in the vistas from the **Tree House** in Kohukohu, a town so nice they named it twice (p. 109).

OFF-THE-BEATEN-PATH Great discoveries are usually unearthed where others simply haven't thought to explore. The town of **Coromandel** was exactly what we expected from New Zealand, just more so (p. 136). **Rangitito,** beautiful Rangitito, made the urban frenzy of Auckland seem a world away (p. 85). The **Marlborough Sounds**—"the coolest, chillest place imaginable"—left us speechless. Well, almost (p. 267). After a few days in the **Catlins,** we never wanted to leave (p. 345).

THE BEST OF THE BEST We hate to be bossy, but trust us on these. **Milford Sound** will take your breath away, and once it's restored you won't be able to shut your big yapper about the place (p. 330). Hiking the **Fox** or **Franz Josef Glacier** makes people happy—just don't stick your tongue onto the ice (p. 300). Hop in the water with the **dolphins** in Kaikoura, and you'll never want to return to dry land (p. 272). Face your fear, hold your breath, and then jump out of an airplane at 14,000 feet. Don't forget to change your undies once you're on the ground (see skydiving, index). The **Milford Track** is the greatest of the Great Walks, and requires a reservation well in advance and a steep track access fee, but it's worth putting aside some cash and planning ahead (p. 322). We've said it once, but we'd really, really hate for you to miss out—indulge yourself at a **Maori hangi** (see Rotorua, p. 185).

ESSENTIALS

PLANNING YOUR TRIP

A vacation is ideally an escape, a spontaneous affair, conceived on a whim and completed without hassle. In today's world, however, escapes are not made without prior planning. Traveling is a complex process, and budget travel is, in many ways, even more difficult—you pay for ease, after all. You can eliminate a lot of surprises by setting aside the time to read through this chapter before you jump into anything. With a little more research you may find better and cheaper ways of doing things. Before you get on the plane, it is a good idea to have at least a tentative itinerary, and to read through Let's Go listings of those towns. These days, even some hostels require reservations, so you can't always fly by the seat of your pants. Don't be afraid to change your plans, though; just remember: the more knowledge you have, the more prepared you will be to be spontaneous.

■ When to Go

The best season for your visit to New Zealand depends on the type of activities you are most interested in (warm or cold weather) and your sensitivity to crowds (if so, avoid major holidays). New Zealand's attractions are spread out and best appreciated over several days; try to budget at least three weeks for your trip. Most of New Zealand enjoys its **high season** in the warmest months (Nov.-Feb.). Certain areas such as the Tongariro region in the North Island and the skifields of the South Island draw the biggest crowds in the winter (June-Aug.), when the **ski season** is in full swing. Major national holidays also add considerable congestion to New Zealand's highways and byways (for dates, see p. 356.) During these times, hordes of pleasure-seeking New Zealand families add themselves to the mix of thrill-hungry tourists from abroad; **be sure to book travel, activities, and accommodations well in advance.** For activities not adversely affected by slightly less-than-perfect weather, a wise idea might be to simply wait a few weeks until low season comes around and the crowds disappear. Some areas and activities shut down during low season, however, so you'll want to read on and weigh your options before you decide. Whenever you go, don't worry—you'll never be at a loss to find beauty and excitement.

GEOGRAPHY AND CLIMATE

New Zealand consists of two main volcanic islands, North Island and South Island, various smaller surrounding island groups, and a few subantarctic island groups to the far south. Virtually the entire country is hilly or mountainous, laced throughout with rivers, dotted with lakes, and broken up by numerous bays and inlets. The North Island enjoys an active volcanic and geothermic life; the Lake Taupo region and the Bay of Plenty, in particular, are home to a plenitude of hot springs and three large volcanoes. The less-populous South Island is known for its rugged, snow-capped mountains, including Mt. Cook (Aoraki), the highest peak in New Zealand. It's also home to numerous glaciers that formed thousands of years ago.

New Zealand has an oceanic, temperate climate—which is really just a scientific way of saying that while its weather changes are never extreme, they are often unpredictable. Weather systems in mountainous areas can change instantaneously, so be prepared. Rainfall in most of the North Island and the northern South Island is heaviest in the winter (June-Aug.) although the infamous summer rainfall in the Westland region of the South Island can total seven or eight meters annually.

For those of you traveling to New Zealand from the Northern Hemisphere, be aware that the **seasons are reversed** from what you are accustomed to. Summer arrives in December and lasts roughly until February; winter is from June to August. Year-round, however, the temperature fluctuation is far from extreme, even from the tip of the North Island to the bottom of the South Island. The following chart gives the average high and low temperatures in degrees Celsius/Fahrenheit during four representative months of the year.

Average Temp. Low-High	January °C	January °F	April °C	April °F	July °C	July °F	October °C	October °F
Auckland	12-24	54-75	13-20	55-68	9-15	48-59	11-18	52-66
Bay of Islands	14-25	57-77	11-21	52-70	7-16	45-61	9-19	48-67
Christchurch	12-22	54-72	8-18	46-64	3-12	37-54	7-17	45-63
Dunedin	11-19	52-66	8-15	46-59	4-11	39-52	7-15	45-59
Invercargill	9-18	48-65	6-15	43-59	1-11	34-52	5-15	41-59
Nelson	13-22	55-72	8-18	46-64	3-13	37-55	7-17	45-63
New Plymouth	13-22	55-72	11-19	52-66	6-14	43-57	9-17	48-63
Queenstown	10-22	50-72	6-16	43-61	1-10	34-50	5-16	41-61
Rotorua	12-24	54-75	9-18	48-64	4-13	39-55	7-17	45-63
Wellington	13-20	55-68	11-17	52-63	6-12	43-54	9-15	48-59

■ Entrance Requirements

A valid **passport** is required to enter New Zealand and to re-enter your own country (see below). To enter New Zealand, your passport must be valid for **three months** beyond the date of your planned departure from New Zealand. Returning home with an expired passport is illegal, and may result in a fine. Citizens of **Canada, Ireland, South Africa,** the **U.K.,** and the **U.S.** do not need a **visitor visa** to visit New Zealand but must apply for a **visitor permit** upon arrival (look out for the yellow arrival card). Only citizens of **Australia** need **neither** a visa nor a permit to visit or work in New Zealand.

To qualify for a visitor permit, you must display a valid ticket to a country to which you have the right of entry; you may also need to display sufficient funds to support yourself during your stay. The visitor permit allows you to visit New Zealand for three months (six months for citizens of the U.K.); to extend your stay, you must reapply at an immigration office before your current permit expires.

Admission as a visitor does not include the right to work in New Zealand, which is usually authorized only by a **work visa or permit.** Entering New Zealand to study in a course of three months or less is covered by a **visitor permit.** For details on longer courses of study or work in New Zealand, see **Alternatives to Tourism,** p. 19.

A **departure tax** of NZ$20 must be paid by passengers leaving New Zealand (children under 12 exempt). Travel agents usually include this tax in the price of the ticket; with other means of booking, inquire as to whether it is included.

■ Embassies and Consulates

Australia: 32-38 Quay St., **Auckland** (Private Bag 92023) (tel. (09) 303 2429; fax 377 0798); 72-78 Hobson St., **Thorndon** (P.O. Box 4036), **Wellington** (tel. (04) 473 6411; fax 498 7118).
Canada: 61 Molesworth St. (P.O. Box 12049), **Wellington** (tel. (04) 473 9577; fax 471 2082).

Ireland: Dingwall Building, 2nd fl., 87 Queens St., **Auckland** (P.O. Box 279) (tel. (09) 302 2867; fax 302 2420).

U.K.: Consulate General, 151 Queens St., **Auckland** (Private Bag 92014) (tel. (09) 303 2973; fax 303 1836). High Commission, 44 Hill St. (P.O. Box 1812), **Wellington** (tel. (04) 472 6049; fax 471 1974).

U.S.: Consular services, General Building, 4th fl., 29 Shortland St. (Private Bag 92022), **Auckland** (tel. (09) 303 2724; fax 379 3722); 29 Fitzherbert Terr., Thorndon (P.O. Box 1190), **Wellington** (tel. (04) 472 2068; fax 471 2380).

■ Documents and Formalities

Applications for visas, passports, and other vital documents should be filed in your home country several weeks or months in advance of your planned departure date. Remember that you are relying on slow-moving government agencies to complete these transactions, and apply as early as possible.

When you travel, always carry on your person **two or more forms of identification,** including at least one photo ID. A passport combined with a driver's license or birth certificate usually serves as adequate proof of your identity and citizenship. Many establishments, especially banks, require several IDs before cashing traveler's checks. Never carry all your forms of ID together, however, or you risk being left entirely without ID or funds in case of theft or loss. Consider carrying several extra passport-size photos that you can attach to IDs you acquire while traveling. If you plan an extended stay, register your passport with your nearest embassy or consulate.

PASSPORTS

Before you leave, photocopy the page of your passport with your photograph, passport number, and other identifying info. Carry one photocopy in a safe place apart from your passport and leave the other at home. These measures will help prove your citizenship and facilitate the issuing of a new passport if you lose the original.

If you lose your passport, immediately notify the local police and the nearest embassy or consulate of your home government. To expedite its replacement, you will need to know all information previously recorded and show identification and proof of citizenship. A replacement may take weeks to process and may only be valid for a limited time. Some consulates can issue new passports within 24 hours if you give them proof of citizenship. Any visas stamped in your old passport will be lost. In an emergency, ask for immediate temporary traveling papers that will permit you to re-enter your home country.

Your passport is a public document belonging to your nation's government. You may have to surrender it to a foreign government official, but if you don't get it back in a reasonable amount of time, inform the nearest consulate of your home country.

AUSTRALIA Citizens must apply for a passport in person at a post office, a passport office, or an Australian diplomatic mission overseas. An appointment may be necessary. Passport offices are located in Adelaide, Brisbane, Canberra, Darwin, Hobart, Melbourne, Newcastle, Perth, and Sydney. A parent may file an application for a child who is under 18 and unmarried. Adult passports cost AUS$120 (for a 32-page passport) or AUS$180 (64-page), and a child's is AUS$60 (32-page) or AUS$90 (64-page). For more info, call toll-free (in Australia) 13 12 32, or visit http://www.austemb.org.

CANADA Application forms in English and French are available at all passport offices, Canadian missions, many travel agencies, and Northern Stores in northern communities. Citizens may apply in person at any of 28 regional passport offices across Canada. Canadian citizens residing abroad should contact the nearest Canadian embassy or consulate. Children under 16 may be included on a parent's passport. Passports cost CDN$60, plus a CDN$25 consular fee, are valid for five years, and are not renewable. Processing takes approximately five business days for applications in person or three weeks for mail delivery. For additional info, contact the Canadian Passport

Office, Department of Foreign Affairs and International Trade, Ottawa, ON, K1A 0G3 (tel. (613) 994-3500; http://www.dfait-maeci.gc.ca\passport). Travelers may also call (800) 567-6868 (24hr.); in Toronto (416) 973-3251; in Vancouver (604) 775-6250; in Montréal (514) 283-2152. Refer to the booklet *Bon Voyage, But...*, free at any passport office or by calling InfoCentre at (800) 267-8376 (within Canada), for further help and a list of Canadian embassies and consulates abroad. You may also find entry and background information for various countries by contacting the Consular Affairs Bureau in Ottawa (tel. (800) 267-6788 (24hr.) or (613) 944-6788).

IRELAND Citizens can apply for a passport by mail to either the Department of Foreign Affairs, Passport Office, Setanta Centre, Molesworth St., Dublin 2 (tel. (01) 671 1633; fax (01) 671 1092), or the Passport Office, Irish Life Building, 1A South Mall, Cork (tel. (021) 272 525; fax (021) 275 770). Obtain an application at a local Garda station or request one from a passport office. The new Passport Express Service, available through post offices, allows citizens to get a passport in two weeks for an extra IR£3. Passports cost IR£45 and are valid for five years. Citizens under 18 or over 65 can request a 3-year passport that costs IR£10.

SOUTH AFRICA Citizens can apply for a passport at any **Home Affairs Office** or **South African Mission.** Tourist passports, valid for 10 years, cost SAR80. Children under 16 must be issued their own passports, valid for five years, which cost SAR60. Allow at least three months for processing. If a passport is needed in a hurry, an **emergency passport** may be issued for SAR50. An application for a permanent passport must accompany the emergency passport application. Current passports fewer than 10 years old (counting from date of issuance) may be **renewed** until December 31, 1999; every citizen whose passport's validity does not extend far beyond this date is urged to renew it as soon as possible, to avoid the expected premillenial glut of applications. Renewal is free, and turnaround time is usually 2 weeks. For further information, contact the nearest Department of Home Affairs Office.

UNITED KINGDOM British citizens, British Dependent Territories citizens, British Nationals (overseas), British subjects and British Overseas citizens may apply for a **full passport,** valid for 10 years (five years if under 16). Applications are available at passport offices, main post offices, many travel agents, and branches of Lloyds Bank and Artac World Choice. Apply by mail or in person (for an additional UK£10) to one of the passport offices, located in London, Liverpool, Newport, Peterborough, Glasgow, or Belfast. The fee is UK£31, UK£11 for children. As of October 1998, children under 16 need their own passports. The London office offers same-day, walk-in rush service; arrive early. The **British Visitor's Passport** has been abolished; travelers over 16 now need standard 10-year passports. The U.K. Passport Agency can be reached by phone at (0990) 21 04 10.

UNITED STATES Citizens may apply for a passport at any federal or state **courthouse** or **post office** authorized to accept passport applications, or at the nearest **U.S. Passport Agency.** Refer to the "U.S. Government, State Department" section of the telephone directory or the local post office for addresses. Parents must apply in person for children under age 13. You must apply in person if this is your first passport, if you're under age 18, or if your current passport is more than 12 years old or was issued before your 18th birthday. Passports are valid for 10 years (five years if under 18) and cost US$65 (under 18 US$40). Passports may be **renewed** by mail or in person for US$55. Processing takes 3-4 weeks. **Rush service** is available for a surcharge of US$30 with proof of departure within 10 working days (e.g., an airplane ticket or itinerary), or for travelers leaving in two-three weeks who require visas. Given proof of citizenship, a U.S. embassy or consulate abroad can usually issue a new passport. For more info, contact the U.S. Passport Information's **24-hour recorded message** (tel. (202) 647-0518). U.S. citizens abroad should contact any passport agency, U.S. embassy, or consulate, or send information requests along with a self-addressed stamped envelope to: Overseas Citizens Services, Room 4811,

Department of State, Washington, D.C. 20520-4818 (tel. (202) 647-5225; fax 647-3000). Additional information is available through the Bureau of Consular Affairs homepage at http://travel.state.gov, or through the State Department site at http://www.state.gov.

CUSTOMS: ENTERING

As an island nation, New Zealand is free from many pests and crop blights, and they'd like to keep it that way. All food, plant, and animal goods must be declared, so look out for the blue declaration of goods forms. Quarantined goods may or may not be confiscated, but they must be declared. **Camping equipment** must also be declared. Customs officials will likely inspect your equipment and if it is used, they may clean it for you.

Personal effects and goods up to a total combined value of NZ$700 are admitted free of duty or Goods and Services Tax (GST). Anything beyond the allowance must be declared and is charged a duty. Visitors over 17 are also allowed to enter with the following concessions duty- and tax-free: 200 cigarettes or 50 cigars or 250g of tobacco, or a mixture of all three not weighing more than 250g; 4.5L of wine (six 750mL bottles) or 4.5L of beer; and one bottle containing not more than 1125mL of liquor. Check with the nearest embassy or consulate for more information.

CUSTOMS: GOING HOME

Upon returning home, you must declare all articles you acquired abroad and pay a **duty** on the value of those articles that exceed the allowance established by your country's customs service. Goods and gifts purchased at **duty-free** shops abroad are not exempt from duty or sales tax at your point of return; you must declare these items as well. "Duty-free" merely means no tax in the country of purchase.

AUSTRALIA Citizens may import AUS$400 (under 18 AUS$200) of goods duty-free, in addition to 1.125L alcohol and 250 cigarettes or 250g tobacco. You must be over 18 to import alcohol or tobacco. There is no limit to the amount of Australian and/or foreign cash that may be brought into or taken out of the country, but amounts of AUS$10,000 or more, or the equivalent in foreign currency, must be reported. All foodstuffs and animal products must be declared on arrival. For information, contact the Regional Director, Australian Customs Service, GPO Box 8, Sydney NSW 2001 (tel. (02) 9213 2000; fax 9213 4000), or visit http://www.customs.gov.au.

CANADA Citizens who remain abroad for at least one week may bring back up to CDN$500 worth of goods duty-free any time, including tobacco and alcohol. You are permitted to ship goods except tobacco and alcohol home under this exemption as long as you declare them when you arrive. Citizens of legal age (which varies by province) may import in-person up to 200 cigarettes, 50 cigars or cigarillos, 200g loose tobacco, 1.14L wine or alcohol, and 24 355mL cans/bottles of beer; the value of these products is included in the CDN$200 or CDN$500. For more information, write to Canadian Customs, 2265 St. Laurent Blvd., Ottawa, Ontario K1G 4K3 (tel. (613) 993-0534), phone the 24-hr. Automated Customs Information Service at (800) 461-9999, or visit Revenue Canada at http://www.revcan.ca.

IRELAND Citizens must declare everything in excess of IR£142 (IR£73 for travelers under 15 years of age) obtained outside the EU or duty- and tax-free in the EU above the following allowances: 200 cigarettes, 100 cigarillos, 50 cigars, or 250g tobacco; 1L liquor or 2L wine; 2L still wine; 50g perfume; and 250mL toilet water. Goods obtained duty and tax paid in another EU country up to a value of IR£460 (IR£115 per traveler under 15) are not subject to customs duties. Travelers under the age of 17 may not import tobacco or alcohol. For more info, contact The Revenue Commissioners, Dublin Castle (tel. (01) 679 27 77; fax 671 20 21; email taxes@iol.ie; http://www.revenue.ie) or The Collector of Customs and Excise, The Custom House, Dublin 1.

SOUTH AFRICA Citizens may import duty-free: 400 cigarettes, 50 cigars, 250g tobacco, 2L wine, 1L of spirits, 250mL toilet water, and 50mL perfume, and other consumable items up to a value of SAR500. Goods up to a value of SAR10,000 above this duty-free allowance are dutiable at 20%; such goods are also exempted from payment of VAT. Items acquired abroad and sent home as unaccompanied baggage do not qualify for any allowances. You may not export or import South African bank notes in excess of SAR25,000. For more info, consult the free pamphlet *South African Customs Information,* available in airports or from the Commissioner for Customs and Excise, Private Bag X47, Pretoria 0001 (tel. (12) 314 99 11; fax 328 64 78).

UNITED KINGDOM Citizens or visitors arriving in the U.K. from outside the EU must declare goods in excess of the following allowances: 200 cigarettes or 100 cigarillos or 50 cigars or 250g tobacco; still table wine (2L); strong liqueurs over 22% volume (1L), or fortified or sparkling wine, other liqueurs (2L); perfume (60 cc/mL); toilet water (250 cc/mL); and UK£145 worth of all other goods including gifts and souvenirs. You must be over 17 to import liquor or tobacco. These allowances also apply to duty-free purchases within the EU, except for the last category, "other goods," which then has an allowance of UK£75. Goods obtained duty- and tax-paid for personal use (regulated according to set guide levels) within the EU do not require any further customs duty. For info contact Her Majesty's Customs and Excise, Custom House, Nettleton Road, Heathrow Airport, Hounslow, Middlesex TW6 2LA (tel. (0181) 910-3602/3566; fax 910-3765) or check the web (http://www.open.gov.uk).

UNITED STATES Citizens may import US$400 worth of accompanying goods duty-free and must pay a 10% tax on the next US$1000. You must declare all purchases, so have sales slips ready. The US$400 personal exemption covers goods purchased for personal or household use (this includes gifts) and cannot include more than 100 cigars, 200 cigarettes (1 carton), and 1L of wine or liquor. You must be over 21 to bring liquor into the U.S. If you mail home personal goods of U.S. origin, you can avoid duty charges by marking the package "American goods returned." For more information, consult the brochure *Know Before You Go,* available from the U.S. Customs Service, Box 7407, Washington D.C. 20044 (tel. (202) 927-6724), or visit the Web (http://www.customs.ustreas.gov).

YOUTH, STUDENT, AND TEACHER IDENTIFICATION

The **International Student Identity Card (ISIC)** is the most widely accepted form of student identification. Flashing this card can procure you discounts ("concessions") for entertainment, accommodation, transport, and other services. It also provides insurance benefits, including US$100 per day of in-hospital sickness for a maximum of 60 days, and US$3000 accident-related medical reimbursement for each accident (see **Insurance,** p. 17). In addition, cardholders have access to a toll-free 24-hour ISIC helpline whose multilingual staff can provide assistance in medical, legal, and financial emergencies overseas (tel. (800) 626-2427 in the U.S. and Canada; elsewhere call collect to the UK office (44) 181 666 9025).

Many student travel agencies around the world issue ISICs, including STA Travel in Australia and New Zealand; Travel CUTS and via the web (http://www.isic-canada.org) in Canada; USIT in Ireland and Northern Ireland; SASTS in South Africa; Campus Travel and STA Travel in the U.K.; Council Travel, Let's Go Travel, STA Travel, and via the web (http://www.ciee.org/idcards/index.htm) in the U.S. When you apply for the card, request a copy of the *International Student Identity Card Handbook,* which lists by country some of the available discounts. The card is valid until December of the following year and costs US$20, CDN$15 or AUS$15. Applicants must be at least 12 years old and degree-seeking students of a secondary or post-secondary school. Because of the proliferation of phony ISICs, many airlines and some other services require other proof of student identity, such as a signed letter from the registrar attesting to your student status and stamped with the school seal or your school ID card. The **International Teacher Identity Card (ITIC)** offers the same insurance coverage, and similar but limited discounts The fee is US$20, UK£5, or AUS$13. For more information on these cards, consult the organization's web site (http://www.istc.org; email isicinfo@istc.org).

Federation of International Youth Travel Organizations (FIYTO) issues a discount card to travelers who are under 26 but not students. Known as the **GO25 Card,** this one-year card offers many of the same benefits as the ISIC, and most organizations that sell the ISIC also sell the GO25 Card. A brochure that lists discounts is free when you purchase the card. To apply, you will need a passport, valid driver's license, or copy of a birth certificate; and a passport-sized photo with your name printed on the back. The fee is US$20. Information is available on the web at http://www.ciee.org, or by contacting Travel CUTS in Canada, STA Travel in the U.K., Council Travel in the U.S., or FIYTO headquarters in Denmark (see **Budget Travel,** p. 25).

YHA CARDS

YHA cardholders can receive reduced fares on a number of transportation and travel options. Your HI card from home will double as a YHA card in New Zealand; for more info, see p. 33. YHA discounts are available on the **bus** companies Newmans Coachlines (30% off adult fares), Intercity Coachlines (30%), Kiwi Experience (5%), Magic Travellers Network (5%), Northliner Express (30%); the **train** company TranzScenic (30%); the **airlines** Air New Zealand (50% off standby fares) and Ansett New Zealand (50% off standby fares); the **rental car** companies Rent-a-Dent (10%), Pegasus Rental (10%), and Shoestring Car Rental (10%). Cardholders receive member rates at YHA-affiliated accommodation.

INTERNATIONAL DRIVING PERMIT

You probably won't need the **International Driving Permit (IDP)** in New Zealand, as long as you have a current license from your own country. A few car rental agencies do require the IDP, however, and it can serve as an additional piece of ID in a tough situation. An IDP, valid for one year, must be issued in your own country before you depart and must be accompanied by a valid driver's license from your home country. Contact the national automobile association in your home country for details.

■ Useful Information

NEW ZEALAND TOURISM BOARD OFFICES

The ever-helpful NZTB can provide you with information galore about any region or aspect of the country that captures your attention. Their web-page **(http://www.nztb.govt.nz)** is easy-to-use and enormously useful, offering concise travel info and nifty links to other travel pages. They have offices in the following countries:

Australia: Level 8, 35 Pitt St., Sydney NSW 2000 (P.O. Box R1546); (tel. (02) 9247 5222; fax 9241 1136).
U.K.: New Zealand House, 80 Haymarket, London SW1Y 4TQ (tel. (0171) 930 1622; fax 839 8928; email charlottem@nztb.govt.nz).
U.S.: 501 Santa Monica Blvd., Suite 300, Santa Monica, CA 90401 (tel. (800) 388-5494 (headquarters) or (310) 395-7480; fax 395-5453).

NEW ZEALAND EMBASSIES AND CONSULATES

Australia: New Zealand High Commission, Commonwealth Ave., **Canberra** ACT 2600 (tel. (02) 6270 4211; fax 6273 3194); New Zealand Consulate-General, Level

14, Gold Fields Building, 1 Alfred St., Circular Quay (GPO Box 365), **Sydney,** NSW 2000 (tel. (02) 9247 1344).

Canada: New Zealand High Commission, Suite 727, 99 Bank St., **Ottawa,** ONT K1P 6G3 (tel. (613) 238-5991; fax 238-5707; http://www.nzhcottawa.org).

U.K.: New Zealand High Commission, 80 Haymarket, **London** SW1Y 4TQ (national tel. (0991) 100 100, international tel. (01344) 716 199; fax (171) 973 0370).

U.S.: New Zealand Embassy, 37 Observatory Circle NW, **Washington, D.C.,** 20008 (tel. (202) 328-4800; fax (202) 667-5227); New Zealand Consulate-General, 12400 Wilshire Blvd., Suite 1150, **Los Angeles,** CA 90025 (tel. (310) 207-1605; fax 207-3605).

INTERNET RESOURCES

Along with everything else in the 90s, budget travel is moving rapidly into the Information Age, with the **Internet** as a leading travel resource. **NetTravel: How Travelers Use the Internet,** by Michael Shapiro, is a thorough and informative guide to cyber-travel (US$25).

The World Wide Web

Search engines (services that search for web pages under specific subjects) are an essential tool for browsing the Web. **Lycos** (http://a2z.lycos.com), **Alta Vista** (www.altavista.digital.com), and **Excite** (www.excite.com) are among the most popular. **Yahoo!** is a slightly more organized search engine; its travel links are at http://www.yahoo.com/Recreation/Travel. Even better is the **New Zealand and Australia-specific Yahoo!,** at http://www.yahoo.com.au. Another good way to explore is to find a site with a good list of links and surf from there. Check out *Let's Go's* own page (http://www.letsgo.com) for starters, or try the following informative New Zealand sites.

The New Zealand Tourism Board (see above)

New Zealand Government Online (http://www.govt.nz). Provides statistics and vital visitor info. Follow their link to the **New Zealand Immigration Service** (http://www.immigration.govt.nz) to find out about the restrictions and requirements of staying in New Zealand.

Akiko: New Zealand on the Web (http://nz.com/NZ). News, cultural essays, and travel info. Recent additions include: a virtual tour of New Zealand; "KiwiChat," a bulletin board of New Zealand questions, thoughts, and travel stories; and "Chat-Tour," a forum where you can talk to fellow Kiwi aficionados in "real time."

Discover New Zealand Magazine (http://www.us.discovernz.co.nz/discovernz) features travel articles, an event calendar, a dining guide, and cultural and historical essays.

The New Zealand Herald (http://www.nzherald.co.nz/dailycom/index.html) is an excellent source of daily news.

Usenet Newsgroups

Another popular source of information is **newsgroups,** forums for discussion of specific topics. **Usenet,** the name for the family of newsgroups, can be accessed easily from most Internet gateways. In UNIX systems, type "tin" at the prompt. There are a number of different hierarchies for newsgroups. The "soc" hierarchy deals primary with issues related to society and culture. The "rec" (recreation) hierarchy is especially good for travelers, with newsgroups such as **rec.travel.air** or **rec.travel.australia+nz.** The "alt" (alternative) hierarchy houses a number of different types of discussion. Finally, "Clari-net" posts AP news wires for many topics. Remember that the quality of discussion changes rapidly and new groups are always appearing.

ESSNETIALS

■ Money

CURRENCY AND EXCHANGE

AUS$1 = NZ$1.18	NZ$1 = AUS$0.84
CDN$1 = NZ$1.31	NZ$1 = CDN$0.76
IR£1 = NZ$2.81	NZ$1 = IR£0.36
SAR1 = NZ$0.32	NZ$1 = SAR3.17
UK£1 = NZ$3.24	NZ$1 = UK£0.31
US$1 = NZ$1.99	NZ$1 = US$0.50

New Zealand's unit of currency is the New Zealand dollar. Coins come in denominations of 5, 10, 20, and 50 cents, $1 and $2; notes come in denominations of $5, $10, $20, $50, and $100. Typical bank hours are Monday through Friday, 9am to 4:30pm.

If you stay in backpackers, prepare your own food, and stick mostly to the free and low-budget natural attractions, you could probably get by on around US$30 per day. Transportation, dining out, and high-adrenaline adventure activities will dramatically increase this figure. No matter how low your budget, you will need to keep handy a larger amount of cash than usual, especially if you are traveling into more rural areas where credit cards might not be widely accepted.

Pickpocketing and petty theft is not a major problem in New Zealand, but you should take precautions anyway. Carry most of your cash on your person; a money belt is the safest bet. Theft from cars has lately become an increasing problem in New Zealand, so do not leave cash, documents, or other valuables in your car.

It is cheaper to buy domestic currency than foreign, so as a rule you should convert money after arriving at your destination. But to avoid getting stuck with no money outside of banking hours it's a good idea to have enough local currency to last for the first 24 to 72 hours of a trip. Watch out for commission rates and check newspapers to get the standard exchange rate; banks generally have the best rates. A good rule of thumb is to go to banks that have only 5% margins between their buy and sell prices. In smaller towns, travel offices may be your only option, and they are usually willing to help in an emergency. Since you lose money with every transaction, try to convert in large sums. Current exchange rates can be checked at http://www.bloomberg.com.

TRAVELER'S CHECKS

Traveler's checks are one of the safest and least troublesome means of carrying funds, as they can be refunded if stolen. Several agencies and many banks sell them, usually for face value plus a small percentage commission. (Members of the American Automobile Association and some banks and credit unions can get American Express checks commission-free; see **Drivers Permits and Car Insurance,** p. 8). **American Express** and **Visa** are the most widely recognized, though other major checks are also often sold, exchanged, cashed, and refunded. Keep in mind that traveler's checks may be less readily accepted in small towns than in cities.

Each agency provides **refunds** if your checks are lost or stolen and many provide additional services. (Note that you may need a police report verifying the loss or theft.) Inquire about emergency message relay services and stolen credit card assistance when you purchase your checks. Also ask about toll-free refund hotlines in New Zealand (such as the **American Express hotline** at (0800) 441 068).

You should expect a fair amount of red tape and delay in the event of theft or loss of traveler's checks. To expedite the refund process, keep your check receipts separate from your checks and store them in a safe place. Record check numbers when you cash them, leave a list with someone at home, and ask for a list of refund centers when you buy your checks. Keep a separate supply of cash or traveler's checks for emergencies. Never countersign your checks until you're prepared to cash them, and always bring your passport when you plan to use them.

Buying traveler's checks in New Zealand dollars can be difficult, as many major check companies do not yet offer them. **Visa** (see below) sells them in Australia and the U.K. Most establishments that accept traveler's checks will accept them in Australian and sometimes U.S. dollars, however.

American Express: Call (800) 25 19 02 in Australia; in New Zealand (0800) 44 10 68; in the U.K. (0800) 52 13 13; in the U.S. and Canada (800) 221-728). Elsewhere, call U.S. collect (801) 964-6665. American Express traveler's checks are now available in currencies including Australian, British, Canadian, and U.S., but unfortunately not in New Zealand dollars. They are the most widely recognized worldwide and the easiest to replace if lost or stolen. Checks can be purchased for a small fee (1-4%) at American Express Travel Service Offices, banks, and American Automobile Association offices (AAA members can buy the checks commission-free). Cardmembers can also buy checks at American Express Dispensers at Travel Service Offices at airports, or order them by phone (U.S. tel. (800) ORDER-TC (673-3782)). Visit their online travel offices (http://www.aexp.com).

Citicorp: Call (800) 645-6556 in the U.S. and Canada; in Europe, the Middle East, or Africa (44) 171 508 7007; from elsewhere call U.S. collect (813) 623-1709. Sells both Citicorp and Citicorp Visa traveler's checks in currencies including U.S., Australian, and Canadian dollars and British pounds. Commission is 1-2% on check purchases. Citicorp's World Courier Service guarantees hand-delivery of traveler's checks when a refund location is not convenient.

Thomas Cook MasterCard: For 24-hour cashing or refund assistance: from the U.S., Canada, or Caribbean call (800) 223-7373; from the U.K. call (0800) 622 101 free or (1733) 318 950 collect; from anywhere else call (44) 1733 318 950 collect. Offers checks in currencies including U.S., Canadian, Australian, British, and South African. Commission 2% for purchases. Thomas Cook offices will cash checks commission-free; banks will make a commission charge. Thomas Cook MasterCard Traveler's Checks are also available from **Capital Foreign Exchange** (see **Currency and Exchange**) in currencies including U.S., Canadian, British.

Visa: Call (800) 227-6811 in the U.S.; in the U.K. (0800) 895 078; from anywhere else in the world call (44) 1733 318 949 and reverse the charges. Sells checks in New Zealand dollars in Australia and the U.K. Any of the above numbers can tell you the location of their nearest office. Any type of Visa traveler's checks can be reported lost at the Visa number.

CREDIT AND DEBIT CARDS

Credit cards are accepted in New Zealand by most businesses, although many backpackers (hostels) only accept cash.

Major credit cards—**MasterCard** and **Visa** are the most widespread—can be used to extract cash advances from associated banks and ATMs in New Zealand. Credit card companies generally get better rates than banks and other currency exchange establishments. Because of steep late payment fees, however, you may want to consider using **debit cards** instead, which carry credit card symbols but draw money directly from your checking account with an extra fee. **American Express** cards also work in some ATMs as well as at AmEx offices and major airports. All such machines require a **Personal Identification Number (PIN).** Call your credit card company for a PIN before you leave home, if you don't already have one.

American Express (U.S. tel. (800) 843-2273) has a hefty annual fee (US$55) but offers a number of services. AmEx cardholders can cash personal checks at AmEx offices. U.S. Assist, a **24-hour hotline** offering emergency medical and legal assistance, is also available (U.S. tel. collect (301) 214-8228). Cardholders can take advantage of the American Express Travel Service; benefits include assistance in changing airline, hotel, and car rental reservations; baggage loss and flight insurance; and personal mail holding at one of the more than 1700 AmEx offices around the world. **MasterCard** (U.S. tel. (800) 999-0454) and **Visa** (U.S. tel. (800) 336-8472; (0508) 724 200 in New Zealand) are issued in cooperation with individual banks and some other organizations; ask the issuer about services that go along with the cards.

CASH (ATM) CARDS

Cash cards, popularly called ATM (Automated Teller Machine) cards, are widespread in New Zealand, even in surprisingly small locales. ATMs in New Zealand are called **cashpoint machines**. Automatic teller machines (ATMs) are fairly widespread in New Zealand, but don't count on them when you head into rural areas (*Let's Go* generally notes towns in which there are none). In most bank systems, you can access your own personal bank account abroad for a fee. (Be careful, however, and keep all receipts–even if an ATM won't give you your cash, it may register a withdrawal on your next statement.) Happily, ATMs get the same wholesale exchange rate as credit cards. Despite these perks, do some research before relying too heavily on automation. There is often a limit on the amount of money you can withdraw per day (usually about US$500), and computer network failures are not uncommon. If your PIN is longer than four digits, ask your bank whether the first four digits will work or whether you need a new number. Many ATMs are outdoors; always be cautious and aware of your surroundings. The two most common types of ATMs in New Zealand are those owned by the **national banks (ANZ),** and the **Bank of New Zealand (BNZ).** Both carry the major international money networks, **Cirrus** (U.S. tel. (800) 4-CIRRUS/424-7787) and **Plus** (U.S. tel. (800) 843-7587) as well as Visa, MasterCard, and Diners Club. Cirrus usually charges **US$3-5** to withdraw overseas; check with your bank. The back of your ATM card will have the symbol of networks with which it is compatible.

MONEY FROM HOME

One of the easiest ways to get money from home is to bring an **American Express** card. To its cardholders, AmEx offers Express Cash, where withdrawals are automatically debited from the cardmember's checking account or line of credit. Cardholders may withdraw up to US$1000 in a seven-day period, with a 2% transaction fee for each withdrawal (min. US$2.50/max. $20). To enroll in Express Cash, cardmembers may call (800) CASH NOW/227-4669. Outside the U.S., call collect (904) 565-7875.

Money can also be wired abroad through international money transfer services operated by **Western Union** (U.S. tel. (800) 325-6000). In the U.S., call Western Union anytime at (800) CALL CASH/225-5227 to cable money with your Visa, Discover, or MasterCard. The rates for sending cash are generally $10 more expensive than with a credit card, and the money is usually available in the country you're sending it to anywhere from 13 to 15 hours later, although this may vary.

In extremely dire emergencies, for a US$15 fee, U.S. citizens can have money sent to the nearest consular office via the State Department's **Overseas Citizens Service, American Citizens Services,** Consular Affairs, Room 4811, U.S. Department of State, Washington, D.C. 20520 (business hours tel. (202) 647-5225, other times (202) 647-4000; http://travel.state.gov). **Non-American travelers** should contact their embassies or consulates for information on wiring cash.

EFTPOS, OR OPENING A BANK ACCOUNT

Two forms of identification are required; your home driver's license and your passport are the most sure-fire bets. Be sure to bring along **home bank statements** from the last three months; although you are allowed to open an account without them, they expedite the process enormously. You can also expect the bank to perform a routine check on your credit history. Accounts can be ready in as little as an hour if you provide bank statements from home. The most compelling reason to open a New Zealand bank account, especially if you anticipate a long stay, is to get an **Eftpos debit card.** Carried by all major New Zealand banks, the Eftpos network is accepted at almost all ATMs and most establishments throughout the country. Get one and you may never have to touch cash again during your stay.

TAXES AND TIPPING

In New Zealand, a 12.5% **Goods and Services Tax (GST)** is applied to all goods and services and is usually included in the displayed price. New Zealanders **do not normally tip** in restaurants or other establishments.

■ Safety and Security

PERSONAL SAFETY

New Zealand enjoys its reputation as a warm and fuzzy tourist haven. As is true anywhere, however, tourists can't help being more vulnerable to crime for two reasons: they often carry large amounts of cash and are not as street savvy as locals. To avoid unwanted attention, try to **blend in** as much as possible. Walking directly into a cafe or shop to check a map beats checking it on a street corner. Better yet, look over your map *before* setting out. **111** is the **EMERGENCY NUMBER** in New Zealand. Especially when traveling alone, make sure someone at home knows your itinerary.

Nightlife in larger cities is rife with tourists and students and is probably safer than in many other countries. But in smaller towns, nightlife may be largely a local affair and can get rough around the edges. If you sense that you are the only tourist around and feel at all uncomfortable, move on. There is no sure-fire set of precautions that will protect you from all of the situations you might encounter when you travel. A good self-defense course can give you more concrete ways to react to different types of aggression, even if it often carries a steep price tag. **Impact/Model Mugging** can refer you to local self-defense courses in the United States (central database tel. (800) 345-KICK/5425). Women's and men's courses vary from $50-400.

OUTDOOR SAFETY

Remember that extreme weather can make hiking in New Zealand more treacherous than you might expect. Outdoor enthusiasts should befriend the **Department of Conservation (DOC),** the government organization that preserves, protects, and promotes New Zealand's park system (for more on the DOC and New Zealand's park system, see p. 34). When undertaking long hikes or other outdoor activities, always sign the **INTENTIONS BOOK** or at least make sure someone knows your plans. Most visitors centers and DOC offices and all those near national parks have intentions books. Sign your name, departure date, and intended return date. DO NOT forget to sign out when you are finished; otherwise a search party will come looking for you. Recently, **car theft** (both of and from) has become quite a problem in New Zealand, especially at trailheads. When hiking, always park in DOC-recommended lots.

Exercise extreme caution when using pools or beaches without lifeguards. Hidden rocks or dangerous currents may cause serious injury or even death. If you rent scuba-diving equipment, make sure that it is up to par before taking the plunge. And speaking of plunges, always consider the risks carefully before undertaking any of the strenuous, potentially risky activities that have made New Zealand an adventurer's paradise, such as bungee jumping, skydiving, and white- or blackwater rafting.

FINANCIAL SECURITY

Don't put a wallet with money in your back pocket. Never count your money in public and carry as little as possible. If you carry a purse, buy a sturdy one with a secure clasp and carry it crosswise on the side, away from the street with the clasp against you. Secure packs with small combination padlocks that slip through the two zippers. A **money belt** is the best way to carry cash. A nylon, zippered pouch with a belt that sits inside the waist of your pants or skirt combines convenience and security. A **neck pouch** is equally safe, although far less accessible. Refrain from pulling out your neck pouch in public; if you must, be very discreet. Avoid keeping anything precious in a small pack worn around the waist. **Photocopies** of important docu-

ESSNETIALS

ments allow you to replace them if they are lost or stolen. Keep some money separate from the rest to use in an emergency or in case of theft. Label every piece of luggage both inside and out. *Let's Go* lists storage availability in backpackers and train stations; storage areas may not be secured, however. Never leave your belongings unattended; crime occurs in even the most demure-looking establishments. If you feel unsafe, look for places with either a curfew or a night attendant.

DRUGS AND ALCOHOL

The **legal drinking age** is 20, although pending legislation may lower the age to 18. The age for tobacco use is 18. First-time drunk-driving offenders can receive three months imprisonment, a $4500 fine, and a six-month suspended license. Illegal drugs are, well, illegal. Possession of marijuana can result in a three-month imprisonment and a $1000 fine, while selling is punishable with a maximum sentence of eight years. Possession of harder drugs can result in a $1000 fine and a six-month imprisonment; selling them can put you in **jail for life.** If you carry **prescription drugs** while you travel, it is vital to have a copy of the prescriptions themselves readily accessible.

■ Health

Common sense is the simplest prescription for good health on the road—eat well, stay hydrated, sleep enough, and don't overexert yourself. Travelers complain most often about their feet and their gut, so take precautionary measures. Drink lots of fluids to prevent dehydration and constipation, wear sturdy shoes and clean socks, and use talcum powder to help keep your feet dry. In New Zealand, it is common for pharmacies to take turns being the town's **late-night pharmacy;** call the local hospital to get the number. A foreigner's office visit to most medical treatment centers costs about NZ$35.

BEFORE YOU GO

For minor health problems, bring a compact first-aid kit, including bandages, aspirin or other pain killer, antibiotic cream, a thermometer, a Swiss Army knife with tweezers, moleskin, a decongestant for colds, motion sickness remedy, medicine for diarrhea or stomach problems, sunscreen, insect repellent, and burn ointment.

In your passport, write the names of any people you wish to be contacted in case of a medical emergency, and also list any allergies or medical conditions you would want doctors to be aware of. If you wear glasses or contact lenses, carry an extra prescription and pair of glasses or arrange to have your doctor or a family member send a replacement pair in an emergency. Allergy sufferers should find out whether their conditions are likely to be aggravated in the regions they plan to visit, and obtain a full supply of any necessary medication before the trip, since matching a prescription to a foreign equivalent is not always easy, safe, or possible. Carry up-to-date, legible prescriptions or a statement from your doctor, especially if you use insulin, a syringe, or a narcotic. While traveling, be sure to keep all medication with you in your carry-on luggage.

Travel to New Zealand does not ordinarily require vaccination against infectious diseases. However, if you are stopping in other countries along the way, you may want to make use of the following resources. The **United States Centers for Disease Control and Prevention** maintains an international fax information service for travelers. In the U.S., call 1-888-232-3299 and select an international travel directory; the requested information will be faxed to you. Similar information is available from the CDC website (http://www.cdc.gov.). **United States State Department** compiles Consular Information Sheets on health, entry requirements, and other issues for all countries of the world. Particularly helpful is the website at http://travel.state.gov. For quick information on travel warnings, call the **Overseas Citizens' Services** (U.S. tel. (202) 647-5225).You can also call the U.S. Centers for Disease Control's 24-hour hotline at US tel. (800) 342 2437.

If you are concerned about being able to access medical support while traveling, contact one of these two services: **Global Emergency Medical Services (GEMS)** has products called *MedPass* that provide 24-hour international medical assistance and support coordinated through registered nurses who have on-line access to your medical information, your primary physician, and a worldwide network of screened, credentialed English-speaking doctors and hospitals. Subscribers also receive a personal medical record that contains vital information in case of emergencies. For more information call (800) 860-1111 (8:30am-5:30pm); fax (770) 475-0058, or write: 2001 Westside Drive, #120, Alpharetta, GA 30201. The **International Association for Medical Assistance to Travelers (IAMAT)** offers a membership ID card, a directory of English-speaking doctors around the world who treat members for a set fee schedule, and detailed charts on immunization requirements, various tropical diseases, climate, and sanitation. Membership is free, though donations are appreciated and used for further research. Contact chapters in the **U.S.,** 417 Center St., Lewiston, NY 14092 (tel. (716) 754-4883, 8am–4pm/EST); fax (519) 836-3412; email iamat@sentex.net; http://www.sentex.net/~iamat), **Canada,** 40 Regal Road, Guelph, Ontario, N1K 1B5 (tel. (519) 836-0102) or 1287 St. Clair Avenue West, Toronto, M6E 1B8 (tel. (416) 652-0137; fax (519) 836-3412), or **New Zealand,** P.O. Box 5049, Christchurch 5.

JETLAG

Many travelers to New Zealand will arrive after a flight of over 12 hours. While it may be tempting to sleep, many people think it is best to force yourself to make it through at least to early evening. If you are arriving in the morning, one strategy is to stay up all night before departure, sleep on the plane, and arrive relatively acclimatized. Some travelers take herbal supplements such as melatonin to help reset their body's clocks. Regardless, immediately adopt local time, give yourself a day or two to rest, and carry on.

PREVENTING DISEASE

You can minimize the chances of contracting a disease while traveling by taking a few precautionary measures. Always avoid animals with open wounds. If you are bitten, be concerned about **rabies**—be sure to clean your wound thoroughly and seek medical help immediately to find out whether you need treatment. When spending time in the outdoors, never drink water from outdoor sources that you have not treated yourself. To purify your own water, bring it to a rolling **boil** (simmering isn't enough) or treat it with iodine drops or tablets. **Parasites** (tapeworms, etc.) also hide in unsafe water and food. **Giardia,** a major concern for outdoor enthusiasts, is acquired by drinking untreated water from streams or lakes all over the world. It can stay with you for years. General symptoms of parasitic infections include swollen glands or lymph nodes, fever, rashes or itchiness, digestive problems, eye problems, and anemia. Boil your water, wear shoes, avoid bugs, and eat cooked food.

HOT AND COLD

Common sense goes a long way toward preventing **heat exhaustion**—relax in hot weather, drink lots of non-alcoholic fluids, and lie down inside if you feel awful. Continuous heat stress can eventually lead to **heatstroke,** characterized by rising body temperature, severe headache, and cessation of sweating. Wear a hat, sunglasses, and a lightweight, long-sleeve shirt to avoid heatstroke. Victims must be cooled off with wet towels and taken to a doctor as soon as possible.

Always drink enough liquids to keep your urine clear. Alcoholic beverages are dehydrating, as are coffee, strong tea, and caffeinated sodas. If you'll be sweating a lot, be sure to eat enough salty food to prevent electrolyte depletion, which causes severe headaches. Less debilitating, but still dangerous, is **sunburn.** Bring sunscreen with you (it's often more expensive in New Zealand) and apply it liberally and often. If you do get sunburned, drink more fluids than usual while recuperating.

> ### Ozone in Godzone
> Unfortunately, there's not much of it. Depleted ozone levels and unpolluted air combine for wicked **sunburns** that zap even people who are naturally darker-skinned and accustomed to the sun. Grab a hat and slather on the suncreen even for a short time outdoors; "burn times" are included in the daily weather forecast, and are usually within 12-15 minutes.

Extreme cold is just as dangerous as heat, because overexposure to cold brings the risk of **hypothermia.** As body temperature drops rapidly, the warning signs are easy to note. You may shiver, have poor coordination, feel sleepy or exhausted, have slurred speech, hallucinate, or suffer amnesia. **Do not let hypothermia victims fall asleep** if in the advanced stages—their body temperature will drop lower, and if they lose consciousness, they may die. Seek medical help as soon as possible. To avoid hypothermia, keep dry and stay out of the wind. In wet weather, wool and most synthetics will keep you warm, but most other fabrics, especially cotton, will make you colder.

WOMEN'S HEALTH

Women traveling may be vulnerable to urinary tract and bladder infections, common and severely uncomfortable bacterial diseases that cause a burning sensation and painful, sometimes frequent urination. Untreated, these infections can lead to kidney infections, sterility, and even death. If symptoms persist, see a doctor. If you develop vaginal yeast infections regularly, take along a sufficient supply of over-the-counter medicine. Refer to the women's health guide *Our Bodies, Our Selves* (published by the Boston Women's Health Collective) for more extensive info specific to women's health on the road. Also see **Women Travelers,** p. 20.

CONTRACEPTION

Contraceptive devices are legal and easily accessible in New Zealand; you might want to bring enough of your favorite brand before you go, as type and quality varies. Women on the pill should bring enough to allow for possible loss or extended stays. Bring a prescription, since forms of the pill vary a good deal. **Abortion** is legal in New Zealand, and requires the approval of two certifying consultants who make an appraisal of the potential damage to the mother's mental and physical health should the pregnancy continue. For more info on contraception and abortion in New Zealand, contact the **New Zealand Family Planning Association (FPA),** P.O. Box 11-515, Manners St., Wellington, New Zealand (tel. (04) 384 4349). You can also contact the **International Planned Parenthood Federation** at Regent's College Inner Circle, Regent's Park, London NW1 4NS (tel. (0171) 487 7900; fax 487 7950).

AIDS, HIV, STDS

New Zealand does not screen incoming travelers for the HIV virus; however, restrictions may apply to those staying longer to work or study (contact your nearest consulate). For more information once in New Zealand, you can contact the **Acquired Immune Deficiency Syndrome (AIDS) National Hotline** (tel. (0800) 802 437 or 358 0099 within Auckland), a 24-hour hotline that offers AIDS counseling and information. The hotline is sponsored by the **New Zealand AIDS Foundation,** P.O. Box 6663, Wellesley St., Auckland (tel. (09) 303 3124; fax 309 3149). In Europe, write to the **World Health Organization,** attn: Global Program on AIDS, 20 Avenue Appia, 1211 Geneva 27, Switzerland (tel. (41 22) 791 2111), for statistical material on AIDS internationally. Or write to the **Bureau of Consular Affairs,** #6831, Department of State, Washington, D.C. 20520. The brochure *Travel Safe: AIDS and International Travel* is available at all Council Travel offices.

Sexually transmitted diseases (STDs) such as gonorrhea, chlamydia, genital warts, syphilis, and herpes are a lot easier to catch than HIV and can be just as dangerous. It's a wise idea to actually look at your partner's genitals before you have sex. Warning signs for STDs include: swelling, sores, bumps, or blisters on sex organs, rectum, or mouth; burning and pain during urination and bowel movements; itching around sex organs; swelling or redness in the throat; and flu-like symptoms with fever, chills, and aches. If these symptoms develop, see a doctor immediately. Sexual health centers and family planning centers, which offer STD testing and treatment, are located in major cities and towns. When having sex, condoms may protect you from certain STDs, but oral or even tactile contact can lead to transmission.

■ Insurance

Visitors who suffer personal injury by accident in New Zealand are covered by the local **Accident Compensation Co-Operation** (known locally as ACC), which entitles them to a claim, irrespective of fault. Some medical and hospital expenses are included in its benefits, but it does not cover lost wages outside of New Zealand.

Beware of buying unnecessary travel coverage—your regular insurance policies may well extend to many travel-related accidents. **Medical insurance** (especially university policies) often cover costs incurred abroad; check with your provider. **Australia** has a Reciprocal Health Care Agreement (RHCA) with New Zealand, which means that Australians are entitled to many of the services in New Zealand that they would receive at home. The Commonwealth Department of Human Services and Health can provide more information. **Canadians** are protected by their home province's health insurance plan for up to 90 days after leaving the country; check with the provincial Ministry of Health or Health Plan Headquarters for details. Your **homeowners' insurance** (or family coverage) often covers theft during travel. Homeowners are generally covered against loss of travel documents (passport, plane ticket, railpass, etc.) up to US$500.

ISIC and **ITIC** provide basic insurance benefits (see Youth, Student, and Teacher Identification, p. 7), and access to a toll-free 24-hour helpline whose multilingual staff can provide assistance in medical, legal, and financial emergencies overseas (tel. (800) 626-2427 in the U.S. and Canada; elsewhere call the U.S. collect (713) 267-2525). **Council** and **STA** offer a range of plans that can supplement your basic insurance coverage, with options covering medical treatment and hospitalization, accidents, baggage loss, and even charter flights missed due to illness. **American Express** cardholders receive automatic travel accident coverage (US$100,000 in life insurance) on flight purchases made with the card; call Customer Service (tel. (800) 528-4800). YHA travel insurance gives a 10% discount on Australian and overseas travel insurance policies.

The Berkely Group/Carefree Travel Insurance, 100 Garden City Plaza, P.O. Box 9366, Garden City, NY 11530-9366 (24hr. tel. (800) 323-3149 or (516) 294-0220; fax 294-1095; http://www.berkely.com; email info@berkely.com). Offers 2 comprehensive packages including coverage for trip cancellation/interruption/delay, accident and sickness, medical, baggage loss bag delay, accidental death and dismemberment, and travel supplier insolvency. Trip cancellation/interruption may be purchased separately at a rate of US$5.50 per US$100 of coverage. 24-hour hotline.

Globalcare Travel Insurance, 220 Broadway, Lynnfield, MA 01940 (tel. (800) 821-2488; fax (617) 592-7720; email global@nebc.mv.com; http://www.nebc.mv.com / globalcare). Complete medical, legal, emergency, and travel-related services. On-the-spot payments and special student programs, including benefits for trip cancellation and interruption. GTI waives pre-existing medical conditions, and provides coverage for the bankruptcy or default of cruise lines, airlines, or tour operators. Also included at no extra charge is a Worldwide Collision Damage Provision.

■ Alternatives to Tourism

STUDY

Exchange programs are available in Auckland, Christchurch, Wellington, Dunedin, and other smaller cities. Foreign study programs vary tremendously in expense, academic quality, living conditions, degree of contact with local students, and exposure to local culture; do some research before you decide.

American Field Service (AFS), 310 SW 4th Avenue, Suite 630, Portland, OR 97204-2608 (tel. (800) 237-4636; fax (503) 241-1653; email afsinfo@afs.org; http://www.afs.org/usa). AFS offers summer, semester, and year-long homestay international exchange programs with New Zealand for high school students and graduating high school seniors. Financial aid available.

Butler University Institute for Study Abroad, 4600 Sunset Ave, Indianapolis, IN 46208 (tel. (800) 858-0229; http://www.butler.edu/www/isa), offers programs at 4 New Zealand universities.

School for International Training, Kipling Rd., P.O. Box 676, Brattleboro, VT 05302-0676 (tel. (800) 336-1616; fax (802) 258-3500; email info@sit.edu). Offers extensive **College Semester Abroad** programs in New Zealand. Programs cost US$9900-11,900, including tuition, room and board, and airfare. Scholarships are available and federal financial aid is usually transferable from home college or university. Write for a brochure. At the same address, the **Experiment in International Living** runs five-week summer programs combining homestays (including stays in Maori villages) with community service in New Zealand (tel. (800) 345-2929 or (802) 258 3447; fax (802) 258-3428; email eil@worldlearning.org; http://www.worldlearning.org). Positions as group leaders are available world-wide if you have experience working with high school students, previous in-country experience, and are a college graduate.

WORK

Officially, you can only hold a job in New Zealand with a **work visa or permit.** To obtain these, you need to be sponsored by a New Zealand employer who can demonstrate that you have skills that locals lack—not the easiest of tasks. Call the nearest New Zealand Consulate or Embassy to get more info.

Many backpackers (hostels) in New Zealand could aptly be termed "working hostels," for they are filled not with vacationers but with travelers and locals who have set up a temporary home near their jobs. In larger cities, travelers help around the hostel in exchange for room and board, and may eventually establish their own residence in New Zealand. In more rural areas, many travelers find seasonal employment fruit picking (see p. 194). Such work is usually arranged through hostel owners—ask around. Despite popular misconception, you do need a work permit to do this. Australian citizens and residents with a current Australian resident return visa do not need a visa or permit to work in New Zealand.

Citizens of Canada, the Republic of Ireland, Japan, Malaysia, and the U.K. aged 18 to 30 are eligible to apply for a place in a New Zealand **working holiday scheme;** contact the nearest New Zealand Immigration Service office for more details (http://www.immigration.govt.nz). If you are a U.S. citizen and a full-time student at a U.S. university, the simplest way to get a job abroad is through work permit programs run by the **Council on International Educational Exchange (Council)** and its member organizations. For a US$225 application fee, Council can procure three- to six-month work permits (and a handbook to help you find work and housing). Contact Council for more info (see **Volunteering,** below).

Transitions Abroad Publishing, Inc., 18 Hulst Rd., P.O. Box 1300, Amherst, MA 01004-1300 (tel. (800) 293-0373; fax (413) 256-0373; email trabroad@aol.com; http://www.transabroad.com). Publishes *Transitions Abroad,* a bi-monthly magazine listing all kinds of opportunities and printed resources for those seeking to study, work, or travel abroad. They also publish *The Alternative Travel Directory*, a truly exhaustive listing of information for the "active international traveler." For subscriptions (US$25 for 6 issues, Canada US$30, other countries US$38), contact *Transitions Abroad*, Dept. TRA, Box 3000, Denville, NJ 07834, or call (800) 293-0373.

VOLUNTEERING

New Zealand provides readily available volunteer jobs, especially for those of agricultural bent. Particularly popular are jobs on organic farms arranged through WWOOF (see below). A helpful resource is the *International Directory of Voluntary Work* (UK£10), from Vacation Work Publications (tel. (01865) 24 19 78; fax 79 08 85).

Council has a Voluntary Services Dept., 205 E. 42nd St., New York, NY 10017 (tel. (888) COUNCIL/268-6245; fax (212) 822-2699; email info@ciee.org; http://www.ciee.org), which offers 2- to 4-week environmental or community services projects in over 30 countries. Participants must be at least 18 years old. Minimum US$295 placement fee; additional fees may also apply for various countries.

New Zealand Wilderness Trust Box 19300, Hamilton, New Zealand (tel. (07) 855 1187; fax 855 1186; email nzwt@clear.net.nz). Takes volunteers for year-round projects in the upper North Island, including habitat restoration and protection, flora and fauna surveys, endangered species protection, track creation and maintenance, and more. Projects begin on Mondays; report in Hamilton no later than the preceding Sunday. Project packages: 1 week $155, 4 weeks $520, additional week $120.

Willing Workers on Organic Farms (WWOOF), P.O. Box 1172, Nelson, New Zealand (tel./fax (03) 544 9890; email wwoof-nz@xtra.co.nz; http://www.phdcc.com/sites/wwoof), distributes a list of names of over 500 organic farmers who offer room and board in exchange for help on the farm. Membership fee is NZ$20 from within the country; from overseas, AUS$25, CAN$25, UK£10, or US$20. Couples discounts available. Include 2 international postal reply coupons with your request or contact them by email.

■ Specific Concerns

WOMEN TRAVELERS

Women exploring on their own inevitably face additional safety concerns, even a country as safe as New Zealand. Be adventurous, but avoid unnecessary risks. Trust your instincts; if you'd feel better somewhere else, move on. Always carry extra money for a phone call, bus, or taxi. You might consider staying in those backpackers (hostels) that offer single rooms locking from the inside. Stick to centrally located accommodations and avoid solitary late-night treks.

Watch out for persistent, too-friendly locals, especially when hitting the pub scene. In general, pubs tent to be havens of New Zealand machismo culture. Wearing a conspicuous **wedding band** may help prevent harassment. Feigned deafness, sitting motionless, and staring away could also do a world of good that angry reactions may not achieve. The extremely stubborn can sometimes be dissuaded by a firm, loud, and very public "Go away!"

Don't hesitate to seek out a police officer or a passerby if you are being harassed. Memorize the **EMERGENCY number** in New Zealand: **111.** Carry a **whistle** or an airhorn on your keychain, and don't hesitate to use it in an emergency. For more on women's concerns, see **Safety and Security,** p. 13, and **Health,** p. 14.

Wander Women, 30 Edenvale Cresent, Mount Eden, Auckland 3 (tel./fax (09) 630 1108), offers guided hiking, climbing, canoe and caving trips for women-only and mixed groups. Also special mother-daughter and mother-son trips.

Handbook For Women Travellers by Maggie and Gemma Moss (UK£9). Encyclopedic and well-written. Available from Piatkus Books, 5 Windmill St., London W1P 1HF (tel. (0171) 631 0710).

Women Going Places is a women's travel and resource guide geared toward lesbians but appropriate for all women which emphasizes women-owned enterprises. US$15 from Inland Book Company, 1436 W. Randolph St. Chicago, IL 60607 (tel. (800) 243-0138; fax (800) 334-3892) or a local bookstore.

A Foxy Old Woman's Guide to Traveling Alone, by Jay Ben-Lesser (Crossing Press, US $11). Information, informal advice, and a resource list for solo travelers on a low-to-medium budget.

OLDER TRAVELERS

Many **senior citizen** discounts in New Zealand, especially transportation passes, only apply to country citizens. As far as activities and accommodations, however, you may be able to finagle a special price if you ask nicely. The following agencies and organizations may offer more consistent deals:

Elderhostel, 75 Federal St., 3rd fl., Boston, MA 02110-1941 (tel. (617) 426-7788; email Cadyg@elderhostel.org; http://www.elderhostel.org). For those 55 or over (spouse of any age). Programs at colleges, universities, and other learning centers in over 70 countries on varied subjects lasting 1-4 weeks.

National Council of Senior Citizens, 8403 Colesville Rd., Silver Spring, MD 20910-31200 (tel. (301) 578-8800; fax 578-8999). Memberships cost US$13 per year, US$33 for 3 years, or US$175 for a lifetime. Individuals or couples can receive hotel and auto rental discounts, a senior citizen newspaper, and use of a discount travel agency.

Unbelievably Good Deals and Great Adventures That You Absolutely Can't Get Unless You're Over 50, by Joan Rattner Heilman. After you finish reading the title page, check inside for some great tips on senior discounts. US$10 from Contemporary Books or online at http://www.amazon.com.

BISEXUAL, GAY, AND LESBIAN TRAVELERS

Male homosexual acts were banned until 1986, when sexual intercourse was finally made legal for persons over 16, regardless of sexual orientation. Intolerance does not need to be unduly feared in major New Zealand cities, many of which feature an active gay culture, with gay-friendly bars, health centers, and bookstores. More rural or remote areas are less accustomed to displays of homosexuality, however. They may be less friendly, but will not likely be openly or unpleasantly disapproving. The following organizations can offer specific tips. Local organizations are listed throughout the book.

New Zealand Gay and Lesbian Tourism Association, P.O. Box 11-582, Wellington 6001 (tel. (04) 384 1877; email nzglta@clear.net.nz; http://nz.com/webnz/tpac/gaynz). This professional, nonprofit organization helps arrange both group and individual travel worldwide, addressing everything from hotel reservations to special tours to transportation needs.

Gaylink Travel Services, P.O. Box 11-584, Wellington 6001 (tel. (04) 384 1877; email gts@clear.net.nz; http://nz.com/webnz/tpac/gaynz/GaylinkTravel.html.)

Travel Desk NZ Ltd., 45 Anzac Ave., Auckland (tel. 377 9031; email out@nz.com.)

Lesbian Line, P.O. Box 11-882, Wellington (tel. (04) 389 8082; open Tu, Th, Sa 7:30-10:30pm).

DISABLED TRAVELERS

New Zealand is overall an accessible and welcoming country for the disabled. Law requires that every motel and hotel provides a certain number of fully accessible rooms. In addition, a number of tramps and walks are wheelchair-accessible; always check with the DOC.

Main taxi companies in major cities and many towns have a **Total Mobility Taxi Service** offering transportation for those with wheelchairs. With sufficient notice, some major **car rental agencies** will offer hand-controlled vehicles at select locations. According to New Zealand's current quarantine policy, **guide dogs** are not allowed into the country. For more details about disabled travel services, contact New Zealand's **Enable Information** (toll-free disability information line (0800) 171 981). The **Deaf Emergency** telephone number is (tel. (0800) 161 616).

Directions Unlimited, 720 N. Bedford Rd., Bedford Hills, NY 10507 (tel. (800) 533-5343; in NY (914) 241-1700; fax (914) 241-0243). Specializes in arranging individual and group vacations, tours, and cruises for the physically disabled. Group tours for blind travelers.

Twin Peaks Press, P.O. Box 129, Vancouver, WA 98666-0129 (tel. (360) 694-2462; fax (360) 696-3210; email 73743.2634@compuserve.com; http://netm.com/mall/ infoprod/twinpeak/helen.htm). Publishers of *Travel for the Disabled,* which provides travel tips, lists of accessible tourist attractions, and advice on other resources for disabled travelers (US$20). Also publishes *Directory of Travel Agencies for the Disabled* (US$20), *Wheelchair Vagabond* (US$15), and *Directory of Accessible Van Rentals* (US$10). Postage US$4 for first book, US$2 for each additional book.

MINORITY TRAVELERS

During New Zealand's European colonization in the 19th and early 20th centuries, land disputes ran rampant between the Maori, the native people of New Zealand, and the encroaching European settlers. Race relations today between Maori and Pakeha (non-Maori peoples) appear to have reached some measure of stability, although tension remains. Debate, protest, and legal reform over the place of Maori culture, history, and land claims in New Zealand continues. (See **History and Current Events,** p. 54, for more details.) The population is mainly Caucasian; the largest minority group is Maori, followed by other Polynesian and Asian peoples. (Also see **The People,** p. 41.) Asian tourism, particularly Japanese or Korean, is becoming common in New Zealand; as a result, prejudice against Asians is increasing. Visitors of Asian descent may possibly be at risk for theft, due to the stereotype of the wealthy Asian tourist. Other minorities may find that they stand out in a crowd, but are more likely to invite curious looks than outright harassment or violence.

As always, however, it is difficult to generalize about how minority travelers will be treated in a foreign country. *Let's Go* asks its researchers to exclude establishments that discriminate for any reason. If you encounter discriminatory treatment in your travels, you should firmly and calmly state your disapproval and make it clear to the owners that another establishment will be receiving your patronage. If the establishment is listed in a *Let's Go* guide, please mail a letter to *Let's Go* stating the details of the incident (see **Helping Let's Go,** p. iv in the front of the guide).

DIETARY CONCERNS

Vegetarians in New Zealand should not have serious problems finding suitable cuisine. *Let's Go* notes restaurants with good vegetarian selections in its city listings. **The International Vegetarian Travel Guide** (UK£2), last published in 1991, provides info on veggie travel. Order back copies from the Vegetarian Society of the UK (VSUK), Parkdale, Dunham Rd., Altringham, Cheshire WA14 4QG (tel. (0161) 928 079; email: veg@minxnet.co.uk; http://www.vegsoc.org).

Travelers who keep **kosher** should contact synagogues in larger cities for info on kosher restaurants. **The Jewish Travel Guide** lists synagogues, kosher restaurants, and Jewish institutions in over 80 countries is available from Ballentine Mitchell Publishers, Newbury House 890-900, Eastern Ave., Newbury Park, Ilford, Essex, U.K. IG2 7HH (tel. (0181) 599 88 66; fax 599 09 84). It is available in the U.S. ($15 plus $3 shipping) from Sepher-Hermon Press, 1265 46th St., Brooklyn, NY 11219 (tel./fax (718) 972-9010; contact person Samuel Gross). If you are strict in your observance, however, consider preparing your own food on the road.

TRAVELING ALONE

There are many benefits to traveling alone, among them greater independence and challenge. Lone travelers in New Zealand do not suffer as much from the robbery and harassment they may face elsewhere. Lone travelers do need to be well-organized and look confident at all times, however. Maintain regular contact with someone at home who knows your itinerary. (For more tips, see **Safety and Security,** p. 13.) The very cautious can contact a number of organizations that will match them up with travel companions. **Connecting: Solo Travel network,** P.O. Box 29088, 1996 W. Broadway, Vancouver, BC V6J 5C2, Canada (tel. (604) 737-7791 or (800) 557-1757; http://www.travel-wise.com/solo), is a bimonthly newsletter with feature articles, travel tips, and listings of singles looking for travel companions. The annual directory (US$7.95) lists tours and lodgings, and is free with membership (US$25 annually). **Traveling On Your Own,** by Eleanor Berman (US$13), Crown Publishers, Inc., lists information resources for "singles" (old and young) and single parents.

■ Packing

The best reason to pack light is that you will have to carry everything. Over time, your pack *will* get heavier. A good rule of thumb is to lay out only what you absolutely need—then take half the clothes and twice the money. (For important tips, also see **Camping and the Outdoors,** p. 34, and **Health,** p. 14.)

LUGGAGE If you plan on hoofing it, a sturdy **backpack** is essential. Many packs (often internal frame) are designed for travelers, others (often external frame) specifically for hikers. Get a pack with a strong, padded hip belt to transfer weight down from your shoulders. Don't sacrifice quality for low prices. Good packs cost anywhere from US$150 to $420. Bringing a **daypack** or **rucksack** in addition to your luggage allows you to leave your big bag behind while you go sight-seeing or daytripping. Guard your money, passport, and other important articles in a **moneybelt or neck pouch,** and keep it with you *at all times.* See **Safety and Security,** p. 13, for more details on protecting you and your valuables.

CLOTHING AND FOOTWEAR Well-cushioned **sneakers** are good for street walking. A high-quality water-proofed pair of **hiking boots** is necessary if you plan to hike—and you probably will, given the gorgeous scenery. **Black shoes** (not sneakers) will get you into clubs and bars with a dress code (there are quite a few). Bring along pants and a button-down shirt to complete your ensemble.

Talcum powder in your shoes and on your feet can prevent sores, and moleskin is great for blisters. As for **bad weather gear,** a waterproof jacket and backpack cover will keep the wet stuff off you and your stuff. Gore-Tex® is a miracle fabric that's both waterproof and breathable. Avoid cotton as outer-wear, especially if you will be outdoors a lot. Always bring warm layers, regardless of the season.

MISCELLANEOUS In New Zealand, the electric current is 230-240 volts AC, 50 Hz, enough to fry any 110V North American appliance. Power sockets are made for three-prong flat plugs. Visit a hardware store for an adapter (to change the shape of the plug) and a converter (to change the voltage). Don't make the mistake of using only an adapter (unless appliance instructions explicitly state otherwise), or you'll melt your radio, and that's no fun.

Important items on the agenda should be: **sleepsacks** (made from a sheet folded lengthwise and sewn up to leave an open edge at the top), a must if you plan to stay in backpackers; a small bar or tube of **detergent soap**; and a **lead-lined film pouch,** because airport security X-rays *can* fog film. **Other useful items** include: sealable plastic bags (for damp clothes and spillables); plastic water bottle; alarm clock; waterproof matches; small sewing kit; pocketknife; padlock; whistle; flashlight; earplugs (for noisy backpackers!); rubber bands; string; toilet paper; electrical tape (for patching tears); garbage bags; string; insect repellent; sunscreen; tweezers.

GETTING THERE

■ Budget Travel Agencies

Students and people under 26 ("youth") with proper ID often qualify for enticing reduced airfares from **student travel agencies.** Most flights are on major airlines, though in peak season some agencies may sell seats on less-reliable chartered aircraft.

Campus Travel, located at 52 Grosvenor Gardens, London SW1W 0AG (http://www.campustravel.co.uk). Forty-six branches in the U.K. Student and youth fares on plane, train, boat, and bus travel, discount and ID cards, travel insurance. Telephone booking service: in Europe call (0171) 730 34 02; in North America call (0171) 730 21 01; worldwide call (0171) 730 81 11; in Manchester call (0161) 273 17 21; in Scotland (0131) 668 33 03.

Council Travel (http://www.ciee.org/travel/index.htm), the travel division of Council, is a full-service travel agency specializing in youth and budget travel. In the **U.S.,** call 800-2-COUNCIL (226-8624) for the agency nearest you. The **London** office is located at 28A Poland St (Oxford Circus), London, W1V 3DB (tel. (0171) 287 3357). Visit the web site at http://www.ciee.org/cts/ctshome.htm.

Let's Go Travel, Harvard Student Agencies, 17 Holyoke St, Cambridge, MA 02138 (tel. (617) 495-9649; fax 495-7956; email travel@hsa.net; http://hsa.net/travel). Railpasses, HI-AYH memberships, ISICs, ITICs, FIYTO cards, guidebooks (including every *Let's Go* at a substantial discount), maps, bargain flights, and a complete line of budget travel gear. All items available by mail; call or write for a catalog (or see the catalog in the center of this publication).

STA Travel, 6560 Scottsdale Rd #F100, Scottsdale, AZ 85253 (tel. (800) 777-0112 nationwide; fax (602) 922-0793; http://sta-travel.com). Student and youth organization with over 150 offices worldwide offering discount airfares for young travelers, railpasses, accommodations, tours, insurance, and ISICs. Sixteen offices in the U.S. In New Zealand, 10 High St, **Auckland** (tel. (09) 309 97 23). STA offices in Australia include: 224 Faraday St, **Melbourne** Vic 3000 (tel. (03) 9347 6911), and **Canberra** ACT (tel. (02) 6247 0800, fast fares 1300 360 960; email traveller@statravelaus.com.au; http://www.statravelaus.com.au/). Open M-F 9am-5pm.

Travel CUTS (Canadian Universities Travel Services Limited), 187 College St, Toronto, ON M5T 1P7 (tel. (416) 979-2406; fax 979-8167; email mail@travelcuts). Canada's national student travel bureau and equivalent of Council, with 40 offices across Canada. Also in the U.K., 295-A Regent St., **London** W1R 7YA (tel. (0171) 637 31 61). Discounted domestic and international airfares open to all; special student fares to all destinations with valid ISIC. Issues ISIC, FIYTO, GO25, and HI hostel cards, as well as railpasses. Offers the free *Student Traveller* magazine, as well as information on the Student Work Abroad Program (SWAP).

Usit Youth and Student Travel, 19-21 Aston Quay, O'Connell Bridge, Dublin 2 (tel. (01) 677 8117; fax 679 8833). In the U.S.: New York Student Center, 895 Amsterdam Ave, New York, NY, 10025 (tel. (212) 663-5435; email usitny@aol.com). Additional offices in Cork, Galway, Limerick, Waterford, Maynooth, Coleraine, Derry, Athlone, Jordanstown, Belfast, and Greece. Specializes in youth and student travel. Offers low-cost tickets and flexible travel arrangements all over the world. Supplies ISIC and FIYTO-GO25 cards in Ireland only.

■ Traveling by Plane

The privilege of spending up to 24 hours on an airplane doesn't come cheap. The **airline industry** attempts to squeeze every dollar from customers; finding a cheap airfare will be easier if you understand the airlines' systems. Call every toll-free number and don't be afraid to ask about discounts. Have knowledgeable **travel agents** guide you; better yet, have an agent who specializes in the region(s) you will be traveling to guide you.

To obtain the **cheapest fare,** buy a round-trip ticket and stay over at least one Saturday. Midweek round-trip flights run about US$40-50 cheaper than on weekends; weekend flights, however, are generally less crowded. Traveling from hub to hub (for example, Los Angeles to Auckland) will win a more competitive fare than from smaller cities. Return-date flexibility is usually not an option for the budget traveler; traveling with an "open return" ticket can be pricier than fixing a return date and paying to change it. When dealing with any commercial airline, buying in advance is best. Periodic **price wars** may lower prices in spring and early summer months, but they're unpredictable; don't delay your purchase in hopes of catching one. Most airlines allow children under two to fly free (on the lap of an adult).

It is not wise to buy **frequent flyer tickets** from others—it is standard policy on all commercial airlines to check a photo ID, and you could find yourself paying for a new, full-fare ticket. If you have a frequent flyer account, make sure you're getting credit when you check in. It's many kilometers to New Zealand, no matter where you're coming from.

Students and others under 26 should never need to pay full price for a ticket. Seniors can also get great deals; many airlines offer senior traveler clubs or airline passes with few restrictions and discounts for their companions as well. Sunday newspapers often have travel sections that list bargain fares from the local airport. Outsmart airline reps with the phone-book-sized *Official Airline Guide* (check your local library; at US$359 per yr., the tome costs as much as some flights), a monthly guide listing nearly every scheduled flight in the world (with fares, US$479) and toll-free phone numbers for all the airlines which allow you to call in reservations directly. More accessible is Michael McColl's *The Worldwide Guide to Cheap Airfare* (US$15), an incredibly useful guide for finding cheap airfare.

Whenever flying internationally, pick up your ticket well in advance of the departure date, have the flight confirmed within 72 hours of departure, and arrive at the airport at least three hours before your flight to ensure you have a seat; airlines often overbook. (Of course, being "bumped" from a flight doesn't spell doom if your travel plans are flexible—you will probably leave on the next flight and receive a free ticket or cash bonus. If you would like to be bumped to win a free ticket, check in early and let the airline officials know.)

Many airlines are now offering ticketing and reservations over the internet, and some award discounts to web reservers. Free worldwide flight schedules are available at http://www.travelocity.com. **TravelHUB** (http://www.travelhub.com) will help you search for travel agencies on the web. The **Air Traveler's Handbook** (http://www.cs.cmu.edu/afs/cs.cmu.edu/user/mkant/Public/Travel/airfare.html) is an excellent source of general information on air travel. Edward Hasbrouck maintains a **Consolidators FAQ** (http://www.travel-library.com/air-travel/consolidators.html) that provides great background on finding cheap international flights. Groups such as the **Air Courier Association** (http://www.aircourier.org) offer information about traveling as a courier and provide up-to-date listings of last minute opportunities. **Travelocity** (http://www.travelocity.com) operates a searchable online database of published airfares, which you can reserve online.

The following programs, services, and fares may be helpful for planning a reasonably-priced air trip, but always be wary of deals that seem too good to be true.

COMMERCIAL AIRLINES

The commercial airlines' lowest regular offer is the **Advance Purchase Excursion Fare** (APEX); specials advertised in newspapers may be cheaper, but have more restrictions and fewer available seats. APEX fares provide you with confirmed reservations and allow "open-jaw" tickets (landing in and returning from different cities). Generally, reservations must be made seven to 21 days in advance, with seven- to 14-day minimum and up to 90-day maximum stay limits, and hefty cancellation and change penalties (fees rise in summer). Book APEX fares early during peak seasons. Look into flights to less-popular destinations or on smaller carriers. Even if you pay an airline's lowest published fare, you may waste hundreds of dollars. For the adventurous or the bargain-hungry, there are other, perhaps more inconvenient or time-consuming options, but before shopping around it is a good idea to find out the average commercial price in order to measure just how great a "bargain" you are being offered.

New Zealand airlines may be a good bet for competitive prices. Approximate fares from Los Angeles to Auckland range from $1900-2000, depending on the season; from Honolulu, $1400-1500. To obtain discounted fares, you should book at least 14 days in advance. Certain perks can be had from flying a Kiwi airline, as well. **Air New Zealand,** for example, offers discounted domestic air passes with the purchase of your ticket to New Zealand.

TICKET CONSOLIDATORS

Ticket consolidators resell unsold tickets on commercial and charter airlines at unpublished fares. The consolidator market is by and large international; domestic flights, if they do exist, are typically for cross-country flights. Consolidator flights are the best deals if you are traveling: on short notice (you bypass advance purchase requirements, since you aren't tangled in airline bureaucracy); on a high-priced trip; to an offbeat destination; or in the peak season, when published fares are jacked way up. Fares sold by consolidators are generally much cheaper; a 30-40% price reduction is not uncommon. There are rarely age constraints or stay limitations, but unlike tickets bought through an airline, you won't be able to use your tickets on another flight if you miss yours, and you will have to go back to the consolidator to get a refund, rather than the airline. Keep in mind that these tickets are often for coach seats on connecting (not direct) flights on foreign airlines, and that frequent-flyer miles may not be credited. Decide what you can and can't live with before shopping.

NOW Voyager, (primarily a courier company; see below), does consolidation with reliability which rivals that of most charter companies (97% of customers get on flights the first time) and prices which are considerably lower. NOW sells tickets over the internet at its web page (http://www.nowvoyagertravel.com).

Not all consolidators deal with the general public; many only sell tickets through travel agents. **Bucket shops** are retail agencies that specialize in getting cheap tickets. Although ticket prices are marked up slightly, bucket shops generally have access to a larger market than would be available to the public and can also get tickets from wholesale consolidators. Generally, a dealer specializing in travel to the country of your destination will provide more options and cheaper tickets. The **Association of Special Fares Agents (ASFA)** maintains a database of specialized dealers fro particular regions (http://www.ntsltd.com/asfa). Look for bucket shops' tiny ads in the travel section of weekend papers; in the U.S., the Sunday *New York Times* is a good source. In Australia, these ads often pop up in the *Sydney Times*. Kelly Monaghan's *Consolidators: Air Travel's Bargain Basement* (US$8 plus $3.50 shipping) from the Intrepid Traveler, P.O. Box 438, New York, NY 10034 (email info@intrepidtraveler.com), is an invaluable source for more information and lists of consolidators by location and destination.

Be a smart shopper; check out the competition. Among the many reputable and trustworthy companies are, unfortunately, some shady wheeler-dealers. Contact the local Better Business Bureau to find out how long the company has been in business and its track record. Although not necessary, it is preferable to deal with consolidators close to home so you can visit in person, if necessary. Ask to receive your tickets as quickly as possible so you have time to fix any problems. Get the company's policy in writing; insist on a **receipt** that gives full details about the tickets, refunds, and restrictions, and record who you talked to and when. It may be worth paying with a credit card (despite the 2-5% fee) so you can stop payment if you never receive your tickets. Beware the "bait and switch" gag: sketchy firms will advertise a super-low fare and then tell a caller that it has been sold. Although this is a viable excuse, if they can't offer you a price near the advertised fare on *any* date, it may be a scam to lure in customers. Also ask about accommodations and car rental discounts; some consolidators have fingers in many pies.

For destinations **worldwide,** try **Airfare Busters,** with offices in Washington, D.C. (tel. (202) 776-0478), Boca Raton, FL (tel. (561) 994-9590), and Houston, TX (tel. (800) 232-8783); **Pennsylvania Travel,** Paoli, PA (tel. (800) 331-0947); **Cheap Tickets,** with offices in Los Angeles, CA, San Francisco, CA, Honolulu, HI, Seattle, WA, and New York, NY (tel. (800) 377-1000); or **Moment's Notice,** 7301 New Utrecht Ave, Brooklyn, NY (tel. (718) 234-6295; fax 234-6450; http://www.momentsnotice.com) offers air tickets, tours, and hotels; US$25 annual fee. **NOW Voyager,** 74 Varick St. #307, New York, NY 10013 (tel. (212) 431-1616; fax 334-5243; email info@nowvoyagertravel.com; http://www.nowvoyagertravel.com), acts as a consolidator and books discounted international flights, mostly from New York, as well as courier flights, for a registration fee of US$50. For a processing fee, depending on the number of travelers and the itinerary, **Travel Avenue,** Chicago, IL (tel. (800) 333-3335; fax (312) 876-1254; http://www.travelavenue.com), will search for the lowest international airfare available, including consolidated prices, and will even give you a 5% rebate on fares over US$350.

ONCE THERE

In most towns, all cities, and many airports, you should watch for the green "i" symbol denoting one of the 81 independently owned and operated **Visitor's Information Network (VIN)** tourist offices throughout New Zealand. Coordinated by the New Zealand Tourism Board, these offices are incredibly useful and will help plan every aspect of your travel from A-to-Z, including booking accommodations, transport, and activities. You can also tune into **88.2 FM,** the 24-hour tourist radio station.

■ Getting Around

Transportation in New Zealand is remarkably easy for tourists, particularly in high season, when local shuttles and backpacker buses come out in full force to supplement the main bus lines. **Booking ahead** will often get you significant fare reductions as well as a guaranteed seat. **Luggage storage** is available at most backpackers; many bus stations and tourist offices will also informally keep your belongings behind the counter for the day. Not all places secure their storage areas, however, so this is not a good option for storing valuables. Transportation can be booked at tourist offices and travel agencies, as well as at many backpackers.

BY PLANE

The two major domestic airlines, **Air New Zealand** (toll-free reservation tel. (0800) 737 000) and **Ansett New Zealand** (toll-free reservation tel. (0800) 267 388), provide connections between major towns and cities. Air New Zealand covers the country comprehensively; a number of smaller companies are also grouped under Air New Zealand Link. "Flightseeing" is another option. Smaller local companies in each area provide beautiful views from the air for rates competitive to those for boat or ferry, starting at NZ$90. See the **Sights and Activities** listings in each town for more details.

DISCOUNTED FARES You can buy special tourist and student/YHA air passes, packages of flight coupons that can be used with a certain degree of flexibility throughout your stay. (For Air New Zealand, you must buy air passes from outside New Zealand in conjunction with an incoming Air New Zealand ticket. Air New Zealand's **Visit New Zealand Passes** allow travel within New Zealand; **G'day Passes,** in conjunction with Ansett, allow travel within New Zealand and Australia and between the two countries.) Inside the country, ask about the special economy fares available; some Air New Zealand flights feature Thrifty (up to 30% off standard economy fare), Super Thrifty (up to 40%), and Real Deal (up to 50%) fares, while some Ansett New Zealand flights feature Saver Plus (10%), Good Buy (30%), Good Buy Special (40%), Good Buy Plus (50%) fares (restrictions apply). To get in on these deals, book as far in advance as possible.

BY TRAIN

A few train routes run between major cities and towns, but skip over almost everywhere else. Although you can't explore, you can see beautiful scenery that would be missed in a car. Train fares are also generally more expensive than bus. **TranzRail** (toll-free reservation tel. (0800) 802 802, daily 7am-9pm) offers **special discounted fares:** for children aged four to 14 (40% off); travelers over 60 (30%); YHA members (30%); ISIC cardholders (20%); and those taking day excursions (30%). Minimum fare is $14 (children $7). Some trains have a backpackers car with less luxurious seating, smaller windows, and cheaper fares. This is a great way to meet your fellow travelers. Economy fares are offered regularly for travel at certain times of day, as well. Reserve all discounted fares well in advance, especially in high season.

BY BUS

Many budget travelers, especially backpackers, choose the bus (or coach, as the Kiwis say) as their transport of choice, especially in more remote areas. Remember that bus schedules can be somewhat flexible, and many buses will leave if you are not at the stop when they arrive. Always show up **15 minutes early,** and do not be alarmed if buses are 20 to 40 minutes late. Visitors centers will have the most up-to-date information about bus schedules and fares, and many offer discounts if fares are booked through them. **InterCity** (toll-free reservation tel. (0800) 731 711), the major bus line, covers both islands extensively. **Newmans** (tel. (07) 578 8103), an InterCity subsidiary, is another large bus company. All buses can be pre-booked by phone, at Travel Centres, or at most visitors centers. In addition, cyclists will be happy to know that buses carry **bikes** for a nominal fee. **Northliner Express** (tel. (09) 307 5873) runs north of Auckland and offers a 30% discount for YHA members.

BY SHUTTLE Local shuttle buses are your best bet for beating the price offered by main bus lines while getting to the same places. These services use vans and often travel to smaller towns not serviced by the main coach lines. However, there is a high turnover in shuttle companies and they can be less reliable and comfortable. Local visitors centers will often have current info on prices and schedules and can do bookings. During winter and in more remote locations, make sure to call ahead.

DISCOUNTED FARES YHA and **VIP** membership offer you 30% off fares for InterCity and Newmans; **ISIC** cards get you a a 30% discount on Newmans and a 20% discount on InterCity. **Children** over four and under 16 travel for 40% off the full economy adult fare on major bus companies. A limited number of Saver (30%) and Super Saver (50%) fares on each bus are also available by **booking early** (at least 5 days prior to travel, with tickets purchased no later than 2 days prior to travel). All discounts are valid only on fares $20 or more. In addition, **Travelpass New Zealand,** P.O. Box 26601, Epsom, Auckland (tel. (09) 357 8400; fax (09) 913 6121), offers **3 in 1 Travelpasses** that combine discounted travel on InterCity, TranzScenic, and the Interislander Ferry. **4 in 1 Travelpasses** add a domestic flight on Ansett New Zealand.

BACKPACKER BUSES In addition to the standard bus companies, a few cater specifically to **backpackers.** These tours have planned itineraries and always stop for the night at prearranged destinations. Generally, if you come to a place that particularly grabs you, you can separate from the bus and stick around town. As each company has a fairly constant stream of buses running the same routes, you can join up with a new touring group when you're ready to move on again. The trade-off is fundamental: you lose the spontaneity that so many backpackers treasure; in return, you meet a busload of starry-eyed young travelers and you benefit from the knowledgeable tour guides. Accommodations are pre-booked, but are not included in the overall price; food is also at your own cost. Many backpacker buses also offer sweet discounts on recreational activities along the route, such as kayak rentals and guided tours. Reservations must be made at least a couple of days ahead of time and confirmed, especially in high season. Some popular backpacker buses include **Kiwi Experience** (tel.

(09) 366 9830; fax 366 1374; open daily 8am-8pm) and **Magic Travellers Network** (tel. (09) 358 5600; open daily 7am-7pm). Kiwi Experience and Magic Travellers offer 5% off fares for HI-YHA members.

BY CAR

CAR RENTAL Avis (tel. in Auckland (09) 526 2847, outside Auckland (0800) 655 111; http://www.avis.com/), **Budget** (tel. (0800) 652 227; http://www.budgetrentacar.com/), and **Hertz** (tel. (0800) 654 321; http://www.hertz.com) are the major **car rental** operators, and offer their services in all main cities and towns. (To find Avis, Budget, and Hertz numbers for your home country, see **RV and Camper Rentals,** p. 38.) Most agencies rent to those age 21 and over, although some agencies require drivers to be 25. Rates vary according to season, as well as duration of rental and condition of car, and generally include automobile insurance and GST. (American Express cardholders, please note that American Express does **not** cover the required Collision and Damage Waiver in New Zealand or Australia, as it does automatically in most other countries.) Expect to pay at least NZ$50 a day for a month's rental from one of these companies; for cars of better condition and make, the price may skyrocket to as high as NZ$130 per day. Smaller operators often offer eye-poppingly low fares, but be cautious—look carefully into the reliability and reputation of the company before committing.

BUY-BACKS Buying a car, then selling it upon departure, may be a smart option for longer stays. Buy-back outlets, such as the **New Zealand Guaranteed Buy-Back Vehicle Associates,** 825 Dominion Rd., Mt. Roskill, Auckland (tel. (09) 620 6587), sell cars specifically for this purpose. Prices range from NZ$3000-7000; you must keep the car for a minimum of a month. At the end of your stay, the buy-back outlet buys back the vehicle minus the depreciation rate.

If you prefer to strike out on your own car-buying spree, Auckland is definitely a hot spot for the best car deals: check out one of its car auctions or the used car section of *The New Zealand Herald* (especially on Wednesdays). The *Trade and Exchange,* another good place to look, comes out on Monday and Thursday.

A car must have a **V.I.C.** (vehicle inspection certificate, sometimes called a W.O.F.), which ensures that it is road safe. Make sure that your potential car has received one within the past month. They are good for six months and cost $25. A car must be **registered** (six months $82.65; one year $157.75) Whenever there is a change of ownership, a **MR13A form** must be completed by the buyer and seller and turned in at a NZ Post Shop. A **MR13B form** must be completed by the buyer as well ($9.20). Insurance is not necessary but highly recommended, as is membership in the Automobile Association (AA). The latter will get you emergency breakdown service, free service for simple problems, and free towing for more serious ones (one-year membership $85).

Before you buy your car, you should have it inspected. Vehicle Inspection Services can be found in the yellow pages under that heading and will do comprehensive prepurchase checks for $60-80. You may want to check out **car fairs in Auckland;** some are **Oriental Markets,** carpark on Beach Rd. in the Central Business District, open Saturday 9am-noon; **Sell Your Own,** 676 Great South Rd., Manukau (tel. (0800) 735 596), open daily 7am-7pm; **Sell it Yourself,** 50 Wairau Rd., Glenfield (tel. 443 3800), open daily 7am-7pm; **Ellerslie Racecourse** (tel. 810 9212), off the Greenlane Roundabout, open Sunday 9am-noon; and **Manukau City Park and Sell** (tel. 358 5000), open Sunday 8:30am-1pm. **Car auctions** are another option; **Turners Car Auctions,** McNab St., Penrose (tel. 525 1920), sells budget cars at 11:30am on Wednesday, and family cars at 6pm on Thursday. **Hammer Auctions,** 830 Great South Rd., Penrose (tel. 579 2344), sells budget cars on Monday, Wednesday, and Friday.

RULES OF THE ROAD Become familiar with the driving laws of the land before you set out; *The Road Code of New Zealand* ($14.95), available at AA offices (see below) and bookstores tells you all you need to know. **Speed limits** are strictly enforced; speed cameras are even set up at the traffic lights of many large towns to catch lead-footed offenders. **Drunk driving laws** are serious business in New Zealand and are strictly enforced. Americans, join your Kiwi companions and drive on the **left hand side** of the road; many accidents arise from tourists who don't give themselves some extra practice driving time to adjust before heading out. **Petrol,** the New Zealand equivalent of what Americans call gas, costs approximately NZ$1 per liter; it can run you an easy NZ$15-20 per day. State highways are abbreviated **SH; **SH2 is in the process of being renamed the Pacific Coast Highway. Members of world-wide automobile associations can enjoy the reciprocal agreement with the **New Zealand Automobile Association (AA)** (tel. (0800) 500 222) to obtain free maps and other services from AA offices in New Zealand. For assistance on the road, The New Zealand **AA hotline** (tel. (0900) 332 22) costs $1 per minute.

BY THUMB

> *Let's Go* strongly urges you to seriously consider the risks before you choose to hitch. Although we try to report accurately on the availability of hitching opportunities in each area, we do not recommend hitching as a necessarily safe means of transportation and none of the details presented here are intended to do so.

Some visitors to New Zealand, particularly backpackers, rely on hitchhiking as their primary mode of transportation, and express satisfaction with its safety and convenience. Others, however, report that hitchhiking is not as safe as it used to be, especially for women traveling alone. A man and a woman are a safer combination; two men will have a harder time finding a ride. No matter how safe or friendly New Zealanders may be, you should always think seriously before trusting your life to a stranger, as you risk suffering from an accident, theft, assault, sexual harassment, or worse. Exercise caution when hitchhiking, particularly women traveling alone: avoid getting into the back of a two-door car; when waiting for a ride, stand in a well-lit, public place; avoid hitchhiking at night; avoid hitchhiking alone. Trust your instincts—if you ever feel unsafe or threatened, do not hesitate to firmly but politely ask to be let off.

Hitching is often reported to be easiest just beyond the end of a town's residential area, but before the open highway. Choose a spot on the side of the road with ample space for a car to pull over. Don't laze by the side of the road; walk backwards in the direction of traffic with your thumb out. Keep your destination secret until after you've found out where a prospective driver is headed; that way, if the driver looks sketchy and you don't want to go with him, you can always bluff and say otherwise. Do not put your backpack in the trunk; you might not get it back.

■ Accommodations

The accommodations and restaurant listings in the book are ranked according to our researchers' assessments. The better accommodations are listed first, and the last entries, while acceptable, may not be the best places to stay a night. Unless we state otherwise, you can expect that every establishment has free hot showers and free linen. Most offer laundry for a standard fee ($1-3), but do not always have automatic dryers. When there is a linen charge, it is usually charged once per stay. **Central heating** is **not** a standard feature in New Zealand, and will be listed wherever found. In our listings, a **twin** contains two single beds; a **double,** one double bed. **Checking in** at hostels in New Zealand can be a remarkably laid-back process; after hours, you may be expected to sign in on a self-check blackboard, or you may be allowed to simply check the listings to see which beds are open and plunk yourself down for the night, making payment in the morning. **Seasonal fares** are flexible, as well. The prices we quote are given by each establishment and should hold true, but some accommodations vary fares at their own discretion. Budget-conscious bedders may also benefit from the variety of **accommodation networks** in New Zealand. Those who plan on doing a lot of camping, for example, may choose to join a network like the **Top 10 Holiday Parks** (membership fee $15 for 2yr.) to reap consistent discounts. **Booking ahead** is a must in high season (usually summer) and major holidays.

BACKPACKERS (HOSTELS)

For tight budgets and those lonesome traveling blues, backpackers (the Kiwi term for "hostel") can't be beat. Backpackers are generally dorm-style accommodations, in large, co-ed or single-sex (especially common in YHA backpackers) rooms with bunk beds, although some backpackers do have private rooms for families and couples. They frequently offer bike rentals, shuttle bus connections, and storage areas; most have central kitchens and laundry facilities. Many are also happy to book local activities. Fees range from NZ$14-20 per night for a dorm-style room. When listing backpackers, we assume that all have no lockout, no curfew, and no key deposit, unless otherwise noted.

Hostels associated with one of the large hostel associations (HI-YHA, VIP, etc.) often have lower rates for members. If you have Internet access, check out the **Internet Guide to Hostelling** (http://hostels.com), which includes hostels from around the world in addition to oodles of info about hosteling and backpacking worldwide. The following are the major hostel networks in New Zealand:

Budget Backpacker Hostels (email bakpak@chch.planet.org; http://www.back-pack.co.nz) is a brochure that claims to include over 80% of the nation's independent backpackers. After surveying guests of all BBH backpackers, BBH publishes a free guide of backpackers listings with satisfaction ratings, available at the Auckland and Christchurch airports, Visitor Information Network offices, participating backpackers, or via email (bakpak@chch.planet.org). In addition, all BBH establishments that recognize discount cards (YHA, VIP, etc.) give equal discounts to those

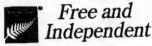

ESSENTIALS

carrying the BBH guide. Average overnight fee NZ$13-14. Advance reservations recommended, especially in high season. Book directly to the backpackers.

Hostelling International-Youth Hostels Association of New Zealand (HI-YHANZ): National Office: P.O. Box 436, 10 Gloucester St., Christchurch (tel. (03) 379 9970; fax (03) 365 4476; email info@yha.org.nz; http://www.iyhf.org/); **National Reservations Centre:** P.O. Box 68 149, Auckland (tel. (09) 309 2802; fax 373 5083; email yhaakbg@yha.org.nz; http://www.yha.org.nz). Because YHANZ is linked to the HI network, your **HI card** from home is recognized at all YHANZ backpackers and at most other establishments that give discounts for YHA membership. Annual membership fee NZ$24. Average overnight fee NZ$14-20. HI-YHA backpackers are inspected annually for quality and service standards; look in the HI-YHANZ Accommodation Guide to see a hostel's quality rating. The privately owned YHA Associate hostels, on the other hand, meet YHA standards, but offer the same rate to all guests. Reservations can be made via the **International Booking Network (IBN),** a computerized system that allows you to make hostel reservations from overseas. You must book at least 14 days in advance, however, and your reservations are accompanied by a NZ$5 booking fee. HI and YHA cards can be bought at most travel agencies (see p. 25), YHA hostels, or HI offices. For more info about HI membership in Canada, call (613) 237-7884 or fax 237-7868; in the U.S., call (202) 783-6161; fax 783-6171; email hiayhserv@hiayh.org; http://www.hiayh.org.

VIP Backpackers Resorts, Like HI-YHA cards, a VIP card obtains discounts from VIP backpackers and other establishments. Annual membership fee NZ$30. Average overnight fee NZ$10-15. Book directly to backpackers (have credit card handy). VIP cards can be obtained from many travel agencies (see p. 25) or VIP backpackers. In New Zealand, contact VIP Backpackers Resorts (NZ), P.O. Box 80021, Greenbay, Auckland (tel. (09) 827 6016; fax 827 6016).

MOTOR PARKS AND CAMPS (HOLIDAY PARKS)

Known as holiday parks, these accommodations complexes vary in size from sprawling compounds to grassy plots, all offering a range of options for the budget traveler. Motor parks and camps usually feature tent sites (from $10) and caravan (RV or camper) sites (from $20); **powerpoints** are what Kiwis call on-site power hook-ups. Some also feature on-site caravans, where you rent a caravan (often with kitchen, sometimes with toilet) nightly. Most establishments charge for tent and caravan sites **per person.** Many also feature cabins or flats with singles (from $20), doubles (from $30), and bunk rooms (from $15), offering varying amenities (kitchens, linens, etc.).

BED AND BREAKFASTS (B&BS)

For a refreshing alternative to impersonal hotel rooms, B&Bs (private homes with rooms available to travelers) can refresh the travel-weary with their homespun hospitality. On the other hand, many B&Bs have steeper prices (doubles from $60) and may not provide phones or private bathrooms. Families may want to look elsewhere, as well, because most B&Bs discourage visits by children under 15.

HOMESTAYS AND FARMSTAYS

An intensely memorable experience, homestays and farmstays in an area are often arranged through the nearest town's tourist office, although some companies also book homestays and farmstays. You stay at a real working farm or orchard, often alone or with a few other guests. The price starts around $100 per person and includes participation in farm activities (more available in winter) and fresh, home-cooked meals. **Rural Tours "Stay in a Country Home" Farmstays,** central booking office at 92 Victoria St., Cambridge (tel. 827 8055; fax 827 7154; email stay@rural-tours.co.nz), books farmstays throughout New Zealand. **American International Homestays,** P.O. Box 1754, Nederland, CO 80466 (tel. (303) 642-3088 or (800) 876-2048; fax (303) 642 3365; email ash@igc.apc.org; www.commerce.com/homestays), has lodgings with host families in New Zealand and all over the world. Many tourist offices book homestays and farmstays in the region, as well.

LONGER STAYS

If you've come in search of employment, go to it—getting a job requires both persistence and savvy. For more info, see p. 19. Once you've got yourself a source of funds, you'll want to open a bank account to store the results in; see **Money**, p. 10, for more details. **Housing** will be the next pressing concern. Look in the daily paper for rental listings or check out real estate agencies who will arrange rentals or leases for you. You might also try college campus noticeboards. Some work programs will help with job placement and housing (see **Volunteering**, p. 20). Obtain a copy of the Residential Tenancies Act 1988 (available from Tenancy Services, the Ministry of Housing) to learn about your tenant rights and obligations in New Zealand. Be sure to check with the nearest New Zealand embassy or consulate to find out about visa, residency, and taxation regulations that could easily thwart your best-laid plans.

Home exchange offers the traveler with a home the opportunity to live like a native, and to dramatically cut down on accommodation fees—usually only an administrative fee is paid to the matching service. Once the introductions are made, the choice is left to the two hopeful partners. Most companies have pictures of member's homes and info about the owners (some will even ask for your photo). Check out the exchange companies below:

Intervac U.S., P.O. Box 590504, San Francisco, CA 94159 (tel. 800 756 HOME; fax (415) 435 7440; email IntervacUS@aol.com). Part of a worldwide home-exchange network. Publishes five catalogs per year. Members contact each other directly. US$78 gets you two of the company's catalogs and inclusion of your own listing in one, plus access to web listings.

The Invented City: International Home Exchange, 41 Sutter St., Suite 1090, San Francisco, CA 94104 (tel. (800) 788-CITY in the U.S. or (415) 252-1141 elsewhere; fax (415) 252-1171; email invented@pacbell.net; http://www.invented-city.com). Domestic and international home exchange agency. Annual membership and access to home-exchange database US$75.

▓ Camping and the Outdoors

TRAMPING IN NEW ZEALAND

With all the national parks, forest parks, scenic reserves, and other assorted protected areas in New Zealand, it is no suprise that the opportunities for overnight wilderness excursions are almost limitless. Backpacking, trekking, bushwalking: whatever you call it back home, it's called **tramping** in New Zealand. There are hundreds of well-maintained tracks scattered all over New Zealand, and copious opportunities for route-finding in remote undeveloped wilderness areas. **Department of Conservation (DOC)** offices are the premier and most well-stocked sources of information for any and all tracks and tramps. Offices are all over New Zealand and near virtually all protected wilderness areas; staff will know all about current track conditions and weather forecasts and can offer plenty of advice. For most tracks, the DOC produces a $1 brochure with a basic but adequate **map** and track information. Detailed topographic maps are also available ($12).

HUTS AND CAMPING New Zealand's tracks are home to a well-developed **hut system.** Essentially backcountry cabins offering overnight indoor accommodation, they can be found on virtually every developed track in New Zealand. Huts are classified and priced according to the facilities available. **Hut tickets** ($4) are available at all DOC offices and usually from park rangers. Nicer huts cost two tickets ($8), and will have mattresses, water, toilets, and occasionally fireplaces, stoves, or gas cookers. More basic huts are one ticket ($4) and may only have water and toilets. For those planning extensive tramping, an **Annual Hut Pass** can be purchased for $65. Children under age 12 can stay in the huts for free, and ages 12-17 are half-price. This hut system does not apply in peak season to any of the **Great Walks.** Huts provide an excellent opportunity for meeting fellow trampers, provide shelter from extreme weather, and make it unnecessary to carry the extra weight of a tent. However, those who prefer alternate accommodation can **camp** on almost all tracks. There is usually a small charge for camping near huts; where permitted, camping is free near the track.

THE GREAT WALKS

New Zealand's most spectacular and popular tramps are classified as **Great Walks** and are administered under a separate bureaucracy. Eight tramps and one canoe trip operate under this separate system. The tracks are well maintained and camping facilities are a step above those on other backcountry tracks. Huts often have cooking facilities, flush toilets, gas lighting, and a helpful DOC warden on hand. Normal hut tickets do not apply; Great Walks Passes must be purchased (huts $6-30; campsites $6-9). Camping is not allowed outside of designated sites on Great Walks. The **Milford** and **Routeburn** tracks must be **reserved** at least a year ahead.

Because of their beauty and natural wonder, hiking these tracks will not necessarily be a remote wilderness experience. The vast majority of trampers on Great Walks are foreign travelers; there are surprisingly few Kiwis. Although you might not be roughing it completely, several of the tramps are strenuous and can be dangerous if you are not properly equipped.

The list below briefly describes and ranks the Great Walks, excluding the **Whanganui Journey** (see p. 160), a 4-5 day canoe or kayak trip down the Whanganui River in Whanganui National Park. Keep in mind that these rankings are subjective and your opinion may differ.

The Milford Track: A four-day tramp through two spectacular glacial valleys and over a mountain pass, dubbed "the finest walk in the world." Located in the northern section of Fiordland National Park in the South Island, the track offers incredible views of mountains, glaciers, and countless waterfalls cascading down sheer rock faces, including the 580m Sutherland Falls, the highest in New Zealand. Although **reservations are required** at least one month and often a year in advance and hiking the track is expensive ($180), it is absolutely worth the planning and money required (see p. 322).

Tongariro Northern Circuit: A three-to-four day tramp winding between and around the three volcanoes of Tongariro National Park in central North Island. The track is almost entirely above the tree line, offering never-ending views of the wild and unique volcanic formations, moon slopes, and technicolor lakes. The huts are all in incredible locations. The **Tongariro Crossing**, "the finest one-day walk in New Zealand," is part of the circuit (see p. 174).

Routeburn Track: A two-to-three day tramp with outstanding alpine scenery. Running between Fiordland and Mt. Aspiring National Park, the track courses high along the side of a glacial valley and over a mountain pass. Alpine lakes, mountain top vistas; and numerous waterfalls are the highlights of the track (see p. 325). **Reservations are required.**

The Heaphy Track: A four-to-five day tramp, this is the longest Great Walk at 77km. Running from east-to-west through Kahurangi National Park in northern South Island, this track boasts greater variety than any other Great Walk, passing through beech forest, vast open expanses of alpine meadows, surreal limestone topography, and dense coastal rainforest. Its length and difficult access make it one of the least-crowded Great Walks (see p. 286).

The Kepler Track: A three-to-four day tramp around and over a mountain range on the shores of Lake Te Anau in Fiordland National Park. The views of the lake and mountains from the open tussockland on the mountain tops are excellent but constitute only about a quarter of the track. The track's easy accessibility and lower cost are definite advantages (see p. 326).

The Abel Tasman Coast Track: A three-to-four day tramp along the coast and beaches of Abel Tasman National Park. This is by far the most popular and crowded of the Great Walks. With golden beaches and turquoise ocean views it is extremely beautiful, but the sheer number of people can spoil the walk, especially from Christmas until the beginning of February (see p. 282).

The Lake Waikaremoana Track: A three-to-four day tramp around Lake Waikaremoana in Te Urewera National Park on the North Island. Highlights of the track include bluff-top views of the lake, lots of virgin forest teeming with bird life, and excellent fishing. The track can be difficult to access without private transportation (see p. 210).

The Rakiura Track: A two-to-three day tramp through the rainforest on Stewart Island winding through mostly regenerating rainforest. It is by far the least hiked of the Great Walks, making it an excellent choice for those seeking a respite from more crowded tracks (see p. 354).

Other Recommended Tramps
There are plenty of other tramps in New Zealand that rival even the Great Walks for natural splendor and will typically have fewer people. These include:

Mt. Taranaki Round-the-Mountain Track, a 55km, 4-day tramp in Egmont National Park that traverses the upper slopes of the volcano, affording excellent views of the surrounding farmland and coast (see p. 150).
Rees-Dart Track: A 72km 4-5 day tramp up a river valley, over a pass, and out another valley. Spectacular alpine scenery with a possible one-day side trip to Cascade Saddle, from which Mt. Aspiring and its glaciers can be seen. Located mostly in Mt. Aspiring National Park (see p. 321).
Greenstone/Caples Tracks: Two separate 2-3 day tracks running through forested mountain valleys south of the Routeburn Track, outside of Fiordland National Park (see p. 321).

CAMPING AND HIKING EQUIPMENT

Purchase equipment before you leave, so you know exactly what you have and how much it weighs. Be prepared for a detailed inspection of all equipment by customs; due to fear of invasions, they may even clean your tent for you. If you want to buy equipment while in New Zealand, check at hostels or used camping stores to find low prices. Spend some time examining catalogs and talking to knowledgeable salespeople to find sturdy, light, reasonably priced goods. Most good **sleeping bags** are rated by "season," or the lowest outdoor temperature at which they will keep you warm. "Summer" means 30-40°F (-1° to 4°C), "three-season" 20°F (-7°C), and "four-season" or "winter" below 0°F (-18°C). Sleeping bags are made of either down or synthetic material (which is cheaper, heavier, more durable, and warmer when wet). Prices vary, but can range from US$65-100 for a summer synthetic to $250-550 for a good down winter bag. **Sleeping bag pads,** including foam pads (from $15) and air mattresses ($25-50), cushion your back and neck and insulate you from the ground. Another good alternative is the **Therm-A-Rest,** part-foam and part-air mattress.

The best **tents** set up quickly; you'll want stakes to survive the weather. Low-profile dome tents are the best all-around. Tent sizes can be somewhat misleading: two people can fit in a two-person tent, but will enjoy life more in a four-person. Good two-person tents start at $150, four-person tents at $400. Seal the seams of your tent with waterproofer, and make sure it has a rain fly. If you intend to do a lot of hiking, you should have a frame backpack. **Internal-frame backpacks** mold better to your back, keep a lower center of gravity, and can flex adequately to allow you to bend and maneuver as needed. **External-frame backpacks** are more comfortable for long hikes over even terrain, since they keep the weight higher and distribute it more evenly. Whichever you choose, make sure your pack has a strong, padded **hip belt.** Any serious backpacking requires a pack of at least 4000 cubic inches. Allow an additional 500 cubic inches for your sleeping bag in internal-frame packs. Sturdy backpacks cost anywhere from $150-500. This is one area where it doesn't pay to economize, so get the best quality you can afford. (For additional information, see p. 23.)

Be sure to wear **hiking boots** with ankle support appropriate for the terrain you are hiking. Your boots should fit snugly and comfortably over one or two wool socks and a thin liner sock. Break in boots *before* hiking. **Rain gear** is more effective in two pieces, a top and pants, rather than a poncho. **Warm layers of clothing** are always important, regardless of the season. **Synthetics**, like polypropylene socks and long underwear, will keep you warm even when wet. When camping in autumn, winter, or spring, bring along a **"space blanket,"** which helps retain body heat and doubles as a groundcloth ($5-15). Plastic **canteens** or **water bottles** keep water cooler than metal ones, and are virtually shatter- and leak-proof. Large, collapsible **water sacks** will significantly improve your lot in primitive campgrounds and weigh practically nothing when empty, though they can get bulky. Bring **water-purification tablets** for when you can't boil water. Although most campgrounds provide campfire sites, you may want to bring a small **metal grate** or grill of your own. In places that forbid fires, you'll need a **camp stove.** The classic Coleman starts at about $30. Other necessities include: a first aid kit, Swiss army knife, insect repellent, calamine lotion, high energy food, and waterproof matches or a lighter. A battery-operated lantern, plastic groundcloth, nylon tarp, waterproof backpack cover, and a "stuff sack," a plastic bag to keep your sleeping bag dry, are also useful items.

WILDERNESS AND SAFETY CONCERNS

Stay warm, stay dry, and **stay hydrated.** The vast majority of life-threatening wilderness problems stem from failure to follow this advice. On any hike, however brief, you should pack enough equipment to keep you alive should disaster befall. Always fill out the **intentions form** at the nearest DOC office before undertaking a hike; also let someone know when and where you are tramping, whether it's a newfound friend, your backpackers, or a local hiking organization. Always get updates on the latest **weather forecasts** from the local **DOC,** which can also help advise you on what walks and hikes are appropriate. Do not try hikes beyond your ability and experience—you could endanger your life. See **Health,** p. 14, for info about outdoor ailments such as giardia and insects. A good guide to outdoor survival is *How to Stay Alive in the Woods,* by Bradford Angier (Macmillan, US$8).

Be aware of insects in wet or forested areas. **Mosquitoes** are most active in the summer from dusk to dawn; the ever-present and ever-annoying **sandflies** make their home in bushy and grassy areas, and are especially populous in the southern parts of the South Island (see p. 323). To guard against both, wear long pants (tucked into socks) and long sleeves, buy a bednet for camping, and use insect repellent. Soak or spray your gear with permethrin, which is licensed in the U.S. for use on clothing. Natural repellents can also be useful: taking vitamin B-12 pills regularly can eventually make you smelly to insects, as can garlic pills. Still, be sure to supplement your vitamins with repellent. Calamine lotion or topical cortisones (like Cortaid) may stop insect bites from itching, as can a bath with a half-cup of baking soda or oatmeal. **Ticks** are responsible for Lyme and other diseases. Brush off ticks periodically when walking, using a fine-toothed comb on your neck and scalp. Do not try to remove ticks by burning them or coating them with nail polish remover or petroleum jelly.

Pay attention to the skies when hiking; weather patterns can change instantly, especially in the more volatile mountainous areas. If the weather turns nasty on a day hike, turn back immediately. Before undertaking **overnight** or **longer hikes,** in particular, always check with the nearest DOC office about the hike's weather and safety rating, as well as the availability of huts along the track.

USEFUL RESOURCES

Whether novice or expert, you can visit your nearest outdoors equipment store to find publications and general info on camping and adventuring in New Zealand, or contact an outdoors publication company. **Adventurous Traveler Bookstore,** P.O. Box 64769, Burlington, VT 05406-4769 (Canada and U.S. tel. (800) 282-3963; international: tel. (802) 860-6776; http://www.adventuroustraveler.com), sells general adventuring and specifically New Zealand titles, such as *101 Great Tramps in New Zealand,* by Pickering and Smith. Order from catalogues (free in Canada and the U.S.; elsewhere US$2), or right off the website. **The Department of Conservation (DOC),** or **Te Papa Atawhai,** P.O. Box 10420, Wellington (tel. (04) 471 0726; fax 471 1082), has the low-down on the seasonal availability and safety of hikes, the regulations and practicalities of adventuring in New Zealand, maps, and more. **The Mountaineers Books,** 1001 SW Klickitat Way, #201, Seattle, WA 98134 (tel. (800) 553-4453 or (206) 223-6303; fax 223-6306; email mbooks@mountaineers.org), has many titles on hiking (the *100 Hikes* series), mountaineering, and conservation.

For **topographical maps** of New Zealand contact **Terralink New Zealand,** 32 Goodshed Rd. (Private Bag 903), Upper Hutt, New Zealand (tel. (04) 527 7019; fax 527 7246; email mapcentre@terralink.co.nz). Once there, you can buy topographical maps from the local DOC office.

RVS AND CAMPERS

Traveling with a **recreational vehicle (RV)** or **camper** (also known to Kiwis as caravans or campervans) is easy in New Zealand, where motor camps and caravan sites abound. Renting a camper will always be more expensive than camping or hosteling, but the costs compare favorably with the price of renting a car and staying in hotels. Rates vary widely by region, season, and type of camper; expect to pay at least $60-80 per day in low season (about $50-70 more in high season), including insurance. In New Zealand, caravan sites cost around $10 per person per night. Check with your local **Automobile Association** or contact a major international firm, such as Avis, Budget, or Hertz, to arrange camper rentals overseas.

■ Keeping in Touch

MAIL

Mail can be sent internationally through **Poste Restante** (the international phrase for General Delivery) to any town. It's well worth using, generally without any surcharges, and much more reliable than you might think. Mark the envelope "Ben <u>EDELSON</u>, *Poste Restante,* CPO, City, Country." The last name should be capitalized and underlined. The mail will go to the central post office (CPO), unless you specify a specific post office. As a rule, it is best to use the largest post office in the area; sometimes, mail will be sent there regardless of what's on the envelope.

Post offices or post shops are generally open Monday to Friday, 9am to 5pm. When picking up your mail, bring your passport or other ID. If the clerks insist that there is nothing for you, have them check under your first name as well. *Let's Go* lists post offices in the **Practical Information** section for each city and most towns.

To send mail within New Zealand, regular postage costs 40¢. Delivery time is approximately two days between major cities, but FastPost stickers expedite the process. To send mail out of New Zealand, use an AirPost sticker or envelope and it will arrive in six to ten days. Medium-sized AirPost letters cost NZ$1 to Australia and around NZ$2 to Europe, North America, and South Africa. Postcards cost NZ$1.

When possible, it is usually safer and quicker (albeit more expensive) to send mail express or registered than by airmail. **Federal Express** (Canada and U.S. tel. (800) GO-FEDEX/463-3339; Ireland (800) 535 800; U.K. (800) 123 800; U.S. International Customer Service (800) 247-4747) is one reliable and widespread company.

Surface mail is by far the cheapest and slowest way to send mail. It takes two to four months to cross the Pacific—appropriate for sending large quantities of items you won't need to see for a while. It is vital, therefore, to distinguish your airmail from surface mail by explicitly labeling "airmail." When ordering books and materials from abroad, always include one or two **International Reply Coupons (IRCs)**—a way of providing the postage to cover delivery. IRCs should be available from your local post office as well as abroad (US$1.05).

American Express travel offices throughout the world will act as a mail service for cardholders if you contact them in advance. Under this free **"Client Letter Service,"** they will hold mail for 30 days, forward upon request, and accept telegrams. Just like *Poste Restante,* the last name of the person to whom the mail is addressed should be capitalized and underlined. Some offices will offer these services to non-cardholders (such as those who have purchased AmEx Travellers' Cheques), but you must call ahead to make sure. A complete list is available free from AmEx (tel. (800) 528-4800) in the booklet *Traveler's Companion* or online at http://www.americanexpress.com/shared/cgi-bin/tsoserve.cgi?travel/index. Check the **Practical Information** section of the city you plan to visit for AmEx office locations.

TELEPHONES

For **emergency assistance,** dial 111. For national **directory assistance,** dial 018. For the **international operator,** dial 0170. For **international directory assistance,** dial 0172. The North Island has several different area codes (see Appendix). Phone numbers that begin with (025) are **cellular phone** numbers and cost more than a standard local call. Phone rates tend to be highest in the morning, lower in the evening, and lowest on Sunday and late at night. Also, remember **time differences** when you call overseas. New Zealand is 12 hours ahead of Greenwich Mean Time. New Zealand observes **Daylight Savings Time** from the first Sunday in October to the last Sunday in March.

New Zealand's three kinds of **pay phones** are color-coded: card phones are green, credit card phones yellow, and coin phones blue. Coin phones are gradually being phased out, however, so don't count on being able to access them everywhere. **Phone cards** can be bought at tourist offices, backpackers, larger hotels, and certain shops; just look inside any phone card booth to see a listing of the places nearby that sell phone cards. **Overseas calling cards,** sold in NZ$5, $10, $20, and $50 denominations, can be used at any kind of phone. Local calls from pay phones start at 20¢ per minute; non-local calls start at 40¢ per minute (international call $3 per min.).

You can place **international calls** from most telephones. To call direct out of New Zealand, dial the international access code (00) followed by the country code (see back cover), the area code, and the local number. Country and area codes may sometimes be listed with a zero in front (e.g., 03), but after the international access code, drop successive zeros (with an access code of 011, e.g., 011-3). **To call New Zealand from overseas,** you must dial the international access code for the country you are in, (011 from the U.S. and Canada, 0011 from Australia, 00 from the U.K. and Ireland, and 09 from South Africa) followed by New Zealand's country code (64), the area code without a zero, and then the local number.

Although operators place **collect calls,** also called reverse charge calls, for you, it's cheaper to find a pay phone and deposit just enough money to be able to say "call me" and give your number (though some pay phones can't receive calls). Some companies, seizing upon this "call-me-back" concept, have created callback phone services. Under these plans, you call a specified number, ring once, and hang up. The company's computer calls back and gives you a dial tone. You can then make as many calls as you want, at rates about 20-60% lower than you'd pay using credit cards or pay phones. This option is most economical for loquacious travelers, as services may include a US$10-25 minimum billing per month. For information, call **America Tele-Fone** (US tel. (800) 321 5817) and **Telegroup** (tel. (800) 338 0225).

A **calling card** is probably your best and cheapest bet; your local long-distance service provider will have a number for you to dial while traveling (either toll-free or charged as a local call) to connect instantly to an operator in your home country. The calls (plus a small surcharge) are then billed either collect or to the calling card. For more info, call your telephone carrier. Within New Zealand, numbers for international carriers are: AT&T (tel. 0911), MCI (tel. 0912), Sprint (tel. 0918), British Telecom (tel. 0944), Mercury (tel. 094), Telstra (tel. 00, followed by 0961), and Optus Australia (tel. 00, followed by 0996). Other international operator numbers are: Canada (tel. 0919), Ireland (tel. 0953), and Hawaii (tel. 0918). Many phone companies also provide legal and medical advice, as well as exchange rate details.

Budget Backpacker Hostels New Zealand (BBHNZ) has a phone card with a **voice message mailbox** that you can access during your visit. Cardholders are assigned a mailbox number which friends and family can call and leave a message; you can access these messages from any phone in New Zealand. Cards can be purchased at BBHNZ hostels. For more information, contact BBHNZ (tel. (09) 638 6545; email bbh@clear.net.nz; http://www.backpack.co.nz).

MEDIA AND OTHER COMMUNICATION

Daily **newspapers,** including the London *Times,* the Sydney *Herald*, and the *New York Times* are available in major cities and airports. The closest New Zealand comes to a national newspaper is *The New Zealand Herald,* published out of Auckland. **Fax** machines are widespread in New Zealand, particularly in large hotels.

THE INTERNET

Electronic mail (email) is another speedy and attractive option. With a minimum of computer knowledge and a little planning, you can beam messages anywhere for no per-message charges. Most towns in New Zealand have an Internet connection, if not at a cafe or backpackers than at least at the visitors center or library. Per hour rates vary from NZ$5-20; shop around. Set up a web-based account before you leave; some good ones are **Hotmail** (http://www.hotmail.com/), **USANET** (http://www.usa.net), and **Traveltales.com** (http://traveltales.com), geared specifically toward travelers.

New Zealand (Aotearoa)

Situated on the farthest corner of the earth, New Zealand's natural diversity and iso-lated wildness make it an island paradise popular with those in search of adventure amid pristine beauty. The landscape of its two islands features lush rolling hills, tow-ering snow-capped peaks, bubbling geothermal activity, thriving rainforest, and pic-turesque golden beaches, all contained within an area not much larger than the United Kingdom. This array of earthly delights is matched only by the number of ways to take it all in, which include hiking glaciers on the South Island's West Coast, swimming with dolphins off Kaikoura, skiing near Queenstown, black-water rafting in the underground Waitomo Caves, tramping one of the Great Walks, and sea-kayak-ing in the Bay of Islands. While the scenery is perfect for contemplation, the adven-turous prefer to witness it in ways that are anything but reflective. Bungy-jumping is quintessentially Kiwi, and tandem skydiving is immensely popular with those who need reassurance that the laws of gravity are still in effect. As a people, New Zealanders (who refer to themselves as Kiwis) are especially outgoing, helpful, and hospitable. The land's original settlers, the Maori, have a thriving cultural life that con-tinues to mingle with and influence the traditions of later European settlers.

THE PEOPLE

The total population of New Zealand is about 3.6 million, with these inhabitants unevenly distributed across the two islands. About one-third of the total population lives in Auckland, the largest city on the North Island, while the South Island is more sparsely settled. Christianity is the dominant religion, with the Anglican, Presbyterian, and Catholic denominations making the largest showings. Maori denominations of Christianity, such as the Ratana and Ringatu churches, were first developed during the missionary era of the late 19th and early 20th centuries in an effort to synthesize traditional Maori beliefs with the precepts of Christianity.

Caucasians make up the majority racial group of the population, but this domi-nance is offset by considerable minority presence. The British and the Irish are the best-represented of European ethnicities, followed by those of Dutch and German descent. New Zealand Maori count as 15% of the population, making them the largest minority ethnic group. Other Pacific Islanders are the next largest group at 6% of the population, the result of large-scale immigration movements that began in the 1970s. In fact, more non-Maori Polynesians live in the greater Auckland area than anywhere else in the world. Asians are also a fast-growing minority group, comprising 5% of the total population in 1996, an increase of 74% from 1991.

■ Language

The cultural mix of Maori and European is reflected in the language—although English is the dominant spoken tongue, the influx of Maori into day-to-day English parlance is immediately striking. The cross-fertilization between English and Maori is evident in phrases from the greeting "Kia ora!" to the fare-well "Haere ra!" For every city named Christchurch and river named Avon, there's a town called Tauranga and a estuary named Waikareao. Some places are even bestowed with dual names: Mt. Cook is also known as

> *The cross-fertilization between English and Maori is evident in phrases from the greeting "Kia ora!" to the farewell "Haere ra!"*

Aoraki or Aorangi, and Taranaki is a more frequently used alternate for Mt. Egmont and the region surrounding it. (For more info, see p. 151 and p. 157.) A more thorough list-ing of both Kiwi English and Maori words and phrases can be found in the **Kiwi**

NEW ZEALAND

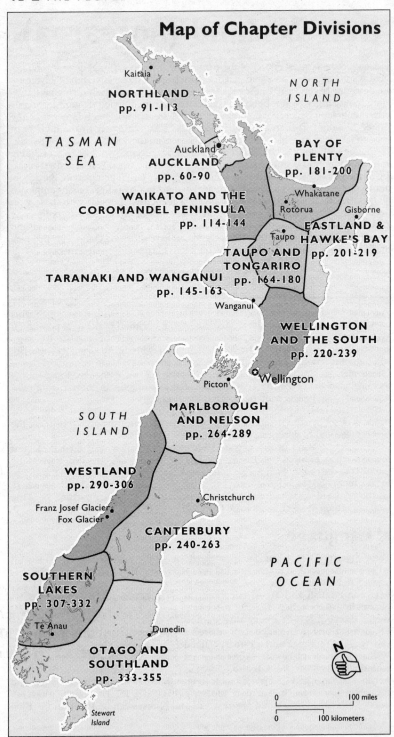

Map of Chapter Divisions

NORTH ISLAND

TASMAN SEA

Kaitaia

NORTHLAND
pp. 91-113

BAY OF PLENTY
pp. 181-200

Auckland
AUCKLAND
pp. 60-90

Whakatane

WAIKATO AND THE COROMANDEL PENINSULA
pp. 114-144

Rotorua

Gisborne

EASTLAND & HAWKE'S BAY
pp. 201-219

Taupo

TAUPO AND TONGARIRO
pp. 164-180

TARANAKI AND WANGANUI
pp. 145-163

Wanganui

WELLINGTON AND THE SOUTH
pp. 220-239

Picton

Wellington

SOUTH ISLAND

MARLBOROUGH AND NELSON
pp. 264-289

WESTLAND
pp. 290-306

Christchurch

Franz Josef Glacier
Fox Glacier

CANTERBURY
pp. 240-263

PACIFIC OCEAN

SOUTHERN LAKES
pp. 307-332

Te Anau

Dunedin

OTAGO AND SOUTHLAND
pp. 333-355

N

0   100 miles
0   100 kilometers

Stewart Island

We All Live in A Never-ending Maze

New Zealanders have long been inexplicably fascinated by mazes. In the early 20th century, there were many hedge mazes throughout the country, but many fell into disrepair during the two World Wars. Then, in the 1970s, Stuart Landsborough and his innovative puzzle mazes spearheaded a sudden revival in maze construction. During the 1980s, Landsborough was involved in nearly 200 three-dimensional wooden maze construction projects in New Zealand (most notably in Wanaka) and around the world. Highlights of his work include mazes in Japan in which the paths are surrounded by water, a dragon maze with stained glass windows, and the Beatles Maze for Liverpool's 1984 International Garden Festival, the centerpiece of which is an 18-ton, 51-foot-long yellow submarine. Today, mazes dot the country; there is an especially popular one in Rotorua (see p. 190).

English and Maori-English Glossary at the back of the book. New Zealanders speak English with a distinctive Kiwi accent and a vocabulary more in sync with British and Australian usage than American. Regional variation adds an extra twist, such as the slightly rolled "r" characteristic of the Scottish-colonized areas.

After decades of efforts to rekindle Maori culture, the Maori language has resurfaced and revitalized itself as a form of everyday communication, rather than solely for ceremonial purposes. Maori was established as an official language in New Zealand in 1974, and is spoken by 4.2% of the population today. First captured on paper by missionaries in the early 1800s, Maori uses only fifteen letters (a, e, h, i, k, m, n, ng, o, p, r, t, u, w, wh), gives each syllable equal stress, and ends each with a vowel. The soft Maori "ng" can appear at any point in a Maori word and sounds similar to the ending of "ring." The sound indicated by "wh" is a difficult sound for non-native speakers to attain, one that is closely approximated by a soft, aspirated "f" sound by some tribes (particularly in the north). As for vowels, there appears to be scholarly linguistic disagreement as to whether or not dipthongs exist in Maori. Successive vowels are generally pronounced with some emphasis, though not with the marked separation heard in some languages. Though some Maori words may appear at first to be tongue-twisting concoctions (see p. 235), most are decipherable with a syllable-by-syllable, phonetic approach.

■ From *Hongi* to *Hangi*

No visit to New Zealand is complete without an evening at a *marae*, the sacred grounds around a Maori meeting house, or *whare nui*. *Marae* protocol is explained on-site, but it helps to know the basics. Upon arriving at the *marae*, a warrior from the village will greet the group with an elaborate set of prowling steps, body movements, and a tongue-protruding facial gesture (it's exceedingly uncouth to return such a gesture). The *wero* ends when a peace offering *(teka)* is proffered and accepted. The entire ritual of arrival and introduction is called the *powhiri* (or formal welcome). The chief of the tribe will welcome your group, and one of your number (your chief) will deliver a brief speech in return. To seal the bond of friendship, both chiefs press noses together in the traditional greeting known as the *hongi*.

> *The chief of the tribe will welcome your group, and one of your number (your chief) will deliver a brief speech in return*

The *tangata whenua* (people of the land) are respectful of their heritage and traditions. The *whare nui* symbolizes the body of a Maori ancestor embracing the *whare:* the spine of the building is the backbone, the front beams are the arms, and the intermediate beams are the ribs. Shoes are not worn inside the *marae*, and pictures may not be permitted, depending on the tribe. After a *karakia* (prayer) is given, the traditional dinner, *hangi*, is prepared by roasting sweet potatoes, meat, mussels, and other goodies in a pit of heated stones until they reach peak smoky delicacy.

NEW ZEALAND

▓ Maori Art

Before the European arrival, the Maori sustained a thriving artistic tradition. From performance arts to craftswork, everyday art was vital in maintaining tribal unity, expressing spiritual beliefs, celebrating important occasions, and honoring one's ancestry. Over the course of European settlement, however, many art forms and traditions grew rare or disappeared altogether. A growing movement today seeks to recover these *wahi ngaro* (lost aspects) of Maori tradition and culture. The Maori Arts and Crafts Institute in Rotorua, for example, trains students in the ancient tribal traditions of wood and jewelry carving. Annual Maori performing arts festivals encourage modern-day Maori to carry on the ancient traditions, as well.

Carving is one prominent early Maori art form still practiced today. Traditional beliefs charged the artist to impart qualities like fear, power, and authority to his or her pieces, in order to transform them from mere material objects to *taonga* (highly treasured, even sacred objects). Each object also accumulated its own body of *korero* (stories) with each successive owner. A design particular to a tribe was passed down from generation to generation, distinguishing itself by its repetition of certain stylistic features and motifs, such as *tiki* (human forms), *manaia* (bird men), and *taniwha* (sea spirits). The most common mediums were bone, wood, and greenstone (also see **A Jaded Perspective,** p. 300). Carvers created items large and small, decorating both towering meeting houses and tiny tiki pendants.

Moko (facial tattooing) is one of the most famous Maori art forms, and has been since the days when 19th-century Europe was transfixed by portraits and photographs of New Zealand "savages" with full facial tattoos. Traditionally, *moko* could only be executed by *tohunga ta moko*, experts trained extensively in using the sharp wooden adze and mallet or birdbone chisel to etch the design into the skin, then using a toothed chisel to fill in the ink dye (a mixture of burned kauri or totara resin and pigeon fat). The *tohunga ta moko* declared the recipient *tapu* (sacred) while the tattoo was healing. Men's *moko* began with a simple design for youths; more spiral flourishes were added as the wearer won prestige in battle. Thus, only older, highly distinguished warriors could sport full facial tattoos. Women's *moko* were more simple, usually surrounding only the lips and the tip of the nose, although some stout-hearted women elected to have their thighs and breasts tattooed as well. The practice of men's *moko* died out by the end of the 1800s, while women's *moko* continued to be practiced until the mid-1900s. Today, performers of traditional Maori arts often recreate the traditional tribal *moko* with face paint.

19th-century Europe was transfixed by portraits and photographs of New Zealand "savages" with facial tattoos

Historically and culturally vital, **haka** (dance) is another art form in revival today. The vigorous arm-waving, foot-stomping *peruperu* is an all-male dance, once performed by armed warriors before battle as a convocation to the god of war. *Taparahi*, on the other hand, are weaponless dances danced by both genders for a variety of reasons: to greet important guests, to honor the dead, or for sheer entertainment. In the *poi*, a dance now performed by women, balls on strings are twirled in elegant synchronicity. (It was originally designed to increase suppleness and flexibility in the wrists of warriors). To see a modern *haka*, head to a *marae* or just glue your eyes to the **All Blacks** (see p. 51) before the beginning of every rugby match.

Traditional Maori **song** and **oratory** also lie at the heart of Maori culture, and particularly ceremonial life. *Tau marae* orations are performed at traditional funeral ceremonies for important chiefs, featuring a chief orator who delivers a formal, stylized tribute to the dead. Another important type of oratory is *karakia* (chants), which were once strictly the property of *tohunga* (priests or specially learned men). *Karakia* imparted *mauri* (spiritual essence) to objects, as in the Maori myth in which Tiki chants a *karakia* in order to bring his clay figurine to life. *Waiata* are the most common type of lyrical song. Two kinds of *waiata* that have survived are the *waiata*

Searching for the Source

Maori legend refers to **Hawaiki** as the place where the first human was created, the origin of all life and the ultimate destination after death. The traditional Maori *tangihanga* (funeral ceremony) tells the dead to "follow the setting sun to their ancestors in Hawaiki." The living have taken this advice to heart as well, making Hawaiki a hot spot of scholarly debate in New Zealand for the last century. In the late 1800s, **Abraham Fornander** was the first to make the linguistic connection between the homelands named in different Polynesian myths: Savai'i in Samoa, Hawai'i in the Hawaiian Islands, Havai'i in the Marquesas Islands, and Avaiki in the Cook Islands. His contemporary **Percy Smith** then spearheaded his own investigation into the location of the Maori homeland. Disregarding traditional scientific modes of inquiry, Smith believed that Hawaiki could be located simply by tracing place-name cognates throughout Polynesia. Although Smith's methodology may be shunned today, modern archaeologists and anthropologists do share his intense desire to locate the elusive homeland. General consensus today seems to locate Hawaiki somewhere in the Society or Marquesas Islands. Conclusive evidence is scarce, however, and experts may well echo the lament of the traditional Maori song: "Who will take me to Hawaiki, far away in the distance?"

tangi, songs of mourning (often composed by women); and *waiata aroha* (solely composed by women), which often dwell upon unrequited love, obstacles in love, and delinquent lovers. In all of these oral arts, tribes nurtured their own traditions, creating specialized mythology and tribal historical accounts.

THE LAND

■ Conservation

New Zealand is hailed worldwide as a leader in conservation efforts, both on land and at sea. Some 28% of the country is set aside as protected land, and a massive international whale sanctuary established in 1994 includes more than 11 million square miles. The Southernmost part of the South Island was recognized as a natural area of international importance and designated the **Te Wahipounamu South West New Zealand World Heritage Area.** The country is covered with 13 national parks, plus numerous other forest parks, groves, and wildlife reserves. The first national park was created in 1887, as a result of the foresight and efforts of Te Heuheu Tukino IV, the high chief of the Ngati Tuwharetoa Maori tribe. Distressed by the morass of European farming and competing Maori tribal claims that was wreaking havoc on the holy mountains, the chief offered the area as a gift to the New Zealand government on the condition that it be kept *tapu* (sacred). The gift has endured in the current Tongariro National Park; over one million blissful nature-lovers descend upon its awe-inspiring volcanoes every year.

The other national parks see an equal share of visitors, many of whom come to tramp one of New Zealand's nine **Great Walks.** Unique to New Zealand, the Great Walks are designated multi-day hikes equipped with extensive overnight huts and camping facilities. (See p. 35 for detailed information on the Great Walks). While reveling in the natural splendor of New Zealand, be considerate and aware of your actions—carelessness destroys.

■ Biodiversity

Nature lovers will find not only a well-developed outdoors-experience infrastructure, but an outstanding display of flora and fauna. New Zealand's geological isolation has resulted in the evolution of countless endemic, unique species and a diversity of life

NEW ZEALAND

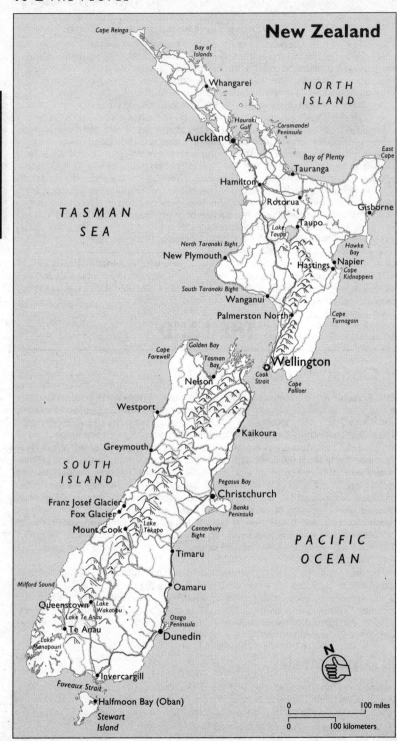

New Zealand

Cape Reinga

Bay of
Islands

*NORTH
ISLAND*

Whangarei

Hauraki
Gulf

*Coromandel
Peninsula*

Auckland

*East
Cape*

Bay of Plenty

Tauranga

Hamilton

Rotorua

*TASMAN
SEA*

Gisborne

Taupo

Lake
Taupo

North Taranaki Bight

*Hawke
Bay*

New Plymouth

Hastings

Napier

*Cape
Kidnappers*

South Taranaki Bight

Wanganui

Palmerston North

*Cape
Turnagain*

*Cape
Farewell*

Golden Bay

*Tasman
Bay*

Wellington

Nelson

*Cook
Strait*

*Cape
Palliser*

Westport

Kaikoura

Greymouth

*SOUTH
ISLAND*

Pegasus Bay

Christchurch

Franz Josef Glacier

Fox Glacier

*Banks
Peninsula*

Mount Cook

Lake
Tekapo

*Canterbury
Bight*

*PACIFIC
OCEAN*

Timaru

Milford Sound

Oamaru

Queenstown

Lake
Wakatipu

Lake Te Anau

Te Anau

*Otago
Peninsula*

Lake
Manapouri

Dunedin

Invercargill

Foveaux Strait

Halfmoon Bay (Oban)

*Stewart
Island*

N

| 0 | 100 miles |
| 0 | 100 kilometers |

unmatched in the world. Isolated from the rest of the earth for the roughly 70 to 100 million years since it split off from the ancient supercontinent of Gondwanaland, New Zealand today is over 2000km away from Australia and Antarctica, and nearly as far from many tiny Pacific Islands. As a result, it was the last major landmass excepting Antarctica to be settled by humans. During this span of time, the plants and animals on the islands evolved in new and unusual directions as they exploited food and habitat niches. Many predators that later evolved on the supercontinent never came into being in ancient New Zealand, and many creatures that went extinct in the rest of the world were able to survive in New Zealand.

NEW ZEALAND

A Lone Twig on the Tree of Life

That metallic lizard-looking critter greasing your palms whenever you slide a New Zealand 5¢ coin across the counter is no ordinary lizard. It's the **tuatara,** a grayish-brown, spiky-spined reptile that zoos and animal parks like to call "New Zealand's living fossil"—the last surviving species of the Mesozoic order Rhynchocephalia. It's been around in this form for some 225 million years, though its nearest relatives went extinct 100 million years ago. While it looks fairly similar to your pet iguana, tuatara have some major differences on their twig of the evolutionary tree: remnants of a third eye (quite rudimentary), the lack of a male copulatory organ, and an egg-formation period that can last up to four years. They're also nocturnal, mature at age 60 with a length of 60cm, and can live to be 300 years old. Having had a fairly long time to work out a routine with their avian neighbors, tuatara share earthen burrows with certain seabirds, occupying them in daylight and leaving them for the birds at night. Sadly far less common than their coinage counterparts, the tuatara have been decreasing in numbers ever since the Maori introduced the Polynesian rat a thousand years ago. At the brink of Darwin-style elimination, the tuatara live on only a few islands off the New Zealand coast, in areas such as the Bay of Plenty, the Coromandel Peninsula, and the Cook Strait. The 150-hectare Stephens Island in the Strait is home to some 30,000 of the reptiles, though only seven of the remaining islands' populations are considered to be in good health. Life's hard when you're an evolutionary relic.

FAUNA

One immediately noticeable facet of New Zealand's wildlife is the preponderance of strange and exotic birds, from the legendary giant **moa** to the country's flightless mascot. Ancient New Zealand's birds evolved to occupy the niches that mammals took elsewhere in the world, gaining stronger legs, increasing dramatically in size, and sometimes even losing their wings. The four different species of **kiwi** demonstrate this phenomenon perfectly, with their straight, thin, brown or gray feathers and slender and probing beaks with external nostrils to help in scrounging by smell for food on the forest floor. Solitary, nocturnal, flightless, tailless, and almost wingless, the kiwi is in a class of its own. Other evolutionary quirks include the fact that it burrows, mates for life, is quite protective of its territory (which can extend up to 40 hectares), lays eggs proportionally larger to their body size than any other bird, and incubates them for 80 days (by the male in some species).

Any visitor to the ski slopes or national parks of New Zealand will quickly realize that the Kea is no ordinary polly, but rather a clever, destructive, and very bold menace

The **kea,** the world's only alpine parrot, is one of the few birds to makes its home in the peaks of the Southern Alps. Any visitor to the ski slopes or national parks of New Zealand will quickly realize that the Kea is no ordinary polly, but rather a clever, destructive, and very bold menace. Keas will not hesitate to rip open any unattended pack in search of food, and also dine quite readily on ski clothing and even car antennas. The **kereru** is the native pigeon (with two subspecies), and the only bird other than the extinct moa able to help disperse the larger seeds of some native plants. Fanciful names for New Zealand's amazing variety of birds abound: the **morepork** (*ruru*, the only native owl), the **muttonbird** *(titi)*, and the **wrybill** (*ngutuparore*, with its slender and twisted beak) among others. Despite the humor of unusual names, however, it's no laughing matter that much of New Zealand's native avian fauna is endangered (see Extinct and Endangered, p. 49). Despite the abundance of flightless birds in New Zealand as compared to the rest of the world, one-third of the avian residents of the islands still return to the ocean for their food, including the Australasian gannet, and New Zealand's 14 species of **albatross**. The Fiordland crested penguin (*tawaki;* one of the world's rarest), the little blue penguin *(korora)*, and the endangered yellow-eyed penguin *(hoiho)*, are also seabirds albeit of a different sort.

There is much more to the animal kingdom of New Zealand than showy birds, however. Three species of **bats** represent the only indigenous land mammals, though there are plenty of marine mammals. Whales, orca, seals, sea lions and dolphins can be found in the waters of the South Island. New Zealand has no snakes, but it does have the coastal katipo spider (a relative of the black widow spider). New Zealand's basket of biological diversity fills to overflowing with over 1500 species of **land snails** (some of which are even carnivorous), 11 species of the heaviest insect in the world (the mouse-sized, grasshopper-esque weta), teeming crayfish *(koura)*, pesky sandflies *(te namu)*, and the ethereal glow-worms *(titiwai)* of the order Diptera (the same group as houseflies; see p. 128).

FLORA

The flora of New Zealand, like the fauna, took several unusual evolutionary turns since the tectonic exodus from Gondwanaland. In the absence of large mammalian grazers and browsers, many plants never had the need to evolve toxic chemicals, tough leaves, or the spikes, thorns, and other defense mechanisms common in many other parts of the world. Amid the musical Maori names and the bouquet of 2700 plants native to New Zealand (of which DOC reports that 80% are endemic), are the canoe-worthy totara, sky-reaching kahikatea, massive **kauri,** steadfast kamahi, reminiscent-of-the-tropics nikau, and the endless variety of understory ferns. Mamaku tree ferns can grow up to 20m in height; the **ponga tree fern,** with its silver-underside fronds, is the national symbol. The **pohutukawa,** often called "New Zealand's Christmas tree" for the bright crimson flowers that bloom in most varieties during late December, is another distinctive species found in the northern regions. Maori tradition holds that when these gnarled coastal trees bloom early there'll be a long hot summer ahead. The rata, while similar to the pohutukawa, adds a peachy-orangish cast to the landscape. In general, **podocarps** (a broad class of conifers similar to the yew family and including totara, rimu, miro, mati, and kahikatea) dominate many of New Zealand's forested regions, but **beech forests** are also common. Numerous other plant species besides trees are unique to the country as well (such as the world's largest buttercup, the Mt. Cook lily), and local DOC offices are often more than happy to talk about the area's special flora.

INVASIONS

For as long as humans have been arriving to New Zealand, other species have been coming with them and establishing themselves on New Zealand soil. From the earliest attempts to grow taro and kumara to current-day outdoors enthusiasts who unintentionally import camping equipment carrying microbes and eggs of unwanted vermin, invasions of exotic species have been a recurring phenomenon for New Zealand, often with quite serious results. Most invasions have taken place as the result of deliberate introductions (e.g., the introduction of trout into waterways around the country), actions often taken long before the rise of modern-day awareness of the long-term ramifications. Chief among the faunal invasions have been those of deer, goats, pigs, rabbits, and possums, introduced to provide sporting opportunities, game, and fur. Moose were also at one point introduced to New Zealand, and sporadic reports of moose sightings from remote areas of Fiordland came in during the 1920s—even though moose were officially eradicated as of the turn of the century.

Chomping down on rainforest bush, exotic animal species can disrupt the balance of New Zealand's many unique ecosystems and cause biological chaos. The end result (often after the passage of decades or even centuries) is all too frequently the endangerment or extinction of unique New Zealand species (see Extinct and Endangered, below). As one prime example of introductions gone awry, the stoats and weasels once brought to the country to serve as predators of rabbits are now believed to turn to feeding on hapless native birds when the local rabbit and possum supply diminishes. It's with good reason that the DOC has declared open-season on most exotic bush fauna, happily distributing hunting permits.

Exotic flora are another area of concern, as they out-compete other native flora for sunlight, space, and nutrients. Many flora introduced from harsher climates have a heyday in New Zealand with the relatively mild year-round climate, and often end up reproducing several times per year. With no native predators, and with introduced predators often feeding on indigenous plant life instead, the end result can be calamitous, disrupting the long-term stability of an ecosystem. Of the 20,000 exotic species introduced to the country, the DOC reports that over 200 are now weeds. Fungal invaders are yet another area of increasing concern.

Possum Problems

Although New Zealand's reputation of having several times more sheep than people still holds true, the fact is that there are now more possum than sheep. By some estimates, over 70 million of the marsupials are chewing tender leaves and damaging the flowers of New Zealand's native trees, carrying diseases, out-competing native birds for food, and steadily consuming much of the country's remaining native bush. If you visit the rare areas of the country where possums have not struck, such as Great Barrier Island, the damage wreaked by the animals in the rest of the country will become painfully evident. DOC's response has ranged from poison-trapping to offering head bounties, but in the wake of each subsequent ineffective solution more and more radical approaches have been tried. The latest is the use of aerial poison bombs. A supposedly natural, biodegradable toxin known as "1080" is being dropped in many of the country's most rugged and intractable forests. Although carrots were once used, their toxin-level variability created problems and the new bait is now cereal-based, colored green, and smells of cinnamon (deterring birds but delicious to the intended victims). DOC insists that studies overwhelmingly attest to 1080's safety, but they do warn surrounding areas before carrying out their aerial missions of eradication.

EXTINCT AND ENDANGERED

The extinct moa is a sad warning for other endangered New Zealand birds. Just 200 turkey-sized, blue-green, and strong-beaked **takahe** remain; the **black stilt** *(kaki)* are down to 70. Fifty nocturnal **kakapo,** the world's heaviest parrot (males can weigh in at 4kg), are still in existence; unfortunately, the DOC states that the kakapo "is, perhaps, the slowest-breeding bird on earth." Intensive conservation efforts are underway for all three species. With the arrival of many Europeans in the 1800s, habitat pressures brought extinctions. Before 1800, 70% of the landscape was covered in forest; today, only 15% of the original lowland forest remains, and only 10% of the original wetlands. Ninety percent of the original kauri forests were harvested. Today, untold numbers of native plants are undoubtedly also being edged out of their niches.

Most estimates calculate that roughly half of the avifauna originally present in New Zealand disappeared within decades of human arrival, as the plump, flightless birds and their large, nutritious eggs made attractive and easy prey. Now-extinct closer relatives of the kiwi included, strangely enough, the estimated 11-to 20-odd species of gigantic moa. Part of the group of **ratites** (which includes the other large flightless marvels like the emu of Australia, ostrich of Africa, and rhea of South America), the largest species of moa, *Dinornis maximus,* stood up to 2½m tall. Even the smallest moa reached the 1m mark for height. The moa are believed to have gone extinct from a combination of factors including climate change and, more dramatically, over-hunting by early Maori (see p. 258). Human settlement of New Zealand affected more than one species at a time: when the moa went extinct, for example, the New Zealand **giant eagle** *(Hapagornis),* with its incredible 3m wingspan, also went extinct because its primary food source was moa carrion.

Even before the arrival of humans 1000 years ago, extinction was a fact of life in New Zealand. Various catastrophes periodically swept the islands, from tidal waves to volcanic eruptions, and countless numbers of species became extinct. With the arrival of the Polynesians, their **dogs** *(kuri)* and their **rats** *(kiore),* the pace of extinction rapidly increased. (Interestingly, both the kuri and the kiore suffered their own twist of fate: the last pure-bred kuri disappeared in the mid-1850s, while the kiore have held out since the introduction of the European rat only on some small offshore islands.)

THE CULTURE

■ Sports

New Zealand loves sports like nobody's business. Almost half the population belongs to the New Zealand Sports Assembly, which represents 150 national sporting associations. In addition to the multitude of outdoor sports that occupy the nation, including skiing, rafting, mountain biking, hiking, and jetboating, New Zealanders also hit the grass in organized sports like cricket, golf, tennis, and field hockey. This active country also likes to sit on the sidelines, especially if the sport being played is rugby, the bloody, rough-and-tumble ball sport invented in England (see below). Kiwi pride swells enormously for the **All Blacks,** the national team whose season runs from April to September. When a crucial match like the **Bledisloe Cup Championships** is being televised (or any Aussie match, for that matter), forget about going out to eat, changing money, or shopping—all the locals will be glued to their TVs, not running businesses. Despite the team's widespread popularity, however, the All Blacks have encountered controversial moments in their history. In 1960, for example, the All Blacks made a vehemently protested national tour of South Africa in which Maori players were excluded. Then, in 1981, the South African Springboks made a tour of New Zealand that some opposed as tacit support of apartheid in South Africa.

In addition to rugby union, there is also rugby league, which features regional teams like the stalwart, ever-popular Auckland Warriors. Another Kiwi favorite is **netball,** a women's sport played in winter. The national team, the **Silver Ferns,** has been steadily gaining in popularity and recognition.

In 1995 the Kiwi sailing team **Black Magic** swiped the Americas Cup from the United States, marking only the second time in 144 years that the cup was not won by an American team. The cup's subsequent mauling at the hands and sledge hammer of a Maori activist drew international headlines. Fully restored, the cup has since made several country-wide tours, and plans are well underway for its defense in 2000. The series will be held in Auckland's Hauraki Gulf, with a record 18 challengers already registered.

New Zealand also keeps certain sporting heroes at the center of national pride, including: Sir Edmund Hillary, the first to climb Mt. Everest in 1953; Jack Lovelock, 1500m gold medalist in the 1936 Berlin Olympics; **Yvette Williams,** long jump champion in the 1952 Helsinki Olympics; **Peter Snell,** 800m gold medalist, and **Murray Halberg,** 5000m gold medalist in the 1960 Rome Olympics.

■ Visual Arts and Literature

A number of prominent and critically acclaimed artists have hailed from New Zealand in the last century. **Frances Hodgkins** (1869-1947) and **Colin McCahon** (1919-1987) are two of the most famous 20th-century New Zealand painters. Hodgkins left New

All Black All Over

Everywhere you turn, from hostel walls to the TV, from the daily paper to bathroom stalls, New Zealand's national rugby team, the **All Blacks,** are there. What may seem like obsessive coverage has strong historical and cultural justifications. Protected with a fierce pride against such abominations as the padded wimpiness of American gridiron, rugby is a source of national unity and honor. Each player must be strong on both offense and defense, quick and powerful, fit enough to last the full non-stop 80 minutes, and most of all, tough. In 1986, Buck Shelford gave new meaning to the phrase "he's got balls" when he almost lost his in a test (international match) against France, leaving the game to receive emergency surgery. Although they lost to South Africa in the 1995 World Cup final, the team has consistently been one of the world's best. For opponents, victory over the All Blacks is an unforgettable event—Welsh club team triumphs over the All Blacks in the 1960s are still commemorated with anniversary neckties (supposedly sent to the All Blacks as well). A loss by the All Blacks is so unexpected that tears from devastated fans mixes with beer in pubs across the country. Such is the power and marketing power of the team that every other national team is spun from their yarn; New Zealand also boasts the All Whites in soccer, the Tall Blacks in basketball, the Black Sox in softball, and the Black Cats in cricket. While it may take Kiwi blood to fully understand the intricacies and meaning of the game, you don't have to jump in the middle of a **scrum** to appreciate the athletic prowess of popular star Jonah Lomu, the intensity of the Maori *Haka* challenge offered to opponents before each game, or the delirious passion of fans at the scoring of a **try.** In New Zealand, rugby is not merely sport, it is love—and in 1999, love will be in the air as New Zealand tries to recapture the World Cup.

Zealand in 1913 for the literary and artistic circles of London, eventually becoming a leading figure in watercolor figurative painting. McCahon retained his base in New Zealand and focused the bulk of his work on the landscapes of the South Island. Today he is considered one of the most important influences on modern art in New Zealand.

New Zealand boasts an active, distinguished literary culture as well. **Katherine Mansfield** (1888-1923), world-famous short story writer, was another World War I expatriate to Britain. Her best-known short story collections are *Bliss* (1920), reportedly dismissed by Virginia Woolf as merely "superficial smartness," and *The Garden Party* (1922). Her childhood home in Wellington has been preserved as a museum (see p. 231). **Dame Ngaio Marsh** (1895-1982), most renowned for her mystery series featuring detective Roderick Alleyn, stayed firmly rooted in New Zealand as a member of the leading artistic group in Christchurch in the mid-1900s. The next literary wave in New Zealand brought poet **James K. Baxter** (1926-1972), renowned for his celebration of the New Zealand wilderness; and novelist **Janet Frame** (b. 1924), best known for *Owls Do Cry* (1957), *A State of Siege* (1966), and her autobiographical trio *An Angel at My Table* (1985; also adapted to film by Jane Campion). Maori writers have surged onto the literary scene as well, often focusing on issues of culture and identity. For example, **Patricia Grace** (b. 1937), of Ngati Raukawa, Ngati Toa, and Te Ati Awa descent, is known for the bittersweet coming-of-age story, *Mutuwhenua the moon sleeps* (1978), about a young Maori girl's love for a Pakeha (non-Maori). **Witi Ihimaera** (b. 1944), of the Te Whanau a Kai tribe, is best-known for *Tangi* (1973), an exploration of father-son relationships. Perhaps most well-known is **Keri Hulme** (b. 1947), a South Islander of Scottish, English, and Ngai Tahu descent, whose novel *The Bone People* won the 1985 Booker Prize.

■ Film

Recent films made in New Zealand have become both popular and critical hits. **Jane Campion's** *The Piano* (1994), a dark, haunting love story about turn-of-the-century European settlers, won two Cannes Film Festival awards and a Best Supporting Actress Oscar for Anna Paquin. Another prominent director is **Lee Tamahori,** whose *Once*

Xena, Warrior Princess

In a country that worships rugby, beer drinking, and other testosterone-derived activities, there is one exception to the overwhelming culture of machismo: Xena, the star of a popular TV show written, produced, and directed by New Zealanders. Set in the golden age of myth (and filmed near Auckland), the show follows the adventures of Xena as she battles capricious gods and greedy humans in order to free all people from tyranny and injustice. Since its debut a little more than two years ago, the show has enjoyed worldwide popularity. Xena landed on the cover of the American feminist magazine *Ms.* and is all over the Internet. Countless Xenites throng pages and chat rooms devoted to all things Xena. In particular, many female fans are inspired by her unapologetic, sexy, self-determined character. The show's producers and Lucy Lawless, the actress who plays Xena, know that having a female hero puts the show in the position of an underdog, but also opens up possibilities for subversion. The show is witty and self-aware, deliberately manipulating the subtext of the relationship between Xena and her sidekick, Gabrielle. While Xena might be fierce, she's certainly not androgynous, dressing in skimpy outfits even as she battles the forces of evil. But as Lawless explains, "she wears those things because they're better to fight in."

Were Warriors (adapted from Alan Duff's book of 1992) has been praised for its stark, honest appraisal of the plight of urban Maori today. A landmark work in Maori representation on the silver screen is **Tangata Whenua: The People of the Land** (1976), the six-part documentary series by Maori filmmaker Barry Barclay. One of the pioneers of the New Zealand film scene was **Len Lye** (1901-1980), kinetic sculptor and modern filmmaker of the 60s. Lye introduced the technique of "direct filmmaking," where images are etched or painted directly onto the film itself. Born in Christchurch, Lye left New Zealand for London in the early 1900s, joining fellow expatriate Frances Hodgkins in London's artsy elite of the 20s and 30s, then moving to New York in 1944. Today his work is shown at the Govett-Brewster Art Gallery in New Plymouth (p. 149).

Music

Today, in the nightclubs of New Zealand's small towns and large cities electronic music reigns supreme, in a range of genres from house to drum and bass. New Zealand's contemporary popular music scene reflects the global shift towards more electronic sounds. Granted, there are still bands rocking out hard: the **Exponents** and **Head like a Hole** are two of the most popular, and consistently pack houses wherever they play. The independent label **Kog** is an umbrella for talent in the Auckland area, spearheaded by the break infested grooves of **Chumbwa** and the full-on funkiness of **DJ Amanda.** Check out **The Fix,** a free glossy mag, for info on the Auckland scene. Down in Wellington, **Mu** tears it up with serious skills on the vinyl, while **Manuel Bundy** criss-crosses the country with rhythmically centered beats, crafting smooth sets time and again. **The Gathering** (http://www.gathering.co.nz) is a multi-day rave in the South Island that celebrates New Year's Eve and draws an international crowd. Perhaps of more interest to Top 40 fans around the world, Maori artists **OTC** (Otara Millionaires Club) have laid claim to the hip-hop, dance music ascendancy. Geographic isolation hasn't disconnected New Zealand from trends of the past, either. Kiwis had **punk** in the 1970s too, a phase that continued throughout the decade with the influential Christchurch label **Flying Nun.** And in the 1980s, The **Split Enz** and its offshoot **Crowded House** enjoyed worldwide popularity as part of **New Wave.**

Food and Drink

From the earliest New Zealanders' dinners of roast moa and kumara, New Zealand's cuisine has always been of the meat-and-potatoes kind. This tendency toward the basic can be seen in the solid triumvirate of fish 'n' chips, cafe fare, and the ever-

Pavlov's Dessert

Sweet and white, creamy and light, pavlova is, was, and forever shall be *the* New Zealand dessert. The soft-centered **mound of meringue** topped patriotically with whipped cream and slices of kiwifruit seems an appropriate national specialty for "the Land of the Long White Cloud." It's also considered by some to be a prerequisite to marriage—if one's spouse can't make a decent pav, he or she just isn't fit to bring little Kiwis into the world. The graceful sugary treat draws its name from the famed Russian ballerina Anna Pavlova, who endeared herself to the world down under during a 1929 tour. But controversy continues to reign over who invented and named the dessert. Some poor misguided souls on the West Island believe they invented the dessert, after the Esplanade Hotel of Perth (Australia) got all the press in 1934 for a dish they called pavlova. Research done by the New Zealand National Library, however, shows that the heart and soul belong to New Zealand: the Esplanade's original recipe lacked the crucial vinegar apparent in a "meringue cake" recipe that surfaced in Wellington, New Zealand, in 1927. The name for the dish itself was the idea of another Kiwi cook, as evidenced by a 1929 recipe for "Pavlova Cakes." To experience the glory of the pav yourself (and make yourself eligible for Kiwi marriage), you'd better start cracking those eggs.

present Chinese restaurant, all serving fried and greasy goodies. Although individual **vegetarian** entrees are not terribly difficult to find (**kosher** fare is rarer), traditional New Zealand food tends to run on the heavy, meaty side, with lamb, venison (called cervena when farm-raised), and pork dominating the menu of traditional establishments. Fresh seafood is another staple, overrunning the menus of coastal towns with fresh fish, prawns (what Americans call jumbo shrimp), crayfish, and more. **Chinese fast food** (or takeaways, as the Kiwis say) serves up all-you-can-eat buffet fare in copious, if not exactly high-quality, form. **BYO** (bring-your-own wine) restaurants without a license to sell liquor are also widespread; some charge a corking fee. Keep in mind that ordering an **entree** will get you an appetizer in New Zealand; to order a main course, look for the **mains.** Restaurant closing hours tend to be flexible; many restaurants simply close their doors whenever business seems to have run dry.

Traditional New Zealand food tends to run on the heavy, meaty side, with lamb, venison, and pork dominating the menu

New Zealand potables are also notable. The wines of the Marlborough and Hawke's Bay regions are world-famous, particularly the Sauvignon Blanc, Riesling, Chardonnay, Cabernet Sauvignon, and Pinot Noir varieties. As for other types of tippling, keep in mind that all New Zealand spirits are double spirits (double doses), unless specifically noted by the bar; hard liquor is less popular because it is more expensive due to import taxes. New Zealand also serves up a good brew, with various national lagers and draughts (such as Steinlager), regional beers (such as the Canterbury Draught), and specialty brews. Some breweries market beer nationally, while others are strictly local gems. Teetotalers may be more likely to gravitate towards **Lemon and Paeroa (L&P),** a popular carbonated lemon drink that is "world-famous in New Zealand," as the advertisements tell you with a wink. For a more refined thirst-quencher, you can enjoy a British-style **Devonshire tea.** The late afternoon (around 4pm) snack traditionally plies you with tea, scones with Devonshire cream or jam, crumpets, and other delectables. **Nutella,** a smooth hazelnut and chocolate spread, offers your toast a silky smooth alternative to the yeasty **Vegemite** or **Marmite** spreads (see p. 249).

Last but not least, don't forget to eat your fruits and veggies—a range of exotic fruit is yours for the taking. **Nashi pears,** for example, a cross-breed of apples and pears, have the shape and texture of an apple, but the mottled color and flavor of a pear. Or, try other options such as feijoas, persimmons, and, of course, kiwifruit.

HISTORY AND CURRENT EVENTS

While New Zealand may be known more for its timeless natural wonders than its history, familiarity with the nation's past can only enhance a visitor's experience. The country today is braided from the remnants of Maori and European settlement, but has become something different than either. Such was not always the case; the Maori layered their civilization over a thriving and unique ecosystem, permanently changing the natural world as they shaped their surroundings. The second wave of European settlers encountered a tribal society that has sunk its cultural roots deep into island soil.

New Zealand's colonization by the British was not so much the result of a planned policy of Empire building, but rather a government's reluctant response to demanding citizens making a go at settlement in an often hostile land. The country's natural resources attracted many a trader on the make, but the Maori were not always cordial to newcomers. As the new settlers established themselves, they began to replicate their home government in the new territory, and the European model of individual property holding and elected government showed little respect for the Maori's tribal society. Conflict was inevitable. Today, New Zealand seems to have brokered an enviable peace between Maori and Pakeha (non-Maori), but tensions still run beneath the surface.

Let's Go can provide only a very condensed account of New Zealand's history—the interested traveler is urged to further explore while in-country.

MAORI SETTLEMENT

As legend has it, the Maori forebears had been living happily for many years in **Hawaiki,** the ancestral homeland, when **Kupe** the explorer set out on a scouting expedition to the east. He stumbled upon a lush, mist-covered stretch of land which he named Aotearoa, "the land of the long white cloud." Years later, when intertribal dispute and strife finally forced the ancestors to leave Hawaiki, they remembered Kupe's lavish praise of the paradisiacal land to the east. In seven mammoth canoes, each carrying the forebear of a different Maori tribe, the ancestors turned their backs on Hawaiki and set sail, destination Aotearoa.

Cook's glowing report of New Zealand, published eight years after he returned to England, quickly spread the world in Europe about the largely untouched land of plenty on the other side of the world

Scholarship holds that the first settlers, the **moa hunters,** came to New Zealand in the late 10th century (for more on the moa, see p. 49). Artifacts dredged from the past provide telling details about the day-to-day life of the earliest New Zealanders. They made their living by fishing and moa hunting, using stone and carved bone tools developed by their Polynesian predecessors. By the 14th century, they were widely practicing horticulture, mainly in the warmer, sunnier climes of the North Island. The *kumara* (sweet potato), one of the most common crops, is still grown today. The early Maori were evidently highly territorial. Tribes kept close watch over their hunting, fishing, and burial lands, as attested by the widespread legacy of weapon artifacts and village *pa* (fortified hillsides) they left behind. This fiercely protective attitude toward land was still in full force hundreds of years later, when they encountered the first Europeans.

THE EUROPEAN ARRIVAL

The first historically certified non-Maori to lay eyes on New Zealand was a Dutchman named **Abel Tasman.** In 1642, Tasman tried to land in what is now called Golden Bay in the South Island, but was rebuffed by a hostile Maori tribe that killed several of his men. After fleeing in terror, he recovered his wits enough to produce the first written account of New Zealand. Several years later, a cartographer used Tasman's description to put the country on the world map for the first time, naming it Nova Zeelandia after a province in the Netherlands.

In 1769, the legendary British explorer **Captain James Cook** cruised in on the *Endeavour*. He managed to break Tasman's precedent and established friendly relations with many of the *tangata maori* ("the ordinary people," as they called themselves) that he encountered. In his tour around the coast of New Zealand, Cook also sprinkled place names right and left and claimed the islands for Britain. Much like Kupe's advertisement to the Maori ancestors, Cook's glowing report of New Zealand, published eight years after he returned to England, quickly spread the word in Europe about the largely untouched land of plenty on the other side of the world.

Sealers and **whalers** were the first to take Cook up on his offer, arriving in droves in the early 1800s to make short work of New Zealand's resources. The seal colonies were practically wiped clean by the 1820s, followed by the whaling waters at the turn of the century. **Missionaries** also made an early appearance, with the first Christian missionary arriving in 1814 from New South Wales. A bevy of earnest reformers followed in his wake, working around the clock to learn Maori so they could teach the precepts of Christianity to the "Indians" and "aborigines," as they were called until "Maori" came into popular usage in the 1830s. Independent **traders** were the next to arrive, seeking flax and novelty items (such as Maori-made trinkets or even preserved heads) in exchange for firearms, metal tools, and other European goods. Forty years later, the next massive rush of settlement came with the **gold rushes** of the Westland and Otago regions in the South Island.

In a pattern familiar to colonized peoples the world over, the trading relationship between the Maori and the Europeans had consequences far beyond the economic sphere. Traders bore the fatal gift of European disease, which killed 25% of the Maori population. Western firepower escalated Maori intertribal violence, culminating in the musket wars of 1820-1835. The situation intensified when European armed trade ships began to participate in tribal warfare without governmental authorization. Soon, early settlers began to fear for the peace and stability of their settlements, and appealed to their governments for protection.

In 1833, Queen Victoria sent **James Busby** as British Resident to keep law and order. While settlers were setting up their own citizen vigilante associations, Busby was struggling to find a way to prevent non-British settlements from declaring their own independent states. He began calling large meetings with local Maori chiefs at his house in Waitangi in the interest of gaining their loyalty and cooperation. In 1835, Busby even persuaded 34 northern chiefs to sign the **Declaration of Independence of New Zealand,** which established the Confederation of United Tribes (but did not actually affect New Zealand's status as a British colony). Unfortunately, Busby's authority was backed by little more than the Crown's good intentions. European settlers soon grew frustrated with his powerlessness, particularly as new settlements began cropping up with increasing frequency in the late 1830s.

THE TREATY OF WAITANGI

In January 1840, dissatisfied with Busby's performance, the British Colonial Office sent **Captain William Hobson,** the first governor, to replace him. Upon royal request, Hobson wrote the **Treaty of Waitangi,** which offered the Maori the rights of British citizens and Her Majesty's protection in exchange for sovereignty over the land. Captain William Hobson shook each chief's hand, proclaiming, *"He iwi tahi tatou"* ("Now we are one people"). The Treaty was then translated into Maori by Henry Williams, an Anglican missionary.

Crucial nuances of meaning were evidently lost in translation, however. In Article One, the English version boldly asked for all "rights and powers of sovereignty over the land," while the Maori heard it as *"kawanatanga"* (government or administration), presumably leaving ultimate sovereignty to Maori chiefs. In Article Two the Maori were merely ensured "exclusive and undisturbed possession of their lands" in the English version, while in the Maori version they were promised *"tino rangatiratanga,"* unrestrained exercise of chiefly authority over lands, villages, and natural treasures.

Unfortunately, these discrepancies were not apparent to the assembly of northern Maori chiefs who gathered at Busby's house to hear Hobson's presentation of the Treaty of Waitangi on **February 6, 1840.** Local missionaries certainly made no effort to clarify, as they sought to persuade Maori chiefs that the treaty was an "act of love" on Queen Victoria's part, an effort to ease tribal conflict and to protect them from harsh domination by some other European nation. Their glowing promises must have been at least partially convincing, since 26 of the 34 chiefs who had signed the Declaration of Independence signed the treaty on this day, with about 500 more signatures gathered on later treaty-signing campaigns on both the North and the South Islands. Notable refusals took place in the Waikato and the center of the North Island, two areas that later bore the brunt of especially violent conflict.

SETTLEMENT AND LAND WARS

In November 1840, Britain responded to the burgeoning settlement in New Zealand by declaring the country a separate colony from New South Wales, Australia, in *The Letters Patent,* usually called *The Charter of 1840.* The support Hobson had won among the Maori quickly disappeared when European settlers began showing more and more disregard for Maori properties. Before long, the Maori began to suspect that they had given up more than they had intended and started to rebel against British authority.

In 1844, Hone Heke, one of the first chiefs to sign the treaty, **cut down the British flagpole** at Kororareka near Russell, which he saw as a symbol of illegitimate land claim. The government tried to re-erect the pole several times, finally giving up the fourth time Heke and his allies cut it down. The Russell incident marked the beginning of the **Maori Wars** between Heke's army and British-led forces, which lasted until 1846.

In 1852, the government passed the **Constitution Act,** which established a settler government with six provincial councils and a national parliament with a Lower and an Upper House. The Constitution Act also gave the vote to men over 25 holding official land titles, a move intended to shut out Maori representation, as Maori land ownership was communal. All hopes of royal intervention on the behalf of the Maori died in 1856, when New Zealand was declared a completely self-governing British colony.

The Maori became increasingly disturbed to see a British government that denied them representation taking shape around them. In the mid-1800s, the **King Movement,** based in the King Country region south of Waikato (see p. 114), sought to centralize Maori support, naming Te Wherowhero of Waikato their king in 1858. In a more moderate strain of resistance, they envisioned the Maori king as a local complement to the faraway British monarch, not a usurper of power. The British government understood their motives differently, however, and refused to recognize the Maori king. When violent conflict erupted once again in Taranaki in 1860, **Governor George Grey** blamed the King Movement and decided to strike at Waikato, the movement's primary stronghold. War exploded across the North Island as a result, with British forces finally withdrawing in 1870.

In 1865, the first **Native Lands Act** set up a court to investigate Maori land ownership and distribute official land titles. While any Maori claimant in a land block could initiate a court investigation, land titles in these disputes usually went to chiefs, making it even harder for individual Maori to hold onto land.

CONFLICT AND CONCESSION

Over the course of the next century, a series of attempts was made to resolve disputes between Maori and Pakeha (non-Maori).

1873 The second **Native Lands Act** split up the land title for a land block among its shared owners. Each individual's share had to then be passed on to all natural heirs,

Universal Suffrage

September 19, 1893, was a day of victory for the New Zealand women's suffrage movement, led by Kate Sheppard. After years of petitions, rallies, and protests, Governor Glasgow signed the bill that made New Zealand the first country in the world to give the women the vote on a national level. This stride toward equality was made 25 years ahead of the rest of the world. In 1902, New Zealand's west-ward neighbor, Australia, was the second country to grant women suffrage.

whittling down the size of the shares more and more with each generation and making it even harder for a tribe to hold onto communal blocks of land.

1877 The **Fisheries Act** sought to recognize Maori fishing territories. Ineffectively enforced and unrecognized by many settlers, it was re-enacted 106 years later, in the spirit of late 20th-century reforms to restore Maori land rights.

1882 Disillusioned with the colonial government, the Nga Puhi tribe sent the first delegation to England to personally petition Queen Victoria. Although they were never given audience, the Maori continued to send representatives until the 1920s.

1907 New Zealand became a **dominion**.

1909 The third **Native Lands Act** set aside funds specifically for Maori land development in order to aid Maori farmers. In an interesting paradox typical of the era, the same amount was also set aside to buy up Maori land.

1915 Enlisted to fight in World War I, the **Australia and New Zealand Army Corps (ANZAC)** were chosen to join the infamous Dardanelles campaign. At **Gallipoli** on April 25, the ANZACs were sent in to attack Turkish forces entrenched in the Dardanelles strait. The battle was a huge military failure, leading to massive Australian and New Zealand casualties.

1922 In a landmark case, the government agreed to compensate the Te Arawa tribe for lost fishing and burial rights in the Rotorua lakes. Four years later, another such agreement was made with the Ngati Tuwharetoa tribe concerning Lake Taupo.

1932 Governor General Lord Bledisloe offered James Busby's former house at Waitangi as a gift to the nation, reflecting renewed national interest in the treaty.

1935 The first **Labour Party** came into government, touting official recognition of the treaty as part of their platform. They established connections with certain Maori political movements, but never came through on their election promise to incorporate the treaty into official law at last.

New Zealand had been a dominion of the British Empire since 1907, but courageous performance in two World Wars helped pave the way to autonomy. Making a final break from Britain, New Zealand was declared **fully independent** in **1947.**

The new nation then had to establish its relationship with the Maori, for independence meant it had a limited liability for the legacy of colonialism but still inherited its problems and tensions. In 1960, the **Waitangi Day Act** made February 6 a national "day of thanksgiving." It was declared an official public holiday 13 years later. Today, Waitangi Day is simultaneously a cause for celebration and a day of protest for those speaking out on perceived continued infringement of Maori rights. By the 1970s, the New Zealand government had emerged as a mediator between its aggrieved Maori citizens and its former rulers. The 1975 **Treaty of Waitangi Act** set up the **Waitangi Tribunal** to hear Maori claims against the Crown. Under the Act, the Tribunal must consider both the Maori and English texts of the treaty in its decisions. In the same year, the **Land March,** a protest against unfair land claim treatment, started at Te Hapua in the Northland and ended at the Parliament building in Wellington.

■ Recent Events

In 1987, Labour Party Prime Minister David Lange committed New Zealand staunchly to the **antinuclear movement** by barring all nuclear-capable vessels from New Zealand harbors and stepping up pressure on the French government to stop nuclear testing at Moruroa Atoll. His action was the culmination of a movement that was marked by the 1985 bombing of the Greenpeace ship, the *Rainbow Warrior,* which was to attend a protest of French nuclear testing (see **Rainbow Warrior,** p. 100). Today, the ship's masts are commemorated in the Dargaville Maritime Museum (p. 113), and New Zealand is still a leader in the antinuclear campaign. As recently as 1995, New Zealand tried unsuccessfully to revive a case against French nuclear testing at the International Court of Justice.

In 1983, the Kiwis and the Aussies established the **Closer Economic Relations Trade Agreement,** which allows free and unrestricted trade between the two nations. After some difficult economic times in the late 1980s, highlighted by a 1986 stock market crash, New Zealand nursed its economy back to health in the 1990s by instituting many free-market reforms. Sheep husbandry is believed by some to have driven the recovery. Now the main global producer of sheep meat, New Zealand is responsible for a staggering 64% of world export trade.

In October 1990, in a landmark victory, the National Party loosened the longtime Labour Party stronghold, as frontman **Jim Bolger** was elected prime minister. Three years later, the majority of New Zealand voted to establish a mixed member proportional representation **(MMP)** system of government, similar to the German system. Under the system, a 120-seat Parliament was established, with a pre-determined number of Maori electorate seats, general electorate seats, and party list seats (in which the elected party selects members). The first MMP election took place in October 1996. Although no party won a clear majority, Bolger's **National Party** captured 35% of the vote and 44 seats. Coming in after the National Party were the **Labour** party (the center-left pro-business party led by Helen Clark), the **Alliance** party (a more left-wing party), and the relatively new party, **New Zealand First,** led by the controversial **Winston Peters,** a part-Maori candidate.

New Zealand politics in recent years has been defined by behind-the-scenes maneuvering, fragile power-sharing arrangements, and allegations of corruption.

New Zealand politics in recent years has been defined by behind-the-scenes maneuvering, fragile power-sharing arrangements, and allegations of corruption

In November 1997, while Bolger was out of the country, National's **Jenny Shipley,** a former schoolteacher and farmer, engineered a "coup" to replace him as their party's leader. Months of secret planning paid off when Bolger resigned in the face of Shipley's leadership bid. She was sworn in as New Zealand's first woman prime minister in December of that year. A primary focus of Shipley's government has been to increase free-market competition and reduce government size. These policies have drawn criticism that, despite her gender, she has ignored concerns fundamental to New Zealand women.

Shipley's term as prime minister was thrown into disarray in August 1998. She inherited a fragile coalition between her own conservative National Party, and the more liberal New Zealand First. This coalition dissolved when Peters, the deputy Prime Minister and Treasurer, led his four fellow New Zealand First ministers out of an emergency cabinet meeting in protest of a planned sale of the Wellington airport. New Zealand First characterized the proposed deal as selling New Zealand assets into foreign control, while Shipley argued it was just good business. She sacked Peters for his intransigence, but then faced the difficult task of ruling as a minority leader.

The other major news story of 1998 was a nine-and-a-half-week power outage in Auckland's business district, an event that unfortunately gave New Zealand a rare place in world headlines. (For more on the outage, see p. 80.) The power failure did severe damage to the country's economy and put hundreds of Aucklanders out of business. A report released in August 1998 concluded that the utility company, **Mercury Energy,** had been negligent in its maintenance of the city's power cables. The report stated that the company had been aware of the potential for breakdown, but had not taken the proper steps to prevent it. More alarmingly, **Transpower,** the national power grid company, stated in August that unless a new power station was built near Auckland, an earthquake or plane crash could disable power in much of the North Island.

Currently, the recognition of **Maori land rights** is an issue of heated governmental debate. Certain tribes in the Wellington area, for example, have made claims on land beneath the Parliament building and the National Museum, touching off a storm of controversy. While many non-Maori New Zealanders feel that they are not responsible for the past and that the country owes no debt to the Maori, the government has generally disagreed. The **Office of Treaty Settlement** is the government organization responsible for mediating between Maori claims and the British crown. In November 1997, the British crown admitted in the **Ngai Tahu Deed of Settlement** that it had acted unfairly and in violation of the 1840 Treaty of Waitangi, but land reparations are another matter.

Within New Zealand, the legal definition of Maori was expanded in July 1998, when the **Te Whanau o Waipareira Trust,** an organization of Auckland area Maori, won recognition as a tribe from the Waitangi Tribunal. Because they are not part of a traditional *iwi* (a common, traceable bloodline), urban Maori were previously unable to access government funds for job training, education, welfare, and health services. Their new status has yet to be approved by New Zealand's High Court and does not grant rights to land reparations or property, but is an important step towards remedying the problems that beset urban Maori.

Also in July of 1998, the Minister of Justice, Doug Graham, announced plans to introduce a bill that would **lower the drinking age** to 18, allow supermarkets to sell beer and wine, and reduce licensing requirements. Similar bills have failed in the past, and the police and leading health authorities remain opposed to this one.

In upcoming years, plans are underway to cash in on the dawning of the millennium. For the 2000 Sydney Olympics in Australia, New Zealand is scheduling concerts, marathons, and a large **Maori Performing Arts Festival** to help pull visitors to the other side of down under. Although Gisborne and Hastings are currently bickering over which city should take official honors, one thing is sure: it will be on New Zealand's shores that the first rays of the next millennium's sunlight fall.

NEW ZEALAND

NORTH ISLAND

Auckland

Situated on the rim of the "Ring of Fire," Auckland is poised to explode onto the global scene. As the Americas Cup 2000 fast approaches, the host city is building and refining in preparation for the world spotlight. In February of 1998, a catastrophic power outage in the city's business district lasted nine and a half weeks and struck hard at the country's economy. Yet this stumble has not lessened Auckland's ambition (or ability) to be a world-class city. A trademark Kiwi hospitality and openness has already made it a multi cultural mecca, with the largest Polynesian population in the world and sizeable European and Asian communities. Despite its large urban sprawl, Auckland center is surprisingly small; its one million residents are constantly crossing paths with friends. For all the focus upon its terrestial area, Auckland's true spirit is captured by the ships that populate its numerous harbors and waterways, making its reputation as the "City of Sails." Perhaps more fitting is the Maori name for Auckland, "the City of 100 Lovers." Join those who have fallen for the city's striking beauty and sought it as their own.

🖐 AUCKLAND HIGHLIGHTS

- In the "City of Sails," where one person in five is a boat owner, landlubbers and veterans alike sail on Waitemata Harbour (see p. 79).
- Great Barrier Island (see p. 88) offers a pristine escape from the burdens and responsibilities of civilization.
- The beaches of Waiheke Island (see p. 86) fill with disciples of sun and surf in the summer.
- The party lasts all night at clubs on Auckland's K Road and High Street (see p. 74).

▉ Getting There and Away

BY PLANE

Swank and smartly renovated, the **Auckland International Airport (AKL)** serves as port of entry to 85% of New Zealand's overseas visitors. It is located a 50-minute drive from central Auckland. The many shuttles that run to and from the airport connect to city accommodations, or stop at several transfer points within the city, including the Sheraton Hotel, the Sky City bus station, the Downtown Airline Terminal, and points in the neighborhoods of Parnell and Newmarket. **Airbus** (tel. 275 7685) runs between these points every 20 minutes from 4:40am-10pm; call for a recording of all departure points. ($10; $16 return; students, YHA/VIP members, seniors $7; children $5; buy tickets from the driver.) **Johnston's Shuttle Link** (tel. 256 0333 or 275 1234) has prearranged pickups, and the **Little Kiwi Airport Shuttle** (tel. 309 0905) runs between the airport and the Downtown Airline Terminal at the corner of Albert and Quay St. (every 20min., 6am-8pm). **Taxis** are $30-$40 to downtown.

At the airport, exchange currency at the **Bank of New Zealand (BNZ)**; this is also where you'll pay the $32 **departure fee.** Those connecting to domestic flights (who have more than 45min. between flights) can check their bags at the airline counters; otherwise, lug them on the blue airport shuttles.

Air New Zealand flies direct daily to Christchurch (2¼hr., 1-2 per hr., $388), Wellington (1 hr., every 30min., $290), Rotorua (45min., 6-11 per day, $200), and Queenstown (4hr., 1 per day, $602). **Ansett New Zealand** and **Mt. Cook Airline** fly to the

North Island

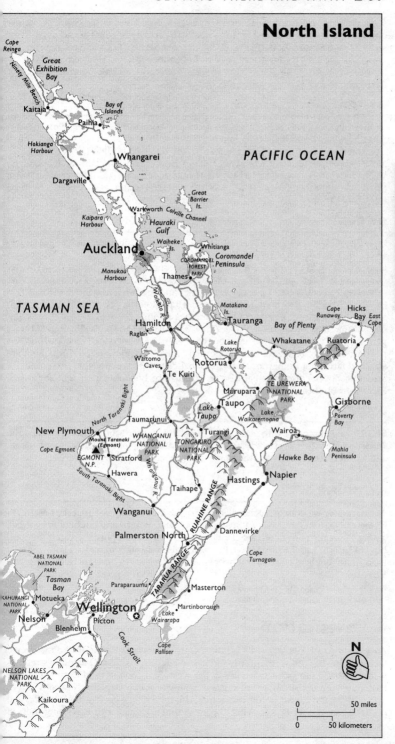

PACIFIC OCEAN

TASMAN SEA

Cape Reinga

Great Exhibition Bay

Ninety Mile Beach

Kaitaia

Bay of Islands

Paihia

Hokianga Harbour

Whangarei

Dargaville

Warkworth

Kaipara Harbour

Great Barrier Is.

Colville Channel

Hauraki Gulf

Waiheke Is.

Auckland

Manukau Harbour

Whitianga

Coromandel Peninsula

COROMANDEL FOREST PARK

Thames

Matakana Is.

Hamilton

Raglan

Waitomo Caves

Te Kuiti

Tauranga

Bay of Plenty

Cape Runaway

Hicks Bay

East Cape

Whakatane

Ruatoria

Lake Rotorua

Rotorua

Murupara

TE UREWERA NATIONAL PARK

Gisborne

Poverty Bay

Taupo

Lake Taupo

Lake Waikaremoana

Taumarunui

New Plymouth

North Taranaki Bight

WHANGANUI NATIONAL PARK

Turangi

TONGARIRO NATIONAL PARK

Wairoa

Mahia Peninsula

Cape Egmont

Mount Taranaki (Egmont)

EGMONT N.P.

Stratford

Hawera

Whanganui R.

Hawke Bay

South Taranaki Bight

Taihape

RUAHINE RANGE

Hastings

Napier

Wanganui

Palmerston North

Dannevirke

ABEL TASMAN NATIONAL PARK

Cape Turnagain

Tasman Bay

Paraparaumu

TARARUA RANGE

KAHURANGI NATIONAL PARK

Motueka

Masterton

Nelson

Wellington

Martinborough

Picton

Lake Wairarapa

Blenheim

Cook Strait

Cape Palliser

NELSON LAKES NATIONAL PARK

Kaikoura

N

| 0 | | 50 miles |
| 0 | | 50 kilometers |

same destinations with similar service and rates. Students and backpackers receive discounts; hefty marked-down prices can also be had by booking ahead or by flying stand-by (see **Essentials: By Plane,** p. 28, for more details). Beyond New Zealand, **Air New Zealand** flies to the Australian cities of Sydney (3½hr., 5 per day, $559, $729 return), Brisbane (3½hr., 2 per day, $559, $729 return), and Melbourne (4hr., 2 per day, $559, $729 return), among other destinations.

BY TRAIN

TranzRail (tel. (0800) 802 802) chugs from the **Auckland Railway Station** (tel. 270 5209) which is located just a bit inland, off Beach Rd. (take Custom St. E past Anzac Ave.) between the Central Business District and the neighborhood of Parnell. (Open M-F 7:30am-6pm, Sa-Su 7:30am-1pm.) Trains head down the main rail line daily to Wellington (11hr., 2 per day, $135) via Hamilton (2hr., $36) and Palmerston North (8¾hr., $108); to Tauranga (3½hr., $54) via Hamilton; and to Rotorua (4hr., $63) via Hamilton. Cheaper fares are available (see **Essentials: By Train,** p. 29).

BY BUS

InterCity (tel. (0800) 731 711 or 913 6100; email info@intercitycoach.co.nz; http://www.intercitycoach.co.nz) arrives at the new travel center of **Sky City,** at Hobson and Victoria St. in downtown Auckland. Service runs north daily to Paihia in the Bay of Islands (4hr., 2-3 per day, $41) via Whangarei (2¾hr., 2 per day, $30), with another service to Paihia (7¾hr., 1 per day in summer and less often in winter, $58) via Dargaville (3hr., $39). Southbound daily runs include Rotorua (3½-5hr., 6 per day, $43) via Hamilton (2hr., 9 per day, $27); Tauranga (3½hr., 2-3 per day, $37); New Plymouth (6hr., 2 per day, $69); Napier (7hr., 2 per day, $75); and Wellington (11hr., 2 per day, $94) via Taupo (4½-5hr., 4 per day, $49) and Palmerston North (9-10hr., 2-3 per day, $69) or Wanganui (8hr., 1 per day, $68). The prices listed throughout are standard fares, but numerous and substantial **discounts** are available (especially for students). Special discounts can also be obtained by booking far enough ahead (see **Essentials: By Bus,** p. 29, for more info).

BY CAR

SH1 is the main route into and out of Auckland. Toward the south, it's called the **Auckland-Hamilton Motorway,** with on-ramps at the top of Hobson St., Symonds St., and Khyber Pass Rd. Toward the north, it's called the **Northern Motorway,** with an on-ramp at Beaumont St. by Victoria Park.

BY THUMB

The collective wisdom of Auckland's backpacker community says that the best **hitchhiking** can be found by taking a bus to the outlying suburbs and hitching from there, asking locals for current advice. To head north, hitchers reportedly catch the local bus at Platform 5 at the downtown bus terminal (every 30-60min.) to Albany ($4). To head south, hitchers take the InterCity/Newmans service to Bombay Hills (1 per day, $10). It is **illegal** to hitch on the freeway; hitchers recommend thumbing from on-ramps that have room for cars to pull over. See **By Thumb,** p. 31, for more information on hitchhiking in New Zealand.

■ Orientation

Auckland spreads out across its isthmus, with **Waitemata Harbour** and the Pacific Ocean billowing out to the north and east while the **Manukau Harbour** stretches southward and the Tasman Sea lies to the west. **SH1** (Southern Motorway) pumps traffic up from the south and diverges downtown. It becomes the Northern Motorway north of the city and converges into **SH16,** stretching west to the Waitakeres and north to Ninety Mile Beach. While the greater metropolitan area is nothing short of

Auckland Overview

sprawling, many visitors within the heart of the city are regularly struck by its extreme compactness—cross over one block into a different district and you'll know it immediately. The quickest way between two parts is usually walking.

As with most major cities, the lifeblood of the city center is money. The fusions of mirrored glass and steel that are Auckland's banks and businesses dominate the **Central Business District (CBD).** Two main thoroughfares run through the CBD: **Queen Street** runs north-south, meeting the sea at **Queen Elizabeth II Square** (perpetually shortened to **QE II Sq.**), while a main cross street, **Victoria Street,** runs east-west from Victoria Park to Albert Park. The **Waterfront** wraps around the CBD along **Quay ("key") Street.** Just on the other side of Quay St. from QE II Sq.'s office buildings and pigeons is the **Ferry Building** (see **Getting Around: By Ferry,** p. 66). Just a bit inland, off Beach Rd. (take Custom St. E past Anzac Ave.) stands the **Railway Station,** between the CBD and Parnell.

The neighborhoods of **Parnell** and **Ponsonby** go their separate ways from mother Auckland. Parnell extends up the east side, dressing in tasteful Victorian buildings and well-versed in wine aesthetics, while Ponsonby takes off to the west, falling in with starving artists, tattoos, and other fixtures of bohemian life. Ponsonby's partner in crime, **Karangahape Rd.** (universally known as **K Road**) rounds out the hipsters' scene with more bars, clubs, and the occasional strip joint.

East of the CBD, Quay St. turns into **Tamaki Drive,** which then swoops along the coast. Skirting subtropical waters and cream-colored sands bordered by stands of pohutukawa trees, it becomes a prime in-line skating, kayaking, and parading venue in the summer months. **Orakei Basin,** off **Hobson Bay,** is home to frequent rainbows and hundreds of pleasure yachts. Hiding around **Bastion Point** from Orakei is **Mission Bay,** a prime parade, carousing, and sunbathing spot with a little stretch of cafes and bars. **St. Heliers Bay,** a few minutes down the shore on Tamaki Dr., has white sand and a tiny shopping district where the *nouveau riche* wage elegant battles with the old money of Paritai Dr. The charming suburb of **Mt. Eden** is 2km south of city center, on a hill overlooking the metropolis.

The Auckland-based **New Zealand Herald** is the country's most comprehensive daily newspaper. **Metro** magazine keeps its finger on the pulse of Auckland's pop culture and politics, while **Express** is the gay and lesbian local paper of choice. **The Fix** has the dope on Auckland's dance clubs.

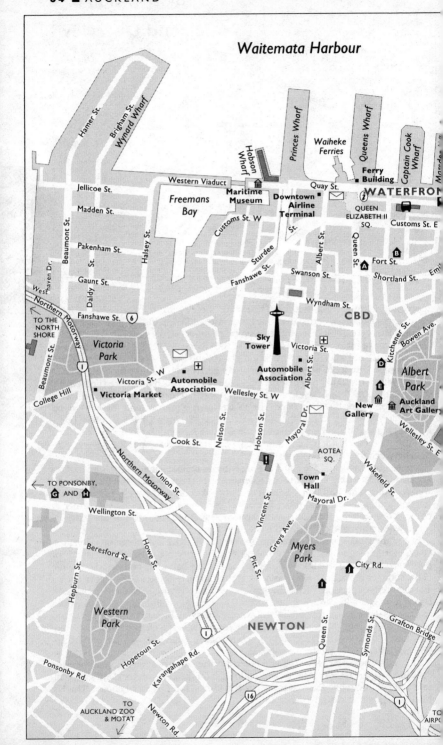

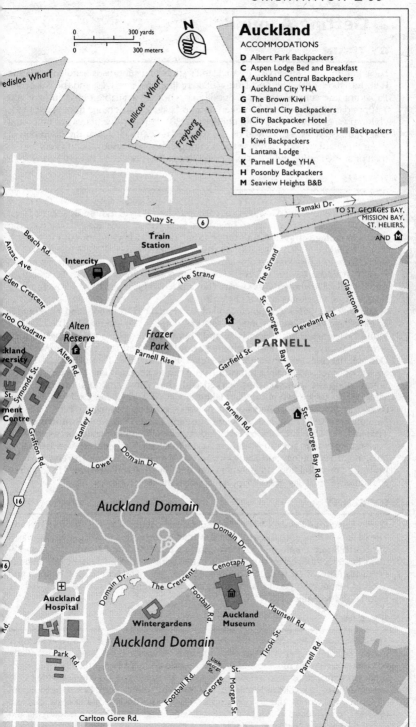

Auckland
ACCOMMODATIONS
D Albert Park Backpackers
C Aspen Lodge Bed and Breakfast
A Auckland Central Backpackers
J Auckland City YHA
G The Brown Kiwi
E Central City Backpackers
B City Backpacker Hotel
F Downtown Constitution Hill Backpackers
I Kiwi Backpackers
L Lantana Lodge
K Parnell Lodge YHA
H Posonby Backpackers
M Seaview Heights B&B

■ Getting Around

BY TRAIN

Local commuter train service to Auckland's sprawling suburbs is handled by **Tranz Rail** (tel. 366 6400). The Auckland-Waitakere line runs east-west and the Auckland-Papakura line runs north-south. Service is generally available between 6am and 7:30pm daily. Each journey is broken up into "stages;" rates range from Stage 1 ($1, children 60¢) to Stage 6 ($4.30, children $2.80). Lower priced fares are only valid after 9am. **Bicycles** are allowed on the trains at no extra charge at the discretion of the train guard, who may refuse them during crowded periods. Buy tickets on the train or at the **station,** which is located off Beach Rd., between CBD and Parnell.

BY BUS

Contact **Rideline** (tel. 366 6400 or (0800) 103 080 outside of Auckland). The major company, **Yellow Bus Co.,** was recently purchased by **CityLine Buses,** so fares, schedules, and routes are apt to be in flux for a while. Fares are calculated by the number of Stages traveled, and range from Stage 1 ($1, children 60¢) to Stage 8 ($7.20, children $4.30). A pass for an day of unlimited travel will also be offered ($6-9, children 40% discount, family rates available; effective after 9am). Ten-trip tickets are also available. Pay the driver (exact change not required). Most city buses can be caught at the **Downtown Bus Centre** (not a place to be at night), or across from QE II Sq., both on Customs St. near Queen St.

The **Link bus** makes a complete loop of the central city in an hour and a half, and is an excellent way to orient yourself (stay on as long as you like for $1). The blue and white buses make both clockwise and counterclockwise loops through Queen Street, Sky City, Victoria Park, Ponsonby, K Rd., Auckland University, the Auckland Domain, the Auckland Museum, Newmarket, Parnell, the Railway Station, and QE II Sq. Though not technically a tourist bus, you can make it into one by getting on anywhere along the route at stops marked with the yellow Link logo in a blue oval. Those eager to see *everything* can take the United Airlines-run **Explorer Bus** (tel. (0800) 439 756), which offers hop-on, hop-off service connecting the Ferry Building, Mission Bay, Kelly Tarlton's, Auckland Museum, Parnell Village, Downtown Airline Terminal, Sky City, and Victoria Park Market. A **satellite bus** operates between October and April that goes to Mt. Eden, St. Luke's shopping center, Auckland Zoo, Museum of Technology and Transport, and the Art Gallery. Buses depart on the hour from the Ferry Building. (In summer 9am-4pm, in winter 10am-4pm; $15, children $7, families $35, 2-day pass $25; purchase from the driver.)

BY FERRY

Ferries leave from **Prince's Wharf** behind the Ferry Building, across from QE II Park. The islands of Rangitoto (see p. 85) and Waiheke (see p. 86) are very accessible, as is the North Shore community of Devonport (see p. 83). The **Pakatoa Cat** (tel. 379 0066; fax 366 3006) leaves from Pier 3 and heads for Coromandel on the Coromandel Peninsula (2hr.; W-Su 10am, F 12:30pm; $31 one way, $59 return). The heliport and hydrofoil launching point for those bound for the remote beauty of Great Barrier Island is in **Mechanics Bay.**

BY CAR

The **Automobile Association,** 99 Albert St. (tel. 377 4660), sits in its own skyscraper in the CBD on the corner of Victoria and Albert St. (open M-F 8:30am-5pm). A plethora of maps (free to members of affiliated world-wide AAs with membership card; moderately priced for non-members) is found here, along with country-wide bookings and travel items like inflatable neck pillows and money belts. Before heading out on your own, you should also pick up a copy of **The Road Code of New Zealand** ($14.95). The *Driver's Guide* brochure indicates all of the CBD's one-way streets and parking areas. The *Minimap* series is quite comprehensive and available from the visitors center on Wellesley St. Alternatively, **Specialty Maps,** 56 Albert St. (tel. 307 2217), can provide some handy cartographic devices for a good price (open M-F 8:30am-4:30pm, Sa 10am-1pm).

Ace Rentals, 39-43 The Strand (tel. 303 3112), in Parnell, rents economy cars from $35 per day for up to 20 days and $25 per day for 20 days or more (includes unlimited km, insurance, 24hr. AA coverage). **Omega Rental Cars,** at the airport (tel. 275 3265), or at 137 Newton Rd. (tel. (0800) 525 210 or 358 3083), starts its budget cars at $39 (min. 4 days; tax, insurance, AA service, and unlimited km included). One-way rentals to joint offices in Wellington, Christchurch, Nelson, Picton, and Queenstown are also offered. **Maui Rentals** (tel. (0800) 651 080), also at the airport, rents campers with showers and kitchens from $70 per day. The worldwide chains are also in Auckland, of course: **Avis** (tel. 526 2847 or (0800) 655 111), **Budget** (tel. (800) 652 227), and **Hertz** (tel. (800) 654 321) have offices at the airport. For important details on driving in New Zealand, please see **Essentials: By Car,** p. 30.

If you'll be in New Zealand for an extended period of time, you may want to consider buying a car. **Car auctions** are one option; **Turners Car Auctions,** McNab St., Penrose (tel. 525 1920), sells budget cars at 11:30am on Wednesdays, and family cars at 6pm on Thursdays. **Hammer Auctions,** 830 Great South Rd., Penrose (tel. 579 2344), sells budget cars on Mondays, Wednesdays, and Fridays. Otherwise, check out the following **car fairs in Auckland** to find a deal when buying or selling a car.

Oriental Markets, at the carpark on Beach Rd. in the Central Business District. Open Saturday 9am-noon.

Sell Your Own, 676 Great South Rd., Manukau (tel. (0800) 735 596). Open daily 7am-7pm.

Sell it Yourself, 50 Wairau Rd., Glenfield (tel. 443 3800). Open daily 7am-7pm.

Ellerslie Racecourse (tel. 810 9212), off the Greenlane Roundabout. Open Sunday 9am-noon.

Manukau City Park and Sell (tel. 358 5000). Open Sunday 8:30am-1pm.

BY TAXI

Alert Taxis (tel. 309 2000), **Auckland Cooperative Taxi** (tel. 300 3000), and **Discount Taxis** (tel. 529 1000) don't gouge on prices. Taxis queue all over the CBD, but large stands can be found at the intersection of Victoria St. E and Queen St., and on K Rd. across from the clubs. Calling ahead for a pickup is a good idea.

BY BICYCLE

Adventure Cycles, 1 Fort Lane (tel. 309 5566 or (0800) 335 566), at Quay St., rents mountain bikes from $25 per day, $90 per week, or $190 per month. Touring and racing bikes pedal from $18 per day, $70 per week, or $180 per month. All gear (such as helmets, water bottles, locks, maps, and tools) is included. **Kiwi Adventure Cycling** (tel. 379 0779), at the corner of Beach Rd. and Anzac Ave., has excellent deals on extended hire (all gear included). One-way hire across the North Island is available, as is free luggage storage.

BY MOTORCYCLE

New Zealand Motorcycle Rentals, 85 Customs St. W. (tel. 358 2252; http://www.nzbike.com), offers motorcycles and scooters with one-way rentals to Wellington and Christchurch. (From $39 per day, includes unlimited km, airport transfers, insurance, 24hr. support service. Open M-Sa 9am-5:30pm; Su 10am-3pm.)

■ Practical Information

TOURIST AND FINANCIAL SERVICES

Visitors Center: Auckland Visitor Centre, 24 Wellesley St. W., CBD, (tel. 366 6888, airport branch 256 8646; fax 366 6893). The headquarters of New Zealand's extraordinary Visitor Information Network is well-outfitted with a complete booking network and every existing brochure and map about New

Zealand. English, French, Japanese, Cantonese, Mandarin, and some German spoken. Message boards advertise everything from cars for sale to flatmates wanted to upcoming gallery events. Open M-F 8:30am-5:30pm, Sa-Su and public holidays 9am-5pm. If you arrive by ferry, the most convenient stop for information is the **branch** in QE II Sq., in the green octagonal kiosk. Open in summer daily 9:30am-5pm, in winter M-F 9:30am-5pm.

DOC: In the Ferry Building on Quay St. (tel. 379 6476). Doubles as the **Auckland Regional Parks Office,** with maps and camping information galore. Open M-W, F 9am-1pm and 1:30-4pm, Th 1:30-4pm. (For more info see p. 34)

Budget Travel: YHA Travel (tel. 379 4224; fax 366 6275), on the corner of Shortland St. and Jean Batten Pl. It's not officially affiliated with the hostelling organization of the same name, but offers some real deals. Open M-F 9am-6pm, Sa 10am-2pm. Proving that Kiwis are not flightless birds, there are **Air New Zealand Travel Centres** (reservations tel. (0800) 737 767) are everywhere you look. Drool over the glossy brochures in the Airport Domestic Terminal (tel. 256 3999), Custom St. in the CBD (tel. 366 2424), or 228 Broadway St. in Newmarket (tel. 520 4035). The **Ansett New Zealand Travel Shop,** 75 Queen St. (tel. 307 5380 or (0800) 800 146, reservations tel. 302 2146), in the CBD, does domestic and international bookings. Open M-F 8:30am-5pm. Otherwise, try the in-house travel centers at **Auckland Central Backpackers (VIP)** (tel. 358 4874) or **Auckland City YHA** (tel. 309 2802). Both are open to non-guests and offer special discounts only available there. The **Flight Centre** (tel. (0800) FLIGHTS/354 4487) has offices at 350 Queen St. (tel. 358 4310) and 2 Fort St. (tel. 377 4655), in the CBD, or at Broadway Plaza (tel. 529 2400) in Newmarket, offering consistently low airfares.

Consulates: Australia, 132-38 Quay St. (tel. 303 2429), in the Union House; **Germany,** 52 Symonds St. (tel. 377 3460); **Ireland,** 87 Queen St. (tel. 302 2867); **Japan** (tel. 303 4106) ASB Bank, corner of Albert and Wellesley St.; **U.S.** (tel. 303 2724), on the corner of Shortland and O'Connell St. on the fourth floor of the General Building; **U.K.,** 151 Queen St. (tel. 303 2973), in the Fay Richwhite Building; **Western Samoa,** 283 Karangahape Rd. (tel. 303 1012), in Newton.

Currency Exchange: Interforex has the best hours around, with two central locations: 2 Queen St. (tel. 302 3031), in the Endeans Building, and 99 Quay St. (tel. 302 3066), in the Ferry Building. Both branches are open daily 8am-8pm. The corner of Queen and Victoria St. in the City Centre is a shrine to New Zealand banking, with the grandiose **Bank of New Zealand (BNZ)** (tel. 379 9900) and its consistently good rates, **ANZ** (tel. 358 9200), and **National Bank,** 45 Queen St. (tel. 357 0040), which charges no commission on cashing traveler's checks and foreign currency. Hours across the board are M-F 9am-4:30pm, Sa 10am-2pm.

ATMs: New Zealand has more ATMs per capita than almost any other country in the world. Walk down Queen, Ponsonby, Parnell, or Broadway and you'll find one every few meters. Most are on the Cirrus, Star, Visa, or MasterCard systems.

American Express: 105 Queen St. (tel. 379 8286 or (0800) 801 122). The office changes foreign currency or traveler's checks without commission. Members' mail held for up to one month. Open M-F 9am-5pm, Sa 9:30am-12:30pm.

EMERGENCY, MEDICAL, AND POSTAL SERVICES

Emergency: 111 is the emergency number for all of New Zealand.

Police: Auckland Central Police Station (tel. 379 4240) is on the corner of Cook and Vincent St. The **Downtown Station** (tel. 379 4500) is on the corner of Jean Batten Pl. and Fort St. Other stations include **Airport International Terminal** (tel. 275 9046), the **Karangahape Rd. Community Constable** (tel. 309 8177), and the **Devonport Community Constable** (tel. 489 4008).

Hotlines: Auckland Central Victim Support (tel. 623 1700). **Lifeline** (tel. (0800) 423 743 or 522 2808) offers 24hr. counseling. The **Auckland Help Foundation** (tel. 623 1700) offers 24hr. aid to victims of sexual assault, as does the **Rape Crisis Centre** (tel. 366 7213). For concerns regarding STDs contact the **AIDS Hotline** (tel. (0800) 802 437), or the **AIDS Foundation** (tel. 303 3124).

Medical Services: Urgent Pharmacy, 60 Broadway St. (tel. 520 6634), in Newmarket, is open M-F 5:30-11:30pm, Sa-Su 8:30am-11pm. On-call daily 11pm-7:30am. The **Auckland Hospital** (tel. 379 7440) sits on the edge of the Auckland Domain on Park St. in Grafton. For less dire cases, **Travelcare,** 87 Queen St. (tel. 373 4621), in the CBD, will immunize, vaccinate, heal, and soothe "Auckland's visitors and hotel guests." **Ponsonby Accident and Emergency,** 202 Ponsonby Rd. (tel. 376 9222), has its own **pharmacy.** Open daily 7:30am-10pm. For alternative medicine, seek out the **Uptown Pharmacy,** 178 K Rd. (tel./fax 373 3552). Open M-W, F 8:30am-5:30pm, Th 8:30am-8pm, Sa 10:30am-1pm.

Post Office: Post shops are scattered throughout the city, but the **Wellesley Street Post Shop (CPO)** in the Bledisloe Building, 24 Wellesley St. (tel. 379 6714), is where you can claim your *Poste Restante* with a valid passport or driver's license. Packages can be forwarded to another post office in the country within 30 days of receipt (from $7). Open M-F 8:30am-5pm, Sa 9am-12:30pm.

Internet Access: Live Wire, MidCity Complex, 239 Queen St. (tel. 356 0999; http:/ /www.livewire.co.nz), has a fast connection for $3 per 15min. Open M-F 9am-10pm, Sa 10am-11pm, Su 10am-10pm. At **Web Work Shop Cyber Gallery,** 195 Symonds St. (tel. 377 6347; email webworks@webworkshop.co.nz; http:// www.webworkshop.co.nz), check your email ($5 per 30min.) and admire original New Zealand art on the walls (open M-F 10am-6pm, or by appointment).

LOCAL SERVICES

Luggage Storage: National Mini Storage LTD, 68 Cook St. (tel. 356 7020), will store luggage for 50¢ a day. For long term storage, **Auckland Central Backpackers,** 9 Fort St. (tel. 358 4877), will store bags for a flat fee (less than 1 month $10, over 1 month $15, bikes and surfboards $15).

Bookstores: Whitcoull's, on the corner of Queen and Victoria St., purveys just about everything made from (or printed on) paper. Three glorious floors and a cafe. Fathom the possibilities in the travel section. **The Dead Poets Bookshop,** 238 K Rd. (tel. 303 0555), offers pre-loved books and specializes in collectibles.

Women's Organizations: Auckland Women's Centre, 63 Ponsonby Rd. (tel. 376 3227; fax 376 1817), is a women-only space offering counseling, a library, and other services. Open M-F 9am-4pm. **Wanderwomen,** 30 Edenvale Crescent, Mt. Eden (tel./fax 630 1108), coordinates weekend adventure trips for women, including kayaking, climbing, and caving. Call for schedules.

Gay-Bi-Lesbian Organizations: Call the **Gayline/Lesbianline** for counseling (tel. 303 3584), or stop into the **The Pride Centre,** 33 Wyndham St., for information, referrals, and a social events calendar. Open M-F 8:30am-5pm.

Ticket Agency: Ticketek (tel. 307 5000) is comprehensive, but a credit card phone booking comes with a $6 surcharge. Book through a music store instead for only $1. Avoid the fees altogether by going in person to the **Countrywide Bank box office** at the Aotea Centre. Open daily 9am-5:30pm; later on performance nights.

Weather Conditions: MetPhone (24hr. tel. (0900) 999 09), 99¢ per minute. **Met-Fax** (0900) 77 999; helpline tel. (0800) 500 669) gives you a visual picture in 10min. You could also check *The New Zealand Herald* or ring the **visitors center** (tel. 366 6888) on Aotea Sq.

■ Accommodations

The sails of Westhaven's yachts aren't the only expensive sheets in Auckland. Centrally located hotels and motels all run $70-90 for a double. Those with cars can try the suburbs of **Remuera** and **Grey Lynn** for cheaper motel options; otherwise, a variety of hostels and backpackers, of a relatively high standard and closer to the action, pick up the slack. Families that don't mind sharing facilities are discovering hostels, and many establishments are responding with rates for family rooms. The **Fort St.** area, while rife with bargains, is probably better suited for younger people, or at least those who don't mind a lot of drunken revelry and the nearby "massage parlours" of the red light district. For peace and quiet, the best option is to head for one of the backpackers in the residential neighborhoods, which still have easy access to the city.

Albert Park Backpackers (VIP), 27 Victoria St. E (tel. 309 0336; fax 309 9474), in the **CBD.** Super-centrally located, the Albert Park is 5 stories of classy, yet lived-in accommodations with black-lacquered bunks. Filled with hip twentysomethings, the kitchen and lounge sport a pool table, a view of the city, and a cordial atmosphere. Jovial staff makes bookings (with credit card). Check out the basement **Mad Dog Music Bar,** where you get a free beer upon check-in, and live music Th-Sa night. Free bike and luggage storage. 10- to 12-bunk dorms $16; 4- to 6-bed shares $17; singles $30; twins and doubles $47. Lockers $1. Key deposit $10. Summer check-in virtually 24hr.; in winter, reception 7am-11pm. To hold a reservation past 3pm, book with a credit card. Check-out 10am.

City Backpacker Hotel, 38 Fort St. (tel. 307 0181 or (0800) 220 198; fax 307 0182; http://www.city-backpacker-hotel.co.nz), in the **CBD,** is for those who dream of having their own apartment in the center of Auckland. Each flat features its own full kitchen, living room with TV, toilet and shower, and intercom. Most suites average 2-4 bunks each, with the largest having 6 bedrooms (most have 3 2-bunk rooms). Bunks $17 per person ($110 per week); singles $25; twins $40; doubles $45. Groups can rent out studio apartments for $150 per night. $20 linen and key deposit (refundable). Free laundry, luggage storage. Check-out 10am.

Downtown Constitution Hill Backpackers (VIP), 6 Constitution Hill (tel. 303 4768, or (0800) 366 1444; fax 303 4766), in the **CBD** and near the Railway Station. The self-proclaimed "smallest hostel in the downtown area" comes through with bungalow coziness in a red cottage bordering the Alten Reserve. Manager keeps things lively, and is very sensitive to maintaining a clique-free environment. Barbecue every Saturday night. Free luggage storage. Free coffee and tea. Dorms $16 summer, $15 winter; doubles $40, with bath $45. Winter dorm special: first 4 nights for $12 each. 4-day max. stay in summer. Check-out 10am.

Auckland Central Backpackers (VIP), 9 Fort St. (tel. 358 4877; fax 358 4872; email backpackers@acb.co.nz; http://www.acb.co.nz), in the **CBD.** An 8-story monument to backpacker partying, its 360 beds are more a place to dump your pack before heading up to the 7th floor bar than a place to quietly de-jetlag. Many people who plan on staying in Auckland work here 14 hours per week in exchange for free accommodation. Travel Centre downstairs. Social lounge and several kitchens (open 6:30am-11pm). Bunks are $16; shares (up to 4) $18 per person; singles $33; twins and doubles $45. Rates rise slightly Nov. 1-Apr. 6. Reservations are highly recommended (with credit card necessary to hold past 4pm). Bunks and shares 6-night max. stay; afterward, upgrade or move on out. Blanket deposit $20. Email $3 per 15min. Reception 24hr. Check-out 10am.

Ponsonby Backpackers, 2 Franklin Rd. (tel. 360 1311 or (0800) 476 676; fax 360 1365), in **Ponsonby.** A blue and white Victorian mansion just around the corner from the electric cafes of Ponsonby. The jumbled lounge is warmed by cushy couches and a big fireplace. Dorms $15; singles $25-30; doubles $38. Tent sites $10. 6-night max. stay in summer. Linen $1. Internet $8 per hr. Reception 8:30am-8pm. Check-out 10:30am.

Auckland City YHA (tel. 309 2802; fax 373 5083; email yhaauck@yha.org.nz; http://www.yha.org.nz), at the corner of City Rd. and Liverpool St., just south of the **CBD.** Housed in a former hotel, City may be big, but it still holds onto that quietly fun YHA atmosphere. The 3rd-floor lounge with outdoor smoking deck and the in-house Tommy's Bistro serve as centers for socializing. Rooms come with linen and writing desks; higher floors have a bit of a view. Friendly staff will help you book your itinerary at the travel center (open daily 8am-5pm). Dorms $19; twins and doubles $44; singles $35. Non-members add $4 per night and $10 key deposit, receiving a "free" membership card at the end of a 6-night max. stay. All prices drop $1 in winter. Check in 24hr., check-out 10am.

The Brown Kiwi, 7 Prosford St. (tel. 378 0191; fax 378 9398; email bookings@brownkiwi.co.nz), in a white colonial home in **Ponsonby.** Clean kitchen, barbecue area with tables. Free storage. Gay friendly. Dorms $17, twins $36, doubles $40. $10 key deposit. $3 duvets, $2 sheets. Internet access $2.50 for 15min.

Seaview Heights B&B, 23A Glover Rd. (tel. 575 8159 or (025) 854 659; fax 575 8155), in **St. Heliers.** Imagine a sleek white house surrounded by roses and azaleas in a neighborhood of million-dollar homes overlooking the ocean with Auckland City shimmering in the distance. If you can also imagine dusting, vacuuming, and doing sundry chores for about 3hr. per day, imagine yourself staying for free (only 1 person per day, however). Courtesy drop-off and flexible check-in and -out. Your bed might be in a little room with the linen and mop closet, but you get access to the same swank lounge, swimming pool, and succulent breakfasts as those in the $160-200 honeymoon suite, or for $100, you and a friend can stay in an awesome room with striped twin beds and a sweeping ocean view from the balcony.

Parnell Lodge YHA, 2 Churton St. (tel. 379 3731; fax 358 4143; email yhaakpa@yha.org.nz). Two-story brick building in pleasant suburban environment 20min. from the city. Free long-term storage if you stay a night upon return. Large kitchen, outdoor barbecue area. Single-sex dorms $17; twins and doubles $40, extra person $9; children $12. Free linen. Check-in before 10pm. Reception 8am-10pm in summer; 8am-noon, 5-10pm in winter.

Central City Backpackers (VIP), 26 Lorne St. (tel. 358 5685; fax 358 4716), in the **CBD.** Recently renovated, CCB is a large hostel (5 floors) with a small hostel feel. Stylish lobby, cafe/bar, and loud nightclub. If you're lucky, you'll be able to have a dance party without ever turning on the stereo and without ever leaving your room. TV lounges on the 1st and 3rd floors. 6- to 10-bed dorms $17 ($90 per week); 1- to 4-bed shares $19 ($102); singles $35; doubles and twins $44. Book from the airport for a discount (dorms $14); first three nights $14 for first-time visitors. Blanket deposit $10. Key deposit $20. Shuttle from airport $9. Check in after 10am; credit card necessary to hold a reservation after 4pm. Check-out 10am.

Lantana Lodge (VIP), 60 St. George's Bay Rd. (reservation tel. 373 4546, guest tel. 373 4616), in **Parnell.** The elegance of this white Victorian home doesn't stop with the gingerbread porch or the flower garden—every square inch of the place is compulsively clean. Plenty of good clean fun with the good-natured guests, too. Free storage. Dorms $17 (in winter $110 per week); doubles or twins from $45 ($245), extra person $11. Key deposit $10. Reception 8am-10pm. Check-out 10am.

Eden Lodge, 22 View Rd. (tel./fax 630 0174), in **Mt. Eden.** A little slice of pristine budget paradise. The 90-year-old palatial home on the slopes of Mt. Eden is family-run, and little bunnies hop about on the wide green lawn. Stretch out on the huge leather couches in the lounge to watch the big-screen TV. Free pickup from the city if you call ahead. Off-street parking. House dorms $15, bunk-house dorms $13, doubles $40. Cash only. One-week max. stay in summer. Reception 8am-noon and 5-8pm. Check-out 10am.

Kiwi Backpackers, 430 Queen St. (tel./fax 358 3999; guest tel. 358 4501). The Kiwi earns points for its central location on mid-Queen St., and for having the cheapest beds in town, if not the country. Lounge has pool table, TV, chess board. There are many guests of diverse nationalities, with no New Zealanders allowed. 10-12 bed dorms $10, 6-8 bed dorms $12, doubles and twins $35. $20 key deposit, linen $2. Free luggage storage for guests. Parking available. Reception/bar open 8am-midnight.

■ Food

Auckland is a bountiful cornucopia of dining options, with authentic foods from all corners of the globe. It is also a city very much aware of healthy eating habits, as the multitude of vegetarian restaurants suggests (though McDonald's is very much a presence). Takeaways are quite common, although deliveries are rare and often have limited coverage. As is to be expected, the food downtown is generally more expensive; it's best to venture up Queen St. and K Rd. to find the best value. See the Cafes section for more dining options.

CENTRAL BUSINESS DISTRICT

Rasoi Vegetarian Restaurant, 211 K Rd. (tel. 377 7780). Prepare yourself for a warm fuzzy peach interior and Indian food that makes you feel warm and fuzzy too. Value is an understatement as deluxe Mali ($8.95) is a small feast, and the all-you-can-eat buffet ($12.95) is fit for the maharajah himself. Savory bags of home-made snack food ($2.50) are perfect for journeys, and mango lassi ($3.50) is a sweet ending. Open M-Sa 11am-9pm.

Pizza Pizza, 57 Lorne St. (tel./fax 309 3333), on the second floor of the giant orange building across from the central library. Funky, laid-back pad placed upon a pizza pedestal by students (who receive 20% discount on small and large pies). Laminated cartoon-covered tables entertain whether you dine upon them or wait for a takeaway. Deep-dish masterpieces range from the carnivorous Meatlovers to the twisted vegetarian Serious Espresso (mushrooms, garlic, capers, olives, asparagus, and green pepper). Personal pizza and a drink for $5; regular pizzas $12.95, large $19.95. Free delivery to Central City area. Open M-W 10:30am-10pm, Th-F 10:30am-10:30pm, Sa-Su 4:30-10:30pm.

The Burgerie, 95 K Rd. Started as a late night stand specializing in vegetarian and vegan fast food. Today they continue the tradition while curing carnivorous cravings. The tempeh burger with peanut sauce and beetroot ($5.40) is quite a combo with kumara wedges ($3). Everything fried in vegetable oil, except the banana or berry soy shakes ($4.20). Eat it at the stand or take it all away. Open M-W 11am-1am, Th 11am-3am, F-Sa 11am-5am.

Cafe Hasan Baba, 466 Queen St. (tel. 358 5308). With a mural of Istanbul gracing an entire wall, authentic Turkish carpets and pictures, and Turkish music wafting in the background, this place has great ambiance and food to match. Meze platters let you sample the goods ($12.50) and takeaway kebabs ($4.50) are choice. Strong Turkish coffee ($2.50) and delicate baklava ($4) offer native flair. Open M-F 11:30am-11pm, Sa-Su 4:30pm-midnight.

Simple Cottage Restaurant, 50 High St. (tel. 303 4599). Lacking much of the pretension of its downtown surroundings, the cottage is haven to novice and maven who together savor the flavor of heaping plates of hot vegetarian food ($8). The box of toys against the wall keeps simple pleasures in mind and easy to find. Open M-Sa 9am-9pm, Su noon-8:30pm, dinner specials 5-8:30pm.

Mexican Cafe, 67 Victoria St. W. (tel. 373 2311). This second-story restaurant and bar comes complete with cactus taps and 23 different tequilas for mad margaritas ($6 glass, $30 jugs) and nachos ($5) during daily happy hour (5-7pm). Munch Mexican mains by mosaic murals; beef, lamb, chicken, or beans wrapped the way you like ($15-20) as the mariachis watch over the kitchen. Open M-W noon-2:30pm and 5-11pm, Th-F noon-2:30pm and 5pm-12:30am, Sa 5pm-12:30am, Su 5-11pm.

Bokcholee, 8 Lorne St. (tel. 375 0032; fax 631 0638). The exotic smells wafting out of this small popular establishment draw you inside, where menu items are displayed in photographic glory. Choose from vegetarian and meat dishes served hot or cold ($6-10). Open M-Sa 10am-11pm.

Food Alley, 11 Albert St. between Customs and Wolfe St. At this popular student spot is a sizeable central eating area surrounded by 14 counters selling large portions of Thai, Korean, Malaysian, Japanese, Indian, Chinese, and Indonesian food (all meals $5-8). A bar and ice cream shop provide a European presence. You could come here every day for two weeks and eat at a different place each time. Open daily 10:30am-10pm.

PARNELL AND NEWMARKET

Al & Pete's, 496 Parnell Rd., at the top of Ayr St., Parnell (tel. 377 5439). Look for the sign with the dual chef profile, and then file inside. They are pros when it comes to fish n' chips ($4.70). Seasoned veterans opt for the potato fritter (60¢). Take it away from this nondescript joint to enjoy in your favorite domain. Open M 11am-11pm, Tu-Th 11am-midnight, F-Sa 11am-2am, Su 11am-10pm.

Kebab Kid, 363 Parnell Rd. and also 166 Ponsonby (tel. 373 4290). Middle Eastern fast food may seem foreign to most, but the kid has your favorite kebab ($6-7), salad and dips ($5.50-6.50), and baklava ($2) ready to go. Take it away into the urban desert, or have them deliver it (limited coverage) right to your palace door. Open Su-M noon-10pm, Tu-Th and Sa noon-11pm, F noon-2am.

PONSONBY

Yuki Sake Bar, 26 Ponsonby Rd. (tel. 360 5050). The sushi sashimi set is served on a wooden bridge connecting two people with a complete experience. Sit down with lacquered wooden chopsticks and frolic over delicate sides. Introduce fish into the rolls and rock your boat with a combi platter ($10).

⊛**Musical Knives,** 272 Ponsonby Rd. (tel. 376 7354). Chef Peter A. Chaplin's creations from organic materials are so crafty that the Material Girl herself took him along as her personal cuisine artist on 2 world tours. Completely non-smoking, though the drinking of organic juices, wines, and sake is permitted and encouraged. Entrees

($8.50-14.50) and mains ($22-23) are dear but near to your heart's content. Go for it at the "only vegetarian restaurant in Auckland where you can truly *dine*." Open daily from 5pm.

Open Late Cafe, 134 Ponsonby Rd. (tel. 376 4466). A gigantic poster of Marilyn Monroe and Tom Ewell in *Seven Year Itch* hangs above the crowds of young party-goers busily devouring nachos big enough to share ($7-11), and very veggie-friendly dishes. The classic Ponsonby after-drinking eating place. Open Su-Th 6:30pm-2am, F-Sa 6:30pm-3:30am.

■ Cafes

Although coffee quality is an important measure of a cafe's worth, in Auckland one must ultimately look at ambiance. The cafe scene is an integral part of the social fabric of the city, and each cafe develops its own character to accommodate those escaping the chaos of the urban landscape or refueling before launching into evenings on the town.

◉Brazil, 256 K Rd. (tel. 302 2677). Cafe of the future and the past, Brazil mixes red vinyl, peeling paint moldings and the rusty service station decor of yesteryear with the underground sounds of electronica. A lethal espresso is made all the more potent with bean-roasting on the premises. Upstairs, rotating resident DJs spin and scratch old skool hip hop, dubby dancehall, and jungle madness. Internet access is $5 per hour. Great breakfasts too. Open M-Tu 8am-8pm, W-Th 8am-midnight, F 8am-1am, Sa 9am-1am and Su 9am-8pm.

The Lost Angel Cafe, 472 K Rd. (tel. 379 3100). The rocket ride out front beckons you to enter this haven from the adult entertainment sector of the street. Inside, gutted televisions suspended from the ceilings highlight an eclectic decorative flair. Cheap eats include 12-inch pizzas ($11), while all coffee drinks are $2.50. Live music on Thursday, slamming poetry on Wednesday after 10pm with the Holy Rev. Stinkfinger. Aspiring DJs take advantage of open decks to craft their sets in front of an audience that enjoys dub-infused drum & bass. B.Y.O.V. (vinyl) and take it out for a spin. Open Tu 10am-5pm, W 10am-2am, Th-Sa 10am-4am, Su 10am-midnight.

Cafe Cezanne, 296 Ponsonby Rd. (tel. 376 3338). Students, dilettantes, and the occasional starving artist all bring a left bank *joie de vivre*. A colorful menu of big beautiful breakfasts, pastas, and salads ($6-12) is complemented by the equally colorful murals on the walls. The *pièce de resistance* is the hot chocolate ($3), escorted by two chocolate fish. Open Su-Th 8am-midnight, F-Sa 8am-2am.

Net Central Cybercafe, 5 Lorne St. (tel. 373 5186; email calum@netcentral.co.nz; http://www.netcentral.co.nz). Brightly lit, simple decor features 15 PCs and five Macs. Solid coffee ($2.80-4) and light meals ($5-9) are somewhat of a pretext; people come here to get on-line with the fastest cafe connection in town. Speed does not come cheap ($1.20 per 5 min.) but soften the blow with a combo (30 min. and a coffee, $8.95). Helpful staff knows their way around a computer, so don't be afraid to ask. Deals available on multiple hours. Open daily 10am-10pm.

DKD, 17 O'Connell St. (tel. 303 4653). Forced to relocate to make room for Planet Hollywood, DKD has moved from its home in the bowels of the civic center to a more visible and conventional spot downtown. The coffee is arguably the city's finest, and the desserts are rich ($3.50-4.50). Short menu has something for everyone (mains $8-12). Open M-F from 10am, Sa-Su from 4pm.

Manifesto Espresso & Wine Bar, 315 Queen St. (tel. 303 4405). The bright blue store front reveals a dimly lit interior exuding a reserved aura with a polished edge. Boasting the most extensive wine list in Auckland, each month features a different special designed to broaden your knowledge of the grape. Off-license allows you to walk out with your favorite. Great selection of sizeable tapas ($3-7) are ideal for sharing among friends. Sunday night jam session downstairs at 8:30pm ($8, free if you bring an instrument). Open daily 4pm-1am.

Raw Power Cafe, 5-7 High St. in the Century Arcade (tel. 303 3624). Bright orange interior with royal blue trim. Serves vegetarian food fit for royalty. A heaping bowl from the salad bar will hold many bean and pasta dishes ($6.50). Breakfast served all day ($6.50-7.50) while lunch mains change daily ($6.50, with salad $9). Many vegan options, including chocolate cake served with orange slices ($3). Sit at the juice bar and choose 4 from a list of 20 fruits and vegetables to squeeze into a fresh juice ($3-6). Open M-F 7am-4pm, Sa 10am-3pm.

The Live Poets Cafe, 238 K Rd., adjacent to **The Dead Poets Bookshop** (tel. 303 0555). A lively spot serving coffee and sandwiches has sprung from the decaying matter of old paperbacks. The shelves end at tables where you can enjoy a flat white ($2.50) and a good book from the shop, which specializes in collectible antiquarian literature and offers exchanges as well. Every Friday night, extended hours inspire an open mic where you can share your folk, jazz, or poetry with a receptive crowd. Open Sa-Th 10am-6:30pm, F 10am-11pm.

Mecca (tel. 309 6300), Upper Vulcan Lane. Make the pilgrimage to this gathering house, which spills into the lane with outdoor seating. The coffee beans are roasted daily, making for sweet smooth mochaccino ($3.50) in a large bowl. Have a big breakfast ($12.50) or a lighter bagel with brie and tomato ($5.50). Lunches have a Middle Eastern flair ($7.50-12.50) while the crowd has a slight pretentious air, but wear some black and you'll fit right in. Open daily 7am-6pm.

Atomic Cafe, 121 Ponsonby Rd. (tel. 376 4954), in Ponsonby. Very little attitude for a Ponsonby cafe makes for simple enjoyment of serious coffee roasted daily. Bins along the brick wall allow you to take your favorite whole beans home, while heaps of magazines and Dr. Seuss books make for intelligent reading for all ages. A cappucino ($2.50) goes well with a large breakfast ($6-12.50) or a slice of cake ($5). Open M-W 6am-6pm, Th-F 6am-11pm, Sa 7:30am-11pm and Su 8am-4:30pm; kitchen closes at 3pm, 2:30pm on Su.

The Other Side, 320 Parnell Rd. (tel./fax 366 4426). "The works" breakfast will have you "fully functioning" with bottomless filter coffee and a vegetarian option ($10). Lunch and dinner entrees ($5.50-12.50) and mains ($14.50-16.50) will satisfy. Open M-F 7am-10pm, Sa-Su 8am-10pm.

■ Bars

English- and Irish-style pubs dominate the scene, and almost everywhere you go domestic beers are the drink of choice. Tap beers like Steinlager, Speight's, Lion Red, DB, and Export Gold are almost invariably higher in quality (and cheaper) than bottled imports. Spirits and cocktails are gaining in popularity, especially with the Ponsonby jet-set. A major trend of the moment is sweet citrus drinks such as KGB and Stolchinaya, which have the alcohol content of beer and the tang of lemonade. Going prices are $3-4 for a pint of beer, $5 for double spirits and premium spirits. Specialty cocktails and fancy shooters can go as high as $6-7 a shot, and a cocktail shaker goes for $20-25. While the **CBD** and **the Waterfront** are mostly pubs and taverns, **Ponsonby** is full of choice places with black-clad yuppies. **Parnell,** while courting students, is also home to the old money crowd.

Margarita's, 18 Elliot St. (tel. 302 2764). The Monday and Thursday night special of 8 beers for $5 (for the first 100 people) packs them in. Descend from the street to discover a spacious wood-floored space with pool tables, air hockey, and arcade games including Top Skater, where you physically board your way to glory. DJ caters to full spectrum of musical tastes, from jazz early to house later. $2.50 pints between 5-7pm and 9-10pm daily. Open daily 4pm-3am.

The Dog's Bollix (tel. 376 4600), at the corner of K and Newton Rd., in Newton. Dublin is alive and well in Auckland. A good-natured Guinness crowd gives the pub a *céilí* atmosphere, especially when the founders (and namesake band) are playing their brand of traditional Irish music. Every night except Monday, there is live music. On Tuesday and Sunday, this is an acoustic jam, with all players welcome. Frequent step dancing and limerick competitions. Handles $4. Open M-Sa 8:30am-midnight, Su noon-midnight.

Corner Bar, on Shortland St. in the De Bretts Hotel, is guaranteed to start your evening right. Eclectic crowds vary from after-work suits to pre-party queens and everyone in between. It all fits together in a warm and cozy candlelit interior tucked away in the corner of the city. Open M-Th from noon, F-Sa noon-3am.

Kiwi Tavern, 3 Britomart Pl. (tel. 307 1717), east of QEII Sq. along Customs St., opposite the Oriental Markets. A 3-story monument to native birds and cheap booze. Tuesday night is 2-for-1 drinks. Live music Tu-F starting after 9pm. DJ Saturday night. Give the bartender a smile and receive a Kiwi Card, good for more drink discounts ($5 jugs). Downstairs, the **Moa Bar** (tel. 307 1919) complements nicely with mellow wine bar atmosphere and daily happy hours 5-7pm (pints, wine $2.50). The "lawn moa" on the wall are a great touch, good for a few laughs over a few drinks. Open daily noon-3am.

The Blue Bar, corner of Parnell and Akaroa Rd. (tel. 367 6821), 2nd floor above The New Exchange. A central bar is surrounded by sculpted couches that break up a pale blue interior. The real draw is the adjacent garden barbecue where you choose your own steak and grill it yourself ($14.50). Open M-Sa 4pm-1am.

Lava Lounge, 17 O'Connell St. Lava lamps and red disco balls create a relaxed mood to enjoy a drink or catch a breath from dancing upstairs. Table top version of Ms. Pacman creates a nice group sitting area. Cool down momentarily but don't solidify here; more incendiary action awaits. Treat yourself to a last drink at dawn on weekends. Open Tu-Th 5pm-3am, F-Sa 5pm-8am.

The Classic Comedy & Bar, 321 Queen St. (tel. 373 4321). The Classic serves up laughs in the back room with a variety of nights ranging from improv (Tu, $5, $3 for students) to amateur open mic (W, $6) to seasoned pros later in the week (cover varies). The bar is open from 4pm and boasts the largest selection of flavored vodkas in New Zealand (try the Wasabe if you dare). The staff is friendly and engineers a mix of great company and good times. Shows start at 8pm. Open Tu-Th 4-11pm, F-Sa 4pm-1am.

Temple, 486 Queen St. (tel. 377 4866). Auckland's "live original music venue" delivers tunes of all kinds 6 nights a week. Mondays at 9pm there is an open mic jam night, all performers welcome. Other nights vary, and there is rarely a cover. Dark interior makes it hard to find much of anything inside. Happy hour from 5-8pm (2 spirits or beers $5). If the music strikes a painful chord, head upstairs to a room only slightly larger than the pool table it features. Open M-Th 5pm-2am, F 5pm-4am, Sa 5pm-3am.

The Voodoo Lounge (tel. 358 4847), on Vulcan Ln., in the CBD. Dripping with all the makings of an incantatous evening—from the bats and scorpions embedded in the bar to potent potions like "dragon's blood" (a shooter of sambuca, chartreuse, Wild Turkey, and Jägermeister). Half of the crowd grooves smoothly to deep, throaty tunes (live music on weekends) while the rest sulk in vinyl booths over wax-dripped skulls or gravitate to the balcony to play pool. $2 cover on F. Open Tu-Th 8pm-1 or 2am, F 7pm-6am, Sa 9pm-6am.

Java Jive (tel. 376 5870), corner of Ponsonby Rd. and Pompallier Terr., in Ponsonby. Drop in at this subterranean blues/jazz/rock club with plenty o' atmosphere and little attitude. Photos of blues greats gaze down approvingly on the happily mixed crowd of all ages. Live bands every night of the week. First note sounds at 8:30pm M-W, 10pm Th-Su; until then, full menu is available. Open nightly; Su-Th from 6pm, F-Sa 6pm-3am.

Eastside, 67 Shortland St. (tel. 373 5434). "Enter the warmth of the womb" and nest under the giant carved eagle spread over the bar. DJ booth behind the head is the ideal vantage point from which to scan for prey in this dimly lit establishment populated by down-to-earth locals. Martini Madness Mondays speak for themselves. Open Sa-Tu from 8pm, W-F from 3pm until late.

The Fat Ladies Arms, 144 Parnell Rd. (tel. 358 2688), in Parnell. "Drinkin' and kissin'," red pool tables, and plenty of good ol' fashioned rock 'n' roll make this American Western-themed bar the hottest saloon in Parnell. Thursday night is the night to come and drink well: starting at 8pm, there is a $5 cover at the door, then $2 drinks thereafter. Live music Sa at 9pm. DJ W-Sa. Full menu daily, as well as $2.50 pints from 6-8pm, $2.50 bourbon from 8-10pm. Open M-Sa 11am-1am.

■ Nightclubs

During the week, the nightlife in Auckland converges upon those venues with special club events. On weekends, the city comes alive with mass movement busting out all over. The downtown **High Street** clubs are generally more relaxed about dress code and attract a younger crowd. Up on **K Road,** style reigns supreme as everyone dons his or her favorite shade of black and joins the queue. Adding color to the scene are the drag queens, who come out at night and stay until the next day.

The two magic numbers in Auckland are 5, the standard cover charge, and 20, which should be your age (at the least) if you want to get in. Carding is strict, so bring your ID; you will get turned away otherwise. To find out what's going on around town, the glossy mag **the Fix** can't be beat, especially since it's free. Pick it up, as well as special events flyers, at **Beat Merchant** on Albert St., **CyberCulture** at 151 K Road, and the mother of all record stores, **Real Groovy**, at 438 K Rd.

Herzog, 324 K Rd. A corrugated metal door slides up to let you enter narrow dark passages leading to the crowded dance floor with an elevated platform in the corner. Rough stone dance floor epitomizes the unpolished edge. Danceable house that refuses to cheese out. A religious experience is a strong possibility with Jesus figures lined up behind the bar and a 12-panel relief sculpture of the crucifix in the adjacent pool room. Attractive bohemian crowd is there for the music.

Buddha, 166B Queen St. (tel. 303 1584), in the CBD. Look for the Buddha head above a black doorway and the big bouncer who enforces a fairly tight dress code, especially on weekends. Downstairs is an alternate universe of deep house and techno. Chill next to the Buddha himself, and leave an offering before you go. Open Th-Sa from 9pm.

Cause Celebre and **The Box,** 33 High St. (tel. 303 1336), in the CBD. Break into the club scene with a young dancing crowd. Unassuming entrance reveals sprawling network of bars and dance floors. Wednesday nights DJ Wanda is the queen of 80s retro classics. Thursday nights feature hip hop grooves while weekends find a balance along the edge of house and techno. $5-10 cover. Open W-Sa 11pm-6am.

Squid, 17 O'Connell St. above DKD Cafe. Although the bar is quite prominent early on because of drink specials, the dance floor dominates as the night goes on and doesn't stop until the wee hours. Creatively eclectic decorations adorn the ceiling and bar, and the plush couches are a great spot to watch a fine light show. Small cover on weekends. Open W-F 10pm-5am, Sa 10pm-3am.

The Kiss Club and Bar, 309 K Rd. (tel. 303 2726). Blacklights reveal quite little given the amount of black being worn in the room. The absence of a cover combined with a steady house beat packs them in on the weekends. While you search for room to dance, admire the photos of drag queens that adorn the walls. Open W-Th 10pm-3am, F-Sa 10pm-5am, Su 10pm-3am.

■ Gay and Lesbian Nightlife

New Zealand fancies itself a tolerant and gay-friendly country, and Auckland is very accommodating to those with alternative lifestyles. Ponsonby is the center of the gay community both in terms of population and nightlife, as gay-run bars and brasseries on Ponsonby Rd. offer numerous opportunities for a night out. Around the corner, K Rd. clubs often cater to the gay set. Scope out the newspaper **Express** newspaper ($2 at newsstands, or free at Surrender Dorothy) for the most current listings.

Taking over Auckland for two weeks, the big **HERO Gay and Lesbian Festival** (Feb. 4-20, 1999) is a carnivalesque celebration of theater performances, film screenings, and outdoor events culminating in a grand parade and lively all-night dance party on the last night. To find out the schedule of events, check out *Express* or find HERO on the web (email herowhatsnewsub@qrd.org.nz; http://nz.com/NZ/Queer/HERO).

Surrender Dorothy, 3/175 Ponsonby Rd. (tel. 376 4460), in Ponsonby. At the sign of the hairy legs and ruby slippers, you'll find an unpretentious and fun watering hole. Even more pairs of glittering pumps and stilettos snake across the ceiling and photos of glamorous drag queens hang from the walls. Predominantly male couples, but lesbian couples and friends of "friends of Dorothy" are more than welcome. Drinks are pricey but you pay for ambiance. Open "for joy and fabulousity" nightly 5pm-12:30am.

S.P.Q.R., 150 Ponsonby Rd. (tel. 360 1710), in Ponsonby. S.P.Q.R. stands for *Senatus populus que Romanus,* which hearkens back to a Roman republic more tolerant of homosexual activity. This ultra-chic cafe and bar, lit by candles and glowing orbs, touts itself as a similar people's forum, attracting quite a mixed crowd. New Zealand wines, beers, and spirits $5-10; pizzas and pastas $14.50-$19.50. Come for a dose of Ponsonby trendiness and exquisite people-watching. Open M-F 10am-2am, Sa-Su from 9am.

Urge, 490 K Rd. (tel. 307 2155). Touting itself as a space for gay males, only those of that persuasion will probably feel truly comfortable here, which is the point. Push aside a heavy black leather curtain as you enter and step into a small dark environment catering more to denim and leather than satin and cashmere. Promotions and musical guests are advertised in *Express,* so check it out if you've got the urge. Open M-Th from 8pm, F-Sa 8pm-3am, Su 6pm-midnight.

Sinners, 373 K Rd. (tel./fax 308 9985). Hard to categorize since in the course of an evening so many people pass through; of course on weekends the night lasts until noon the next day. Around 4am, the crowd exudes a strong gay vibe, with a sizeable contingent of shirtless sculpted men dancing to hard uplifting house on the large dance floor. Later in the night/day, the crown evolves into a varied mix of hyper-stimulated insomniacs. Amazingly, this is when the club is most crowded, as people come to recover their sanity and melt into the morning. Open W-Th midnight-7am, F-Sa midnight-noon, Su midnight-7am.

■ Entertainment

Auckland offers much in the way of entertainment. With seven major theaters in the downtown area, there is always a performance to attend. The 2256-seat **ASB Theatre** in Aotea Centre is the most majestic, home to the **New Zealand Royal Ballet,** the **New Zealand** and **Auckland Philharmonics,** and world-class productions that arrive for limited engagements. **Ticketek** (tel. 307 5000) has its box office here; book in person to avoid paying hefty surcharges (open daily 9am-5pm and until showtime). At the other end of the theater spectrum stands the **SiLO** (tel. 373 5151; email sharyn@sinesurf.co.nz; http: //www.silo.co.nz), Lower Greys Ave., behind Town Hall, an underground experimental theater managed and staffed by art students and their friends. Amenities include free use of Sony Playstation in the funky lobby while you wait for the show to begin or during intermission; more active types can borrow the hacky sak from the bar, and kick it for a while. (Tickets are around $10. Cash or check only, reserve by phone, or wait until one hour before the show for door sales.) For a more grass-roots theater experience, consider **Pumanawa,** a recently formed collective of Maori artists whose performances incorporate elements from the stories of their cultural heritage. Contact Taamati Rice (tel. 528 6472) for more information. In mid-July, the **Auckland International Film Festival** (tel. 377 7420; http://www.enzedff.co.nz) captures the attention of movie buffs with two weeks of screenings from all over the world. Films are shown in the **St. James Theatre,** 312 Queen St. (tel. 377 4241). (Tickets are generally $10, students $8, seniors $6, children $5.) The main theater also accommodates theatrical productions. Across the way on Queen St., the historic **Civic Theater** is being rebuilt into a modern entertainment complex which will house an **IMAX** theater and a Planet Hollywood restaurant.

For a more active evening of entertainment, the **Ponsonby Snooker Centre,** 106 Ponsonby Rd. (tel. 360 2356), is the classiest pool hall in Auckland. There are three full size snooker tables and no coin-operated tables. Reservations are necessary at night (all tables $10 per hour). For those who prefer games of chance to games of skill, **Sky City** is the destination of choice, with casinos for all levels of gamblers. For those who want to improve their chances, free gaming lessons are available from the casino. Across the street is the **Palace,** on Victoria St., the only bar in Auckland that matches the casino by staying open 24 hours.

On those rare occasions when they pass through Auckland, big name bands generally play at the **Powerstation** or the **North Shore Event Centre.** Check at **Real Groovy,** 438 Queen St. (tel. 302 3940), for schedule and ticket info. (Open Sa-Th 9am-5:30pm, F 9am-9pm.) For a more refined musical experience, head for the **Auckland Town Hall Concert Chamber** in the town hall, which stands opposite the Aotea Centre. Recently renovated, this space has great acoustics and is home to the **International Chamber Music Festival** (tel. 445 1863; email music.fest@xtra.co.nz) in July. Older teenagers may be interested in a recent phenomenon in Auckland, the emergence of **Rib Clubs.** These underage clubs serve up plenty of fun without alcohol and run until late. The music varies, but generally **Beat City,** corner of Hobson and Victoria St. (tel. 373 3551) plays more R&B and hip-hop (open F-Sa from 6pm, $5 cover) while **Platinum 104,** 104 Fanshawe St., plays more trance and happy hardcore, for serious energy release.

In late January, the **Auckland Anniversary Regatta** displays that famous Kiwi sailing finesse to the Waitema Harbour and Tamaki Dr., while in early March you can admire the vigor of the human body during the **Rangitoto-St. Heliers Masters Swim,** St. Heliers Beach. In early December, the **Auckland Open Tennis Championships** bring sport and refinement to the ASB Tennis Centre. And of course, in 2000, don't forget about the **Americas Cup.**

■ Sights

VANTAGE POINTS

Visual learners and the gotta-see, gotta-do crowd can sate their desires in multiple ways in Auckland. Volcanic hills rise up around the city and provide keen lookouts: **Mt. Eden** and **One Tree Hill** are two of the more famous vantage points. To reach Mt. Eden and its parks, take bus #274 or #275, across from the Downtown Bus Terminal. To get to One Tree Hill, as well as its park and observatory, take bus #30 or #31 from the corner of Victoria and Queen St. At the base of One Tree Hill, **Auckland Observatory** (tel. 624 1246) offers one-hour viewing sessions of the cosmos through the EWB 50cm telescope on Tuesday, Thursday, and Saturday at 7:30 and 8:30pm. Bookings are essential. The observatory offers a Stardome Planetarium show where a guide will take you on a tour of the universe. *(2-6 per day. $9, children $4.50; seniors and students $7, families $22.50.)*

Rising above the steel and glass of the CBD is the dominating feature of the city skyline: the brand-new **Sky Tower,** bounded by Hobson, Wellesley, Federal, and Victoria St. With a good map in hand and its red lights overhead, you'll never lose your sense of direction anywhere in the Auckland area with the 2m-taller-than-the-Eiffel-tower behemoth around. The steel, glass, and Maori carving-adorned **lobby** overflows with modern conveniences, with everything from 24-hour phones to ATMs to visitor information (call (0800) SKY CITY/759 2489 for all information, open 24hr.). The **observation deck** boasts a 360° view. The **Sky Deck** is 34m higher, and offers essentially the same views, but without all of the mayhem of the main deck. *(Open Su-Th 8:30am-10pm, F 8:30am-11pm, Sa 8:30am-midnight, last elevator up runs 30min. prior to closing. $15; children $7.50, 10% discount to families, groups and seniors. Sky Deck $3 more.)* The vertigo-unaffected can even step out onto the glass floor in the outer ring. The interactive computers and the inlaid compass rose add class, bearings, and regional history all in one fell swoop. Or take a separate elevator to **Orbit,** the upscale rotating restaurant.

THE CENTRAL BUSINESS DISTRICT

The city center is very much in transition; major construction projects to improve the downtown infrastructure are in various stages of completion. The landscape changes daily and the final shape of the skyline is anyone's guess. This part of the city is still recovering from the power outage in February and March, and many restaurants and shops have gone out of business. Regardless, high powered execs glued to their cell phones still run off to power lunches, as international shoppers peruse the shops and malls of lower Queen St.

Glancing up Victoria St. E from Queen St., a tall, free-standing rock and metal arch fronts a wall of green, marking the main entrance to **Albert Park.** A short, steep walk past shady trees ideal for climbing yields a grassy knoll with a commemorative gun battery and ample room for a picnic or sunbath. Sitting regally at the southern end of the park on the corner of Wellesley and Kitchener St. is the prim, white **Auckland**

Art Gallery (tel. 307 7700). Peruse the standing collection of 19th-century Maori portraiture on the ground floor (free), or head into the rest of the gallery to view one of the traveling shows (admission varies). As the curators have displayed the works without notes, you can either enjoy the art purely on its own terms, or pay $3 for an audio guide, and lend it some historical context and analysis. The sister to this "old" gallery is the **New Gallery** (tel. 307 4540), a block down on the corner of Wellesley and Lorne St. *(Open daily 10am-5pm. Admission $4, children, students, seniors $2.)* Half the fun is strolling through the steel and glass space, listening to profound comments made by Auckland's artistically elite on eclectic exhibits which may challenge you to find their aesthetic merit. Both galleries also sport cafes, though neither is particularly inspiring, especially at prices far from bohemian.

As you cross Albert Park, it's impossible not to notice the 54m tower of the **Old Arts Building,** 22 Princess St. Built in 1926, the tower was inspired by that of Christ Church College, Oxford (England). It has also come to symbolize **Auckland University,** the largest of New Zealand's seven universities. The university occupies the better part of four large blocks centered about Symonds St. The main campus **library** stands on the corner of Princess St. (the east edge of Albert Park) and Alfred St. Open to the public, the view from the top floor will distract anyone from Katherine Mansfield's books. Opposite the library is the **Maidment Arts Centre,** 8 Alfred St. (tel. 308 2383), which offers some of the best performances in Auckland. *(Theater performances $16-20; students $12-16.)* During term-time there are free music recitals on Fridays at lunchtime. At the corner of Princess St. and Waterloo Quadrant, nestled in the university's park grounds, stands the Classical **Old Government House,** built in 1856. Until the capital was moved to Wellington in 1865, this building served as the residence of the fledgling nation's seat of government.

PONSONBY

Ponsonby has emerged from its dubious past as the slum of Auckland to become the affordable and hip place to live. Populated by students, artists, and a substantial part of the city's gay and lesbian community, Ponsonby Rd. caters to all of their tastes and then some. Both sides of the street are lined with ethnic eateries and trendy cafes and bars, mixed in with little shops peddling second-hand clothes and delicate crafts. When the weather warms, outdoor seating and strolling are prime. Connecting Ponsonby to the top of the city, K Rd. still bears the signs of its adult entertainment industry, which has slowed considerably and is far from threatening, even at night. The **Trash and Treasures Collectibles Market** (tel. 625 5322), in the K Rd. carpark, level 5, off Mercury Lane, happens every Sunday from 6am to 11am.

THE WATERFRONT

Graceful white yachts set off the blue of **Waitemata Harbour** every day of the year. **QE II Square** is at the base of Queen St., where the CBD runs into the sea. To one side is the Novotel, easily spotted by the enormous sign or the lunchtime crowds watching the occasional person jump off the side of the building as part of the famous **Urban Rap Jumping** (tel. 373 3559). Similar to abseiling or rappelling, urban rappers move face-first down the side of the building attached to a rope, with bursts of free fall for those so inclined. *(11am and 2pm daily, weather permitting; $50.)*

Stroll along **Westhaven Drive** on any weekend morning and you'll have no trouble seeing how Auckland got its nickname as the City of Sails. One in five Aucklanders owns a boat and, as the forest of masts attests, most are moored at **Westhaven Marina,** the largest man-made marina in the Southern Hemisphere. The **Marina Office** (tel. 309 1352), at the end of Westhaven Dr. by the Harbour Bridge, can answer questions and provide information on charter sailings. Continuing down Westhaven Dr. along the arm of the Marina are the uppercrust **yacht clubs,** where

AUCKLAND

The Day Auckland Went All Black

The first cable shorted out on January 20, the second on February 2. By February 20, 1998, all four of the power cables supplying power to Auckland's central business district failed, plunging 120 blocks of the city's commercial heart into darkness. The company responsible, Mercury Energy, didn't even try to make excuses. Chairman Wayne Gilbert said bluntly: "It is a dark day for us. I don't seek to blame others. It is our issue and we need to fix it. We are extremely sorry and this is an enormous setback to our reputation." While generators were flown in from around the world to support emergency and national defense services, power was not fully restored for over nine weeks. Residents were urged to leave town, and a general confusion settled in as pointmen directed traffic, hotels hired extra staff to help guests through darkened corridors, and businesses relocated operations to the suburbs. Outsiders blamed the failure on Mercury Energy's preoccupation with a takeover attempt, pointing out that over the past few years it had fired half its workforce and had neglected to maintain its equipment. Several years ago the former state-run enterprise had become a private company, and some took the failure as an example of the free market's misplaced emphasis on profit rather than performance. Whatever the reason, the outage was a disaster for Auckland's businesses. Retailers were hit the hardest, as their customers no longer came to work and tourists and outsiders did not come through the area as frequently. Losses due to the outage were estimated to be at least $1 million a day. Only businesses with their own generators or that could cope without lights had a chance at surviving. In the face of such a situation, good old-fashioned Kiwi ingenuity kicked in. Groovy Records flew a plane over the city advertising that they were open. Making the best of a bad situation, businesses discovered a whole new marketing theme. Newspapers filled with ads featuring prominent graphics of lightbulbs and floodlights and new slogans like "we have power!" Blackout sales and specials became common, and previously unassuming goods such as batteries, flashlights, candles, and kerosene lamps flew off the shelves.

crews return from civilized competition to enjoy a civilized drink (or six). The **Royal New Zealand Yacht Squadron,** at the end closest to the city and water, is one of the oldest and fanciest. Continuing back along Westhaven Dr. toward the CBD, **Pier Z** juts out on the left and contains all things boat-related in a series of specialty shops. **Charter services** line the street and loads of boat rental shops lie a bit farther down.

On the other side of **Wynard Wharf,** all of the Viaduct Basin's rusty scupper fishing boats are getting the boot to make way for new development for the **Americas Cup 2000.** Euphoria and pride in victory over the Yanks has been replaced with a fierce determination to retain possession of the Cup, and development of the next boat is well underway (though very top secret). On the other side of the Viaduct Basin is **Hobson Wharf,** at the base of which sits the superb **New Zealand National Maritime Museum** (tel. 358 3010), with meticulously crafted exhibits on New Zealand's dance with the sea, all enhanced with true-to-life settings and sounds. *(Open daily in summer 9am-6pm, in winter 9am-5pm. Admission $10, students $5.)* Part of the museum was actually built around the sleek yacht (in dry dock) that is the fastest ever to race in an Americas Cup. Technically, it lost to the American Dennis Connor's *Stars and Stripes* in that race, though the latter had the unfair advantage of being a catamaran (a point of serious contention among Kiwis). The **Cup** itself is also on display following a national tour of the country in winter the of 1997, delayed somewhat while the Cup was being repaired in London after **violent vandalization** at the hands and hammer of a Maori activist. Other highlights include a walk-through ship's hold that rocks back and forth in demonstration of a 19th-century trans-Pacific crossing, plush chairs in the captain's cabin that play recorded oral histories of the sea, and the mainsheet of New Zealand's victorious Americas Cup yacht. If the museum isn't interactive enough for you, it also administers the **Rangitoto Sailing Centre** (tel. 358 2324) next door. No experience is necessary and everything from a three-hour morning sail to a three-day course can be arranged. *(Rates start from $20 per hr.; bookings essential.)* To hearken back to the days of yore, join the crew on-board the elegant tall-ship, **Søren Larsen** (tel. (0800) 767 365). Packages range from three-hour sails ($45 per person) to voyages to Fiji, Tonga, and New Caledonia ($180-250 per day). (Due to these extended trips, she isn't always in port for daytrips; call ahead.)

The crown jewel of the waterfront is the beautiful 1912 **Ferry Building,** at 99 Quay St., constructed for £68,000. Steam cleaning in the late 1950s restored the rich red and tan tones of the sandstone, brick, and Coromandel granite (the ornate Edwardian Baroque style is the work of architect Alex Wiseman). Inside, you'll find snooty restaurants, the downtown DOC office, a currency exchange, and the main office for **Fuller's ferries.** Their ferries offer service to the islands of Waiheke (p. 86), Rangitoto (p. 85), and Great Barrier Island (p. 88), as well as across to the North Shore community of Devonport (p. 83). Fuller's also runs **harbor cruises,** the cheapest being the **Coffee Cruise** (1½hr., 2 per day, $25) for the grand tour, a roll, and coffee or tea. Most of your questions can be answered by the **Harbour Information Office** (tel. 357 6366), a kiosk a bit closer to the water on the right. *(Open daily 9am-3pm.)*

The Ferry Building is also the start or end point of one of Auckland's most popular activities, the **Coast to Coast Walk** (4hr.; 13km). The walk runs between Waitemata Harbor and Onehunga Beach (Manukau Harbor), the first two European settlements in Auckland, and is a wealth of historical and natural wonder. Maps are available at the information center.

ORAKEI, MISSION BAY, AND ST. HELIERS

Quay St. continues past the wharves and **Mechanics Bay,** the home of the Coast Guard heliport and Great Barrier Airlines. At this point, Quay St. turns into pohu-tukawa-lined **Tamaki Drive.** In December, the white sand beaches are accented by the scarlet carpet of dropped blossoms being trampled underfoot by health-conscious joggers, cyclists, and skaters. Head to **Ian Ferguson's Marine,** 12 Tamaki Dr. (tel./fax 529 2230), should you need **in-line skates** (first hr. $10, $5 each additional hr., $25 per day), or **kayaks** (singles $10 per hr., $35 per day; doubles $20 per hr., $70 per day). One-on-one kayak coaching is available ($40 per hr., $60 from Olympic gold-medal-winner Ian). Fit romantics might enjoy a **moonlight kayak trip** to Rangitoto Island (6-11pm, $45 per person, bookings are essential; shop open daily 9am-6pm). **St. George's Bay,** inland from Tamaki Dr., is a pretty little pool good for a quick paddle at the base of Parnell. Otherwise try the yacht-filled **Orakei Basin,** sailing grounds of the rich of **Paritai Drive.** Auckland's wealthiest street, it's part of a gated community of million-dollar mansions. Orakei is also home to the **Orakei Marae** (tel. 521 0617), just as exclusively located, and up a hill with fantastic views. If you're interested in visiting, call ahead and be sure to respect *marae* protocol (see **From Hongi to Hangi,** p. 43). It was here in 1978, on Bastion Point, that the first Maori land claims were made, and tensions eventually escalated into military intervention by the New Zealand government.

Deep beneath Tamaki Dr., 6km east of the CBD, lurk the stingrays, eels, and sharks of **Kelly Tarltons Underwater World,** 23 Tamaki Dr. (tel. 528 0603), possibly the most ingenious use ever of converted sewage tanks. *(Open Nov.-Mar. 9am-9pm, last entry 8pm; Apr.-Oct. 9am-6pm, last entry 5pm. Admission $20, students and seniors $16, under 13 $10, age 4 $6, under 4 free.)* A dry-erase board at the entrance serves as a fishy tabloid of who's being fed, who's been born, and who's mating with whom. A moving walkway transports guests into the marine world of rays, sharks, and fish; it only takes a moment to adjust to moving underwater through a plexiglass tube. The newest exhibit is the **Antarctic Encounter,** which features a colony of live king penguins whose playful antics counteract the unfortunate animatronic plastic orca used to illustrate the food chain (it eats an even more unfortunate plastic seal).

Escape to dry land east of Kelly Tarltons at the **Michael Joseph Savage Memorial Gardens,** a poppy-dotted park that pays homage to New Zealand's first Labour Party Prime Minister. The view out to Rangitoto and the Gulf is simply stunning. The golden sands wrap around to a series of small coves, the first of which is **Mission Bay,** named after an 1859 Anglican stone mission (now an upscale French restaurant); the tiny parking lot next door brims in summer with cars of sun-worshippers. The restaurants, bars, and sands of Mission Bay are rivaled only in popularity and accessibility by the next cove, **St. Heliers Bay.** A quiet town throughout the winter, summer brings hordes of people to throng Tamaki Dr. and St. Heliers Bay Rd. The #769 and #765 buses go to both Mission Bay and St. Heliers Bay. The shoreline fun continues to **Music Point,** the site of New Zealand's first international air arrival in 1937.

AUCKLAND DOMAIN, PARNELL, AND NEWMARKET

To the east of the CBD lies the vast expanse of grass and trees that is the **Auckland Domain.** Best accessed from the Grafton Bridge which extends off K Rd. over the motorway, or by walking up from the waterfront (Quay St.) once you reach the train station, the Domain has many roads and trails great for biking. The duck pond is in the center, and a nearby gazebo often holds jazz bands playing free concerts on summer weekends. East of the pond is the main attraction, the **Auckland Museum** (tel. 379 9956), which holds court to a host of Polynesian, European, and natural history exhibits. *(Museum open daily 10am-5pm. Admission by donation.)* The museum's pride and joy are the downstairs galleries that feature Aotearoa's Maori heritage. The center gallery is home to the last completely original war canoe in existence, as well as the **Hotuni whare,** a complete meeting-house on loan from the Tainui tribe of the Thames area. Its elaborately carved beams took three years to complete (1875-1878). Dismantled in 1925, it was reassembled inside the museum four years later. The whare is still considered a sacred space, guests are asked to remove their shoes before entering.

Hotuni is also the venue for the **Pounamu Maori Performance Group** (tel. 306 7080). *(Daily 11am and 1:30pm. $7, children, seniors, and students $5.)* The blast of a conch shell announces the start of this amazing cultural show of music, dance, and weaponry. Just across from the Domain are the **Wintergardens** (tel. 379 2039), a collection of glass houses surrounding a Victorian lily pond. *(Open daily in summer 9am-7pm; in winter 9am-5pm. Free.)* The **Cool House** offers seasonal floral displays while the **Tropical House** is a collection of plants from the tropics, including the victoria lily in the summer. The **Fernery** houses the distinctive ferns native to the Waitakeres. On the other side of the tracks (the Newmarket Beach Railway) is the neighborhood of **Parnell,** home to old money estates and historic buildings. The most notable architecture is a group of Victorian homes-turned-gift boutiques, along the side of Parnell Rd., known as **Parnell Heritage Village** (look for the fleet of tour buses outside). At the top of the road on the opposite side sits Auckland's Anglican **Cathedral of the Holy Family,** which was moved intact in all of its 19th-century glory to make room for a larger church. The free and lovely **Parnell Rose Gardens** at the base of the hill burst into bloom from November to March. If the smell of the roses is mingled with hops, that's because they're downwind of the **Lion Breweries,** 5 Kingdon St., Newmarket (tel. 377 8840), the birthplace of what many consider to be New Zealand's best lager, the inimitable Steinie. *(Free tours and tastings Tu-Th 10:30am and 2pm; bookings essential.)*

Everything you need to create a little Parnell in your own home can be purchased in its sorority sister neighborhood, **Newmarket,** which intersects Parnell at the top of the hill. Both new and market-oriented, it bustles with shops along Broadway St. that tend to stay open late on Friday nights (usually until around 8 or 9pm).

WESTERN SPRINGS

The mainly residential suburb of **Western Springs** is home to two of Auckland's big name attractions: the zoo and MOTAT. The **Auckland Zoo** (tel. 360 3800), on Motion Rd., recently added Rainforest and Pridelands sections. *(Open daily 9:30am-5pm; last entry 4:15. Admission $12, students $9, seniors $8, children $7, families $32.50.)* The kiwi and tuatara exhibits are both worth a look, as are the red panda and the Wallaby Walkabout. A classic streetcar connects the zoo to its gear-head neighbor, the **Museum of Technology and Transport (MOTAT),** 805 Gr. North Rd. (tel. 846 0199). *(Open daily*

10am-5pm. Admission $10, students, seniors, and children $5, families $20.) Bring your science-bent young ones for the hand-on physics experiments; it's also appropriate for those who live and die for steam engines and antique cars. The admission fee also gets you into **MOTAT II,** a collection of classic aircraft and seaplanes in Sir Keith Park Memorial Airfield (500m past the zoo on Motions Rd.) To get to Western Springs, take the yellow bus #045 Point Chevalier, across from QE II Sq. ($3).

GREATER AUCKLAND AREA

■ The Waitakeres

Gorgeous and undertouristed, the Waitakeres await those who have exhausted Auckland's wild nightspots, harbors, and shops. Occupying a tract of land between the **Manokau Harbour** and the **Tasman Sea,** hundreds of bush-covered acres await exploration by way of over 250km of walking and tramping tracks. The **Arataki Visitor Centre** (tel. 303 1530; fax 817 5656) on Scenic Dr. has comprehensive information to help you plan your route (open daily 9am-5pm). Getting there without a car is difficult, though buses from the city go to Titirangi, 6km down the road. Hitchhiking in these parts is also a dim prospect. If you can get a car, the coastline offers some amazing beaches. **Karekare** is perhaps the most scenic and was the backdrop for the film *The Piano.* A great waterfall here is accessible by a short walk from the carpark on the approach to the beach. A bit farther north, **Piha** offers excellent surf but is often more crowded. At the southern tip right at the entrance to Manukau Harbor from the ocean is **Whatipu,** which has great fishing and cool caves accessible from the beach. Farther inland along the harbor, **Cornwallis** offers calmer waters well suited for swimming and a beach that's perfect for picnics. For people without access to cars, **Bush and Beach Ltd.** (tel. 478 2882, bookings tel (0800) 4BEACH) offer guided wilderness tours that take in many highlights of the region, including a rare gannet bird colony at Muriwai beach, one of two such colonies in the world. Half-day trips run year-round ($55, children $27.50; 12:30pm-5pm), while full-day trips run September through April. ($99, children $49.50; 9:30am-5pm daily). There is no maximum group size, and free pickup from your city accommodation is provided, along with free wine tastings at the end. **Auckland Adventures** (tel. 379 4545 or (025) 855 856) offers trekking and mountain biking trips that take in Muriwai Beach as well as Mt. Eden at a relaxed pace. Trekking options include the afternoon adventure ($55, 12:45-6pm) or wilderness adventure ($75, 9am-6pm), while the Mountain Bike Adventure ($75, 9am-6pm, $20 less if you have a bike) covers more ground. Additional options are the beach barbecue ($10 per person) and group overnight camping on the beach ($15 per person, all equipment and breakfast included).

■ The North Shore

To the north of "Auckland City" lies the **North Shore,** home to family beaches and suburban shopping centers. Tailor-made for pleasant afternoons, the North Shore is all about seagulls circling lazily in the sky as families sun on the golden sand and couples picnic on the green. Subdivisions in the area really took off after the completion of the **Harbour Bridge,** and today the North Shore is home to vast numbers of business commuters. As the suburbs spread, the bridge soon became so clogged with traffic that the city contracted a Japanese company to come and install extensions (affectionately called "nippon clip-ons") on either side of the bridge, expanding the meager four lanes to eight. **Devonport** is a popular weekend destination for Aucklanders in search of a little peace, or a piece of artwork. And even when the museums and galleries lock up and the sun sets over the beaches, Devonport's theaters and Takapuna's bars are just beginning to wake up. **Link Buses** (tel. 366 6400) runs service between Devonport and Takapuna, departing five minutes after the ferry lands ($2.20, children $1.30). **Ferry** service to Devonport is operated by Fullers (15min.; departs Auckland daily every 30min. 6:15am-7pm and every hour 7pm to 11pm; $7, children $3.50, families $15).

▓ Devonport

With tranquil blue waters in its harbor and multi-colored Victorian rooftops, Devonport remains "the marine playground," domain of ferryboats and pleasure yachts.

PRACTICAL INFORMATION The chummy info hive of the **Devonport Visitor Information Centre** (tel. 446 0677) stands in the shade of "Albert" (the Moreton Bay fig tree). It's on Victoria Rd., in Devonport's Windsor Reserve adjacent to the library (open daily in summer 9am-5pm; in winter 10am-4pm). The **Devonport Explorer Bus** (tel. (0800) 868 774 or 357 6366) is a hop-on hop-off day tour of Devonport's sights that leaves from the wharf daily every hour (between 10:25am-3:25pm, $22 including ferry return). **North Shore Taxis** (tel. 486 1799) offers more direct transportation to your destination of choice. You can also see Devonport by **TukTuk** (tel. (025) 739 445)—you'll know one when you see it. Up to three people can each pay $7 for the standard tour, $10 for a broader coverage of prime viewing locations, or $3 for transport to a single destination (book ahead). Or, experience the eight-horsepower thrust of **Town and Country Clydesdales** (tel./fax 238 6675 or (025) 346 400). Driver Dan Dufty will take as many as 20 people "up, down and all around town" to the clippity-clop of his cart ($4), with pickup from the Devonport wharf. For $10 he will drive you out to the stables and give you a tour too. **Public toilets** are adjacent to the visitors center. **Shorecare Accident and Medical Centres** (tel. 486 7777) will direct you to the doctor on call. **Wigmore's Devonport Pharmacy,** 33 Victoria Rd. (tel. 445 0061), handles your prescription needs (open M-F 8:30am-6pm, Sa-Su 9am-5pm). **Gentronics** at 53a Victoria Rd. (tel. 445 3740) offers **Internet access** ($5 per 15 min., $10 per hr.; open M-F 9am-5:30pm, Sa 10am-2pm). The **post office** is on 18 Clarence St. (open M-Tu, Th-F 9am-5pm, W 9:30am, Sa 9am-1pm). The **police** (tel. 489 4008) are based out of the visitors center.

ACCOMMODATIONS, FOOD, AND NIGHTLIFE The name of the accommodation game in Devonport is Bed and Breakfasts, with over 25 to choose from. The visitors center has a complete listing. One exceptional option is the **Esplanade Hotel,** 1 Victoria Rd. (tel. 445 1291; fax 445 1999; email reservations@esplanadehotel.co.nz; http://www.esplanadehotel.co.nz), which commands a spectacular view of the harbor and city (doubles with private bath $120-195).

Rooms in Devonport are expensive, so budget travelers should strongly consider making it a daytrip. Food prices are much more reasonable, with **Abide in the Vine Cafe,** 41 Victoria Rd. (tel. 445 0478), leading the way. Lunch quiches and frittatas are vegetarian-friendly and wallet-friendly, too ($3-5). The self-proclaimed "best coffee in town" goes down well with a $3 slice of cake (open daily 6am-4pm). At night, head over to **Oscar's Bar,** 48-56 Victoria Rd. (tel. 445 4470), adjacent to the movie theater. An old-fashioned Wurlitzer jukebox cranks out the hits when the live band isn't playing on Friday and Saturday nights, and pints cost $4.50. (Happy hour 5:30-6:30pm. Open M-F 4pm-1am, Sa-Su noon-1am.)

SIGHTS AND ACTIVITIES A look to the left off the Devonport Wharf reveals the base of the **Royal New Zealand Navy,** which supports a fine **Navy Museum** (tel. 445 5186), full of nautical artifacts from Cook's 1769 voyage up to the present day. (Open daily 10am-4:30pm. Admission by donation.) The oral histories on tape are particularly interesting. If the weather is fine, a stroll through the Victorian elegance of downtown Devonport uncovers a host of galleries. The **Devonport Museum** (tel. 445 2661), located just off Vauxhall Rd., is one of the stops on the walk. (Open Sa-Su 2-4pm. Admission by donation.) The museum perches on the side of **Mt. Cambria,** one of three extinct volcanoes in town (lopped off from the 1920s through the 50s as a result of quarrying). Mt. Cambria's taller neighbor to the west, **Mt. Victoria,** offers panoramic 360° views and can be reached by foot or vehicle.

Concrete tunnels snake through the third volcanic cone, **North Head.** Building on the Maori idea to use the peak for a *pa (*a lookout and fort), gun magazines and militia bunkers were installed in the late 1800s during the Russian Scare (they came into play again in WWI). Urban legend holds that the first aircraft built by Boeing is stored deep inside one of the tunnels. The reserve is open daily from 6am to 10pm, but the vehicle gates close at 6pm. The summit of North Head affords million-dollar views of the **Hauraki Gulf** and the coastline.

The **Devonport Food & Wine Festival** is the last weekend in February.

■ Takapuna to Whangaparaoa

North of Devonport, sprawling suburbs blend slowly into the natural beauty of the coast. To Takapuna, Milford, and beyond, the coast is characterized by curving sandy beaches separated into little bays by outcroppings of basaltic tuft. Some bays are protected areas, and huge fines (up to $5000) for pocketing shellfish are enforced; check the posted signs. **Cheltenham Beach** (a protected area) curves gracefully away just north of North Head, cupping calm waters are a favorite of beach-going families and pleasure summers. Head to **The North Shore Visitor Information Centre,** 49 Hurstmere Rd. (tel. 486 8670), for local highlights (open M-F 9am-5pm, Sa-Su 10am-3pm). Around the Takapuna Head is **Narrow Neck Beach,** ill-named for being both longer and wider than Cheltenham, with barbecue and picnic facilities. **St. Leonard's Beach** slides into **Takapuna Beach,** creating an immense playground for young sun- worshippers, windsurfers, and families in summertime, and joggers and *tai chi* practitioners in the grey of winter. The bus from Devonport to Takapuna gives access to the bars, bistros, and breweries of **Hurstmere Road.**

Windsurfing is popular in the volcanic crater of **Lake Pupuke,** a clear blue lake with a reedy shoreline. A coastal walk from Takapuna north through **Thorne Bay** to **Milford Beach** features awesome **volcanic rock formations** and the man-made Algie's Castle (from the 1920s). **Long Bay** is a marine reserve (DOC ranger tel. 303 1530, after hours tel. 473 9534). Jutting off into the open seas from the top of Long Bay is the lofty **Whangaparaoa Peninsula,** where in two years' time hundreds of sightseers with binoculars will convene to watch the latest battle for the Americas Cup.

■ Hauraki Gulf

Boasting 57 islands of various terrain and settlement, the Hauraki Gulf has a destination for everyone. **Fuller's Ferries** (tel. 367 9111) is your *uber-host* to the region, running everything from standard transportation to wine tastings and specialty cruises. The **Coffee Cruises** take in the scenic highlights from the comfort of a sleek catamaran (1¾hr., 3 per day, $20, children $10, families $50), while the **Explorer Super-ticket Cruise and Sightseeing Pass** covers most of the Hauraki Gulf. The pass includes guided bus tours of Devonport, Rangitoto Island, and Waiheke Island, plus all ferry tickets, a bonus cruise, and special discounts at several Auckland tourist attractions and restaurants. (Valid for 5 days; $69, children $49.)

■ Rangitoto Island

Te Rangi i totongia a Tamatekapua ("the day the blood of Tamatekapua was shed") is a long name for a little volcano to bear—and so the mount is known simply as Rangitoto. In 1854, the Crown grudgingly shelled out £15 for what seemed a mere lump of rock, and it's been a premier picnic spot for Auckland daytrippers almost ever since. Most folks head out to Rangitoto by ferry. **Fullers** (reservations tel. 367 9111, timetables tel. 367 9102) runs from Auckland's Pier 3 via Devonport (M-F 2-3 per day, daily Dec. 26-Mar. 1), returning from the Rangitoto Wharf (45min., round-trip $18, children $9). Of course, the more adventurous could always kayak on over. At the Rangitoto ferry landing, you'll find a coin phone to call the **resident ranger** (tel. 372 7348), or, in case you miss the boat, the **DOC stranding phone line** (tel. 307 9279).

Once there, most visitors foot it to the top. The **Summit Walk** (about 1hr. one-way) winds through lunar-like fields of volcanic rock and through arboreal glens higher up. During hot summers, walking the track is akin to hiking on charcoal briquettes. Those who don't wish to walk can take Fullers' **Volcanic Explorer** "safari." The narrated four-wheel-drive tram ride drops its passengers at the base of the 900m boardwalk leading to the summit. Cruise and volcanic explorer packages are available ($35, children and seniors $17.50). At the top, you can take a peek into the perfectly inverted cone of the **crater.** Green pohutukawa and rewarewa trees flourish where red hot lava once flowed. The **lava caves** are a side trail option (20min. return). Bring a flashlight and wear durable clothes if you plan to explore the jagged passageways formed by hot lava flowing through cooling volcanic rock. For local tracks, head to the **DOC office** (tel. 366 2166) in the ferry building (open in summer daily 8:30am-6pm, in winter M-F 8:30am-5pm). If there's time, the stroll down the mountain to **Islington Bay** yields secluded swimming beaches (arrange for a ferry pickup, or plan for the 1½hr. walk back). The Islington Bay area is also where barren Rangitoto meets agrarian and pastoral **Motutapu Island,** the **DOC office** (tel. 372 2060), and the area's only **campground,** located at Home Bay. Rudimentary facilities include toilets, running water, and barbecue sites ($5 per night, children $2).

■ Waiheke Island

For its 8000 permanent residents, many of whom have moved away from the city and built their dream home, Waiheke is a haven from the urban grind, yet separated from downtown Auckland by only a 35-minute ferry ride. For the summer inhabitants, who push the population well over 30,000, it is an accessible location with a laid back lifestyle and active artistic community. And for the daytrippers and weekend adventurers who trickle in during winter and arrive in hordes during summer, it offers numerous sandy beaches for soaking up sun and maximizing relaxation.

ORIENTATION AND PRACTICAL INFORMATION Waiheke lies 24km west of the Coromandel Peninsula and 17km northeast of Auckland, just east of Rangitoto in the Hauraki Gulf. Most of the 134km of coastline buckles and warps, folding into secluded rocky coves where waters lap at private shores. The vehicle ferry puts in at **Kennedy Point** near the villages of **Surfdale** and **Ostend,** while the Fullers ferry arrives at **Matiatia Bay** nearest to the town of **Oneroa,** the main center of shops and services on the island. The other major town on Waiheke is **Onetangi,** on the central north coast.

The most common transport is the **Fullers ferry** (tel. 367 9111, timetable info tel. 367 9102). The sleek cats depart from Auckland's pier several times daily (35min., $23 round-trip, bicycles $4). Those with their own vehicles can use **Subritzky Shipping Line Ltd.** (tel. 534 5663), which runs three vehicle ferries departing from Half Moon Bay in Pakuranga on the Auckland waterfront. (Daily hourly departures from 7am-4pm. 1hr. $100-120, bookings essential.) The **Waiheke Island Visitor Information Centre** (tel. 372 9999; fax 372 9919; email waiheke@iconz.co.nz), is in the Artworks Centre on Korora Rd. in Oneroa (open daily 9am-5pm; in winter 9am-4pm).

Once on the island there are numerous transportation options. The **Waiheke Bus Co.** (tel. 372 8823) meets all ferries and makes a loop around the island ($1-3; M-F 6am-8:15pm, Sa-Su 6:30am-8:15pm). Be prepared to wait if you decide to take a bus at any time other than right when you get off the ferry. **Waiheke Taxi** (tel. 372 8038) and **Dial-A-Cab** (tel. 372 9666) go when you want to go, though you'll pay for it. The **WIS Shuttle** (tel. 372 7756) is also available for charters; book ahead. Fullers offers an excellent package deal, the **Island Explorer Tour,** which includes return ferry, a 1½hr. scenic highlights tour of the island, and an all-day bus pass good on any island bus ($34, children $18.50; bookings essential in summer). Renting a vehicle is the surest way to traverse the island, but locals, especially truck drivers, don't cut visitors much room on the roads. **Waiheke Rental Cars** (tel. 372 8635), at the ferry landing in Ostend, rents from $45 per day (overnight $50, plus 40¢ per km). Motorbikes can be hired from $35 per day. **Waiheke Auto Rentals** (tel. 372 8998) also provides motor vehicles at competitive rates. Bicycles can be hired from **Rats Wharf Bike Hire** in the Matiatia Wharf car park (full day $25, half-day $15). The **visitors center** in Oneroa also has bikes ($30 full day, $20 half-day; tandems $30/$25) and will also store luggage ($2 per bag). **Medical centers** are in Ostend (tel. 372 5005) and Oneroa (tel. 372 8756). In Oneroa, an **ATM** is at the corner of Ove St. and Oceanview Rd. The **BNZ** (tel. 372 7171) is on Oceanview Rd. on the next block (open M-F 9am-4:30 pm). **Internet access** is available at **When the Bike Comes In,** located in the Surfdale Arcade ($3 per 15min., $5 per 30min.). In an **emergency,** dial 111. The **police** (tel. 372 8777) are on Waikare Rd. (available M-F 8:30am-4pm). **Mail Delivery Service** (tel. 372 7802) handles your postal needs.

ACCOMMODATIONS Places to lodge are sprinkled all over the island, though they generally gravitate toward one of the beaches. The **Palm Beach Backpackers,** 54 Palm Rd. (tel. 372 8662), is near enough to its namesake that you can hear the crashing surf from the sprawling wooden lodge. Relax in the lounge and game room, or really relax in the meditation gazebo tucked among the backyard trees. (Dorms $16; doubles $40; tent sites Oct.-Apr. $12, May-Sept. $10. Key deposit $10. Kayaks $20 per day.) YHA-affiliated **Waiheke Island Youth Hostel** is on Seaview Rd. (tel./fax 372 8971; email robb.meg@bigfoot.com). A steep staircase up the hill from Onetangi Beach leads to a colorful dolphin mural that beckons guests from all walks of life into this small but cozy hostel. Check yourself in if nobody's there. (Dorms $17 summer, $14 winter; twins and doubles $38. $10 key deposit. 50% discount on shuttle from ferry.) Near the beach are the **Onetangi Beach Apartments,** 5 Fourth Ave (tel. 372 7051; fax 372 5056; email bfw@iconz.co.nz), self-contained units with bathroom and kitchen plus an indoor spa and outdoor pool. (Studios Dec.-Apr. $95 for 2, May-Nov. $85. Free laundry and email.) At the other end of the spectrum is the **Fossil Bay Lodge (VIP),** 58 Korora Rd. (tel./fax 372 7569), near the beach in Oneroa. Guests can work in exchange for food and accommodation as part of WWOOF (see p. 20), or can stay in wood cabins with a French country flair (doubles $40), backpacker rooms ($15), or a spiffy copper A-frame that sleeps five in the top unit ($60 for 1-3, extra person $15) and eight in the lower unit ($80 for 1-6, extra person $15). **Campers** can trek out to the little-frequented but lovely **Whakanewha Regional Park,** on the southeast corner of the island ($5 per person; advance reservation required; phone Parksline at 303 1530).

FOOD Eating establishments are generally concentrated in the towns, ranging from simple cafes to fine wining and dining. **Salvage** (tel. 372 2273) on Oceanview Rd. in the Pendragon Mall, Oneroa, commands a supreme view of the harbor from covered outdoor seating. Smart lunch items run $3-5 while brunch ($4.50-12.50) and dinner ($12-20) options are pricier. Outstanding blueberry chocolate muffins ($2.50) will warm you. (Open Su-Th 7am-11pm, F-Sa 7am-midnight.) **The Dolphin Cafe,** 147 Ocean View Rd. (tel. 372 9393), serves up large burgers ($5-8) and hearty spiced wedges ($3) in an informal, laid-back setting. Eat on checkered tableclothed tables or takeaway (open from 9am daily). Ciao down at **Caffe da Stefano** (tel. 372 5309), in Surfdale village. They offer "truly Italian" pizzas ($11.50-14.50) and stuffed focaccias ($4.80-6), but Italian coffee is their specialty. (Open W-Su 9am-3pm and 6-8:30pm.)

SIGHTS AND ACTIVITIES Waiheke's prime attraction is its many beaches, especially in the summer, when warm temperatures and high humidity make a dip in the ocean a very alluring activity. **Onetangi Beach** is the largest stretch of sand but is also the most crowded. **Oneroa Beach** has fewer people even though it is closer to town. **Palm Beach** is another lovely spot, and just to the west is the aptly named **Nudie Beach.** To enjoy the coast from another perspective, consider **Waiheke Yacht Charters** (tel. 372 9579 or (025) 764 753), which runs ecotours from their 36-foot craft (half-day $45, full day $65; max. 10 people). **Waiheke Tours** (tel. 372 7262 or (021) 667 262) does kayaking trips. *(1-3hr. tour plus use of kayak all day. $40-55 depending on number of people. Backpacker specials available.)* They provide all equipment and free

AUCKLAND

return taxi from your accommodation or the wharf. For **fishing** charters, try any one of the fleet of fancifully named boats: the **Doolittle** (tel. 372 6163), **Miss Fleur** (tel. (025) 963 918), or **Mermaid Marine** (tel. 372 7185).

When you grow weary of the waves there are excellent walking tracks on the island, particularly in the lush **Whakanewha Regional Park.** The **visitors center** has an excellent guide with maps and descriptions. Several cycling loops provide some breathtaking views. Also, the DOC oversees **Stony Batter,** a reserve on the northeast end of the island that was once a WWII gun emplacement. Bring a flashlight and a map if you're going to romp through the tunnels.

Back on dry land, **galleries** and **craft shops** are the main attraction. The solar plexus of island creativity is the **Artworks Centre** (tel. 372 6900), in Oneroa on Korora Rd., with two floors to peruse and a **community theater** that brings the best of Broadway and the West End to the Hauraki Gulf. *(Center open daily 10am-4pm.)* Also in the Artworks Centre resounds the tuneful glory of **Whittakers' Musical Museum** (tel. 372 5573). Every day except Tuesday, Lloyd and Joan Whittaker travel through 500 years of musical history playing their extensive collection of instruments, many of which they have personally restored. *(Open daily 10am-4pm. Show from 1-2:30pm. Admission by donation. Show $7, children and seniors $5.)* Explore the wonderful world of wine at the **Stoneyridge Vineyards,** 80 Onetangi Rd. (tel. 372 8822). *(Summer tours run at 11:30am and 4pm; in winter 3pm.)* Fullers also runs a **Vineyard Explorer tour and ferry** (tel. 367 9111), which visits three vineyards in addition to the sights. *(Departs Auckland W-Su noon, in winter Sa-Su only. Returns by ferry at 5pm. Optional return sailings, $55.)*

■ Great Barrier Island

The largest and most remote of the Hauraki Gulf islands, Great Barrier Island (Aotea) maintains the most tenuous of connections with the mainland. Officially a part of Auckland, the island is very much its own world, with its own weather patterns (it can be sunny here while it rains in the city) and its own laid-back lifestyle. The island is a naturalist's dream, with lush forests and marsh lands covering the terrain, and silky white sand beaches breaking up the rocky coastline. In fact, thanks to the complete absence of any possums, and the efforts of conservationists, the forest has been allowed to regenerate after fierce logging through the 1940s. Several of the 1000 permanent residents suggest that Great Barrier Island is the closest today's New Zealand comes to approaching the untainted beauty of its past.

ORIENTATION AND PRACTICAL INFORMATION To get proper bearings on the Barrier takes more than knowing that it lies 90km northeast of Auckland, just off the northern tip of the Coromandel Peninsula—it requires a new state of mind. Time passes much more slowly here than on the mainland, rendering appointments and schedules virtually meaningless. There is **no power** on the island, so residents generate their own electricity via diesel or gas generators (usually from dusk until 10 or 11pm), resulting in mighty quiet nights. In short, bring a **flashlight.** Roads are graded, **unsealed** in many places, and about 1½ lanes wide. As there are no sidewalks, **pedestrians** should keep to the outside of curves, so vehicles can see them coming. There are four main settlements on the island: **Tryphena,** where the ferries arrive, **Claris,** where the airport is located, **Whangaparapara,** and **Port Fitzroy.**

The **Great Barrier Island Visitor Centre** (tel. 429 0033; fax 429 0660) is located at the Claris airfield (center open in summer M-F 8:30am-6pm, Sa-Su 8:30am-5pm; in winter M-F 8:30am-4:30pm, Sa-Su 9am-4pm). The **Fullers Information Office** (tel. 429 0004; fax 429 0469), next to the Stonewall Store in Mulberry Grove, keeps more extensive listings of activities on the island and is more convenient for ferry passengers arriving in Tryphena (open daily in summer 8am-5pm, in winter 9am-4pm). If you're seeking serious hiking, see the **DOC Field Centre** (tel. 429 0044, after-hours tel. 429 0046), at Akapoua Bay in Port Fitzroy. There are **no banks** on the island, and credit card-friendly shops and services are not common, so bring your cash or Eftpos card. The **Community Health Centre** (tel. 429 0356) is in Claris by the airfield.

Pigeongram, Ma'am

For nearly 500 years, our feathered friends the carrier pigeons were at the forefront of rapid delivery postal service. Today, the species have been driven nearly to extinction by hunting and international courier services; only two pigeon post services remain in use. One is the **French Foreign Legion,** which keeps a squadron of pigeons ready for important communiques, should more conventional means of communications be severed in time of war. The other is the **Great Barrier Pigeongram Service** at Port Fitzroy. For $20, your message will be strapped to the bird's leg, wing its way to a loft in Auckland, and from there be forwarded via surface mail anywhere in the world (usually encrusted with bird doo by the time it arrives). Established in 1898, the service sent its most memorable message on Sept. 30, 1900, when a young boy ran from Tryphena to Okupu in order to save his brother's life by pigeongramming an emergency message. Sent in duplicate via the two best birds, one was lost in a storm, but the other, "Velocity," made it through to medical help. You don't have to run to Okupu to send a pigeongram today—just call **Pigeon Post** (tel. 429 0242) in Claris or the **Pigeon Post Outpost** in Pa Beach to have your note happily winged away.

Great Barrier Pharmacy (tel. 429 0006) is just out of Claris. **Laundry facilities** can be found in the **Tryphena Shopping Centre** and on the other side of the island, at the **Great Barrier Lodge** (tel. 429 0488) in Whangaparapara. **Bob's Taxi** (tel. 429 0988) will cart you around at your convenience, though at a steep price. The **post office** (tel. 429 0242) is on Hector Sanderson Rd., Claris. The **police** (tel. 429 0343) are on Kaitoki-Awana Rd., Claris.

The transport of choice for most visitors is a **ferry.** The swank **Fullers** ferry (bookings tel. 367 9111, timetable tel. 367 9117) is the fastest, departing Auckland's Pier 2 at the ferry building and putting in at Tryphena, Whangaparapara, and Port Fitzroy (2hr.; 4 per week, 2 per week in winter; $89 return). **Gulf Trans** (tel. (0800) GULF TRANS/485 387), operates the **M.V. Tasman** once per week to transport "bulk, chilled and frozen freight, vehicles, and passengers." (6hr., departs Tu 7am, $40 return) They also run a ferry that can transport your car. One step up in comfort and price is the **M.V. Sealink** (3½hr., departs 9am W-F, Su-M, $65 return). Air travel to Great Barrier is popular. **Great Barrier Airlines** (tel. (0800) 900 600 or 275 9120) is the major carrier with at least two flights per day to Claris connecting with Auckland, Whitianga, Whangarei, and Paihia. All flights are $89 one-way, $169 return, except Paihia ($120/$240). There is also a "fly one way, ferry the other" package in conjunction with Fullers for $115. **Northern Air** (Auckland tel. 256 899, Great Barrier tel. 429 0909 or 025 744 767) also flies to and from Auckland.

ACCOMMODATIONS AND FOOD

Lodgings on Great Barrier allow for a broad range of living experiences, from bush camping to a family-style self-contained chalet. While reservations are only essential in the summer, they are advisable year-round, especially since many places will arrange for a free shuttle from the airport or ferry.

The **Stray Possum Lodge (VIP)** (tel. (0800) POSSUM/767 786 or 429 0109), in Tryphena, is the Barrier's most-talked-about backpackers, standing in its own exquisite bush-clad valley. Mountain bikes can be rented for $20 per day, or $10 per half-day. Free transport to and from the ferry is offered, as well as free pickup from Claris airfield for those on the **Possum Pursuits Activities Pass** (daytrip $20, $45 for your stay at the lodge). Check-out is at 10am (credit cards and Eftpos accepted).

Another attractive option is the **Pohutukawa Lodge,** Tryphena (tel. 429 0211; fax 429 0117; email Plodge@xtra.co.nz), located in the center of town next to the Fullers information center. The lodge has 24-hour power, a communal kitchen, and a simple but cozy lounge. (Flexible check in and check-out. Backpackers dorms $15. Ensuites ($75-95) have their own bathrooms and include breakfast at the adjacent Irish Pub, **The Currach.**) This is the only backpackers in town that serves food, with the pub offering burgers and hearty chowders ($4.95-6.50), while rich desserts such as Death by Chocolate ($6.50) offer opportunities to indulge. Every Thursday night is a musical jam session starting at 9pm (pub open daily from 4pm). Puriri Bay in Tryphena is home to **Tipi and Bob's Holiday Lodge** (tel./fax 429 0550), an impressive complex with self-contained units, several with fabulous views of the ocean (summer 1-bedroom $100, 2-bedroom $125, winter $85-100, extra person $20). There is a bar and upscale restaurant on the premises. The latter specializes in fresh fish catches, with entrees ($7.50) and mains ($21-26). The bar serves big meals ($6.50-14.50) and also offers takeaways (burgers $4-8.50, chips $3). (Open in summer daily 8am-10pm, in winter M-Tu, Th-Su 8am-10pm.) The **Medlands Beach Backpackers** (tel. 429 0340) on Mason Rd. overlooking Medlands Beach, sits in an eden of eucalyptus trees and camellia flowers. Well-worn, clean rooms are a five-minute walk from the white-sand beach, and beach equipment is available. (Dorms $20 in summer, $14 in winter; twins $24/$16; singles $30/$20; linen $5; check-out 10am.) Couples and groups staying a week or more may find it cheapest to rent a cottage. **DOC** maintains six **campsites** ($6) and two guest **cottages:** one isolated at the beach at Okiwi (sleeps 8) and one convenient to bush walks at Akapoua (sleeps 10). Both are $50 for two people in summer ($30 in winter; extra person $10). Rudimentary **huts** which sleep up to 24 people are also maintained at Whangaparapara and Kaiaraara ($8, children $4).

ACTIVITIES The most popular activity on Great Barrier Island is doing absolutely nothing. The east coast beaches of **Whangapoua, Haratonga, Kaitoke,** and **Awana** are noted for their **surfing.** Most accommodations have some boogie boards floating around for guest use. **Medlands Beach,** with its graceful white sand dunes, sapphire water, and blissful breezes, is the island's most popular beach (though in island lingo that translates into maybe 20 people in the height of summer). The west coast is quieter and more popular for yachts. Tryphena Harbour's beaches at **Puriri Bay, Pa Beach,** and **Mulberry Grove** are good for snorkeling and swimming. **Aotea Kayak Adventures** (tel. 429 0664) runs guided kayak tours ranging from an introductory tour to a twilight paddle ($25-65). Kayak maven and long-time Barrier resident Wayne can also add snorkeling, fishing, and bushwalks (prices negotiable). He may even help you catch a lobster dinner (book through the Stray Possum Lodge, tel. 429 0109). **GBI Adventure Horsetreks** (tel. 429 0274) will take you up hill and down dale for $20 per hour. Chartered **fishing trips** (tel. 429 0110) from $45 can be arranged through Tryphena.

Whangaparapara serves as an excellent base for challenging **mountain biking** on the Whangaparapara-Port Fitzroy Rd., accessible by a left-hand turn-off before reaching the Stamping Battery (closed to all non-DOC vehicles). Past the Stamping Battery on the left side of the road is the entrance to the **Hot Springs Walk** (1½hr.). The main pool is formed by a dam at the junction of two rivers, and smaller pools of varying temperatures are farther up the left hand stream. Just across Whangaparapara Rd. from the mountain bike track is the entrance to the **Te Ahumata Track** (2hr.), also known as the "White Cliffs Walk" for the gorgeous quartz crystals in the stream beds in the lower reaches. The 398m summit offers expansive views of the ocean, Mt. Hobson, and the Coromandel Peninsula. For an even bigger rush, try the feisty five-hour **Windy Canyon-Mt. Hobson-Kaiarara Stream Track.** Beginning from the main road on the way to Okiwi, the track ascends steeply through untouched subalpine forest to the island's highest point, **Mt. Hobson (Hirakimata).** From the 621m summit, descend to the swimming-hole-friendly Kaiarara Stream and spend the night at the **Fitzroy Hut** (bunks $8). A bit past the hut, the track intersects the forest road that runs north to Port Fitzroy. Ask at the visitors center for information on other tracks.

Northland

The long jutting piece of land that stretches up from Auckland and the main body of the North Island is Northland proper, an enchanting world of verdant valleys, dramatic cliffs, and silky beaches. Home to the first landings of legendary explorers Kupe and Captain Cook, Northland is often called the cradle of both Maori and European civilization in New Zealand. The sparkling Bay of Islands on the east coast is a collection of small towns and settlements admired every summer by tourists and seasonal residents. The west coast shelters the quiet beauty of the Kaipara and Hokianga Harbours. At the very top, the Aupouri Peninsula and Cape Reinga stretch out to the edge of the island with hauntingly empty beaches.

Your mode of transportation in Northland is key to your enjoyment of the region. If you have the means, rent a **car,** since it gives you the freedom to explore at your own pace. Keep an eye on fuel levels, because petrol pumps are few and far between. If you travel by **bus,** strongly consider buying a pass that lets you get on and off as often as you like. **Hitchhikers** on the east coast encounter sparse traffic and consequently long waits once they get past the Bay of Islands. On the west coast, **SH12** is also very much the road less traveled, but the locals are said to be more accommodating. **Cyclists** should consider heading up the west coast first, as the east coast has many nasty hills and headwinds on the way up from Auckland. **Campers** should note that Back Country hut passes do not apply in the Northland, and that you must book in advance for all huts and lodges.

🏔 NORTHLAND HIGHLIGHTS

- The Bay of Islands (see p. 96) is a marine paradise, where visitors can swim with dolphins, sea-kayak among the mangroves, or take a leisurely (or high-speed) cruise.
- Scuba diving around the Poor Knights Islands (see p. 95) is some of the world's best.
- The giant kauri of the Waipoua Forest Park (see p. 110) tower over the landscape.
- A guided day-tour is a rugged, captivating way to take in the remote Aupouri Peninsula and Cape Reinga region (see p. 106).

▮ Whangarei

The name Whangarei ("Fahng-a-ray") means "cherished," and that is an apt description of local and tourist attitudes toward the largest city in Northland (pop. 46,000). Situated on the banks of the **Hatea River** at the deepest point of a narrow harbor, Whangarei takes better advantage of its strategic location at converging waterways for pleasurable recreation than commercial gain. Inland, many curious and colorful activities vie for travelers' attention, while offshore, flashes of tropical fish dart about the underwater formations of top-notch diving sites. Jacques Cousteau even rated nearby **Poor Knights Island** (see p. 95) one of the top ten diving spots in the world. With much to do and little pressure to do it all, it's not surprising that visitors stay an extra night or two.

ORIENTATION AND PRACTICAL INFORMATION

Whangarei wraps around the **Whangarei Harbour,** 167km north of Auckland along **SH1** on the east coast. The main drag, **Bank Street,** intersects commercial **Cameron Street,** with a pedestrian mall that buzzes during business hours. The **Whangarei Visitors Bureau,** 92 Otaika Rd. (tel. 438 1079; fax 438 2943; email wrevin@nzhost.co.nz), in Tarewa Park, is at the southern entrance to the city. It is easily accessible by car, and buses will drop off by request. (Open M-F 8:30am-5pm, Sa-Su

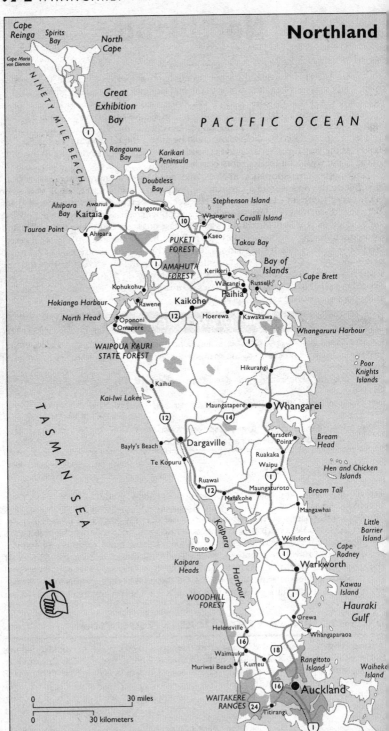

Northland

PACIFIC OCEAN

TASMAN SEA

Cape Reinga
Spirits Bay
North Cape
Cape Maria van Diemen

NINETY MILE BEACH

Great Exhibition Bay

Rangaunu Bay
Karikari Peninsula

Doubtless Bay

Ahipara Bay
Awanui
Kaitaia
Mangonui
Stephenson Island
Whangaroa
Cavalli Island

Tauroa Point
Ahipara
PUKETI FOREST
Kaeo
Takou Bay

AMAHUTA FOREST
Kerikeri
Bay of Islands
Cape Brett

Kohukohu
Waitangi
Paihia
Russell

Hokianga Harbour
Rawene
Kaikohe

North Head
Opononi
Omapere
Moerewa
Kawakawa
Whangaruru Harbour

WAIPOUA KAURI STATE FOREST
Poor Knights Islands

Hikurangi

Kaihu

Kai-Iwi Lakes
Maungatapere
Whangarei

Bream Head
Marsden Point
Ruakaka
Waipu
Hen and Chicken Islands

Bayly's Beach
Dargaville
Te Kopuru
Bream Tail
Mangawhai
Little Barrier Island

Ruawai
Maungaturoto
Matakohe

Pouto
Wellsford
Cape Rodney

Kaipara Heads
Warkworth
Kawau Island
Hauraki Gulf

WOODHILL FOREST
Orewa
Whangaparaoa

Helensville
Little Barrier Island

Waimauku
Kumeu
Rangitoto Island
Waiheke Island

Muriwai Beach
Auckland
WAITAKERE RANGES
Titirangi

Kaipara Harbour

N

0   30 miles
0   30 kilometers

10am-4pm; Dec. 25-Jan. daily 8:30am-6:30pm.) Otherwise, buses roll into the **bus stop** at **Northland Coach and Travel,** 11 Rose St. (open M-F 8am-5pm). Book buses at either location; with one day's notice they will also pick up at either location. **Northliner** (tel. 438 3206) and **InterCity** (tel. 438 2653 or (0800) 731 711) head to Auckland (3hr., 4 per day, $31); Kaitaia (4hr., 2 per day, $38), via Paihia (1½hr., 4 per day, $18). To get to Dargaville, hop on the workers' shuttle run by **Dargaville Taxi Charters** (tel. 439 7066; M-F 5:10pm), which leaves from Northland Coach and Travel. Advance booking is essential. **Hitchhiking** to Auckland is considered easiest from the visitors center in Tarewa Park; those heading to the Bay of Islands often try from SH1 (Western Hills Rd.) before traffic picks up to 70kph. Whangarei city buses are run by **JB buses** (tel. 437 5261 or (025) 857 446), and offer limited service (time-table available at visitors center). The most useful service JB operates is to Whangarei Falls. (Tu and Th, departs from bus stop at 9am and 11am, leaves falls at 11:20am and 3:15pm, $3.20 one-way.) For a cab, call **Kiwi Carlton Cabs** (24hr. tel. 438 2299); the company also runs sightseeing tours on the side ($12 return to the falls). The **DOC Visitors Centre** (tel./fax 430 2007) is in the regular visitors center and has info on all of Northland, as well as a fantastic souvenir shop. The visitors center also houses **public toilets** and a cafe. **Banks** in town radiate from the pedestrian mall.

In an **emergency** dial **111.** The **police station** (tel. 438 7339) is on Cameron St. The **White Cross Accident & Medical Clinic,** 121 Bank St. (tel. 430 0046), is open daily from 8am to 10pm. The **Whangarei Care Chemist** (tel. 438 7767) is in the same building (open daily 9am-1:30pm and 2:30-9pm). The **post office** (tel. 430 2761) is at Rathbone St. at Robert St. (open M-F 8:30am-5:30pm and Sa 9am-1pm). The **library** on Rust Ave. in front of the carpark offers **Internet access** ($5 for access card, then $5 per 30min.; open M-F 9am-6pm, Sa 9am-5:30pm). The **telephone code** is **09.**

ACCOMMODATIONS

In summer it is a good idea to reserve a day before you arrive. The nearest (but by no means close) **DOC camping grounds** are at **Uretiti Beach,** behind the sand dunes at Bream Bay to the south, and on the **Whananaki beachfront** at Otamure Bay, 2km past Whanaki Village on Rockwell Rd. ($6, children $3; water, toilets, and cold showers; reservations recommended).

Bunkdown Lodge, 23 Otaika Rd. (tel. 438 8886; email bunkdown@xtra.co.nz). This 100-year-old villa feels like home, with a plush living room and wood fire. Fresh herbs and vegetables grow in the courtyard for you to pick and cook with in the small kitchen. Sturdy 4-bed bunk rooms have individual lights, and twin rooms have desks. Bikes, Internet access ($5 per 30min.), a telescope, and massages are available. Bunks $15; twins and doubles $40. Free pickup.

Hatea House Hostel (VIP), 67 Hatea Dr. (tel. 437 6174; fax 437 61 41), is a compact home that maximizes every bit of space. Ask about cave and coast tours and kayak rental. Outdoor breakfast area. Dorms $15; singles $30; doubles $36; double cabin $40. Laundry $3. Cash only.

Whangarei YHA Hostel, 52 Punga Grove Ave. (tel./fax 438 8954), is a 15-20min. up the hill from the bus station, opposite the town basin off Riverside Dr. Call for (potential) free transportation to this fern-covered residential area. Perks include Friday potlucks, free fishing tackle, and snorkeling gear. The only heat in winter is a stove in the comfy lounge—you'll likely want one of their hot water bottles at night. Dorms $14; singles $28; doubles $32. Reception 8-10am and 5-7pm. Check-out around 10am. Off-street parking. Ask about winter deals and longer stays.

Whangarei Falls Caravan Park (tel. 437 0609), on Ngunguru Rd. on the way to the falls, north of the city center in Tikipunga. Call ahead for free pickup. Swimmers can work their muscles in the pool or under the falls themselves, refueling afterward in the communal kitchen. Bunks $13; 6-bed cabins with kitchenettes $32 for 2, extra person $10. Caravan and tent sites $9. Linen $2.

FOOD

Food sources adorn the main avenues and walkways. The **Pak 'N Save** market (tel. 438 1488), at the Walton St. Plaza across from the town basin, is cheap (open M-F 8:30am-8pm, Sa-Su 8:30am-7pm).

Taste Spud, 3 Water St. (tel/fax 438 1164). This hot potato and curry spot hits the mark with cheap stuffed spuds ($4.30-5.50) and burritos ($3.50-5). Deals rotate to include pakoras and melts ($1.50). Chill out with fruity soft serve ice cream or frozen yogurt ($1.50). Open M 8am-7pm, Tu-Th 8am-8pm, F 8am-8:30pm, Sa 11am-8pm, Su 4-8pm. Takeaway available.

Cafe Paparazzi (tel. 438 2961), on Quality St. between Vine and Cameron St. Mediterranean flair with murals of beach front villas and live ivy. Outside in the candlelit courtyard, the fountain gushes and an accordion player sometimes serenades. Tasty muffins ($2.50-3) for breakfast, fresh pastas ($5-7.50) for lunch, and live music all day Saturday. Open M-Sa 8am-5:30pm, F 8am-11pm. Reservations advised.

Caffeine, 4 Water St. (tel. 438 6925). The name says it all regarding this espresso cafe's focus. They do caffeine well, and in your favorite style ($2.50). Local artists display their work on the wall of this cheery terra cotta and green spot. Muffins ($2.50) are filling, while the veggie croissant ($5) is a tasty light meal.

Bogarts (tel. 438 3088), at Walton and Cameron St. Of all the coffee joints in all the world, you have to walk into this one. The wood-fired pizzas ($10-20) don't amount to a hill of beans in this crazy world, but they're darn good, sweetheart. Open M-F from 11:30am, Sa 5pm-1am, Su 6-11pm.

NIGHTLIFE

Planet Earth B.C., 27 Bank St. (tel. 430 8000). Modern interior with a couch for lounging and enjoying happy hour (M-F 5-6pm), live bands (F-Sa nights), and 16 gourmet burgers ($9-13.50) ranging from vegetarian to the Prawn, Bacon and Banana burger. Open M-Th 10:30am-midnight, F-Sa 10:30am-3am.

Oliver's Cafe and the Dickens Inn (tel. 430 0406), on the corner of Cameron and Quality St. More a den of friends than Dickensian debauchery. Ale is definitely the drink of choice (handles $3.50), though food is a specialty. The Hearty Pickwick Club Sandwich ($8.90) and Fagin's garlic bread ($2.50) will have you asking the waiter, "Please sir, might I have some more?" Come for lunch; dinner prices will pick your pocket. Saturdays have live classical guitar, Fridays a DJ cranks the tempo after 9pm. Open M-Th 8am-10pm, F-Sa 8am-1am, Su 9am-11pm.

Red Iguana Bar (tel. 438 4279), in the Grand Hotel at Rose and Bank St. Follow the droves of beer- and band-lovers to this unpretentious little watering hole with an American Wild West flavor and well-trodden floorboards. Live rock, jazz, and R&B Th-Sa 9:30pm. Happy happy hour M-F 5:30-6:30pm, with $2.70 handles (normally $3.50) and $2-2.50 glasses of wine (normally $3). Open daily from 11am.

Metro Bar, 31 Bank St. (tel. 430 0446). For a younger crowd that enjoys dancing more to DJs than to bands, this is the place to be. Play pool, or chill out upstairs. Happy hour M-F 5-6pm. Open M 11:30am-7:30pm, Tu-Th 11:30am-9:30pm, F 11am-1am, Sa 5:30pm-1am.

SIGHTS AND ACTIVITIES

Whangarei's primary attraction in town is a series of curious museums linked by paved walkways that collectively comprise the **Town Basin.** The most compelling of the former is the **Clapham Clock Museum** (tel. 438 3993), identifiable by the gigantic bronze sundial out front and the mural depicting advancements in time-keeping from the early Greeks to the 19th century. *(Open daily 9am-5pm, extended hours in summer. $5, students and seniors $4.50, children $3, families $12.)* The collection began in 1900 with one man's fascination with the gears of a music box, and became a 1500+ piece tribute to timekeeping. Ask for a free tour, and they'll turn on every cuckoo, bell, and whistle in the joint. The **Museum of Fishes** (tel. 438 5681) is "the best, biggest, and brightest display of mounted fishes in New Zealand." *(Open daily 10am-4pm. Admission $3.50.)* And if that's not enough to entice, come bat your eyes at Eel MacPherson. If you run through the museum fast enough, the fish just might appear to be swimming. The third of the three unique museums is **Di's Doll Museum and Studio** (tel. 438 5181), where 2000 dolls of all shapes, sizes, and ethnicities are segregated according to national uniforms or skin tone. *(Open M-Sa 9am-4:30pm, Su 10am-4pm. $3.50, students $2, children $1.50, families $8.)* The shop's handmade porcelain dolls are for sale. West of downtown Whangarei is the **Heritage Park,** which houses the **Whangarei Museum,** the **Clarke Homestead,** and the **local Kiwi House** (tel. 438 9630), three attractions that can be packaged together (each $3, all three for $7). Back in town, walk through the rose gardens of **Cafler Park** to discover the **Fernery** and the **Snow Conservatory.** The former is the largest public collection of ferns in the country, including some giant ones appropriate for a Brontosaurus' breakfast. Despite its name, the focus of the conservatory is the desert and its diverse cacti.

For those people looking to escape to the outdoors, Whangarei offers numerous **walking tracks** through the reserves that border the town. In particular, the **Whangarei Falls** are worth checking out (from the car park there is a 30min. loop trail). The climb up **Mount Parahaki** offers great views of the city; automobiles can also make the ascent up the side of New Zealand's largest *pa* and see a WWII memorial with a glowing neon red cross. Those who want to escape farther should explore the **Whangarei Heads,** where **Ocean Beach** offers great surf and bursts of rocky coastline, and the view from **Mount Manais,** with its castle-like peaks, will drive you crazy with 360° panoramas. For more organized activities, **The Bushwacka Experience** (tel. 434 78 39 or (025) 578 240) offers two tours. The "Basic Tour" takes you on bushwalks through rock crevasses, on the "waterfall express," and then to glowworm caves, with tea, barbecue, and four-wheel drive safari transportation. The "Adventure Seekers" tour adds abseiling and rock climbing. Both tours wind up at the **farm base,** where you can milk cows and shear sheep. *(Free pickup from the city. Tours on demand with a 1-day notice. Basic tour 2hr., $45. Adventure seekers 4hr., $75. Discounts available for large groups.)* **Northland Coastal Adventures** (tel. 436 0139 or (025) 271 8891) allow you to arrange a full day of diverse outdoor activities; you can explore five different regions along the east coast north of Whangarei that you can explore ($65 or 2 people $120, lunch not included). Bill of **Hatea House** (tel. 437 6174) runs tours of the **Abbey Caves** as well. *(1-cave tour lasts 1½hr., $12; 2-cave tour, 3hr., $35; discounts for Hatea House guests.)* Whangarei is also home to a vibrant artistic community. **The Quarry,** managed by the **Northland Craft Trust** (tel. 438 1215), is a loose collection of artists that shares studio space, and opens to the public and other artists over the Labor Weekend (Oct. 23-25, 1999). Also, **Collaborationz '99: Hooked on Art** brings artists together 20 minutes north of Whangarei in McGregor's Bay to integrate their crafts. *(Feb. 19-23, 1999; registration $300, optional accommodation and meal packages, all materials supplied.)*

■ Near Whangarei: Poor Knights Islands

Eleven million years ago, eruptions off the coast of Northland gave birth to a string of islands, including the Poor Knights Islands. The Ngatiwai tribe called them home for a spell, naming them Tawhiti Rahi and Aorangi Islands. In the early 1800s, however, a string of invasions and deaths earned the islands the distinction of being *tapu* (forbidden). Today, landing on the islands without a permit is also *tapu* (but by decree of the DOC, not the local tribe). Lack of human interference on the islands make them a haven for all sorts of rare creatures, including tuatara and giant weta. **Fishing** and **shellfish collecting** are strictly prohibited on or around Poor Knights Islands.

The real action here is under the sea, and the big draw is world-class diving; **Jacques Cousteau** has rated the island area one of the ten best diving sites in the world. Special mooring buoys off the coast serve as landing points for the scores of scuba, snorkel, and kayak trips run out of the coastal town of **Tutukaka** (30km east of Whangarei). The cliffs drop away 100m underwater, but the face is far from sheer. Sea caves both above and below water make for awesome sea kayaking and snorkeling among moray eels, stingrays, and subtropical reef fish. Pleasure cruisers and recreational divers are best suited to the **Knight Line Cruises** (bookings tel. (0800) 288 882, information tel. 434 3733 or (025) 810 826). Their boat *El Tigre* departs the Tutukaka New Marina Complex daily at 8:30am, returning at 4:30pm (snorkeling equipment, kayaks, DOC swim-with-dolphins permit supplied). Guided trips pass through sea caves by boat, kayak, or snorkel, and Knight Line even offers a scuba tour of the "wall of mouths." *(Full-day $80, children $45; diving with all scuba gear $140. Bookings essential. Max. 6 people.)* More serious divers should contact the **Dive Shop** (tel. 438 3521) on Water St. The Dive Shop will take four or more people out on their boat (with full scuba gear $60), and also runs introductory diving sessions for novices ($130-150). Free pickup is available from your accommodation. To participate in a cool conservation program, contact the **Friends of Matakohe/Limestone Island** (tel. 438 4639). The group is making the little island in the Whangarei Harbour into a nature reserve. They are in search of volunteers to help with replanting and the construction of walking trails, shelters, and viewing platforms. In return for hard labor, you can camp on the island.

BAY OF ISLANDS

A tremendously popular summertime destination, the Bay of Islands has long attracted visitors with its temperate climate and beautiful coastline. The most celebrated visitor was Captain Cook, who dropped anchor here in 1769. Cook got along well with the Maori and sent word back to England, setting the wheels in motion for the Bay's permanent European settlement. He named the region after the 144 islands that create pockets of tranquility for maritime enthusiasts and exploration options for landlubbers. The best way to get a feel for the region is to get on board one of the all-day cruises. Or, jump into the water and see the Bay from a different perspective.

■ Paihia

Paihia is the principal center of commercial activity and nightlife in the Bay of Islands. In the summer, its population of 4000 skyrockets to nearly 20,000. It is also the transportation hub of the region, as all of the buses arrive and depart from the **Maritime Building.** You can book virtually any water-based activity from this building.

ORIENTATION AND PRACTICAL INFORMATION

Marsden Road runs along the waterfront and is the main artery. **Paihia Wharf** is roughly in the middle of town, opposite the commercial center of **Paihia Mall** and bordered by **Williams** and **Bayview Road.**

Buses: Northliner Coaches (tel. 402 7857) and **Intercity** (tel. 357 8400) arrive at the Maritime Building, contract through **Pioneer Coachlines,** and run to Auckland (4¼hr., 2 per day, $42) via Whangarei (1¼hr., $18); also to Auckland via Waipoua, with a stop to see the forest (8hr.; in summer 1 per day; in winter M, W, F, Su, $58); and to Kaitaia (2¼hr., 2 per day, $28) via Kerikeri (30min., $8).

Ferries: Fullers Passenger Ferry (tel. 402 7421) departs for Russell daily on the half-hour (15min.; in winter 7:30am-6:30pm, in summer 7:30 until 10:30pm; $3). Buy tickets on board, or at the Fullers desk in the Maritime Building. The **vehicle ferry** departs from Opua (about 10km south of Paihia) for Russell every 10min. (5min. 6:50am-9pm. Cars $7, camper vans $12, motorcycles $3.50. No fee for driver, extra passenger $1.)

Taxis: Haruru Cabs (tel. 402 6292) covers local requests. **Paihia Taxis and Tours** (tel. 402 7506) offer 'round-the-clock shuttles to the airport ($15 per person). More creative transportation options include the **Tuk Tuk Shuttle Service** (tel. (025) 866 071), which goes to Waitangi ($5), Haruru Falls ($8), or both ($12). **Lily Pond Farm Park** gives wagon rides to up to 8 people around town ($2 per person), or to Waitangi ($5 per person).

Car Rentals: Paihia is the ideal location to rent a car for a trip up to Cape Reinga. **Budget Rentals** (tel. 402 7811) is in the **Paihia Holiday Shop** at the corner of Williams and Selwyn Rd.

Hitchhiking: Hitchhiking to Kerikeri or points north is best accomplished near the rotary at the end of Marsden Rd. Those headed south do best to wait at Paihia Rd. at the edge of town.

Visitors Center: Information Bay of Islands (tel. 402 7345; fax 402 7314; email: fndcboi@xtra.co.nz), in the white octagonal pavilion to the left of Paihia Wharf. Understaffed but helpful. Also offers **Internet access** ($5 per 30min.). Open daily winter 8am-5pm, summer 8am-8pm.

Banks: Banks such as **ASB** and **BNZ** cluster around the Paihia Mall, have 24hr. **ATMs,** and are open M-F 9am-4:30pm.

Emergency: Dial 111.

Medical Services: Bay View Medical Centre is located at 7 Bay View Rd. (tel. 402 7132) and open by appointment M-F 9am-5pm. For emergencies and after-hours, contact the **Bay of Islands Hospital** in Kawakawa (tel. 404 0280). **Paihia Pharmacy** on Williams Rd. (tel. 402 7034) stocks a fine array of sunscreens (open M-F 8:30am-5pm, Sa 8:30am-noon).

Telephone code: 09.

ACCOMMODATIONS

The number of beds in Paihia has been steadily increasing for quite some time, with almost every summer bringing the introduction of a new backpackers. Reservations are essential in summer. **Kings Street** is the mecca for budget travelers.

Mousetrap Backpackers (VIP), 11 Kings Rd. (tel. 402 8182). An eclectic mix of potted plants, backpackers' art on the walls (and ceiling), and the hostess' *joie de vivre* make this into a funky and comfy abode. The soul of this backpackers is the balcony with an ocean view, which has transformed many well-intentioned active visitors into "balcony bums." Longer stays encouraged. Outdoor wood barbecue. Daily rental of bicycles ($10) and kayaks ($25). Dorms $16; twins and doubles $39. Look for winter discounts.

Pipi Patch Lodge (VIP), 18 Kings Rd. (tel. 402 7111; fax 402 8300; email pipipatch@acb.co.nz; http://www.acb.co.nz). Brought to you by the folks at Auckland Central Backpackers, the Pip continues a tradition of partying excellence (especially in the summer), with a bar on the premises and a stream of Kiwi Experiencers to fill it. A swimming pool, free spa, well-equipped lounge, and outdoor basketball hoop complete the amenities. Dorms $16; singles, doubles, and twins $40; family units with full kitchen $40 for 2, extra person $15, max. 5. Key deposit $20. Linen $1. Reception in winter 7:30am-7:30pm; in summer 7:30am-8:30pm.

Peppertree Lodge, 15 Kings Rd. (tel./fax 402 6122; email: peppertree.lodge@xtra.co.nz). A sparkling, good-natured place with white clapboard siding and a little pepper tree out front. Well-designed with backpackers in mind. Bicycles and a tennis court with balls and rackets available. 6-8-bed dorms in summer $16, in winter $15; 4-bed dorms with private bathroom in summer $18, in winter $15. Doubles and twins in summer $45, extra person $15; in winter $40, extra person $10. Self-contained studio double in summer $75, winter $50.

Lodge Eleven (tel./fax 402 7487), at the corner of King and MacMurray Rd. Two stories of motel-style units are well maintained by a hospitable owner. Each unit has its own bathroom, with an adjacent kitchen and lounge. Dorms $16; 4-bed dorms $18; singles $30; twins and doubles in winter $40, in summer $44. Highly popular 6-bed Swedish log cabin in back ($90). Key deposit $10. Linen $1. Laundry $4. Bicycles $10 per day; tennis equipment $5 for use on nearby courts. Reception 8am-8pm. Check-out 9:30am.

FOOD AND NIGHTLIFE

Paihia has a wide array of attractive restaurants. The **Four Square** market (tel. 402 8002), on Williams Rd., has a strong wine-and-cheese selection for picnics (open in summer M-F 8am-8pm, Sa-Su 8am-6pm; in winter M-F 8am-6pm, Sa-Su 8am-5pm;).

NORTHLAND

Basrah, towards the Selwyn Ave. edge of the Paihia Mall (tel. 402 8544). Tucked away in the corner of the shopping arcade lies this Middle Eastern oasis, with overflowing pitas stuffed with lamb, beef, chicken, or falafel. Turkish coffee ($3) is a kicker, and sweet Turkish delights (50¢) send you home smiling. Open in summer Su-Th 11am-9pm, F-Sa 11am-10:30pm; in winter for lunch daily 11am-3pm, for dinner Tu-Su 5-9pm.

Ruffino's (tel. 402 7964), 39 Williams Rd., above the Four Square. Some of the area's best pizza hidden in a sanitary white office building. Generous personal-size pizzas are choice goods ($7.50-10); salads ($4) and pastas ($10-11) are good too. BYO. Takeaway available. Open daily in summer from 5:30pm; in winter from 4:30pm.

Caffe Over the Bay, on Marsden St. across from the wharf (tel. 402 8147). Savory scents entice you to the balcony facing the bay. Friendly service, mellow jazz, and cute round tables inside. Vegetarian soup of the day with garlic bread ($8.90). Hazelnut pancakes ($10) highlight all-day breakfasts ($6.50-12.50). Lunch pastas and salads ($10-13). Open daily in summer 8am-8pm; in winter 8am-3:30pm.

Blue Marlin Diner (tel. 402 7590), on Marsden Rd. at the mall. Saddle up in the swiveling seats at the blue bar, or sit at booths along the wall while you enjoy the staple fish and chips ($4.95). Opt for light snacks or more conventional meals of steak and fish fillets ($12.50-14). Takeaway available. Open daily in summer 7:30am-8:30pm; in winter 8:30am-6pm.

Saltwater Cafe, 14 Kings Rd. (tel./fax 402 7783). Blue neon sign reels them in to the Northlands' top restaurant for two years running (and it's only been around 2 years). Chef Trent Warren sculpts food into beautiful works of visual art, and then gives you the pleasure of breaking them down. Delicate entrees ($8-13), succulent mains ($18.50-29.50), and wicked desserts ($8.50-10) are too unique to pick representatives. Open daily from 5:30pm.

The Lighthouse Black Boat Bar (tel. 402 8324), on Marsden Rd. opposite the wharf carpark, is Pahia's primary night spot. This place hops on summer weekends, when the queue leads out the door, down the stairs, and around the block. DJ is on by 9:30 each night, spinning a wide array of tunes in the spacious interior. Happy hour M-F 9-10pm ($2 pints). Handles $3.50. Open M-Sa noon-2am.

SIGHTS AND ACTIVITIES

Paihia is the center for modern-day activities in the Bay of Islands, and the **Maritime Building** at the wharf is the meeting point for many of the tours and trips (building open daily in summer 6:30am-9pm; in winter 7am-7pm). In summer, expect crowds of fellow tourists on any activity you choose; advance booking is key. In winter, many activities require minimum numbers. Always ask about backpackers' discounts, as they are not always advertised. Many of the trips listed here will also pick you up in Russell; inquire when booking.

Cruises

The focal point of most of the sightseeing cruises is the **Hole in the Rock,** an island at the extreme end of the bay that ships can pass through. Trips offered by different companies vary significantly; don't let price and duration be the only criteria for your decision. **Fullers** (tel. 402 7421; fax 402 7831; email reservations@fullers-northland.co.nz) runs a Cape Brett trip to the Hole. *(4hr. Daily at 9am, in summer also at 1:30pm. $55, children $28.)* The **Cream Trip** meanders in and out of the smaller bays, delivering the mail (it is one of the few official Royal Mail runs left in New Zealand). *(5½hr. 10am daily in summer; in winter M, W, Th, Sa. $65, children $33.)* You may also combine the two trips into a **Supercruise.** *(6½hr. 9am daily in summer; in winter M, W, Th, Sa. $85, children $45.)* None of Fullers' cruises include lunch, so bring your own. **Kings** (tel. 402 8288) also offers a cruise with a route similar to the Supercruise. *(6hr. 10am daily Oct-May. $75, children $45. Lunch $10.)* They also offer a year-round Hole in the Rock Cruise. *(3¼hr. 2 per day. $50, children $25.)* For an evening cruise, contact **Darryl's Mini Cruises** (tel. 402 7848 or 402 7730). Although they don't make it to the Hole in the Rock, dinner is included as part of the cruise—call for the schedule of departures. *(2½hr. $35, children $11.)*

Adventure Cruises

For those who want to feel the adrenaline rush of shooting across the waves, several faster cruising options are available. The **Fast Boat Company** (tel. 402 7020) offers "more of the bay in less time," with two exciting possibilities. The **Excitor** travels at speeds of up to 35 knots, is suitable for all ages, and goes out to the Hole in the Rock—bring a camera. *(1½ hr. Runs daily in summer every 2hr. 8:30am-9pm; in winter 10am and 2pm. $50, children $25.)* A step up in intensity is the **Excitor Extreme,** which is the fastest boat of its type operating in New Zealand, and is the kind used by special armed military services throughout the world. *(1½hr. $70.)* Capable of speeds of over 50 knots, the trip is only suitable for adults in excellent health. In inclement weather, both of these trips may modify their routes, taking in more territory at slower speeds. **Kings** (tel. 402 8288) has also gotten into the adventure cruising market with their **Mack Attack** boat. *(Operates Sept.-May. 1½hr. $50, children $25.)*

Swimming with Dolphins

DOC licenses select companies to go out in search of playful pods, and in the right conditions you can slip into the water and frolic with the slick grey creatures. There is no guarantee of sightings, though some companies will let you try again the next day; check before booking. When spotted, the dolphins must be left alone if feeding or if they are accompanied by baby dolphins. **Dolphin Discoveries** (tel. 402 8234) in the Maritime Building, has been spotting dolphins since 1991 and has the highest success rate. *($85, children $45.)* The ubiquitous **Fullers** (tel. 402 7421) has a **Dolphin Encounters** trip that includes an underwater microphone to hear all the whistles and clicks. *(4hr. Daily 8am, also in summer at 12:30pm. $85, children $45.)* They have a special safety net that allows passengers not confident in their swimming skills to get in the water. **Bay of Islands Heritage Tours** (tel. 402 6288), also in the Maritime Building, puts a Maori spin on the dolphin tour with a traditional welcome, and plenty of stories about Tangaroa, the god of the sea. *(8am and 1pm. $85, children $45.)* **Carino** (tel. 402 8040 or (025) 933 827), a 40- by 30-foot catamaran sailing charter, offers a full day of sailing, sunning, fishing, island beach stops, bushwalks, and swimming with dolphins, all for $60. If you don't find any, console yourself with the $6 barbecue lunch, or drink your marine mammal blues away at the on-board bar.

Fishing and Sailing

In addition to being the cheapest option for swimming with dolphins, charter boats are a great way to see the islands and get in a little fishing on the side. Naturally, each skipper and boat has a distinct character. The good folk at **Charter Pier** (tel. 402 7127 or 402 7125 or (0800) 2GOFISHING/ 246 437 4464), halfway down the wharf on the left, are familiar with every operator and handle all the bookings. *($45 per person for large boats, max. 22 people; $65 for small boats, max. 8 people.)* After a brief conversation, owner Karen will match you with a boat and guide. Generally, trips are four hours long, and there are opportunities for big game fishing. You can also hire self-drive boats for a less structured experience. For a more offbeat sailing experience, **She's A Lady** (tel. 402 8119 or (025) 964 010) focuses on passengers having a good time. *(7-8hr. 9am. $65, includes lunch.)* **Fullers** (tel. 402 7421) operates the **R. Tucker Thompson,** a majestic tall ship with a basic bar that endeavors to experience the bay in much the way as Cook and Co did. *(7hr., daily Nov.-May. 9:30am. $75, children $40.)*

Sea Kayaking and Rentals

Rugged individualists who want to paddle their own way can explore the mangrove forests, Haruru Falls, and the intricacies of the outlying islands via kayak. The trademark image of a woman drifting serenely through mangroves is highly visible throughout the region, and belongs to **Coastal Kayakers** (tel. 402 8105). They offer independent kayak rentals ($10 per hr., $25 per half-day, $40 per day) and also a mask and snorkel combo ($10 per day). They also do package tours and hard-core **wilderness expeditions**. *(2-3 days, Nov.-May. From $110. Bring a sleeping bag.)* **Bay Beach Hire** (tel. 402 7905), on Marsden Rd. opposite the Edgewater Motel, has both individual and tandem kayaks. *($10 per hr., half-day $25, full-day $35.)* They also have catamarans, windsurfers, dinghies, and fishing tackle.

Flying, Falling, and Diving

Those who would prefer to see the bay from above can take a scenic flight around the islands, Cape Brett, and the Hole in the Rock with **Salt Air** (tel. 402 8338), located in a kiosk just to the south of the Maritime Building. Their 1946 seaplane will take you around for 20 minutes ($85 per person) or 30 minutes ($95 per person). They also run tours to Cape Reinga. *(Daily in summer 8am and 2pm; in winter 10am. $239 per person, max. 8 people. Free pickup from accommodation.)* **SkyHi Tandem Skydive Ltd.** (tel. 402 6744 or (025) 756 758) drops you out, not off. Departing from Watea Airfield, they offer free pickup from your accommodation, and from wherever you land, too. *(3000m $185, 4000m $225.)* **Paihia Dive** (tel. 402 7551) on Williams Rd., offers a Discover Scuba Course for novices. *(2 dives, backpacker special $150.)* They also offer a two-day dive trip to the **Rainbow Warrior.** *($125 with all the gear.)*

Rainbow Warrior

The battered hull of Greenpeace's *Rainbow Warrior* rests off-shore in Matauri Bay, the end result of a dark series of events. After the French resumed nuclear testing in the South Pacific, Greenpeace dispatched the *Rainbow Warrior* to carry out a **mission of protest.** The French Secret Service got wind of the highly publicized endeavor and, on July 10, 1985, **bombed the ship** in Auckland Harbour. The event became instant international news. A bird reserve near Thames (see p. 134) was established in memory of Fernando Pereira, the on-board photographer who was killed, and the episode remains a sticking point in Kiwi-Franco relations to this day. The hull of the sabotaged ship was moved to the Bay of Islands in 1987 and **sunk in Matauri Bay,** where the haven for subtropical fish now plays host to world-class divers in an eco-friendly maritime park, an unexpected, but not altogether unfitting, end for the environmentalist vessel.

On the Ground

Although it may be hard to imagine, there are land-based activities in Paihia as well. **Bay Beach Hire** (tel. 402 7905) rents mountain bikes ($5 per hr., $15 half-day, $20 full day) with which you can explore the inland hills. Several walking tracks in these hills lead to scenic views of the waterfront. For a completely unique Paihia experience, visit the **Lily Pond Farm Park** (tel. 402 6099) on Puketona Rd. on the way to Kerikeri. *(Open daily from 10am. $5, children $3.)* Although it's a bit difficult to reach without a car, those who get there are greeted by black swan salutes, and a chorus of chickens, pheasants, emu, ducks, peacocks, and pigs. Activities include horse and pony rides (5-15 min., $1), feeding the animals ($1), milking the cow at noon, a swimming hole, and a bush walk to a small waterfall. A small stand sells hamburgers ($3.50), toasted sandwiches, and chips ($2.50). For a more substantial horse ride, **Ginny's Horse Treks** (tel. 405 9999) has a great summer option of five hours of riding, glow-worm caves, and swimming holes. *(Nov.-Apr. Free pickup in Paihia, 9am at the base of the wharf. $55, bring your own lunch.)* They also offer shorter treks in the winter, but no free pickup. *(2hr. $35.)* For those singing a different tune, the **Bay of Islands Jazz & Blues Festival,** now in its 14th year, usually takes place over three days in early August and features internationally acclaimed musicians as well as local talent. *(Admission $30, children free.)*

■ Russell

It's hard to believe that Russell once merited the title "Hell Hole of the Pacific," and was notorious for seedy sailor activity and Maori-Pakeha clashes. In time it straightened itself out, and today retains a quiet charm year-round. In summer it is especially appealing as a break from the Paihia crowds. Consider this place if you feel overwhelmed; the prescription for your malaise is to take two days in Russell.

ORIENTATION AND PRACTICAL INFORMATION The **Strand** runs along the water's edge from the **Russell Wharf.** All the shops are within a two block radius of each other, just south of **Long Beach Road.**

Kings runs the **Russell Visitor's Centre,** which is in a kiosk right on the wharf (open daily in summer 8am-8pm). In the winter, the building is stocked with brochures, but there is no attendant. Queries should be directed to the **Bay of Islands Maritime & Historic Park Visitor Centre** (tel. 403 7685; fax 403 7649) on the Strand. This is also the main **DOC office** for the Bay of Islands (open daily in summer 8:30am-5pm; in winter 8:30am-4pm). **BNZ** on York St. (tel. 403 7821) has painfully short hours (open M-F 10:10am-2pm), as does **Westpac Bank** (tel. 403 7809) on Cass St. near the Strand (open M-F 10am-1:45pm). **Fullers Passenger Ferry** (tel. 402 7421) departs for Paihia daily on the hour (15min.; in summer 7am-10pm, in winter 7am-7pm; $3, children $1.50). Buy tickets on board, or at Fullers' desk in the Maritime Building. The **vehicle ferry** departs from Okiato (about 8km south of Russell) for Paihia every 10min. (Sa-Th 6:40am-8:50pm, F 6:40am-9:50pm. Cars $7, campervans $12, motorcycles $3.50. No charge for driver, extra passengers $1.) **Russell Taxi** (tel. 403 0760) offers local service. In an **emergency,** dial **111. Russell Medical Services** (tel. 403 7690) is in the Traders Mall, between York and Church St. (open M-F 9am-4:30pm). The **Doctor on Call** (tel. 404 0328) can be reached daily in summer 24hr. (in winter M-Friday 7pm-10am, Sa-Su 24hr.). **Russell Pharmacy** is at 21 York St. (tel./fax 403 7835; open M-F 8:30am-5pm, Sa 9am-noon). The **post shop** is in the Russell Foodmarket on York St. (open M-F 8:30am-6pm, Sa 9am-1pm). **Internet access** is available at **Innovation** (tel. 403 8843 or (025) 814 811; email jacqui@igrin.co.nz), on York St. in the Traders Mall, for $5 per 15 minutes (open M-F 8am-5pm). The **telephone code** is **09.**

Capital Confusion

Contrary to popular belief, today's Russell was *not* the first capital of New Zealand. That honor belongs to the town of **Okiato,** across the waters from Opua. Okiato was originally named Russell in 1840 (in honor of the British Colonial Secretary), and was established as the capital almost immediately after the signing of the Treaty of Waitangi. This Russell flourished for several months before succumbing to a fire, after which the capital was moved to Auckland (in 1841), along with most of the local industrial base. The ensuing economic downfall angered local Maori, who razed Russell. Its smoking embers were designated "Old Russell" (now Okiato), and most of the land is a nature reserve today.

ACCOMMODATIONS Russell's accommodation options are plentiful, and well suited for escaping the party atmosphere of Paihia and actually getting some sleep at night. **The End of the Road,** 24 Brind Rd. (tel. 403 7632; email 100373.344@compuserve.com), is at the top of Robertson Rd. and then left down the hill to the end of Brind. It's more home than hostel, with amazing views of Matauwhi Bay, a lemon tree track to the wharf (10min.), and an easy walk to Long Beach (15min). Unfortunately there are only six beds. (Dorm $18, in winter $16; twin and double $40, in winter $36.) **Russell Holiday Park** is on Long Beach Rd. (tel. 403 7826; fax 403 7221). Flowering plants and trees abound on this sprawling complex that caters to families. Industrial-strength facilities include timed coin-op showers and a large communal kitchen, though no utensils. (Powered and tent sites $12, in winter $10; cabins $60, in winter $30; cabins with kitchen $70, in winter $40; flats with kitchen and bathroom $100, in winter $50.) The **Russell Lodge** is at the corner of Chapel and Beresford St. (tel. 403 7640; fax 403 7641), situated close to the shops. It has a communal kitchen, a rec room, and an outdoor pool shaded by trees. (Dorms $18, in winter $16; deluxe doubles with TV and kitchenette $75 for 2, extra person $10; motel units with private bathroom and eating area $125 for 2, extra person $10. Laundry $2.) **The Duke of Marlborough Hotel** (tel. 403 7829; fax 403 7828; email: the.duke@xtra.co.nz), is on the Strand. The oldest hotel in New Zealand, the Duke retains its charm from years gone by. Tassled lamps and big band swing music in the dining room hearken back to another era. Each room is unique and has its own bathroom, TV, and coffee and tea. Many have wicker furniture, while the suites have couches and sitting rooms. (Singles $95-100; doubles $135-175; suites $235.)

FOOD AND NIGHTLIFE Orca's Cafe (tel. 403 7589), on the Strand, has a beautiful beachfront view from the bar seating at the front window and an enclosed outdoor courtyard out back. Dine on pleasing veggie-friendly options such as toasted sandwiches ($4-9.50) and salads ($4.50-8.50). Breakfast options include muffins topped with a lemon slice ($2.50). Dinner is served in the summer (mains $10-20). (Open in summer daily from 8am; winter Tu-Su 9am-3:30pm.) **York St. Cafe** (tel. 403 7360) in the Traders Mall is a simple place serving full meals at low prices. Mains for lunch ($12.50-15) and dinner ($15-23) span the range of culinary delights, while takeaway burgers, chicken sandwiches, and fish and chips ($4.50-6.50) make for affordable dining options. (Open daily in summer 8am-11pm; in winter 9am-11pm.) The **Duke of Marlborough Tavern and Bistro** on the corner of Chapel and York St. is actually two separate establishments connected by a common bartender. The Bistro has a nautical theme with fishnet overhead and a dinghy in the corner. Lunch specials such as steak, slaw, and fries are $9.50, while all-day breakfasts are $10. Dinner mains ($16.50-19.50) are meaty. (Open M-Sa noon-3pm and 6-9:30pm, Sunday afternoons during high season.) The adjacent **Tavern** is your standard sports bar, with pool tables and big-screen TV (open M-Th 9am-11pm, F-Sa 9am-midnight).

SIGHTS AND ACTIVITIES Russell offers travelers historical treasures as well as outdoor pleasures. The best collection of the former is at the **Russell Museum** (tel. 403 7701) on York St., which has a functional scaled replica of Cook's *Endeavor*, as well as articles ranging from the ridiculous (cow hairballs and swordfish eye sockets) to the sublime (an excellent video on the turbulent history of the Bay of Islands). *(Open daily 10am-4pm, Jan. 10am-5pm. Admission $3, children 50¢.)* The **Russell Heritage Trail** is a self-guided walk around town that introduces you to many old buildings. *($1 map available at the DOC office.)* The Anglican **Christ Church,** on the corner of Baker and Robertson Rd., is New Zealand's oldest standing church, built in 1814. Charles Darwin attended services here while the *HMS Beagle* was anchored in the bay; he made a substantial contribution to the help fund the church that was later to attack his theory of evolution by natural selection. Not to be outdone by the Protestants, Bishop Pompallier arrived in 1838, and his posse of Catholic missionaries soon followed suit. Although the church is gone, the 1841 **Pompallier House** (tel. 403 7861), on the esplanade at the end of the Strand, is open to the public and displays such artifacts as the mission tannery, printing house, and book bindery—the Bible was even translated into Maori here. *(Open daily 10am-5pm, tours 10am-4pm. Admission $5.)* For a more comprehensive tours of the area, **Russell Mini Tours** (tel. (025) 904 738), in the Fullers shop on the Strand directly opposite the wharf, offers tour that depart daily from the wharf and cover sites not accessible by foot. *(In winter 5 per day, in summer 7 per day. $12, children $6.)* The **Russell Film Society** (tel. 403 7048) screens movies every Thursday night at 7:30pm in the Russell Town Hall. *($6, children $3.)*

Outdoor lovers will appreciate several nice spots near town. Mirroring Pompallier House on the opposite side of Russell is **Flagstaff Hill.** A short walking track ascends to the site where **Hone Heke,** the man who felled the symbol of British rule (the flagpole) four times in 1844-1845, displayed his axe-wielding skills (see p. 56). When the tide is out, the hill can be approached along the beach at the north end of the Strand; otherwise take the signposted route off Flagstaff Rd. Lovely **Long Beach** of Oneroa Bay lies just over the hill at the end of Wellington St. (which becomes Long Beach Rd. at that point) and offers plenty of opportunities to sun and swim. You can go kayaking with **Kaptain Kayak** (tel. 403 7252 or (025) 280 5466), who offers half-day, full-day, and multi-day tours of the coast line. Trekkers come from all over to walk the **Cape Brett Lighthouse Track,** an eight-hour medium grade walk in each direction. *(Track fee $15, children $8, payable at DOC office in Russell.)* The old lighthouse keeper's house has been turned into a hut with a gas cooker, running water, and toilets, but no utensils (hut fee $8, children $4). You must book ahead at the DOC office in Russell. The start of the track is an hour's drive from Russell; return shuttles are available through the DOC office ($30). Maori guides are available for the track and will introduce you to the history of the region (prices negotiable). A popular option is to be dropped off at the lighthouse by sea, and then hike back, so as to enjoy the coast and save a day. The DOC office has more information. They can also tell you about the **campsite** on the island of **Urupukapuka,** right at the beach with running water and cold showers, but no toilets ($5, children $2.50).

■ Waitangi National Reserve

Across the mouth of the Waitangi River lies a beach with a past. On February 6, 1840, more than 500 Maori, settlers, traders, dignitaries, and missionaries came ashore on the pebbled beach of Waitangi to witness the signing of the single most important document in New Zealand's history—the **Treaty of Waitangi** (see p. 55). Today, the treaty is the focal point of hotly debated Maori land rights grievances. Yet despite the demonstrations and legal battles linked to this place, the **Waitangi National Reserve** (tel. 402 7308) is a remarkably serene and verdant place. To reach the reserve from Paihia, follow Marsden Rd. over the Waitangi Bridge, and then head up the hill. Alternatively, you can take the scenic route (if you have a car) and check out **Haruru Falls** on Puketona Rd. The falls can also be reached by way of the **Waitangi National Trust Mangrove Walk,** a 2½ hour stroll from the visitors center.

NORTHLAND

> ### Kiwi Carnage
>
> Man's best friend can be less than a bosom buddy to New Zealand's native fauna, especially when Fido turns out to be a serial killer in disguise. In 1987, one such carnivorous canine went AWOL from his owners in the Waitangi State Forest, in the Bay of Islands. On a systematic rampage, he managed to slaughter as many as 500 kiwi—at least 50% of the area's population—before meeting a bullet-induced death. Keep your dog well-fed and leashed, or you'll bear the guilt of kiwi carnage, and some stiff legal action besides.

The grounds include the **Treaty House,** an exercise in prefabricated Victorian architecture that is now a museum. From 1832 to 1844, it was home to the Crown's first watchdog "British Resident," **James Busby** (see p. 55). To the left of the lush lawn that leads to the water is the **Whare Runanga,** a Maori meeting house for all tribes, constructed by a team of master carvers in 1940 for the treaty's centennial celebration. Two 10 minute sound and light presentations illustrate the stories behind the intricate carvings inside (daily on the half hour, 9am-4:30pm). The world's largest war canoe, *Ngatokimatawhaorua,* is on display a short walk away from the Treaty House in the opposite direction. The 35m canoe is hauled out by 80 warriors and paddled around the bay every February 6th to celebrate Waitangi Day. The **Visitors Centre** has another multimedia presentation (25min.) giving a rather candy-coated version of the story behind the treaty. Pay here for access to all buildings. (Open daily 9am-5pm. $8, children free.) Access to the grounds is free, and several of the exhibits are out in the open and accessible to anyone. The cafe down the path from the visitors center has coffee and pricey food.

See the bits and pieces of ill-fated New Zealand voyages at **Kelly Tarlton's Museum of Shipwrecks** (tel. 402 7021), which floats at the mouth of the Waitangi River by the bridge. The collection of over 1000 artifacts was salvaged from the watery graves of 20 wrecks. The fully licensed cafe on board operates after the museum closes, and features an improvisational music jam session every Sunday night. (Museum open daily 10am-5pm, in the summer extended hours; $6, children $2.50, group discounts with advance notice. Cafe open from 5pm.) **Te Ti Beach** at the mouth of the river on the other bank is a popular spot in summer.

■ Kerikeri

Kerikeri is the hub of one of the most fertile regions in the whole of New Zealand. Sitting to the north and west of Paihia, the town center is slightly inland of the coast, and is still considered part of the Bay of Islands. Craft shops and organic fruit stands line the roads leading into the town, which has close access to the water. In addition to its small permanent population, the area provides work for a substantial number of transient farm workers, especially around harvest time when work is available for anyone willing to put time in the field.

ORIENTATION AND PRACTICAL INFORMATION Kerikeri Road is the main street in town, leading from **SH10** all the way to the water. Most of the services are clustered within the triangle it forms with **Hobson Avenue** and **Cobham Road.** The **Visitor's Centre** in Paihia handles most Kerikeri queries, though info can be found in the **library** (tel. 407 9297; http://www.kerikeri.co.nz) on Cobham Rd. The **Kerikeri Medical Centre** is on Homestead Rd. and **Kerikeri Pharmacy Ltd.** is on Kerikeri Rd. (open M-F 8:30am-5:30pm, Sa 9am-12:30pm). The **post office** (tel. 407 9721) is on Hobson Ave. **Internet access** is available at **Kerikeri Computers,** 88 Kerikeri Rd. (tel. 407 7941) for $1 per 5 minutes. In an **emergency,** dial **111** or call the **police** (tel. 407 9211) on Kerikeri Rd. near Clark Rd.

ACCOMMODATIONS Budget accommodations in Kerikeri are geared toward backpackers who are looking for seasonal work at one of the many orchards and farms in the area. Farms contact worker's hostels, which then list the job postings. The **Kerikeri YHA,** 144 Kerikeri Rd. (tel. 407 9391; fax 407 9328), just past the edge of town toward the water, is a pleasant hostel in several pieces. Identical male and female bunkhouses are on either end of bathroom building, with single-sex facilities. It is a five-minute walk through bush to the fairy pools, a popular swimming spot. (Dorms $14, $70 per week; twins $34.) To get to the **Hone Heke Lodge (VIP),** 65 Hone Heke Rd. (tel./fax 407 8120; email honehekelodge@hotmail.com), turn off Kerikeri Rd. and then go left up the hill at the sign of the backpacking orange. This low-lying motel-style structure is a worker's hostel featuring a TV lounge with a wood fire, a rec room with pool and ping-pong tables, and two small kitchens. Bikes ($5 half-day, $10 full-ay) are reasonably priced, while laundry ($6) is not. (Dorms $14, $70 per week; doubles $40; twins $34; doubles and twins have fridge, hot pot, and toaster; 3 tent sites $10 each. $10 key deposit. $5 blanket deposit.) The **Hideaway Lodge** (tel./fax 4079793), on Wiroa Rd., is very sociable, though slightly grungy. At the SH10 rotary, go in the opposite direction from Kerikeri and look for the sign. The sprawling hostel attracts many workers by offering free transport to and from the fields. The lounge is worn but cozy with a wood fire, TV, pool table, and keg every Friday. The swimming pool is open 24 hours. To whip up gourmet grilled cheese in one of the two kitchens, get utensils upon check-in. (Bunks $12, $70 per week; doubles $30, $160 per week; deluxe doubles $35, $170 per week; tent sites $7.50, $45 per week, powered $8, $49 per week.)

FOOD AND NIGHTLIFE The **Rocket Cafe** (tel. 407 8688), on Kerikeri Rd. between the town and SH10, has glass doors along all four walls. The veggie-friendly menu includes Fabulous Breakfast Bagels ($5.50) and a hearty soup of the day with garlic bread ($6.50). The back doors open onto an expansive lawn with games amid the organic kiwi vines overhead. (Open daily 8am-5pm.) The **Fishbone Cafe,** 88 Kerikeri Rd. (tel 407 6065 or (025) 914 067), has a warm ambience in the center of town with reasonably priced menu items. Breakfasts and lunches are plentiful and affordable ($5.50-8.50); dinner is more expensive (entrees $6.50-12, mains $16-19), and reservations are necessary. (Open M-W 8:30am-4pm, Th-Sa 8:30am-9pm.) Beneath the Fishbone, accessed from Homestead Rd. behind Kerikeri Rd., is **Excess,** a small pub that gets crowded when rugby is on. (Open W-Su from 2pm; in winter F-Sa 4:30-11pm.) For your supermarket needs, turn to the symphony of foods at **New World** (tel. 407 7440), at the corner of Homestead Rd. and Fairway Dr. (open Sa-Tu 8am-6pm, W-F 8am-8pm).

SIGHTS AND ACTIVITIES Kerikeri is steeped in history. Both the Maori and Pakeha sides of the story are represented at the north end of town, around the picture-perfect **Kerikeri Basin**, which is a 20-minute walk from town down Kerikeri Rd. toward the water. Near the happy little yachts and dinghies bobbing playfully in the water is a trinity of Anglican missionary power: **St. James Church,** the graceful white **Kemp House** next door (which claims to be the oldest standing European building in the country), and **Stone Store** (constructed in 1832-1836 to house supplies for the Church Missionary Society). Cross the footbridge over the **Kerikeri River** and you will find yourself several centuries back in time at **Rewa's Village** (tel. 407 6454). *(Admission $2.50, children 50¢.)* The replica structures of this pre-European Maori fishing village create a worthwhile glimpse into the age of chiefs Hongi Hika and Rewa. Other cool water-based activities include swimming in the **Fairy Pools,** magical swimming holes by the Kerikeri River. The pools can be reached via an access road near the YHA. Alternatively, walk along the river away from the ocean or drive along Waipapa Rd. 2.5km east of SH10 to the **Rainbow Falls.**

THE FAR NORTH

■ Kaitaia

Armed with heaps of kauri wood and some powerful preaching, the soon-to-be Rev. Joseph Matthews came cruising in one balmy November day in 1832, on the lookout for a new mission site and troubled souls to save. Feeling there was the Lord's work to be done in the wee burg of Kaitaia, he sent sermons and supplies flying. By the 1850s and 60s, the missionaries handed over the reins of modern convenience-building to the local Maori and immigrant Dalmation communities (both of which flourish today). Billed as the "Gateway to the North," Kaitaia sits at the base of Cape Reinga and Ninety Mile Beach, and is an ideal place for refueling and restocking.

ORIENTATION AND PRACTICAL INFORMATION For answers to all Cape queries, seek out the **Northland Information Centre** (tel./fax 408 0879; email katvin@nzhost.co.nz), in Jaycee Park on South Rd. (open M-F 8:30am-5pm, Sa-Su 9am-1pm). The **DOC Kaitaia Field Centre,** 127 North Rd. (tel. 408 2100; fax 408 2101), can answer questions about camping on Cape Reinga (open M-F 8am-4:30pm). Commerce St. buzzes with **banks. InterCity** buses head south daily to Auckland (7hr., 10:20am, $62) via Whangarei (4hr., $37) and Paihia (2hr., $27). In an **emergency,** dial **111.** The **police** (tel. 408 0400) are on Rodan Rd. **Kaitaia Hospital** (tel. 408 0010) is on Rodan Rd. After hours, there is a **doctor on call** (tel. 408 3060). **Amcal Chemist,** 89-91 Commerce St. (tel. 408 1425), is the local pharmacy. (Open M-Th 8:30am-5pm, F 8:30am-6pm, Sa 9am-noon and 7-8pm, Su 10am-noon and 7-8pm.) The **post office** is at 101 Commerce St. (tel. 408 3100; open M-F 9am-5pm), and has **Internet access** ($5 per 30min.; open M-Th 8:30am-4:30pm, F 9am-3:30pm).

ACCOMMODATIONS, FOOD, AND NIGHTLIFE The **Hike and Bike Kaitaia YHA,** 160 Commerce St. (tel. 408 1840), offers neither hikes nor bikes, but does have clean, well-maintained facilities. (Dorms in summer $15; in winter $14; singles $25; twins $32; doubles $36; tent sites $10; non-YHA $4 more). If bikes are what you're after, then check out **Main Street Backpackers,** 235 Commerce St. (tel. 408 1275 or 0508-MAINST/ 624 678), New Zealand's first Maori-run hostel. Members of the community come to teach guests traditional bone carving ($10). Bikes, dune boards, and camping gear are available. (Dorms $13-16; singles $30; twins and doubles $34; tent sites $10.) Host Peter also runs **Tall Tale Travel 'N Tour** (tel. 408 0870), a learning experience about Maori protocol and culture that includes a visit to **Karawa Marae** (2hr., by arrangement, $40). In the center of town, the **Kaitaia Hotel,** 15-33 Commerce St. (tel./fax 408 0360), boasts a steak restaurant, the **Flame Grill,** and a traditional pub, plus standard rooms (singles $35; doubles $52; triples $58). Upstairs, from September to June, **Scandals** nightclub has a DJ spinning eclectic dance music (F-Sa 9pm-2am). For lighter fare, **Maisey's Main Street Cafe,** 14 Commerce St. (tel. 408 4934) does takeaway specials including fish, chips, coleslaw, fritters, and mussels ($5). **Pak N' Save** (tel. 408 2700), on Commerce St., has groceries (open M-F 8:30am-7pm, Sa-Tu 8:30am-6pm).

■ Kaitaia Surroundings and the North Coast

The attractions around Kaitaia are best accessed with a car. Both Kaitaia and its ocean-facing neighbor **Ahipara** offer scenic walkways that serve as windows into the kauri industry of yesteryear, most notably the **Kaitaia Walkway** (45min.; expandable into a 9km track suitable for experienced trampers). The Ahipara **Gumfields** spread over most of the peninsula out to **Tauroa Point,** southwest of Kaitaia, and are littered with remnants of 19th-century gum digging (trenches, dams, and an old gum diggers' shack). A mountain bike track goes down to the ocean.

For more extensive trails, head to the **Karikari Peninsula,** 20km northeast of Kaitaia between **Rangaunu Harbor** and **Doubtless Bay,** where the **Lake Ohia Gumholes** await. Leave the swimming togs at home—the lake was drained in the early 1900s. Fossilized remains of a kauri forest still poke out of swampland, while rare ferns and orchids flourish on the banks. The **Ancient Kauri Kingdom Ltd.** (tel. 406 7172) on SH1 in Awanui makes an enterprise of digging up Kauri logs that were felled in the swamp 30-50,000 years ago, and finishing the perfectly preserved wood into high-quality crafts and furniture (open daily). Farther east, along the base of the Karikari peninsula, sits **Coopers Beach,** offering sunbathing and good surfcasting in Doubtless Bay. The beach is flanked by Maori *pa* sites. To the west is the **Taumarumaru Reserve,** a majestic grassy headland pockmarked by three *pa*. To the east lies **Rangikapiti Pa,** on an incredibly strategic spot overlooking both Doubtless Bay and the **Mangonui Harbour.** Farther up the peninsula is a popular DOC campground at **Maitai Bay.** Facilities include cold showers, running water, toilets, and a well-placed boat ramp (tent sites $6, children $3; reserve through DOC in Kaitaia). Pushing farther east along SH10, one arrives at **Whangaroa Bay,** a narrow inlet with a snaking coastline. On the eastern shore is the town of **Whangaroa,** which is home to the **Sunseeker Lodge** (tel. 405 0496), on Old Hospital Rd. A steep hill brings you to this charming accommodation and its brilliant views of the bay. Spacious and clean dorm rooms are $15 ($70 per week), and the private double is small but secluded ($36). With a two-night stay, kayaks and lessons are free. (Well-appointed motel units for 2 are $90 in summer, $65 in winter. Two-night stay required for laundry, $6. Call for free pickup from the bus station in Kaeo.)

■ Aupouri Peninsula and Cape Reinga

The **Aupouri Peninsula** extends from the northern coast like a delicate finger, pointing the way for the spirits of the dead, whom the Maori believe take this final route overland before arriving at **Cape Reinga** and diving into the ocean to return to the mythical homeland of Hawaiki.

The path to the afterlife is gilded on the west by the golden sands of **Ninety Mile Beach,** more poetic a name than "ninety kilometer beach" or "fifty-six mile beach," both of which would be more appropriate. Near the top of the beach, the sands are interrupted by the **To Paki Stream,** which empties into the ocean. This is part of the **To Paki Reserves,** administered by the **To Paki DOC Field Centre** (tel. 409 7521), off **SH1.** With many walking tracks, the reserves offer a meditative serenity punctured in the summer by the screams of thrill-seekers coasting on their boards down the 100m-high sand dunes. Don't venture out to the very tip, which is sacred and protected Maori land. On the opposite side of the peninsula, the boarders boogie in the ocean waters of **Tapotupotu** and **Spirits Bay,** while landlubbers lie on graceful curves of sand. Slightly south along the side of the peninsula is **Great Exhibition Bay,** which, despite the name, entertains more boaters and fisherfolk than nude bathers. The bluff is capped with a **lighthouse** that perches over the churning waters where the Pacific and the Tasman meet. **Cape Maria van Diemen** to the west and the **North Cape** to the east have just as breathtaking, if less celebrated, scenery.

TOURS Most people elect to take a **guided day tour** in a specially designed sand-and-surf-worthy craft out of Paihia or Kaitaia. It makes for a long day, but it's a safer option for navigating the changing sands of an extremely remote region. If you have your own car, don't try to be a hero and impress your friends. You will get stuck. In fact, guided trips pass not only beautiful scenery but the rusting automobiles of adventurous yet substantially less-skilled drivers. Rental car companies have caught on and explicitly forbid such excursions.

Though Paihia's tours can sometimes seem more plastic or commercial than those of Kaitaia, they tend to include a stop in the **kauri forest** at Puketi. Out of Paihia, one good bet is **Northern Exposure Tours** (tel. 402 8644, (021) 588 098, or (0800) 573 875), whose "small bus with attitude" (max. 9 people) stops to hug the kauri in Puketi, dig for *tua tua*s on Ninety Mile Beach, get sandblasted tobogganing on the dunes at Te Paki, get spiritual at Cape Reinga, and thrash around in the surf of Tapotupotu Bay (10½-11hr.; $65, includes lunch). The **4x4 Dune Rider** (tel. 402 8681), also of Paihia, runs a similar tour with lunch in a rugged, air-conditioned Mercedes Benz bus (max. 20 people) with air-brushed cartoons of passengers on the side. (Free pickup daily from Paihia at 7:30am and Kerikeri at 8:15am. $75, children $55; 10% backpackers/family/AA discount.) They offer another trip for the same price which explores the base of the peninsula including the **Anipara Sand Dunes.** For a livelier experience, join the party-hard crowd on board **Kiwi Experience** (tel. 366 9830), which offers a special Cape Reinga trip (departs Paihia 7:30am, $69; max. 28 people). **Kings** (tel. 402 8288) offers an "express" trip that stops at the Ancient Kauri Kingdom but not the forest (9½hr., departs Paihia 8:15am; $60, children $40). The "scenic" trip that takes in the forest as well as the **Wagener Museum** in Houhora (11hr., departs 7:30am; $79, children $40; max. 40 people). Rounding out the Paihia trips, **Fullers** (tel. 402 7421) runs several comprehensive tours, focusing either on Maori culture or the natural surroundings. (11hr., departs Paihia 7:30am, $79, children $40, lunch $10 extra). Out of Kaitaia, two additional operators offer nearly identical packages. **Sand Safaris** (tel. 408 1778) offers small, anecdote-embellished tours that hit all the major spots on the peninsula and around Kaitaia ($45, children $25, includes lunch). **Harrison's** (tel. 408 1033 or (0800) CAPE REINGA/ 2273 734 642) cape runner tour covers the same ground and attractions ($40, children $20, lunch included).

ACCOMMODATIONS DOC maintains two **campsites** in the area of the Te Paki Reserve. **Tapotupotu Bay,** just south of the Cape region, flaunts sheltered golden sands accessible by a posted turn-off 3km before the end of the road to the cape (camping $6, children $3). The other is at **Kapowairu** along the east coast of Spirits Bay ($5, children $2.50); both are first-come, first-camped; the latter has 200 sites. DOC also maintains a third campsite, approximately in the middle of the Aupouri Peninsula at **Rarawa.** Sites can be found amid pine trees, a stone's throw from the white-sand beaches of Great Exhibition Bay. Follow the signs 1km north of Ngataki on SH1 ($6, children $3; open Labour Day-Easter). All three sites feature the DOC hallmarks of minimalism: cold showers, running water, and toilets.

Travelers looking for slightly more material comfort in their accommodations should head to **Pukenui** (pop. 1000), the population center of the peninsula. There awaits the **Pukenui Lodge (YHA/VIP)** (tel. 409 8837; fax 409 8704; email pukenui@igrin.co.nz), on the corner of SH1 and Wharf Rd. Enjoy a swim in the pool or a turn in the spa ($5 for 4 people). (Dorms $15.50; singles $35; doubles and twins $40.) Slightly out of town on Lamb Rd., the **Pukenui Holiday Camp** (tel./fax 409 8803) has a communal kitchen and bathrooms, plus a lounge with TV, stereo, a pool table, and a library. (Bunks $15; basic cabins $40 for 2 people; tourist cabins with kitchen $50 for 2; flats with bathroom and kitchen $55 for 2; extra person in cabins and flats $10.) To get away from it all, head 9km north of Pukenui to the **Northwind Lodge Backpackers** (tel./fax 409-8515) on Otaipango Rd., Henderson Bay. Remote is an understated description, but guests like it that way. (Dorms $15; singles $15; doubles $30.)

NORTHLAND

THE HOKIANGA

Every summer, refugees from the full-blown commercialism of the Bay of Islands escape to the cool green obscurity of Hokianga. Adventure activities give way to bushwalking, fishing, and meditating. Hokianga, or *Te Hoki anga hui o Kupe* ("the place of Kupe's return"), is hailed as the last spot the great Maori navigator Kupe put into port before departing for Hawaiki. A long-standing Maori tradition holds that Kupe (as well as everyone else who pays a visit) will one day return. But there's no rush—time passes slowly in Hokianga. As evidence, check out the "Opo the Dolphin" T-shirts for sale in the superettes, commemorating the region's only tourism claim to fame. A friendly blue-nosed dolphin wandered in to the harbor and set up a sideshow residence near the Opononi Wharf for a time. Mind you, Opo's antics took place in the summer of 1956.

PRACTICAL INFORMATION The **Hokianga Visitor Information Centre** (tel./fax 405 8869) is in **Omapere** on **SH12**, 450m out of "town" in a shady glen. You can watch comical 1950s newsreels about Opo the Dolphin in the "museum" upstairs (open daily 8:30am-5pm). There are **no banks, ATMs, or cash advances** in the Hokianga, so bring your Eftpos card or cash from Dargaville or the Bay of Islands. In an **emergency,** dial **III. Hokianga Health** (tel. 405 7709) is located on SH12 just outside of Rawene; call before coming. The **telephone code** is **09.** Both **Northliner** (Auckland tel. 307 5873, Northland tel. 438 3206) and **InterCity** (tel. (0800) 401 500) contract out to **Pioneer Coachlines** in the region. Service is sketchy at times, particularly in the winter, and runs on "Hokianga time," which means prior reservations are necessary (even if you have a pass). It also helps to make yourself obvious to the driver. From Paihia, buses run daily in the summer, and on Monday, Wednesday, Friday, and Sunday in the winter, departing at 9am for Kaikone (30min., $9) and running through the Hokianga region (2hr., about $20), then the Waipoua Forest (3¼hr., $35) and eventually on to Auckland (8¼hr., $55). Buses from Auckland arrive in Omapere by 2:30pm. Because the buses are sporadic and relatively expensive without the **Northland Wanderer pass** ($80, available through Intercity), many consider **hitchhiking** a viable alternative. Hitchers can be seen standing on the straightaways or approaching drivers at markets and post offices; those heading north or south take the Rawene-Kohukohu ferry and find a ride from the cars on board.

KAIKOHE Stop in this gateway town to linger in the **Ngawha Hot Springs** (tel. 401 0166). They're located 6km north of Kaikohe center, at the end of Ngawha Hot Springs Rd., in the sulfur-smelling **Ngawha Hot Springs Village.** Locals, arthritics, and travel-weary tourists soak in the separate wood-lined thermal pools, each with its own name, fluctuating water temperature, and unique mineral content. **Bulldog** and **Kotahitanga,** the two hottest, are touted as cure-alls. **Solomon** reportedly treats skin complaints, **Tanemahuta** is good for burns, **Doctor** supposedly cures arthritis, and **Waikato** and **Favorite** are for pure relaxation and watching **Baby** change color. The dark water is not treated at all, and the strong smell will not come out of your clothes even after repeated washings—you may want to hire towels ($1) and togs ($1). (Open daily 7am-9:45pm. Admission $2, children $1.)

RAWENE Rawene's centrality made it vital to the Kauri shipping industry of yore. Today, ferries rather than ships predominate, carrying passengers and vehicles to the other shore. Ferries depart every hour on the half-hour (15min.; 7:30am-7:30pm; passenger $1.50, motorcycle $4, car $13, campervans $20). For traveler's assistance above and beyond the call of duty, drop into the **Far North District Council** (tel. 405 7829) on upper Parnell Rd. (open M-F 8am-5pm). For assistance of a caffeinated sort, **The Boat Shed Cafe** on the water, down a bit from the ferry landing, makes great espresso (open daily 9am-5:30pm). **The Wharf House** (tel. 405 7713), also by the waterfront, makes tall burgers (open daily 7am-4:30pm). In the other direction, past the service station on the waterfront, are the much-celebrated **musical loos** of Hokianga. The fully automated, self-cleaning toilets play lovely piano music and feature mechanical toilet paper dispensers. Don't get too comfortable, though, as the doors fly open after 10 minutes (there is luckily a 1min. countdown). **The Four Square** at the Waterfront has a **post center** at one end of the counter (mail operates M-F 9am-5pm). The **store** is open later for your grocery needs (M-F 7:30am-5:30pm, Sa-Su 8:30am-5pm).

KOHUKOHU Most practically known as the other end of the Hokianga ferry (departing for Rawene daily at 7:45am, 8:30am, 9am and then every hour on the hour until 8pm, same rates as above), Kohukohu is also distinguished by one of its accommodations. **The Tree House** (tel. 405 5855; fax 405 5857) is a sprawling wooden-planked network of decks and rooms by a duck pond in a 17-acre forest. Activities include a walking track (10min. to a lookout point), mountain bikes ($2.50 per hr., half-day $10, full day $16), and lounging in the TV-free common space. It's hard to predict when you will leave. A small shop at the front desk sells food basics and phone cards. (Dorms $16; singles $25; doubles and twins $38; tent sites $10. Linen $2. Duvet $2.50.) Call from Rawene for free pickup from the ferry landing, or from Kohukohu if you arrive from points north. Reservations are essential for everything (even tent sites) in the summer; in winter, call ahead for doubles and twins.

To get a feel for untouched Hokianga, you'll need to barge farther upstream. **The Alma** (tel./fax 405 7704 or tel. (025) 997 450), a 1902 flat-bottomed kauri ship, swapped its twin masts for twin diesel motors and now runs tours up the harbor in the summer from Rawene (daily, call for departure times), as well as a fishing trip from Opononi on Fridays at 6pm. Meals are served on board ($5-15) with fresh crayfish as an option ($22.50, children $11.25).

OPONONI In the four decades since Opo the Dolphin put it on the map, **Opononi** has progressed about four years, evolving from a fun-in-the-sun small resort town of the 50s into an "Age of Aquarius" spiritual center of the 60s. Kupe's monument (an anchor stone and commemorative plaque) sits at the top of a hill on the harbor side of SH12 between Opononi and Rawene, while the grave of **Opo the Dolphin** is located in front of the South Hokianga War Memorial. Kupe may someday return to Hokianga to fulfill the myth, but Opo isn't going anywhere soon.

A scant 3km up from Omapere on **SH12** and 23km from Rawene, the town's wharf ties it to the harbor. If you're planning on spending the night, head to the epitome of Hokianga serenity (no TV, no guest phone, no clocks) at the **House of Harmony** (tel./fax 405 8778). A deck overlooking the harbor makes for fine breakfasts. There is free pickup from the bus station. First-come, first-harmonized. ($15; tent sites $8). Stop in at the **Opo Takeaway** (tel. 405 8065) for the dolphin-safe Opo Burger ($4.50), served with chicken breast, cheese, and pineapple. Bread is baked fresh every day. (Open daily 10am-7pm).The **Opononi Resort** is the pub in town, a spacious room featuring two pool tables and an elevated platform for live music Friday and Saturday nights in summer, and Saturdays in winter (open M-F 11am-11pm, Sa 11am-3am). **The Four Square** supermarket is open Monday through Saturday 7:30am-6pm, Sundays 8am-5:30pm, and has a **post shop** inside (open M-F 9am-5pm).

OMAPERE Keeping watch over the mouth of the Hokianga Harbour, Omapere is a good pit stop before heading south to Waipoua or eastward to Kaikohe and the Bay of Islands. A formidable sand bar at the mouth of the harbor keeps the waters in a relative calm, interrupted only by the crash of sand-boarding tourists careening 160m down dunes into the water. You'll need a water taxi to join in, as the sledding takes place on the dunes of the far shore. **Hokianga Express** (tel. 405 8872), **Harbour Explorer** (tel. 405 8033), and **Sierra** (tel. 405 8702) all offer comparable service and rates. They loan you boards and pick them up at the end of the day ($15-20). Catch the scene in Hokianga with **CTSH** (tel. 405 8181) on a scenic tour from the Omapere Tourist Hotel to the Hokianga and Waipoua Forest (departs 8am M, W, F; $10). They also run charters to the Bay of Islands and Kaitaia, and a shuttle to Paihia (Monday at

NORTHLAND

8am, $15) and Kaitaia (2hr., Tu, Th at 8am, $21). If you choose to stay in Omapere, **Globetrekkers (VIP)** (tel./fax 405 8183), off SH12, makes a good home. The simple backpackers cottage has all the basics. (Dorms $15; singles $20; doubles $35. Free linen, blankets, and pickup from bus at visitors center. Check-out 10:30am.)

■ Waipoua Forest Park

Remoteness and inaccessibility protected the virgin kauri forests of the Waipoua region from 19th-century axe-blades. Although the area came under the control of the crown in 1876, nobody knew what to do with it. Synthetic varnishes saved the trees from the kauri-chomping gum industry of the 1930s, but World War II proved to be a more daunting foe. The 1940s demand for shipbuilding timber stirred up controversy that resulted in the largest primary forest in New Zealand being declared a sanctuary in 1952. Although the DOC didn't enter the picture until 1987, Waipoua (north of Dargaville on Northland's western coast) is New Zealand's least-logged and best example of primary kauri forest.

Along with the kauri giants, Waipoua is home to the **Waipoua Forest Visitor Centre** (tel. 439 0605; fax 439 5227; open in summer M-F 8am-4:30pm, Sa-Su 9am-4:30pm; daily in winter 9am-4:30pm), several walking tracks, and a **campground.** The latter curls up on the banks of the Waipoua River, with tent and powered caravan sites ($7, children $3.50). Self-register at the communal kitchen/shower/toilet building, and do your laundry in the tub with your own soap. For the less rugged individualist, little green two-bunk cabins named for different tree species come with crockery and cutlery ($28, children $7). For groups of people, there are four-bunk cabins which offer sinks and electric stoves ($40, children $5). Obtain cabin keys from the visitors center or, after hours, check in with the caretaker who lives in a little cabin of her own. Open flames of any kind are strictly forbidden. As the kiwi-crossing signs on SH12 attest, this is kiwi country—dogs and cats are not welcome. Do not leave valuables in your car.

Almost everyone who comes to the forest—young or old, wheelchair-bound or avid tramper—is there to see "the big tree" in the northern Waipoua. A brief walk from the carpark off SH12 leads through dense and dripping bush to the 1200-year-old, 52m-high, 14m-wide **Tane Mahuta.** Nicknamed "Lord of the Forest," it is the world's largest living kauri and New Zealand's biggest tree. The boardwalk separating admirers from the trunk maintains a respectful distance and protects the Lord's delicate, shallow root system. Back at the car park, a caravan sells coffee, tea, sandwiches, and postcards (open in summer daily 8am-6pm; in winter daily 10am-3pm). **InterCity buses** will stop here long enough for you to snap some photos.

Waipoua's other "big trees" are also easy to visit. From the labeled carpark a few kilometers south of Tane Mahuta on SH12 towards the visitors center, paths lead to the 30m **Te Matua Ngahere,** "Father of the Forest," the second largest living kauri (20min. walk); the close-knit **Four Sisters,** two double-trunked trees side-by-side (10min.), and the **Yakas Kauri** (30min. walk). Although the Maori began the tradition of naming individual trees, not all bear solely Maori monikers: witness **Darby** and **Joan,** flanking either side of a bridge on SH12 north of the visitors center. For those with time to explore, the **Yakas Track** (3hr.) connects the campground and visitors center to Yakas Kauri Carpark, wending through all sorts of trees and fording the Waipoua River. The **Waiotemarama Walk** (6hr.) begins off Waiotemarama Gorge Rd. near Omapere, reaching a spectacular waterfall within 15 minutes and ending at the base of Mountain Rd. **Okopako Lodge/ The Wilderness Farm** (tel./fax 405 8815), which has panoramic harbour view and farm animals, is at the end. Halfway through at its steepest point, the walk connects with the **Waima Main Range Route.** This is a serious three-to-four day walk that passes over the highest point in Northland (and often through low-lying clouds); trampers should possess good wilderness skills and be well equipped for foul weather. A less taxing walk along mostly flat beach is the two-to-three-day **Waipoua Coastal Walkway,** which links Hokianga Harbour with the Kai Iwi Lakes.

Another pocket of kauri stands 17km south of the Waipoua Forest (40km north of Dargaville) at the 450-hectare **Trounson Kauri Park** (open Labour Weekend-Easter). The **Kauri Coast Holiday Park** (tel./fax 439 0621), on Trounson Park Rd. in Kaihu, runs guided night walks through Trounson past glow-worms and calling Kiwis (1hr., $10, children $7). The Holiday Park offers scenic horse rides ($15 per hr., $24 for 2hr., $30 half-day). Pleasant accommodations by a river include basic cabins ($30 for 2, extra person $12) and tourist cabins with shower, toilet, and basin ($42 for 2, extra person $12). They also have tent and powered sites right by the water ($9.50).

■ Dargaville

Part entrepreneur in the Kauri timber and gum trade, part visionary and city planner, Joseph Dargaville literally put this place on the map. Realizing that the geographic center of the Kauri industry was destined to shift to the confluence of the Wairoa River and Kaihu Creek, in 1872 he purchased 171 acres at that very location. Within two years, his homestead, (which still stands) was built, and within a decade, his prophecy was fulfilled as 2000 inhabitants of the surrounding settlements gravitated toward the town he had designed for them. While the Kauri industry has died, the town's geographic position is equally advantageous for tourism. Surrounded by beautiful beaches, forests, and lakes, Dargaville is an excellent place to replenish supplies before heading into the wild.

ORIENTATION AND PRACTICAL INFORMATION

Dargaville borders the **Wairoa River,** 187km north of Auckland on the west coast. **Normanby Street** is the main road by which **SH12** traffic passes through town. One street over toward the river is **Victoria Street** and most of the shops.

Buses: InterCity (tel. (0800) 731 711) contracts out to **Pioneer Coachlines,** which runs to Auckland (3½hr., M-F 3 per day, Sa 1 per day, Su 2 per day; $39) and north to Paihia (4¼hr.; daily in summer, 3 per week in winter; $32) via the Waipoua Forest Park (1¼hr., $15). They also service the Hokianga towns of Omapere, Opononi, and Rawene (2½-3hr., $17-25), and Kaikohe (3¾hr., $29).

Taxis: Dargaville Taxis and Charters (tel. 439 7066) run around town, and do a daily shuttle to Whangarei (runs 7:30am-3:30pm; $13; departs from the visitors center; book there ahead of time).

Hitchhiking: Traffic along the Waipoua Forest Road in either direction is fairly regular. Conventional wisdom says to wait at the edge of town.

Visitor Center: Dargaville Visitor's Information Centre, 65 Normanby St. (tel./fax 439 8360; email dgrvin@nzhost.co.nz). Open M-F 8:30am-5pm, Sa-Su 9am-4pm, extended summer hours.

Currency Exchange: All of the major New Zealand banks can be found on Victoria St., most with **ATMs.** Get plenty of money here, as there are **no banks** further north in the Hokianga.

Library: (tel. 439 7057) on Hokianga Rd. Offers an email service that allows you to send email for free, and receive it on their account (open M-F 9:30am-5pm, Sa 9am-noon).

Public Toilets: In the park adjacent to the library.

Emergency: Dial 111.

Medical Services: Dargaville Medical Centre (tel. 439 8079), on Hokianga Rd., is open M-F 8am-5pm, Sa 9am-noon; after hours, the phone message will refer you to the doctor on call. **Kaipara Unichem Pharmacy,** 18 Hokianga Rd., has their own monogrammed pens and is open M-F 8am-6pm, Sa 9am-1pm, Su 9:30am-12:30pm.

Police: (tel. 439 8399), on Portland St. across from the YHA.

Post Office: In the **Terartz Stationary Shop,** Victoria St. (tel. 439 6051). Open M-F 8am-5pm.

Telephone Code: 09.

ACCOMMODATIONS

Just about everyone comes to see the areas that lie *beyond* Dargaville's minimal hub, so there's usually no dire need to book ahead. One exception is during the peak of summer (Dec.-Jan.), when the campgrounds teem with those destined for kauri meditation or Kai Iwi recreation.

The Greenhouse (YHA/VIP), 13 Portland St. (tel. 439 6342), is a breath of fresh air. Comfy dorms have room dividers for extra privacy, as well as potted ferns and eco-murals. Attentive and generous owners have posted helpful info, including menu recommendations at the local restaurants. Free bikes, fishing tackle, and organized fishing trips by arrangement. Polish your own kauri gum pendant ($5-12), play pool, or chill by the TV in the congenial lounge. Dorms $15, $70 weekly, 3rd night half-price; singles $25 ($20 in winter); doubles and twins $36; tent sites $8. Laundry $5. Reception 8:15am-9:30pm. Check-out 10am.

Northern Wairoa Hotel (tel. 439 8923; fax 439 8925), on the corner of Hokianga Rd. and Victoria St. Recent restorations accentuate the solid kauri glory of the woodwork and turn-of-the-century velvet luxury, all available at backpacker prices. The linen and china restaurant downstairs fills up on "cheap and cheerful" Mondays, serving lavish dinners. Rollicking pub features bands and karaoke on weekends. Single room with plush linen and wash basin ($15). With private bath, singles $30; doubles $60; triples $90.

Baylys Beach Motor Camp, 22 Seaview Rd. (tel./fax 439 6349). Adorable cabins on a grassy green, edged with pohutukawa trees. Crawling with families once the weather warms. Communal kitchen with dishes and pots dispensed (7am-10pm). Tent sites and powered sites $9, children $4. Basic double cabins $30 (extra adult $10, child $8). Double cabins with bath $45 (extra adult $12, child $8). Linen $3.

Kai Iwi Lakes Camp (tel. 439 8360), on Kai Iwi Lakes Rd., is booked through the visitors center. Divided into two parts, the larger **Pine Beach Camping Ground,** on Lake Taharoa, accommodates up to 500 campers. Rudimentary blocks of showers, toilets, and basins, and coin-op barbecue (50¢ for 6min. of gas). **Promenade Point** is even more basic, with only toilets and basins. Water taps, but no power for caravans. Advance reservations essential in summer. $6 per person, children $4.

FOOD AND NIGHTLIFE

Dargaville has a number of smart, new eateries. The aroma of fresh-baked bread wafts from **Woolworths** (tel. 439 7269), on Victoria St. at Gladstone St. Fresh locally grown kumara highlights the wide produce selection (open Sa–W 8am-7pm, Th-F 8am-8pm).

Blah Blah Blah Cafe & Bar, 101 Victoria St. (tel. 439 6300). For lunch, fresh baked panini ($6.50) and $8 meals are the fare, while the eclectic cafe dinner menu changes every 6 weeks, though the prices are stable (entrees $6.50, mains $12-15). Kitchen closes by 9-10pm; bar snacks available until close. 10% discount for YHA/VIP members. Open in summer daily 8am-midnight; in winter M 8am-5pm, Tu-Th 8am-midnight, F-Sa 8am-1am, Su 4pm-midnight.

UNC Restaurant & Bar, 17 Hokianga Rd. (tel. 439 5777). The premier restaurant in town serves lunch and dinner in a spacious rust-colored glass fronted interior. Stuffed potatoes ($5.50) for lunch can't be beat. Dinner mains range from veggie stir fry ($15.50) to leg of venison ($22.50), with inventive entrees such as potato pumpkin gnocci ($7.50) to get you started. Pleasant chef will ably accommodate non-menu requests. Friday and Saturday nights, a dance floor opens up around 9:30pm when the kitchen closes. Open daily 11am-1am.

Belushi's, 102 Victoria St. (tel. 439 8866). Sunny orange-painted bricks liven this daytime cafe serving lighter fare and all things espresso, including smooth shakes ($4). Toasted sandwiches on bread ($3) or more creative combos on bagels ($3-5). In summer, Monday nights after hours bring chess players of all abilities (6-9pm). Otherwise, open M-F 8am-5pm, Sa-Su 9am-3pm.

Seaview Cafe (tel. 439 4549), on the corner of Seaview and Baylys Coast Rd., services the guests of the motor camp. General store, cafe, liquor store, and takeaway all in one. Burgers ($3-5) and chips ($2-3) are representative of the menu. Open daily 7:30am-10pm.

SIGHTS AND ACTIVITIES

With much pomp and circumstance, Dargaville recently unveiled an imposing bronze statue of a Dalmation **gum digger** at the intersection of Victoria St. and Hokianga Rd. He stands in jaunty tribute to the thousands of immigrants lured to the Kaipara district from the former Yugoslavia in the 1870s and 80s, who exchanged civil unrest and famines for a life of lumber and gum digging. You can get the digs on the whole kauri story at **Kauri Museum** (tel. 431 7417) on SH12, 45km south of Dargaville in Matakohe. *(Open daily Nov.-Easter 9am-5:30pm, Easter-Oct. 9am-5pm; $7, children $2.50.)* Exhibits about the mighty tree include delicate amber carvings in the sparkling **Kauri gum collection,** impressive outlines of felled kauri trunks that absolutely dwarf Waipoua's Tane Mahuta, and bizarre kauri gum hair extensions. For those without a car, a shuttle runs between the museum and Dargaville daily, leaving town at 9am and 2pm and returning at 1pm and 4:05pm ($15 return). No afternoon shuttle runs on Sunday.

Just outside of town, the **Dargaville Maritime Museum** (tel. 439 7555) rounds out the picture of the Kauri industry with a history of the ships that transported both logs and loggers. *(Open daily 9am-4pm. Admission $4.)* To get there, take Victoria St. south to the River Rd., and from there to Mt. Wellesley Rd. Follow the signs up to the museum's perch, atop Mt. Wellesley in Harding Park. The museum has an extensive collection of local shipwreck artifacts, culled from the 115 reported shipwrecks along the Kaipara coastline. Outside, draped with strands of flashing lights, stand the masts of the famed **Rainbow Warrior** (see p. 100 for more on the ship). The museum's most recent feather-in-the-cap addition is the *Poutu Rangomaraeroa,* a 2.7m pre-Maori wood carving of a woman found on Kaipara's North Head.

For an excellent trek, the volcano **TokaToka** offers panoramic views of the region from its summit, 17km south of Dargaville. A track begins behind the Tokatoka Tavern, a 15 minute drive south along SH12. The 30 minute ascent is very steep.

The **Kai Iwi Lakes** are rimmed with pure white silica sand and are a summertime mecca for water enthusiasts of all sorts. **Lake Taharoa** is the largest of the three and the best bet for swimming. Water-skiing is the sport of choice on **Lake Waikere.** The smallest and most serene is **Lake Kai Iwi** itself, trafficked solely by sails and dinghies, and offering excellent fishing. **Buses** make it to the turn-off on Omamari Rd., 24km north of Dargaville on SH12, but you'll need to be resourceful to cover the remaining 11km to the first of the lakes. Closer waters lap the expanse of **Baylys Beach** (also known as Dargaville Ocean Beach or Ripiro Beach), which at 100km is New Zealand's longest beach. Astonishing in breadth as well as length, its vanishing point is often obscured by mist, as are the tops of the nearby cliffs. Perhaps more remarkably, the beach is officially a public highway; road rules apply, though it's best to have a four-wheel-drive vehicle and knowledge of conditions. To explore the beach in full, consider **Taylor Made Tours** (tel. 439 1576 or (025) 361 543), which go to shipwreck relics, visit the 1884 **Kaipara Lighthouse,** and arrange sand tobogganing. *($45 per person, lunch included.)* Although surfing is quite popular here, an equally thrilling ride through the surf is available with **Baylys Beach Horse Treks** (tel. 439 4531), who will pick you up and drop you off at the Greenhouse YHA hostel. *(2½hr., usually 3 per day, $33 with 10% discount for Greenhouse guests.)*

NORTHLAND

The Waikato and the Coromandel Peninsula

The Waikato and the Coromandel Peninsula appeal to outsiders not with exotic and unbelievable natural wonders, but with the invocation of a life that much of the developed world has left behind. Neither region offers high profile, photogenic attractions like volcanoes or glaciers; their charms are more subtle. With a rural bent and a pragmatic attitude, the Waikato is one of the primary agricultural centers of New Zealand. Visitors with an appreciation of the farming life or those lucky enough to stumble upon the annual extravaganza of National Fieldays will witness the pride residents take in the region's productive capabilities. Inhabitants of the Coromandel are similarly disinclined toward the rushed frenzy of modern life. Less agrarian and more artistic, peninsula dwellers welcome the visitor who feels as they do the draw of the cerulean sea, endless beaches and coves, and kauri forest.

ⓦ WAIKATO AND COROMANDEL HIGHLIGHTS

- A scenic drive along the coast of the Coromandel Peninsula (see p. 131) unveils magnificent coastal vistas and striking natural beauty.
- Black-water rafting in the Waitomo Caves (see p. 127) allows curious spelunkers to explore New Zealand's mysterious underworld.
- The small towns of the Coromandel Peninsula (see p. 131) are an ideal place to indulge in a worry-free existence.
- Raglan offers some of the world's finest surfing (see p. 123).
- At Hot Water Beach (see p. 142), beach bums can dig their own jacuzzi in the sand for the ultimate soothing experience.

THE WAIKATO AND KING COUNTRY

Tranquility settles over the lush pastureland and lazy streams of the Waikato and King Country today, but life in these parts did not always come so easily. In the 1840s and 50s, the Maori tribes of the Waikato banded together to resist the threat of encroaching European settlement, finally proclaiming Potatau Te Wherowhero the first Maori King in 1859. The king's signature white top hat was passed on to his son, King Tawhiao, who used it during the Waikato War of 1863-1864 to make a legendary gesture of defiance, casting his "crown" onto a map of the North Island and proclaiming grandly, "There, I rule!" As a result, his people called the region *Rohe Potae,* "the brim of the hat." To the settlers, however, it was simply "King Country," in grudging deference to the Maori dominance that lasted until the 1880s.

Modern times brought a different kind of power to the region. With 12 power stations along its length, the Waikato River churns out 50% of the North Island's electricity. The longest river in New Zealand, it is also the defining geographical feature of the region as it winds through small agricultural communities providing recreation for visitors and locals alike. As it makes its way toward the coast, the river passes through population centers varying from the arboreal charm of Cambridge to the urban bustle of Hamilton, before reaching the end of its journey and the surf of Raglan Harbor.

▩ Hamilton

The largest inland city in New Zealand (and the fifth-largest overall), Hamilton suffers from a shortage of astounding geographical features, offering instead a central loca-

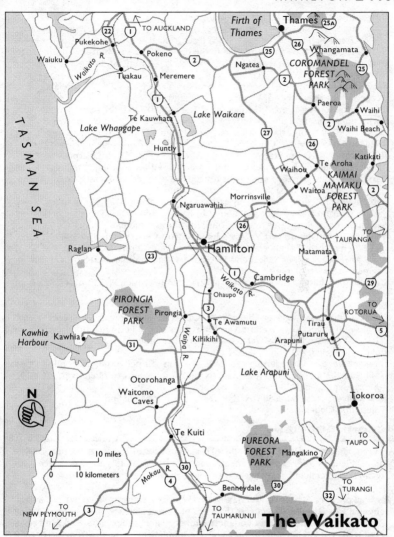

Firth of Thames
TO AUCKLAND
Pukekohe
Waiuku
Pokeno
Tuakau
Meremere
Ngatea
Thames
Whangamata
COROMANDEL FOREST PARK
Paeroa
Waihi
Waihi Beach
Te Kauwhata
Lake Whangape
Lake Waikare
Huntly
Waihou
Te Aroha
Waitoa
KAIMAI MAMAKU FOREST PARK
Katikati
Morrinsville
Ngaruawahia
Hamilton
Matamata
TO TAURANGA
Raglan
Cambridge
Waikato R.
Ohaupo
PIRONGIA FOREST PARK
Pirongia
Te Awamutu
Tirau
Putaruru
TO ROTORUA
Kawhia Harbour
Kawhia
Kihikihi
Arapuni
Lake Arapuni
Otorohanga
Waitomo Caves
Te Kuiti
PUREORA FOREST PARK
Mangakino
Tokoroa
TO TAUPO
0   10 miles
0   10 kilometers
N
Mokau R.
Benneydale
TO NEW PLYMOUTH
TO TAUMARUNUI
TO TURANGI
The Waikato

TASMAN SEA

WAIKATO & COROMANDEL

tion. Half of the North Island and its terrestrial wonders is accessible with a drive of a few hours, making Hamilton an ideal hub. After returning from the spokes, you can retire to any of the numerous restaurants and cafes to rejuvenate.

ORIENTATION AND PRACTICAL INFORMATION

Hamilton lies just off **SH1**, and is bisected by the **Waikato River.** Most of the commercial activity and nightlife is on the west bank. **Victoria Street** is the main drag, with the stretch between **Ward** and **Hood Street** particularly prime for daytime shopping and nighttime carousing. **East Hamilton** is more residential, housing **Waikato University** and many cafes.

Trains: TranzScenic heads daily to Auckland (2hr., 4 per day, day $36, night $32); Tauranga (1½hr., 8:06pm, $29); Rotorua (2hr., 10:09am, $40); and Wellington (8½hr., 2 per day, $108, night 98) via Palmerston North (6½hr., $83, night $74).

Buses: InterCity heads daily to Auckland (2hr., 6 per day, $27), Gisborne (7hr., 1 per day, $73), Wellington (8½hr., 4 per day, $53) and Rotorua (2½hr., 4 per day, $24). **Pavlovich buses** (tel. 847 5545) head to Raglan from the Transport Centre (1hr., M-F 4 per day, $4.70 payable to the driver). **Creswell Motors Ltd.** heads to Cambridge from Collingwood St. near Victoria St. (30min., M-Th 3 per day, F 5 per day; $4.50 to driver).

Taxis: Red Cabs (tel. 839 0500) and **Hamilton Taxis** (tel. 847 7477) are abundant, especially at the corner of Victoria and Collingwood St.

Car Rental: Rent-a-Dent, 383 Anglesea St. (tel. (0800) 736 822), rents economy cars with unlimited distance for $49 per day. **Waikato Car Rentals** (tel. 856 9908 or (025) 990 350), on Brooklyn Rd., rents cars from $25 per day (1 week min.), and vans from $69 per day. Open M-F 7:30am-5:30pm, Sa 8am-1pm, Su 8:30am-1pm.

Bike Rental: R&R Sports, 943 Victoria St. (tel. 839 3755), at Liverpool St. Rents trade-in mountain bikes, canoes, and kayaks (about $25 per day). Also skis, boots and poles ($20 per day) or snowboard and boots ($40 per day). Open M-Th 9am-5:30pm, F 9am-8pm, Sa 9am-2pm, Su 11am-2pm.

Hitchhiking: Hitching is reportedly easiest to Raglan along SH23. North to Auckland, many try from SH1 past the junction of Te Rapa St. and Avalon Dr. (though they say it's best to take a city bus from the outskirts of town and hitch from there).

Visitor Center: Hamilton Visitor's Information Centre (tel. 839 3580; fax 839 3127; email hlzvin@nzhost.co.nz), in the Transport Centre at the corner of Ward and Anglesea St. Open year-round M-F 9am-4:45pm, in summer Sa-Su 10am-4pm, in winter Sa-Su 10am-2pm.

Currency Exchange: BNZ is across Victoria St. from Garden Pl. **Thomas Cook** is on Garden Pl.

Emergency: Dial 111.

Medical Services: Anglesea Clinic, at the corner of Thackeray and Anglesea St. (tel. 858 0800). Open 24hr. **Hamilton Pharmacy** (tel. 834 3444), open daily 8am-10pm. **Waikato Hospital** (tel. 839 8899), on Pembroke St.

Police: (tel. 838 0989), on Bridge St.

Internet Access: At the **library** ($6 for first 30min., $4 per additional 30min.) Open M-F 9am-8:30pm, Sa 9am-4pm. Also try the more expensive **Mailboxes, Etc.,** 101 Alexander St. (tel. 838 2998), $20 per hr.

Post Office: 346 Victoria St. (tel. 838 2233). Open M-F 9am-5pm.

Telephone Code: 07.

ACCOMMODATIONS

Accommodations in Hamilton are spread out, so call ahead and arrange a ride. During National Fieldays prior bookings are absolutely essential. Motels are everywhere, but you can find excellent backpackers with a little persistence.

✪J's Backpackers, 8 Grey St. (tel./fax 856 8934, email ropb@wave.co.nz). Set in residential East Hamilton, J's covers the ABCs of a successful stay. Backpackers have a whole house to themselves, complete with cozy lounge, spacious deck, and small but well-kept kitchen offering free coffee. Complimentary pickup from bus or train station. Dorms $16; twins $40. Linen $2. Laundry $5. Internet access $5 per 30min. Kayaks $35. Ride to town $2. Bikes are free with two-night stay, otherwise $5. Luggage storage available.

The Flying Hedgehog (VIP), 8 Liverpool St. (tel./fax 839 3906). From the visitors center, turn left onto Victoria St., then turn right on Liverpool St. Little cartoon hedgehog signs spout mildly obscene words of wisdom with pointers on how to survive at this hostel. The young, international crowd mixes in the co-ed rooms and undersized kitchen. Pleasant owners have helpful tips when reception is open (8:30am-8pm). Dorms $18; doubles and twins $40; $1 off VIP. Laundry $4. Bike rentals $5. $1 credit card service charge. Check-in 11am, check-out 10am.

Commercial Establishment Accommodation, 287 Victoria St. (tel. 839 4993; fax 834 2389; email coassess@wave.com.nz). Stay down in the thick of things in a little slice of late 1800s Hamilton. Pub and restaurant downstairs. Lounge with TV, pool table. Singles $39, with bath $49; doubles $55, with bath $85; twins with bath $69. Laundry $4. Reception 8am-10pm. Check-out 10am.

Helen Heywood YHA Hostel, 1190 Victoria St. (tel. 838 0009; fax 838 0837). Head north up Victoria St., and past Ulster St. on the right is this white and blue cinderblock house. Quiet, reserved, and slightly crusty, with a large, well-equipped kitchen. Lounge has comfy couches, TV, and $2 lockers. Dorms (sometimes co-ed) $15; singles $26; doubles and twins $36; non-YHA $4 more. Laundry $2.

FOOD

Restaurants specializing in every imaginable exotic cuisine beckon with glowing interiors all along Victoria St., mostly between Garden Pl. and Hood St. Takeaway eaten on the grass of Garden Place is choice on a sunny day. **Food Town** (tel. 838 2739), on the corner of Bryce and Tristram St,. is the most central market.

Planet Burger, 206 Victoria St. (tel. 839 1444). If McDonald's and the Star Wars cantina got together, the result would be this black lit, sculpted-rock-walled joint serving up burgers that are out of this world. Portions are huge: a basic Comet Burger ($5) and order of fries ($3) can easily feed 2 people, a deal on any planet. The more adventurous might try the sizzling Solar Burger with Tandoori chicken ($9) or attempt to make Contact ($7.20) with vegetarian life forms breaded and fried. Open M-F 11:30am-2pm and 5-10:30pm, F-Sa 5pm-4am, Su noon-10:30pm.

Rocket Espresso Lounge (tel. 839 6422), on the corner of Victoria and Hood St. Outdoor seating and an eclectic bohemian clientele make this an ideal spot to refuel. Potent espresso ($2.50) guaranteed to overcome inertia and power you through the day. Heavenly muffins ($2.50) go fast; panini sandwiches ($4.50) and bleu cheese pizza ($4) complete your mission. Open daily 9am-5pm.

Gourmet Sushi (tel. 838 3500), in the Marketplace (corner of Hood and Alexandra St.). The name says it all about the food, if not the prices. Spartan interior is well lit and clean. Vegetarian rolls for under $1, inventive tofu-wrapped rice pieces $1.50. Fresh salmon Nigiri ($1.50, 6 for $8). Open M-Sa 11am-6pm.

Bayon Cambodian Cafe, 783 Victoria St. (tel. 839 0947). Blinking Christmas lights lead you to this softly lit spot with soothing Cambodian music in the background. Picture book menu is helpful in deciding, though vegetarians have all of one choice. Spicy mains ($7-12). Takeaways available. Open daily 11am-9:30pm.

Metropolis Caffe, 211 Victoria St. (tel. 834 2081) From the outside, it blends in with the other storefronts, but walk in and enter a simple green-walled space with creative flourishes. Spiraling corrugated steel mazes and wavy copper arrows provide accent, and there is a main seating area supplemented by elevated gaming section and upstairs chilling area with funky plants. Black clad staff serves wines and coffees primarily, but also items from creative menu such as onion bhujia with fruit chutney and raita ($5.50) (open daily from11am).

Sahara Tent Cafe and Bar, 254 Victoria St. (tel. 834 0409). Experience an Arabian night of authentic turkish and middle eastern cuisine in a warm dark wooden interior that radiates with candles and mid-east melodies. Entrees ($7) and mains ($13-17) include all of the standards prepared with a flourish. Groups of 4 or more can enjoy all you can eat feast of 5 entrees, 5 mains, 3 desserts, and coffee for $28 per person. Reserve a cushiony place under curtains in the back. Lawrence never had it so good.(open M-F 5:30pm-11:30pm, Sa-Su 11am-11:30pm).

NIGHTLIFE

Hamilton seems deceptively quiet at night, but don't despair, there is still life out there somewhere. The key is to tap into the scene; *City Happenings,* published by the City Council and available at the visitors center, is a good place to start.

Biddy Mulligan's Irish Pub, 742 Victoria St. (tel. 834 0306). Biddy must have done right by St. Patrick somewhere along the way—back in '93, this became the first pub in New Zealand to have Murphy's Irish Stout on tap (pints $5). DJ on Thursday nights plays hits from the 60-80s. Friday and Saturday nights, a live Irish band livens up the scene. Open Su, Tu 11am-11pm, W 11am-midnight, Th-Sa 11am-2am.

Fiberglass Cows and Electric Sheep

As anyone who has ever tried to book a room in the greater Hamilton-Cambridge area during the middle of June will attest, the country's **National Fieldays** are a huge deal. For four days (June 16-19, 1999), 120,000 people descend on the tiny burg of Mystery Creek (situated between Hamilton and Cambridge) for the Southern Hemisphere's largest A&P (agricultural and pastoral) show. Billed as a celebration of agricultural excellence, Fieldays offer travelers a unique glance at agrarian culture. With chainsaw carving demonstrations, head-to-head tractor pulls, builder competitions, and a fashion show of clothes made from recycled farm materials, there is truly something for everyone. Witness the latest advances in sheep-dipping, bloat-drenching, and bovine-enhancing biotechnology. Any mental paradigm of the simple farmer will be shattered anew with each invention you encounter along the event's 57 hectares. (Admission $9, children $5; call 843 4499 for more information.) Come to get a taste of real, rural Godzone, and pick up some inexpensive wool sweaters, gumboots, and oilskins while you're at it.

X-tatic, 188 Victoria St. (tel. 839 0045). The best dance music in Hamilton. DJs work it in the **Sweat Box,** where music varies from house to trance to jungle and a young crowd gets into it. The room with the bar is a versatile space; sometimes it has live acts, other times comfy couches, but always excellent visual stimulation. Outdoor deck area provides a breather with a light show bouncing off the trees. After midnight $2 cover, more for special events. Open W-Sa 9pm-3am.

JBC Bar and Cafe, 270 Victoria St. (tel. 839 7202), in the basement. The idea behind this dimly lit jazz blues concept is to provide live entertainment five nights a week and vegan friendly food. Performers vary from folk, to hardcore, to you at the open mic. Monthly art exhibitions. Cover $5-10; discounts available for students, VIP, seniors. Open M-F 10am-3am, Sa 5pm-3am.

Liquid Lounge, 21-23 Hood St. (tel. 834 2181). A chill bar that plays tribute to its Heineken sponsorship with a backlit row of green bottles glowing above the bar and a neon red star over the pool table. The gin and tonic ($5) is one smooth liquid, while antipasto platters ($13-$15) provide substance and house music provides structure. Open Tu-Th from 5pm, F-Sa from 4pm.

The Outback Inn, 141 Victoria St. (tel. 839 6354). Hamilton's largest bar (1000 person capacity) attracts a young crowd that grooves to MTV-style video music on a sawdust-covered dance floor, with a gaming arcade on the other side of a large bar. Vegetarians beware: on weekends this place is a veritable meat market. Open Su-M 11am-11pm, Tu 11am-2:30am, W-Sa 11am-3am.

Theater

Hamilton boasts numerous theaters, many affiliated with Waikato University. The most dynamic and impressive is the **Meteor,** 1 Victoria St. (tel. 834 2472). Once a roller skating rink, then an indoor wholesale car showroom, it is now a versatile space for performances, raves, and other special community events. The **National Street Theater Festival** occurs in December (call 856 4421 or email coprso@ihug.co.nz for exact dates).

SIGHTS AND ACTIVITIES

Not surprisingly, much of the leisure activity in Hamilton is centered around the river. Paths on each side are ideal for joggers and cyclists, while canoes and kayaks are perfect paddling options. If your accommodation does not provide these amenities, check **R&R Sports** (see Practical Information, above) for rental options. Ramps from Victoria St. allow wheelchair access to lovely vantage points of the river. The fully enclosed paddlewheeler replica **M.V. Waipa Delta** (tel. (0800) 472 3353 or 854 9415) offers three daily trips, plus lunch (12:30-2pm, $30), afternoon tea (3-4pm, $20), and dinner (7-10pm, includes live entertainment, $40). *(Book ahead on weekends. During the week arrive 15min. early at the landing on the eastern bank of the river, just north of Victoria Bridge.)*

If you're stuck for cash on your travels, don't panic. Millions of people trust Western Union t

transfer money in minutes to 153 countries and over 45,000 locations worldwide. Our record c

safety and reliability is second to none. So when you need money in a hurry, call Western Unio

WESTERN UNION | MONEY TRANSFER®

The fastest way to send money worldwide.®

MCI Spoken Here

Worldwide Calling Made Simple

For more information or to apply for a Card call: **1-800-955-0925**

Outside the U.S., call MCI collect (reverse charge) at: **1-916-567-5151**

International Calling As Easy As Possible.

The MCI Card with WorldPhone Service is designed specifically to keep you in touch with th people that matter the most to you.

The MCI Card with WorldPhone Service....

- Provides access to the US and other countries worldwide.
- Gives you customer service 24 hours a day
- Connects you to operators who speak your language
- Provides you with MCI's low rates and no sign-up fees

For more information or to apply for a Card call:
1-800-955-0925

Outside the U.S., call MCI collect (reverse charge) at:
1-916-567-5151

Pick Up the Phone, Pick Up the Miles.

You earn frequent flyer miles when you travel internationally, why not when you call internationally? Callers can earn frequent flyer miles if they sign up with one of MCI's airline partners:

- American Airlines
- Continental Airlines
- Delta Airlines
- Hawaiian Airlines
- Midwest Express Airlines
- Northwest Airlines
- Southwest Airlines
- United Airlines
- USAirways

Your MCI Worldphone Access Numbers

COUNTRY		WORLDPHONE TOLL-FREE ACCESS #
#Singapore		8000-112-112
#Slovak Republic (CC)		00421-00112
#Slovenia		080-8808
#South Africa (CC)		0800-99-0011
#Spain (CC)		900-99-0014
#Sri Lanka	(Outside of Colombo, dial 01 first)	440100
#St. Lucia ÷		1-800-888-8000
#St. Vincent		1-800-888-8000
#Sweden (CC) ♦		020-795-922
#Switzerland (CC) ♦		0800-89-0222
#Syria		0800
#Taiwan (CC) ♦		0080-13-4567
#Thailand ★		001-999-1-2001
#Trinidad & Tobago ÷		1-800-888-8000
#Turkey (CC) ♦		00-8001-1177
#Turks and Caicos ÷		1-800-888-8000
#Ukraine (CC) ÷		8▼10-013
#United Arab Emirates ♦		800-111
#United Kingdom (CC)	To call using BT ■	0800-89-0222
	To call using C&W ■	0500-89-0222
#United States (CC)		1-800-888-8000
#Uruguay		000-412
#U.S. Virgin Islands (CC)		1-800-888-8000
#Vatican City (CC)		172-1022
#Venezuela (CC) ÷ ♦		800-1114-0
Vietnam ●		1201-1022
Yemen		008-00-102

Automation available from most locations.
(CC)   Country-to-country calling available to/from most international locations.
÷   Limited availability.
▶   Wait for second dial tone.
◄   When calling from public phones, use phones marked LADATEL.
■   International communications carrier.
★   Not available from public phones.
♦   Public phones may require deposit of coin or phone card for dial tone.
●   Local service fee in U.S. currency required to complete call.
▲   Regulation does not permit Intra-Japan calls.
÷   Available from most major cities

And, it's simple to call home.

1. Dial the WorldPhone toll-free access number of the country you're calling from (listed inside).

2. Follow the voice instructions in your language of choice or hold for a WorldPhone operator.
   - Enter or give the operator your MCI Card number or call collect.

3. Enter or give the WorldPhone operator your home number.

4. Share your adventures with your family!

The MCI Card with WorldPhone Service... The easy way to call when traveling worldwide.

MCI — Calling Card
123 456 7890 1234
J.D. SMITH
WorldPhone

For more information or to apply for a Card call: 1-800-955-0925

Outside the U.S., call MCI collect (reverse charge) at: 1-916-567-5151

Please cut out and save this reference guide for convenient U.S. and worldwide calling with the MCI Card with WorldPhone Service.

COUNTRY		WORLDPHONE TOLL-FREE ACCESS #
American Samoa		633-2MCI (633-2624)
#Antigua		1-800-888-8000
	(available from public card phones only)	#2
#Argentina (CC)		0800-5-1002
#Aruba ÷		800-888-8
#Australia (CC)	To call using OPTUS ■ ◆	1-800-551-111
	To call using TELSTRA ÷	1-800-881-100
#Austria (CC) ◆		022-903-012
#Bahamas		1-800-888-8000
#Bahrain		800-002
#Barbados		1-800-888-8000
#Belarus (CC)	From Brest, Vitebsk, Grodno, Minsk	8-800-103
	From Gomel and Mogilev	8-10-800-103
#Belgium (CC) ◆		0800-10012
#Belize	From Hotels	815
	From Payphones	557
#Bermuda ÷		1-800-888-8000
#Bolivia (CC) ◆		0-800-2222
#Brazil (CC)		000-8012
#British Virgin Islands ÷		1-800-888-8000
#Brunei		800-011
#Bulgaria		00800-0001
#Canada (CC)		1-800-888-8000
#Cayman Islands		1-800-888-8000
#Chile (CC)	To call using CTC ■	800-207-300
	To call using ENTEL ■	800-360-180
#China ◆	For a Mandarin-speaking Operator	108-17
		108-11
#Colombia (CC) ◆		980-16-0001
	Collect Access in Spanish	980-16-1000
#Costa Rica ◆		0800-012-2222
#Cote D'Ivoire		1001
#Croatia (CC) ★		0800-22-0112
#Cyprus ◆		080-90000
#Czech Republic (CC) ◆		00-42-000112
#Denmark (CC) ◆		8001-0022
#Dominica		1-800-888-8000
#Dominican Republic		1-800-888-8000
	Collect Access in Spanish	1-800-888-8000
#Ecuador (CC) ÷	Collect Access in Spanish	999-171
#Egypt (CC) ÷	(Outside of Cairo, dial 02 first)	355-5770
El Salvador		800-1767

— FOLD —

COUNTRY		WORLDPHONE TOLL-FREE ACCESS #
#Federated States of Micronesia		624
#Fiji (CC)		004-890-1002
#Finland (CC) ◆		08001-102-80
#France (CC) ◆		0800-99-0011
#French Antilles (CC)	(includes Martinique, Guadeloupe)	0800-99-0019
#French Guiana (CC)		0-800-99-0011
#Gabon		00-005
#Gambia		00-1-99
#Germany (CC)		0-800-888-8000
#Greece (CC) ◆		00-800-1211
#Grenada ÷		1-800-888-8000
#Guam (CC)		1-800-888-8000
Guatemala ◆		99-99-189
Guyana		177
#Haiti ÷	Collect Access in French/Creole	193
		190
#Honduras ÷		8000-122
#Hong Kong (CC) ◆		800-96-1121
#Hungary (CC) ◆		00 ✰ 800-01411
#Iceland (CC) ◆		800-9002
#India (CC) ◆	Collect Access	000-127
		000-126
#Indonesia (CC) ◆		001-801-11
Iran ÷	(SPECIAL PHONES ONLY)	1-800-55-1001
#Ireland (CC)		1-800-55-1001
#Israel (CC) ◆		1-800-940-2727
#Italy (CC) ◆		172-1022
#Jamaica ÷	Collect Access	873
		1-800-888-8000
#Japan (CC) ◆	(from Special hotels only)	0066-55-121
	To call using KDD ■	00539-121
	(from public phones)	
	To call using IDC ■	0066-55-121
	To call using ITJ ■	0044-11-121
#Jordan		18-800-001
#Kazakhstan (CC)		8-800-131-4321
#Kenya ÷	(Special hotels only)	080011
#Korea (CC)	To call using KT ■	009-14
	To call using DACOM ■	00309-12
	Phone Booths÷	00369-14
	Press red button, 03, then ★	
	Military Bases	550-2255
#Kuwait		800-MCI (800-624)

— FOLD —

COUNTRY		WORLDPHONE TOLL-FREE ACCESS #
#Lebanon	Collect Access	600-MCI (600-624)
#Liechtenstein (CC) ◆		0800-89-0222
#Luxembourg (CC)		0800-0112
#Macao		0800-131
#Macedonia (CC)		99800-4266
#Malaysia (CC) ◆		1-800-80-0012
#Malta		0800-89-0120
#Marshall Islands		1-800-888-8000
#Mexico (CC)	Avantel	01-800-021-8000
	Telmex ▲	001-800-674-7000
	Collect Access in Spanish	01-800-021-1000
#Monaco (CC) ◆		800-90-019
#Montserrat		1-800-888-8000
#Morocco		002-11-0012
#Netherlands (CC) ◆		0800-022-91-22
#Netherlands Antilles (CC) ÷		001-800-888-8000
Nicaragua (CC)	Collect Access in Spanish	166
	(Outside of Managua, dial 02 first)	
	From any public payphone	✰2
#Norway (CC) ◆		800-19912
Pakistan		00-800-12-001
#Panama		108
#Papua New Guinea (CC)		05-07-19140
#Paraguay ÷		00812-800
#Peru		0-800-500-10
#Philippines (CC) ◆	To call using PLDT ■	105-14
	To call using PHILCOM ■	1026-14
	Collect Access via PLDT in Filipino	1237-77
	Collect Access via ICC in Filipino	1026-15
#Poland (CC) ÷		00-800-111-21-22
#Portugal (CC) ÷		05-017-1234
#Puerto Rico (CC)		1-800-888-8000
#Qatar ★		0800-012-77
#Romania (CC) ÷		01-800-1800
#Russia (CC) ◆ ÷	To call using ROSTELCOM ■	747-3322
	(For Russian speaking operator)	747-3320
	To call using SOVINTEL ■	960-2222
#Saipan (CC) ÷		950-1022
#San Marino (CC) ◆		172-1022
#Saudi Arabia (CC) ÷		1-800-11

At the corner of Victoria and Grantham St. is the **Waikato Museum of Art and History** (tel. 838 6606), where you can admire towering Maori carved wooden totems, an epic Kauri wood canoe, and rotating exhibits. *(Open daily 10am-4:30pm. Admission by donation.)* More eccentric is the wall of bees behind plexiglass at the **Exscite** (EXplorations in SCIence and TEchnology) **Centre.** *(Open daily 10am-4:30pm. Admission $5, children, students, seniors $3.)* The center is full of hands-on displays such as the inertia chair, three-dimensional tic-tac-toe, and a chaotic pendulum. The museum cafe is open for lunch during museum hours, and also for dinner (Tu-Sa from 6:30-9pm) with live jazz every Thursday night and periodic wine tastings. Other activities in Hamilton include a trip to the **Hamilton Zoo** on Brymer Rd. (tel. 8383 6720), which has an environmental conservation theme and the largest aviary in New Zealand. *(Open 9am-5pm daily. Admission $7, children $3, seniors $5.)* A walk through the **Hamilton Gardens** (tel. 856 3200) can be a highlight. For a creative outlet, consider a night of art at the **Russel Studio Gallery,** 225 Victoria St. (tel. 025 289 5986). Call ahead, then drop by and create ($10 plus materials). **Vilagrad Winery** (tel. 825 2893) offers tours by appointment. Venturing slightly out of Hamilton to Kihikihi, you'll encounter **Wharepapa South,** some great rock formations for climbing (Rob from J's Backpackers can organize climbing gear; see Accommodations, above).

∎ Cambridge

In many ways, Cambridge is a microcosm of New Zealand, balancing the refined civility of its English ancestry with the down-to-earth charm of its Kiwi geography. Priding itself upon its reputation as the "town of trees," Cambridge roots itself firmly by the banks of the Waikato River, and then branches out into farms that speckle the surrounding volcanic hills. The town's quiet pastoral grace is tossed aside in earnest only once a year for **National Fieldays** held in neighboring Mystery Creek, when a four-day extravaganza of agricultural technology captures the attention and imagination of the entire community.

ORIENTATION AND PRACTICAL INFORMATION Cambridge is located 24km east of Hamilton on **SH1. The Waikato River** runs through town, and **Te Kouto Lake** is a short walk from the **village green.** Many restaurants can be found on **Victoria Street.** The **Cambridge Information Centre,** 23 Wilson St. (tel. 827 6033), has been in a transitional phase but should still be able to help travelers. Pick up some petty cash at the **BNZ,** 51-53 Victoria St. (tel. 827 6122; open M-F 9am-4:30pm). **InterCity** runs buses daily to Auckland (2½hr., 6 per day, $30) via Hamilton (15min., $8), and to Rotorua (1hr., 6 per day, $21), Wellington (8½hr., 3 per day, $70), and Taupo (2½hr., 4 per day, $25). Bookings can be made at **Cambridge Travel,** 74 Victoria St. (tel. 827 5096). The **bus station** is right around the corner on Alpha St. under a green and tan awning. **Cresswell Motors LTD** (tel. 827 7789) also runs local service to Hamilton, stopping at the corner of Victoria and Commerce St. (M-Th 4 per day, F 6 per day, $4.50.) Many **hitchhikers** headed for Hamilton walk out along Hamilton Rd. (which becomes SH1), and then stick their thumbs out before the 50km sign.

A sweet-smelling and fully attended **public toilet** sits on the corner of Victoria and Queen St., on the village green. (Toilets 20¢, showers with soap $1, with towel $2. Open daily in summer 7:30am-6pm, in winter 8:30am-5pm; after-hours the toilets are free.) During hours, free toilets can also be found in the **Hally's Lane Carpark** off Victoria St. **Boyce's Pharmacy** (tel. 827 7358) can meet your prescription needs (open M-Th 8:30am-5:30pm, F 8:30am-6pm, Sa 9am-noon). After hours, call the **Citizen's Advice Bureau** (24hr. tel. 827 4855) for info regarding chemist or doctor on call. **Waikato Hospital** (tel. 839 8899) is on Pembroke St. **Cambridge Taxis** (tel. 827 5999) operate 24hr. M-Sa, and on Sunday by appointment at least one day prior. **Four Seasons Mowers and Cycles,** 42 Victoria St. (tel./fax 827 6763), rents bicycles for $30 per day and also specializes in bike repairs. **Bubbles Laundrette** (tel. 827 5303) is in the Hub Shopping Mall at the corner of Anzac and Alpha St. (open M-F 8:30am-5:30pm, Sa-Su 9am-2pm). The **library** is at 23 Wilson St. (tel. 827 5403) in the same building as the visitors center and offers **Internet access.** ($5 per 30min. Open M and Th 9am-5pm, Tu 9:30am-5pm, W and F 9am-8pm, Sa 9:30am-noon.) In an **emergency,** dial **111.** The **police** (tel. 827 5531) are on Dick St. across from the town square. The **post office** is at 43 Victoria St. (tel. 827 5066; open M-F 9am-5pm). The **telephone code** is **07.**

ACCOMMODATIONS Cambridge brims with enchanting little B&Bs (many of which come with not-so-enchanting little price tags). To find out about farmstays both locally and nationwide, contact **Rural Tours** "Stay in a Country Home" Farmstays, in back of the Cambridge Country Store (open M-F 8:30am-5:30pm; for more info see p. 33). For roughly $100 a night, they will organize a short-term stay at a host farm, with all meals included. Book early for lodging during National Fieldays (June 16-19, 1999).

You can taste rural life in the midst of a five-acre hobby farm at the **Cambridge Country Lodge,** 20 Peake Rd. (bookings tel. 827 8373; guest tel. 827 5762), located 2km north of Cambridge on SH1. The low-lying lodge is a series of adjacent units that have been converted from stables into well-appointed rooms with very comfy beds. There is free use of the bicycles, and free pickup and drop-off in town. (2-4 bed dorms $15. Self-contained units with shower, toilet, and kitchen $45 for 2, extra person $10. Checkout 10am. Breakfast available.) Just around the corner from the bus station sits the **National Hotel** (tel. 827 6731; fax 827 3450), at the corner of Victoria and Alpha St. Licensed since 1865, the present building is in the register of historic places. Pressed tin ceilings and intricate woodwork accent the 14 rooms, all of which come with electric blankets; some have pleasant balconies overlooking Victoria St. Hallway bathrooms have bathtubs. Downstairs there is a sports bar, a casino, and a genuine old world New Zealand pub. (Singles $35; twins and doubles $60, extra person $10. Flexible check-in and check-out.) **Karapiro Domain Motor Camp** (tel. 827 4178), at the end of Maungatautari Rd. by Lake Karapiro has a great location by the lake. (Dorms $12, with kitchen, shower, toilets; bunkhouse $6.50, no facilities. No linen. Tents sites $5.50, powered $6.50.)

FOOD AND ENTERTAINMENT If the weather's bad, wrap yourself in a cappucino at one of Cambridge's little cafes. On a sunny day, nothing beats a picnic on the shores of Lake Te Koutu. **Fran's Cafe,** 62C Victoria St. (tel. 827 3946), cuddles teapots, country crafts, and the work of local artisans in its triangle of peach-colored walls. Self-serve sandwiches range from salmon, brie, and avocado to beef dagwoods ($1-3). Or try hot lunch specials like the vegetarian lasagna ($4, with salad $6) or the sumptuous desserts ($2-3; open M-F 7am-5pm, Sa 7am-3pm). **Sazaracs,** 35 Duke St. (tel. 827 6618), has a duck-shaped overhead fan with beak blades and a variety of other quirky decorations. Happily, this attention to detail carries over to the rich coffees ($2-3) and desserts ($5-8) as well as the wide variety of mains ($10-15). (Open Tu-F from 6pm, Sa-Su 10am-4pm and from 6pm.) **The Gallery,** 64C Victoria St. (tel. 823 0999; fax 823 0997), has a light interior with high ceilings, open rafters, and skylights. Lunch items include quiches ($3.50) and other light mains ($7). At dinner the chefs have the freedom to create truly artful delicacies; presentation is half of the experience with delicate entrees ($9-12) and exquisite mains ($20-25), including lamb dishes that have received national recognition. (Fully licensed. Open M 9am-5pm, Tu-Sa 9am-11pm.) **Prince Albert English Pub,** 75 Victoria St. (tel. 827 7900), is in the Victoria Plaza. Here at Cambridge's only real night spot, you can quaff draught beers (handles $3.50, pints $4.50), shoot pool or play air hockey in the arcade hall, or hear live bands on Friday and Saturday. Bar meals are available. (Open M-W 11am-midnight, Th-F 11am-2am, Sa 10am-2am, Su 10am-10pm.) **Countdown Foods** (tel. 827 7616), on the corner of Kirkwood and Lake St., is the place to stock up for those long-distance journeys or communal kitchen excursions (open Sa-Tu 8:30am-7pm, W-F 8:30am-8pm). **Pumpkin Planet** (tel. 827 5442), on Victoria St. between Queen St. and Hamilton Rd., has bountiful produce and free recipes (open M-F 8am-6pm, Sa-Su 8am-5pm). Next door, **Ma Bakers** (tel. 827 7858) offers a large loaf of fresh hot bread for $1.50 with any other purchase (open daily 6:30am-4pm).

SIGHTS AND ACTIVITIES Cambridge has built a highbrow reputation as a place of crafts, antiques, and thoroughbred horses. While these pastimes attract the monied elite of the Waikato and Auckland for weekends of indulgence, they can also be enjoyed by budget travelers who can appreciate the beauty without taking it home at the end of the day. The **Cambridge Country Store,** 92 Victoria St. (tel. 827 8715), has an amazing selection of all things New Zealand housed in its 1898 church frame. The **All Saints Cafe** upstairs offers muffins and scones ($2) and lunch items ($4-5) to be eaten on nice antique wooden furniture. *(Open daily in summer 8:30am-5:30pm, in winter 8:30am-5pm)* At the other end of the crafts spectrum, **Tribal Art Collectors & Traders,** 89 Victoria St. (tel. 827 8848), feels like a museum, but you can buy what you like. *(Open M-Sa 10am-5pm.)* The staff is happy to tell you about the amazing collection of art from around the world. Saturday afternoons from October to May, **cricket matches** transpire on the lawn in the town square.

Equine sports lie a bit farther out of town. Throughout the year (apart from July) those 18 and over can slap down $1 or more on the pony of their choice at the renowned **Cambridge Raceway,** 47 Taylor St. (tel. 827 5506). Food concessions cater to those making an evening of it. *(Races run M-Sa 6:15-10:30pm, Su noon-5pm. Basic stand ticket $4.)* **Cambridge Thoroughbred Lodge** (tel. 827 8118), on SH1 6km south of Cambridge, offers special horse shows that encourage audience participation, and involve many breeds of horses. *(Open daily 10am-4pm, show runs Tu-Su at 10:30am, afternoon shows by arrangement for groups of at least 10. Tickets $12, children $5, families $25.)* To ogle the studs working out, head out to **Matamata Raceway** (tel. 888 4442), New Zealand's largest thoroughbred training center. Daily from 6 to 8am, breakfast while watching the jockeys train the horses or the amateurs riding before work. Races take place about once a month. A walk or bike ride down **Racecourse Road** in Cambridge will take you past many stud, deer, and other hobby farms.

Cambridge is aptly called "The Town of Trees" for the arboreal splendor that locals have cultivated since the town's inception. The **Cambridge Tree Trust** maintains the many "Tree Trails" around Lake Te Koutu on the edge of town. **Walking tracks** dart back and forth between riverbank and residential road on either side of the water and are accessible from the Victoria St. bridge. Alternatively, climb to the top of nearby **Sanitarium Hill** and observe the green canopy from above. The **Cambridge Museum** (tel. 827 3319) in the Old Court House at the south end of Victoria St. is packed with relics of eras gone by. *(Open Tu-Sa 10am-4pm. Admission by donation.)*

■ Raglan

The inhabitants of the tiny coastal town of Raglan (or Raglan-by-the-sea) make relaxation mandatory and "no worries" a way of life. The left-handed break at Manu Bay is touted as the world's finest and can be seen in all its splendor in the 1966 classic surfing movie, *The Endless Summer.* Join the stampede of surfers that cruise here from around the world every summer in search of the perfect wave.

ORIENTATION AND PRACTICAL INFORMATION Forty-eight kilometers of mountain road **(SH23)** winding around extinct volcanoes separate Raglan from Hamilton. The town itself sits back in the harbor 6km from the coastline and all the good surfing points. The **Raglan Visitors Information Centre** (tel. 825 0556; fax 825 7054) is on the corner of Bow St. and Nero St. The petite office also serves as the AA and **DOC office.** Call for weather and road conditions, as well as high tide information. (Open in summer M-F 10am-5pm, Sa-Su 9am-4pm; in winter daily 9am-4pm; go next door to the council office if no one is there.) Currency can be exchanged at **WestPac Trust Bank** (tel. 825 8579), at the top end of Bow St. where the palm trees start (open M-Tu and Th-F 9am-4:30pm, W 9:30am-4:30pm). **No ATM** is available, so take care of banking in Hamilton before heading to Raglan. The **petrol station,** across from where Main St. becomes Norrio St., does accept Eftpos cards. The only public transportation service to Raglan is the **Pavlovich buses** (tel. 847 5545), whose departure schedule is designed primarily for those who live on the coast but work or study in Hamilton.

Buses head to Hamilton from West Raglan, pausing right in front of the information center about five to 10 minutes later (6:50am, 7:20am, 9:30am, 3:30am; $4.70 payable to the driver). There's no weekend service, but a weekend in Raglan might be just what you need if you're that concerned about strict schedules. **Hitchhiking** is practiced regularly along SH23, at the edge of town before the traffic picks up to 100kph. The most-used spots are up at the top end of Bow St. by the water tower (look for the giant surfing mural) or at the Te Uku outpost dairy. The **library** is next door to the visitors center; it currently has **Internet access,** but may discontinue the service soon. There are **public toilets** on Cliff St. behind Seagull's Takeaways and also on Wainui Rd. past the surf shop. For medicine or millions of dollars, head to **Raglan Pharmacy LTD & Lotto** (tel. 825 8164; open M-F 9am-5pm, Sa 9am-7pm). **After Hours Doctors** are on call (tel. 825 0007). **Raglan Medical Centre** is at 2 Wallace St. (tel. 825 8822; open M-Tu and F 9am-4:30pm, Th 9am-7pm, W 9am-3pm and 6:30-8pm, Sa 10am-1pm, Su 10am-noon.) If you left yours at home, you can rent a board for $20-25 per day from **Raglan Surf Co.,** 3 Wainui Rd. (tel. 825 8988); they will also rent wetsuits for $15 per day (open daily 9:30am-5pm). Check here for an update on the daily **surf conditions,** or alternatively, call up "The Rock" 93 FM (tel. 838 2693). In an **emergency,** dial **111.** The **police** (tel. 825 8200) are on Nero St., in a little clapboard house. The **post office,** 39 Bow St. (tel. 825 8007), is next to Town Hall (open M-F 9am-5pm). **Theft** of and from cars has become a problem lately. If you have a car, make sure you lock it when you are at the beach.

ACCOMMODATIONS Raglan's population of 2500 increases by half during the summer. In the winter, expect to find a number of visitors who came for a weekend and stayed for the season, as the surf is consistently good year-round. Tucked away at the end of a cul-de-sac, right around the corner from the information center, you'll find a little slice of beach heaven at **Raglan Backpackers and Waterfront Lodge,** 6 Nero St. (tel. 825 0515). All the smartly appointed rooms open onto an airy inner courtyard complete with hammock, flowers, and surfers lazing in the sun. Some of the rooms have gorgeous views of the harbor and the reading lounge stays perpetually toasty on winter nights, thanks to a fireplace and plush couches. A separate TV lounge and tidy kitchen round out the premises. Free surfboards, kayaks, bikes, and drop-off to beaches and walking tracks are available, and the owner Jeremy might just join you in the ocean to show you where and how to catch a wave. (Co-ed dorms $14; doubles or twins $32. Cash only. Linen $2.) **Marcus's Magic Mountain Lodge, Farmstay, and Backpackers,** 334 Houchens Rd. (tel. 825 6892 or (025) 756 276; fax 825 6896), in nearby Te Mata, is "the only place in the world where you can see four volcanoes and three lagoons only two minutes walking from your doorstep." You can also go horse-trekking, fishing, or hunting for wild boar in the bush, celebrating the kill with a glorious pig roast at the end of the day. For $20 and half-a-day's work on the farm, you'll get a comfy bed in the homestead and home-cooked meals; otherwise the price is $70. (B&B option: singles $45; doubles $75; group house which has 3 doubles and 2 singles $140; cash only. Free pick-up from Raglan with notice.) **The Raglan Kopua Camping Ground** (tel. 825 8283; fax 825 8284), on Marine Parade next to the Aerodrome and airstrip, is a vast flat expanse of land that in peak season can easily accommodate 1000. The TV lounge can accommodate 20 at best, but who needs TV when you've got surf? The communal kitchen has no utensils, but the communal single-sex bathrooms have showers and toilets. (Tent sites $8, in winter $7; powered $9/$8. 4-person chalets $10 per person, $20 min. 5-person cabins with full kitchen and TV, $40 for 2, extra person $12. 4-person tourist flat, full kitchen, shower, toilet, $50 for 2, $12 extra person, children $5. Laundry $3.)

FOOD AND ENTERTAINMENT Farmers and surfers chow down at the **Tongue and Groove** (tel. 825 0027), on the corner of Bow St. and Wainui Rd. Local art inspired by the beach and ocean graces the walls, and information about both is readily dispensed by the friendly staff. The veggie-friendly menu includes breakfasts served until 2pm ($5-10) and dinner mains beginning at 6pm ($15). In between and during those hours, snacks and sandwiches such as the marinated tofu with Thai peanut sauce ($6.50) are the fare. On weekend nights, the Tongue occasionally grooves to live music or DJs, and happy hour specials have been known to surface from time to time. (Open Tu-W 8:30am-4pm, Th-M from 8:30am.) In 1847, scores of prefab kauri woodcottages were deposited in Raglan in anticipation of a crush of immigrants. The only one remaining was retro-fitted a few years back to become **Vinnie's,** 7 Wainui Rd. (tel. 825 7273), with sparkling stained glass windows, a new deck, and some of Raglan's best grub. Originally a pizza pad (pizzas $4.50), the menu has taken off recently, with fresh fish fares ($10-15) and bean burritos with homemade salsa ($9.50) among the diverse offerings. (Open daily from 11am, in the winter Tu-Su only.) **Petchells Supermarket** (Four Square), 16-18 Bow St. (tel. 825 8300) is a market, auto supply, and sundry shop all in one (open M-F 7:30am-5pm, Sa-Su 7:30am-4pm).

SIGHTS, SAND, AND SURF Whether you're seeking an endless summer of your own or arriving in the dead of winter, be you a surfing maniac or a sedate stroller, Raglan's black-sand beaches are more than worth the trip. The most accessible is **Te Kopua Beach,** which can be reached via the footbridge at the base of Bow St. Accessibility has its price, as this beach is overrun with families and screaming children in the summer. Te Kopua also occupies a perfect harbor location for wind surfing. Catching a ride to the coast is a fairly straightforward task as beach-bound vehicles are easy to spot in town. Fine swimming and more space can be had at **Ocean Beach (Ngaranui Beach).** Watch out for strong undertows; only the west end of the beach is patrolled by lifeguards. The strong winds make it ideal for wind surfing.

Hard-core surfers head to **Manu Bay (Waireke).** If the conditions are right, the world's most perfect wave could be yours. Farther down the coast is **Whale Bay (Whaanga),** where green surf and rocky shore are accessible by a walking path from the cul-de-sac at the end of Calvert Rd. that goes over volcanic rocks to the black sand beach. The surfing here can be awesome in autumn. In April and May, there are often professional surfing competitions. If you're in search of a holy grail (or a red herring), somewhere between Manu Bay and Ocean Beach the elusive **Tatooed Rocks** can be found. Years ago, an unknown artist chiseled his way to local fame by sculpting two large rocks on the beach. They are only accessible at low tide, and some locals have searched for years without success. Farther down the coast, **Ruapuke Beach** offers rugged coastline and good surf casting. The less crowded **Cox's Bay** and **Puriri Park (Aro Aro Bay),** to the east of the town center, are ideal for children, picnics, or both. Walk along Wallis St. away from the information center to reach them.

Although the surfers might lead you to believe otherwise, Raglan does have more to offer than the ocean. If you can't catch a wave, go sit on the inactive volcanoes of **Mt. Karioi** and **Mt. Pirongia** in **Pirongia Forest Park.** One glance at Mt. Karioi's curvaceous silhouette and it's no wonder that in Maori legend it is referred to as "the sleeping lady." Mt. Karioi also boasts terrific mountain biking on the gravelly **Whaanga Road,** which wraps around the mountain's coastal side. Refrain from careening around the curves during the week—the one-lane road carries a considerable amount of traffic, and vehicles seem to be perpetually going over the edge. Mt. Pirongia is further from Raglan, but is larger and has more walking options. Another great view of the ocean can be had from **Te Toto Gorge,** which has recently become infamous as the place where car thieves dump the carcasses of their booty.

Freshwater wonders also await. The locals are mighty proud of **Bridal Veil Falls** and the fact that it is higher than its Niagara counterpart (though not quite as wide). Its thin, delicate spray is best photographed from a lookout that's a 20-minute walk from the carpark on Kawhia Rd. The bold can abseil down beside the falls with the help of a trained professional (contact Marcus Vernon, owner of the Magic Mountain Lodge; see Accommodations, above). You can soak out many of life's aches and pains at the **Waingoro Hot Springs** (tel. 825 4761), north of Raglan on SH22. With the proper DOC permits, you can also hunt wild pigs or go fly-fishing for rainbow trout in the **Kaniwhaniwha Stream.** On a rainy day, contact the secretary of the **Raglan Museum** on Wainui Rd. (tel. 825 8129) to see its photographic chronicle of the town's surfing legacy (open Sa-Su 1-3:30pm or by appointment; free).

■ Otorohanga

Otorohanga's literal meaning, "food for the long journey," originates with the legend of a great Maori king who paused in his journey to multiply his few supplies into enough to sustain his trek. Today, the nearly half-million tourists who pass through the town en route to Waitomo use their ATM and Eftpos cards to do essentially the same thing. Aside from visiting the Kiwi House, travelers come to Otorohanga primarily to refuel, restock, and relax before hitting Waitomo.

ORIENTATION AND PRACTICAL INFORMATION Maniapoto Street is the central road in town where most commercial activity takes place. The **Visitor Information Centre,** 87 Maniapoto St. (tel. 873 8951; fax 873 8398), is located at the intersection with **Wahanui Crescent,** where the **bus** arrives and departs. Keep an eye out for Wiki, the giant kiwi who greets visitors. **InterCity** (tel. (0800) 731 711) heads to Auckland (2½hr., 3 per day, $39) via Hamilton (1hr., $16); and to Wellington (8hr., 2 per day, 1 on Sa, $86) via Wanganui (5hr., $45) and Palmerston North (7hr., $50). The **train station** is at the other end of Wahanui Crescent.

Otorohanga was the first stop on the main trunk railway when the King Country was opened to Europeans and their descendants in the 1880s and 1890s. Today, **TranzScenic** (tel. (0800) 802 802) still stops here, on its way to Auckland (2½hr., 2 per day, 1 on Sa, $42 day/ $37 night) via Hamilton (1hr., $20/$18), and to Wellington (7hr., 2 per day, 1 on Sa, $99/$88) via Palmerston North (6hr., $72/$64). To get to Waitomo, take Bill Millar's **Waitomo Shuttle** (tel. (0800) 808 279) from the visitors center and learn more about the history of Otorohanga and the King Country in ten minutes than a guidebook could print in 50 pages. The shuttle drops off at accommodations (5 per day, $7; between 8am-8pm additional shuttles by arrangement, $18; during all other hours, $26). Bill also operates **Otorohanga Taxis** (tel. (0800) 808 279) for your other local transportation needs (open Su-Th 8am-11pm, F-Sa 8am-1am). **Hitchhiking** opportunities are said to be best from the visitors center, at the end of Maniapoto St. before the bridge, or at the intersection of Waitomo Caves Rd. and SH3. The only **ATM** (servicing MasterCard and Cirrus) is at **WestPacTrust Bank** on Maniapoto St. Card users on other systems should bring cash from Hamilton, Rotorua, or points south. Fill up at one of the three **petrol stations** in town as there is no petrol station in Waitomo. The **public library** is in the Council building (tel. 873 8199) and offers **Internet access** ($5 for 30min.; open M-Th 10am-5pm, F 10am-6pm, Sa 10am-noon). There are **public toilets** on Wahanui Crescent, around the corner from the visitors center. The **doctor on call** can be reached (tel. 873 8399) all day. In an **emergency,** dial **111.** The **police** are available at the Community Constable's office, 36 Maniapoto St. (tel. 873 7399; open daily 9:30am-3:30pm). After hours calls should be directed to the Te Kuiti police (tel. 878 8111). The **post office** is inside King's Paper Plus (tel. 873 8816), on Maniapoto St. (open M-F 8:30am-5pm, Sa 9am-7pm). The **telephone code** is **07.**

ACCOMMODATIONS, FOOD, AND SIGHTS By night, the cry of the kiwis from the nearby breeding pens echoes through Otorohanga's best budget accommodations. At the **Oto-Kiwi Lodge,** 1 Sangro Crescent (tel. 873 6022; fax 873 6066; email oto-kiwi@xtra.co.nz), the energetic hosts welcome "backpackers, globetrotters, and musicians" to their compound at the end of the cul-de-sac. Bikes ($10 per day), hotties, and shovels for digging thermal pools at Kawhia (40min. drive west to the coast) are available. Best of all, in one of the buildings, proprietor/bassist/vocalist John Rothery has set up a complete studio for jam sessions. (Bunks $15; doubles $37; beds in recording studio $12; tent sites $7.50. Key deposit $10. Internet access $4 for 30min. Laundry $3. 10% discounts to Kiwi House and Waitomo Down Under.) Adjoining the town's famous Kiwi House is the **Kiwi Town Caravan Park and Motor Camp.** To contact the proprietor, Bill of Waitomo Shuttle (tel. (0800) 808 279), use the phone in the communal kitchen or catch him as he drives the Waitomo Shuttle into town at 8:30am or 6:30pm. Simple but clean facilities include a communal kitchen, toilets and showers, and laundry ($1.50 per load). Those staying here will hear the kiwis next door thrice daily: 30min. after sunset, during a 2hr. window centered about midnight, and just before daybreak. (On-site caravans $27 for 2; caravan sites $15 for 2, extra person $7.50; tent sites $6.50.) For hotel lodgings, try the brown splendor of the **Royal Hotel** (tel. 873 8129; fax 873 8744), at the corner of Turango and Te Kanawa St., where singles are $40 while doubles and twins are $60 (extra person $15; hall bath). For an inexpensive sit-down meal, consider the **Otorohanga Club Restaurant** (tel. 873 6543), at the south end of Maniapoto St., where steak dinners are $10 (lunches $4-8; open daily 11:30am-3pm and from 5pm). **Price Cutter,** at the south end of Maniapoto St., is the market of choice (open M-Th 8am-6pm, F 8am-7pm, Sa 9am-3pm, Su 10am-2pm).

As Wiki, the overstuffed town kiwi welcoming committee, will tell you: No stop in Otorohanga would be complete without a pilgrimage to the **Otorohanga Kiwi House and Native Bird Park** (tel. 873 7391), on Alex Telfer Dr. Although the birds spend only four hours of the day awake, a sighting in the "moonlit" kiwi house is guaranteed as kiwi couples are awake in shifts throughout the day. Outside you'll find New Zealand's original walk-through aviary (don't look up), with tuataras, geckos, and cave wetas (Open daily Sept.-May 9:30am-5pm; June-Aug. 9:30am-4pm; $7.50). John of Kiwi House fame also runs the **Oto-Kiwi Eco-Tours** (tel. 873 6022), with one- and two-day trips ($40 per person.) Groups of up to six people decide from a range of trips and activities such as fishing, hiking, abseiling, caving, and mountain biking.

If you are looking for a unique traveling companion, every Wednesday between 10:30am and 3pm cattle, pigs, and sheep (and farm implements) are sold at a **farmer's market**. This is one of the larger stock sales in New Zealand; consult the visitors center for the exact location and other details. For a unique overstock experience, visit **Haddad's,** 65-71 Maniapoto St. (tel. 873 8377), just a few doors down from the bus station on Maniapoto St., where the brother owners offer the lowest price in New Zealand on many staples of brand-name farming attire and your other wardrobe needs (open M-Th 8:30am-5pm, F 8:30am-7pm, Sa 9am-noon).

■ Waitomo

It was 1887 when Maori chief Tane Tinorau and European surveyor Fred Mace chose to leave Maori legend behind and explore the depths of the local river cave. Although no gods were found, that day the two spelunkers were treated to an other-worldly display of bioluminescent blue, courtesy of thousands of glow-worms. Within a year, Tinorau had opened up the cave to visitors and was guiding them inside to experience the ethereal wonder. One hundred years later, though the glow-worm population has remained stable, the number of tourists has soared to nearly 500,000, putting this minuscule hamlet (pop. 250) squarely on the map. While most visitors come for the "light show," nearly one-tenth are now attracted by the adventure caving industry, which offers trips of varying degrees of difficulty, consistently low degrees of water temperature, and considerably high degrees of pleasure.

PRACTICAL INFORMATION

The Museum of Caves Information Centre (tel. 878 7640; fax 878 6184; email waitomomuseum@xtra.co.nz), is just inside the entrance to the **Museum of Caves** in Waitomo Village. The front desk functions as a base camp for everyone living in, passing through, or even thinking about coming to Waitomo. Aside from booking any cave-related activity you would ever desire, the ultra-helpful staff can give detailed first-hand accounts of just how wet you'll get or how many glow-worms you'll see. Be warned that there are **no banks or ATMs** in Waitomo. In emergencies consult the front desk. Card phones are just outside, as are after-hours public toilets. The information center also offers the lowest prices on groceries in the village (albeit a limited selection), as well as disposable cameras and film. (Open in winter daily 8:15am-5pm, in Jan. 8:15am-8pm, all other months 8:15am-5:30pm.)

Nearly 70% of visitors to the caves arrive by coach. **InterCity** runs daytrips from Auckland (9am, $45 one-way) and Rotorua (9:30am, $37 one-way); the bus returning to each departs Waitomo at 2pm. The **Waitomo Wanderer** (tel. 873 7559) offers loop service to and from Waitomo from Rotorua (2hr., 7:30am) and back, leaving Waitomo at 4pm for Taupo (4pm, 3½hr.) via Rotorua (2hr.), returning to Waitomo at 9:15pm. Wandering will run you $25 one-way, $15 for children (round-trip $45, 25). Booking ahead is required, with pickup and dropoff available at all hostels. Bike transport is $10. The **Waitomo Shuttle** (tel. (0800) 808 279; fax 873 8214) is the best option for those making **InterCity** or **Tranzscenic** connections in Otorohanga (4 per day, 10min., $7). Trips after 8pm can be arranged ($18 one-way), and pickups are made from any of the Waitomo hostels (with a free history lesson along the way). **Hitchhiking** from Otorohanga is reportedly fairly easy; hitchhikers often hang out at the visitors center until they find a fellow tourist with a car, or else walk out along Waitomo Caves Rd. Apparently, hitchhiking into Waitomo is best accomplished by standing at the junction of Waitomo Caves Rd. and SH3. In an **emergency**, dial 111. Call the **search and rescue hotline** (tel. 878 6219 or 878 8384), or the **Otorohanga Medical Centre** (tel. 873 8399). The **post office** is located in the visitors center at the museum (see above). The **telephone code** is **07**.

ACCOMMODATIONS

Bedding down in Waitomo runs the gamut from the great outdoors to the great indoors of a B&B. In the summer season, bookings are essential.

Waitomo Caves Hostel (YHA) (tel. 878 8204; fax 878 8205), behind the Waitomo Caves Hotel in Waitomo Village, overlooking the Museum of Caves. Brightly painted rooms and clean spacious facilities all located just up the hill form the center of "town." Dorms $17 (non-members $20); twins and triples with bath $20 per person. Linen $5. Check-in at the hotel after 10:30am. Check-out 9:30am. **Waitomo Caves Hotel** is more upscale, though singles without bathrooms are $25.

Juno Hall (tel./fax 878 7649), on Waitomo Caves Rd., 1km from the visitors center. Low-lying brown lodge with a warm, toasty interior. Well-stocked spice rack in the kitchen inspires savory breakfasts, while free linen and duvets promote sweet dreams. Free pickup and dropoff to village or hitchhiking points. Dorms $16; doubles $39; extra person $9. Suites with TV, shower, toilet $49, extra person $9 (up to 4). Tent sites $7.50 per person. YHA/VIP $1 off. Check-out 10am.

Cavelands Waitomo Holiday Park (tel./fax 878 7639), across the street from the Museum of Caves. A well-maintained accommodation complex of the utmost convenience. Communal kitchen, showers, and toilets for all guests. Free flashlights for Ruakiri Walk. Self-contained tourist flats with TV, kitchenette, bathroom $70 for 2, extra adult $10, extra child $5. Tent sites $7.50, children $4.50; powered $9, children $5. Laundry $2. Linen $3. Check-in noon, check-out 10am.

Dalziel's Waitomo Caves Guest Lodge B&B (tel. 878 7641; fax 878 7466), next door to the general store in the village. Pet goat watches over a hillside of well-appointed and landscaped private units, each with bathroom facilities, heater, and TV. Continental breakfast, complimentary coffee. Singles $50; doubles $70, extra person $20. "The Cottage" is a slightly smaller twin for $60. Check-out 10am.

FOOD

Dining establishments in Waitomo are few and far between, and given the limited selection of overpriced groceries in the village, travelers would be best served stocking up at the markets of Hamilton, Otorohanga, and Rotorua. The best prepared food in town can be found at the **Black Water Cafe** (tel. 878 7361), in the main Black Water Rafting building 1km east of the village. Currently, diners and those waiting for their rafting trips all mill about together, generating a slightly hectic environment, though renovations will soon create a separate space for eating. In the meantime, the kitchen offers large breakfasts ($5-10), and savory lunch items ($3-5). The pot of soup and basket of bagels by the fireplace are for post-rafting munchies. (Open June-Aug.

8:30am-5pm, Sept.-May 7:30am-8:30pm.) The **Cavelands Brasserie and Bar and General Store** (tel. 878 7700) is the large building next to the Museum of Caves. This is a good place to get a meal while you wait for your caving trip to leave (the only food you may get for the next 5hr.). They will rush meals and grant takeaways if you are running late for your adventure. Burgers ($8.50-10.50) and fries ($2-3) are standard, while mains ($12.50-17) for dinner in the summer are slightly fancier. The **general store** is overpriced and should be used as a last resort in emergencies (open daily in summer 8am-9pm; in winter 8am-6pm). The **Waitomo Caves Tavern** (tel./fax 878 8448), located below the Waitomo Caves Hotel, is *the* watering hole for all of Waitomo, and the only place serving dinner in Waitomo during the winter months. Hearty pub grub is available at very reasonable prices—including burgers or steaks with fries and salad (small $6.50, large $7.50). (Open for dining daily noon-2:30pm and M-Sa 6-9pm, Su in summer 5:30-8:30pm, Su in winter 5:30-7:30pm. Bar open M-Sa 11am-11pm, Su in summer 11am-10pm, Su in winter 11am-8pm.)

ADVENTURE CAVING

The scores of holes littering the lush green pastureland around Waitomo are gateways to a mystical world where time and temperature cease to exist as we know them. Centuries become measured in centimeters rather than years, and the caves remain constantly dark and cool regardless of conditions top-side. New adventure trips are constantly springing up to satisfy growing demand (often offering low introductory prices until they become established) and some only advertise in Waitomo. Given this labyrinthine array of caving possibilities (including climbing, canoeing, sight-seeing, strolling, and glow-worm sighting), the best advice is to book ahead to some extent, but to allow for the option of staying an extra day or two.

Always go caving with a guide; never cave solo, even if you consider yourself an experienced spelunker. Aside from safety issues, virtually all of the caves in the area are privately owned, and trespassing can be risky business. Safety is always a top concern with Waitomo's many professional companies; in tiny Waitomo, even the slightest breath of faulty gear or injuries can put a caving company out of business. Standard protocol for "adventure caving" is to slap on a full wetsuit and some coveralls (or just the coveralls if it's a "dry" trip), a hard hat with a head lamp, and a pair of gumboots. Many adventure caving trips also include at least one abseil, so the ever-so-stylish ensemble is usually accessorized with a seat harness and brake bar. After zipping up, buckling up, and being checked over repeatedly, it's off to the paddocks where the extremely patient guides will walk you through the basics of single-rope technique (SRT), much to your own amusement and that of the sheep and cows around you. Before you suit up and head out, you may want to consider testing yourself for claustrophobia in a caving situation. If the company running your tour doesn't already require it, head on over to the **Museum of Caves,** explain your situation, and ask to try the cave "crawl-through." It's much darker and about three times smaller than any of the squeezes on commercial tours, and gives a good indication of your potential for freaking out. In selecting a caving trip, it's a good idea to sit down first and figure out what your priorities are. Each trip or tour is unique and has its own personality and pace—there is no absolute "best."

Waitomo Adventures (tel. 878 7788 or (0800) WAITOMO; email bookings@waitomo.co.nz; http://www.waitomo.co.nz) deals out a great hand of options. **Haggas Honking Holes,** so-called because the caves are on Farmer Haggas' property, includes three waterfall abseils, plenty of climbing and squeezing, and admirable formations all at an action-packed clip. "The Honk" combines the intensity of boot camp, the aesthetics of an art museum, and the camaraderie of summer camp to create the most adrenaline-packed excitement available for first-time cavers. (Trips daily 11:15am and 4:15pm, to coincide with the Kiwi Experience and Waitomo Wanderer schedules; 4hr; $125.) In the summer additional trips may be added; generally groups have up to nine people and two guides, though this can expand to 12 and three if necessary. A swimsuit and towel are essential; polypropylene thermals, thick wool socks, and soap are advisable. Waitomo's other blockbuster trip is the **Lost World,** a 100m free-hanging abseil into an ethereal world of mist and miniature ferns not entirely unlike a land of Spielberg dinosaurs. An awestruck reporter from the *King Country Chronicle* in 1906 dubbed it "a fairyland without the fairies." You descend in tandem with your guide; the umbilical-like connection ensures that your guide goes wherever you do. Don't wear jeans. (Trips daily at 7am and 11:30am; 4hr.; $195; extra trip at 4:30pm in the summer.) You can combine both the Honk and Lost World into the **Gruesome Twosome** for $295. In addition, Waitomo offers **Tumu Tumu Toobing,** a rafting trip that features more caving and less tubing than comparable trips. (Daily at 11am and 3:30pm; 4hr.; $65, $45 if packaged with one of Waitomo's other adventures.) Waitomo offers a 10% discount on all trips to students, as well as to YHA and VIP members (office open daily in summer 7:30am-9pm, in winter 9am-5pm). All trips depart from the Museum of Caves parking lot.

Starry Night

Over the eons, humans have looked heavenward in search of inspiration and answers; standing inside a glow-worm cave, however, the answers might not be what you'd expect. Indeed, few pause to consider the sordid but fascinating details of this little creature's life. The glow-worm (*Arachnocampa luminosa;* in Maori *titiwai*), is actually not a worm at all, but the larva of a fly. After hatching, the baby flies set about the business of excreting sticky threads to make a "hammock" and "fishing lines." On each of the 70 lines (from 1-50cm long) controlled by each worm is a drop of shiny stuff—the worm's waste product, lit up by the light of the bioluminescent larva itself (with the brightness of one-billionth of a watt). After months of trolling with poo for flying midges and the like, the glow-worm undergoes metamorphosis and becomes an adult fly. Evolution was so busy figuring out how to make the glow-worm's stool shine that it forgot to develop a digestive tract. After only a day or two of adult life—flying, mating, and laying eggs—the fly dies of starvation (or from being oversexed). The next time you gaze up in awe at the greenish stars in the nighttime sky of a cave's ceiling, remember that the speck of light is a tail-glowing maggot fishing for its lunch with a glob of excrement. Ain't nature grand?

Black Water Rafting (BWR) (tel. 878 6219 or (0800) CAVING; email bwr@black-water-rafting.co.nz), begun in 1987, is the granddaddy of all adventure caving in Waitomo. To the usual array of wetsuit, helmet, and boots add some stylish purple "eel pants" and an innertube, and you're ready to float into the world of the glow-worm. **BWI** is the classic tour and involves a gentle float and the obligatory glow-worms ($65; allow 3hr., mostly for the ritualistic dressing procedure; 1 guide per 6 tourists). **BWII** gets flashier with an added abseil, rock climbing, and the option of an adventurous escape through a waterfall ($125, lunch and snacks provided; 5hr.; 1 guide per 6 tourists). Both BWI and II depart from and return to the Black Water Cafe, where a delicious hot shower (bring soap, towel and bathing suit), as well as free soup and bagel await. BWI is suitable for seniors, and all trips can be modified to fit special needs; just ask ahead of time.

Waitomo Down Under (WDU) (tel. 878 6577 or (0800) 102 604; fax 878 6565; email waitomo.du@xtra.co.nz) offers four different tours, frequently guided by direct descendents of Tane Tinorau. **Adventure 1** is a float through which features formation and worm spotting ($65; 3hr.; bring swim gear and towel), and runs five times a day (9am, 10am, 12:15pm, 1:30pm, 3pm; max. group size is 12, min. is 3). **Adventure 2** is a "dry" abseil 50m into an absolutely stunning cave known as the "Baby Grand." The adventurous can choose to lock off their ropes and then swing, flip, and dangle in mid-air ($65; 2hr.; no jeans). Similar dress rules apply for **Adventure 3**, which features all spelunking, all the time. Guests squeeze, climb, get grubby, and generally have a good time ($50; 2hr.; bring towel and soap). **Adventure 4** is basically Adventure 2, done under the cover of darkness at 7:30pm. Once reaching the free hang, the lights are turned out for a spacewalk in a galaxy of glow-worms ($65; 2hr.; no jeans). All trips depart from the WDU building next to the museum. (Pickup and drop-off available from area hostels; 10% discount available for students, YHA and VIP members, and groups of 6 or more.)

For a less commercial approach with excellent value, try an independent operator like Simon Hall's **Waitomo Wilderness Tours** (tel. 878 7640; email waitomomuseum@xtra.co.nz; after hours tel./fax 873 8012, email simon_hall@xtra.co.nz). Smaller groups (max. 6) partake in five different activities. A 27m abseil down a ferny rock slope takes you to the water, where the floating options of **cave canoeing** (by canoe) or **Long Tomo rafting** (by inner tube) await. Each trip is tailored to fit the group's interests. ($65; 5hr.; trips run daily at 9am and 2pm, Nov.-Apr. also 11am and 4pm; bring a towel, t-shirt, swimsuit, socks, and camera.)

SIGHTS AND ACTIVITIES

Any visit to Waitomo should include a visit to the **Museum of Caves** (tel. 878 7640). *(Open daily 8:30am-5pm. Admission $4, children under 18 free.)* Learn about how the caves were formed, learn about the wildlife that now resides there, and take in a multimedia spelunking experience in the small theater. **Black Water Rafting** provides a complimentary museum pass as part of their adventure, and **Waitomo Down Under** will provide one on request.

If you are curious to see where all of those tour buses are headed, get on down to the **Glow-worm Caves** (tel. 878 8227), 500m around the bend west of Waitomo Village on Waitomo Caves Rd. *(Tours run every 30min. in summer 9am-5:30pm and 8pm, in winter 9am-5pm.; $17.50, children $10.)* Not without cause, this is the cave that everyone keeps talking about. Stroll along the stage-like boardwalk alongside dramatically lit formations for a truly theatrical experience. "The Cathedral" has served as a performance venue for the likes of Kenny Rogers, the Vienna Boys Choir, and Maori opera diva Dame Kiri Te Kanawa. The Disney-esque boat ride at the end is breathtaking, and probably the only time you'll find silence anywhere in the tourist-filled cave. Hear only the drip of dark water as the boat slips under a mantle of glowing stars. Independent travelers are advised to come at either end of the day. Take a midday tour (45min.) and you will almost assuredly become an appendage to a large coach tour. Nearby **Aranui Cave** holds a treasure trove of formations that you don't even have to get your feet wet to see. *(Tours run daily 10am-3pm on the hour, same prices as above. Both caves: $27, children $14. Family pass: 1 cave $50, both caves $65.)* The most natural caving expedition also happens to be free; at the museum, you can pick up a guide to the **Waitomo Walkway,** a DOC-maintained trek (3hr. round-trip) that takes you mostly through bush, but at its farthest point leads you into the **Ruakiri Natural Tunnel.** At night, put on some sturdy shoes and grab a flashlight and a friend to find another cache of glow-worms to ogle. Entry points are across the road from the museum, at the rotary intersection of Waitomo Caves and Te Anga Rd., and the car park of the Ruakuri Scenic Reserve on Tumutumu Rd. From this latter point, the tunnel can be experienced in one hour.

Amazingly enough, there *are* activities in Waitomo that don't involve wetsuits or worms. One of the more interesting topside activities is the bush trek (1hr. round-trip) to the **Opapaka Maori pa.** As the trail winds through excruciatingly beautiful forest, placards along the way describe local plants, their medicinal uses, and Maori legends. At the crest of the hill, barbed wire separates the trail from the *pa* (or more accurately, where it used to stand—use your imagination); you are allowed to cross over the fence with the makeshift bridge, but mind the livestock. The walk begins from the carpark located just west of Juno Hall on Waitomo Caves Rd.

Farther down along Waitomo Caves Rd. toward Waitomo Village is the turn-off for **Woodlyn Park** (tel./fax 878 6666). Farmer, historian, and globe-trotting sheepshearer Barry Woods puts on a thoroughly entertaining and refreshingly authentic **Pioneer Show,** detailing Waitomo's European history with lots of animal antics and audience participation. *(Daily in summer 1:30pm; book ahead in winter. $9.50, children $4.50, families $28.)* Try your hand at everything from sheep-shearing to jigger-chopping. For an even more hands-on experience, try **Barry's U-Drive Jetboat.** Although the inexperienced at handling a jetboat might turn it into "U-Crash," safety equip-

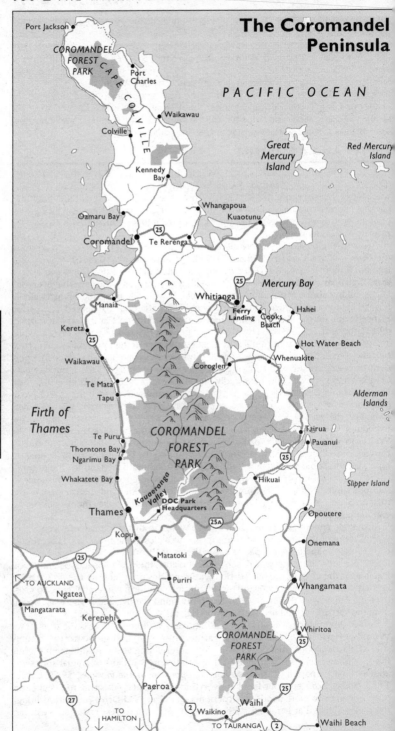

The Coromandel Peninsula

ment abounds and the sloping walls of the water course are lined with tires. *(Open daily 9am-5pm, in summer also 6:30-8pm. 8 laps $27; book ahead.)* At the other end of spectrum is **Waitomo Horse Trekking** (tel. 878 7659), departing from Juno Hall and led by their multi-talented staff. *(Treks $30 per hr., $40 per 2hr., half-day $60, full day $100, overnight $200 per day; meals included; book in advance.)* Hunting outings can also be organized. Lastly, a unique and free experience is **The Shearing Shed** (tel. 878 8371), also on Waitomo Caves Rd., where there is a daily shearing show at 1pm (show up at 12:45pm) in which the stars of the show are not the usual sheep, but Angora rabbits. Afterwards, browse the gift shop for something soft and fluffy.

COROMANDEL PENINSULA

Removed from the standard tourist loop, this peninsula of largely untouched natural beauty takes visitors back in time to how New Zealand once was. With lush, subtropical forest, rugged hills, and close-knit, friendly communities, the Coromandel's greatest virtue is its distinct lack of commercialization. The winding, often harrowing coastal road will lead you along beach and through bush back to the basics. Before you set out, adjust your clock to "Coromandel time" so you can unwind properly while leisurely browsing craft shops, soaking in your personally dug hot pool on the beach, hugging a powerful kauri tree, or just listening to the song of the Tui bird. From the transportation gateway of Thames, you can trace the very edge of the coast to the charming, artisan town of Coromandel. Cutting inland and occasionally turning to gravel, the roads from Coromandel bring more inspiring vistas, and eventually give way to Whitianga. At Hot Water Beach, Hahei, and magical Opoutere, life becomes even simpler and more relaxing, and Coromandel time seems to stand still. When you've finished with the surfer beach town of Whangamata, you may desperately want to do it all over again. While the peninsula, a favorite Auckland getaway, explodes during Kiwi holidays (avoid it altogether in the few weeks after Christmas), in the low seasons and the winter, it's no tour buses, no crowds, and no worries.

Public transportation on the Coromandel's winding, often gravel roads can be a little sparse at times, especially in winter when some services make limited runs. Check with the local visitors centers for current options. If you can't drive it yourself, consider buying a **Coromandel Busplan** from **InterCity** to circuit the peninsula in a clockwise direction from Thames to the town of Coromandel to Whitianga and back to Thames. **The Loop Pass** ($49) allows unlimited segments in the one-way loop, while the **Busplan Pass** ($79) includes the loop plus a starting leg from Auckland and a final leg to Auckland or Rotorua. (Passes valid for 3 months; book each leg the day before. Loop runs daily Oct.-Apr. and in winter Tu, Th, F, and Su.)

■ Thames

Arriving in this small, sunny town of 6500, you'd never guess that it was briefly the country's largest city in the 1870s, with over 18,000 inhabitants, 100 hotels, and rows of bars serving up whiskey to streams of miners and prospectors. The gold rush is recalled in the pared-down town today only by some old hotels and buildings, a shopping mall called Goldfields, and a surfeit of bright yellow signs around town marking various bonanza sites and mines. No longer resounding to the pounding of stamper batteries nor the drunken revelries of miners, the closest Thames gets to such excitement today is the hum of car motors and the shouts of inebriated students when summer holidays hit. Just under two hours from Auckland by car, Thames is the main access point to the Coromandel and the service center for the tiny communities of the peninsula.

ORIENTATION AND PRACTICAL INFORMATION

From Auckland, **SH25** (the new Pacific Coast Highway) wraps around the **Firth of Thames** before heading up and around the tip. Thames itself lies on a flat between the Firth and the upsweep of the gold-mine-riddled Coromandel Range. Most of Thames's shops and services stretch out along the 1.6km **Pollen Street**. Parallel and seaward is **Queen Street,** the in-town name for SH25.

Airplanes: Air Coromandel (tel. (0800) 275 912) flies to Auckland (8am, 3pm; $90) from Thames, Coromandel, Whitianga, Pauanui, or Matarangi; the company also flies to Great Barrier Island from those locations (W, F, and Su noon; $75) as well as Rotorua ($100) and Tauranga ($75).

Buses: InterCity heads from the visitors center to Auckland (summer 2 per day, winter 4 per week, $20), Tauranga (2hr., same buses with a transfer, $20), Coromandel (1¼hr., daily in summer and 4 per week in winter, 10:15am, $14), and Whitianga on a non-loop run (1¾hr.,10:15am, $14). **Turley Murphy** buses go to Coromandel (in summer daily 3:30pm, in winter Su-F 3:30pm), as does the new **Coromandel Bus Service** (M-Tu, Th-F 10am and 2:30pm, Sa 10am, Su 4pm; $14, $25 round-trip).

Car Rental: Worth considering, particularly if you want to reach the remote tip or stop at various kauri groves and beaches scattered on and off the road. Confident drivers only, as roads can be hairy. **Rent-a-Dent,** 503 Queen St. (tel. 868 8838 or (0800) 736 822), starts at $40 per day plus 20¢ per km. Discounts after 3 days.

Bike Rental: Bike touring is an excellent and popular way to see the Coromandel, if you've got the legs for it—many roads are hilly, unsealed, and winding. **Price and Richards** ("Sports Cycles Mowers"), 430 Pollen St. (tel. 868 6157 or (025) 714 971), rents 21-speed mountain bikes ($20 per day, $15 for 3 or more days) with all necessary gear. If you have the desire but not the legs, rent a power cycle (motorized mountain bike) from the visitors center for $40 per day (discounts for multiday; deposit $80; carrier bags $8).

Taxis: Thames Gold Cabs (tel. 868 6037). Open M-Th 8am-late, F-Sa 8am-2am.

Hitchhiking: Thumbers report that it's usually no problem catching a ride to Coromandel, even in winter.

Visitors Center: The **Thames Information Centre** (tel. 868 7284) is in the Old Railway Station on Queen St., at the end of Willoughby St. Open in summer M-F 8:30am-5pm, Sa-Su 9am-5pm; in winter M-F 8:30am-5pm, Sa-Su 7am-4pm.

DOC: Kauaeranga Valley Field Centre (tel. 868 6381), 13km out of town, is open daily 8am-4pm (see Coromandel Forest Park, p. 134).

Currency Exchange: BNZ (tel. 868 6020), at the corner of Sealey and Pollen St. Open M-F 9am-4:30pm. Get sufficient money in Thames, as there are only four other **ATMs** farther up the peninsula.

Emergency: Dial 111.

Medical Services: Thames Medical Centre (24hr. tel. 868 9444), on Rolleston St. just down from the hospital's side entrance. A **pharmacy** (tel. 868 9095) is in Goldfields Mall. Open M-Th 8:30am-5:30pm, F 8:30am-8pm, Sa-Su 9am-4pm. The **Thames Hospital** (tel. 868 6550) is on MacKay St., parallel to Pollen St.

Police: On Queen St. across from the Mall (24hr. tel. 868 6040).

Post Office: On Pollen St. between Mary and Sealey St. (tel. 868 7850). Open M-F 8:30am-5pm, Sa 9am-1pm.

Telephone Code: 07.

ACCOMMODATIONS AND FOOD

B&Bs and homestays come out from the wallpaper in the summer holiday season, when you need to book far, far ahead (ask at the visitors center). Several motor camps are along the coastal road between Thames and Coromandel, and DOC runs eight campgrounds in the Kauaeranga Valley (see Coromandel Forest Park, p. 134).

Sunkist Lodge (VIP), 506 Brown St. (tel. 868 8808). Veer onto Brown St. off Queen St. at the Mall, and head up about 4 blocks. This former gold-rush hotel comes with its own resident ghost. Sturdy bunks and a terrific second-floor front deck. Info, free multi-day luggage storage, and Internet access. Large dorms $14; 4-bed shares $16; doubles or twins $35.

Dickson Holiday Park (YHA) (tel. 868 7308; fax 868 7319), on Victoria St. 3km north of town off SH25. A bit far, but you can always borrow one of the free bikes or get a free pickup. Streamside location with great walks, game room, solar heated pool, and both a regular indoor and outdoor "pioneer" kitchen. Metered showers. Mixed dorms $15; simple tourist cabins and on-site caravans with kitchenette ($38 for 2). Tent sites $20 for 2 or $9 per person.

Action Backpackers Coromandel, 476 Pollen St. (tel. (0800) 2THAMES or 868 6200). Formerly the Old Pioneer Hotel, this new and centrally located hostel, known as ABC for short, is run in conjunction with the backpacker-friendly **Holy Cow Bar** next door. Extensive renovations will bring internet access as well as large kitchen and lounge area. Dorms $15 (over bar $13); doubles $40.

Brooksby Motel, 102 Redwood Ln. (tel. 868 6663). From Pollen St., turn on Sealey St. and walk to Rolleston St. (2 streets over). Turn left, veer up Karaka St., and soon Redwood Ln. is on the left. Nicely set next to a stream and backing into bush, yet only a few minutes from town. Well-equipped and extremely clean, though uninspired rooms (4 units) with kitchens, TVs, electric blankets, and separate bedrooms. Singles $60; doubles $68; $5-7 more in summer. Compact studio room without kitchen ($50 for 1, $60 for 2).

The lion's share of takeaways and cafes is found in the **Mall** (food court) and on **Pollen St.** Hotel bars often have affordable, standard dinners. Nearby, the pleasant **Food for Thought,** 574 Pollen St. (tel. 868 6065), serves healthy vegetarian fare. The lunch selection includes a kumara bake or veggie pizza (under $5), topped off with bulky muffins ($1.50) and a better-than-average herbal tea and coffee selection (open M-F 7:30am-4:30pm). The **Thames Bakery** (tel. 868 7088), on Pollen St. by Mary St., proffers cheap fresh bread, hot pies, and tasty cakes (open daily 6am-5pm). There's nothing shocking about the menu, but **Holy Cow** (tel. (0800) 2THAMES) on Pollen St. has excellent standard meals at great prices. After the curry and rice ($5) or the lamb steaks ($15), you can happily moo-ve on to the night's first (or fifth) beer (try a Coromandel Draught) from the popular weekend bar (open daily for food and drink 11am-2am). And don't dare leave the Coromandel without trying the flounder, oysters, mussels, or scallops, all of which are locally caught. Save some cash and fill up your trundler at the **Pak 'N Save** (tel. 868 9577) in Goldfields Mall (open M-Th 8:30am-6pm, F 8:30am-8pm, Sa-Su 9am-5pm).

SIGHTS AND ACTIVITIES

Thames's history provides much of its present attractions. The local goldfields, discovered in 1867, were declared open in August of that year, despite the difficult nature of the extraction. (Coromandel gold is found only in quartz and requires hardrock processing; see p. 134). In the peak year of 1871, over $3 million was gleaned from the tunnels riddling the surrounding hills. By the time mining slowed around WWI, over $2.6 billion (2.4 million oz. of bullion) had been extracted.

Even the marginally interested should check out the **Gold Mine and Stamper Battery** (tel. 868 7748), on SH25 at the north end of town. You can tour the claustrophobic tunnels that miners (represented by mannequins the guide refers to by name) chipped out by hand for eight hours a day, six days a week. (Complex open for tours Dec. 26-Jan. 31 daily 10am-4pm, Feb.-May daily 11am-3pm; and winter weekends with variable hours; 30 min. Tours $5, children $2.) If you still aren't impressed, wait until the stamper battery is cranked up to a full deafening roar. A photo history museum and an opportunity to pan for gold (only in Jan., $2-5) are open in the summer. The **Thames Historical Museum** (tel. 868 8509), at the corner of Pollen and Cochrane St., provides a less interactive look into the past with a display on the massive mining and kauri logging industries. (Open daily 1-4pm.)

The Hard Rock Blues

If you've got visions of kiwi-sized nuggets of gold plopping into Thames miners' hands, think again—though the hills were rich, it was never an easy process to extract the gold of the Coromandel Peninsula (it's found only in quartz rock and not in separate veins). Eking it out of such hard rock required use of massive rods called **stampers** that weighed as much as 450kg and could hammer down quartz chunks over 60 times per minute. The resultant powder was ejected with water onto a shaking table where the grains of quartz, fool's gold, and the real aurum were separated by weight. The refuse was dumped into the local waters, and built up so much that many houses are now built on the extended coast. Workers who didn't labor in the death-hastening mines could expect to go deaf manning the stamper batteries (the noise quotient would put even the most vigorous modern rock concert to shame). At its peak, from 1870-71, there were over 800 stampers running 24 hours per day, six days per week in Thames, and rumor has it that none could sleep on Sundays when the mind-numbing clamor ground to a halt.

The **WWI Peace Memorial** atop Monument Hill, lit up at night, gives exciting views of both the town and the Firth (up Waiotahi Rd., where Pollen St. meets Queen St. at the north end of town). The **Karaka Bird Hide,** which was built with compensation funds from the French government for the bombing of the *Rainbow Warrior* (see Rainbow Warrior, p. 100), stands just past Goldfields Mall. A short walk through the mangroves takes you to the shelter to look for shorebirds on the extensive mud flats. The best two hours are on either side of high tide.

Though most people head up the **Kauaeranga Valley** for tramping, several other area walks are also worth noting. Best is **Rocky's Goldmine Trail** (about 3hr. loop), which starts and ends at the Dickson Holiday Park, with great views, green bush, and refreshing streams. The area, however, is riddled with old and dangerous mine shafts. Stay clear, and stay on the path as some are hidden. The track emerges on Tararu Creek Rd. From there, turn left to go back or right to reach a well-kept secret, the 3m **Black Hole Waterfall** that slides over into the deep pool below (about 2.6km up Tararu Creek Rd. from the entrance to the **Dickson Holiday Park;** ask there for more specific directions).

One of the loveliest activities in Thames is leaving it, only because the winding, narrow, and scenic 55km drive to Coromandel, with rocky inlets and small bays, is so tempting. The views over **Coromandel Harbour** when the road turns inland will undoubtedly make you pull over. Notable trees on the way can be found at the **Waiomu Kauri Grove,** one of the peninsula's finest old-growth stands (a 1hr. walk through farmland and bush from the end of Waiomu Creek Rd., 15km from Thames). About 5km further is the turn-off for the **Tapu-Coroglen Rd.,** which cuts across the peninsula to rejoin SH25. Head up it for a few kilometers and look for the sign marking a steep 10-minute walk through gorgeous native bush to the 1200-year-old "square kauri tree," 15th largest in the Coromandel. It's worth the quick detour.

■ Coromandel Forest Park

The jagged hills of the discontinuous 72,000-hectare Coromandel Forest Park are thick with regenerating bush, tangled with creepers, and sluiced by high waterfalls and small fern-lined creeks. Hiding deep within the hills that stretch up the peninsula's volcanic backbone are many of the old kauri dams and mine shafts, side by side with the few remaining patches of original forest. Active replanting efforts of native species are underway, as are rigorous pest management techniques (especially in the north, where possums have not fully infiltrated). You'll find plenty of walks in the Kauaeranga Valley east of Thames, as well as some remote walkways in the peninsular fingertip (see p. 138).

Fallen Giants

As gorgeously scenic as it may be, the Coromandel is in many ways a case study in human rapacity—its very name is taken from a Royal Navy vessel that collected massive kauri logs from the peninsula in 1820. The knot-free wood and huge, straight trunks of these noble trees were coveted for ship masts and buildings. By the 1870s, the last of the easily extractable stands disappeared, and logging moved into the area's mountainous ridges, where the insatiable quest for timber led to ever-more-elaborate innovations in tree removal. To get trees off the remote hilltops, logs were dragged, trammed, or rolled into streambeds where they accumulated behind dams. As water built up, loggers tripped the dams, releasing floods of trees that crashed down the valleys in a wasteful process that damaged the logs and gouged out the streambed. Between logging and burning the land for farming, less than 1% of the region's forest survived the short-sighted exploitation. Although today you can see more of the original kauri wood in San Francisco and Auckland buildings than in the forest, much of the irreparably altered (but regenerating) landscape on the peninsula has been set aside as part of the Coromandel Forest Park.

The **Kauaeranga Field Centre** (tel. 868 6381) lies 13km up Kauaeranga Valley Rd., a winding half-paved job that branches off at the BP station at the south end of Thames (open daily 8am-4pm). Stop in before you head up to clarify your plans or fill out help forms. There's also a small **DOC office** with irregular hours in the town of Coromandel. Getting up Kauaeranga Valley without your own transportation is a mild pain, especially at non-peak times (though on weekends year-round and in summer it's generally hitchable). Thumbers are sure to arrange a return ride before hitting the trails, or they run the risk of getting stuck 9km from park headquarters at the end of the road where most trails start. **The Sunkist Lodge** occasionally runs a shuttle service ($36 round-trip). **Thames Gold Cabs** can also take you up for a heady $36 one-way. With your own car it's no problem—just don't leave those passports on the dashboard.

DOC campgrounds are liberally scattered in the park, with eight off the road up Kauaeranga Valley and four at the tip (see p. 138). The **Kauaeranga** sites are basic ($5). The only hut in the park is the **Pinnacles Hut,** a rugged Ritz with views, a year-round warden, wood stove, gas cooking (bring your own utensils), 80 mattresses with fitted sheets, solar lighting, and toilets ($12, book in advance; annual or other hut passes not applicable). It's about a three-hour climb from the road end, including swing bridges and 1080 steps carved into rock. Three other primitive, remote areas for camping are in the vicinity ($6).

Numerous trails criss-cross the Coromandel and signs of human influence (including old mine shafts and deteriorating kauri dams) are everywhere, making much of the park historic as well as naturally attractive. **Kauaeranga Valley** is the most hiked spot, with walks heading off the road. A five-minute hop from the visitors center leads to an old intact kauri dam and the bludgeoned streambed it helped carve out. A trip from the **Wainora campground** (2-3hr. round-trip) leads to two of the valley's only surviving large kauri. **The Kauaeranga Kauri Trail** heads up to Pinnacles Hut and the **Pinnacles** themselves, sheer jagged bluffs like fins arcing out of emerald water. It's well worth the 1000-plus stairs through fern-laden regenerating bush, by deep gorges, and over swing bridges. Atop the Pinnacles, an hour from the Hut, the views all across the peninsula will take away any breath you have left after scrambling up ladders and a steep rocky trail. Some do it as a day hike, others as an overnight. The **Kauaeranga River,** running along the road up the valley, sports tons of swimming holes. Find your own, or check out **Hoffman's Pool,** a two-minute walk down the Nature Walk with deep greenish waters and jumping rocks. Rockhounds get a big kick out of the Coromandel: geological hammers are allowed in the park (undoubtedly the first thing you packed) and up to 2kg of surface rock can be removed per day (check with DOC for details).

■ Coromandel

The isolated town of Coromandel is home to artisans, individualists, and country bumpkins united in their love of location. With the mesmerizingly blue waters of Coromandel Harbour dotted with little isles and the deep greens of the hills sweeping up above town, there's not much else to do in town but be visually stimulated by the environs and aesthetically pleased by the plethora of little craft shops. New Zealand's first gold was found in them thar hills in 1852, but the prospects proved less than boundless: though at one time there were over 10,000 residents, the town never quite reached Thames's gaudy proportions.

ORIENTATION AND PRACTICAL INFORMATION Most shops and services lie right where **Tiki Rd.** (SH25 from the south) meets **Kapanga Rd.,** which turns into **Wharf Rd.** on its western side to wrap around the harbor, and into **Rings Rd.** at the other end to snake on up the peninsula. The **Coromandel Information Centre** (tel. 866 8598) lies on Kapanga Rd. just across the creek. Staffed by a volunteer force, it's well organized and friendly (open in summer daily 9am-5pm, in winter M-F 9am-5pm, Sa-Su 10am-2pm). The small **DOC office,** with irregular hours, is in the same building. The local **BNZ** (tel. 866 8876), at the corner of Tiki and Kapanga Rd., is the only bank (**no ATM**; open M-F 10am-3pm). The two-man pink cottage of a **police station** (tel. 866 8777) is next to the information center. Send a hand-crafted postcard from the **post office,** 190 Kapanga Rd. (tel./fax 866 8865; open M-F 9am-5pm). The **telephone code** is **07.**

Like most of the Peninsula, transport services change rapidly and vary considerably by season—check with the information center for up-to-date schedules. The **Coromandel Busplan** InterCity bus passes through to Whitianga (1hr., in summer 11:30am daily, in winter 4 per week, $14 if not part of Busplan), continuing to Thames (3hr., $14) but you can go direct to Thames with **Turley Murphy** (1hr., 7:30am, in summer daily, in winter Su-F; $12), and on to Hamilton (3½hr., $34). **Coromandel Bus Service** runs to Whitianga Monday, Wednesday, and Friday at 8:30am ($13) and to Fletcher's Bay Monday, Wednesday, and Friday at noon ($17). The **Pakatoa Cat Ferry** runs daily in summer (about 4 per week in winter) to Auckland (2hr., one-way $31, children $15.50, bicycles $10). The ticketing office is at 24 Kapanga Rd. (tel. 866 7084; open daily 9am-5pm, or earlier, depending on ferries). **Hitchhiking** is reportedly easy to Thames and only slightly more difficult to Whitianga. The 25A Rd. that turns off just past the fire station on Tiki Rd. is more heavily traveled and considered a better spot than the 309 Rd. Hitching northward in winter is difficult, and you may get stranded. Several local accommodations rent bicycles.

ACCOMMODATIONS AND FOOD Coromandel has quite a few good backpackers and motor camps in secluded bays. Homestays spring up in the holiday season, often in the homes of local artists trying to supplement their incomes. Book ahead in January and February, or you certainly won't be sharing the town's relaxing vibes after hours of searching for a bed. **Summer/winter rates** are listed.

About 1km north, at the corner of Rings Rd. and Frederick St., sit the three airy white cottages of **White House Backpackers (VIP)** (tel. 866 8468). Owner Richard organizes driving and fishing trips (under $50; daytrips for 3 or more to Castle Rock, Hahei, and Hot Water Beach $35) and group trips anywhere. The backpackers offers free pickup from town. (4-bed dorms $14; 2-bed dorm $16.50 per person doubles $30.) Up a steep little hill on Alfred St. off Rings Rd., 1km from the town center, sits **Motel Celadon** (tel. 866 8058). You'll never want to leave the lovely, self-contained cottage, glowing with shiny wood, original artwork, and unbeatable views. Hospitable owner Ray Morley even gives pottery lessons. (Cottage $80/$70 for 2, extra person $10. Bed and breakfast unit $70/$60. Studio unit that sleeps 3-4 $70/$60. 10% discount with copy of *Let's Go* book.)

Tidewater Tourist Park (YHA), 270 Tiki Rd. (tel. 866 8888), is fresh and immaculate, with venetian blinds and a small kitchen. Sauna and mountain bike rentals are available ($10 per day). Compact shares are $15; twins and doubles $34. Try not to track mud into the spacious white tourist flats. (Singles $60/50; doubles $70/60, extra person $12/10.) Book far in advance December-March for beds, though there's generally a bit of room on the grass expanse for tents ($9). In peak months you'll be good buddies with the tent next door, at **Long Bay Motor Camp** (tel. 866 8720), 3km out on Wharf/Long Bay Rd., you can always resolutely look out into the blue waters or march through acres of bush to the secluded back-to-basics **Tucks Bay** campground (metered showers. Tent sites $9; powered $11; Tucks Bay tent sites $8). **Tui Lodge,** 600 Whangapoua Rd. (tel. 866 8237), from Kapanga/Wharf Rd. turn on to Tiki Rd. by the BNZ, then left on to Whangapoua Rd. The lodge is 500m on the right, down a gravel drive. With sheep grazing in the front pasture and an orchard in back, adjustment to Coromandel time is made easy. Stroll the grounds with a free cup of tea or coffee to the musical accompaniment of the tui birds or explore the town (5min. ride) on one of the free bikes. (Free laundry and in-season fruit. Sauna $2. Dorms $14; doubles/twins $28; tents $8; private, self-contained camper unit is $12 bargain.)

The Pepper Tree Restaurant and Bar (tel. 866 8211), on Kapanga Rd. in the town center, specializes in fresh seafood and organic beef. You'll have to shell out a bit, but the food gets better with every bite. (Scallop and steak dinners $19-24, delicious mussel fritters under $13.) Eat by the open fire, or outdoors where live entertainment fills the gazebo in summer. (Open daily in summer from 9am, in winter from 11am.) For veggie options or more affordable dinners, head to **The Deli** on Wharf Rd. The colorful secret garden out back is great for sitting and savoring Monday night pizza specials (small $8, large $12) and those infamous soy milk lattes (open daily from 9am; all day breakfasts). Be sure to check out the (witch) crafts shop next door. If bread is all you need to survive, the **Bakehouse** on Wharf Rd. has a full range of cheap rolls and large loaves as well as hot pies ($2) and tasty pastries (open daily 7:30am-4pm). Stock up at **Price Cutter** (tel. 866 8669), on Kapanga Rd. just before the bridge. (Open M-F 7:30am-6pm, Sa 7:30am-4pm, Su 9am-2pm, with longer hours in the holidays.) Organic produce is sold at **Myrrh and Cinnamon Health Foods,** 65 Wharf St. (tel. 866 7553).

SIGHTS AND ACTIVITIES The crafty side of things is unavoidable in Coromandel; luckily, that's not such a bad thing. Local artists create and display their pottery, weaving, embroidery, sculpture, woodwork, and more in the area's many shops. **Weta Shop** (tel. 866 8823) on Kapanga Rd. is the best of the lot, offering quality over quantity with both local and national art, crafts, and sculpture in the outdoor courtyard. Aside from crafts, Coromandel's biggest attraction is the **Driving Creek Railway** (tel./fax 866 8703), 3km north of town. Begun as a pet project in 1975 to extract clay and pinewood kiln fuel from his hills, owner and potter Barry Brickell has spent 20 years developing a narrow gauge railway snaking up through glowingly green regenerating forest, through tunnels, around spirals, and over bridges to the views from the terminus. *(Rides $12, children $5, families $22. Backpacker/student discount $1. Rides at 10am and 2pm in winter, hourly in summer.)* Although the rail is mostly a tourist attraction (over 35,000 people came along for the hour-long trip last year), it's still used to transport kauri seedlings up and clay down to the potters who work and sell wares at the base shop. The **Coromandel Gold Stamper Battery** (tel. 866 7186), on Buffalo Rd. off Rings Rd. north of town, is operational and set in a suitably verdant nook with a short bush walk and New Zealand's largest working water wheel. *(Open in summer daily 10am-5pm; in winter ask at the visitors center before heading up. Admission to the displays $2; tours, by arrangement, cost a bit more.)* Relive the way it never was panning for "guaranteed" gold ($5.)

A short but terrific stroll (25min.) through the **Long Bay Scenic Reserve** to a grove of young kauris starts at the Long Bay campground. It winds back along the rocky waters of the bay where the walk can stretch into a lazy afternoon of sunning and exploring. Pay your respects to the **Waiau Kauri Grove,** 8km down the horrifically narrow and gravely **309 Rd.,** which branches off 4km south of town to cross over to Whitianga. Walk for ten minutes to join other gape-mouthed visitors in this cathedral of soaring trees that once covered the peninsula, and is now preserved only in such scattered pockets of grandeur. If you have no transport, try **Carter Tours** (tel. 866 8045 or (025) 937 259), which runs trips just about wherever. *(Four hour trips $30-40; min. 2 people.)* The climb up to **Castle Rock** (2hr. round-trip), an exposed vertebra of the peninsula's volcanic backbone, offers panoramas to which a camera can't do justice. The trailhead is 2km up a forest road that turns off the 309 Rd. just past Waiau Waterworks. The trailhead is a two-hour bike ride from Coromandel Town.

■ Near Coromandel: The Northern Tip

North of Coromandel, no posh lodgings cater to rich city slickers and no quaint craft shops or heavy-duty gold stamper batteries dot the region. Here, the wealth is of unmitigated natural beauty: jumbled green hills, deserted crescents of bays, and a wild coastline broken up only by sheep placidly gnawing on undulating farmland. The spectacular **Coromandel Walkway,** between Fletcher Bay and Stony Bay, is worth any effort it takes to get there.

The quality of roads in the region is inversely proportional to the "gasp" factor— the harrowing, narrow gravel roads add to the charm, though they have a tendency to flood out in rain. One road winds up the west side to Fletcher Bay at the tip of the tip; another branches off just past **Colville** (28km north of Coromandel), and finds its way to Stony Bay. Public transport is slim. Before heading out in your own rental car, make sure there's no fine print in your rental agreement about this area. **Coromandel Buses** (tel. 866 8468), in Coromandel, runs a shuttle up to **Fletcher Bay** (M, W, F; $17). Winter **hitchhiking** in the Northern Tip is all but impossible, though some hitch in summer (once past Colville thumbers should be sure that their ride is going all the way). Mountain biking is a great but very strenuous way to circuit the tip on the track connecting Fletcher Bay and Stony Bay.

Fletcher Bay Backpackers (tel. 866 8989) has an enviable location, next to the Coromandel Walkway trailhead. Within spitting distance of the ocean, Fletcher's is a base for tramps into the bush or along the coast as well as prime territory peaceful meditation. Owned by DOC, Fletcher's has 16 beds; bookings are essential (dorms $13). DOC manages five basic campgrounds in the northern region ($5). Check in with **DOC** (tel. 866 6852) to book the one at **Waikawau Bay** during the summer holidays. The well-stocked **Colville General Store** (tel. 866 6805) is the last place for groceries and gas in the tip. (Open in winter M-F 8:30am-5pm, Sa 9am-5pm, Su 9am-4:30pm, later in summer.)

The peninsula's crowning track, the 10.7km **Coromandel Walkway** (3hr. one-way) explores lonely bays and coves, passes turquoise waters along the coast between Fletcher and Stony Bays, and dips into inlets and bushy valleys. Other than a few short, stiff climbs, it's not difficult, though it can be a bit hairy in winter before it's cleared for the summer season (it overgrows quickly). You can return from the walkway by the same route, on the masochistic 7km mountain bike track, or have someone pick you up at the other end. **Carter Tours** (tel. 866 8045 or (025) 937 259) will do drop-offs and pickups in summer ($50, min. 2 people). Another great hike goes up the peninsula's tallest mountain, 892m **Mt. Moehau.** As the top is Maori land, you're requested to turn back just as you get tantalizingly close. Approachable from several points, the peak is perhaps more easily reached from **Te Hope Stream,** 12km north of Colville (5hr. return). The more strenuous **Stony Bay** route follows an exposed ridge (taking most of a day).

■ Whitianga

Whitianga ("fit-ee-ANG-guh") is the Coromandel's second major town (pop. 4000) after Thames. Located in attractive **Mercury Bay,** the scenic area is enough to inspire a little land lust in just about anyone. A small town born of timber (over 500 million feet of kauri were cut in 60 years), Whitianga is now the Coromandel's main resort town, surviving on tourism. Its population increases tenfold during the summer, when it seems like every angler, boater, and beach bum from Auckland descends on

Whitianga to plumb its rich, deep-sea fishing waters, explore its nearby marine reserve, or loaf on its many beaches.

ORIENTATION AND PRACTICAL INFORMATION Whitianga sits where **Mercury Bay's** sweep of palm-studded beach meets the calm waters of **Whitianga Harbour.** The route to **Hahei, Hot Water Beach,** and points beyond is a lengthy detour around the harbor, but the ferry crossing takes only a minute. **SH25** runs along the beach as **Buffalo Rd.,** and turns south to become **Albert St.,** the town's main drag.

The **Whitianga Information Centre,** 66 Albert St. (tel. 866 5555; fax 866 2205), is run under the umbrella of the Business Association—non-member outfitters don't get mentioned. (Open Dec.-Mar. M-Sa 8am-6pm, Su 8:30am-5:30pm; Apr.-Nov. M-F 9am-5pm, Sa-Su 9am-1pm except July and Aug. when closed Su). The **Westpac Trust Bank** (tel. 866 5246), on Albert St. by Monk St., has a **24-hr. ATM** (bank open M-Tu, Th-F 9am-4:30pm, W 9:30am-4:30pm). Book transportation at the **Information Centre** or through **Travel Options** (tel. 866 4397), diagonal from the information center (open M-F 9am-5pm, Sa 10am-noon). **Air Coromandel** (tel. (0800) 900 600) flies from the airstrip off SH25 south of town to Auckland (2 per day, $89) and Great Barrier Island (30min., 2 per week, $75). More flights and destinations may be added during the summer season. The **ferry** (tel. 866 5472) heads across the harbor's neck to Ferry Landing. (In summer 7:30am-11pm; in winter 7:30am-noon, 1-6:30pm, limited evening service; $1.50 round-trip.) Buses leave from the information center. The **Coromandel Busplan** buses leave for Dalmeny Corner (in summer 2 per day, in winter 3 per week, 1:15pm) with a connection to Hahei and Hot Water Beach, and on to Thames (1hr., $24). To get to Whangamata, take the bus to Hikuai (1:15pm) to be picked up by **Whangamata Tours** (tel. 866 4397; InterCity affiliate) at 2:15pm (1½hr., $29). **Mercury Bay Taxis** (tel. 866 5643) will also do a run to Coromandel for $50 per van load (van fits 10).

Whitianga Mowers and Cycles, 15 Coghill St. (tel. 866 5435), a block from the information center, rents mountain bikes. (Half-day $10, full-day $20; $25 deposit. Open Dec.-Jan. daily; Feb.-Nov. M-F 8:30am-5pm, Sa 9am-noon.) In an **emergency,** dial **111.** Your friendly neighborhood **police** (24hr. tel. 866 4000) are on Campbell St., around the corner from the **post office** (tel./fax 866 4006; open M-Tu, Th-F 8:30am-5pm, W 9:30am-5pm). The **telephone code** is **07.**

ACCOMMODATIONS AND FOOD As a summer resort town, Whitianga has more than its share of motels, motor camps, and other lodgings. There are three good hostel options, though the steady flow of Kiwi Experience buses affects each differently. The independent traveler's choice, about 1km from downtown, is **Coromandel Backpacker's Lodge,** 46 Buffalo Beach Rd. (tel./fax 866 5380), a sea-green abode with smart, well-heated accommodation in winter, and the cheapest ocean views in town year-round. Airy dorms upstairs have window seats to watch the breeding dotterels in the bird reserve across the street; downstairs twins and doubles offer privacy and separate communal areas. Gracious owners, a courtesy van, and a miniature visitors center are welcome amenities. Rent a bike ($15 per day) or enjoy free use of kayaks, surfboards, fishing rods, and shovels for Hot Water Beach (dorms $15; doubles or twins $17.50 per person; linen, towel included). A javelin toss from the town center off Albert St. lies the **The Cat's Pyjamas Backpackers Lodge,** 4 Monk St. (tel./fax 866 4663). Two immense ginger cats and one black one sidle around this unassuming hostel with a simple residential house feel. Ask Buster, the affable owner, about yacht trips ($50) and scenic flights in the plane he built out back. (Dorms $15; doubles or twins $17.50 per person.) Catering almost exclusively to the busloads of Kiwi Experience bar hoppers, **Buffalo Peaks Lodge,** 12 Albert St. (tel. 866 2933), shows none of the wear and tear you might expect. Bright and clean with an internal courtyard, spa, and lively murals of New Zealand icons, Buffalo Peaks may be worth the reservation it will likely take to arrange a bed. (Dorms $17.50; doubles $38.) **The Mercury Bay Motor Camp,** 121 Albert St. (tel. 866 5579), is a half a kilometer south of the town center, with standard motor camp facilities. Showers are metered in summer. Close to the marina, if not the beachfront, they rent kayaks ($20 per day) and mountain bikes ($10 per day). Compact cabins cost $25 per adult (extra person $10, in peak season min. $55); spiffy tourist flats run $38 per adult (in peak season $95, extra person $12); grassy tent and caravan sites are $9 ($20min. Dec. 24-Jan. 31).

Dining out is essentially a contradiction in terms in Whitiaga. There is, fortunately, a diamond in the rough—the little overgrown cottage housing lovely **Cafe Nina** (tel. 866 5440), on Victoria St. at the back side of the park. The savory fruit muffins will melt in your mouth. Lunches ($6-9) have some veggie fare, as well as takeaway sandwiches and cakes. (Open M-Sa 8am-6pm, Su 8am-4pm; lunch served noon-2:30pm.) There are a few standard takeaway and pub options. Locals recommend **Pratty's Takeaways** (tel. 866 5557), on the corner of Buffalo Beach Rd. and Albert St. by the water, for fresher fish at better value (fish 'n' chips for $4.30; open M-Th 11am-9pm, F-Sa 11am-10pm). Head to **Four Square** (tel. 866 5777), on Albert St. by the information center, for groceries (open M-F 7am-6pm, Sa 8am-6pm, later hours in summer). Fruits and veggies can be had at **W. Fresh** across the street (open M-F 7:30am-5:30pm, Sa 7:30am-1pm).

SIGHTS AND ACTIVITIES An excellent option for the painful day after too much sun and too little sunscreen is a chance to do your own bone carving. Maurice of **Bay Carving** (tel. 866 4021), at Aotearoa Lodge on Racecourse Rd. (turn left off Buffalo Beach Rd. 1km out of town, or call for a pickup) will help you choose from an array of designs or create your own, plunking you down in the studio with a chunk of beef bone, dentist's drills, files, and sandpaper. The end result, from tracing paper to polished pendant in three hours or so, is amazingly satisfying. Designs (and tutelage) cost $25-45 (call ahead to schedule, especially in summer; open daily 9am-9pm).

Head across the river on the ferry to follow the path in the small **Scenic Reserve** just to the right, leading along the water's edge up to the 24m bluff of **Whitianga Rock** (a historic Maori *pa* from which stone for the old ferry landing wharf was taken). The walk from **Ferry Landing** up to the **Shakespeare Lookout** is worth the hour or so it takes (you can also drive). Named for a certain resemblance to the Bard in its rocky profile, it's a jaunt along **Front Beach** to the crescent of **Flaxmill Bay,** and a steep meander up from the sign on the pohutukawa at the far end. The view from the top is expansive and includes as a bonus a clear view of **Lonely Bay** below—the only legal nude beach on the Coromandel. Isolated from any unsightly view of buildings and roads, the pristine little cove's golden sands and turquoise surf are accessible only by boat, or by the steep footpath down from Shakespeare Lookout. The next beach over is **Cooks Beach,** a shallow 3km stretch of prime swimming. **Buffalo Beach,** directly on the shores of Whitianga, is named for the HMS Buffalo that wrecked there in 1840 while collecting kauri for England.

The untouched beauty of the peninsula is the perfect setting for a horse trek. **Twin Oaks** (tel. 866 5555), 9km north of town on the road to Kuaotunu, offers two-hour saunters for riders of any skill through farmland and to the top of a ridge with dramatic 360° views of the peninsula. *($25. Three per day in summer; less consistent in winter. Transport possible; call ahead.)* **Purangi Winery** (tel. 866 3724) is perfectly situated on the main road between Ferry Landing and the Hahei and Hot Water Beach area (Hot Water Beach ConXtions stops here). The rustic, all-organic winery makes 23 varieties of fruit wines, ports, and liquors, and you can taste them all in succession. *(Open for tastings daily in summer 9am-9pm, in winter 10am-5pm.)* The passionfruit liquor and boysenberry port are must-tastes.

It's that blue, blue water and what's in it that draws most people to the Mercury Bay area. With **Cathedral Cove Marine Reserve** nearby, the cluster of the Mercury Bay Islands off the coast, and thriving ocean life, every kind of water activity from snorkelling to banana boating can be found here. Whitianga is one of New Zealand's best bases for big game **fishing** from December to March. Ask around locally for recommended outfitters if you're planning on fishing, kayaking, or seeking Flipper and other marine mammals. There's even a glass-bottomed boat or two. If rough seas turn your sights inland, abseiling and scenic flights are also possibilities. **Air Coromandel** (tel. (0800) 900 600) flies all over the peninsula from $30 for a 15-minute hop to hour-long $99 flights up to the Northern Tip.

■ Near Whitianga: Hahei

The name sounds like a combination of the sigh of inevitable contentment and the exclamation of finger-pointing glee that you'll likely utter while here: Hah-hey! In reality, it stems from chief Hei of the Arawa canoe that docked somewhere off the coast, a contraction of a name that in full means "the outward curve of Hei's nose." A nose by any other name would smell just as sweet in this blissful swath of sand made pink by crushed shells. **Hot Water Beach ConXtions** (tel. 866 2478) has great service to these parts, making a circuit between Ferry Landing, Hahei, Hot Water Beach, and Cooks Beach, with narration and short stops for lookouts on the way. (In summer 2-3 per day from 7:30am to 5:30pm. If low tide at Hot Water Beach is early, they arrange for a special earlier ferry run. A $15 Explorer Bus Pass lets you on and off all day, or you can travel each segment independently.) The drivers can help you figure out when to get the bus you want. ConXtions also meets the **InterCity** bus from Whitianga to Thames to bring people into Hahei or Hot Water Beach ($15 round-trip to the bus; $6 more as an add-on to the Explorer Pass).

   Tatahi Lodge (tel. 866 3992; fax 866 3993) is almost reason enough to stay here instead of Whitianga. Its lovely glowing wood lodge, plush couches, lounge, and numerous windows are meant for post-beach bliss. Bikes are also for hire. (Dorms $15; doubles or twins $36.) Not quite as spiffy is the equitably priced **Hahei Holiday Resort** and its accompanying **Cathedral Cove Backpackers Lodge (VIP)** (tel. 866 3889; fax 866 3098), at the end of Harsant Ave. off the town's main road. The dorms ($15) are behind Japanese screens, which are classy but don't quite meet the ceiling, while doubles or twins ($18) are more soundproof. There's almost always room for international travelers, but call ahead. Best of all, it's just over the dune from the beach. (Tent sites $9.50, powered $11; campervan sites $10. Double cabins $34-43.)

   Hahei's beach, sheltered by offshore islands, is reportedly great for swimming but bad for surfing—many surfers instead head to Hot Water Beach. Once you get tired of tanning, point those feet in either direction and start walking. To the south rises a dramatic bluff, **Hereheretaura Point,** an understandably ideal spot for an old defensive Maori *pa;* cross the creek at the beach's end and follow the path up to the *pa* (30min.) for 360° views. To the north, around a green hill, gaze out at the small islands speckling the ocean and amble down to the Coromandel's ultimate poster: the **Cathedral Cove Marine Reserve (Te Whanganui-a-Hei).** You can either walk from the beach or turn left past the general store to reach the hour-long track (45min. from the carpark atop the hill) to the cove. The track passes through pastures and descending hundreds of steps, wending along through bush, toward the jewels that make the track one of New Zealand's most visited. The white sands and lapping turquoise waters of **Gemstone Bay** and **Stingray Bay** beg a wade or a snorkel in their lucid waters but are themselves merely preludes to their neighbors: **Mare's Leg Cove** (so named by Cook for the now washed-away soaring 10m archway), and **Cathedral Cove** itself. With its pristine beach and arcing rock formations, it's an idyllic spot of subtropical water hemmed by high white bluffs accessible only though a stone archway carved out by the sea (which can fill to the waist at high tide). You can swim out to the warped stone formations, like forgotten sculptures in the shallows, or stand under the freshwater falls trickling over the white cliffs.

   Nigel and his **Hahei Explorer** (tel. 866 3910) will help those unable to make the trek to Cathedral Cave by foot. *(Dec.-Feb. $12.50 one-way, $20 round-trip.)* At any time of year you can take one of his spectacular scenic trips (1hr., $35), to explore the local islands, hidden caves and archways, and a spectacular 30m blowhole. Though the little rigid-hull inflatable boats fit only seven and bounces in high waves, they can go anywhere, and you'd surely never find all the excitement (or pull 360°s) on your own (4 per day in summer, usually on demand in winter). He also rents mountain bikes ($25 per day) and snorkel gear ($25 per day).

■ Near Whitianga: Hot Water Beach

Imagine a beach hidden on the eastern side of the Coromandel, where you could take a little shovel, dig a little hole, and watch hot water fill in to create your own ocean-side thermal pool. Now stop imagining—it's true. Proving once again that Mother Nature can outdo the resort industry any day, the 30-50m golden crescent of steaming sands is a free spa, percolating with water as hot as 65°C. Rent a cheap shovel from the beachfront store (open daily 9am-5pm), and for two hours on either side of low tide you can soak in your own dug-out series of pools while watching for dolphins or surfers off-shore. Although cyclones in early 1997 removed several meters of sand, bringing out the "Hot" in "Hot Water Beach," the absolute must-do of the Coromandel is building up again. In summer yours probably won't be the only set of legs poking up out of the sand, as 1500 people try to dig or hijack pools in the somewhat limited space at once. (Avoid coming in January if you can; it's delightfully empty the rest of the year and always a toasty treat.) The beach is beautiful, but the rips, reefs, and sandbars that give good surfing breaks also make for treacherous swimming. **Hot Water Beach ConXtions** (tel. 866 2473) runs by several times daily on its circuit ($15 Explorer pass), and also picks up from the holiday park to meet the **InterCity** at Dalmeny Corner on its way to Thames (1-2 per day, $15 round-trip or $21 including the Explorer Pass). They rent shovels for $2, as well. You can have dibs on the best holes at the beachfront at **Hot Water Beach Holiday Park** (tel. 866 3735), a small and tree-lined park that can cram up to 400 in its tent, caravan, and campervan sites ($12 in summer, $8 in winter). Tourist flats (max. 8) are $80-100. If it's high tide, there's consolation at the indoor thermal pools.

■ Whangamata

Best known for the swath of beach even longer and prettier than its name (Wahn-ga-mah-TAH), Whangamata's four kilometers of white sand sweeping around an island-studded bay are known from here to Raglan as one of the North Island's top surf spots. Outside the summer crunch of surfers and vacationers, with more beachfront and thick-on-the-hills bachs (holiday homes) than people, small Whangamata remains sleepily residential, carefree, and full of easygoing locals. You'll always be within a board's length of beach and bush here.

ORIENTATION AND PRACTICAL INFORMATION Snug against its boomerang of beach at the mouth of the long and narrow **Whangamata Harbour** (for which a controversial and snazzy new marina has been proposed), the town is a maze of residential streets. Any and all action centers on **Port Rd.**, the main street that runs into SH25 at either end. Moored at 616 Port St. is the **Whangamata Information Centre** (tel. 865 8340), a low-key volunteer center (open M-Sa 9am-5pm, Su 10am-1pm). Not far up the street is **Westpac Trust Bank** (tel. 865 9771; open M-F 9 or 9:30am to 4:30pm). The **post shop** (tel./fax 865 8230) is on Port St., by the bank (open M-F 8:30am-5pm, Sa 9am-noon). The **telephone code** is **07**.

Whangamata's ring of hills currently deters major bus lines from coming up the winding roads, but the situation is set to change shortly. Call the visitors center for the most recent update, or **Whangamata Travel and Services,** 640 Port St. (tel. 865 8776), to make bookings (open M-F 9am-5pm). At least until the changes take effect, **Whangamata Tours** (tel. 865 7088) offers a shuttle out to the bump in the road of Hikuai as well as to Opoutere ($8, students $6) to meet the **InterCity** bus to Thames (30min.; in summer daily, in winter 4 per week; $12, students/YHA $9); or to Waihi (30min.; in summer M-Sa 2 per day, in winter M and F 2 per day; $12, $9) for connections to Tauranga and points further afield. Trying to get to Whitianga from here entails waiting three hours at Hikuai for the 4pm bus from Thames—don't try to defy the Coromandel's clockwise transport system.

ACCOMMODATIONS AND FOOD You could imitate the local surfers and hole up in your car, or you could take your pick of Whangamata's lodgings. The pine-green dome at the brand new **Bedshed** (tel. (0800) 659 580), on Port St. 500m from the town center, houses the most upscale backpackers lodge you're likely to see, with wall-to-wall carpeting and a surround-sound video theater. The owner doesn't take bookings so she can pick out the "right people" who will obey the strict no-alcohol policy around the summer holidays. (Shares from $18; doubles from $40; motel units start at $129 for 2 for 2 nights in winter. Linen $2.50 per night.) By the beach on Beverly Terr., and behind the Pricecutters on Ocean Rd., you'll find the **Whangamata Backpackers Hostel** (tel. 865 8323). You won't be afraid to toss a wetsuit over the mismatched chairs and beds in this tired but comfy house with the ocean a minute away. Low-key owners Barbara and Pauline will agreeably give out sporting gear. (All beds $15.) Park your tent across the fence from chomping sheep at the **Pinefield Holiday Park** (tel./fax 865 8791), 1km or so south on Port St. Standard communal facilities, a swimming pool, and usually a few campervan sites are open for international travelers. (Caravan and tent sites $11; basic cabin shares $15; well-sized cabins for 2 with kitchen $45; terrific chalet doubles start at $65.)

Vibes Cafe (tel. 865 7121), spreads good ones with great espresso, cheap vegetarian melts, pitas and burgers (under $5), and the only sushi on the Coromandel ($5 for 6 pieces). Sit back and ponder the local artwork, joke with the sociable staff, or wait for an old surfing great to drop in. (Open M-Sa 9am-ish-5:30pm-ish, and also Su in summer.) Those with picky palates will find a friend at **Ginger's Health Foods and Cafe** (tel. 865 7265), where you can get your vegan wheat- or gluten-free products. Made-to-order sandwiches from $2.60 feature options like tahini, hummus, guacamole, or good ol' chicken. They pack lunches for $6-9—call the night before your hike or cruise. (Open daily 7am-5pm.) Revel in the classically unauthentic nature of **La Hacienda** (tel. 865 8351), where $3.50 tacos overflow into their paper sack, and burritos and nachos ($5) can be devoured on the patio (open 24hr. in peak; daily 11am-8pm in summer; weekends only in winter). Get your groceries at the **Four Square** at Port and Ocean Rd. (open daily 7am-7pm), or **Quarry Orchards** (tel. 865 8282), next to the post office, with veggies and bulk food (open in summer daily 7:30am-6pm, in winter M-Sa 8:30am-5:30pm).

ACTIVITIES Most come to Whangamata for the beach: to marinate, to take low-tide wades out to the hulk of **Hauturu Island** just off-shore, to check out shorebirds in the estuary reserve at its south end, or just to play in the big waves that draw surfers from all over. Especially good breaks are found near the harbor mouth. **Whangamata Surf Shop**, 634 Port St. (tel. 865 8252), is owned by a long-time surfer who makes new rental boards every winter ($18 per half-day, $25 per day), and rents boogie boards and fins ($12, $18), as well as wetsuits ($5 per day; open daily 9am-5pm). Surfcasting and game fishing for off-shore tuna and marlin are also good around Whangamata.

Whangamata is surrounded by green hills and close to the good trails and biking opportunities of the 11,500-hectare **Tairua Forest**, north of town. The forest is mostly a pine timber plantation, with roads rugged enough to please any mountain biker for a few hours. Whangamata's premier natural area is the **Wentworth Valley,** on the turn-off 3km south of town on SH25. The river valley's several walks are strewn with mine shafts and relics from turn-of-the-century days. A telegraph line between Auckland and Wellington was diverted here during the Waikato land wars of the 1870s. A walk (1hr.) leaving from the basic campground ($6 sites) heads up to **Wentworth Falls.** The sea tunnel at **Pokohino Beach** leads at low tide to a rocky little cove where you can relax on isolated white sand. It's reachable via a short but steep walk from a carpark at the end of Pokohino Rd., a forest road that branches off Onemana Rd. 6km north of Whangamata on SH25.

Long before the buzzword ever got tossed about, **Kiwi Dundee** (a.k.a. Doug Johansen), based in Whangamata, was running one of New Zealand's most recognized ecotourism operations. *(Half-day trips $80 per person, full days $116; group rates available.)* His title was won in a country-wide contest to find a Kiwi to match the Aussies' Crocodile; today, Doug and his partner Jan Poole use the name for their adventure company (tel. 865 8809 or (025) 746 219). Each trip is tailored to your interest

WAIKATO & COROMANDEL

and ability, and all come with a passionately enthusiastic stream of superlatives, humor, and tidbits of natural history born of Doug's lifetime of exploring and fighting for conservation on the Coromandel.

■ Near Whangamata: Opoutere

Come live by the estuarine tides for a day or three and remember what silence can be, punctuated only by the shrieks of shorebirds, the chortles of tui and bellbirds, and the wash of surf along kilometers of one of the last utterly undeveloped beaches in the Coromandel. This is Opoutere, a magical nowhere, a 15-minutes drive north of Whangamata. The only lights between the YHA and the phone down the road are the constellations of glow-worms in the banks, the shining diamonds in the sky, and the sparkling phosphorescence in the water.

Lying on a harbor estuary at the mouth of the Wharekawa River, Opoutere (Oh-poh-tury) isn't a town—it's just a place, home to an idyllic hostel, motorcamp, and little else but 5km of perfect, lonesome beach. The **Wharekawa Harbour Sandspit Wildlife Reserve** here is one of New Zealand's few remaining nesting places for the threatened New Zealand dotterel (30-50 of the remaining 1200-odd individuals make their home here), and for the similarly scarce variable oystercatcher, a large black bird with shockingly pink extremities. During the nesting season (Oct.-Feb.), DOC tries to fence off and guard the ridiculously exposed sand where these birds nest (they require close to a 360° view of their environs). You can watch kingfishers dart above herons stalking their prey, digging with the oystercatchers for pockets of clam-like pipis to supplement dinner. Or ponder the waves and the jagged line of the **Alderman Islands** far offshore. Diving into the bush will scare up flighty fantails (small sparrow-like birds that the Maori believed brought death upon entering a home), as well as the other numerous native birds that constantly clamor around Opoutere, en route to the summit of **Maungaruawahine** *pa.*

Capitalizing on this oasis from civilization is the appropriately peaceful **Opoutere YHA Hostel** (tel. 865 9072), 4km in from the Opoutere turn-off from SH25 (follow the light of the glow-worms), north of Whangamata. Housed in a group of older school buildings, it's a communal oasis unto itself. There's no TV to interrupt the night—just a guitar for songs around the potbellied stove, and a big kitchen with solid redwood tables. Try some homemade yogurt, or take a free kayak out on the shallow estuary at high tide. (12-bed dorms $13; smaller shares $15; doubles or twins $18; tent sites $10; non-members $4 more.) About 1km down the road is the **Opoutere Park Beach Resort** (tel. 865 9152), at the far end of the estuary (open Sept.-May). Tent and caravan sites ($9.50) are afforded a bit of privacy by pine plantings; tourist flats for three ($48, 10% discount for 2 or more nights) and chalets ($66, same discount) are set near massive old pohutukawas some 200m from the beach through a pine forest. Although both places have limited stores, you should buy groceries before you come. **Whangamata Tours** (tel. 865 7088) runs through Opoutere from Whangamata on its connection with the **InterCity** bus from Whitianga at Hikuai (in summer daily, in winter 4 per week).

Taranaki and Wanganui

The looming mountain in the center of the North Island's westernmost outcrop defines its surrounding region, both in ancient mythology and contemporary tourism. Disagreement about its name underscores the difficulty of rapprochement between traditional Maori culture and European settlers, a semantic trouble that is shared with the city of Wanganui. (For more on the name of this looming mountain, see p. 151.) Mythology speaks of Taranaki as a restless, sorrowful place, and it is true that the mountain has the natural instability of a volcano. But superficially at least, the sorrow of legend is replaced with the joy of both visitors and residents greeting the area's many attractions. Year-round relaxation is afforded by Taranaki's balmy summer weather and gentle, wintry charm; life here is slow...and darn good. The rugged green slopes are among the richest dairyland in the world; Taranaki just might deserve its unofficial title as "the Udder of New Zealand." But it's also much more, for a unique mix of surf, snow, and river rescues Taranaki and Wanganui from bucolic blandness and places them on par with the best adventuring spots in the country.

💧 TARANAKI AND WANGANUI HIGHLIGHTS

- Egmont National Park (see p. 150) is host to excellent tramping and skiing.
- The Whanganui River (see p. 160) provides a mix of serenity and adventure for intrepid canoeists.

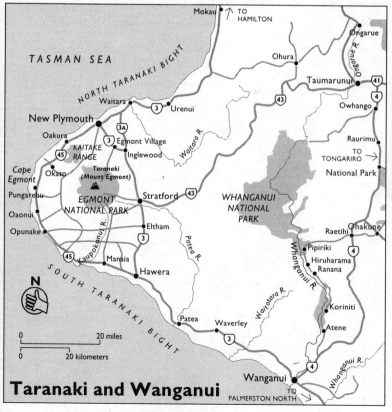

Taranaki and Wanganui

■ New Plymouth

Residents of New Plymouth love to point out that in one hour here, you can go from surfing in the Tasman to skiing on the slopes of Taranaki. While this is indeed an exciting proposition to outdoor sports enthusiasts, the city itself gets lost somewhere in between the sea and the snow. In fact, New Plymouth itself has quite a lot to offer, including excellent museums, mouth-watering cuisine, numerous outdoor public spaces, and lively weekends. The city is a walker's paradise; take the time to explore the interior before heading for the great outdoors.

PRACTICAL INFORMATION

Airport: Flight information (tel. 755 2250).
Buses: Depart from the **Travel Centre,** at the corner of King and Queen St. Open M-F 7:30am-5pm, Sa 7:30-8:10am and 1:30-2:45pm, Su 1:30-5pm. Free luggage storage for the day. **Intercity** (tel. 759 9039) and **Newmans** (tel. 757 5482) depart for Auckland (6¼hr., 2 per day, $69) via Hamilton (3¼hr., $46); for Wellington (6¾hr., 2 per day, $59) via Stratford (30min., $12); Hawera (1¼hr., $17), Wanganui (2½hr., $29) Palmerston North (4hr., $39), and Rotorua (6hr., 1 per day, $69).
Taxis: Queue at corner of Brougham and Devon St. **New Plymouth Taxis** (tel. 757 5665), **Egmont City Cabs** (tel. 754 8801), and **Energy City Cabs** (tel. 755 3365).
Bike Rental: Coronation Cycles and Mowers, 207 Coronation Ave. (tel. 757 9260). Mountain bikes from $25 per day. Lawnmowers rented on request.

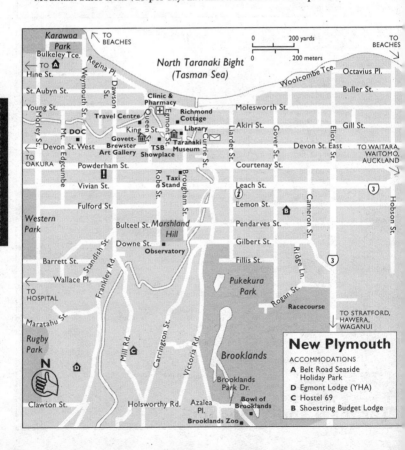

New Plymouth

ACCOMMODATIONS
A Belt Road Seaside
    Holiday Park
D Egmont Lodge (YHA)
C Hostel 69
B Shoestring Budget Lodge

Hitchhiking: Hitchhiking toward Wanganui around the east side of Egmont is reportedly easiest in the nebulous zone on the outskirts of town on SH3, before the traffic picks up to 70kph. More traffic usually heads this way than heads up SH3 toward Otorohanga, Hamilton, and Auckland.

Visitors Center: New Plymouth Information Centre (tel. 759 6080; email nplvin@nzhost.co.nz), at the corner of Leach and Liardet St. Open M-F 8:30am-5pm, Sa-Su and public holidays 10am-3pm.

DOC: 220 Devon St. W. (tel. 758 0433; emergency mobile tel. (025) 438 956; fax 758 0430). Bevy of brochures on both Egmont National Park and Sugarloaf Marine Park; fishing queries also answered. Open M-F 8am-4:30pm.

Currency Exchange: Thomas Cook, 55-57 Devon St. E. (tel. 757 5459). More banks on the corner of Devon and Currie St.; **BNZ** offers good exchange rates. Take your pick of **ATMs** all along Devon St.

Women's Centre: 32 Leach St. (tel. 758 4957).

Laundry: Devon Laundrette, 282 Devon St. E. (tel. 758 8264).

Emergency: dial **111.**

Police: (tel. 757 5449), Powderhorns St.

Medical Services: Accident and Medical Clinic White Cross Taranaki (tel. 759 8915), in Richmond Centre on Egmont St. Open daily 8am-10pm.

Hospital: Taranaki Base on David St. (tel. 753 6139).

Pharmacy: Care Chemist (tel. 757 4614) in Richmond Centre on Egmont St. Open daily 8am-9pm.

Library: Brougham St. (tel. 758 4544), offering **Internet access.** $5 per 30min. Open M, W, F 9am-8:30pm, Tu, Th 9am-5:30pm, Sa 10am-3pm; closed public holidays.

Post Office: (tel. 759 8931) Currie St. Open M-F 8:30am-5pm, Sa 9am-1pm.

Telephone Code: 06.

ACCOMMODATIONS

For a city of only 50,000 people, New Plymouth provides warm beds for more than its fair share of travelers. Shuttles to "the mountain" (Taranaki) run from all accommodations, but it's difficult to get to town after dark without a car.

Shoestring Backpackers (VIP), 48 Lemon St. (tel./fax 758 0404), in a residential neighborhood 5min. from town center. Amiable hostel has a full kitchen and dining area with a table large enough for all guests to eat from at once (which does happen occasionally). Capacious lounge with TV (CNN), fireplace, and adjacent sun room for reading. Outdoor deck for smoking, and even a Finnish sauna ($4 per use). Dorms $14; singles $20; doubles $32, with TV $36. Laundry $2. Linen $4. Meets your transportation needs with bicycles, mountain shuttle, and free pickup from the travel center.

Hostel 69, 69 Mill Rd. (tel./fax 758 7153; email peter.pan@taranaki.ac.nz). At the end of Dawson Rd., take the left fork (Mill Rd.); hostel is 300m up the hill on the left. On a clear day, this is the only hostel in town from which you can actually see the mountain. Those who make the hike are rewarded with a funky lounge (with fireplace), bright kitchen, Internet access ($3 per hour) and a backyard disguised as a rainforest. Dorms $15; doubles $28. Tent sites in the jungle clearing out back $8. Linen $2. Laundry $1. Mountain shuttle $15. Flexible check in and checkout.

Egmont Lodge (YHA), 12 Clawton St. (tel. 753 5720; fax 753 5782). Take Frankley Rd. at the Dawson St. fork and follow the signs, or else call and arrange for free pickup. Away from the din of the city, enjoy the sound of Waimea Stream flowing through the backyard and help feed the nearly 2m long pet eel who lives there. Inside, you'll find an accessible kitchen with a deck, and clean, comfy accommodations below. Dorms $15; singles $25; doubles and twins $36. Tent sites out back $10. Linen $3. $10 key deposit. Free bikes; numerous activities can be arranged at the front desk (open sporadically; guests should just make themselves at home).

Central City Lodge, 104 Leach St. (tel. 758 0473; fax 758 6559; email amber-court@xtra.co.nz). As the name implies, this place is right in the heart of town. Ask for the backpackers. Dorms $15; singles $30; doubles $40. Communal kitchen and lounge. Linen (duvet, towel, and soap) $5. Use of indoor pool and spa $2 for the whole stay. Key deposit $5. Check-in before 10pm preferred. Check-out 10am.

Belt Road Seaside Holiday Park, 2 Belt Rd. (tel./fax 758 0228), on prime oceanfront real estate. The closest beach is within 1km, while city center is a 5-10min walk. Backpackers $17-22. Tent sites $8.50 per person, powered sites $17 for 2, $10 extra person. Cabins $25-45, with high end "suites" having their own bathroom and linen. Bedding $5. Communal toilets and kitchen (use of pots and utensils $5).

FOOD

New Plymouth offers many opportunities to escape the meat and potatoes lifestyle of the Taranaki region, though **Devon Street** still offers many temptations of the flesh. Explore and consume according to your heart's desire. Or, cobble together your own creation after a stop at **New World,** on the block bounded by Leach, Courtenay, Liardet and Gover Streets, the closest market to the hostels (open daily 8am-9pm).

Simply Read Cafe and Bookshop, 2 Dawson St. (tel. 757 8667). This cheery red, green, and purple 50s-style bungalow serves up truly elegant food with an ocean view. Light pastries and casseroles filled with all sorts of goodies are $5.50, including a julienne side salad. Purchase a novel from the array of New Zealand fiction in the living room and devour it with coffee and a scone. Open W-Su 10am-5pm.

⊛**Agra Indian Restaurant,** 151 Devon St. E. (tel. 758 0030). Bask in the candle-lit glow of reddish walls decorated with swaths of Indian fabric and posters of Bangladesh. Later, bask in the afterglow upon finishing your savory dinner. Traditional Indian food done right, with large portions and multiple vegetarian options, all at a reasonable price (mains $8-15). Takeaways available. Open daily from 5:30pm, also Friday for lunch noon-2pm.

E.S.P.resso (tel. 759 9399), adjacent to the Govett-Brewster Art Gallery (see p. 149). Museum cafe serving artful and affordable creations. Delicate filos filled with meats or vegetables are representative of the mains ($9.50 with a side salad). Cakes and pastries ($2-3) go well with a smooth bowl of latte ($4) and a slice of pretension (gratis). Open daily 8am-4pm.

Steps Restaurant, 37 Gover St. (tel. 758 3393), nestled unassumingly in a little white cottage. Step up to gourmet cuisine at prices that won't lead you above and beyond your budget. Diverse lunch items rotate through the ever-changing menu ($9-12.50), while elegant dinners belie the casual atmosphere inside ($20-22). Open for lunch Tu-F noon-2pm, dinner Tu-Sa from 6pm.

NIGHTLIFE

Early in the week, the nightlife in New Plymouth resembles that of Taranaki's rural towns, in that there is none. The weekends are another story, as people emerge from the mountain and sea to party hard 'til the stroke of three.

Mayfair, 67 Devon St. W. (tel./fax 757 4739). On Friday and Saturday nights, hundreds of people pack inside to soak up the techno pumped out by the epic 5000 watt sound system. You have to feel it to believe it. A movie theater when it was first built, the seats were removed and the ceiling lowered to create an entertainment complex with free pool tables and bar towards the entrance, and a large dance floor with light show farther in. Open W-Sa 11am-3am.

⊛**X Bar & Cafe,** 40 Powderham St. (tel. 758 7723). The weekend starts on Thursday night at this laid-back haven for the surf and snowboard set. Alternative music is accompanied by biking, surfing, and snowboarding videos on several strategically placed monitors. Happy hours and promotional nights throughout the weekend and big food served cheap for lunch and dinner. Open Tu-Su from 11am. Upstairs at **Comet** (tel. 759 4093), snowboard shop and coffeehouse synergize thanks to an ultra-cool staff and the best java in town. Open M-F 10am-6pm, Sa 11am-3pm.

Grapevine Wine Bar & Cafe, 36C Currie St. (tel. 757 9355). Come here to hear all about it at this upstairs spot catering to a slightly more sophisticated set. The ornate bas-relief on the ceiling won't make you forget the Sistine Chapel, but it adds a nice touch. Curvaceous bar serves up more vintages than an antique show, as well as "Stiff Dicks." Go easy on the latter or you may end up with a better view of the ceiling than you bargained for. Live music F-Sa 10pm-3am. Open Tu-Sa from 5pm, also Friday for lunch 12 noon -2pm.

The Mill, 2 Courtenay St. (tel. 758 1935). Impossible to miss at the end of Currie St., The Mill has been around since 1868 when it was actually a functioning flour mill. Today, the grinding involves not wheat stalks, but rather people grooving to video music in the basement dance area dubbed **CrowBar** (open F-Sa 9pm-3am). On the ground floor, classic rock inspires karaoke and occasional dancing on the bar. Leave your studded leather and ripped jeans at home if you want to swim with the mainstream. Open M-Th from 11am, F-Sa 11am-3am.

Elevate, 55A Egmont St. (tel. 758 1112). Look for the arrow on the door pointing up, and elevate yourself inside to this second-floor cafe and bar offering style on a budget. Soft lighting, warm brown tones and vaulted ceilings create an ambient atmosphere highlighted by acid jazz and intelligent drum and bass. Mellow out with a drink and light mains ($7.50) and watch the world go by in the street below. Open Tu-Sa from 6pm.

SIGHTS AND ACTIVITIES

A stroll down **Devon Street** reveals New Plymouth's 19th-century heritage, as evidenced by artful moldings and dates embossed on the upper levels of the downtown shops. The city serves as the only real roost for Taranaki's culture vultures, harboring fine museums, galleries, and theaters, as well as access to some of the nation's most spectacular beaches and mountains. For a shot in the arm of the region's history, clear out an hour or two for the **Taranaki Museum** (tel. 758 9583), on Ariki St. between Brougham and Egmont St. *(Open M-F 10:30am-4:30pm, Sa-Su and holidays, 1-5pm. Free.)* Across the street from and operated by the museum is the **Richmond Cottage,** a historic dwelling place of New Plymouth's earliest Parliamentary movers and shakers. *(Open Nov.-May M, W, F 2-4pm, Sa-Su 1-4pm; June-Oct. F 2-4pm, Sa-Su 1-4pm. Admission $1.)* The porch of the cottage opens onto **Pukeariki Landing.** Once the entry point for people and goods traveling by sea, it is now a lovely green spot adorned with cool Maori sculptures.

For a modern take on art, cruise the **Govett-Brewster Art Gallery** (tel. 758 5149), at the corner of King and Queen St. *(Open daily 10:30am-5pm. Donations accepted.)* Although your fellow patrons are as unapproachable as royalty, the rotating collection of art and visiting exhibitions are quite accessible. The work of **Len Lye** (see p. 51) is featured, including videos of all his films and kinetic sculptures. Curl up on the couches upstairs with the latest art magazines; downstairs get the obligatory caffeine fix at **Cafe E.S.P.resso** (see p. 148). At night, those of refined tastes may enjoy a theater or opera excursion at the **TSB showplace,** 94 Devon St. W. (tel. 758 4947). Call for schedules or check out the box office in person (open M-F 11am-4:30pm). For a more intimate experience, the **Little Theatre** on Aubrey St., between Morley and Edgecombe St., lives up to its name.

Flocks of joggers experience souped-up nature at the semi-automated wilds of **Pukekura Park** at the top of Liardet St. (no bicycles allowed). *(Open daily 8:30am-4pm, though the gates to Pukekura Park are open 8:30am-6pm, until 7pm during daylight savings Time.)* Amid the towering trees and bounteous rhododendrons, take a peek at the coin-operated illuminated fountain and the push-button waterfall. If the weather cooperates, visit the calla lilies in Stainton Dell or the green grandeur of the leg-stretching walk to **King Fern Gulley.** No matter what it's like outside, the **Fernery** and display houses warmly await hushed footfalls on a carpet of cedar chips. Adjacent to Pukekura Park is yet another confederation of structures and gardens, the **Brooklands.** Attractions here include the **children's zoo.** *(Open daily 8:30am-5pm. Free.)* If you are in town anytime from the week before Christmas 1999 to February 6, 2000 (Waitangi Day), walk through and see the park illuminated for the **Festival of Lights.**

New Plymouth also offers several scenic walkways of various lengths and grades. Detailed printed guides are available at the visitors center. The **Te Henui Walkway** is one of the best, following the Te Henui stream through 5.9km of natural splendor down to the sea. The coastal walkway offers dramatic views of the sea crashing

When Life Imitates Art...

Len Lye's landmark "direct film" *Tusulana* (1929) was based upon the life of the Australian **witchetty grub,** although he himself never actually saw one. In the film, a monster that is a cross between a spider and an octopus attacks a segmented worm-like creature—what Lye called "the totem of individuality." The behavior of the monster bears striking resemblence to that of a **macrophage,** a microscopic organism that attaches itself to the wall of a living cell and then attempts to pierce and inject it with its own genetic fluids. Amazingly, Lye first learned of macrophages 20 years after the film's completion. Furthermore, in a 1960s *Life* magazine article, Lye read about antibodies that protect cells from invaders and whose behavior matched that of his witchetty grub. Yet his grub evolves into a macrophage in the course of the film. Could science explain that as well? Not surprisingly, in the 1970s, research into antibody behavior determined that in certain situations, the antibodies suffered from immunization problems, causing them to align with the macrophage and attack the cell, mirroring the plot of the 40-year-old movie. Lye explained this uncanny phenomenon as a manifestation of what he called his **Old Brain,** capable of tapping into unconscious truths about external reality, and a case of the "fine art myth being inadvertently backed up by science—a sort of genetically informed model of sociological import."

against the rocky coastline. Follow this path south past industrial areas and arrive at **Paritutu,** a prominent rock at the edge of the shore (in Maori, *pari* is cliff and *tutu* is to stand erect). Those brave enough to scale its 154m track (deservedly rated "hard") are treated to epic views of the coast and on a clear day, the mountain as well.

■ Egmont National Park

Rolling green hills on the plains below bow like a temple of green-robed disciples to their master and maker, majestic Mt. Egmont (Taranaki). Everything within a 10km radius of the nearly symmetrical volcanic peak was declared part of New Zealand's second national park in 1881, restraining the vigorous logging boom of the time and preserving area farmlands. Today, three paved roads serve as arteries into the park: **Egmont Road,** from New Plymouth through Egmont Village to the North Egmont Visitor Centre; **Pembroke Road,** from Stratford to the Stratford Mountain House and the Manganui Skifield; and **Manaia Road,** from the Manaia/Hawera area to the Dawson Falls Visitor Centre. With more than 140km of prime tracks, Egmont remains New Zealand's most accessible national park.

Easy access to the park is all too often equated with easy going on the slopes. In fact, climbing Mt. Egmont (Taranaki) is far more than a leisurely walk in the park. The mountain has claimed the lives of 54 people, making it the most dangerous peak in New Zealand. Although the threat of this dormant volcano erupting is small (the last major awakening took place in 1755), other dangers are still plentiful: the upper slopes are prone to dramatic and sudden weather changes, and chilling rain can fall at any elevation at any time of year. Maori forays into the region were made only occasionally, and with great respect and careful preparation; the same principle still holds today. All but the most hardened mountain climbers are strongly advised to take along a guide. Climbers are advised to assemble proper gear and check the mountain forecast before setting out. Regardless of the season ("dry" months are Dec.-Apr.), weather-proof clothing is essential, as is a sturdy pair of hiking boots. In the winter, standard equipment includes an ice axe and crampons. Chris Prudden's **Mountain Guides Mt. Egmont** (tel. 758 8261 or (025) 474 510), based in New Plymouth, will take one person for $250 and groups of two to four people for $300.

The **Around-the-Mountain Circuit,** with views, bush, and alpine gorges, normally takes three to five days and can be begun from any of the several main entrances to the park. During the summer, the trail can be shortened substantially by taking shorter routes at higher altitudes. In the spring, water runoff from the mountain and

A Mountain by Any Other Name

A quick guide to the many names of the mountain:

Taranaki is what the Maori call it.

Mt. Egmont is the name the English settlers bestowed upon the mountain. Their descendents and the national media have continued to use this name in order to distinguish mountain from park.

Mt. Taranaki is what politically correct people call it, in order to recognize Maori culture while distinguishing it from the region as a whole (which misses the point that to the Maori, the mountain *is* the region.

Tara is what the mountain guides call it, in order to sound cool.

Keep all this in mind and be understood, whether you are in a *pa*, on the peak, in a parliamentary debate, or on TV.

rains can often cause the height of rivers and streams to rise, making for difficult crossings. Hikers are best off waiting for levels to subside, as the flows are fast and deceptively deep. There are *endless* trail options in the park; visit DOC and make your own hiking plans. DOC accommodations are simple and rustic, but sufficient; always call ahead. Notable is **Syme Hut** on Phantom's Peak (1900m), arguably the best place to watch the sun rise or set; however, the hut's prime location also means that it is exposed to wind and ice. Camping is not permitted in Egmont National Park, but goat and wild pig **hunting** is (with a DOC permit).

NORTHERN EGMONT The **North Egmont Visitor Centre** (tel. 756 8710) is the port of entry for most of the park's adventurers (open in summer daily 9am-4:30pm; in winter Th-M 10am-4pm). DOC officials point trampers in the right direction with the aid of a color-coded relief map. Those planning to hole up in the huts can see photos of all nine and purchase hut tickets ($8, children $4) after getting an eight-minute audiovisual tour of the park. There are also three private huts on the mountain, each run by one of the three mountain clubs in the region. The **Tahurangi Lodge,** owned and run by the Taranaki Alpine Club, offers kitchen facilities and a great location at 1520m. Prior booking is essential; inquire at the visitors center, or write P.O. Box 356, New Plymouth ($15 per night).

For a short but sweet walk, the **Connet Loop Track** (30min. round-trip; depart from the base of the North Egmont car park). Winding its way through the "goblin forest," the track is an ethereal world of fern and moss when clouds hang low on the slopes. The **Ngatoro Loop Track** (30min. round-trip) navigates through stately cedars to the wing beats of native birds. For a 1½-hour pure bush experience, hit the **Veronica Loop Track.** Hard-core botanists might want to make the full day trek to the **Ahukawaka Swamp,** home to unique lichen, mosses, and microbes. **Bells Falls,** best reached from **Holly Hut,** is also worth checking out. Great views of New Plymouth and beyond can be had from the north side of the volcano; the route to the **summit** from northern Egmont is purportedly safer than that from the other entry points (4-5hr. up, 3hr. down).

In Egmont Village, just outside the park and east of New Plymouth on Egmont Rd., hoof it over to **Missing Leg Backpackers,** 1082 Junction Rd. (tel. 752 2570). The name comes not from a horrific tramping incident, but from Eric, the resident three-legged dingo. Reserve ahead to stay at the stylish mountain lodge with horses, mountain bikes, and camping gear for hire. (Dorms $13; doubles $30.) Free pickup from Inglewood; a shuttle from New Plymouth to Inglewood is $5 (ask at visitors center).

SOUTHERN EGMONT AND DAWSON FALLS Roughly 15% of park pleasure-seekers enter the perimeter by way of Stratford, arriving at the **Stratford Mountain House,** with its easy access to the **Manganui skifields** in winter, and several trails in other seasons. Trips to the summit can also be attempted from this side, but the route is longer (9-11hr. return) and more treacherous. For accommodation consider **Man-**

TARANAKI & WANGANUI

ganui Lodge, the private hut run by the Stratford Mountain Club. Advance booking is required; contact the club president (tel. 752 7471). Also from the south, access to the park can be gained by means of Manaia Rd., 8km of pavement that leads to the **Dawson Falls Visitor Centre** (tel. (025) 430 248), a stylish Swiss chalet with easy access to skifields and dozens of bush walks (open in summer daily 8:30am-4:30pm; in winter W-Su 9am-4:30pm). From the center, you can hike to **Wilkies Pools** (1½hr.), a series of terraced plunge pools that spill into each other. Just remember that the water is ice-cold. The DOC runs the bare-bones **Konini Lodge** (tel. (025) 430 248). The expansive kitchen and common room areas improve the situation. Prior booking is required ($12; BYO linen). Also nearby is the **Kapuni Lodge,** which rounds out the trio of private huts on the mountain. This one is maintained by the Mt. Egmont Alpine Club of Hawera and offers gas cooking, running water, and 18 bunk beds ($10); book ahead of time by contacting Paul Adowd (tel./fax 278 4765) and arrange to collect a hut key in Hawera.

■ Stratford

An Ode to Stratford
> *If inland travel is the path you tread,*
> *And mountain exploration is your game,*
> *The town of Stratford beckons you instead.*
> *With rural charm and streets that bear the name,*
> *Of characters from Shakespeare's major plays,*
> *Like Hamlet, Regan, Lear, and Juliet.*
> *Here you can pass up Egmont on those days,*
> *When it is raining, else you'll get quite wet.*
> *Yet be forewarned (of this you can be sure):*
> *Insomniacs rejoice! This town's your cure.*

ORIENTATION AND PRACTICAL INFORMATION 'Ware, lest you wander from the main thoroughfare, **Broadway St.** (SH3), the source of local sustenance, spirits, and slight revelry. **InterCity** departs from the information center and heads to Auckland (7hr., M-F 5 per day, Sa-Su 2 per day, $74) via New Plymouth (45min., $12), and to Wellington (5½hr., M-F 4 per day, Sa-Su 2 per day, $52) via Hawera (30min., $11), Wanganui (1½hr., $23) and Palmerston North (3hr., $35). **Central Cabs** (tel. 765 8395) are available for your local transport needs. **Bicycles** can be rented from Excelsior House, 182 Broadway (tel. 765 6254) for $20 per day. **Hitchhikers** report that hitchhiking to New Plymouth and Wellington gets easier along SH3 the farther you get from the center of town.

The **Stratford Information Centre** (tel./fax 765 6708) is on Broadway South (open M-F 8:30am-5pm, Sa-Su 10am-2pm). The **DOC office** is on Pembroke Rd., RD 21 (tel. 765 5144; fax 765 6102; open M-F 8am-4:30pm). Change money at **BNZ** (tel. 765 7134), located in the middle of Broadway St. (open M-F 9am-4:30pm) with multiple **ATMs** to either side. The **Stratford Public Library** is at Prospero Pl. (tel. 765 5403; open M-Th 9:30am-5:30pm, F 10am-6pm, Sa 9:30am-noon). **Public toilets** are at the information center and also on Broadway, behind the **clock tower.**

In an emergency, dial **111.** The **hospital** is on Miranda St. between Romeo and Celia St. (tel. 765 7189). The **police** (tel. 765 7145) are on Broadway St., and the **post office** (tel. 765 6009) is on Miranda St. at Prospero Pl. The **telephone code** is **06.**

ACCOMMODATIONS Stratford serves as a gateway to the ski resorts of eastern Taranaki, but those destined for the slopes should consider staying on the mountain itself in order to maximize their skiing time. In Stratford proper, the **Taranaki Accommodation Lodge,** 7 Romeo St. (tel. 765 544; fax 765 6440) is the largest of its kind in the region, with 50 individual rooms sleeping one, two or three people. Find a communal kitchen, showers and toilets on each of the two floors. The lodge also has TV lounges and laundry ($2 per load), as well as free use of the outdoor pool and tennis

The Axeman Cometh

One of the winningest sportsmen in New Zealand history, axeman Ned Shrewry competed in a time when a wood chopper could become a national hero. Born in Stratford in 1889, Ned's career as a wood chopper lasted from 1910 to 1934, truly the glory days of the sport. He was the dominant chopper of the era, capturing three world titles as well as countless New Zealand and Australian crowns. His career was interrupted when he fought in World War I, where he was twice injured and won the Military Medal—in his opinion "because I kept the cookhouse supplied with kindling wood." Actually, the medal was for surviving a shell explosion that buried him alive, but also knocked his helmet off his head and over his face, keeping the dirt out and creating an air pocket that kept him alive until he could be dug out. He returned to New Zealand after the war and traveled around, chopping at shows throughout the 20s. He died in 1962, but recieved immortality in 1996 when he was voted into the New Zealand Sports Hall of Fame.

courts. (Singles $18; shared rooms $16 per person. Group discounts available.) The other affordable option in town is the **Stratford Holiday Park,** 10 Page St. (tel./fax 765 6440), which is a motel, backpackers, and campground all rolled into one. The kitchen and bathrooms are communal; the dorm in the lodge has a separate kitchen and lounge. (Bunks $16; 2-person cabins $33-42, extra person $12. Double motel rooms with own facilities $70, extra person $15, max. 6. Tents sites $9, powered $10. Duvet and linen $5. Bicycle hire $20 per day. Check-out 10am.)

FOOD AND NIGHTLIFE Broadway St. does not suffer from a shortage of cheap and greasy takeaways, though finding quality fare is another matter. Those camping or graced with kitchens might be better off gathering supplies at the **New World** supermarket (tel. 765 6422), on the corner of Orlando and Regan St. (open M-Tu 8am-6pm, W-Th 8am-8pm, F 8am-7pm, Sa-Su 9am-6pm). One exception to this rule is the little red-walled bistro the **Backstage Cafe,** 234 Broadway St. (tel. 765 7003). Enter stage left for food that is right on. Enjoy a huge slab of veggie pizza ($3) along with other inexpensive lunch options. At night, yuppies arrive in waves to feast on succulent mains ($20-25) and drink wine. (Open M 10am-4pm, Tu-Sa 8am-10pm.) The **Axeman's Inn,** 305 Broadway St. (tel. 765 5707), pays tribute to the region's prolific logging industry 'round the turn of the century. Black and white photos of loggers in action adorn brick walls, and the bar is covered with a wood shingled roof. Read all about the life of Ned Shewry (see p. 153) or enjoy live music every Thursday night. Upstairs is the restaurant, serving up standard pub fare at reasonable prices ($7-15). Downstairs is the bar. Overlooking it all from the rafters is the Axeman himself, one of Nigel Ogle's finest (see Tawhiti Museum, p. 155). The inn is open daily from 11am to 2am, with dining only on Sundays.

SIGHTS AND ACTIVITIES With Mt. Egmont looming in the background, it's little wonder that **skiing** is the main attraction of the area. The **Manganui Ski Field** (snowphone: 765 7669; general info tel. 765 5493) is the only field on the mountain and has open season from June through October. One T-bar and three rope tows offer access to several expert runs as well as two natural half-pipes for snowboarders. *(Adults $30, students $20, children $15, over 60 free; half day rates available.)* Those armed with a flashlight and a pair of sturdy boots can go **glow-worm hunting** for free in the ferny overhangs on the banks of the Patea River, which runs directly through town. For more complex bush excursions, try **Off the Beaten Track Adventures** (tel./fax 762 7885 or tel. (025) 241 2837). Adventurer Paddy Gooch and his wife Margaret will help you put together a choose-your-own-adventure day or two. *($25 per hr., $50 per half-day, $85 per full day; food included.)*

Although Stratford is best known in tourists' minds for providing back-door access to **Egmont National Park** (see p. 150), there are still a few noteworthy sights in the vicinity. Taranaki's pioneer history is celebrated at the **Taranaki Pioneer Village** (tel.

TARANAKI & WANGANUI

765 5399), just outside of Stratford on SH3, a conglomeration of 50 turn-of-the-century buildings fully restored and decorated. *(Open daily 10am-4pm. $5.)* Periodically, the village holds workshops of anachronistic activities such as weaving, pottery, and wood chopping. For a more tranquil experience, visit the **Hollard Gardens** (tel./fax 764 6544), on upper Manai Rd. Begun as an unassuming patch on a dairy farm in 1927, today the gardens are the centerpiece of the annual **Taranaki Rhododendron Festival** (Oct.-Nov.) which was started in Stratford 10 years ago and now includes nearly 40 gardens. To get a real flavor of Taranaki, visit **O'Neill's Brewing Company,** 4281 Mountain Rd. (tel. 764 8335), off SH3 toward Eltham. *(Open M-Sa 11am-6pm, by appt. to eat as well.)* Brian and Helen O'Neill have converted an old service station into a microbrewery (and cafe) that produces Ngaere Draught and Black Peat Lager. Stratford SH5 is at one end of the **Heritage Trail** along SH43 (see p. 162). Numerous scenic walks and drives leave from and return to Statford—ask at the visitors center.

■ Hawera

Hawera, which means "the burned place" in Maori, derives its name from a fire that consumed a nearby *pa* in Whareroa. Yet from the ashes has risen not a phoenix but a heifer, symbolizing the dairy industry which now dominates the region. Today, Hawera's tourism industry continues to suckle at the teat of the immortal cow, offering multimedia tours of the dairy center, and hands-on farmstays to travelers, who may soon find themselves caught up in the early-to-bed, early-to-rise rural lifestyle.

ORIENTATION AND PRACTICAL INFORMATION The main street running through town is **High Street.** At the west end of High St., **Waihi Road** (SH3) is the primary northern route. **South Road** becomes the coastal route to New Plymouth (SH45) in one direction and to Wanganui (SH3) in the other.

    InterCity (tel. (0800) 731 711) and **Newmans** (tel. (0800) 777 707) leave daily for New Plymouth (1hr., 3 per day, $16) and Wanganui (1hr., M-F 4 per day, weekends 3 per day, $19) continuing on to Palmerston North (2½hr., $28) or Wellington (5hr., $48). **Southern Cabs** (24hr. tel. (0800) 282 822) has a stand on Victoria St. near High St. Or you could burn some calories and rent a used bicycle (when available) for $15 per day from **Seavers Cycles,** 18 Regent St. (tel. 278 6046; open July-Aug. M-F 8am-5pm; Sept-June 9am-noon). **Hitchhikers** often find a ride on High St. between Argyle and Albion St. or at the junction of SH3 and SH45 (South Rd. and Waihi Rd.). Most cars head to **New Plymouth** or **Wanganui** via SH3; hitchhiking to the coastal beach communities of western Taranaki along SH45 can be more difficult.

    The **South Taranaki Visitor Information Centre,** 55 High St. (tel. 278 8599), is located at the base of the **water tower,** along with the bus station and the public toilets. This is also the place to buy hut tickets. (Open Feb.-Nov. M-F 8:30am-5pm; Dec.-Jan. M-F 8:30am-5pm, Sa-Su and public holidays 10am-3pm.) **ATMs** abound all along High St. Change money at **BNZ** on Princes St. (open M-F 8am-4:30pm). The **Hawera Library** is at 46 High St. (tel. 278 8406; open M-T, Th 9am-5:30pm, W 9:30am-5:30pm, F 9am-6pm, Sa 9am-noon). In an **emergency,** dial **111**. The **hospital** is on Hunter St. (tel. 278 7109). The **police** are located on Princes St. (tel. 278 8066); the **post office** is at 74 Princes St. (tel. 278 8680; open M-F 9am-5pm). The **telephone code** is **06**.

ACCOMMODATIONS, FOOD, AND NIGHTLIFE Deep in New Zealand's dairyland, it only seems appropriate to get out onto a farm, jump into a pair of gumboots, and experience everything the paddocks and pastures have to offer. At **Wheatly Downs Farmstay** (tel. 278 6523; fax 278 6541), on Ararata Rd., guests are very much encouraged to get involved. Fifth generation farmer Gary Ogle offers such hands-on experiences as riding horses, herding cattle, or shearing sheep. On a clear day, enjoy a perfect view of **Mt. Egmont (Taranaki)** from the living room couch; for a closer look, fly around the mountain in a plane that picks you up right in front of the farmhouse ($50 for a 40min. flight; ask Gary to arrange it). Free laundry and pickup from Hawera center (with advance notice) are provided as well. (Dorms $15; singles $25; doubles $36. Cash only.) At the **Taranaki Ohangi Backpacker Farm** (tel./fax 272 2878), on Urupa Rd. 10km from town, the savvy hosts will gladly show you around their 400-cow working dairy farm in English, German, or French. The backpackers bunkhouse offers clean rooms, a communal kitchen and TV lounge, and a deck with great pastoral and mountain views. Activities include horse riding, cow milking, possum hunting, swimming, and lawn tennis. Pickup from town is free with advance notice; borrow a free bike to wheel around the farm. ($14 per person, cash only. Full bedding $2.) For those adventurers not quite ready to beat their swords into plowshares, **King Edward Park Motor Camp**, 70 Waihi Rd. (tel. 278 8544), is an affordable spot just outside the center of town. The maximum stay is 30 days in this land of communal showers, kitchen, and toilets. (2-person cabins and onsite caravans $28, $10 per extra person. Tent sites $8, powered sites $9. Checkout 10am.)

The **Rough Habits Sports Bar and Cafe,** 79-81 Regent St. (tel. 278 7333) may imply a smoky dive, but this place has a polished edge that attracts a predominantly young crowd. Large starters ($8-12) are good for sharing among friends, or else feast on meaty mains ($15-18) and wash it all down with a $3 handle (open M-Sa from 11am, Sun 11am-11pm).**Barry's Street Bar and Restaurant** (tel. 278 4998), on Princes St. by the post office, caters to a more eclectic crowd. An extensive menu features a selection of gourmet pizzas including "The Egmont"—marmalade, spinach, pine nuts, brie, sun-dried tomatoes, and dollops of sour cream—which do the region proud ($16). DJ or live music on weekends. (Open M-F from 11am, Sa-Su 11-3am.) Let **New World,** 307 High St. (tel. 278 8528), be your grocery haven (open M-F 8am-8pm, Sa-Su 9am-6pm).

Sex and Violence in a Small Town

"I hope I'm not another one of those poor buggers who get discovered when they're dead." Such are the sadly prophetic words of Hawera's own semi-illustrious novelist, **Ronald Hugh Morrieson** (1922-1968). Spending his entire life in a small weatherboard house on Regent St., at age 41 he quit his career as a music teacher to write tales of small town perversion. His two most famous books, *The Scarecrow* (1963) and *Came a Hot Friday* (1964), entertained modest success in Australia, but were largely misunderstood and ignored in New Zealand. Only recent film versions have helped to draw him from obscurity in his native land. Embittered by disappointing critical response and the death of his mother, Morrieson turned to the bottle, succumbing to cirrhosis of the liver in 1968. A few diehard fans salvaged the fixtures from his home when it was demolished in 1993, and used them to decorate their new **Morrieson Cafe and Bar,** 60 Victoria St. (tel. 278 5647), which is around the corner from where his house used to stand. This is one place where you are actually encouraged to eat off the floor (the tables are constructed from the floorboards of his house). Other artifacts include the vestiges of a fireplace and the staircase, which now leads to nowhere. Raise a toast in his memory for $3. (Open daily 11am-1am.)

SIGHTS AND ACTIVITIES Living up to its name, Hawera has burned down three times in its history (1884, 1888 and 1912). After the third fire, residents wised up and built a **water tower;** then they built a visitors center at its base. *(Open M-F 9am-4:30pm, Sa-Su and holidays 11am-11pm. Adults $2, children $1, groups $5.)* Climb the 215 steps for a scenic view of the countryside or use it as a navigational beacon at night, when it is lit up with red neon. For a truly unique experience, venture out of town to the **Tawhiti Museum,** 47 Ohangi Rd. (tel. 278 6837; call for directions). *(Museum open Jan. daily 10am-4pm, Feb.-May and Sept.-Dec. F-M 10am-4pm; June-Aug. Su 10am-4pm.)* Artist Nigel Ogle has perfected the technique of casting life-size fiberglass figures from human models, thus adding a human element which makes the artifacts from Maori and English settlements come alive. Also on the premises is the **Chew Chong Memorial,** an eye-opening examination of Taranaki's most famous Chinese immigrant/entrepeneur. Chew Chong made a name for himself in the dairy industry but perhaps more interestingly in recognizing and then exporting the medicinal **woodear fungus.** For an ear of a different sort, consider sending Nigel's trademark souvenEAR to that special someone back home ($5). Van Gogh would be honored. For a cheesier museum experience, check out **Dairyland** (tel. 278 4537), at the corner of SH3 and Whareroa Rd., by the giant fiberglass cow and giraffe. *(Exhibit and cafe open daily 9am-5pm; cafe also open for dinner Th-Sa from 6:30pm.)* Learn all about the multiple uses of milk, watch live footage from **Kiwi Dairies** (see below), and experience the tactile pleasure of a **simulated milk tanker** with your animatronic driver Darryl. Afterwards, enjoy a bite to eat, or better yet, a frothy shake ($2) in the revolving cafe. Dairyland is actually the visitors center for Kiwi Dairies, looming just down the road, the largest multi-milk processing plant in the world and global supplier of Pizza Hut's mozzarella.

For a different kind of cheese, head down "Lonely Street" (actually, it's just 51 Argyle St., around the corner from High St.) to the **Elvis Presley Memorial Record Room** (tel. 278 7624), marked by a large Graceland mural on the side of the private home. *(Open by appointment only; donations appreciated, uh-huh, thank ya very much.)* For 37 years, proprietor, Elvis-invoker, and self-proclaimed "geriatric rock 'n' roller" Kevin D. Whatley has amassed all things Elvis-encrusted for his impressive garage shrine. His opinion? Died in '77. As Whatley says, "it's just about a man and his music."

■ The Taranaki Coast

Proffering a laid-back lifestyle of catching rays on black sand beaches and catching waves of quality year-round surf, the Taranaki coast from **New Plymouth** to **Hawera** remains an unbelievably beautiful and relatively undiscovered destination. **Hitchhiking** is sporadic at best, and in winter frequent rains make the experience all the more unpleasant. Generally, it's better to hire a car or a guide. You can circumnavigate Mt. Egmont (Taranaki) and travel along the coast in two ways. For an excellent **scenic journey** (1½hr.) offering easy access to various bush walks and the best views of the Taranaki Bights and the Tasman Sea, take Carrington Rd. from New Plymouth to Okahu Rd. and then circle around. The **coastal route** (3½hr.) is best done on **SH45**, but unless you stop and walk to the shore, expect only glimpses of the ocean (much of the view in this route is obscured by either hedges, great distance, or both).

Just outside of New Plymouth to the west, a chain of volcanic plug gnomes is home to over 600 seals in Sugarloaf Marine Park. One good way to gape is with **Chaddy's Charters** (tel. 758 9133). Tours on the classy 1953 mahogany, oak, and teak boat go out on demand. (Adults $20, children free; 1hr. round-trip.) Hop aboard at Chaddy's shed on the ocean side of Ocean View Parade by Ngamotu Beach.

A one-horse town with an awesome beach that is wide, flat, and family-filled in summer, the town of **Oakura** is representative of the population "centers" that dot the coast. It is also home to the **Burnt Toast Cafe and Restaurant,** on Main South Rd. (tel. 752 7303). The specialty here is huge pizzas; for $30 the "Mumbo Jumbo" will feed you and six of your closest friends. (Open W-F 6pm-10pm, Sa-Su 10am-10pm.) The point at the end of **Ahu Ahu Road** yields an amazing surf that is the *raison d'être* for the **Wavehaven** hostel (tel. 752 7800; email wave.haven@taranaki.ac.nz). Chill out here year 'round, staying warm by the fireplace as you watch big screen TV. Surfboard and kayak rentals ($15 a day, $10 for half a day) with wetsuits are available, and surfing lessons for novices can be arranged. There is a climbing wall and volleyball court for landlubbers, while websurfers can send email. (Dorms in separate bunkhouse $10, in main house $15; singles $25. Linen and laundry $3.) The stretch of road between Okato and Opanake has been dubbed the **surf highway** in reverence to the killer waves that pound the coast; this region is consequently host to frequent surfing and windsurfing competitions. In the summer, it is possible to camp in the area for free, though be prepared for swarms of other tourists with the same idea in mind.

The abusive winds, churning seas, and storm-drenched skies that often grace **Cape Egmont** suit the solitary steadfastness of the Cape Egmont **lighthouse,** a navigational aid that the early Maori and Captain Cook surely would have appreciated. Along the highway, round green storage tanks appear from time to time like giant push-buttons in the foothills. Owned by Methanex and Maui Gas, the tanks show that milk isn't the only marketable liquid pumped out of the area. Take a tour at the **Maui Gas Production Station** in Oaonui to check out the scale models of ships and off-shore oil rigs (open daily 7:30am-5:30pm).

Opunake, the closest the coast comes to a bustling metropolis (pop. 1587), harbors both the dramatic cliffs of Middleton's Bay and the pleasantly swimmable Opunake Beach, with its teeming campground. Run the whole gamut of rooms in sprawling cinderblock glory at the **Opunake Motel and Backpackers,** 36 Heaphy Rd. (tel. 761 8330; fax 761 8340; dorms $18; cottage $20 per person, max 8; motel units $55, $70 for 2, extra person $13). Nab supplies for cheap at **Beau's Supermarket,** 59 Tasman St. (tel. 761 8668; open M-Th and Sa 7:30am-6pm, F 7:30am-8pm, Su 7:30am-5pm). Check out the locally renowned smorgasbord at the **Club Hotel.** On the south end of Cape Egmont hides the little town of **Manaia,** which boasts scrumptious croissants (6 for $2) from **Yarrow's Bakery** (tel. 274 8195), on South Rd. (open M-F 8am-4pm). Locals will also point you to the **pharmacy** on 47 Main St. (tel. 274 8200) to see a collection of teddy bears so big it's even billed as a museum (open M-Th 8:30am-5pm, F 8:30am-6pm, Sa 9:30am-noon).

■ Wanganui

Due to its strategic position near the mouth of the Whanganui River, Wanganui was one of the earliest English settlements in New Zealand in the mid-19th century. More of a large town than a city, present-day Wanganui is in transition as it seeks to establish itself as a viable tourist destination. This phenomenon is clearly demonstrated by river activity, which has shifted in the last half century from commerce to recreation. The area is also steeped in a rich Maori heritage (especially if one travels upstream a bit) that is quite accessible to visitors. Yet a slight underlying tension persists between the indigenous and European cultures that call this place home. This is perhaps best reflected in the grass roots movement among locals to restore the "h" to the town's name, which was "accidentally" Anglicized in the early 20th century. Regardless, Wanganui remains a pleasant stop as you travel to points north or south by land or water.

ORIENTATION AND PRACTICAL INFORMATION

Wanganui is located at the junction of **SH3** and **SH4**; the latter is called the **Anzac Parade** within the city limits and runs along the length of the Whanganui River (**Taupo Quay** and **Somme Parade** follow a similar course). They meet at **Victoria Ave.,** which runs perpendicular to the river and is the main street in town.

Transportation

Airport: (tel. 345 5593) Four arrivals and departures daily. Consult **Air New Zealand** (tel. (0800) 737 000) for precise schedules. Open daily 6:30am-7pm.

Buses: Newmans and **InterCity** stop at the **Wanganui Travel Centre,** 156 Ridgway St. (tel. 345 4433; fax 345 3370). Open M-F 8:30am-5:15pm. Buses leave daily for Wellington (4hr., 3 per day, $34); Palmerston North (1½hr., 4 per day M-F, 3 per day on weekends, $15); New Plymouth (2½hr., 2 per day, $29); Rotorua (6hr., 2 per day, $56) and Auckland (8hr., 4 per day, $68) via Hamilton (6hr., $61).

Public Transportation: Wanganui Taxi Bus (tel. 343 5555), for both taxi and bus transport in town. Their little white vans head to Castlecliff Beach and the suburbs. All buses depart from Maria Pl. between Victoria Ave. and St. Hill St. daily except Sunday (7am-6pm; $2; students, disabled persons, and seniors $1.30, children $1. Must have ticket to receive discounts.) Runs 24hr.; call for service.

Car Rental: Rent-A-Dent, 3 Churton St. (tel. 345 1505). $40 per day plus 20¢ per km. **Affordable Rentals** (tel. 343 9288), on the corner of Anzac Parade and Jones St. 1-3 days: $61.90 per day, 200 free km, 28¢ per additional km; 4 or more days: unlimited km and decreasing rates.

Bike Rental: Wanganui Pro Cycle Centre, 199 Victoria Ave. (tel. 345 3715). $20-25 per day for basic bikes, $35 per day for mountain bikes.

Hitchhiking: Many thumbers head to the outskirts of town where the traffic still flows at speeds less than 70kph. People going toward Taranaki do so by way of the

Great North Rd.; toward Ruapehu by way of the Anzac Parade; and toward Wellington by way of the Main South Rd.

Tourist and Financial Services

Visitor Center: Wanganui Visitor Information Centre (tel./fax 345 3286), on the corner of Guyton and St. Hill St. Open in summer M-F 8:30am-6pm, Sa-Su 9am-3pm; in winter M-F 8:30am-5pm, Sa-Su 10am-2pm.

DOC: At the corner of St. Hill and Ingestre St. (tel. 345 2402). Heaps of information on the Whanganui National Park and more. Open M-F 8:30am-4:30pm.

River Tours: Rivercity Tours (tel. 344 2554) in Wanganui. 2-5 day canoe and jet boat packages in conjunction with the Mail Run (see **River Road,** p. 162).

Budget Travel Office: (tel. 348 8190) Trafalgar Square, Taupo Quay. Open M-F 8:30am-5:30pm, Sa 9am-1pm.

Currency Exchange: Money ebbs and flows across Victoria Ave. **BNZ, ANZ, Westpac Trust,** and **National Bank** are there (with ATMs). Open M-F 9am-4:30pm.

Local Services

Library/ Internet Access: Wanganui District Library (tel. 345 8195), in Queens Park. Internet access $5 per 30min. Open M-F 9am-8pm, Sa 9am-4:30pm.

Laundromat: Wanganui Laundrette, 43 Hatrick St. (tel. 345 3980). $6 wash and dry. Drop it off in the morning, pick it up later. Open M-F 8am-4:30pm.

Public Toilet: St. Hill St., next to Cook's Garden.

Showers: Polysport Health and Fitness Center, 32 Wilson St. (tel. 348 8223). $2 per shower, open M-Th 6am-9pm, F 6am-8pm, Sa 8am-1pm, Su 8am-noon.

Emergency and Communications

Emergency: Dial **111.**

Police: Wanganui Safer Travel Centre (tel. 348 1968), on Victoria Ave. at Majestic Sq. Main station (tel. 345 4488) on Bell St.

Pharmacy: Wicksteed Pharmacy, 214 Wicksteed St. (tel. 345 6166). Open daily 8:30am-8:30pm. After hours, call pharmacist on duty.

Medical Services: Wanganui City Doctors, 163 Wicksteed St. (tel./fax 348 8333). Doctors on call 5pm-8:30am and 24hr. on weekends and holidays. During weekdays, they will direct you to an appropriate doctor. The **Wanganui Hospital** (tel. 348 1234) is on Heads Rd.

Post Office: 60 Ridgway St. (tel. 345 8343). Replete with Art Deco Maori faces carved into the facade. Open M-F 9am-5pm.

Telephone Code: 06.

ACCOMMODATIONS

Hostels and backpackers are rooted alongside the English oaks on the banks of the river, but the seeds of alternative accommodations have been spread throughout the city and as far as the sea.

The Tamara Backpackers Hostel, 24 Somme Parade (tel. 347 6300; fax 345 8488; email tamarabakpak@xtra.co.nz). Well-equipped kitchen and 3 lounges. Free VCR movies and bikes. Some rooms with river views; all with blankets and heaters. Dorms have 4 beds max. and are centered around a large back yard. Dorms $14; singles $22; doubles or twins $30-32. Reception open 8am-8pm, though check-in anytime. Check-out 10am. Key deposit $10.

Riverside Inn (YHA Associate), 2 Plymouth St. (tel./fax 347 2529). A century-old pink and mauve Victorian house with antique bureaus and basins; backpacker bunks are in a newly renovated room or out in the back building. The former are packed together closely, but the huge kitchen/dining room helps to compensate. B&B singles $45; doubles $70. Backpacker dorms (co-ed and women's) $15; shared doubles in the out-building $35 per person. Check-in, check-out anytime.

The Grand Hotel (tel. 345 0955; fax 345 0953; email THE-GRAND-HOTEL@xtra.co.nz), on the corner of Guyton and St. Hill St. Built in 1927 in the heart of Wanganui, The Grand is just that. Rooms are colorful and plush, especially the suites. Freebies abound: laundry, parking, baggage storage, jacuzzi, and pick-up from bus station or airport. Three bars, casino, and restaurant. Doubles $70; quads $90; suites start at $100, extra person $10. Check in 24 hr., check out 10am.

Castlecliff Holiday Park, 1a Rangiora St. (tel. 344 2227; fax 344 3078; toll-free (0800) 25 454 7275; email tokiwipark@xtra.co.nz), at Castlecliff Beach. Not exactly Camelot, but roll out of bed onto the black sand beach. Communal kitchen, showers, and toilets. Free pickup from the bus station; taxi bus stops across the street. Backpackers cabin $15. Tent sites $7.50; powered $10, $16 for 2. Caravans $16; standard cabins $35; extra person $7.50. Check-out 10am.

FOOD AND NIGHTLIFE

Wanganui sticks with the basics and does them well. Eateries cluster around **Victoria Ave.** and its side streets from the river to **Guyton St.** Or, whip up your own dish after a stop at **Food Town** (tel. 345 8720), at Taupo Quay and St. Hill St. (Open M-Tu and Sa 8:30am-7pm, W and F 8:30am-9pm, Su 8:30am-6pm.)

⊛**Red Eye Cafe,** 96 Guyton St. (tel. 345 5646). Peruse the local art on the walls, play with the giant wooden ball, or lose yourself in the backyard mosaic mandala—just don't forget to come back for your food. Choose from a variety of hearty breakfasts ($5-9), imaginative pizzas and quiches ($3-5) for lunch, and exotic dinner entrees such as Thai green curry with mango chutney ($8.50-13.50). Open Tu-Sa 9am-10pm (kitchen closed 4-6pm), Su-M 10am-4pm.

Amadeus Riverbank Cafe, 69 Taupo Quay (tel. 345 1538). Experience a harmonious meal by the banks of the Whanganui composed most-artfully by a friendly and talented ensemble. Savory stuffed potatoes ($3-5) and sumptuous sandwiches ($6-12.50) abound. As a finale to your meal, select something sweet from the Calorie Gallery ($2-4). Open M-Tu 8:30am-4pm, W 8:30am-9pm, Th-F 8:30am-10pm (from 7am on summer weekdays), Sa 10am-10pm, Su 10am-6pm.

Jabie's Kebab on the Avenue, 168 Victoria Ave. (tel. 347 2800). "Real food...unreal flavour" promises Wanganui's one-stop kebab shop. Try a kebab of lamb, veggie, chicken, or falafel ($4-8.50 per plate). Pita, hummus, salads, and yogurt go for $3.50-6.50. The $2 baklava may induce shimmying, but that's okay...the spray-painted belly dancer mural proclaims "auditions anytime." Open M-W 11am-9pm, Th-Sa 11am-10pm, Su 4-9pm.

Rutland Arms (tel. 347 7677), on Ridgway St. at Victoria Ave. Join the crowds of locals at this traditional English pub, complete with roaring fireplace, antlers, and beer labels nailed to the open-timber construction. The food here is big—meat lasagna ($4.50) is considered a "snack." Main courses for $13-23, and large selection of draught beers and 50 imported malt whiskies. Open daily from 9:30am.

While more empty than not during the week, pubs are all the rage in Wanganui on the weekends and attract locals and tourists alike. At **The Red Lion Inn,** 45 Anzac Parade (tel. 345 3831), watch people from all walks of life skulling (that's "chugging" to some) handles of the namesake brew ($3.20; live entertainment on Saturdays; open daily 11am-3am). It can be a walk, but the music at **The Celtic Arms,** 432 Victoria Ave. (tel. 347 7037), makes the trip worthwhile. Moderately priced food ($7.50-15) includes all of what you'd expect at an Irish bar, but most people come here for the other staple of Irish pub culture. Open daily noon-1am.

SIGHTS AND ACTIVITIES

Those wanting to spend a day or two in town before heading out into the wilderness might head to the **Whanganui Regional Museum** (tel. 345 7443), in **Queens Park.** Its Te Atihau forum (a place for all peoples to "anchor their canoes"), houses the largest surviving *waka taua* (war canoe) in the Wanganui area. Another exhibit in the permanent collection displays the instruments used in the tribal art of *moko* (see p. 44). *(Open M-Sa 10am-4:30pm, Su 1-4:30pm. Admission $2, children 60¢.)* Also in Queens Park at the top of the hill, the **Sargeant Gallery** houses a permanent collection of local art from the early 20th century, as well as visiting shows. *(Open M-F 10:30am-4:30pm, Sa-Su and holidays 1pm-4:30pm. Donations appreciated.)* Just south of **Queens Park,** one block east of Victoria Ave. on Market Pl., are the deceptively quiet **Moutoa Gardens.**

These gardens were the site of a visible **Maori land rights demonstration** (see **Recent Events,** p. 57) several years ago. Adjacent to the gardens on Rutland St. is the **Quay School of the Arts,** the third largest institution of its kind in New Zealand. A variety of student art is on display in the gallery. To the west of Queens Park, on Maria Pl., are the **Cooks Gardens.** No kitchen herbs here—just a rugby pitch, New Zealand's wooden cycling velodrome, and a running track that was the site of Peter Snell's world-record mile.

    Castlecliff Beach, where the river meets the sea, is noted for its black sand and good surf. **The Sport Shed,** 63A Victoria Ave. (tel. 347 6508), can recommend local surfing mavens if you want to learn the fine art of catching a wave. To get to Castlecliff, take Quay St. W. to Heads Rd. and continue 9km. Alternatively, head for Maria Pl. in town and catch the #3 or #4 Taxi Bus. Farther up the coast, **Kai Iwi Beach** attracts locals who wish to avoid the crowds, but is less accessible by public transportation. Get a bird's-eye view of it all from the top of the **Durie Hill Lookout Tower.** The journey begins from Anzac Parade at the base of Victoria Ave. where a long tunnel takes you 219m into the hill. Then an elevator whisks you up 66m *through* the hill, depositing you at the top. Climb the 300m shell rock tower (built in 1919) and you have reached the pinnacle. *(Open M-F 7:30am-6pm, Sa 10am-6pm, Su 10am-5pm. Elevator is $1 one-way.)* For more adventure (and more money), swoop over town in the dashing Tiger Moth biplane flown by the **Wanganui Aero Club** (tel. 345 3994). Goggles, a souvenir photo, and wind to whip through your hair are all included. *(Operates during daylight hours, weather permitting. 15min. flight $70.)* The more pioneer-minded can let an engine do the paddling for them on the *Otunui,* New Zealand's only paddlewheel boat. A one-hour coffee cruise ($15) departs from the end of Glasgow St. The longer four-hour cruise ($25) departs from the city marina at the base of Victoria Ave. (tel. 343 6343 for schedules and bookings). The other paddlewheeler in town, the *Waimarie,* sank in her moorings back in 1952 and is now housed in the **Whanganui Riverboat Centre,** 1a Taupo Quay (tel. 347 1863). Riverboatabilia and photos galore await inside. *(Open M-F 9am-4pm, Sa 10am-2pm. Free.)*

■ Whanganui National Park

At times seeming almost primeval, the Whanganui River basin is a place of moss-swathed *rimu, kanuka,* and *manuka* mingled with luxuriant ponga ferns. Secluded *marae* and missions still flourish upstream, and even the tiniest communes of artisans and farmers in the tributary valleys seem to be on a higher plane. The eel weirs and riverboats of yore may be gone, but the river endures—with the longest navigable course (200 km) in the North Island (second in overall length only to the Waikato). The Whanganui starts as a trickling stream on the slopes of Tongariro and opens its mouth wide to empty into the Tasman Sea.

    Traditional points of access to the river are **Taumarunui, Ohinepane, Whakahoro,** and **Pipiriki.** Below Pipiriki, the river is accessible by car at key points (see **The River Road,** p. 162). The heart of **Whanganui National Park** (established 1987) is comprised of the forest adjoining the central and lower stretches of the river. The park's remote interior is accessible only to those hardy trampers bold enough to venture forth from the river's edge (see **Whanganui Tracks**). Information about existing trails is available at DOC Field Centers in Pipiriki, Wanganui, and Taumarunui.

THE WHANGANUI RIVER JOURNEY

The Whanganui River can provide anything from a spiritually serene kayak or canoe trip, to the adrenaline-induced stupor of a jetboat ride. Generally, most people travel down the river as far as **Pipiriki,** since past that point the scenery becomes less interesting and the paddling more difficult. From **Taumarunui** the journey is usually five days, while those who begin further downstream at **Whakahoro** can expect three days of paddling. Although it is classed as a "beginner's river," as many as 239 rapids between Taumarunui and the sea ensure plenty of opportunities for weary travelers to commune with the combative side of nature. During the canoeing season (Oct.-Apr.), this river sojourn becomes a Great Walk and requires a **hut and campsite pass** from the DOC. The pass is good for seven days and six nights and can be purchased from DOC Field Centres or from local visitor's centers for $25. Alternatively, it can be purchased for $35 from a patrolling warden who catches you without one. All huts and campsites are first-come, first-serve. The huts can sleep up to 30, but bring a tent just in case and be aware that all camping within 250m of the river must be at a designated campsite. Campsites are free in the **off-season,** while huts revert to a ticket system based on an honor code. Deposit tickets in a clearly marked receptacle in the hut (adults $8, children $4). Overnight visitors traveling by boat can purchase a **one-night pass** from the usual sources (canoe $6, jetboat $8).

The water journey from Taumaranui begins at idyllic **Cherry Grove,** where the Ongarue and Whanganui rivers meet, making an ideal picnic area with a barbecue, campsite, and **DOC Field Centre.** The crafts hit rapids immediately out of Taumarunui into the first stretch of river, which is surrounded mostly by roads and paddocks. Legend holds that if travelers don't place a sprig of green on the **Taniwha Rock,** a river guardian will smite them for their insolence. The first opportunity to stop and camp (after approx. 4 hours of paddling) is at **Ohinepane,** where there is a campsite with potable water. An imposing sight a bit farther downstream are the carved *niu* poles at **Maraekowhai,** where Hauhau warriors used to pray before embarking for battle.

One hour down from Maraekowhai sits **Whakahoro,** one of many *pa* (fortified hillsides) on the banks of the river. A gong on a nearby bluff used to resonate with alarm in time of attack. High banks close in like a muddy maw from here to Pipiriki. The only indication that the area around Mangapurua and Raetihi was intended for use as a World War I rehabilitation site is the monolithic **Bridge to Nowhere.** The 1936 bridge may be a token reminder of the failed settlement, but it's now also part of the picture-perfect **Mangapurua Track.** The unforgettable **Tieke Marae,** just 12½km from Pipiriki, welcomes river travelers for an overnight stay (although the Maori now run this hut, passes and tickets still apply). Respect for protocol is requested, including participation in the *powhiri* welcoming ceremony (instructions are given on location). Don't forget that one representative from the group must give a brief speech, laying money, food, or a small gift (*koha*) on the ground afterwards. Another exceptional accomodation option is the Flying Fox homestay (see p. 162). Tours of the river tend to be based out of Taumarunui near the northern end of the park, or in Wanganui at the extreme southern end (prices range from $30-1500 and trip from 1hr. to 3 days).

WHANGANUI TRACKS

The **Mangapurua Track,** when combined with the **Kaiwhakauka Track,** turns into a 40km, 20-hour, three- to four-day endeavor. It takes off from the Mangapurua Landing on the Whanganui River, then goes over the **Bridge to Nowhere,** through the Mangapurua Valley, and past vast sections of farmland. The track climbs to the **Mangapurua Trig,** offering panoramic views of Mt. Tongariro, Mt. Egmont (Taranaki), and the junction with the **Kaiwhakuaka Track.** Then it's down through the Kaiwhakauka Valley past bush and farms to the **Whakahoro Hut** ($8). This is the only hut along the whole track, though flat campsites are plentiful. From here, a road leads back to Owhango or Raurumu.

The other major trail in the park is the **Matematlaona Track,** which tempts diehard hikers with 42 km of serpentine trail leading deep into the bush along an old Maori trail. The path leads from the **Kohi Saddle** on Upper Mangaehu Rd. well east of **Stratford** (p. 152), to the Whanganui River just downstream and across from the Tieke Marae. The three- to four-day journey stops at three huts ($8) and overall the grade is much flatter than the Mangapurua Track. For a good daytrip out of Wanganui, the **Atene Skyline Track** is a six to eight-hour hike that takes you in almost a complete loop, accessible by a 36km drive up the **River Rd.** (see below) with views of Mt. Ruapehu, Mt. Egmont (Taranaki), and the Tasman Sea.

THE RIVER ROAD

After a 30-year construction fraught with floods and mudslides, 1934 saw the opening of the aptly named **River Road**. Dancing a *pas de deux* with the bushy banks of the Whanganui River, the road allows the only automobile access to the settlements upstream from Wanganui. In fact, it was the completion of the road that signaled the end of the paddlewheel boat as a viable transportation method, as a 10-hour boat ride between Manganui and Pipiriki was reduced to a 1½-hour drive. The River Road parallels SH4 some 15km to the east, connecting Wanganui to **Pipiriki.** From Pipiriki, the road continues out of Whanganui National Park to meet up with **Raetihi** (27km), less than 15km from the ski town of **Ohakune** (p. 178). The northern extremes of the park can be reached from **Whakahoro** via roads from **Owhanga** (south of Taumarunui, p. 162) or **Raurimu** (just north of the town of National Park, p. 177), both on SH4. If you don't have your own car, riding along with the **mail run** (tel. 025 443 421) is a great way to get into the heart of the river valley and meet locals at the same time. (Pickup 7:15am from Wanganui with advance reservation; otherwise, show up early behind the post office, 60 Ridgway St.) The run returns to Wanganui around 2 or 3pm, or you can ask to be dropped off anywhere along the way and be picked up on a different day ($25).

Travelers heading up the road from Wanganui soon see the **Oyster Cliffs,** which take a large white bite out of the river as a reminder of a time when oceans enveloped this valley. A bit farther up, there's riverside camping at the **Otumarie Campsite** (the only DOC campgrounds on the Wanganui side of Pipiriki). Those who continue upstream arrive at one of the most singularly wonderful homestays in New Zealand, **The Flying Fox** (tel./fax 342 8160), 44km up the River Rd. from Wanganui. Truly off the beaten track, the Flying Fox is accessible only by boating up the river or via an aerial cableway—a "flying fox" in Kiwispeak—suspended 20m above the river. En route river travelers are most welcome, too, as cool drinks in the shade of the English oaks are a hospitable tradition. Stay the night in the secluded private bush cabin or in the burlap-walled loft above the microbrewery. Self-proclaimed hippie proprietors Annette and John may feel personally insulted if you don't stop in for a beer or a freshly baked muffin. (Loft or cabins $20 per person; campsites $8. Mountain bikes $10 per day, canoes $35 per day. Advance booking absolutely required. Free laundry and linen.)

A trio of villages with Christian names and a Maori populace stand farther upstream. **Corinth** (formerly Koriniti) features the Opeiriki *pa* (never once taken in battle), a lovely *marae,* and the first Anglican church on the river (est. 1840). **London** (Ranana) is one of the bigger villages on the river, and retains traces of its past as a traditional center of agriculture. **Jerusalem** (Hiruharama) is home to a French Marist Mission and the poet James K. Baxter. Just before Jerusalem is Mautoa Island from which Maori followers of Hauhauism (a xenophobic religious sect, see p. 209) launched ritualized battles against the tribes of the lower river. Continuing upstream, find the cascading beauty of **Omorehu Waterfall.** An alpha-omega of a town, **Pipiriki** is at the end of the River Road and is also the beginning for many jetboat rides and two walking tracks. The **Pukehinau Walk** loops 1km to the Pukehinau crest, once a Hauhau outpost with strategic (and gorgeous) views of the river valley. **Wairua Hikoi Tours** (tel. 345 3485) is a unique tour with a spiritual emphasis on Maori culture that offers shorter one-day canoe trips to The Flying Fox ($45, vehicle transfer included). You must find your own way to Jerusalem (see the mail run, p. 162).

■ Taumarunui

Although undeniably a small town by all physical accounts (pop. 7,668), Taumarunui offers access to much of the surrounding region, thus living up to its reputation as the "Heart of the King Country." Situated at the confluence of the Ongarue and Whanganui Rivers, it is the logical starting point for expeditions down the latter. It also lies at the junction of SH4 and SH43 (the **Stratford-Taumarunui Heritage Trail),** serving as a crossroads for those traveling through the Taranaki and Ruapenu regions or to Whanganui and Tongariro National Parks. Regardless of your destination, this is a good place to gather supplies and information before hitting river, road, rail, or trail.

Taumarunui sits along the **Main Trunk Railway** and **SH4** (called Hakiaha St. within the town limits), 43km north of the town of National Park (p. 177), 129km east of Stratford (p. 152), 82km south of Te Kuiti, and 65km west of Turangi (p. 173). **Tranz-Scenic** (tel. (0800) 802 802) heads to Auckland (4½hr., 2 per day, $52-59) and Wellington (6½hr., 2 per day, $72-84), while **InterCity** (tel. (0800) 731 711) sends one train each day except Saturday to Auckland (4¾hr., $72-81) and Wellington (6hr., $64). **Pioneer Jet Boat Tours Ltd.** (tel. 895-8074) has a bus to Hamilton (M-F 8am, $26). Toward National Park, most **hitchhikers** try the area past the Main Trunk Cafe by the Hakiaha St. railyards. Toward Te Kuiti, they often try the Ongarue River Rd. (SH4). Once in town, **Silver Cabs** (tel. 895 5444) and **Taumaranui Taxis** (tel. 895 8877) will help you get around. The **Visitor Information Centre** (tel. 895 7494; fax 895 6117) is conveniently located in the railway station (open M-F 9am-4:30pm, Sa-Su and holidays 10am-4pm). Amuse yourself with a working model of the Raurimu spiral traintrack while you wait. Take a nature walk through Cherry Grove to get to the **DOC Field Centre** (tel. 895 8201; after hours tel. (025) 946 650; open M-F 8am-4:30pm, and during canoe season (Oct.-Apr.) also open Sa-Su 8:30-9:30am.) **ANZ** (on Hakiaha St.), **BNZ**, and **Westpac Trust Bank** (both one street over on Miriama St.) are ready to serve with **ATMs** (banks open M-F 9am-4:30pm). The **library** is on Hakiaha St. In an **emergency**, dial **III** or call the **hospital** (tel. 896 0020). The **police** (tel. 895 8119), are on Hakiaha St. The **post office** (tel. 895 8149) is on Miriama St. (open M-F 9am-5pm). The **telephone code** is **06**.

Taumarunui Camping Ground (tel./fax 895 9345) is 2km east of town in Manunui. (Tent sites $7, powered sites $8. 2-person cabins $25. One flat, max. 12 people, $15 per head.) Those searching for a few more creature comforts at a budget price can try the **Taumarunui Alpine Inn**, 4 Maral St. (tel. 895 3478; fax 895 3477; http://www.middle-of-nowhere.co.nz). Choose from a variety of comfy singles, doubles, twins or one triple. Amenities include a TV lounge, free laundry and kitchen use, and the only **internet access** in town (for a small fee). Those planning a trip downriver can take advantage of secured off-street parking and free bag storage. All rooms are $16 per person, $6 extra for linen and towels. (Front desk open 7am-10pm; check-out by 10am.) If you're looking for a bed and not much more, the **Grand Lodge Hotel** (tel. 895 6444) is conveniently located across the street from the train station. (Singles start at $15, twins and doubles $37. Linen and blanket $4. Laundry $5. Limited kitchen access.) At the **Tattles Motel,** 23 Marae St. (tel./fax 895 8063) rooms are huge, family style, and wheelchair accessible. Doubles and twins range from $55 to 60; family units start at $80. Parking is available. Quality dining establishments are scarce in Taumarunui, though the **Rivers II Cafe,** 43 Hakiaha St. (tel. 895 5822), stands out. Patrons can enjoy breakfast, lunch, or dinner in a spacious, brightly lit interior or outside at tables along the sidewalk. The French toast with banana ($9) deserves special praise (open daily 7:30am-10pm.) For a quick bite before you catch a bus or train, or to cure a case of the late-night munchies, the **Main Trunk Cafe** on Hakiaha St. is your best bet. Look for the flashy red railway cars to the left as you step out of the train station (open Su-W 8am-midnight, Th-Sa 24hr.). The most comprehensive supermarket is the **New World** (tel. 895 7634), located at the northern end of Hakiaha St. (open M-Sa 8am-7pm, Su 9am-5pm).

Apart from the broad array of outdoor recreational activities, visitors are drawn here to see the serpentine **Raurimu Spiral.** A mighty feat of engineering, this 1908 section of railway track loops and twists and at one point doubles back on itself as it climbs onto the central plateau. The best way to experience the stomach-churning glory of the spiral is to take a **scenic train ride,** which departs Taumarunui daily at 1pm, returning at 3pm ($28 round-trip). Or, gaze upon its loopiness from the lookout 37km south on SH4 at Raurimu. Drivers can also traverse the **Taumarunui-Stratford Heritage Trail,** a 150km stretch of SH43 established in 1990 to provide travelers with a chance to learn about the history of the region. Teal and yellow signs mark sites along the trail, which include several lookout points and historic sites. Also, just off the trail (10km) in Ohura, is a **white-collar prison,** where approximately 90 "guests of Her Majesty" are *invited* to serve their time.

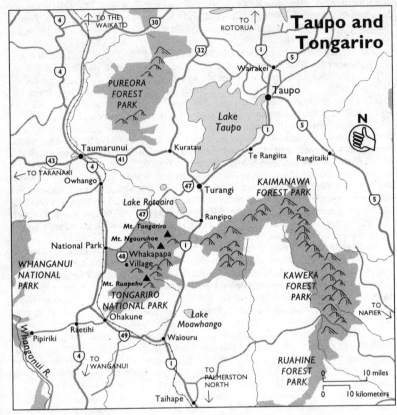

Taupo and Tongariro

With fire and brimstone burning at its core and snowcapped giants towering at its center, the Taupo and Tongariro region uneasily awaits further volcanic tantrums. The lightly snoozing peaks of Ruapehu, Ngauruhoe, and Tongariro provide the energy for the region's geothermal valleys and keep the North Island's heart thumping. Lake Taupo, the country's biggest lake, fills a crater formed from a monumental explosion some 26,000 years ago. Its placid, shimmering waters reflect the peaks of Tongariro National Park (a World Heritage Area), where skiers careen down mountain slopes to the base towns of Whakapapa Village, National Park, and Ohakune. Mellow lake cruisers enjoy the area's choice trout fishing, sailing, and boating in summertime. Despite all the excitement, you can relax here—and not just after a skydive.

🐾 TAUPO AND TONGARIRO HIGHLIGHTS

- Rugged volcanic terrain and steaming turquoise pools enthrall trampers on the splendid Tongariro Northern Circuit (see p. 174).
- The trout in Lake Taupo (see p. 169) attract anglers from around the world.
- Taupo Skydive (see p. 170) gives a birds-eye view of the region's splendor—for those who can take it in at terminal velocity.

■ Taupo

Maybe it's something in the water. Possibly it's the ever-present views of great volcanoes rising beyond sparkling waves. It could be the relief after surviving a morning
skydive and bungy jump combo. Or it might be the happy-go-lucky vibes from the
residents of this sunny community (pop. 21,257) who preside over the largest lake in
New Zealand (616km²) and its population of fat trout. Whatever it is, smiling comes
easy in Taupo. The town lies at the origin of the **Waikato River** and on the same belt
of smoking geothermal activity that powers Rotorua, and offers its attractions to
unsuspecting visitors who may have initially planned on merely passing through. If
you've dreamed of catching a giant trout or covet a hot springs soak, Taupo awaits.

ORIENTATION AND PRACTICAL INFORMATION

Tucked into a corner made by the **Waikato River** as it gushes from the northeast
bulge of Lake Taupo, the city radiates like a streaking comet. Its head is at **Tongariro Street** aimed at the visitors center and the **Boat Harbor,** and its outer tail
angles away along **Lake Terrace** and the river on **Spa Road.** Taupo's center of
gravity lies between **Tongariro** and **Ruapehu Street.** The wayward streaks of SH1
and SH5 exit across the Waikato to Rotorua or Auckland, and the other way to
Turangi and Napier.

   Buses: InterCity/Newmans leave from Gascoigne St. They head daily to Auckland
   (5hr., 2-4 per day, $40-50); Hamilton (3hr., 2-3 per day, $20-30); Rotorua (1hr., 2-4
   per day, $20-25); and Wellington (6hr., 2-4 per day, $63-66). InterCity/Newmans

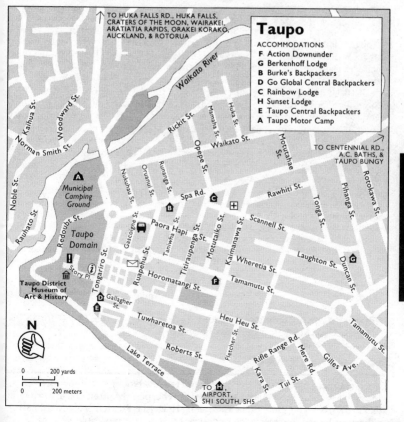

Taupo

ACCOMMODATIONS
F Action Downunder
G Berkenhoff Lodge
B Burke's Backpackers
D Go Global Central Backpackers
C Rainbow Lodge
H Sunset Lodge
E Taupo Central Backpackers
A Taupo Motor Camp

TAUPO & TONGARIRO

and **Kiwi Shuttles** (tel. (025) 503 654) go daily to Napier (2hr., 1-3 per day, $24-35). InterCity connects daily with Turangi's Alpine Scenic Tours to get up to National Park and Whakapapa Village (2hr., 2:30pm, $29). **Waitomo Wanderer** (tel. 873 7559) goes to Waitomo ($40 round-trip). **Taupo Ski Shuttle,** organized by local ski shops, runs daily to the skifields of Tongariro ($25). Book InterCity/Newmans at Taupo Travel Centre on Gascoigne St. (tel. 378 9032), off Tamamutu St. or at Taupo Visitor Centre.

Shuttles: Adventure Link (tel. 025 459 698) runs shuttles between most of Taupo's spread out area attractions (day pass $10).

Taxis: STOP Cabs (24hr. tel. 378 9250) and **Taupo Taxis** (24hr. tel. 378 5100).

Hitchhiking: Taupo is the crossroads of the North Island; finding traffic is not a problem, but getting far enough out of town (especially to go south on SH1) may be. To head north on SH1, many thumbers cross the Waikato.

Visitor Center: The Taupo Visitor Centre (tel. 378 9000; fax 378 9003) is on Tongariro St. Open daily 8:30am-5pm.

DOC: More of a field center than a source of information. Way out at 115 Centennial Dr. (tel. 378 3885), an extension of Spa Rd. Open M-F 8am-noon.

Currency Exchange: Banks! Banks! Everywhere banks! **ASB Bank** (tel. 378 8060), at Tongariro and Horomatangi St., exchanges M-F 9am-4pm; open until 4:30pm.

Rentals: R&R Sports, 17 Tamamutu St. (tel. 377 1585), buys and sells used backpacking gear; they also rent mountain bikes (half day $18, full day $28), fishing poles ($10-20 per day), ski equipment packages ($20) and snowboards with boots ($38). Taupo has cheaper ski rentals than the on-the-mountain shops. **Pointons Ski Shop** (tel. 377 0087), has skis, boots, and poles packages ($15) or snowboard and boots ($40).

It's a Bird, It's a Plane, It's...

Your one-stop potty shop, the **SuperLoo,** next to the visitors center, was voted "the best loo in New Zealand" by Keep New Zealand Beautiful. The country is full of automated public toilets, but nothing quite compares to SuperLoo. Inside the stalls, exclamations of "this really *is* a super loo" can be heard. Kids heading into the toilets spread their arms out and while swooping inside like an airplane, yell "SUUUUUPER LOOOO. Here I come to save the day!" Originally called "The Super Pooper," in 1992 the mayor of Taupo advocated a name change to "The Loo-Pee." Compromise was reached, and thus "Super Loo" was christened in January 1993. A mini-festival marked the occasion, with events such as bobbing for apples in the toilets (to show how clean the water was), anti-graffiti lectures, distance and endurance contests (need we explain?), toilet paper flag football, and a free year of SuperLoo use for the first person to take a poop. The next time nature calls in Taupo, step inside and see for yourself what all the fuss is about (toilets 20¢, 4min. shower $1).

Emergency: Dial 111.

Medical Services: The Taupo Health Centre, 117 Heu Heu St. (tel. 378 7060), is open M-F 8am-6pm. After hours the phone will give you an emergency contact, or check the *Taupo Times* for the on-duty doctor. **Main St. Pharmacy** (tel./fax 378 2636), corner of Tongariro St. and Heu Heu St., is open daily 9am-8:30pm. The **hospital** (tel. 378 8100) is on Kotare St.

Police: The 24hr. station (tel. 378 6060) is behind the visitors center in Story Pl.

Post Office: At the corner of Horomatangi and Ruapehu St. (tel. 378 9090). Open M-F 8:30am-5:30pm, Sa 9am-noon.

Internet Access: Computer Kingdom, 15 Tamamutu St. (tel. 378 4546) $6 per 30min. Open M-F 8:30am-5pm, Sa 9am-3pm.

Telephone Code: 07.

ACCOMMODATIONS

Older, cheaper finds are clustered in the streets a few blocks east of town center. As always, book ahead in summer. Otherwise, the cheapest riverfront bed in town is on **Reid's Farm Rd.** a bit south of the Falls, along Huka Falls Rd. (north of town off SH1), with free camping. Summer/winter rates are listed, where applicable.

⊕**Rainbow Lodge,** 99 Titiraupenga Rd. (tel. 378 5754; fax 377 1568; email rainbow@clear.net.nz), just off Spa Rd. There may be no pot of gold here, but there is a bottomless pot of free coffee. On a residential street, Rainbow's colorful decor and atmosphere brightens even the darkest day. Sauna and pool table. Close to town, though free pickups are still offered. Off-street parking, mountain bike and fishing rod hire. Dorms $15; singles $26; doubles or twins $36.

Action Downunder (YHA) (tel. 378 3311; fax 378 9612), at the corner of Tamamutu and Kaimanawa St. Shiny, new, and clean, from its glossy, native-timber dining room tables to the bustling unisex bathrooms. Hospitable Ken and Allison will either arrange it, give you a voucher, or tell you how to do it. Small TV lounge; the kitchen is ship-shape. Compact, sunny dorms $16; singles $25; doubles or twins $36. Central heating. Bikes for hire ($15 per day, $10 deposit).

Go Global (VIP) (tel. 377 0044; fax 377 0059), at the corner of Tongariro St. and Tuwharetoa St. With a restaurant and Axis Party Bar downstairs, there's no need to go global when you can stay inside the comfortable confines of this large and new hostel, though the noise might drive you out. Nice views of the lake. Adequately spacious rooms, most with own bathroom. Expansion plans for the small TV lounge and tiny kitchen area. Dorms $17; twins $17; doubles $40. Key deposit $10.

Sunset Lodge, 5 Tremain Ave. (tel. 378 3206). Turn off Lake Terrace onto Hawai St. For a more low-key stay, the smallest hostel in Taupo offers lake front ambiance and legendary homemade banana bread. Free bike, pickup and shuttle to "Craters of the Moon." Dorms $15; doubles and twins $34.

Burke's Backpackers, 69 Spa Rd. (tel. 378 9292; fax 378 9092). Hidden behind car dealerships, this old peach motel has the private bathroom advantage (though the rooms were never intended for quite so many bunks). Well-kept grounds make for nice sun bathing. Decent kitchen/dining area, TV. Dorms $15; doubles and family rooms sharing private bathrooms $18 per person, with bath $20. Stylin' spa pool $1, free basic breakfast between 8-9am. Key deposit $10. Bikes for hire.

Berkenhoff (VIP) (tel./fax 378 4909), at the corner of Duncan St. and Scannell St., a 15min. walk from town center. With thatched roof reception, gorgeous thousand-dollar palm and free spa and pool, this nicely self-contained lodge offers quality resort-like amenities. The impressive bar, named "Jake's Place" after its mellow, ice cream-loving, 80 kilo black dog, has Sky TV. Free breakfast, bikes and pickups; daily dropoffs and BBQ dinners ($5-$8). Dorms $15; twins and doubles $36.

Taupo Central Backpackers (VIP) (tel. 378 3206; fax 378 0344), at the corner of Tongariro and Tuwharetoa St. Two-and-a-half reasons to stay: 1) it's central, 2) the in-house bar/deck has sweet views, 2½) if you wake up early enough, there's free weetbix and toast (8-9am). Full of Kiwi Experience busloads. Rooms are adequate, with a sufficient private bathroom. Inadequately sized kitchen. Bunks $18; twins and doubles $42. Key deposit $10.

Taupo Motor Camp, 15 Redoubt St. (tel./fax 377 3080). Go a brief hop up Tongariro St. from the visitors center, then turn left. So central it needn't be fancy. Bunks in summer $15 (winter $12); elementary cinderblock cabin singles $35/$20; doubles $40/$35. Grassy, riverside campgrounds under nice big trees $10/$9.50 per person. The kitchen is basic. They go chocka during holidays, but leave room for internationals. Key deposit $10.

Orakei Korako Geyserland (tel. 378 3131; fax 378 0371), 35km from Taupo. If you've got your own transport, this hidden lakeside lodge across the water from Taupo's best geothermal site is unbeatably scenic and peaceful. Rev up the jukebox and slip into the front deck spa. Bring bedding and food (limited daytime cafe). Rustic communal lodge and bunks you can tell were once trees ($20). Tourist flats (up to 6) with kitchenettes $20 per person mid-week (min. 3). Flats are charged at their full 6-person rates Sa-Su, so if you can't fill the beds, you pay the difference.

FOOD

Taupo isn't known for its middle-range restaurant options. Each of the **nightlife listings** for Taupo offers affordable and decent meals, often with backpacker or nightly specials. For the true Taupo experience, delight in some trout. While it can't be sold over the counter, a few places around town will prepare your catch (for a fee); ask around. The **Pak 'N Save** (tel. 377 1155) is at the corner of Ruapehu and Tamamutu

St. (open M-F 8:30am-8pm, Sa-Su 8:30am-7pm), while **Maxis 24hr. Food,** on Roberts St. near Ruapehu St., has your 3am burger, soda, tobacco, or band-aids.

☀**Pasta Mia,** 5 Horomatangi St. (tel. 377 2930), supplies restaurants around the country with fresh pasta and offers a limited lunch in its home base of Taupo. A mouth watering single serving of pasta is only $5.50 ($10.50 for double)—choose from various types of pastas and sauces to make your perfect combination. You can also take away the raw ingredients. For only $13, you'll have enough uncooked pasta and sauce to make new life-long friends at the hostel (faster than water comes to boil). Open M-F 10am-5:30pm, and Sa 10am-2pm.

Replete Delicatessen and Cafe, 45 Heu Heu St., (tel. 377 3011). Crockery bowls filled with well-prepared, gorgeous and inventive dishes (including veggie options) make for lunchtime eagerness among the crowds that clog the ordering area. You can't go wrong, with most items under $7. Take your unforgettable smoothie or latte in its Grecian-style urn to the open front windows for prime people-watching. Open M-F 8:45am-5pm, Sa 9am-2:30pm, Su 10am-mid-afternoon.

Holy Cow, 10 Roberts St. (tel. 378 0040). This backpacker bar mecca is the best value, with backpacker meals from $5. Mains like couscous and vegetables or spaghetti bolognaise (from $5) are good, hot, and too big to finish. Retains a family-style atmosphere in early evening (before 9pm-ish).

Nonni's (tel. 378 6894), at the corner of Tongariro St. and Lake Terr. A local favorite, Nonni's prime lakefront location is well served by outdoor seating and superb service in an unhurried atmosphere. All-day bruch menu ($8-12) with a large Mediterranean selection. Open daily for lunch 7am-3pm and F-Sa for dinner from 6pm.

NIGHTLIFE

Every backpacker and her mother heads to the bar of Taupo, **Holy Cow,** 10 Robert St. (tel. 378 0040). With burly bouncers spouting world wisdom, belching DJs, and rumps shaking to pumping commercial music, it's a rollicking time. (Open daily 5pm-3am; happy hours 5-7pm and 9-10pm.) Bust out the button-down for a Speight's at the schmoozy **Rockefeller's** (tel. 378 3344) on Tuwharetoa St., where Taupo's business class admires itself in the brass fittings and gleaming bar. Its a good place for a quiet beer during the week and offers free ale with your quarter-kilo steak ($9.95) from Sunday to Tuesday. Taupo's not big on live music, but you can find some at **The Hobler,** 42 Tuwaretoa St. (tel. 378 0830), a popular restaurant and bar (open daily from 11:30am) or at the **Red Barrel** (tel. 378 0555), on Lake Terr. near Tongariro St. Thursdays have a band and $1 spirits from 8 to 10pm (sometimes $2 cover; open daily 10:30am-2am or earlier). Several other bars and a dance club cluster in the area near the lake end of Tongariro St.

GEOTHERMAL SIGHTS

If you ever get bored with the rippling lake and horizon of Tongariro, Ngauruhoe, and Ruapehu, turn your feet inland for Taupo's host of other attractions. Though its geothermal attractions may not get as much press as those of Rotorua, they lie along the same belt of primeval geological action. A 1954 explosion from the drilling of a geothermal bore collapsed several acres of land into a steaming pock-marked landscape called **Craters of the Moon,** now a free DOC-managed Scenic Reserve only a few kilometers north of town on SH1. *(The gates remain open all the time; don't leave valuables in your car.)* The haunting, decidedly active place is alive beneath the thin crust of earth upon which your feet tread. As small vents collapse and become blocked, minor eruptions can occur at any time. The landscape remains surprisingly green with mosses, lichens, and native bushes that love the warm, moist conditions. On chilly mornings and evenings, whirling steam adds a ghostly, otherworldly feel, enveloping and sometimes even obscuring any vista of the craters and roiling mud pools. **Walter's Tours** (tel. 378 5924) provides informative, user-friendly tours of various hot spots around Taupo, such as Craters of the Moon, Huka Falls, Orakei Korako (3hr. tour $20), or to more distant points in Rotorua and even the Waitomo Caves (from $50). **Kiwi Tours** (tel. 378 9662) goes to similar destinations, including the Tongariro Crossing ($30).

Wairakei Park, a slightly bizarre amalgamation of sights, recreational activities, a geothermal power station, a geothermally heated prawn farm, shops, and lodgings, lies across the **Waikato Bridge** on SH1. At its north end, 8km from town, sits the world's first geothermal power station, the **Wairakei Geothermal Power Development** (built 1959-64). From the **Bore Lookout,** at the end of the road turn-off, take in the post-apocalyptic terrain of massive, steaming, stainless-steel tubes worming along the ground to feed Taupo's energy needs. The **Wairekai Visitor Centre** (tel. 378 0913), at the SH1 turn-off, is a worthwhile stop (open daily 9am-4:30pm). Head south back toward town to the Huka Falls Rd. turn-off to reach the lava-red **Taupo Volcanic Activity Centre** (tel. 374 8375), the public side of the observatory next door where researchers monitor the whole volcanic zone. *(Admission $5, children $2.50.)* The Centre recently became more interactive with the introduction of a model geyser, earthquake simulator, and even a tornado machine. Check out the seismograph readings of Ruapehu and recent eruption film footage.

The zinger of attractions on the same road is, according to locals, New Zealand's most visited natural attraction. Join bus loads of camera toters who flock to **Huka Falls** to witness the 100m wide, 4m deep Waikato River force itself into a 15m wide, 3m deep rock chute, shoot breathlessly below a footbridge over the channel, and eject into a roiling pool below. It's definitely worth a look, even if you might have to elbow a few other gawkers out of the way first. The falls are accessible for those without wheels of their own with a little foot-power. The cheapest (and most aerobic) way to make the falls part of your roll of film is via the riverside **Huka Falls Track** (1hr.), leaving from Spa Thermal Park off Spa Rd. Rapids enthusiasts can continue up the path along the Waikato another hour to the stretch of the **Aratiatia Rapids,** a sight once continually impressive and now so only at 10am, noon, 2pm (and 4pm in summer), when the hydroelectric plant's gates are opened to appease visitors.

Far away (and inaccessible to those without their own wheels or a tour) is the dramatic and undeveloped private geothermal reserve of **Orakei Korako** (tel. 378 3131), which can be reached via a sign-posted road that winds through hill and deer farms off SH1 about 25 minutes north of Taupo. As steam wafts up the hidden green valley, a shuttle boat crosses the small, idyllic, dammed lake during the day. *(Open in summer 8am-4pm; in winter 8am-4:30pm.)* On the far side lie pockets of glistening silica terraces, spurting geysers (including a fascinating horizontal geyser), colorful mineral crusts, and deep, scaldingly hot cyan pools. Don't miss the spectacular fern-lined amphitheater of Aladdin's Cave with its warm mineral pool. Jewelry can reportedly be naturally cleaned in the pool in three minutes while its owners gaze at the postcard view from the cave's mouth (entrance fees and boat ride $12.50). If you're captivated, stay for a meal at the local cafeteria or even spend the night at the nearby lodge or cabin.

After a long day of touring, you'll probably want to pay a visit to one of Taupo's two popular hot springs. **De Bretts Thermal Resort** (tel. 377 6502) on the Taupo/Napier Highway, only five minutes from town, includes private pools ($8), a main pool ($7), and a giant waterslide ($4 unlimited use) in a tranquil setting. *(Open daily 7:30am-9pm.)*

ON THE WATER

Lake Taupo's blue waters fill the crater of a volcano whose eruptions were some of the most disruptive the world has ever witnessed. Its final blast, 1800 years ago, ejected 110km^3 and distributed ash and pumice meters-thick over much of the North Island. It even caused blood-red skies to be recorded in ancient Chinese and Roman literature.

The world-famous Taupo **trout,** both brown and rainbow, were introduced from California in the late 1800s and continue to draw novice and experienced anglers from across the world. The apex of the phenomenon is **ANZAC Day** (April 25, 1999), when the great fishing-fest of the ECNZ International Trout Fishing Tournament takes over town with anglers eager to take the biggest, the prettiest, the superlativest of the lake (in 1998 entries were limited to 500). Most catches average around 1½kg. Lake fishing at Taupo is relaxed, scenic, and popular. The lake trout are fat and relatively easier to catch than their more aerobic soulmates of the area's rivers. Spinning and fly fishing is permitted in the lake year-round; on the rivers, only fly fishing is allowed. All the other legal details are printed on back of the fishing license you have to purchase for any line you drop ($12 per day, $25 per week); get one at the visitors center, a sports shop, or one of the offices down at the harbor. Fishing options in Taupo are literally boundless. A group of people can charter a boat with guide and all tackle supplied, for anywhere between $50-130 per hour. Private guides are also available to teach the basics of fly fishing. Inquire at the visitors center.

The western shores of **Acacia Bay** end at cliff and bush, with an undulating edge of isolated rocky inlets and bays. A set of spectacular (if not ancient) Maori carvings have been chiseled into the rock faces at **Mine Bay,** on private land and accessible by boat only. You can approach the lake scenery with your own rented boat, or take advantage of the several outfitters with relatively cheap narrated cruises. **Taupo Scenic Kayaks** (tel. 378 1391) offers half day trips to the carvings and other sights ($40). Many cruises include the carvings, the Western Bays, Hot Water Beach, and a wide expanse of lake itself. Contact the **Charter Office** (tel. 378 3444) at the harborfront to book. The sexy,1920s sailing yacht panache of the **Barbary,** once owned by none other than Errol Flynn (2½-3hr., 2-3 per day, $20) has a strong reputation.

If cruises are too serene for the speed and danger junkie lurking in your heart, the **Huka Jet** (tel. 374 8572) is a heart-racing jetboat blast down the Waikato, performing 360° turns for the Kodak-heavy crowds at Huka Falls. *(Boats run every 30min. from Wairakei Park or the visitors center; $49, children $25.)* Or raft the 2½-hour Grade 3 Tongariro, the half-day backcountry whitewater of the Grade 3-4 Rangitaiki (also accessible from Whakatane, p. 175), or the pure excitement of the half-day Grade 4-5 Wairoa (26 days per year, due to hydroelectric control). A simple, placid float on the Waikato is always an option. Several outfitters run all or some of these rivers; check with the visitors center for details.

Punch's Place (tel. 378 5596), down at the harborfront, has a host of watersports and fishing possibilities. Putter around in a self-drive run-about ($30 per hr., fits up to 4) or get your speed buzz with a seadoo jet-bike ($50 per 30min.). Punches also provides for waterskiing and that ultimate Taupo combination of water, air, and adrenaline known as parasailing (8-12min., $40).

PLUMMETING OUT OF THE SKY

If you've been dying to learn about that whole falling-out-of-the-sky thing, Taupo is the place to be. The town is long-established as the North Island capital for hurtling out of a plane at 3000m or plummeting toward water with only an elastic cord hooked to your feet. Taupo's death-wish appeal may be the result of the scenery: if you're going to go, your last seconds had better look good. **Taupo Bungy,** 202 Spa Rd. (tel. 377 1135), runs a highly professional operation that, since December 1991, has sent over 65,000 off "the plank" 47m above the hauntingly crystalline Waikato, recovering them in fine shape to buy memento T-shirts, pictures, and even videos after the shaky walk back up. For $89, you can hook up and ponder either the sheer cliffs, the impending water, or the tiny pick-up raft below. Call ahead so you don't have to stand around and wait, especially in summer. *(Open daily in summer 9am-7pm, in winter 9am-5pm.)*

If plummeting from 47m is child's play, freefalling from 3000m for 30 seconds at 200kph, and then floating, suspended above the earth for 4 minutes, might do you better. Tandem skydiving in Taupo is cheaper than anywhere else (doubtless because of the sheer number of jumps–over 35,000), and the views on a clear day are spectacular, stretching from Ruapehu to Taranaki to Tarawera. It's not exactly cheap per se, but the sensation has been likened by the keen (and blunt) to be the next best thing to sex—judge for yourself. **Taupo Tandem Skydive** (tel. 377 0428 or (0800) 275 934) has been sending people up since 1990, and though the preparation is disconcertingly brief, the reassuring Tandem Masters do everything but scream for you. *(100kg weight limit; weather dependent; call ahead.)* You can jump from 3000m for $165 or from 3500m for $185. A complementary instant digital photograph is taken on the plane's wing, right at the moment of truth.

Rock 'n Ropes (tel. 374 8111), located at Deerworld off Highway 5 just north of Wairekai, has an arousing array of ropes and adventure exotica including the chicken walk, criss crotch, floating log, vertical playpen, and giant swing. Other, less interactive aerial activities include scenic helicopter and airplane **flights** ranging from local jaunts to circling the Tongariro plateau; check with the visitors center for a complete listing. **The Taupo Gliding Club** (tel. 378 5627) meets each Sunday at Centennial Park, 6km up Spa Rd., and will take you up for a 20-minute glide ($45).

TERRA FIRMA

Your feet can say hello to the ground for a change as you take one of the area walks; some of the nicest are over near **Acacia Bay.** In the aftermath of your most recent scalding, catch, or plummet, catch a free viewing at Taupo Bungy—it's worth the short walk and at least a few vicarious minutes. More sedate experiences await in Taupo itself: if you have time to kill, wander over to the **Taupo District Museum of Art and History** (tel. 378 4167), a regional memorabilia collection that resembles a historical garage sale. *(Open daily 10:30am-4:30pm. $1-2 donation welcomed.)*

■ Turangi

Proclaiming itself the "Trout Fishing Capital of the World" when Taupo is looking the other way, Turangi is famed among the many anglers who come to tackle the rainbow and brown trout of the area's teeming waters. Built in the 70s for workers constructing the hydroelectric Tokaanu Power Station nearby, Turangi unapologetically offers few in-town attractions. Many residents don't contest this state of affairs, and instead simply sweep an arm at the surrounding mountains of Tongariro, the remote Kaimanawa range, and the trout-filled Tongariro River, gathering force from its trickling origin in the valleys of the volcanoes, and spilling into Lake Taupo a few kilometers away.

ORIENTATION AND PRACTICAL INFORMATION Some 4km from Lake Taupo on **SH1,** Turangi boasts no lakefront view. SH1 continues both north around the lake to Taupo, and south (where it's known as the **Desert Road**). **Ohuanga Road** is the main road through town, and virtually all essential shops and services are in the nondescript **Town Centre** complex, a short diagonal walk from the bus stop. The **Turangi Information Centre** (tel. 386 8999) is just across from the Town Centre. Check in here in winter to make sure the Desert Road is open before heading south (open daily 8:30am-5:30pm). For more in-depth park information and before attempting any serious Tongariro walks, stop by the **DOC** office (tel. 386 8607) on Turanga Pl. at the south edge of town (open M-F 8am-5pm). **National Bank** (tel. 386 8967) can be found in the Town Centre (open in summer M-F 8am-5pm; in winter M-F 9am-noon and 1-4:30pm), as can the **Turangi Pharmacy** (tel. 386 8565; open M-F 8:30am-6pm, Sa 9am-2pm, Su 10:30am-1:30pm) and the **post office** (tel./fax 386 8778; open M-F 8:30am-5pm, Sa 9am-12:30pm). In an **emergency,** dial **111.** The **police station** is 100m or so down Ohuanga Rd. (tel. 386 7709); the phone outside the station connects to Taupo police after hours (open M-F 8am-4pm). The **telephone code** is **07.**

InterCity stops at the Travel Centre (tel. 386 8918) and heads daily to Wellington (5½hr., 1-3 per day, $60) via Palmerston North (3hr., $30-35); and Auckland (6hr., 1-2 per day, $60) via Hamilton (4hr., $40) and Taupo (45min., $15). The laid-back folks of **Alpine Scenic Tours** (tel. 386 8918 or (025) 937 281), also at the Travel Centre, run daily shuttles to Whakapapa Village or, if the road is okay, straight to Whakapapa (45min., 2 per day, $15 round-trip), and in summer also to the endpoints of the Tongariro Crossing ($20 round-trip). Alpine heads daily to National Park (1-2 per day, $15 one-way) and to Taupo (3 per week, $14 one-way). **The Bellbird Lodge** (tel. 386 8281) runs a shuttle to skifields and an early bird (6:30am) shuttle to the Tongariro Crossing ($15 round-trip). **Turangi Taxis** (24hr. tel. 386 7441) are there for in-town transport. **Hitchhiking** to Taupo is reportedly not too difficult for those heading north on SH1 who stand at the corner of Pihanga Rd., near the information center. Traffic is lighter going south, however.

ACCOMMODATIONS AND FOOD Well organized and often providing shuttles, Turangi's accommodations will set you up with discounts for affiliated area outfitters. A quiet yet familiar atmosphere reigns in the three houses making up the **Bellbird Lodge** (tel. 386 8281) in the residential north end of town on the corner of Ohuanga and Rangipoia Rd. (call for pickup). It has cozy communal space, and owners who will get you psyched about Turangi. Mountain bikes are available for hire, along with fishing tackle and tramping clothes. (Dorms \$15-16; doubles or twins \$34; tent sites \$9.) The massive complex of **Club Habitat (YHA/VIP)** (tel. 386 7492; fax 386 0106) on Ohuanga Rd. just up and across from the information center, gets the Magic Bus crowd and lots of big groups. Don't mind the pseudo-resort name—though you may need a map to find your serviceable dorm bunk (\$16) or made-up double (\$48), you'll also be able to find good kitchen facilities, drying rooms, a sauna/spa, and the in-house restaurant and bar. Plush tourist cabins for two or motel units come with kitchenettes, TVs, and/or baths and start at \$62; tent sites are \$7. Cloning is alive and well at the **Turangi Holiday Park** (tel./fax 386 8754), off Ohuanga Rd. at the south end of Turangi, where an impersonal shantytown of 96 identical cubicle cabins aligned in neat treeless rows carries on the interior decorating style of the 1970s. (Cabins sleep 1-4, \$15 per person; on-site caravans \$35 for 2; tent sites \$9.)

Culinary pickings are slim in Turangi. The **Grand Central Fry** (tel. 386 5344) on Ohuanga Rd. is a cut above the typical take-away, with excellent burgers and fish 'n chips. (Daily specials \$4-6. Phone in your order to avoid the wait. Open daily 11am-8:30pm.) The restaurant at **Club Habitat** (tel. 386 7492) can do overpriced standard fare (mains \$10-15), with a good buffet breakfast (\$6) offered daily from 7-9:30am; dinner is served from 6-9pm. The bar at Club Habitat is one of the few in town and not half-bad if you're not far past the legal drinking age. Happy hour is from 5 to 7pm, with \$2.20 pints (doors close at 10pm). Set sail to discover the **New World** supermarket (tel. 386 8780; open M-F 8:30am-6pm, Sa-Su 9am-5pm).

SIGHTS AND ACTIVITIES The **Tokaanu Thermal Pools** (tel. 386 8575) are off the main road of tiny Tokaanu Village down SH41 from Turangi. Douse yourself in small, covered private pools (\$5 per person per 20min.) or in a slightly cooler public pool (\$3; open daily 10am-9pm). The free DOC-managed park and walkway outside is an appetizer for the geothermal wonderlands of Taupo and Rotorua, with its gurgling mud, steaming vents, and ever-appealing parfum de sulfur in the air.

The **Tongariro River** is ideal for two things: boating down or fishing up. Several operators raft down the Grade 3 upper section (2½hr.), over 60-odd rapids closed in by walls of bush. Garth at **Tongariro River Rafting** (tel. (0800) 101 024) will ease your passage down "the Bitch" and other suitably overwrought rapids, or let you do it yourself (under supervision) for \$75. Just bring your swimsuit and towel (call ahead). Docile "family floats" on the lower stretch are also available. Turangi's fish are a sure-fire bite: husky 1½- to 2kg trout lurk all over. Fishing guides for the river and lake range from \$40 to \$65 per hour. The increasingly popular **EcoTours** (tel. 386 6409) offers two-hour journeys into Taupo's natural wetlands.

Turangi's other big attraction is its proximity to large tracts of uninhabited bush, both a disjunct northern chunk of **Tongariro National Park** (see p. 151), and the rugged hills rising east of Tongariro that constitute part of the **Kaimanawa Forest Park.** Mainly for the stout of heart (and limb), Kaimanawa is hard to access and not developed for visitors, as it's primarily used for multi-day hunting and fishing trips (only 4 backcountry huts exist, and these are usually reached by air). Easier possibilities include dabbling around the park's edges on foot or mountain bike on any of several trails branching off Kaimanawa Rd. which splits off SH1, 15km south of Turangi. The **Lake Rotopounamu walk,** which leaves from a sign-post 11km up SH47, does an easy 5km loop through native fern forest around this small lake hidden at the base of **Pihanga** (the 1325m extinct volcano towering over Turangi). Farther along SH47, just past the junction with 47a, is the trailhead to **Te Porere Redoubt,** the poorly designed fortification built by Te Kooti's forces in 1869 for what turned out to be the final battle of the land wars. Te Kooti escaped the failed final stand here, but 37 others did not (see p. 187).

■ Tongariro National Park

Standing alone at the roof of the North Island are the three larger-than-life volcanoes of the central plateau: massive **Ruapehu** (2797m), elegantly conical **Ngauruhoe** (2291m), and the lower **Tongariro** (1968m), an amalgamation of ancient craters and ridges. Reaching improbably high, these active volcanoes were considered so sacred that all but the highest-born Maori shielded his or her eyes against the grandeur. Today, Tongariro and its neighbors constitute the heart, if not the soul, of New Zealand's park system: Tongariro was the country's first national park, and the world's fourth. The first national park in the world to be recognized as a World Heritage site for both its natural and cultural significance, Tongariro is a wind-swept land encompassing New Zealand's only desert (the desolate **Rangipo,** lying in the mountain's shadow), native forests of beech in lower areas, and hardy alpine shrublands across the lava-built slopes. The **Tongariro Northern Circuit Great Walk,** which includes the day-long **Tongariro Crossing,** is one of the country's most popular and spectacular hikes, passing through the park's lunar landscapes of smoking vents, gemlike crater lakes, and mineral springs.

ORIENTATION AND PRACTICAL INFORMATION

Tongariro is all about options, and access to the park comes from any of the base towns of **National Park, Whakapapa Village, Turangi,** and **Ohakune. SH1,** the **Desert Road** (frequently closed due to snow and ice), streaks by to the east through the **Rangipo Desert** en route to Lake Taupo. **SH49,** splitting off at the army base town of **Waiouru,** runs south of the park through Ohakune, while **SH4** cuts along the west side and continues to **Taumarunui** toward Auckland. The perfunctorily named tiny village of National Park sits at the junction of SH4 and **SH47,** the latter tracing the park's northern edge onward to Turangi to join SH1. A discontinuous chunk of park sits at the northern end beyond the dammed lake of **Rotoaira.**

Ohakune (at the park's southern edge), and the little settlement of **Whakapapa Village** (in the park on **SH48,** which branches off SH49) are the two major access points both to trails and the skifields. Secure parking is available at the park headquarters in Whakapapa Village. Base yourself in Whakapapa Village or National Park, as many excellent hikes (including the Northern Circuit Great Walk and the Tongariro Crossing) begin there, and convenient shuttles run from both towns. More than one frustrated backpacker has arrived in Ohakune eager to start the crossing only to realize that there's no cheap way around the mountain.

Alpine Scenic Tours (tel. 386 8918 in Turangi, 378 7412 in Taupo) runs several shuttles a day during the summer from Turangi to Whakapapa Village ($25 one-way), making stops at the Highway 47A access point, Mangatepopo, and National Park. From Whakapapa Village, **Tongariro Track Transport** (tel. 892 3716) runs a daily service in summer that is designed for those doing the Crossing. The shuttle departs park headquarters in summer daily at 8am, dropping people off at Mangatepopo, and picking people up after the hike at Highway 47A (4:30 or 6pm; return fare $15). Even if you have a car, DOC recommends parking your car in the secure lot at park headquarters to avoid vandalism and theft. Hitching can be a slow process along Highway 47 and on the way to Whakapapa Village, and is very difficult to Mangatepopo.

There's a **DOC office** at the base of Ohakune Mountain Rd. (tel. 385 0011; fax 892 3814). Park headquarters are at the **Whakapapa Visitor Centre** (tel. 892 3729; fax 385 8128), with two high-tech audiovisual shows (for a small fee), as well as plainer, free displays on the park's history. A brochure including a map of the track and crossing costs $1, and the office will store your luggage for the duration of your hike ($3 per bag; open daily 8am-5pm, later in summer). The DOC runs two campgrounds in the area: **Mangawhero,** 2km up the road from the Ohakune Field Centre, and **Mangahuia** off SH47 (passes $4 per night). Eight **huts** pepper some of the park's multi-day tracks, providing chateau-like lodging in the moonscape with toilets, rain water, and heat from gas or wood burners. Great Walk huts also have gas cookers in summer (but there is no cookware or silverware). All are considered backcountry huts in winter. From October to May, the four huts on the Northern Circuit, including one on

Tongariro Crossing for those doing it as an overnighter, become **Great Walk Huts** ($12), and are first come, first served. Buy your hut pass at a DOC office or pay the hut wardens 25% more on-site. Camping is permitted 500m from the track. As for food, it's definitely cheaper to buy your noodles in the good supermarkets of Ohakune or Turangi, rather than at National Park's limited dairy or at the desperate-hiker store of the Whakapapa Holiday Park. In case of an accident, be aware that the nearest **hospital** is in Taumarunui (tel. 895 7199) or Taupo (tel. 378 8100). For lodging and food options in Tongariro, see the listings for the base towns below.

Equipment

Enjoy the park's beauty, but do not spite Tongariro. If you plan to do any hiking at all, make sure you are well-prepared. Weather conditions can be extreme; blazing sun may change in minutes to freezing wind-driven rain. Even for just a day on the Crossing, it is imperative to carry a good **waterproof and windproof raincoat** and at least one warm fleece or wool layer. Conditions are severe enough to prevent the growth of any plants higher than the knee, and an unprepared tramper won't fare much better. Other highly recommended items are a waterproof pack liner, **sunscreen** and sunglasses, and extra food. A warm hat, gloves, waterproof overtrousers, and a first aid kit are additional bonuses. Consider carefully the strength of your tent before deciding to bring it along. If your tent is only marginally waterproof, you will likely end up soaked and unhappy; however, pass upgrades in order to stay in a hut are $6. All of the huts have water and gas stoves that campers may use, but they have no cooking utensils, so carry along any you may need.

TONGARIRO NORTHERN CIRCUIT AND TONGARIRO CROSSING

Winding in and around the park's defining trinity of volcanoes, the **Tongariro Northern Circuit Track** is among the country's best hikes. The track affords tremendous views of the windswept, lunar landscape pocked with steaming vents, technicolor lakes, and bizarre rock formations, all overshadowed by the perfect cone of Mt. Ngauruhoe, the jumbled mass of Mt. Tongariro, and the slumbering snow-covered volcanic beast of Mt. Ruapehu. The stretch of the track between Mangatepopo and Highway 47A doubles as the **Tongariro Crossing,** a popular day hike. The Crossing is spectacular, but the views are often obscured by clouds, so wait for a clear day if you can. Most people hike from the Northern Circuit west to east, which puts the steepest climbing behind you early and allows a gradual descent to Highway 47 with a view of Lake Taupo to the north.

Due to its high altitude and extreme exposure to the elements, the best hiking season runs from early December through March, as the trails are clear of snow and the weather cooperates to some degree. Although it is possible to do the track year-round, snow on the trail makes it into a technical tramp requiring a great deal more equipment and experience. The peak period of track use runs from Christmas until the end of January. The circuit forms a loop running around Mt. Ngauruhoe and can be accessed from **Highway 47A** north of Mt. Tongariro, from **Highway I** along the Desert Road, from the end of Mangatepopo Rd. 6km off Highway 47, and from **Whakapapa Village.** By far the best location for planning and starting either the Northern Circuit or Crossing is Whakapapa Village; park headquarters, a secure parking lot, and frequent shuttles are here. Both the Circuit and the Crossing can be hiked from either direction; for the circuit, weather is the determining factor. If hiking the entire Circuit, try to do the Crossing portion of the track on a day with a clear forecast, so that you may see the views. If you are only doing the Crossing, from west-to-east is the most popular direction as it puts the most strenuous and steepest climbing behind you early on and allows for a gradual descent with views of Lake Taupo.

The beginning section of the track, from park headquarters in Whakapapa Village to **Mangatepopo Hut,** has good views but is extremely rutted and muddy. Even those planning to do the entire circuit may want to skip this section. Shuttles run to the Mangatepopo carpark, 20-30 minutes from the hut. The hut itself is in a magnificent location with views of Mt. Tongariro, Mt. Ngauruhoe and the ridge that connects them. The hut has four high-powered gas burners, 26 bunks, water, a good communal area, and the current weather report. Next to the hut are eight designated campsites in an exposed area. It's a while to the next water, so fill up your water bottle. The Mangatepopo Hut marks the beginning of the **Tongariro Crossing.**

From the hut, the track ascends toward the ridge and then winds along a stream full of small tumbling waterfalls, traversing over several recent lava flows before reaching the base of the ridge. From here, a short 15-minute side trip leads to the pretty wispy waterfalls of **Soda Springs.** Back on the circuit, the track up the ridge is quite steep; at the top, a cold wind blows across a Martian world scoured almost clean of plant life. Another side trip from the track takes the aspiring mountaineer to the top of **Mt. Ngauruhoe** (3hr.; 2291m). The track continues across the broad, flat expanse of the south crater before ascending to the top of **Red Crater,** the highest point on the track (1886m), and an area that is sometimes buffeted by an unnervingly strong wind. From the top, peer down into the active crater on the right and admire the **Emerald Lakes** below. Much less strenuous than climbing Ngauruhoe is the two-hour round-trip up **Mt. Tongariro** (1967km), a gradual climb on a well-marked trail.

Diverging from the Circuit, the Crossing continues straight across the central crater while the Circuit forks to the right and heads down the **Oturere Valley.** Even those doing the Circuit should consider following the Crossing to **Ketetahi Hut** in order to catch the transcendent views of Red Crater framed by Ngauruhoe and Tongariro, with the Emerald Lakes and ant-like specks of hikers toiling in the distance. Ketetahi Hut has four self-lighting gas stoves and is somewhat cramped, with exposed tent sites. The nearby Ketetahi Hot Springs are on private land and off-limits.

Back at Emerald Lakes, the Circuit track drops steeply down into the Oturere valley and then winds along a steady route decorated with towering chunks of lava twisted into bizarre shapes and pinnacles. Several waterfalls cascade down the cliff faces that cradle the valley and expose layers of ash, lava, and sediment. At the end of the valley is unremarkable **Oturere Hut,** complete with standard amenities. From here, the track is pretty easy tramping; Mt. Ruapehu appears again and hovers about the horizon for the remainder of the track. Two hours past Oturere Hut, the track ascends into beech forest, allowing the first respite from the wind that characterizes the rest of the track. Shed some layers before you ascend as you'll quickly heat up once out of the wind, and enjoy yet another flashy vista from the top of the ridge. Ten minutes beyond is **Waihohona Hut,** which boasts several single beds and quality amenities. The prime campsite is pleasantly located 200m from the hut by a stream.

The final five-hour stretch back to Whakapapa Village monotonously winds upward through tussock. **Old Waihohona Hut,** a few minutes off the track, was once a stopping point for stagecoaches and affords a glimpse of turn of the century tramping. After **Tama Saddle,** side trips to **Upper Tama Lake** and **Lower Tama Lake** lie just to the north; both are good options for a day trip from Whakapapa Village. The track heads down to Whakapapa Village in a final one-hour stretch, which can be taken by an upper route through tussock terrain or along a lower forest route.

OUTDOORS

Multi-day tramps are not the only option in Tongariro; the park can be digested in smaller pieces as well. The **volcanic craters** at the top of Mt. Ruapehu can be reached from Turoa's carpark on the south side, from the top of Bruce Rd. at the base of the Whakapapa skifield, or from higher up beyond the top of the ski lifts (5-6hr.; check with DOC before attempting). Climbers should be aware of gases and potential volcanic activity. Ice and snow can make the trip a risky one, and several people have died doing it. **Whakapapa Skifield** (tel. 893 3738) offers guided walks to the lake in summer ($40).The south side of the park is much quieter, but less accessible without a car, and many of the tracks begin far up Ohakune Mountain Rd. The less-crowded **Round-the-Mountain Tramp** is an accurately named four- to five-day hike around cranky Ruapehu, traversing windswept slopes, crossing a deep gorge, and passing along the edge of the haunting, forsaken Rangipo Desert (there are several huts along the way). Check with DOC, and then try the tramp from Whakapapa Village (or the Ohakune Mountain Rd., if you have transport).

Lair of the Lahar

On December 24, 1953, the debris build-up holding back Ruapehu's Crater Lake collapsed and sent a violent **lahar**—a fast, flowing stream of mud and ash debris—down a valley, sweeping away a railroad bridge. Minutes later, a train carrying 151 people arrived at the non-existent bridge, and hurtled into the gorge below. On September 18, 1995, Ruapehu roused itself again from fitful slumber to begin a month of the most dramatic explosive activity since it blew its top in 1945. Locals cast a watchful eye to their suddenly barren ski slopes. The new eruption sent ash as far as the east coast, emptied out Crater Lake, and then stopped—just in time for the skifields to reopen for the end of the season. Ruapehu remained quiet all summer, raising hopes for a peaceful and profitable winter. But on June 17, 1996, the day before the Turoa and Whakapapa skifields were to open, it spewed ash with a vengeance onto the pristine skifields well into July, disrupting air traffic in Auckland, and coating homes in Gisborne with grit. Although the fields reopened in August, the already shortened season and further ashfall in September ensured that the year's take was less than 20% of usual. After two years of multi-million dollar impacts, locals don't like to talk much about the eruptions. Most people shrug and say that it only happens every 50 years. The advertisements of the skiing industry are quick to assure that the eruptions are over, while Ruapehu offers a more equivocal response, occasionally puffing out plumes of steam.

While most come to Tongariro for one big, volcanic reason, plenty of outfitters in the area have tons of other adventure ideas. Mountain biking is not allowed in Tongariro National Park, but the **Tongariro Forest Conservation Area,** just to the north, is home to the **42 Traverse,** one of the country's most famously satisfying mountain bike trails. An organ-jiggling ride along old logging trails with a stream crossing and a 570m descent, it's not for beginners.

SKIING First tried in 1913, skiing in Tongariro draws well over half of its visitors today in the winter months, with the help of the two commercial skifields hugging Ruapehu's slopes. As they're on DOC land, **Whakapapa** and **Turoa** have to abide by numerous regulations to minimize the impact of thousands of people carving down the mountain. Floodlights for night skiing are not allowed, and putting in new lifts requires nothing short of a major negotiation. Whakapapa and Turoa are nonetheless among the largest and most developed ski resorts in the country. While South Islanders may scoff, the Tongariro skifields attract huge crowds (and can, in fact, get frustratingly crowded at peak holiday times). Both Whakapapa and Turoa have long seasons, usually opening in late June or early July and closing in late October or even November. Unfortunately, Ruapehu attracts bad weather like a 2797m magnet—due to gale-force winds and storms, the fields can be closed almost a quarter of the time. Both fields offer a weather guarantee, however, allowing refunds or credits if lifts have to close.

Whakapapa (tel. 892 3738, snowphone 892 3833), at the top of Bruce Rd. from Whakapapa Village, has killer views of distant Mt. Egmont (Taranaki) on clear days. It's also the country's largest skifield, with six chairlifts, eight T-bars or platters, seven rope tows, a gentle beginner's area (Happy Valley), and 30 groomed, patrolled trails. There's good open terrain for off-piste as well. Snowboarders are welcome (but seem to prefer Turoa). Whakapapa has five cafeterias and a ski shop that rents full ski gear ($26 for skis, boots, and poles), or snowboards and boots ($47). The towns of National Park and Whakapapa Village also have their share of rental places ($25-40 for a snowboard and boots is standard). All-day passes are expected to run around $49, while five-day "anytime" passes are about $225. Whakapapa also runs **scenic lift rides** to "the highest cafe in New Zealand" (Mid-Dec.-Apr.; $15, children $8).

Slather on the sunscreen, strap on the Oakleys, and hit the slopes of **Turoa** (tel. 385 8456, snowphone (0900) 99 444), Okahune's lifeblood, accessible via the Ohakune Mountain Rd. Boasting the country's longest vertical drop (720m) and 400 hectares of patrolled snow, Turoa is known for its wide open terrain, long runs (4km is the longest), five chairlifts, three T-bars, four platter lifts, and one rope tow, as well as a beginner's area at the base, and a large number of intermediate runs (the highest lift runs up to an elevation of 2300m). Snowboarders love Turoa for the natural half-pipes in its gulleys and its lack of any major flats—almost half of the slope at any given time is covered with bleached-blond, styled-out boarders. Turoa also has some excellent off-trail skiing possibilities; it's even possible to haul gear up to Crater Lake and ski down (always check with the Ski Patrol first). Turoa's slopes are usually open daily 9am-4pm. Daylift passes cost around $48 (5-day "anytime" available). You can rent all skiing ($25) or boarding ($40) equipment on the mountain, but be aware that there may be a better selection of both the budget and higher-quality equipment at one of Ohakune's many shops (prices roughly equivalent to those on the mountain).

■ National Park

National Park would be just another podunk village were it not for the spectacular set of three volcanoes towering above it on the plateau. As it is, it's still a podunk village, albeit with as many residents as accommodations (all of which fill with skiers in winter and trampers in summer). Little more than a cluster of buildings at the junction of SH4 and SH47, National Park's main drag, **Carroll St.,** has a dairy and takeaway (tel. 892 2758) that serves as **post office, bus stop,** and town center. (Open in winter M-Sa 7am-8pm, Su 7am-7pm; in summer M-Sa 7:30am-7pm, Su 8am-5pm.) In an emergency, dial **111.** The little **police station** (tel. 892 2869 or (025) 454 627) is on McKenzie St. The **telephone code** is **07.**

TranzScenic and **InterCity** roll through on the way north to Auckland (5½hr., 1-2 per day, $50-70) via Hamilton (3½hr., $30-40), and south to Wellington (5½hr., 1-2 per day, $60-70) via Ohakune (30min., $10-20). TranzScenic's southward route includes Palmerston North (3½hr., 1 per day, $39-43), while InterCity heads to Wanganui (2½hr., $27). Book at either the Ski Haus or Howard's Lodge. The Travel Centre books **Alpine Scenic Tours** (tel. 386 8918 or (025) 937 281), and their daily shuttles to Whakapapa (1-2 per day, $6) and Turangi (1-2 per day, $15). Steve of **Whanganui River Jet** (tel. 895 5995) runs on request in winter to Whakapapa Village ($15 round-trip), Ohakune ($25, min. 3), or trailheads. Catering as they do to trampers and skiers, the accommodations in National Park make things easy by hiring out gear and by supplementing **Whakapapa Shuttles** with their own transport year-round. (To Whakapapa $15 round-trip; to Turoa $25; to Tongariro Crossing $15-16. See Whakapapa Village, below, for more on Whakapapa Shuttles.)

Howard's Lodge (tel./fax 892 2827), on Carroll St., is an excellent and clean accommodation with a spa. They'll hire out skiing, climbing, or tramping gear and bikes ($7 per hr., $40 per day), and will run a shuttle to the endpoints of the **42 Traverse** ($20 round-trip) in winter. (Dorms $18, in summer $14; doubles and twins $70, in summer $40. No linen. Rooms with bedding and bath start in winter $90, in summer $65.) Many of the same services are offered for a higher price at the bustling **Ski Haus** (tel. 892 2854) across the road, with its ski hire, sauna, drying room, central heating, in-house restaurant, and bar complete with sunken fireplace (open year-round). The B&B option costs $10 more. (Dorms $34 during winter weekends, $23 mid-week. In summer, dorms $20; doubles $50; and tent or caravan sites $5, plus $8 for each adult). Somewhat less of a one-stop überhostel is the **National Park Lodge** (tel. 892 2993), two minutes up Carroll St. It's clean, if not inspiringly decorated, with a TV lounge and a small kitchen for the four-person shares (in winter $20-25, in summer $15; doubles in winter $60, summer $40). An eight-bed bunk dorm comes with its own kitchen, TV, and bathroom (in winter $20, summer $13). BYO bedding in summer. Two stones' throws from SH4, **National Park Backpackers** (tel. 892 2870), on Finlay St. has an excellent indoor climbing wall as well as modern, tidy dorms (in winter $17, summer $15, with bathroom $20).

■ Whakapapa Village

Situated on the slopes of Ruapehu, Whakapapa Village is the highest settlement in the country to have a permanent population. The small town is mainly a base for the ski operations of nearby Tongariro National Park. The **telephone code** is **07,** different than nearby Ohakune. For those looking to simply zoom in and out, **Mountain Air** (tel. (0800) 922 812 or 892 2812) runs a daily air shuttle to and from Auckland and Whakapapa Village and Turangi (7am, returning 4:45pm, $99 one-way) with a special $35 lift pass and shuttle. The more ground-bound can take **Alpine Scenic Tours** (tel. 386 8918 or (025) 937 281), which leaves Whakapapa Village for National Park (2-3 per day, $6), Turangi ($15), and the Tongariro Crossing endpoints at the Ketetahi and Mangatepopo carparks. Service can be rather flexible, so be sure to call and ask about any transport dilemmas. **Whakapapa Shuttles** (tel. 892 3716) runs during winter to the Whakapapa skifields ($10 round-trip); its alter-ego, **Tongariro Track Transport,** runs during the summer to Mangatepopo (daily 8am) and picks up from Ketetahi at 4:30 and 6pm ($15 round-trip). **Whakapapa Express** (tel. 385 4022) provides service to and from Ohakune (1 per day; $15 round-trip). If you are traveling with a car, don't leave your valuables behind at the isolated trailhead carparks. **Hitchhiking** in Tongariro is dubious—traffic can be sparse at any time of year. Those determined to get up Bruce Rd. (past Whakapapa Village) or Ohakune Mountain Rd. often start early to catch skifield employees, and are never seen waiting until dark to try their luck going down. The Holiday Park has a small **store,** but you'll find little else in the village except for the post office in **Fergusson's Cafe** (open daily in winter 9am-5pm).

Set next to a rushing stream, the **Whakapapa Holiday Park** (tel./fax 892 3897), just across the road from the visitors center, offers small but private tent and caravan sites carved out of the native bush ($8), and good kitchen facilities. Thin-mattressed bunks populate the spartan backpackers lodge ($12.50; summer only). Cabins are $35 for two people (BYO bedding and utensils). To get to the perky **Skotel** (tel. 892 3719; fax 892 3777), turn left just before the visitors center. Boasting all the amenities (spa, sauna, drying room, cushy mattresses, and small communal kitchen), its functional shares are $20 in summer, but are sold as twins, triples, and quads during winter (starting at $72 per room, with bath). Wood-paneled, airy, deluxe doubles start at $82-115 in summer and only get higher come ski season.

Save your pennies and sip a vicarious coffee in the lobby of the refined, historic, and decidedly non-budget **Grand Chateau** hotel. Both the Skotel and the Chateau have in-house restaurants and bars; **Fergusson's Cafe** (tel. 892 3809, ask for the cafe), does brisk business with soups, hot quiches ($3.50), sandwiches ($2.50-3) and coffee (open daily in winter 7:30am-6:30pm, shorter hours in summer). Sandwiches at the store at the Holiday Park aren't too expensive ($2.50), but willpower-weakening French pastries ($2.50) are cruelly set right by the register (open daily 7am-6pm).

■ Ohakune

At one end of Ohakune lies the massive snow-covered time-bomb whose slopes turn the burg into a dynamic ski town. At the other end, and only slightly less impressive, sits Ohakune's symbolic alter-ego—a giant, tubby, painted statue of a carrot that serves as a reminder of the quiet farming center the town reverts to after the winter snows melt. Its rich volcanic soils produce world-class veggies and its sheep and cattle placidly munch away. The 1300-odd residents (who all seem to know each other) put away their ski poles come spring to relax, wait, and pray for another season of heavy snow (and a silent mountain), even as a quieter summer hiking season gets underway. The 1995-96 eruptions were not easy on Ohakune, highly dependent as it is on ski dollars—but you wouldn't know it from the upbeat residents who wouldn't give up their charmed life for anything so paltry as an active volcano.

ORIENTATION AND PRACTICAL INFORMATION The south end, where **SH49** comes in, has most services (like the grocery store and pharmacy) and is active year-round. The north end, known as the **Junction,** lies 3km up toward where the railroad tracks, and bursts into life during the winter with seasonal chalets and jumping nightlife. It also marks the start of the **Ohakune Mountain Rd.** up to **Turoa. Goldfinch Street/Mangawhero Terrace** runs between the two (20-25min. walk). Ohakune is the most significant town of the area, aside from Turangi on the northern side of Tongariro National Park.

The **Ohakune Visitor's Centre,** 54 Clyde St. (tel. 385 8427; fax 385 8527) has a 3-D relief map of Tongariro National Park (center open in winter daily 9am-5pm; in summer Sa-Su 9am-3:30pm). The **DOC office** (tel. 385 0010; fax 385 8128), just beyond the railroad tracks on Ohakune Mountain Rd., is one of Tongariro's two field centers (open daily 8am-3pm, holidays 8am-4:30pm). Change your money at **Westpac** (tel. 385 8310) in the shopping plaza on **Goldfinch St.** (open M-F 9am-4:30pm).

Ohakune is served by several major transportation lines, but as it's halfway between Auckland and Wellington, arrivals and departures are virtually all in the middle of the day or the middle of the night. **TranzScenic** and **InterCity** run to Auckland (5½hr., 1 per day, $55-75) via National Park (30min., $10-20); and to Wellington (5hr., 1-2 per day, $50-65) via Palmerston North (3hr., $30-40). To go to Taupo, either take the train to Waiouru and catch a bus at 5:10pm, or find your way to Turangi to make the connection. **Hitchhiking** is reportedly not too difficult between Ohakune and National Park or Waiouru, but it's no fun to be stuck in Waiouru trying to hitch across the Rangipo Desert.

The **Mountain Transport Service** (tel. 385 9045 or (025) 445800) and **Whakapapa Express** (tel. 385 4022 or (025) 971 066) run to Turoa ($10-15 round-trip); Whakapapa Express also goes to trailheads in summer ($25 round-trip). The transport-meisters at **Snowliner Shuttles** (tel. 385 8573 or (025) 435 550) run on demand to Turoa ($8, $15 round-trip), and will run to Whakapapa ($16, $27 round-trip) if Turoa is closed, and to trailheads during the summer. Hitchhiking up the mountain is reportedly easier in the morning, but success depends on your amount of gear. National Park and Whakapapa Village make better bases for those without their own car, while those with cars often prefer Ohakune for life outside of their lodging.

Dr. Perera (tel. 385 8356), the town's one-man **medical service,** has an office on Goldfinch St. The **Ohakune Photo Pharmacy** (tel. 385 8304) is next to the bank (open M-F 9am-5:30 or 6pm; during ski season also Sa 9-noon) for all those remedies you'll need after one too many black diamond runs. The **post office** is in a shop at 5 Goldfinch St. (tel. 385 8645; open M-Sa 7am-6 or 7pm). The **telephone code** is **06.**

ACCOMMODATIONS As one big bedroom for Turoa, Ohakune has an outlandish number of accommodations per capita. Almost 20 motels, ski lodges and hostels are here, and a fair number are either open only in winter or jack up their prices from hostel to B&B. Booking ahead during ski season, even by several weeks, is essential. The following places are all open year-round, but prices seriously fluctuate by season—**winter/summer rates** are listed. Up at the Junction end of town, at the upper edge of the ski zone, is the **Rimu Park Lodge (VIP),** 27 Rimu St. (tel. 385 9023). Free bus pickups are offered, with mid-week price cuts. The classic wood-lined lodge has a kitchen and crackling open fire (bunks $30/$15; doubles or twins $35/$17). Compact cabins are comfortable (doubles $60/$40; triples $75), and units in the old wooden train car are made from solid old rail ties (doubles $100/$80). For $65, you can receive board, breakfast, and a ski pass to Whakapapa. The owner is also the town's source of **car rentals:** four-wheel-drives run from $50 per day. The **Ohakune YHA** (tel. 385 8724) on Clyde St., has plain rooms off a lovely veranda, with a woodstove, communal kitchen area, and lounge. Charismatic manager Kuini could take the piss out of the Queen Mother without offense. (Dorms $16/$15; twins $36/$34; mountain bike rentals available). The popular **Alpine Motel and Lodge,** 7 Miro St.

(tel. 385 8758), near the corner of Clyde St. and Raetihi Rd., offers small bunk rooms in its nifty, silo-like backpackers lodge ($20/$15 midweek, weekends $25; 2-day min. stay on weekends in peak season). Well-heated double studio units with bath and TV are also available (weekdays $85/$70; weekends $110/$70; extra person $15). It all comes with a spa, free train pickup, and a drying room. On the street that turns off just before the YHA, next to a brook is the **Ohakune Holiday Park** (tel./fax 385 8561), with a small kitchen, TV lodge, and 18-hole putt putt. It has tentsites and powered sites ($9.50), tiny backpacker cabins and caravans ($16.50, $12-14 extra person; min. 2 in winter), and two new doubles with kitchens and showers ($55).

FOOD AND NIGHTLIFE Many of Ohakune's lodgings have in-house restaurants, though they're usually a bit pricey. Of the other restaurants, usually only the south side eateries are regularly open in summer. The **Mountain Kebabs Cafe**, 29 Clyde St. (tel. 385 9047), has filling meat and vegetarian kebabs (medium $6.50; open daily 10am-10pm). A few doors down is **Utopia,** an excellent lunch cafe with carrot cake you can't imagine. Junction-area eateries open in winter include **La Pizzeria** (tel. 385 8558), next to the Turoa Ski Lodge on Thames St., which offers terrific gourmet pizzas—mamma mia!—for gourmet prices ($12.50 and up; open daily in ski season from 4pm; in off-season, open F and Sa from 4pm). Hit **Margarita's** (tel. 378 9909), on Rimu St. just past Thames St., for Mexican food in an après-ski lodge atmosphere. Half-price heaping Mexican mains (normally $14.50 and up) are offered on Wednesday nights (open in ski season daily from 4pm). Save your money and get your groceries at **New World** (tel. 385 8587), at the corner of Goldfinch and Clyde St. (open daily 8:30am-5pm).

The après-ski scene rages in Ohakune: long after midnight, the Junction bars and the flash **Hot Lava Niteclub** on Thames St. do their best to ensure no one's on the slopes too early the next morning. Most of the ski season hotspots are right on Thames St. Follow your ski instructor to the bar of the **Turoa Ski Lodge** (tel. 385 8274), where just about everyone stops by once a night. Half-price cocktails are on Thursdays, and a DJ is around on Saturdays. Gaggles of dry-docked snowboarders replace the families after dinner hours at the endlessly popular **Margarita's.** Brighten your cheeks by the fire, or with the nightly happy hours (5-7pm and 9-10pm; pints $2.50). Down south, the **Ohakune Country Hotel** (tel. 385 8268), on Clyde St., has a three-bar complex, recently renovated to include the stylish **O-Bar,** and the tourist-frequented **Summit Bar.** The latter requires decent dress and has Sunday night cook-your-own-steak barbecues ($10). The public **Pioneer** bar has no such standards and its occasional live bands draw a more rambunctious local crowd.

OUTDOORS Ohakune has recently awakened to the idea that life exists outside of skiing, and a growing number of summer activities are popping up. The area around the park has some top mountain biking opportunities. The sealed 18km **Ohakune Mountain Rd.** itself makes for a wickedly exhilarating and scenic bike ride when ski traffic is gone. The road is occasionally closed due to ice and snow. Ron Rutherford's **Ride the Mountain** (tel. 385 8257) operation rents bikes and runs to the top ($45). The **Powderhorn Shop and Ski Hire** (tel. 385 8888) in the grand chalet of the same name at the bottom of Mountain Rd., also rents bikes ($25 per half-day, $35 per full day) and climbing, tramping, and in-line skating equipment (open daily 9am-6pm).

From October to April, Ohakune is a point of departure for **canoe trips** on the Whanganui River, a mostly tranquil river running through the heart of the wilderness (see p. 139). Check with the visitors center for outfitter options. Horse trekking, canoeing, four-wheel-drive motorbike tours, and more civilized pursuits like golf and squash abound around town. Whatever you do, treat yourself at the end of the day to a piña colada in the heated pool of the **Powderhorn Chateau** (tel. 385 8888; open year-round 9am-9pm; $6, children $5, guests free).

Bay of Plenty

At the junction of natural wonders, cultural spectacles, and excessive cashflow, the Bay of Plenty is one of the North Island's more popular regions for both travelers and Kiwis. Led by tourist hotspot Rotorua, the bay curves eastward from the Coromandel Peninsula with coastal towns Tauranga and Mt. Manganui offering sun, sky, and water to their many visitors. Deep in the region's geological heart, an ominous tectonic tripwire stretches from the lakes of the Rotorua district out to the sun-warmed coast and White Island. Rotorua, the regional heart of Maori culture, has long been celebrated as a place to plumb the rich depths of Maori tradition. Thanks to its geothermal effects, it has also become the unofficial hot springs capital of the country, serving up a therapeutic bit of the bubbly year-round. Farther south, the rough-edged Opotiki serves as a gateway to the more remote, uncompromising East Cape and its intense natural beauty.

BAY OF PLENTY HIGHLIGHTS

- A Maori *hangi,* or feast, is an incomparable culinary and cultural experience (see p. 185).
- The earth breathes and murmurs at lively geothermal sights around Rotorua (see p. 186).

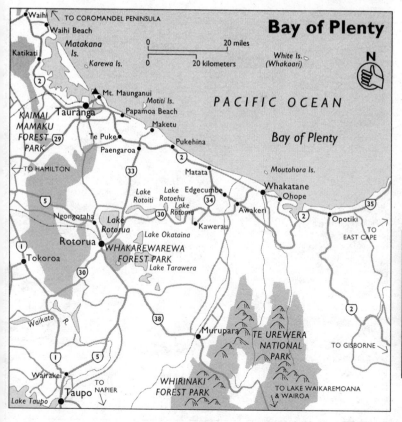

■ Rotorua

You'll know you've hit Rotorua by the omnipresent waft of vaguely rotten-smelling sulfur, and the constant hum of large tour buses which bring close to a million visitors in and out of the gorgeous lake district each year. The North Island's single most popular destination is a place of disparate attractions, as geothermal wonders, agricultural shows, and enlightening Maori offerings all vie for visitors' attention. Tourism is an industry in every sense of the word in the district. Sulfur-searchers come to Rotorua with good reason: the region's geothermal areas are most impressive, as steaming craters and bubbling mud pools boil within sight of calm, azure, trout-filled lakes. Breathe deeply (before you get here), put in some effort, and you'll undoubtedly find beauty beneath the hype.

ORIENTATION AND PRACTICAL INFORMATION

Although the city of Rotorua lies at the southern end of **Lake Rotorua,** local geothermal and recreational attractions are dispersed on **SH5** and **SH30** over an area wide enough to support a thriving shuttle and tour bus industry. Downtown is delineated by **Fenton, Ranolf, Arawa,** and **Amohau Streets,** with the crossroads of **Tutanekai** and **Hinemoa Street** serving as an effective center, home to stores, cafes, and banks.

Transportation

Airport: The Rotorua Airport is off SH30, around the east side of Lake Rotorua. **Air New Zealand** (tel. 347 9564), at the corner of Hinemoa and Fenton St., and

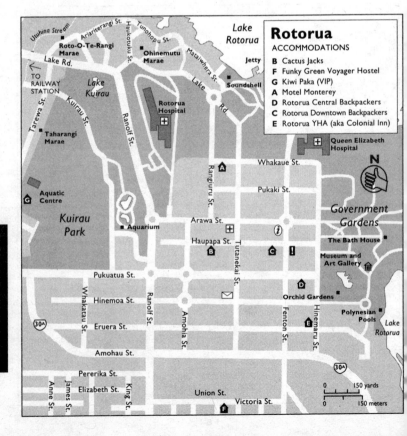

Rotorua

ACCOMMODATIONS

B Cactus Jacks
F Funky Green Voyager Hostel
G Kiwi Paka (VIP)
A Motel Monterey
D Rotorua Central Backpackers
C Rotorua Downtown Backpackers
E Rotorua YHA (aka Colonial Inn)

Ansett, 113 Fenton St. (tel. 349 0146), have 2-4 flights per day to Auckland (45min., $190), Wellington (1hr., $223), Christchurch (2hr., $340), and Queenstown (2½hr., $580). **Alpha-Xpress** (tel. 346 1606) runs an airport shuttle service ($8 for 1 person, $10 for 2).

Trains: TranzScenic tracks end a few kilometers from city center off Lake Rd. Trains leave daily for Auckland (4hr., 1:20pm, $63) via Hamilton (2¼hr., $40). The **Sightseeing Shuttle** leaves Tourism Rotorua daily for the train station (12:20pm; $2).

Buses: All buses come and go from Tourism Rotorua. **Newmans, InterCity** and **Starlighter Express** (tel. 349 0590) all depart daily for Auckland (3¾hr., 3-5 per day, $42-45), via Hamilton (1½hr., $22-24); Napier (4½hr., 3 per day, $50-53); and Wellington (7¼hr., 2-3 per day, $75) via Taupo (1hr., $20). **Waitomo Wanderer** (tel. 873 7559) also goes to Taupo and Waitomo (2 per day; 7:30am and 6:15pm, $25), with pick-up and drop-off.

Local Buses: Rotorua City Buses (24hr. tel. 349 2994, ext. 2902) are cheap and run M-F 7am-5:15pm. Most destinations are no more than 2 sections: 1 section $1.60, 2 $2.20. Main stop is Pukuatua St. between Tutanekai and Amohia St. The green Ngongataha route goes to Rainbow Springs, blue to Whakarewarewa.

Taxis: Fastaxis (24hr. tel. 348 2444) or **Rotorua Taxis** (24hr. tel. 348 1111). In Rotorua, even the cabs do tours (Rotorua Taxis: $32 per hr.).

Car Rental: All the major establishments can be found in Rotorua, and renting a car can be a good alternative to endless tours and shuttles. Cheaper rates (though watch the per-km charge, as sights can be rather far from downtown) include **Link Rentals,** 108 Fenton St. (tel. 349 1629), with "super saver" cars at $25 per day and 18¢ per km; and **Rent-A-Dent,** 14 Ti St. (tel. 349 3993), off Fenton St. past Big Fresh ($55 per day with 100km free).

Bicycle Rentals: Lady Jane's Ice Cream Parlour (tel. 347 9340), at the corner of Tutanekai and Whakaue St., rents city bikes for $15 per day (deposit $20), or dilapidated tandems for $7 per hr. Mountain bikes $8 per hr., $28 per day ($30 deposit). **Pin Cycles,** 161 Fenton St. (tel. 347 1151), also rents used mountain bikes with front shocks or full suspension ($25-35 per half-day, $50 per day).

Hitchhiking: There's always traffic leaving Rotorua. South toward Taupo, many hitchers start past Amohau St. and work toward Whakarewarewa. Amohau St. is also the branch point for SH5 north and SH30 east; many thumbers head a few blocks away from Pak 'N Save to go east. Catching a ride north is reportedly easier no farther from town than Rainbow Springs, after which traffic speeds up.

Tourist and Financial Services

Visitor Center: Tourism Rotorua (tel. 348 5179; fax 348 6044) on Fenton St. between Arawa and Haupapa St. Service is excellent in this busy hub. Cafe, **currency exchange,** as well as accommodation, tour, and travel bookings. Open daily 8am-5:30pm.

DOC: On Amohau St. (tel. 349 7400; fax 347 9115; open M-F 8am-4:35pm). The **Map and Track Shop** (tel. 349 1845), in the Tourism Rotorua complex, has a complete selection of park maps and DOC brochures and sells hut tickets and permits. Open daily 8am-6pm; in winter 9am-5:30pm-ish.

Currency Exchange: Bank branches line Hinemoa St. **Westpac** (tel. 348 1079), at the corner of Tutanekai St., is open M-F 9am-4:30pm. **Thomas Cook** (tel. 347 0111) is in the **Air New Zealand** office at Hinemoa and Fenton St. Open M-F 8:30am-5pm and Sa 9:30am-12:30pm.

American Express: Galaxy Travel, 411 Tutanekai St., P.O. Box 2149 (tel. 347 9444), is an AmEx representative. They won't cash checks, but they do hold mail for members and give advice. Open M-F 8:30am-5pm.

Emergency and Communications

Emergency: dial 111.

Medical Services: Lakes PrimeCare Pharmacy (tel. 348 4385), with the big turquoise sign at Arawa and Tutanekai St. Open daily 9am-9:30pm. **Lakeland Health Centre** (tel. 349 7977) is Rotorua's public hospital on Pukeroa St., off Arawa St., at the northeast corner of the city center. **Lakes PrimeCare** (tel. 348 1000), next to the **Lakes Care Pharmacy.** Open daily 8am-11pm; 24hr. doctor on call.

Police: Diagonally across Fenton St. from the visitors center (24hr. tel. 348 0099).

Internet Access: Vegas Cyber Cafe (tel. 348 5899) above the comic book shop; $3 per 15min.
Post Office: 81 Hinemoa St. (tel. 349 2397), near Tutanekai St. Open M-F 7:30am-5:30pm, Sa 8:30am-4pm, Su 10am-2pm.
Telephone Code: 07.

ACCOMMODATIONS

Rotorua has no shortage of beds, though it may feel that way on a summer weekend if you neglect to call ahead. **SH5**, both at **Fenton St.** and the northeast side of town, has its share of motels; some relatively budget options sit along **Ranolf St.** If you're desperate, contact the visitors center. Overnights with a Maori family or on a *marae* are possible, but are more easily booked for larger groups. And don't be too impressed by "thermal pool" signs—practically every place has one.

⊛Funky Green Voyager, 4 Union St. (tel. 346 1754; fax 347 0078). Walk down Fenton St. to Victoria St. and turn right; Union St. is 2 blocks down. It's hard to find fault with this clean and green hostel at the quiet edge of a residential neighborhood. Small, but with a terrific sunroom, kitchen, and lounge, and tastefully decorated designer toilet seats. After a long day of touring Rotorua, at home—shoes off—with the infectiously friendly Funky Green family is just where you'll want to be. Close to supermarket. Dorms $15; doubles or twins $36. Cash only.

Kiwi Paka (VIP), 60 Tarewa Rd. (347 0931). About 1km from town center. Walk west on Pukuatua St. past Kuirau Park, turn right on Tarewa St. The family-run Kiwi Paka is its own busy quasi-resort, with cafeteria, bush-theme bar, and extensive information and discount bookings. Requisite thermal pool (albeit with a classy kidney shape). Everything shuts down by midnight. Shuttles between bus and hitching points. Dorms $15-17; singles $21; doubles or twins $36; tent sites $8.50.

Rotorua Central Backpackers, 1076 Pukuatua St. (tel./fax 349 3285). From the bus station, turn right down Fenton St. and left on Pukuatua St. This immaculately clean, classic 1936 wood apartment building offers a relaxed stay. Offering separate reading and TV lounges, a roomy kitchen, and extensive information on area attractions, new managers Neil and Catherine seem like old pros. Dorms $15; twins $32; doubles $36. Indoor spa. Bikes $15 per day. Off-street parking.

Cactus Jacks (VIP), 54 Haupapa St. (tel. 348 3121). It's hard to escape the over-the-top American southwest ranch decor of this intensely themed hostel. While the murals are goofy, the obliging management is serious about making your time in Rotorua fun. Courtyard, spacious kitchen, Sky TV, video library, pinball machine, and a thermal pool make up for flaws like small rooms and slightly dim lighting. Dorms $15.50; singles $30; doubles $38; twins $35. Cash only. Bikes $15 per day.

Downtown Backpackers, 1193 Fenton St. (tel. 346 2831), next to Tourism Rotorua Visitor's Center. You could hop off the bus, skip twice, and jump right into a clean bed at this large, new and tidy hostel. Location and adequate standard facilities are the main virtues now as identity and character remain to be forged. Dorms $15; 4-bed dorms $16; doubles or twins $36.

Rotorua YHA, a.k.a. Colonial Inn, (tel. 347 6810; fax 349 1426), at the corner of Hinemaru and Eruera St. Few distinguishing characteristics, though it does have that good old thermal pool and central location. Plentiful and clean toilets and showers. Well-supplied info and booking center. A perfectly fine, if mildly sterile, stay. Dorms $15-17; doubles or twins $20. Off-street parking.

Motel Monterey, 1204 Whakaue St. (tel. 348 1044; fax 348 2644). Quiet, airy rooms with wicker chairs, couches, TV, and kitchenette. A heated pool overhung with orange trees and a hidden, greenery-lined gazebo for the spa. Courtesy pick-up and drop-off. Off-season singles $55; doubles $60 (in season $5-10 more). Family doubles $75 (extra person $12). Continental breakfast $7, cooked $12. Free laundry.

Cosy Cottage International Holiday Park, 67 Whittaker Rd. (tel. 348 3793). About 2km from town, off Lake Rd. Burping mud-hole, hot stream, thermal mineral pool, and natural steam cooker balance tired feel of communal facilities. Double flats with toilet and kitchenette (no linen) $46 (extra person $11). Cabins with kitchenettes $40 for 2 (extra person $10). Tent sites $10; campervans $11 ($20 for 2).

FOOD

A fantastic exception to Rotorua's standard restaurants are Maori *hangis*. Although the meals (which come with cultural evenings and/or concerts) are hardly inexpensive, they shouldn't be missed (see A Maori Evening, below). Rotorua's small cappuccino cafes and several good upscale restaurants line the lake end of **Tutanekai St.,** near **Arawa Street;** vegetarians may be forced to search and settle. Your market choices are **Pak 'N Save,** at the corner of Fenton and Amohau St. (tel. 347 8440; open M-F 8:30am-9pm, Sa-Su 8:30am-8pm) or fruit and veggie wholesaler **Pumpkin Planet** (tel. 348 1442), down Fenton St. a bit at Ti St. (open daily 7am-6pm).

Tastebuds Mexican Cantina, 93 Fenton St. (tel. 349 0591). Impossible to resist, with the invitation of the sombrero-wearing stuffed peasant outside the door and the endless recommendations of locals. Possibly Rotorua's best value, the narrow cantina is always full with patrons bumping elbows to dig into plates of burritos, enchiladas, and tacos (all $4-8). Open M-Sa 10am-8 or 9pm, Su 11am-7:30pm.

Fat Dog Cafe and Bar, 69 Arawa St. (tel. 347 7586), does its roly-poly namesake justice with bright walls, a playful atmosphere, and drinks that make it the latte-lover's best friend. Breakfasts, creative mains, and sandwiches $5-10, but it's the irresistible desserts (under $4) that'll make you a Fat Dog. Open daily 9am-late.

Chez Bleu Cafe, 1262 Fenton St. (tel. 348 1828), by Hinemoa St. A Mediterranean cafe offering decent burgers (under $7) and luscious desserts ($5-6). Pool table and jukebox in the corner make it a pleasant night option. Outdoor dining. Open Su-W 8:30am-midnight, Th-Sa 8:30am-3am.

Chopsticks, 45 Amohau St. (tel. 347 8011), near the corner of Fenton St. A gurgling pool with bridge landscaped into the foyer, and a pagoda in the main dining room. Reasonably authentic; most takeaways are under $10. With two mains, they will deliver 6-10pm. Pay somewhat high prices (most mains start at $14.50) for an oddly post-modern experience as you watch the 7pm Maori cultural group while dipping into chicken and cashews. Open daily 10:30am-2pm and from 5pm.

NIGHTLIFE

Far less memorable than Rotorua's Maori cultural offerings are its nightclubs, pubs, and upscale cafes. These are sustained by the quantity of tourists rather than the quality of the establishments. The late nightlife can be a little rough around the edges. Hog a bar stool at the ever-popular **Pig and Whistle City Bar** (tel. 347 3025), at the corner of Tutanekai and Haupapa St. A former police station and probation office, patrons nowadays are less degenerate, though weekends with live bands can still get rowdy ($2 cover). Pub fare under $10 is served until 9:30pm (open daily from 11:30am). From a wilder part of the animal kingdom comes **Monkey Jo's** (tel. 346 1313) on Amohia St., where the loud and drunk get primitive on the sawdust floor and outdoor patio overlooking the jungle of central Rotorua. There are occasional live bands, frequent long lines, and required tidy dress (open daily from 3pm). At **Grace O'Malley's Irish Bar,** on Hinemoa St. by Ranolf St., play a game at the pointless round pool table, or jounce along to rollicking Irish and retro bands on weekends at this local pick (happy hour 5-7pm; no cover). Those enamored of young foreign drunks flock to the pumping music over at **Lava Bar,** part of Hot Rocks Backpacker at the corner of Ranolf and Arawa St., to dance on the patio or couch with herds of Kiwi Experiencers (open from 4pm).

A MAORI EVENING

As one of the most accessible places to learn about Maori culture, the classic form of entertainment in Rotorua is participation in a Maori *hangi,* or feast. Many offerings are commercial evenings that tread a delicate line among entertainment, education, and exoticization. The many options fall on a wide spectrum: some emphasize learning about Maori history and traditions, while others consist solely of song and dance. Some *hangi* are held on real *marae,* some in specifically built commercial locations, and some in plush motel restaurants. Although the cameras flashing and the sensation

The Arawa of Rotorua

Part of the ancestral lands of the people of the great Te Arawa canoe (one of the canoes of the Great Migration), Rotorua was also New Zealand's first real travel destination. Confident in their ability to control their own destiny, the Arawa did not at first sign the Treaty of Waitangi. But by 1860 they realized that such an alliance would help to protect them from rapidly increasing numbers of settlers and give them increased access to tourists. In the late 1860s, after the land wars had died down, several hotels and a network of Maori guides sprang up. They catered to Rotorua's tourists, who came to see the "8th wonder of the world," the spectacular Pink and White Terraces (frozen cascades of silicate awash with hot water above Lake Rotomahana). Today the Maori have transformed themselves into the tourist attraction; what might first appear at selling out has in fact enabled Maori-owned enterprises to thrive and hints at the possibility of future autonomy. The lands around Tarawera are currently going through extensive Waitangi tribunal hearings, and some may soon revert to Maori hands.

of "culture on display" can be disconcerting, this may be your best chance to move beyond postcard images of tongue-protruding tattooed Maori warriors to get a glimpse of the beauty, power, and richness of the Maori tradition. The *hangi* is a damn good meal, too (see p. 43).

Full evenings offered by the several Maori-owned tour operators usually include an introductory communication protocol, challenge and welcome ceremony, concert, and *hangi;* all will pickup and drop-off from any accommodation (book directly or through the visitors center). Evenings last three to four hours. **Rotoiti Tours** (tel. 348 8969), of the Ngati Rongamai tribe, does one of the most authentic evenings in the Rakeiao *marae*, on the shores of impossibly scenic Lake Rotoiti. *(Adults $49, under 12 half-price.)* Groups get no larger than 80 to 100 on peak summer nights. Winter groups may be under 20, but are not available every night, so call ahead. **Overnights** are also possible, but mainly for groups of more than 10. *(Bedding, kitchen facilities, breakfast supplied. Prices start from $60, based on group size.)* Rotorua's most popular and polished Maori experience is a flashbulb-filled evening with **Tamaki Tours** (tel. 346 2823). *(Evening $55, children half-price.)* From each of the several busloads of people, a chief is chosen to represent his canoe (tour bus). After the welcoming, groups walk through the impressive, model *pa* built for the purpose of viewing age-old customs performed by well-paid modern Maori. Then there is a fascinating cultural group concert and magnificent *hangi*. **Mai Ora** (tel. 348 9047) is also highly recommended and performed year-round. *(Begins at 6pm in summer and 5pm in winter; $60, child $30.)* Based at a pre-European village overlooking the **Whakarewa Thermal Reserve,** your *hangi* will be prepared by the underground heat of the natural hot water.

For a mighty cultural performance, head to the gorgeous and historically significant *marae* **Tamatekapua Meeting House** at Ohinemutu. The hour-long performance, called **Magic of the Maori** (tel. 349 3949), runs nightly at 8pm. *(Admission $15, children $5. Tickets available at the door.)* Whakarewarewa (see p. 188) also offers a daily concert.

GEOTHERMAL ACTIVITIES

Rotorua's famed thermal activity is caused by a volcanic fault line running from **White Island,** 50km offshore from Whakatane (see p. 196), to Mt. Ruapehu in Tongariro National Park (see p. 173). The tectonic plates have created spectacularly unstable mountains and the bizarre landscape of the region's several major geothermal parks and innumerable small steaming pools, craters, and vents—that's life on the geological edge for you.

Just 30km south of Rotorua on SH5, the amazingly beautiful **Wai-O-Tapu** is probably the single finest geothermal spot. Private operators lease it from the DOC as "Thermal Wonderland" (tel. 366 6333); admission is $11 (children $4, families $27). A self-guided tour weaves among boiling mud pools, an expansive silicate terrace, brilliantly hued pools, craters, and (you're in Rotorua) crowds of tourists. While frustratingly veiled in steam all too often, the stunning ochre and turquoise of the bubbling **Champagne Pool** could convert even a teetotaler. **Frozen Bridal Veil Falls** looks as though a pail (or ten) of daffodil-yellow paint was tipped over its edge. Erupting up to 21m each day at precisely 10:15am, **Lady Knox Geyser** is another major Wai-O-Tapu attraction. *(Open daily 8:30-5pm.)* Mother Nature isn't really that regular: the geyser gets an unhealthy dose of soap every morning to disperse the upper level of water and relieve surface tension (prisoners discovered this handy trick in 1896 when trying to wash clothes).

The **Waimangu Volcanic Valley** (tel. 366 6137), 23km from Rotorua off the Tupo Highway, is the southern end of the rift created by Tarawera's 1886 eruption. *(Admission to valley $13, including the terraces $31; open daily 8:30am-5pm.)* Along its trail, the **Echo Crater** is home to the world's largest hot springs (by surface area), where dancing steam creates fanciful patterns on the gleaming water. The gorgeous, ice-blue, and extremely acidic (pH 2.1) inferno crater lake is actually a geyser, living on a 38-day cycle. The path also passes the site of **Waimangu**, once the world's largest geyser. The white cross nearby marks the site where four overeager tourists were blown away in 1903. You can also take a one-hour guided cruise to the former sites of the Pink and White Terraces and steaming cliffs (several per day).

Abandon all hope, ye who enter into the dark underworld of geothermal wonders, also known as **Hell's Gate** (tel. 345 3151), 15km east of Rotorua on SH30. With 10 hectares of seething mud, pools, and rocks, there is basically one true attraction: the largest steaming, hot waterfall in the Southern Hemisphere. Evil-doers never had it so good (open daily 9am-5pm; admission $10, children $5). Capitalizing on its devilish reputation, it's now even open at night (6-10pm), with eerie illumination and a light, sound, and fire performance at 8pm.

TOURS

Since Rotorua's attractions are widely spread out, a sightseeing tour might be your best option. The **Rotorua Sightseeing Shuttle** (tel. 348 0408) caters to tourists on a time budget and makes daily runs from the visitors center. *(Shuttles run 8:15am-4:40pm. Most cost $4-10. Half-day pass $10, full-day pass $16.)* Get tickets and a timetable from the visitors center or from the driver. **Carey's Sightseeing Tours,** 18 Haupapa St. (24hr. reservations tel. 347 1197) offers a bewildering array of half-, three-quarter-, and full-day tour options including pickup, admissions, and in-coach commentary. The half-day "Grand Tour" runs $60 (children $35), while the "Waimangu Round Trip" is a full-day journey costing $100 (children $50). A branch of Carey's, **Carey's Capers,** caters to backpackers with tours covering all the standard sights, but adding in spicier activities, such as a swim in an isolated hot bush stream, rides up Mt. Tarawera, raft-

Prophet of Doom

The flax had not flowered. Streams had been abruptly gushing and drying. But more troubling to the Maori living under Mt. Tarawera were the events of May 31, 1886. Guide Sophia Hinerangi and her boat of tourists returning from a day at the fabled Pink and White Terraces had seen a spectral war canoe, its warrior paddlers wearing ominous symbols on their heads, emerge from a bend in the lake and disappear again. These were the signs foretelling something cataclysmic. The old priest Tuhoto had seen it coming; he had warned his people in Te Wairoa that their departure from the ancestral ways would lead to punishment sent by the spirit Tamahoi, buried within the mountain. The night of terror came on June 10, 1886, when the three domes on this now flat-topped volcano blew and rent the mountain asunder, ripping a 17km wound of otherworldly red, white, and black scoria-lined craters. The largest eruption in 500 years, it blasted away the bed of Lake Rotomahana, burying Te Wairoa and other nearby villages in mud, rock, and ash. The famed terraces were shattered into splinters, forests burned all around, and roars were heard as far as Christchurch and Auckland. When the search parties finally uncovered Tuhoto's house, days later, they found the old man still alive. Tamahoi had protected his prophet.

ing the Kaituna, and bushwalks. *(Day tour $70.)* Sometimes, they'll even run trips for just one person. **The Pink Coach** (tel. 345 4096) is less of a guide and more of a transport service; it does half-day trips to Wai-O-Tapu, Waimangu, Hell's Gate, the Buried Village, and Lake Tarawera ($20-45).

SIGHTS

Rotorua's single most visited sight is a combo of its trademark geothermal and cultural attractions: **Te Whakarewarewawatangaoteopetauaawahiao** (tel. 348 9047), often referred to simply as Whakarewarewa or even Whaka. *(Open daily 8am-5 or 6pm. Admission $11. Daily cultural performances offered 12:15pm, $11. Another at 5:15pm includes full welcome and hangi $39.50; combined park admission and cultural evening $48.50.)* Whaka is located about 2km south down Fenton St. (SH5), between the city and the state Forest Park. Reachable by foot, the sightseeing shuttle, or the public bus, it incorporates the **New Zealand Maori Arts and Crafts Institute** and the **Te Whakarewarewa Thermal Reserve.** Whaka also contains a Maori village, boiling mud pools, a kiwi house, several geysers, and carving, weaving, and crafts demonstrations during the week. The most famous and largest geyser in New Zealand, **Pohutu,** spurts as high as 30m several times per day. Since the village and geothermal reserve don't have many explanatory signs, you may want to aim for the free hourly guided tours that leave from the institute between 10am and 4pm.

A visit to **Ohinemutu,** the lakefront Maori village of the Ngati Whakaue tribe, affords a glimpse of Maori culture. Off Lake Rd. (just walk down Tutanekai St.), you'll come to one of the Arawa people's most symbolically important buildings, the **Tamatekapua Meeting House.** Rich red and speckled with paua shells, its carvings

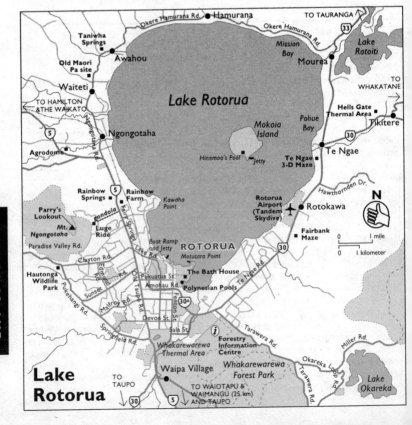

are a maze of figures tangled into figures. The interior is closed to the public, except for nightly concerts (see A Maori Evening, p. 164). Across the way is **St. Faith's Anglican Church** with a Tudor outside and a Maori interior. It serves as a potent focus of cultural history, and continues to hold services (the original St. Faith's housed Rotorua's first Christian service in 1831). The pulpit is supported by carved figures of five Maori ancestors, while an etched window panel shows Christ clad in the cloak of a Maori chief—from the right angle, he appears to be walking on Lake Rotorua.

The **Government Gardens** on Hinemaru St. are worth a wander. The terrific **Rotorua Museum of Art and History/ Te Whare Taonga o Te Arawa** (tel. 349 8334) can be found in the impressive neo-Tudor Bath House in the Gardens. *(Open daily 9:30am-5pm. Admission $4, backpackers $2, children $1, families $8.)* A former luxury spa, the elegant wings today house excellent permanent exhibitions on the former spa itself, the Tarawera eruption of 1886, area geology, and a collection of well-curated treasures of the Te Arawa people; there are also temporary art exhibitions.

The **Agrodome** (tel. 357 4350), 10km north of town on SH5, is for those who have a burning desire to see 19 different breeds of sheep strut their stuff. *(5 shows per day. Admission $9.)* Live sheep shows are offered daily, as are tours of a working farm (9:30, 11am, and 2:30pm). Similar to the Agrodome (but with only 17 breeds of sheep) is the **Rainbow Farm Show**, on SH5 about 5km north of town, next to the Skyline Gondola. Two "farmers" shear sheep, perform a mock auction, lead sheep-dog trials, and let the camera-happy (many with translation headphones) pet baby lambs. *(4 shows per day; $10, children $5.)* The surrounding complex has some baby animals to ooh and ahh over, and a wool-heavy gift shop. Or, combine your show ticket with the entrance to neighboring **Rainbow Springs** (tel. 347 9301) for only $16.50 (children $8), which has various animal life among beauteous springs.

ACTIVITIES

Rotorua has an abundance of both man-made commercial activities and lakes, forest, and hills for more natural activities if you want to escape the world of brochures and concrete. **Skyline Skyrides** (tel. 347 0027), four to five kilometers from the city center and next to Rainbow Springs on SH5, is an elaborate complex responsible for making Rotorua the semi-official **luge** capital of the country. *(Rides $3-4.50 each or $20 for a 5-ride pass.)* After ascending in a scenic, if not thrilling, gondola ride ($11), the luge lets you hurl yourself back down part-way on a three-wheeled plastic cart. Other attractions at the top include a sidewinder toboggan, shooting gallery, nine-hole golf, a ride simulator, and a skyline ride where you fly down like Batman on a wire.

Adrenaline junkies in search of their next hit will thrill to the short but sweet **Kaituna River,** with its infamous, over-7m-high **Otere Falls** drop, spilling out of **Lake Rotoiti.** *(Kaituna usually costs about $60 for 40min.)* The dramatic canyon trip, along with trips to other area rivers including the Rangitaiki, Wairoa (26 days per year), and Tongariro, are offered by umpteen different companies. The original company, with strong local recommendation, is **Kaituna Cascades** (tel. 357 5032). Three times daily they'll pick you up and run the rush ($58).

Otherwise, fulfill your free-fall dreams with **Tandem Skydiving Rotorua** (tel. 345 7520). Painstaking safety precautions, a 3200m fall, and spectacular lake district scenery balance the $180 price tag (book ahead). Getting up Tarawera by foot is possible, but the access point from **Ash Pit Rd.** near Lake Rerewhakaaitu south of town is nearly impossible to reach without your own transport. The land is Maori-owned, so obtain permission in advance (and pay the $2 fee) from the **Rangitauira and Co. Trustbank building** (tel. 348 0032) on Hinemoa St., and get further advice from the Map and Track shop. Tarawera can also be climbed in a jouncing, four-wheel-drive vehicle with **Mountain Magic** (tel. 348 6399), a Maori-run company. They'll even let you clamber around the crater and do slides down into it. *(Half-day $70, children $30.)* Other options include full-day bush trips to the isolated **Tarawera Falls** and thermal springs for a swim ($140, children $60). **Mount Tarawera 4WD Tours** (tel. 348 2814; fax 347 8147) also offers trips with good commentary on the region. *(Half-day $65, children $35.)*

Of the many scenic flight helicopter and plane rides leaving Rotorua, only two companies have permission to land on Tarawera. **Tarawera Helicopters** (tel. 348 1223) is a Maori-owned business operating out of Whakarewarewa. *(45min. flight $245; $185 for 30min. without the landing.)* Other flights include the wickedly cool and even more wickedly priced White Island landing tour. *(4hr., $650 per person, including guided walk.)* **Volcanic Air Safaris** (tel. 348 9984), based at the waterfront, also lands on Tarawera. *($225 for 45min. landing trip; $550 for a White Island landing.)*

Lose yourself (your stodgy, grown-up self, at least) in the **Fairbank Maze** (tel. 345 4089), a large hedge maze right out of Alice in Wonderland, located opposite the airport. *(Open daily 10am-5pm. $4, children $2.)* If you can't get enough, you can head to **Te Ngae Park's 3-D Maze** (tel. 345 9565), a wooden maze located 3km past the airport on SH30. *(Admission $4, children $2.)*

With all its lakes (and purportedly more trout per capita than even Lake Taupo), the Rotorua district is an angler's paradise. Fly guides begin at $70 per hour (typically with a 2hr. minimum); contact the visitors center for a listing of operators and to get a license ($12 per day). Lakes Rotorua and Okareka are open year-round; other fishable lakes in the district are open October through June. If fishing doesn't interest you but the azure lakes themselves do, **kayaking** is probably your best bet, especially on **Lake Okataina** (the only lake completely surrounded by lush fern and thick native bush, regrown since the 1886 eruption). **Adventure Kayaking** (tel./fax 348 9451) does full-day guided trips ($75) or two-day Lake Tarawera trips ($210); they also rent kayaks if you can already wield a paddle ($35 per day). **Waka Hikoi** (tel. 362 7878) offers guided trips and bushwalks with Maori flavor. *($49 per half-day, $79 per full-day.)*

Lake Rotorua itself offers an appealing alternative to bubbling and steaming pools. The **Motutara Walkway,** a tame gravel track, ambles along the lakefront. If you'd rather cruise than walk, the **Lakeland Queen** (tel. (0800) 862 784 or 348 6634) offers a musical-worthy paddle-steamer. *(1hr., 12:30pm, full buffet cruise $26; tea cruise $16.)* Call ahead to find out when full buffet or tea cruises are offered, and to book ahead. **Mokoia Island,** in the middle of the lake, is the mythic home of the legendary young lovers Hinemoa and Tutanekai (whose names grace decidedly less mythic streets in town today). Today, the unfortunately named **Scatcat** (tel./fax 347 9852) takes you out to the island (also a wildlife reserve), with a tour and a dip in the pool. *(Every hr. 10am-2pm; $25, backpackers $22.50.)* Scatcat cruises also run to Rotorua's more scenic neighbor, **Lake Rotoiti** (3:30pm, 2hr., $48). The most futuristic way to see Lake Rotorua is on the **Hovershuttle** (tel. 347 0100), which runs trips on both Lakes Rotorua and Rotoiti. *(Flexible schedule, call ahead. $25 per hr.)*

It may not be native bush, but the 5667-hectare exotic pine plantation otherwise known as the **Whakarewarewa Forest** still draws visitors. Although managed for forestry, the woods have been growing long enough to offer a lush understory and it's free. Check in at the **Visitor Centre** (tel. 346 2082) on Long Mile Rd., a short drive or bike from city center off the road to the airport. *(Open M-F 8:30am-5pm, Sa-Su 10am-4pm.)* The Whakarewarewa forest is known for its awesome mountain biking, some of the country's finest—a well-marked, well-built 15km of tracks is waiting. **Mountain Cats** (tel. (0800) 871 187) hires out mountain bikes and will drop them at the visitors center for you; or, pick one up from the **Golden Glow Motel** on Fenton St. *($15 for 1hr., $10 for each additional hour; $35 per half-day, $45 per full-day.)* Bikes with front- or dual-suspension are available for stiffer prices.

The great cultural melting pot of Rotorua is the grand **Polynesian Spa** (tel. 348 1328), outdoors on the lakefront, at the Government Gardens end of Hinemoa St. *($9, children $3; adults-only pool $9.)* Where else can you don your swimsuit, soak in ecstasy, and comfortably chat with travelers from around the globe? You may never want to leave. The **Radium** and **Priest Springs,** ranging from 33 to 43 degrees, are famed for their supposed healing powers. Don't slip into one of the hottest pools first; seek your comfort zone. Private pools where you can control the temperature are ideal for romantics. Entrance to the **Lake Spa,** a luxury landscaped terrace of caves and waterfalls is a whopping $25, but has water-jet massages (open daily 6:30am-11pm).

■ Tauranga

Tauranga's temperate climate and commercial conveniences have made it one of New Zealand's fastest growing cities. This growth has resulted in an overlay of modernity upon remnants of the 19th century past, a strange mixture that infuses the town with a youthful flavor and energy. One of the earliest sites of Maori habitation, the former "resting place for canoes" is today the resting place for ships, serving as one of the nation's busiest ports. Only a short paddle from Mount Maunganui and its beaches, Tauranga attracts party-goers both young and old, especially during the summer months. Tauranga is also the hub of kiwifruit country and sends the world massive amounts of the tasty little green fuzzballs every year. Many wayward backpackers find employment picking kiwifruit from mid-April to June (with plenty of packing and pruning available in the subsequent months). The communal spirit in the hostels during kiwifruit season is worth experiencing, but don't overestimate the back-aching "fun" of the labor—it's not the easiest way to become a millionaire.

ORIENTATION & PRACTICAL INFORMATION

Downtown Tauranga is located on a narrow northward-pointing peninsula in **Tauranga Harbour.** The main tourist area lies north of **Elizabeth St.,** and is particularly concentrated on **the Strand,** facing Waipu Bay. Streets downtown are named; cross-streets south of Elizabeth St. are numbered in a southward ascending order. **Fifteenth Ave.** is the continuation of **SH2.**

Tauranga

ACCOMMODATIONS
D Bell Lodge (VIP)
A Duck's Nuts Hostel
B Strand Motel
C YHA Hostel

Trains: TranzScenic (tel. 0800 802 802) heads daily to Auckland (3hr., 8am, $54) via Hamilton (1hr., $29). Discounts for students and backpackers with ID.

Buses: Station at the Tourism and Travel Centre by the harbor bridge roundabout. **InterCity** and **Newmans** head daily to Auckland (4hr., 2-3 per day, $37); Hamilton (2hr., 1-2 per day, $23); and Rotorua (1hr., 11:20am, $15-22; transfer here for points in the East Cape). **Supa Travel** (tel. 571 0583) runs to Auckland (3hr., M-F 9am, Su 11am; backpackers $27).

Ferries: From **Coronation Pier** to Mt. Maunganui in summer (tel. 578 5381; every hr., $4).

Hitchhiking: Hitchhikers heading to Auckland or the Coromandel Peninsula believe Waihi Rd. (SH2), just past Jonathon St. and about 500m beyond the Otumoetai Rd. roundabout, to be a good spot. Eastward thumbers to Whakatane or Rotorua often start at the Turret Rd. (SH29) roundabout just across Waimapu Estuary.

Public Transportation: Newlove's Bus Service (tel. 578 6453) crosses into Mt. Maunganui (M-F every hr., $3) and neighboring suburbs. **City Travel** (tel. 544 5494) runs buses M-F along Cameron Rd. into nearby suburbs.

Taxis: Tauranga Taxis (tel. 578 6086), **Bay City Cabs** (tel. 577 0999), and **Coastline Taxis** (tel. 511 8333) are all open 24hr.

Visitors Center: Tauranga Tourism and Travel Centre, 80 Dive Crescent (tel. 578 8103; fax 577 6235), located at the bus station by the harbor bridge roundabout, is the main office for Bay of Plenty tourism. The office is a 10-minute walk from the Strand. Open M-F 7am-5:30pm, Sa-Su 8am-4pm. **DOC:** 253 Chadwick Rd., West Greerton (tel./fax 578 7677). Somewhat far from town, but staff can answer inquiries about area hikes. Open M-F 8am-4:30pm.

Currency Exchange: BNZ (tel. 578 5840; fax 578 6537), on the corner of Willow and Wharf St., and **National Bank** (tel. 578 2049; fax 578 3700), at the corner of Spring and Grey St. are both open M-F 9am-4:30pm.

Emergency: Dial 111.

Police: (tel. 578 8199), on the corner of Willow St. and Monmouth St.

Medical Services: John's Photo Pharmacy (tel. 578 3566), on the corner of Cameron Rd. and 2nd Ave. is your best bet in the evenings. Open daily 8am-9pm. The **hospital** is on Cameron Rd. between 17th and 18th Ave. (tel. 577 8000).

Post Office: On Grey St. (tel. 577 9911), open M-F 9am-5pm.

Telephone Code: 07.

ACCOMMODATIONS

With some foresight, finding a comfortable bed in Tauranga shouldn't be a problem. While those without vehicles will want to stick close to downtown, more mobile visitors will find an array of motorparks and motels along **Waihi Rd.** (coming from Auckland) or **Turret Rd./15th Ave.** All the hostels in town offer free pick-ups and drop-offs and coordinate with each other to ensure that any homeless travelers find a place to stay. The hostels are far and away the best bet for kiwifruit pickers (the season runs mid-April through May). Several could aptly be termed "working hostels," for kiwifruit contractors frequently look to hostels to supply labor, and the majority of guests may be working rather than on holiday.

YHA Hostel, 171 Elizabeth St. (tel./fax 578 5064). Located on a cul-de-sac past the Cameron Rd. intersection, a convenient 10min. walk from the Strand. The Kiwi mantra "No Worries" finds absolute affirmation here with hard working and amiable hosts Danny and Jo at the helm. Discounts for area activities, informed advice, and employment help offered along with spacious kitchen, a small shop, and rental bikes. Dorms (mostly single-sex quads) $15; doubles $32; tent sites $8. Reception open 8-10am, 1:30-10pm (but ring any time, of course). Credit cards accepted.

Just the Ducks Nuts (VIP), 6 Vale St. (tel. 576 1366), in Otumoetai. Take Chapel St. from Tauranga. The free pick-up in the hand-decorated station wagon takes you to a homely hostel with a great glassed-in conservatory, fireplace, pool table, and even a graffiti wall. Rental bikes available. Ask for the front twin with superb views of Mt. Maunganui and the harbor. Singles $15 (weekly $84); twins or doubles $36 (weekly $132); tent sites in backyard $10 (weekly $56). Credit cards accepted.

Bell Lodge (VIP), 39 Bell St. (tel. 578 6344; fax 578 6342), near the Otumoetai Rd. roundabout off Waihi Rd (or SH2). A van makes the several km trip from town. Relaxed and secluded, in a green residential setting with view of the surrounding hills, it offers modern white-and-wood rooms with sliding glass doors overlooking a patio and small courtyard. Amenities include a TV lounge, mini pool table, and large kitchen. Singles $15 (weekly $80); twins with bath $34; doubles with bath $36, with TV $42; tent sites $9. Reception open 8am daily (just ring the bell). Linen $1, free in rooms with bath. Credit cards accepted.

Strand Motel, 27 the Strand, (tel. 578 5807), is centrally located and typical of the motel offerings, though a bit cheaper. Ample parking. $58 for adequate double with shower, bathroom, and TV. Call ahead.

Apple Tree Cottage, 47 Maxwell St. (tel. 576 7404), in Otumoteai. From Tauranga, cross Chapel Bridge, and it's immediately on the left. While the facilities (set up in small buildings and sheds around the apple trees in the backyard) leave a bit to be desired, as you'll note walking outside to the bathroom, the rough-around-the-edges Apple Tree prides itself on a no-pressure atmosphere that may appeal to some travelers. 8-person bungalow dorms $13 (weekly $85); 2 twins $31; 2 doubles $35 per person. Limited tent sites $8.

FOOD

Many of Tauranga's better restaurants are clustered along **the Strand** and the downtown end of **Devonport Rd.** For fast food, **Cameron Rd.** and its surrounding streets offer major Americana.

⊛Shiraz Cafe, 12 Wharf St. (tel. 577 0059). The cream of Tauranga's cafe crop, offering unbeatable taste for your dollar, from hummus ($5) to kebab ($6.50). Outdoor seating in front and pleasant courtyard in back. Serves lunch and dinner ($15). Fully licensed. Open M-Sa 11am-2:30pm, and 5-9pm (closing time flexible).

The Sunrise Natural Cafe, 10 Wharf St. (tel. 578 9302). Vegetarian-oriented sandwiches, hot dishes, and tantalizing desserts for those looking for refuge from the deep-fried delights of Kiwi cuisine. Shares outdoor seating with the Shiraz. Open M-F 8am-3:30pm, Sa 9am-2pm.

The Hobler, 116 Cameron Rd. at Wharf St. corner (tel. 577 9177). The stellar food, fireplace, decorated mantle, and friendly service are bound to cure both hunger and any traveling blues. Find out what time it is at home by checking the clocks set to different time zones while tucking into hearty fare such as club chicken sandwiches ($8-$15) or special two-for-one ribs on Sundays and Mondays ($18.95). Dinner daily 5-10:30pm, and lunch M-F noon-2pm.

The Captain's Table, on Coronation Pier. Delight in a view of the harbor along with standard soup and sandwiches or fish 'n' chips. Most fare under $7. Open Tu-Su 7:30am-4pm.

Chamomile Cafe, 51 Victoria Ave. (tel. 345 6891). A cozy country kitchen of a cafe complete with quilts hanging from the walls, wicker baskets suspended from the ceiling, and dried flowers on the tables. A wide selection of muffins (blueberry white chocolate, $1.50) and scones ($2-3) for breakfast, as well as light lunch items ($2-4) that won't wilt your wallet. Open M-F 8am-2pm, Sa 9:30am-2pm.

NIGHTLIFE

Tauranga provides the West Bay's night with life, attracting the area's drinking and dancing crowds with its relatively new bars and clubs.

Oak and Ale, (tel. 577 1305), on the corner of Spring and Grey. Featuring live music every weekend and table service—shake your booty or leave it pasted to the stool for the entire night. Either way, the $3-5 pints, bar food, or daily happy hour (5-7pm;$3.20 pints) will satisfy. No cover. Tidy dress. Open daily 10:30am-3am.

Grumpy Mole Saloon, 41 the Strand (tel. 571 1222). Although it has a set worthy of Hollywood, John Wayne never knew this playground version of the Wild West with its separate cigar parlor, adjoining courtyard, pulsing music, and giant TV. No fists swinging here, only the twentysomethings. The dress code is almost as long as the bar (just avoid black jeans and biker wear). Pints $3.50. Happy hour 4-7pm and 9-10pm. Open M-Sa 4pm-3am.

Flannagan's, 14 Hamilton St. off the Strand (tel. 578 9222). Nostalgia for the Emerald Isle abounds at this popular Irish pub that caters to a slightly older crowd. Live music most weekends, with a restaurant upstairs. Happy hour Tu, Th, Sa 4-6pm ($2 pints). Open daily11-3am.

SIGHTS AND ACTIVITIES

While Tauranga has a notable history, don't expect to spend the day marveling at architecture or museums—people come here for what's around Tauranga (read: the beach). But if the line at the **Bungee Rocket** (see below) is too long, some historical buildings and parks clustered around the north end of town give a deeper context of cultural place and time. At the end of the Strand sits **Te Awanui,** an intricately carved replica Maori canoe. The small greenhouse and rose gardens of **Robbins Park** have a view of the harbor and less-than-picturesque shipping industry. Up Cliff Rd. and left on Mission St. you'll find the beautiful grounds of the **Elms Mission Station** (tel. 578 7444), established in 1835 as Tauranga's first mission. *(Open "fine" Sunday afternoons from 2-3:30pm, but grounds open anytime.)* Walk the small path through the reserved and beautiful grounds where ripe kiwifruit and tangerines hang down by the chapel in late fall.

Activities and adventure options abound in the burgeoning tourist mecca of Tauranga. Most involve water, but landlubbers can explore the local wineries, a nearby *marae,* and various local hikes. For the more reckless, there is skydiving, gliding, and, in a bizarre manifestation of the Kiwi obsession with all things bungy, the **Bungee Rocket** (tel. 578 3057). Situated on the Strand right on the waterfront, the contraption shoots its hapless passenger 50 meters into the air in 1.3 seconds. *(Open daily in the summer 10am-10pm, later on weekends; winter hours same, weather permitting. $30.)* **Bent Hills Farm Park** (tel. 542 0972), in Papamoa off Welcome Bay Rd., provides horse trekking, four-wheel-drive bikes, grass skiing, and 160 acres of pastoral land with superb vistas for viewing and picnics. The sight of the community of pigs, roosters, wild turkeys, and cattle at the farmhouse immediately redeems the 15-minute drive from town. Visionary farmer Malcolm's plans for his land, including a death-defying dirt luge track, would make Walt Disney jealous. Inquire at hostels and the visitors center for more information.

Tauranga is not far from the **Wairoa River** and its gut-wrenching Grade 5 rapids. The river is only raftable 26 days per year from January to March, however, when the dam on its upper reaches is opened. **Woodrow Expeditions** (tel. 576 2628 or 577 0817) does one-hour jaunts up the Wairoa (\$65 per person). Whether it's deep sea fishing or reefer-game, most trips are booked at and leave from the **Fishing and Boat Charters office** on Coronation Pier (tel. 577 9100). Swim with the dolphins with **Gemini Galaxsea Charters** (evening/off-season tel. 578 3197, or (025) 272 8353; \$80 per person; gear provided) or **Dolphin Seafaris** (0800 326 8747) which both have had great success in recent years. For those with an aversion to water, there are other fish in the proverbial sea of activities. You can act out your death wish in a 2500m fall (\$190) with **Tandem Skydiving** (tel. 576 7990). Slightly less precipitous for both body and budget is gliding: the **Tauranga Gliding Club** (tel. 575 6768) offers three height levels of flights on weekends and Wednesday afternoons. *(\$45, \$75, \$115.)* Celebrate your flight afterwards at the **Mills Reef Winery,** 143 Moffat Rd. (tel. 576 8800) off Waihi Rd. on the way out of town, where both kiwifruit and grape wine are made; tastings flow for free. *(Open daily 10am-5pm.)*

If you've run out of money from one too many rocket bungees, head over to the DOC and learn about the area's hikes. Otherwise, you'll have to duke it out with the joggers on the boardwalks around the popular **Waikareao Estuary.** The **McLaren**

Money Doesn't Grow on Trees

New Zealand's fuzzy unofficial mascot has endeared itself to many a visitor, but before such attractions lead you to a career as a kiwifruit picker, consider the following. Although the idea of alternately backpacking and picking one's way across the North Island may be appealing, the job is far from glamorous. Those who work in the orchards do it not for the love of the fruit, but because they need the cash. Kiwifruit contractors assemble groups of 9 to 15 pickers, who earn about \$12.50 for each bin they pick. Depending on the speed of their team, pickers can earn anywhere from \$60-100 a day. Because picking is a group effort, one slacker can ruin both the speed and paycheck of an entire team. Workers must wear gloves, and those working in T-bar kiwi trees must climb into branches after their elusive quarry. The days are a grueling nine hours long, and rain means an automatic day off. Although the teamwork and bonding under stress create a distinct culture, the payoff might not be worth the mental frustration of such a job.

Falls Park tracks, a 15-minute drive down SH29 toward Hamilton, are pleasantly pastoral. *(For bunkhouse accommodation at the park, call 543 3382.)* For more mobile travelers, the **Kaimai Mamaku Forest Park,** its hills stretching away to the west of town, provides 37,140 hectares of forests and rivers laced with trails. It's basically an extension of the **Coromandel Forest Park** but doesn't get the same crowds. Even fewer people make it out to the 24km of beaches at nearby **Matakana Island.** Stretching across the entrance to Tauranga Harbour and absorbing the blows of the Pacific, the island makes for one of the Bay of Plenty's best surf spots. Thirty-five kilometers offshore lies **Mayor Island,** an isolated and undeveloped volcanic region under Maori ownership. Snorkeling and diving grounds abound, but the island has no amenities besides a rugged campground, and you must obtain permission to land beforehand. **MV Manutere** makes seasonal runs to the island—more information can be found at Coronation Pier.

■ Mt. Maunganui

From the mists of Tauranga Harbour rises Mt. Maunganui, an extinct volcanic cone that is visible from kilometers away. Formerly used by local Maori as both a residence and a stronghold, the mountain now reigns over the mellow seasonal town that bears its name. If the tiled sidewalks, palm trees, and turquoise-painted street lamps lining the main road don't scream "beach town" to you, the crashing waves and expanses of fine sand most certainly will. Just across Waipu Bay from Tauranga, "the Mount" explodes in the summer months.

ORIENTATION AND PRACTICAL INFORMATION When in doubt, head toward anything with the word Maunganui in it: the town's main drag is **Maunganui Rd.,** and the center of town is almost directly below the Mount. **Marine Parade/Ocean Beach Rd.** runs along the ocean and toward the fine sands of **Papamoa Beach Reserve. The Mall** runs on the harborside of downtown. **Buses** stop at the Bayfair Shopping Center, 3km from town and next to the McDonalds before Prince St. on Maunganui Rd. **InterCity** (tel. 575 4669) and **Newmans** go daily to Tauranga (15 min., every 1hr., $3). In the summer, take the ferry to Tauranga from Salisbury Wharf (every hr. 9am-5pm, $5). Stop in at the **Information Centre** (tel. 575 5099), on Salisbury Ave. (Open daily in summer 8:30am-5:30pm; in winter M-F 8am-5pm, and Sa-Su 9am-4pm.) **Thomas Cook,** 194 Maunganui Rd. (tel. 575 3058; fax 575 0099), is open Monday through Friday 8:30am to 5pm and, blessedly, Saturday from 10am to noon. In an **emergency,** dial 111. The **police** (tel. 575 3143) are next door to the information center. (Open M-F 8am-4pm). Drop off postcards at the **Post Shop and Copy Centre,** 155 Maunganui Rd. (tel. 575 8180; open M-F 9am-5pm). The **telephone code** is **07.**

ACCOMMODATIONS AND FOOD Most of what you'll need is clustered in the few blocks under the Mount's shadow. Prices go up and space goes down for most accommodations in summer. Phone well in advance if you want to stay at the **Maunganui Domain Motor Camp** (tel. 575 4471) at the base of the mountain. They have 274 powered tent or caravan sites stretching from the harborside to the beachfront, as well as one tourist cabin with a kitchenette. The location is prime, but the most likely view will be of your neighbor 30 meters away (tent sites from $10; vehicles or caravans from $10 per person; under 15 $4). You can't miss **Mount Backpackers,** 87 Maunganui Rd. (tel./fax 575 0860), the sunny yellow hostel in the town center. Space is quite tight throughout, but the beds are cushy, the hosts are laid back and helpful, and it's a stone's throw from the beach and the best bars in town. Free pick-ups (singles $15 Su-Th, $16 F-Sa; doubles $40, weekly $100). Prices may increase during summer (singles $20). If you're looking for space, bright blue **Pacific Coast Backpackers,** 432 Maunganui Rd. (tel. 574 9601), provides enough room for a large game of hide and seek inside its massive kitchen, game room, communal areas, and camouflaging murals, but is somewhat far from the center of town. (Singles $15. Doubles and twins $19. $10 key deposit.) Across the street from Mount Backpackers, **Ship to Shore Fish**

Supplies (tel. 575 5942) provides a cheap, fresh meal of the daily catch (giant meals $5-6). The proprietors love backpackers and make sure to dole out extra big portions if they know you're on a tight budget. (Open daily in summer 9am-9pm; daily in winter 10am-7:30pm.) Totally vegan and totally mellow is the **Zucchini Cafe,** 79 Maunganui Rd. (tel. 574 4149), a coffeehouse and restaurant serving breakfast, lunch and dinner with local artwork and couches begging you to sink into them—totally. Snacks like hummus or the ever-popular wedges go for $4.50; yummy vegetarian dinners run around $14. Fully licensed with a decent wine selection (open daily in summer 9am-11pm; daily in winter 10am-10pm). **Price Cutters** at the corner of Pacific Ave. and Maunganui Rd. has beach snacks (open M-Sa 7:30am-6pm, Su 7:30am-5pm).

SIGHTS AND ACTIVITIES It doesn't take a bloodhound to sniff out the attractions in the Mount—they stick out like, well, an extinct volcano rising 232m from sea level. Follow **Adams Ave.** or **The Mall** out to where they peter out into a paved lot and a well-maintained track around the base of the volcano (it's even wheelchair-accessible; ask at the motor camp office for access keys). The track is an easy and dramatic 45-minute walk with fantastically warped rocks and crashing surf on one side, and munching sheep and tangled forest on the other. You can start from the other side as well, by following the motor camp road around to the ocean side and going though the marked gate. Routes go up the mountain at several spots off the base track. It's a strenuous 45 minutes, but the view is almost as dizzying as the climb up. There's also a short jaunt out onto the misnamed peninsular **Moturiki Island** that juts into the main beach, and the nearby **Blow Hole.** The Mount's other major draw is the **hot saltwater pools,** nestled at the base of the mountain. Your back will thank you for the $2.50 investment (children $1.50) when you splash into the main pool and its 39° welcome. A more tepid lap pool, private pools ($3.50 per 30min., children $2.50), a small water slide, storage lockers, massages, and multi-trip passes are all available (open M-Sa 6am-10pm, Su 8am-10pm). The main beach with the best surfing is right up against the mountain, but white sand stretches away to the east for kilometers and there are more sheltered waters just across the peninsula in **Pilot Bay.** In the three weeks following Christmas, the main beach comes alive with concerts, surf championships, runs, and more. Get a schedule booklet from the visitors center.

■ Whakatane

Whakatane (FAH-ka-taw-nee) struggles to complement the wealth of natural offerings that directly surround it, from White Island to Ohope Beach. Visitors come mainly for the beaches, the climate (the town enjoys more days of sun than almost anywhere else in New Zealand), and White Island, the ominously smoking volcanic island 50km offshore (and the town's single largest draw). As transportation options are limited, it's a good idea to rent a car to reach the surrounding attractions, using Whakatane (pop. 14,400) as a base.

ORIENTATION AND PRACTICAL INFORMATION Whakatane is situated on drained wetlands between high bluffs and the final bend of the Whakatane River. The main commercial center is pushed up against the bluffs along **the Strand,** with **Boon St.** and **Richardson St.** branching off it. **Landing/Domain Rd.,** the western entrance of SH2, and **Commerce St.** against the bluffs are the main routes in and out of town. **InterCity** (tel. 308 6169) leaves from Pyne St. daily for Rotorua (1hr., 1-2 per day, $24) and Gisborne (3hr., 1 per day, $48) via Opotiki (45min., $16). **Thumbers** often head immediately across the Whakatane River Bridge. The roundabout where Gorge Rd. branches off of Commerce St. towards Ohope is considered by many to be the best spot for those going east. For rental cars, **Hertz,** 105 Commerce St., (tel. 308 6155) is the most accessible from downtown. **The Whakatane Information and Promotions Centre** (tel. 308 6058) is on Boon St. (open M-F 9am-5pm, Sa 9am-1pm, Su 10am-2pm; 7am-7pm daily in Jan.). Change money at the **WestpacTrust Bank,** on the Strand between Boon and Commerce St. (open M-Tu and Th-F 9am-4:30pm, W

9:30am-4:30pm). In an **emergency,** dial 111. The **hospital** (tel. 307 8999), is west on Domain St., left on King St., and right on Stewart St. The Whakatane *Beacon* lists the **pharmacy** on-duty. In an emergency, call the **police** (24hr. tel. 308 5255). Pick up your care packages from the **post office** (tel./fax 307 1588), on Commerce St. at the Strand (open M-F 9am-5pm, Sa 9am-noon). The **telephone code is 07.**

ACCOMMODATIONS AND FOOD Whakatane's accommodations, while relatively cheap, tend toward the old and dark; its motels, found along Landing/Domain Rd., are generally nondescript. For beachfront views at comparable prices, the transportationally advantaged should head over the hill 7km to the campground or motels at Ohope Beach. In town, **The Whakatane Hotel,** (tel. 307 1670) at George St. and the Strand, is the closest thing to a hostel. The second floor is for backpackers and is clean and centrally located with a kitchen and lounge area. Dorm beds (in doubles) are $16 per person (singles $30). Next door, the **Why Not Cafe and Bar** serves a delicate lunch and dinner including tenderly prepared quesadillas, lamb salad, or steak sandwiches ($10-12). Take your beer into the comfier lounge next door with its large-screen TV and fireplace (open from 10am). You're certainly not paying for the view at the **Camelia Court Motel,** 11 Domain Rd. (tel. 308 6213), scenic as the KFC may be, but the price is made up for by soft beds and a relatively central location in a modern and attractive colonial-looking motel. Extras include a trampoline, a game room, and free pick-up and drop-off at the bus depot or airport (singles $65; doubles $73, extra person, $10; 4-person family unit with queen-sized bed and 2 singles $100). Like its straightforward name, the **Whakatane Motor Camp and Caravan Park** (tel. 308 8694) pulls no punches. Follow Beach Rd. to the end of McGarvey Rd., 1km from the town center, to find typical cement-floored campground bathrooms, a kitchen, and a TV lounge with worn chairs. A game room and decently sized swimming pool help to liven things up. (Tent sites, caravans, vehicles $10 per person. Anemically furnished cabins $20 for 1 person, extra person $10. Tourist cabins $30 for 1 person, $35 for 2, extra person $10.) If you're in the mood for a quick bite, let the blinking marquee lights be your beacon to **Neptune's Takeaways,** 64 Boon St. Eat the burgers and toasted sandwiches (under $5) behind beaded curtains while admiring the intricacies of the Little Mermaid-esque ocean mural—just hope it doesn't come alive and take revenge if you're eating the fish 'n' chips (open Su-W 9am-9pm, Th 9am-9pm, F 9am-midnight, Sa 10:30-1am).

SIGHTS AND ACTIVITIES By far the two largest attractions in the area are trips to **White Island** (see below) and swimming with the resident dolphins that congregate in the offshore waters. **Dolphins Down Under,** based out of 19 Quay St. (tel. 308 4636), is the main operator. They provide all equipment, instruction, refreshments, and even hot showers for the three- to four-hour trip. Depending on the tides and weather, there can be as many as five trips per day during the summer ($85, under 14 $50). Don't leave Whakatane without taking at least a few of the bush walks in the area. There are three **scenic reserves** in a small area: **Kohi Point,** atop the hill over Whakatane, with its panoramic views; **Ohope Scenic Reserve,** home to one of New Zealand's largest remaining pohutukawa forests; and **Mokorua Bush Scenic Reserve,** a recovering pasture land. The walk around the hill between Whakatane and nearby Ohope Beach is especially fantastic. A long walk (over 20km), **Nga Tapuwae o Toi** (the Footprints of Toi), connects all three; it can be done in one day, but many split it into three shorter segments. Also try the one-hour walk to the **Tauwhare Pa,** built several hundred years ago, or the **Mt. Tarawera Crater Walk,** a difficult but rewarding two-hour walk up a dormant volcano (see Rotorua: Geothermal Activities, p. 166). Access may be restricted during the summer, due to the danger of fires. The **Information Center** on Boon St. has pamphlets with more information and departure points on area walks. A huge, hulking, fern-covered rock reposes in its own green park along the Strand at the center of town. That's **Pahaturoa,** a sacred Maori ceremonial site that now bears a plaque to the Maori who died serving in World War I. One quick turn off the Strand, the **Wairere Falls** drop impressively from the bluffs above. If the falls inspire, you may want to stroll down the riverbank to where the river meets the sea. On the large rock on the other side stands a bronze statue of **Wairaka,** the female trailblazer whose bravery gave the town its name. On a rainy day, the small **Whakatane District Museum and Gallery** (Te Whare Taonga; tel. 307 9805), at Boon St. near Pyne St. promises an interesting hour.

■ Near Whakatane: White Island

Fifty kilometers off the coast of the Bay of Plenty, sheathed in its own cloud of steam and gas, sits Whakaari, "that which can be made visible, uplifted to view." Captain Cook, in his circuit around New Zealand, called it White Island for the steam cloud forever hanging above its volcanic peaks. Actually composed of three distinct cones, two of which are now extinct, White Island is a landscape of lunar dimensions, with its craters and steaming vents, boiling sulfuric acid pools, and sinuous flows of solid rock. Even in such an inhospitable place, ever-resourceful humans have attempted to eke out profit with a sulfur mine that operated intermittently throughout the late 1800s and early 1900s. This evidently did not please the gods, as a violent explosion and landslide killed 10 men in 1914. Today, a more successful way of exploiting White Island has been found in the pockets of visitors eager to experience the geologic adrenaline rush of visiting this otherworldly isle. For a price, anyone can brave the noxious sulfur fumes and make their own offering to the volcanic gods. Although the island is a privately owned reserve and relatively inaccessible (to put it mildly), there are several options for those wanting to visit. Most affordable is the boat approach; **PeeJay Charters** (tel. 308 9588; fax 308 0303) were named "guardians" of White Island (5-6hr. round-trip; $95 per person, lunch included; weather- and tide-dependent). **Te Kahurangi** (tel. 323 7829) runs daily trips in the summer, and Saturday and Sunday trips in the winter ($85). Boat landings are occasionally stymied by wind, so don't count your volcanoes before they explode. Another option is a thrilling if slightly more vicarious fly-over. Both **Bell-Air** (tel. 308 6656) and **East Bay Flight Centre** (tel. 308 8446) offer trips over White Island as well as other nearby sights (50min. round-trip, $95-110 per seat). The visitors center charges a commission to book any of these; it's cheaper to get a brochure there and book on your own.

■ Near Whakatane: Ohope Beach

Ohope Beach is just that: 11km of spectacular unbroken beach blessed with rolling azure waves and views of the rugged East Cape sweeping away to the northeast. The narrow strip of land ends in an undeveloped **recreational reserve** and the entrance to **Ohiwa Harbour,** a historically rich shell-fishery for th e Maori of the area and a modern resting place for wayward golf balls from the Ohope Beach Golf Course. Marinate in sun and sand, or take a worthwhile hike around the hill between Ohope and Whakatane.

The residential town strings out along the sea. **West End Rd.,** branching off at the base of the highway down the hill, leads to the best surf spot up against the steep bluffs. The Whakatane Information Centre staffs a beachfront **hut** off West End Rd. from December to February. **Buses** on the way to Opotiki stop across from the Mobil Station on Pohutukawa Ave., about 300m down from the West End turn-off (around 3:45pm daily, but book in Whakatane). **Thumbers** who head to Ohope Beach report that hitchhiking prospects are fairly good.

There are some lovely beachfront lots in Ohope Beach that could be yours if you're willing to spend the cash (prices start at $300,000). But if you already blew the inheritance, the **Ohope Beach Holiday Park** (tel./fax 312 4460), located somewhat far up the beach, offers similar views for a slightly less exorbitant price. Mini-golf, a pool with a waterslide, a food shop, and sporting equipment rental are all part of the bargain. There are 200 tent sites ($9), 200 powered sites ($9), and cabins or flats with a range of possible amenities (doubles start at $36). Most of the motels are found on West End Rd., and it's the same seasonal story. The **Ohope Beach Resort,** 5 West End Rd. (tel./fax 312 4692), while not quite a resort, is quite a complex with accommodations, bar, restaurant, and hopping night club appropriately separated from each other. The rooms are well appointed with small beds in sunny rooms with beach views and kitchenettes. A room with a double and two singles is $75 ($100 in Jan.). One backpackers room features nose-bleed triple-decker bunk beds and large lockable storage cupboards ($14 per person). There's a small pool (though shame on those who swim in a kidney-shaped pool when the Pacific is within spitting distance) and a volleyball net. The native Kauri timber glows at the **Kauri Kafe and Bar** downstairs. Feast on Kiwi culinary delights like steak or seafood dinners ($20), or less expensive bar snacks (open daily Nov.-May noon-midnight; May-Nov. bar open 3pm-2am, Kafe from 5pm). Upstairs you'll find **The Local,** a lovely attempt at an olde English pub on the beach with ivy on the walls, polished wood tables, wraparound windows, and even an outdoor balcony. It also features pool tables and mega-speakers that shake the small dance floor with your jukebox choices (free selection Su-W). Tuesday night is karaoke night (open from noon in summer, from 3pm in winter).

■ Opotiki

Poorer and more raw than its neighbor Whakatane, Opotiki ("o-PO-tah-kee") can sometimes seem as if the isolation and wildness of its surroundings have seeped into the town limits—but it's for that wildness and wilderness that most visitors come. As the gateway to the East Coast and the last town of any real size (pop. 9600) before the remote, rugged beauty and the isolated Maori settlements along the spectacular coast, Opotiki straddles the history and presence of two cultures—and bears the battle scars to show it. From the earliest resistance to missionaries in the 1800s to the series of battles ignited by the 1865 murder of Rev. Karl Volker in his still-standing Hiona St. Stephen's Anglican Church, Opotoki has accumulated a fascinating and tumultuous history. Today, surf, isolation, and several well-placed budget accommodations make it a worthwhile stopping point.

It's anyone's guess why the original settlement was placed where it was (an evenly spaced grid boxed between the confluence of the **Waioweka** and **Otara** Rivers) when the ocean was so close, but so it went. Ponder the possibilities at the **Information Centre** (tel. 315 8484; fax 315 6102), at the intersection of St. John and Elliott St. (open M-F 8:30am-4:30pm, daily in summer with extended hours). The **DOC** office is in the same place (open 8am-4:30pm year-round). Be sure to pick up the super helpful *Opotiki and the East Cape* brochure. Just about anything else you need is on Church St. There's a **BNZ** on the corner of Elliott and Church St. (open M-F 9am-4:30pm). The **post office** is on Church St. (open M-F 8:30am-5pm, Sa 9:30am to noon.) **InterCity** leaves from the **bus depot** (tel. 315 6350) across the street from the Information Centre for Gisborne (2hr., 1-2 per day, $35) and Rotorua (2hr., 1-2 per day, $24) via Whakatane (1hr., $16).

You can almost skip a rock across the surf from the porch of the **Opotiki Beach House Backpackers** (tel. 316 5117), on Appelton Rd. at Waiotohi Beach (5km west of town on SH2). Although the stairs are steep and the toilet is across the yard in a corrugated metal shed, there are ultra-comfy futon-style beds. The weather-beaten barn-style dorm is spartan—but oh baby, what a location. Sit on the deck (an informal cafe in summer) and watch White Island smoke, or borrow a free surf kayak or surfboard and hit the secluded beach. (Dorms $12; doubles $30; tent sites $11. No linen. Free bikes available to get into town. Cash only.) Though the outside has seen better days, the inside of **Central Oasis Backpackers,** 30 King St. (tel. 315 5165), with high ceilings and a homey kitchen, is well kept and decorated with the owner Klaus's marvelous paintings. The endearingly sagging veranda boasts a cornucopia of old chairs overlooking the kind of garden every cottage should have. Bread is baked fresh twice a week. (Dorms $12; doubles $16; twins $14; tent sites $8.) There's an old yesteryear feeling to the Art Deco-ish **Masonic Hotel** (tel. 315 6115), at the corner of Elliott and Church St., that even baby blue walls and high ceilings can't disguise. Maybe it's the small rooms or the 19th-century reproductions on the walls. Maybe it's downtown Opotiki. Still, it's central and clean. (Singles $30; doubles or twins $45.) The quick answer to what the choices are for eating and going out in Opotiki is: not many. Once you've cruised Bridge St. on the way into town and seen the Elliott and Church St. blocks, you've seen your options. The **Elliott St. Bar and Grille** (tel. 315 5780), on Elliott St., serves up bar snacks like nachos ($7) or full-fledged meals like fettucini with mushrooms ($15), with a palm tree in one corner and mounted boar heads in the other. (Open daily 4:30pm-1am.) Elliott's is one of the more pleasant places in town for a drink—many of the other bars in Opotiki are quite rough and are best left to the locals.

Most of Opotiki's attraction is its beach and wilderness (which can be difficult to access without your own vehicle). Entertain yourself only on a very rainy day at the **Opotiki Heritage and Agricultural Society Museum,** 123 Church St. (open M-Sa 10am-3:30pm, Su 1:30-4pm; $2, children 50¢, families $3), or head across the street (ask at the museum for a key) to the **Hiona St. Stephen's Anglican Church.** The Rev. Karl Volkner was brutally murdered here in 1865 during a Maori-Pakeha conflict. One popular attraction 7km from town is **Hukutaia Domain,** an 11-acre park with a great labeled collection of New Zealand's native plant species. It's worth going to if only for the **Taketakerau,** a huge hollow puriri tree that was sacred to the local Whaka-torea tribe. Bones of the deceased used to be dug up after a few years and placed in the hollow to keep them safe from enemies. Today the bones have been moved to another site.

Eastland & Hawke's Bay

Eastland and Hawke's Bay are blessed with the boundless optimism of those first to see the sun. The entire coast is sun-drenched, from the sunbursts of Napier's Art Deco buildings to the home of the world's first dawn, Gisborne's Mt. Hikurangi. (Or does the sun strike first on Hastings' Te Mata Peak? See p. 197.) Smiling on the soil of the "Fruit Bowl of New Zealand," the sun's rays give rise to orchards and fields overrun with luscious produce and grapes. Wineries and award-winning Chardonnays draw visitors to both easterly Gisborne and cosmopolitan Napier. Attractions of a wilder sort perch at the southern tip of Hawke Bay, where hordes of gannets (takapu) make Cape Kidnappers their home. Wilder yet, the stubborn streak of the East Coast's personality appears in the remote East Cape and the dense inland wilds of Te Urewera National Park, magnet for stalwart hikers and the North Island's largest remaining chunk of native forest. A land of timeless forests and timely arrivals (Cook bumped along the coast in 1769), the eastern coast doesn't make it easy to penetrate its mysteries. But it's still well worth the effort to explore the gamut of possibilities, from refined to rough-hewn, hokey to holy.

EASTLAND AND HAWKE'S BAY HIGHLIGHTS

- The streets of Napier (see p. 212.) are rife for casual exploration of all things Art Deco.
- Gisborne will initiate world-wide celebrations of the year 2000 (see p. 205.)
- The lonely East Cape (see p. 206) affords a glimpse of tourist-free, yet tour-worthy lands.

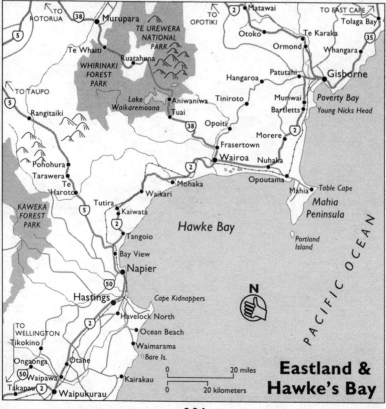

Eastland & Hawke's Bay

EASTLAND

■ Gisborne

Greeting the dawn has become something of an industry for Gisborne (pop. 30,000), which markets itself as the first city to see the sun each morning. Preparations are already underway to welcome the new millennium, with the annual First Light New Year's celebration approaching epic proportions (see p. 205). Overall, it's not a bad place to begin the next 1000 years. The town is small and friendly, with stellar beaches offering excellent surfing and swimming. Surrounding bluffs give great vistas across the sea, and the relatively mild, sunny climate makes for ideal farmland. The site of Captain Cook's first landing in 1769, Gisborne remains a fantastic spot for Cook enthusiasts: the city won't let you forget its history, no matter how hard you may endeavour.

ORIENTATION AND PRACTICAL INFORMATION

Gisborne is laid out where the **Taruheru** and the **Waimata** Rivers join to form the **Turanganui** (at 1200m, one of the world's shortest rivers). **Gladstone Road (SH35,** which turns into **Wainui Road** over the Turanganui Bridge) is the main drag; orient yourself by the **clock tower** sitting at Gladstone and Grey St., alongside the mock-up of the Endeavour. The **Esplanade** runs along the Wainui Rd. side of the river, while **Awapuni** and **Salisbury Road** run parallel to the main beaches.

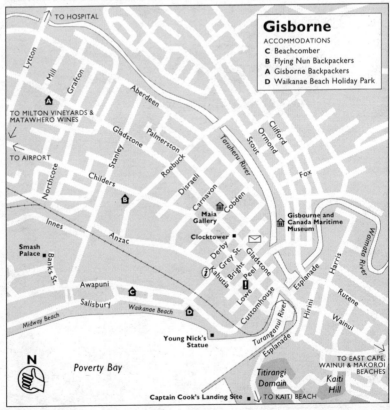

Gisborne

ACCOMMODATIONS
C Beachcomber
B Flying Nun Backpackers
A Gisborne Backpackers
D Waikanae Beach Holiday Park

Airport: West of the city, at the end of Chalmers Rd. off Gladstone Rd. **Air New Zealand Link** (tel. 867 1608) has bunches of daily direct flights to Auckland (1hr., $215) and Wellington (1hr., $228). Fare reductions possible. Book direct or use the **ANZ office,** 37 Bright St., (tel. 876 9768). Taxi to the airport runs around $7.

Buses: Buses (tel. 868 6196) all arrive at and depart from the visitor center. **InterCity** departs daily for Auckland (9hr., 1-2 per day, $89) and Rotorua (4hr., 1-2 per day, $70) via Whakatane (3hr., $48) and Napier (4hr., 1 daily, $33). **Coachrite Connections** (tel. 868 9969) goes to Napier (3-6 per week, 3hr., $30-35) and points further south via Wairoa ($15-20). See p. 206 for transport around the East Cape.

Taxis: Gisborne Taxis (tel. 867 2222), **Sun City Taxis** (tel. 867 6767), and **Eastland Taxis** (tel. 868 1133) are 24hr. servers.

Car Rental: Scottie's, 205 Grey St. (tel. 867 7947), next to the visitor center and part of Ray Scragg Motors, offers cheaper rates than the major chains in town. Standard economy vehicle $28 per day plus 19¢ per km or $55 per day (unlimited distance).

Bicycle/Surf Rental: Maintrax Cycle, at the corner of Roebuck and Gladstone St., has bikes ($10 per day, $50 deposit). **Sungate,** 55 Salisbury Rd. (tel. 868 1673), has hourly, half day, and daily rates on surfboards, body boards, and more ($5-40).

Hitchhiking: To head to the surf beaches at Wainui or Makorori, many hitchhikers start out along Wainui Rd. Hitchers going southwest toward Wairoa or north to Opotiki head to the end of SH35/Gladstone Rd. at Makaraka Rd., where the highway branches off to its respective destinations.

Visitor Center: Gisborne Information Centre, 209 Grey St. (tel. 868 6139; fax 868 6138). Headquarters for East Cape tourism and an 18-hole mini-golf course out back. Open daily 7:30am-7:30pm; in winter 7:30am-5:30pm.

DOC: 63 Carnarvon St. (tel. 867 8531), between Gladstone and Palmerston St.

Currency Exchange: Westpac (tel. 867 1359), at the corner of Gladstone Rd. and Peel St. Open M-Tu and Th-F 9am-4:30pm, W 9:30am-4:30pm.

Emergency: Dial 111.

Police: (tel. 867 9059), at the corner of Peel St. and Gladstone Rd.

Medical Services: David Moore Pharmacy (tel. 868 9510) at the Kaiti Medical Center, is open daily 8am-8pm. Call for emergency advice (tel. 867 9099) or go to one of the local medical centers. **Kaiti Road Medical Center** (tel. 867 7411) is at the corner of Turenne and De Lautour Rd., off Wainui Rd. Open M-F 8am-8pm, Sa-Su 9am-6pm. For **urgent care** only, look to the **hospital** on Ormond Rd. (take Lytton Rd. north from Gladstone Rd.; follow the signs).

Post Office: The Gisborne Post Shop (tel. 867 8867) on Grey St., does faxes and telegrams. Open M-F 8:30am-5pm, W 9am-5pm.

Internet Access: Verve Café, 121 Gladstone Rd. (tel. 868 9095). $3-7 per 30min.

Telephone Code: 06.

ACCOMMODATIONS

Watch out—Gisborne's beachfront places can charge $10-20 more than those just across the street. In the off-season, hostels attract large numbers of permanent boarder-types who rent out rooms for months at a time, creating a very different atmosphere from the summer. Call ahead in summer.

Flying Nun Backpackers, 147 Roebuck St. (tel. 868 0461), off Gladstone Rd., at the corner of Childers and Roebuck Rd. Once a convent, the dorm is in the nuns' old sewing room, and you can wait your turn for the pool table by sitting in a confessional in the chapel-cum-lounge replete with stained glass windows. Free local phone calls. The stream of squeals and giggles from nearby children's schools might drive some insane (or others to confession?). Dorms $14; singles $21; doubles $37; under 14 $7.50; tent sites $8. $10 key deposit when busy. Linen free; bedding hire is $3. Cash only.

Gisborne Backpackers, 690 Gladstone Rd. (tel. 868 1000; fax 868 4000). Many years of exhausted backpackers haven't entirely managed to erase the sterility of this former orphanage and rest home. Small, clean, motel-like rooms overlook the well-kept grounds (help yourself to the citrus fruit in season). 2km from downtown, but free pickup from bus station or airport. Dorm singles $15; private singles $20;

twins $32; doubles $35; tent sites $8 per person. Sheet and blanket $4. Weekly rates available.

Waikanae Beach Holiday Park (tel. 867 5634; fax 867 9765), end of Grey St. Fronting the beach and central to downtown. Facilities galore. Tent and powered sites granted privacy by rows of Norfolk pines. Tourist flats $50; cabins $24. Tent sites $16 for 2, powered $18. Extra person $8-10. Prices rise $2-4 in summer.

Beachcomber Motel, 73 Salisbury Rd. (tel. 868 9349; fax 868 6974). You could bounce off one of their trampolines right onto the beach, though you'll need 10 minutes to walk to the town center. Complimentary newspaper, kitchen facilities, and TV. Singles $75; doubles $85.

FOOD AND NIGHTLIFE

Find respite from the usual artery-clogging budget cuisine at downtown Gisborne's nicer cafes and quality restaurants, or at the small eatery complex down at the wharf. The **Pak 'N Save,** a block up from the clock tower on Gladstone Rd., is fat with options. Open M-F 8:30am-8pm, Sa-Su 8:30am-7pm.

Fettucini Brothers (tel. 868 5700), Peel St. near Palmerston Rd. Menu descriptions alone will make you salivate, and the pastas in a heaping main size ($16) or smaller but sufficient entree ($10) have a variety of enticing vegetarian or meat sauces. Extensive wine menu. Credit cards accepted. Open M-Sa from 6pm.

Verve Café, 121 Gladstone Rd. (tel. 868 9095). Hip without being overbearing, the airy Verve has local artwork on the walls, couches in the back, and a public Internet access (see above). Decent espresso drinks ($2.50), and fulfilling fare like Rewena Pesto Sandwiches ($9) or grilled sandwiches with a choice of meat ($7). Open daily 9am-10pm; in winter M-Sa 9am-10pm, Su 9am-3pm.

⊛**Mega Bite** (tel. 867 5787), on Peel St. by Palmerston Rd. Backpackers from across the globe find home-cooking sanctuary here—just read the personal testimonies written on the walls. You'll be writing home to mom after creating your own sandwich masterpiece for only $2.50 or enjoying a BLT or burger for under $5. Free coffee or espresso with *Let's Go* book. Open daily 6:30am-5pm.

⊛**Smash Palace Wine and Food Bar,** 24 Banks St. (tel. 867 7769). Follow Awapuni Rd. west into the industrial district. A zany event unto itself, the Smash Palace is a must-do. You can consume local brews such as Gisborne Gold ($3 pint) or Parker Wines ($3 glass) while experiencing the surreal post-industrial atmosphere and trove of junk decor, from the antique cars suspended in mid-air to the old DC-3 flying into the roof. Occasional free wine tastings. Open daily noon-late.

The Irish Rover (tel. 867 1112), on Peel St. Snag a $4 Guinness and sit by the fire in this welcoming and popular barn-style pub. Weeknights are low-key, but weekends often feature live music with a $2 cover. Handles on tap $3; bar snack or dinner menu. Open M-Sa 11am-3am (may close earlier).

The Balcony (tel./fax 868 1555), 5th floor of the Post Office building. Enter through Bright St. On top of the city's highest building and jumping with karaoke and disco on Thursday nights, this is the last stop for locals and tourists alike before crashing for the night. Best views in town. $5 cover, $3 pints. Bar open M-Sa 11am-late.

SIGHTS

Titirangi Domain, also known as **Kaiti Hill,** is a good starting place for seeing Gisborne sights. Once across the river, follow the signs from Hirini Rd. At the base of the hill sits **Te Poho-o-Rawiri,** the largest traditional *marae* built from modern materials in New Zealand. It's cavernous and stunningly crafted, with painted roof rafters, woven tukutuku reed panels, and intricately carved dark wood panels with iridescent paua shell eyes. Step back and watch the tangle of swirling lines resolve into faces, birds, and bodies unfurling and weaving into one another. The large panels, *pou pou,* tell a stylized Maori genealogy: each figure represents an ancestor—figures with grotesquely long tongues recall a verbose elder, for example. Be sure to ask permission at the office first and remove your shoes before entering. Nearby sits **Toko Toru Tapu,** a small Maori church nestled on the hillside.

Continue up the hill—it's a steep one, though popular with masochistic local joggers—for a series of phenomenal views across the city and Poverty Bay to the white cliffs of **Young Nick's Head,** named after Captain Cook's cabin boy Nicholas Young who first sighted New Zealand from the Endeavour. Midway up the hill is a statue of Cook. Kaiti Hill can also be tackled via a path winding up from the base of the Cook Landing Site (accessible from the Esplanade along the river).

Back across the Turanganui, at the end of Waikanae Beach, sits the dutifully rendered (if not particularly stunning) **Young Nick's Statue,** where the spacey-looking young lad points eternally at his eponymous bluffs. The museum complex on the Taruheru offers slightly greater stimulation. **The Gisborne Museum and Arts Centre,** 18 Stout St. (tel. 867 3832), has both a changing art gallery and several displays on natural and cultural history (admission $3.50). Just behind the Centre on the riverbank sits the **Star of Canada Maritime Museum** (free entrance), the transplanted bridgehouse of a British steamer that grounded on Kaiti Beach in 1912. (*Both museums open M-F 10am-4pm, Sa-Su 1:30-4pm.*) For contemporary art-in-progress, head to the **Maia Gallery** (tel. 868 8068), on Cobden St., between Gladstone Rd. and Palmerston St. This airy space is both showroom and workshop studio for students in the Toihoukura (Maori Visual Arts) course at the local Tairawhiti Polytechnic. (*Open M-F 8:30am-5pm. Free.*)

The **Eastwoodhill Arboretum** (tel./fax 863 9800) is a popular attraction 35km northwest of the city on the Ngatapa-Rere Rd. (*Open daily 10am-4pm.*) Laid out by an obsessive collector, the 64-hectare place is one of the finest assortments of authentic genetic plant material from the Northern Hemisphere (around 500 genera), all "inspired by English gardens." Even if you don't care about the science involved, it's spectacularly beautiful. There's a 45-minute walk with great views of both flora and grander scenery. Unfortunately, you must find your own transportation.

Gisborne 2000

Officially, the Chatham Islands (500 miles east of Auckland) will be the first place in the world to see the sun of the new millennium. But it's Gisborne that plans to welcome the event city-style; after all, the 750 Chatham Islanders can't put on a show to compare with seasoned Gisborne. For years, the city has marketed itself as the place to welcome the new year, but now the stakes are a little higher. In light of the global celebrations gearing up for the year 2000, the Events Gisborne office is already putting in overtime. Festivities will include a massive outdoor party, a bicycle race, a music festival, and the arrival in Gisborne harbor of 50 sailing ships and *waka huaroa* (ocean-going canoes) from around the world. (For more on this topic, see p. 218.)

ACTIVITIES

For the area's safest and most convenient waters, try **Waikanae Beach,** stretching from the end of Grey St. Sandy and excellent, it gets a bit crowded at peak times. The shore becomes **Midway Beach** a little farther along Poverty Bay, with soft sand and a prime surf spot at its western end. While the bay beaches have their golden wave moments, many surfers with more experience head north of the city to the coastal beaches at **Wainui,** about 6km out on SH35, and **Makorori,** another 4km along. These beaches are pretty safe for swimming as well, but have been known to have riptides. **Kaiti Beach,** at the base of the self-same Hill, is rocky and unpatroled, but the exposed location provides great gusts for windsurfing.

If you're thoroughly pickled from beach time, there are some land-based leisure options as well. The Gisborne district has bunches of grapes and vineyards—so many, in fact, that the area accounts for 34% of New Zealand's total wine production. Several vineyards offer tours in the summer months (by appointment in winter), and most have at least a cellar shop or tastings (contact the visitor center for more information). You can try the strictly organic **Milton Vineyard** (tel. 862 8680) in Manutuke, on Papatu Rd. off SH2 towards Wairoa. **Matawhero Wines** on

Riverpoint Rd. (tel. 868 8366; fax 867 8856) has tours. And don't miss **Smash Palace,** home to the Parker Winery vintages (see Food and Nightlife, above). **The Sunshine Brewing Co.,** 109 Disraeli St. (tel. 867 7777), off Gladstone St. makes Gisborne Gold, Sundowner, Moonshine and other naturally brewed beers (open M-Sa 9am-6pm). Call ahead for a free tour.

If you're around in October, the annual **East Coast Wild Tastes Festival** (Oct. 23, 1999), up the coast in Tolaga Bay, is where you can sample bizarre bush foods. Taste, if you dare, the chocolate-dipped huhu grubs that are the avian kiwis' favorite, or the wild pork burgers. The next day is the **Gisborne Wine and Food Festival,** with buses making the winery circuit.

■ The East Cape

New Zealand's final frontier of tourism, the East Cape juts out into the Pacific, greeting the world's first daylight each morning. The area is dominated by the **Raukumara Mountains** and thinly populated, with most settlements lying near the coast. Many of the towns, while picturesque, are the economic casualties of a collapsed whaling industry. The vast majority of the people are Maori and have left their artistic marks on many churches in beautiful and intricate carvings. The wild, uninhabited interior of the cape is a haven for pig hunters and hard core trampers, and rewards travelers of the adventurous stripe.

Most towns along the East Cape have at least one store, takeaway, gas station, and postal service, often all combined into a single business. Pick up the extremely comprehensive free guide *Opotoki and East Cape,* which lists nearly all traveling resources, at the visitors centers in Opotiki or Gisborne. Accommodations on the East Cape are primarily backpackers and rugged campgrounds, usually mercifully tourist free. Access to the region is via **SH35,** a well-maintained and fully paved 350km stretch of road that runs the perimeter of the cape. Without your own vehicle, transportation is difficult as buses bypass the cape; **courier services** provide the only option. These mini-vans deliver parcels and supplies from Opotiki and Gisborne to the various settlements and farms, allowing passengers to see much that would be missed from the main highway. Check in at the visitors center in Gisborne (tel. (06) 868 6139) for updated information. **Matakaoa Transport** (tel. 868 1933) and **Cook's Couriers** (tel. 864 4711) depart from the visitors center for **Hick's Bay** (M-F 1-2 per day, $20). Book ahead and ask about backpacker discounts and luggage fees. On the weekends, try **Fastway Couriers** (tel. 868 9080), at Grey St. and Awapuni Rd. in Gisborne (departs Sa 9:30am, Su 7:30am).

From Hick's Bay to Opotiki, the **Apanui Pony Express** (tel. (07) 325 2700 or (025) 872 120), based in Te Kaha, is the only service. It runs from Opotiki to Te Kaha (in summer one per day, 10:30am; in winter M-F 10:30am; $15) and to Hick's Bay (3-6 per week, $25). This service must be booked in advance. From Hick's Bay, Pony Express goes on demand to Te Kaha (M-F 6am, $16.50) or Opotiki (same time, $35). Call ahead. Hitchhikers find rides around the cape in summertime; late in the afternoon is peak traffic time, as people return from Gisborne or Opotiki. In winter, increased rain and greatly reduced traffic makes hitching a dubious prospect at best.

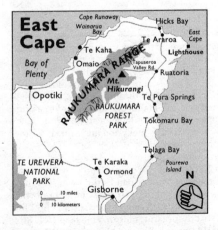

■ Opotoki to Hicks Bay

The highway that skirts the lush, vegetation-cloaked west coast most of the way from Opotiki to Hicks Bay offers the Cape's most spectacular views, especially in December, when the numerous pohutukawa trees explode with red flowers.

In **Omaio**, the **Omaio Store** (tel. 325 2873) welcomes intrepid East Cape trippers with a free cup of tea or coffee with any purchase (open daily 8am-6pm). Free camping is available 1km from town on an oceanside, manure-littered bluff at the **Hoani Waititi Reserve.** One of the better places to stay is **Te Kaha Holiday Park and Motel** (tel. 325 2894), in **Te Kaha.** A new and modern dormitory with kitchen facilities, TV, and colorful striped carpeting waits at the end of a flower-lined driveway ($15; tent sites $9, powered $10.) Play a round of budget golf at the neighboring nine-hole, par 64 course with ocean views ($10 per round; club hire $5).

In **Wainarua Bay** the **Rendezvous on the Coast Holiday Park** (tel. 325 2899) has an expansive, well-maintained campground with a full range of leisure equipment: ping-pong table, pool table, dart board, and trampoline. Adventuring is encouraged with bike rental ($40; helmet and water bottle included), kayak rental, boat hire, and fishing charters. (Dorms $11; tent sites $8, powered $9.) Next door, **Robyn's Backpackers** (tel. 325 2904) welcomes travelers to a luxurious house complete with a lounge deck, an ocean view, excellent music, and a friendly and intimate atmosphere (dorms $15; one double $35). South of "town" a short hike follows the Whanarua stream from the road, passes through several streams, and culminates in a gushing, 12m waterfall in the middle of dense bush.

Shortly after Wainarua Bay, the highway heads inland for 40km until it reaches Hicks Bay. Approximately 2km off the highway along a gravel road chills the **Hicks Bay Backpackers Lodge** (tel. 864 4731), another place to mellow away a few days. Located next to a good swimming and surfing beach, the lodge offers 15 dorm beds ($15), a double room ($45), and tent sites ($9). Find your thrills early in the morning rather than late at night by booking a trip to see the sunrise at the lonely East Cape **lighthouse** (departs 4:30am; $25, 2 person min.). Courier services running from Gisborne and Opotiki arrive and depart from the lodge daily.

■ Hicks Bay to Gisborne

Immediately after Hicks Bay, the landscape begins to transform. Lying in the shadow of the Raukumara Range, the eastern part of the coast receives considerably less precipitation than the western side during summer, and patches of dry brown vegetation intrude upon the endless expanses of green. The road leaves the coast, making for a much less scenic drive. However, diminished scenery comes with a corresponding increase in accommodations quality.

Just past Hicks Bay, the **Te Araroa Holiday Park** (tel. 864 4873; fax 864 4473) is situated on 14 acres and garnished with a stream. A deserted beach with pounding surf is just a short walk away. (Dorms $12; tent sites $7.50, powered $8.50.) Facilities include a kitchen, a washer and dryer, a small store, and the **world's easternmost cinema.** New releases can be seen in the homestyle movie theater complete with Dolby surround sound, 70 seats, couches, and popcorn. Drawing loads of people from around the area, the theater is truly a unique experience.

The unremarkable town of **Te Araroa** marks the turnoff for the East Cape lighthouse, a 42km round trip along a gravel road. In addition to Hicks Bay Backpackers, **East Cape 4WD Sunrise Tours** (tel. 864 4775) does the early morning run to the lighthouse for $25 per person. In downtown Te Araroa, the world's largest pohutukawa tree will make you feel insignificant beneath its 40-meter-wide span of branches; alas, attempting to pronounce the tree's name, Te Waha o Rerekohu, is the main activity in town.

Although breathtaking views of the coast are absent after Te Araroa, **Mount Hikurangi** (1752m) can be spotted. Unlike most of the area, its upper reaches are exposed rock, a striking contrast to the surrounding green. Access to the base of the mountain is available from the town of **Ruatoria,** 20km south of Te Araroa. If you want to hike the mountain, follow the **Tapuaeroa Valley Road** 20km inland from Ruatoria until it terminates at **Rip Station,** a homestead that sleeps up to 30 people. A track that can be hiked in one day begins opposite the homestead. Consult the DOC about conditions before climbing the mountain. If you want to stay at Rip Station ($8) you must book in advance at the Gisborne DOC (tel. 867 8531).

Twenty-five kilometers farther along SH35 is the East Cape's only real **visitors center** (tel. 864 6853), in **Te Puia Springs** (open M-F 8am-noon and 1-4:30pm). Keep going until you reach the best backpackers on the east coast, the **House of the Rising Sun** (tel. 864 5858) in **Tokomaru Bay.** Rest in a pink-trimmed dormitory half a block from the beach or pitch your tent under a lemon tree in the middle of the lawn (dorms $14; tent sites $9). The town's beach is the most accessible on the East Cape, with low surf and easy swimming.

The last point of interest before reaching Gisborne is **Tolaga Bay,** where a 600m wharf juts into the sea. The longest wharf in the southern hemisphere, it is popular with fishermen and also marks the start of the 5km **Cooke's Cove Walkway,** a hike that leads to the next deserted bay with excellent sea and cliff views en route. The wharf and walkway hide out at the end of Wharf Road, a 1.5km detour off the main highway. **First Light Motel and Backpackers** (tel. 862 6425) offers unexciting backpackers accommodation (dorms $16; tent sites $8). Although quite nice, the local beach is a hearty hike from town. Finally, approximately halfway between Tolaga Bay and Gisborne, a stretch of coast can be camped on for free from mid-October until Easter. It is easily identified by the rows of caravans on long-term holiday. There are no facilities.

■ Te Urewera National Park

Te Urewera National Park is a land of acute beauty, laced with streams and lakes, its tilted ridges smoothing into hidden valleys of unbroken green. Cries of the brown *kaka* (bush parrot) and bellbird shrill through this vast tract of native forest. A verdant tangle of lowland *tawa* and podocarp set off by higher reaches of rimu and beech trees, the land of Urewera has long been central to New Zealand's people. Urewera's isolated bush was the historic home of the fierce **Tuhoe Maori,** the legendary "Children of the Mist." The Tuhoe, accustomed to their harsh and remote lifestyle, resisted Pakeha intrusion with greater force and success than many other tribes. In addition to the region's isolation and harsh conditions, this made Urewera an ideal place for several Maori leaders to flee to during the East Cape uprisings of the 1860s.

At the southern end of Te Urewera lies **Lake Waikaremoana,** a 5500-hectare expanse shaped by several inlets. By far the park's most visited spot, the lake is home to one of New Zealand's renowned Great Walks: the 46km Lake Waikaremoana Track, a relatively easy and beautiful three- to five-day walk. Far from being a well-kept secret, the track gets approximately 7000 visitors annually. During summer, it can be as bustling as a Dunedin pub on a Friday night. At other times of the year, however, you might go a day without so much as finding the trail mix crumbs of another tramper. Many streams hop with trout if it's angling you're after, forests brim with deer and pigs if you're the rifle-toting sort, and great expanses of water await for kayaking or floating if you've got that land-locked feeling. Come for several days. Don't rush yourself—let Te Urewera seep in slowly.

PRACTICAL INFORMATION

Te Urewera can be accessed by **SH38,** which winds upward from **Wairoa** on the east coast, eventually exiting the park at **Murupara,** close to the center of the North Island. From Murupara to Lake Waikaremoana the highway becomes gravel for about 75km. It winds around the eastern part of Lake Waikaremoana, passing through the trailhead at **Onepoto,** the visitors center at **Aniwaniwa,** and the trailhead at **Hopuruahine.** Facilities for travelers can be found within the park at the **DOC motor camp** at the eastern end of the lake, and in Murupara, Wairoa, and **Frasertown.**

"Like a Rat Rooting Dung"

Urewera has long been the locus of intense religious and military fervor. One notable figure claiming divine revelation was Te Kooti, who expounded the doctrine of **Ringatu,** the Upraised Hand. Escaping from his exile in the Chatham Islands in 1868, Te Kooti returned to Poverty Bay and killed 70 Maori and Pakeha in the Poverty Bay Massacre, after which he and his followers fled into the dense bush of Urewera. He was doggedly pursued by the Armed Constabulary, who set up their redoubt at Onepoto on the edge of Lake Waikaremoana. Stalemate ensued during the next few years, during which Te Kooti sent venomous letters to his pursuers: "This murderous purpose of yours is like a rat rooting dung. You must give it up. Send a man to tell me to come out into the open where we can fight. That would be fair..." The standoff ended in 1872 as the Tuhoe tribe, worn down by three years of strife, agreed to acknowledge the Crown. Te Kooti fled Urewera, took refuge in the impenetrable King Country south of the Waikato, and was later pardoned. Government troops withdrew from Urewera, but along the way devastated the lake shore area, burning the homes and crops of the resident Tuhoe people and sending them into bitter years of hunger and hardship.

Te Urewera has two ranger stations. The **Aniwaniwa Visitor Centre** (tel. (06) 837 3803; fax 837 3722), at Lake Waikaremoana, is the headquarters for the park, suppling detailed information on the area's ecology and hikes (open daily 8am-5pm). The **Rangitaiki station** (tel. (07) 366 5641; fax 366 5289) on SH38 at Murupara, is the check-in place for the northern end of the park (open M-F 8am-5pm). **Urewera Shuttle Service** (tel. (06) 838 7960), run by Tipi Backpackers in Frasertown, goes to and from Wairoa and the park (Su, W, Th, Sa 11:45am) with stops at Onepoto ($16), the Waikaremoana motor camp ($19), and Hopuruahine ($25). It also runs to Rotorua (Su, Th; $65). The shuttle heads the other direction from Hopuruahine (M, W, F 2pm) and Rotorua (M, F 11am). Call at least a day in advance and arrive early, as schedules are far from rigid. From the lake itself, operators go to the Great Walk starting points or other points on shore by arrangement. **Waikaremoana Guided Tours** (tel. (06) 837 3729), has ferries that connect the DOC motor camp and the Great Walk end points at Onepoto ($10) and Hopuruahine ($12). The ferries run two to three times per day from approximately December 16 to January 31, and on demand in winter. Pickup at three of the lakeside huts is also available (Waiopaoa $80, Marauiti $70, Te Puna $60). **Hitching** to and within Te Urewera is a difficult proposition as cars are full of camping gear and vacation toys, but those with patience report success. **Parking** is available at Onepoto and at the DOC Motor Camp ($3 per day per vehicle). Although the DOC takes no responsibility for vehicles, the lot is generally safer than the trailheads, where vandalism and theft have occurred. The only **petrol** between Wairoa and Murupara is also at the DOC motor camp. The main access town to Te Urewera, nearby **Wairoa,** has a relatively anemic supply of **camping equipment** stores, so beg or borrow your gear before you arrive. **Stirling Sports** (tel. 838 8677), at the corner of 200 Marine Parade Rd. near the corner of Lock St., stocks a spartan selection of camp supplies. **Bay Kayaks** (tel. 837 3737; in winter based in Gisborne, tel. 868 4151) rents kayaks ($25 per half-day, $50 per full day, guide fee $100).

ACCOMMODATIONS AND FOOD

Those not hiking the Great Walk have lodging choices near or within the park. Beautiful, central, and with all the amenities is the DOC-owned **Waikaremoana Motor Camp** (tel. 837 3826; fax 837 3825) in a gem of a location on the lake shore. It has dock facilities and a petrol station (dorms $16; 2-person cabins $30; 2-person chalets or motels $55. Tent sites $7.50; caravan sites $9. Prices rise $5-10 during holidays; deposits required. Call ahead. Luggage storage $3 per bag.) An excellent base for planning explorations of the park is **Tipi Backpackers** (tel. 838 7960) in Frasertown, a German-run hostel that offers lodging in a giant tipi on the lawn ($11), a yellow-walled dormitory ($14), or a double room ($35). Tent sites are $9. Tipi also has free pickup from Wairoa, and hiking gear for rent by the night (gas cooker and fuel $2;

sleeping bags $5; backpacks $5). DOC runs several more primitive campgrounds within the park, including those at Mokau, Hopuruahine, Aniwaniwa, and Rosie Bay (tent sites $2-3 per person; toilets, no showers). There is free camping all around the lake, as long as tents are pitched more than 500m from water and not on private land (clearly marked on most maps). Overflow campers head to **Tuai,** the small town just outside the southern entrance, and stay at the **Big Bush Motor Camp** (tel. 837 3777).

More than 40 huts are conveniently located along the park's spider web of trails. All huts and campgrounds have potable water, covered shelters, and outhouses. To use huts off the Lake Waikaremoana Track, get a **Great Walks pass** before you go ($6 per night; $2 penalty for riff-raff caught on the trail without them). Passes for the back-country huts are $4 per person per night (children $2). During the Christmas holidays, it is wise to carry a tent as the huts occasionally fill up, but there are usually vacancies the rest of the year. Hut bunks are nothing more than foam mattresses laid side by side; those who crave privacy would be better off **tenting.** The **campgrounds** on this track are excellent, with all the facilities available at the huts. Although pitching a tent more than 500m from the trail and lake is free, it is essentially impossible to find tent sites in the dense brush. Stick to the designated campgrounds.

As for food, bring it with you. There's a limited selection at the **Waikaremoana Motor Camp Store** (open daily 8am-noon, 1-5pm). Tuai and Murupara have general stores, but it's best to shop in advance in Wairoa or Rotorua, where prices aren't as jacked up for desperate trampers. Bring a stove and gas as well.

OUTDOORS

The pristine native podocarp and beech forests stretch as far as the eye can see, and are home to vibrant and noisy bird life as well as two species of bats, New Zealand's only native mammals. But it's the landscape that people really come for: myriad fern-lined waterfalls, cobalt-blue lakes, and mythic trees. The Te Urewera network of trails allows any brand of tramper to pay homage. Most people come for the **Great Walk,** which arcs around the western side of Lake Waikaremoana, starting at Onepoto and ending at Hopuruahine Bridge (see below). Other tracks also exist, but if daytrips are more your style, take a lunch up to the beach at **Lake Waikareiti** ("little rippling waters"), improbably set on an lush green hilltop and full of little islands. The islands beg exploration and the DOC rents rowboats at Lake Waikareiti ($10 per half-day or overnight with a $40 deposit). There's also a popular hut at the lake. The dramatically tiered **Papakorito Falls** are only 2km up the road from the visitors center. Check with DOC for fishing and hunting permits.

THE LAKE WAIKAREMOANA TRACK

The track's five **huts** and five **campsites** make it possible to split the walk up into as demanding or as leisurely a trip as you have time and desire for; most people do it in two or three nights. Check in with the Aniwaniwa Visitor Centre (tel. (06) 837 3803) for trail and weather conditions—it may be four-star-style tramping, but you're still nowhere near a doorway when the weather turns bad. The track can be completed year-round, although it becomes quite boggy and cold in the off-season. The best period for the hike runs from mid-October to the end of March. A helpful map complete with brief descriptions of the track is available at the motor camp and area visitors centers ($1). You can start from either end, but beginning at Onepoto puts almost all of the climbing out of the way right off the bat. This is the best choice for early starters, since the first hut is a strenuous four-to-five-hour hike away. From Hopuruahine, the first hut is only two hours away on an easy, flat section of trail, making this a better place for late-day starts.

Beginning at Onepoto, the trail heads up a wide grassy track for 10 minutes until reaching a fork for **Lake Kiriopukae.** A 10-minute detour, the lake makes a nice picnic spot but is otherwise not worth visiting. From the fork, the track makes a calf-burning ascent up **Panekiri Bluff** to the first hut, a 600m, four-to five-hour climb. There is no water on this section of the trail, so top off the water bottle before you begin. The steepest section comes in the first hour, after which the track evens out as it skirts the bluff edge. Try to drag your eyes away from the root-laced, rutted trail every now and then to check out dizzying views of the lake some 500-600m below and the stunted forest of the windswept ridge.

Located at 1180m, the highest point along the Panekiri Range, **Panekiri Hut** is the first option for an overnight stay. The hut's 36 bunks are somewhat cramped and there is no camping; you may want to push on to the next campground or hut, making the second day a little more leisurely. The hike to Panekiri also makes a good day-hike from Onepoto for those who only wish to see the lake from on high.

From Panekiri Hut, the track traverses the ridge for two hours before dropping steeply down towards the lake. **Waiopaoa Hut and Campground** are three and four hours away, respectively. The hut is cramped and far from the lake, but the campground is spacious and has several secluded sites nestled right by the lake. Watch out for vicious **black flies,** which tend to cluster at the lake shore.

A flat stretch of lakeside trail leads to the turnoff for **Korokoro Falls,** a worthwhile one-hour detour. The trail to the 20m waterfall is well marked and crosses the stream at one point. The unremarkable **Korokoro campsite** is shortly after the turnoff for the falls. After the campground the shoreline becomes quite steep and the track leaves the lakeshore, reaching **Maraunui campsite** in two hours. This campsite is the least desirable on the track, but shortly after it is the **Marauiti Hut,** peacefully blending into the surrounding nature. The bunks are spacious and the hut is located on the edge of a beautiful blue inlet with plenty of excellent fishing spots.

The portion of the track following the Marauiti Hut is a comfortable cruise with plenty of opportunities for swimming. Take a break or spend the night at **Waiharuru campsite,** a long rectangular patch of grass with one end bordering what could almost be called a beach. After crossing a stream chock-full of immense, lazy brook trout, the trail hits **Te Puna Hut,** a smallish hut which has few perks except a nice lounging deck outside. The last bit of real climbing follows as the track crosses the **Puketukutuku peninsula.** The DOC is undertaking a predator-control program on this peninsula, to help the kiwi fend off the murderous onslaughts of stoats, possums, and other interloping species (see p. 48). After crossing the peninsula the track leads to the small and undistinguished **Tapuaenui campsite.** Another hour of mostly flat hiking along some of the most striking inlets of the lake leads to the final accommodation, **Whanganui Hut.** Graced with bright yellow pillars on its lounge deck, the hut rests next to a creek but has minimal lake access. From here, it's another hour of flat hiking through grassy fields and up a river valley to the **Hopuruahine track entrance.** SH38 is another 2km up the road from the trailhead.

■ Whirinaki Forest Park

Its 60,900 hectares of scenery aren't as dramatic as those of its eastward neighbor **Te Urewera National Park,** nor is its size as vast as the Kaingaroa pine plantation (the largest in the southern hemisphere), marching away toward the northwest. What Whirinaki has are great soaring stands of rimu, totara, miro, matai, and kahikatea, whose cathedral canopy shelters a lush understory of ferns and supports native birds like the tui, kaka, blue duck, and kiwi. The stands of Whirinaki were grand enough to be the focus of an acrimonious battle in the late 70s and early 80s. The rage over the replacement of old-growth podocarps with exotic plantation species culminated in the cessation of logging in 1987, and the establishment of New Zealand's newest forest park, 88% of which is still in native cover.

Whirinaki's rolling lowland, rugged hills, and remote river canyon get comparatively few visitors (especially foreign ones), simply because the park is so difficult to access. Some 70km southeast of Rotorua, its main access point is the tiny Maori village of **Minginui,** reached from a turn-off onto unsealed gravel at **Te Whaiti** from SH38. The small and less than prosperous Maori settlement of **Murupara,** on SH38, is home to the **DOC Te Ikawhenua Visitor Centre** (tel. 366 5641), where the management of Whirinaki and part of Te Urewera is based (open M-F 8am-4:30pm). The **Map and Track Shop** in Rotorua also has extensive information on Whirinaki. Murupara also sports a fully serviced campground and a small motel. From Te Whaiti, Gary and

Sherrilyn of Whirinaki Forest Holidays (tel./fax (07) 366 3235) can pick you up and take you to their lodge near town, with meals available or use of the communal kitchen (dorms $15; self-contained doubles $70). They watch cars for hikers, do drop-offs and pickups ($30-35), and run horse trekking, hunting, and fishing trips.

Whirinaki is home to several basic **DOC campgrounds** with river water (boil or iodize it), pit toilets, and sometimes a barbecue (pay $2-6 at honesty box); three campgrounds are in the vicinity of Minginui. A total of ten backcountry **huts** ($4; buy tickets from the DOC) and several access roads dot Whirinaki, allowing for easy multi-day tramping. Several day hikes also lead out from the Minginui area, including a short wheelchair-accessible path, a hike to the gorgeous gash of **Te Whaiti-Nui-a-Toi Canyon,** and a trip to the rain-fed **Arahaki Lagoon** (3-4hr.), filled with frog song and lined by the buttresses of skyscraping kahikatea. The park is also home to good biking trails and a year-round hunting season for deer, pigs, and possums.

HAWKE'S BAY

■ Napier

You know you've hit Napier when the cafes outnumber the takeaways, and even the McDonald's is McDeco. The city is an Art Deco overload of sunbursts, zigzags, bubbling fountains, neon-lit clock towers, and clean geometric lines, all in riots of confectionery colors. A sunny, seaside place with impossible-to-resist charm, Napier isn't made for walking—it was designed for promenading: down busy Marine Parade, with its stately Norfolk pines and touristy sights, and through the bustling streets of the city center, with their modern stores and lively cafes. Napier is a bit more relaxed than its northwestern neighbors Taupo and Rotorua, a city meant more for mature outdoor-cafe sitting and serene moonlit beach strolling than for heart-pounding skydiving. Though jam-packed during the summer holidays and event-filled February, Napier looks simply marvelous at any time of year.

ORIENTATION AND PRACTICAL INFORMATION

Marine Parade and **Hastings Street** lie parallel to each other, stretching southward along the bay. Central Napier's streets lie up against the bluffs. Be careful about meandering through the bricked and palm-lined **Emerson Street**—despite the misleading landscaping, it's a main traffic thoroughfare. **Tennyson** and **Dickens Street** parallel it on each side; the gardens of **Clive Square** mark the edge of the town center.

Airport: The Hawke's Bay Airport (tel. 835 1130), north of Napier on SH2, rests on land that was upraised in the 1931 earthquake (see p. 216). **Air New Zealand Link** (tel. 835 3288) has many daily flights to Auckland ($227) and Wellington ($203). Book with the **ANZ Travel Centre** (tel. 835 1171), at Hastings and Station St. Open M-F 8:15am-5pm, Sa 9:30am-12:30pm. The **Supershuttle** (tel. 879 9766) offers door-to-door service to the airport ($7, $18 to Hastings). A taxi costs $10-15 (from Hastings $40-45).

Trains: TranzScenic departs from Munroe St. daily for Wellington (2:05pm, 5hr., $70) via Hastings (2:05pm, 25min., $15) and Palmerston North (3hr., $44).

Buses: All buses leave from the train station. Those heading south pass through Hastings. **InterCity** and **Newmans** both depart daily for Wellington (6hr., 1 per day, $58) via Palmerston North (3hr., $37); Auckland (7hr., 1 per day, $79) via Taupo (2hr., $34) and Rotorua (1hr., $53). InterCity and **Coachrite Connections** (tel. 868 9969 or (025) 469 867) both head to Gisborne (4hr., 1-2 per day, $30-40) via Wairoa (2hr., $20-25).

Public Transportation: Nimon and Sons run the **Nimbus** (tel. 835 0633; runs approximately M-F 7am-5:30pm between Napier and surrounding suburbs). Buses to **Hastings** run almost every hour (M-F 9am-3pm, $4). All leave from Dalton St. near Dickens St. To get to Hastings on the weekend, catch an **InterCity** or **Newmans** bus heading south ($5-10).

Taxis: StarTaxis (tel. 835 5511) or **Napier Taxis** (tel. 835 7777 or (0800) 503 577).

Car Rental: Metro Rent-A-Car (tel. 835 0590) is based in Napier at the corner of Corunna Rd. and Hyderabad Rd., but serves all of Hawke's Bay.

Bike Rental: Napier Cycle World, 105 Carlyle St. (tel. 835 9528), rents in summer for $19 per day (includes helmet and lock).

Hitchhiking: Those heading south report that getting rides is easier when walking along Marine Parade; a few hundred meters past the Aquarium, it becomes SH2 and picks up more traffic. For those heading north, the best spot is reputed to be just across the Pandora Rd. Bridge. Most traffic heads to Taupo, however; those going to Wairoa or Gisborne ask the driver about his or her destination, or ask to be let off where SH5 branches off.

Visitor Center: Napier Information Centre, 100 Marine Parade (tel. 834 1911; fax 835 7219). Book winery tours or gannet trips here, as well as ground travel. Pick up Backcountry (but not Great Walk) hut passes. Open Dec. 26-Jan. 31 daily 8:30am-7pm; Feb.-Nov. M-F 8:30am-5pm, Sa-Su 9am-5pm.

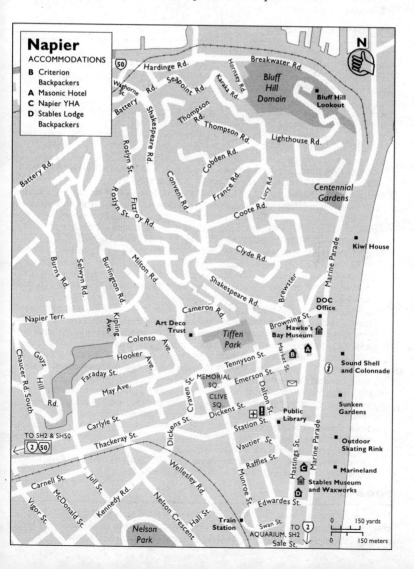

Napier
ACCOMMODATIONS
B Criterion Backpackers
A Masonic Hotel
C Napier YHA
D Stables Lodge Backpackers

DOC: 59 Marine Parade (tel. 834 3111), past the brightly colored museum on Marine Parade. Come here for maps, brochures, advice, and Great Walk hut passes for the Lake Waikaremoana Track in Te Urewera National Park. Open M-F 9am-4:15pm.

Currency Exchange: Change money and sightsee under the beautifully painted ceiling panels at the **ASB Bank** (tel. 834 1240), at Emerson and Hastings St. (The pattern design is called *kowhaiwhai*, with molded spearheads at the corner of each panel.) Open M-F 9am-4:30pm.

Bi-Gay-Lesbian Organizations: Gayline (tel. 843 3087) has information on current goings-on. Dances hosted the third Saturday of each month at the Bay City Club on Milton Rd. (part-way up Bluff Hill, off Tennyson St.). Cover $5.

Emergency: Dial 111.

Police: On Station St. (24hr. tel. 835 4688).

Medical Services: The City Medical Center (24hr. tel. 835 4999), on Station St., just past the police station. Open daily 8am-9pm. They can direct you to a pharmacist.

Post Office: At Dickens St. and Hastings St. (tel. 835 3725). Open M-F 8am-5pm.

Telephone Code: 06.

ACCOMMODATIONS

Napier doesn't lack for good hostel options. You'll either stay far from the center of town, or in the middle of it—there's precious little in between. Parking can be a problem downtown, especially in summer when the town's hopping (and accommodations must be booked ahead).

Criterion Backpackers, 48 Emerson St. (tel. 835 2059). A 1930s Spanish mission-style misfit in the land of Art Deco, the refurbished ultra-central Criterion has an eye-popping carpet that just might spark psychedelic flashbacks. Spacious lounge with 3 fireplaces opens onto a balcony above the bustle of Emerson St. The noise from the bar downstairs, while reportedly under control, has been known to thrum right through guests pillows on weekends. Dorms $12; shares $14; twins and doubles $15. Linen $1. Key deposit $10. Cash only.

◉**Stables Lodge Backpackers,** 321 Marine Parade (tel./fax 835 6242). With affable dog Max making the rounds, community and goodwill abound at this environmentally aware hostel. Plenty of information on local wildlife and ecotourism, as well as daily summertime barbecues. Free fruit, tea, bikes, and book exchange. Dorms $15; doubles $36; 3rd day half price. Duvets $2. Parking on Hastings St.

Napier YHA, 277 Marine Parade (tel./fax 835 7039), at the corner of Vaultier St., in a noisy area. Sleepily sip your coffee and watch the sun rise over the water in the new lounge area of this well located cottage. Inside, colored-window panels set aglow a bewildering variety of wallpaper and fabrics. Bikes for rent. Dorms $15; singles $22; twins and doubles $36. Reception open 8-10am and 4-8pm.

Masonic Hotel (tel. 835 8689; fax 835 2297), corner of Marine Parade and Tennyson St. The classic exterior offers the allure of an original grand old Art Deco hotel, but it isn't the 30s anymore in these rooms with TVs, minifridges, phones, and mattresses so springy you might sleep right through the next 'quake. Patio balcony, restaurant, bar, and a slightly kitschy Irish house pub with a "kasino" downstairs. Free laundry. Singles $60-80 at peak periods; doubles $65-85; on weekends, some rooms cheaper due to noise.

Aqua Lodge, 53 Nelson Crescent (tel./fax 835 4523). From the bus station, turn right on Munroe St., right onto Sale St. across the rail, and the hostel is a block down on the right. Walk through the stucco arch and into the heart of this quintessential suburban backpackers, right down to its courtyard with passion-fruit vines and semi-indoor pool. Quiet and 5 minutes from the town center, it's a favorite with long-term visitors. The owners will help find transport and work in season. Free pickup, and off-road parking. Dorms $15; singles $23; doubles $36 (winter prices negotiable). Weekly bed $90. Key deposit $10. Linen $2.

FOOD

Marine Parade and the main downtown streets are lined with eateries from cheap to chic. A serviceable market can be found in **Countdown Foods**, at the corner of Dickens and Station near Thackeray St. (open M-F 8am-9pm, Sa-Su 8am-8pm).

Mabel's Café (tel. 835 5655), Hastings St. by Dickens St. Despite its pink frosted windows, awning, and walls, there's no salon stylist waiting to beehive your hair at Mabel's. There is a health-conscious proprietor, however, who makes everything on the premises each morning and dishes up pastas and delicious quiche in bubbling casserole dishes ($3.30), heaping salads from earthenware bowls ($3.70-$7.20), and the crockpot soup of the day. Sandwiches under $4. Natural sweet pastries, muffins, carrot cake, pure juices, and $1.50 bottomless cups of coffee. Breakfast served 6-9:30am. Open M-F 6am-3pm.

Shelbe's Café (tel. 835 0474), on Market St. If the wine-bottle candles and richly colored decor of this chill cafe don't clue you in that it's no franchised hut, the pizzas will: thin-crusted heaping pies with wonderfully unorthodox topping combinations. From squid to cranberry to Brie, they put anything on: small ($7-10), medium ($14-16), and large ($18-22). Hawke's Bay wines available. Open Tu-W 3-9:30pm, Th noon-10pm, F noon-11pm, and Sa 3-11pm.

Restaurant Indonesia, 409 Marine Parade (tel. 835 8303), by Sale St. near Pizza Hut. Don't let the simple name or plastic placemats fool you into thinking this might be another run of the mill takeaway. Authentic and absorbing decor prepare you for the similarly elegant cuisine and offer a refreshing break from the standard cafe and grille food. The chicken soup ($4), or mains ($16-$18) such as the pork loin or vegetables on fried rice will not disappoint. "Selamat Makan" (Have a nice meal). Open daily from 6pm. Reservations recommended.

Thorps, 40 Hastings St. (tel. 835 6699), by Tennyson St. You'd think that Mother Nature herself prepared the healthy sandwiches ($4-$6). With 7 breads, 7 meats (including salmon) and over 20 dressings to design from, only the indecisive should dodge this upscale coffee shop. Open M-Th 8:30am-3pm, F 8:30am-5pm, Sa 9am-2pm, Su 10-2.

SIGHTS AND ACTIVITIES

The color-laden symmetry of the buildings is perhaps itself the main sight in Napier. Look up, look down, and look around—even the manhole covers can't escape the craze. It may be the most fun just to wander and explore for yourself the leaded glass windows, Deco doorknobs, and unexpected details that pepper the city, as well as the larger and more dramatic buildings. **Tennyson Street** has a row of classic structures. Check out the Maori Deco of the **Antique Centre,** the Shamrock Deco of the **Munster Chambers,** and the Deco-overload of the **Daily Telegraph** building. **Market Street** has terrific glass windows; the peach and green **Countrywide Bank** building on Dalton and Emerson St. is frothily impressive. And don't forget to check out the Greco Deco of the **Colonnade** and the **Sound Shell.** For a walking guide (1.5km) to Napier's Deco, head to the **Art Deco Trust** (tel. 835 0022) at 163 Tennyson St. for a well-informed tour. *(Tours W, Sa, and Su 2pm, or by arrangement; 2hr. Morning tours in summer. $10.)* The Trust's brochures (available at the shop or visitor center) provide a middle ground between aimless wandering and a full-on tour.

If you've begun to overdose on Deco, head to **Marine Parade.** Interspersed among manicured gardens, burbling fountains, and statues like Pania of the Reef (a distinctively toothy mermaid) are some big visitor draws, including an in-line skating rink, a public pool, and animal attractions. At the north end is the octagonal **Kiwi House** (tel. 834 1336), home to two of the nation's pride-and-joy northern brown kiwis. *(Open daily 11am-3pm. $3, children $1.50, families $7.50.)* A daily talk is offered at 1pm, when a kiwi is brought out from the glassed-in exhibit and enticed into activity with scrumptious huhu grubs. A bit farther down and on the other side is the **Hawke's Bay Museum,** 65 Marine Parade (tel. 835 7781) with its impossible-to-miss large colored cylinders. *(Open daily 10am-4:30pm. Admission $4, children free.)* It has art exhibits as well as displays on colonial history, the earthquake, the East Coast Ngati Kahungunu Maori, Hawke's Bay dinosaur fossils and, of course, Art Deco.

After that brief cultural oasis, follow the sound of barking marine mammals down Marine Parade to **Marineland** (tel. 834 4027) and its zoo-like exhibits and shows. *(Admission $4-10, children $3-5.)* Sealife at the **Hawke's Bay Aquarium** (tel. 843 1404), ranges from giant hawk-billed turtles and coy seahorses to smug piranhas and sinister

Napier's Rebirth

Once a small town on a narrow spit of seaward hills, a massive 7.9 **earthquake** rocked Napier for two minutes on February 3, 1931, killing 258, lifting over 4000 hectares of seabed several meters above water, and destroying almost every building in the process. The terrible loss was architecture's (and tourism's) gain, however, as the massive rebuilding undertaken over the subsequent three years created what is arguably the world's most concentrated collection of **Art Deco** buildings in the world today. The cheap, sturdy, and reinforced concrete of this style was well-suited to a Depression-hit, collapsed town, and the bright color and symmetry lent comfort and sparkle to the optimistic era of rebirth. A different sort of rebirth is going on today, however, as tacky modern stores are refusing to conform their design to the Art Deco style. Many aesthetically-conscious residents of Napier bemoan the situation and are calling for action. Perhaps this encroachment bespeaks the beginning of yet another metamorphosis—earthquakes are not the only means by which towns are altered forever.

sharks. *(Open daily in summer 9am-9pm, in winter 9am-5pm. Admission $7, children $3.50, families $18.)* As always, the question is "who's gawking at whom?" You'll even find tuatara (see Fauna, p. 47), reptiles surviving from the Mesozoic era. The daily feeding frenzy in the main tank is at 3:15pm (also at 11:15am in summer).

Back on dry land, Napier sits at the edge of the vineyard-studded Hawke's Bay plains, one of New Zealand's major wine-producing regions. Originally set up by priests for religious use, **Mission Estate Winery** (tel. 844 2259) is New Zealand's oldest winery. *(Open M-Sa 8:30am-5:30pm, Su 1-4pm. Tours offered M-Sa 10:30am and 2pm.)* **Ngatarawa Wines** (tel. 879 7603) is a small winery in a restored stable with lovely grounds. The winery offers tastings of their sweet dessert wines daily from 11am to 5pm. For those without private transport, several tour operators drive around some of the wineries, offering short guided tours and tastings. **Wine Tour Trails** (tel. 877 5707; fax 877 5129), **Bay Tours Midi Coachlines** (tel. 843 6953; fax 843 2046), and **Vince's Vineyard Tours** (tel. 836 6705; fax 844 4940) offer four- to five-hour tours for about $30 (free pickup). Book at the visitor center.

If you have a few rainy hours, consider visiting **Classic Sheepskins,** 22 Thames St. (tel. 835 9662), off Pandora Rd. (SH2 north) for free tours of the tanning factory at 11am and 2pm. Gain insight into what really happens to those ubiquitous fluffy herbivores of the New Zealand countryside. A courtesy van makes pickups.

ENTERTAINMENT

Napier is a fine place on warm evenings. Wax poetic under a glowing crescent of moon as you sit by a fire on the black-sand beach. Ponder the molten color of the Tom Parker Fountain at the top of Marine Parade, illuminated at night with shifting lights. Wander through one of the many antique shops or meander from one cafe to the next, sipping espresso or a Hawke's Bay wine under the umbrellas at the outdoor seating of the places lining the central streets. Many clubs and bars are found near the intersection of Hastings and Tennyson St., or farther up Hastings St. on Shakespeare Rd. Follow your ears.

O'Flaherty's Irish Pub, 37 Hastings St. by Emerson St. (tel. 834 1235) is an unassuming and authentic tavern for both casual and veteran drinkers. Just staring at the splendid murals is worth the price of a pint ($2 during daily 5-7pm happy hour; open daily 11am-late). Live music every weekend, fresh home-made pies, and above average bar food. Follow the herd to **Grumpy Mole Saloon** (tel. 835 5545), on the corner of Hastings and Tennyson St. The sign at the door reads "all livestock must be left outside" because on a Saturday night you'll be the one squeezing into this enormous paddock (if you can pass the "no scruffiness" test at the door). This night club saloon with its loud music, hot twentysomethings, and American West decor is an odd but popular hybrid choice (open Tu-Sa 4pm-3am).

Napier rocks in February (the month of its earthquake) with festivals. Dust off your "zoot suit" for the glam **Ford Art Deco Weekend** (Feb. 18-22, 1999) and its endless series of stylish, and generally expensive, events: from balls and cafe crawls to champagne breakfasts and country house tours. There's somewhat less to do if you're short on cash, but you can still check out the museum exhibitions and the vintage car rally, find some free jazz, marvel at the costumes, and pack a hamper for Sunday's **Great Gatsby Picnic** on the beach (which is followed by the concluding Thanksgiving service in the Anglican Church to celebrate Napier's rise from its own ashes). There's also the **Harvest Hawke's Bay Wine and Food Festival** (first weekend in February), a weekend of similarly upscale revelry. Local wineries are packed with shuttle tours and tasters all weekend long. The **International Mission Estate Concert** in February at the Mission Estate Winery is a big regional deal in a gorgeous setting. At any time of year, there might be impromptu jazz concerts at the wineries or other entertainment in the soundshell.

■ Near Napier: Cape Kidnappers

Conjure up a bird on a nest, multiply that image by several thousand, put the duplicates in row formation, plunk the whole picture down on a remote cliffpoint in the Southern Pacific, and you've got Cape Kidnappers. The vertical toothy cliffs of Hawke Bay's southern tip strike a dramatic profile at any time of year, but from September to March they are home to the world's largest mainland nesting grounds of the **Australasian gannet.** Fifteen thousand of the large tawny-headed, white and black birds arrive en masse in October and set up their nests in quasi-orderly rows at the three colony sites encompassed by the 13-hectare **Cape Kidnappers Gannet Reserve.** The rocks may look frosted white by snow, but you know better. Chicks hatch in early November and mature through the summer before flying the coop on their ambitious maiden air voyage of 2800km across the Tasman Sea to Australia. In the meantime, it's a scene straight from Alfred Hitchcock: male gannets wheeling and bearing down like 747s toward the teeming colony, then stopping on a dime to drop nesting material to their Mrs. Gannet below. And if they misjudge their landing, hell hath no fury like a lady gannet wronged.

The area is closed to the public between July and October, when the birds are in the tenuous early nesting stage. At other times you are free to visit the masses of gannets (and big masses of gannet, ahem, residue). It's a stunning walk at any time of year, even in winter when the birds are gone. Check with the Napier Visitor Centre for local outfitters and hiking trails among soaring stone and crashing surf. (Trips usually 4-5hr., $17-38.)

■ Hastings

Hastings may be known as Napier's twin city, but the likeness is strictly fraternal. Only 12km away, it was victim to the same earthquake that felled Napier, but was partially rebuilt in Spanish Mission style instead. Its architecture never reached the same gaudy heights as the Art Deco explosion of Napier and little effort has been put into promoting or developing the style further (though the Municipal Theatre on Hastings St. is impressive). There are many kiwifruit orchards in the area, and consequently a lot of fruit pickers in town during the season. Essentially a contented working town, most visitors to Hastings head out: to the wineries, Cape Kidnappers, the beaches, Te Mata Peak, and all the natural attractions of Hawke's Bay to which Hastings is undeniably central.

ORIENTATION AND PRACTICAL INFORMATION Flat and orderly Hastings is momentarily perturbed by the slant of the railway track that slices through the heart of the city center. **Heretaunga Street**, the main road, turns prettily pedestrian for a block on either side of the railway (a herd of ceramic sheep flock at the Market St. end of this stretch). An Art Deco **clock tower** and fountain adorn the town square. Streets are tagged west to one side of the railway and east to the other; south and north designations split at **Heretaunga Street.**

Book activities or travel arrangements at the **Visitors Information Centre** (tel. 878 0510; fax 878 0512) on Russell St. North (open M-F 8:30am-5pm, Sa-Su 10am-3pm).

The **BNZ** (tel. 878 0839) is on Heretaunga St. next to WestpacTrust (open M-F from 9am to 4:30pm). All buses and trains to and from Napier take about 30 minutes to one hour to travel the distance. **InterCity, Newmans, TranzScenic,** and **Coachrite Connections** all leave from the **Hastings Travel Centre** (tel. 878 0213), at the end of Russell St. North (bookings M-F 7:45am-4:45pm). Fares are generally $2-3 different than those from Napier. The local service, **Nimon and Sons** (runs approximately M-F 7am-5:30pm), leaves from Eastbourne St. by the Russell St. corner, or from the Kmart by the Visitor Center (for details see Napier, p. 189). **Hitchhikers** going south often head out just past the 30kph zone beyond the racecourse; those going to Napier thumb up Karamu Rd. North, while those heading to Taupo or Wairoa and Gisborne take the route that bypasses central Napier by getting rides from Pakowhai Rd. The **police** (24hr. tel. 878 3007) are on Railway Rd. The **post office** (tel. 876 03300) is at the corner of Queen and Russell St. The **telephone code** is **06.**

ACCOMMODATIONS Hastings has basically two options: hostels or pricey motels, with very little in the middle. Some hostels are only open from November to May, and survive by helping to arrange work for fruit-picking backpackers. Small and very chill is the cute English villa of **AJ's Backpackers,** 405 Southland Rd. (tel. 878 2302), just off Southhampton St. Owners Jackie and Alan are very hospitable, and their two spastic boxer dogs pick up where their owners leave off. Free pickups are available. Simple rooms have bunks and paper ball shade lanterns (dorms $14; weekly $80 if you're employed).At the summer-only **Hastings Backpackers,** (tel. 876 5888) on Lyndon St. between Hastings St. and Willow Park Rd., both work and play are available (open Nov.-Apr.). Pick fruit at an orchard, sign up for a day trip to area attractions, or, if you're lucky, score the "love shack" in the garden corner. Dorms are $13 ($75 weekly). **The Hastings Holiday Park** (tel. 878 6692; fax 878 6267), out by Fantasyland on Windsor Ave., has lots of park-like green space, large trees, and a duck-filled creek. Basic plyboard-walled sleeping cabins sleep two and cost $38, or opt for tent and caravan sites ($9). Peak rates apply. Rub your lantern and wish for a room at the **Aladdin Lodge,** 120 Maddison St. (tel. 876 6322; fax 876 6736), off Willowpark Rd. South. Close to town and off the noisier main streets, all rooms are nicely outfitted with SKY TV, phones, and kitchenettes. There's a covered spa pool, a tiny plunge pool, and a playground with trampolines, not to mention free laundry. Standard units ($76 for 2 people) have a separate double bedroom and pull-out couches; one small unit with two single beds ($60) is behind the laundry room.

The Race to See the Sun

Hastings catapulted from relative anonymity to potential world-wide fame in 1997, when Terralink, the government surveying department, determined that the 399m Te Mata Peak (right outside of Hastings) would see the sun before Gisborne's Kaiti Hill. Hastily reinventing itself as "The Millennium 2000 City," Hastings began gearing up for the celebration. Although plans are still being formulated, things will doubtless be pumpin' on December 31, 1999 at the Te Mata Peak lookout, where untold numbers of drunken revelers will crowd the tiny parking lot and spread over the windy, treacherous summit. In the meantime, Hastings defends itself staunchly against all of Gisborne's pretensions—after all, there's no glory in being the second city to see the sun. (For more on this topic, see p. 205).

FOOD Though there are a few trendy restaurants, don't expect much in the way of fine dining in Hastings. Undoubtedly your peak culinary experience will be the rich and fruity scoops at **Rush Munroe's Ice Cream Gardens,** 704 Heretaunga St. West (tel. 878 9634). They've been around since 1926 and have had over 70 years to perfect flavors from classic vanilla to loads of luscious fruity flavors (including feijoa). A green oasis in the midst of auto dealerships and tire centers, lick your $1.60 cone (or the bargain $1.90 double) under the trellis. **The Corn Exchange** (tel. 870 8333), out in the old Farm Products Cooperative building on Maraekakaho Rd. (off Heretaunga

St.), is a-maize-ingly chic, with smooth wood, a central fireplace, and outdoor seating. The menu changes every few months but tends to feature fringe meats like venison, duck, and bison (they've even done kangaroo), as well as steak and chicken standards. Mains are pricey (from $20) but servings are beefy, and entrees like the wood-fired oven-baked pizzas are sizeable and reasonable ($14.50). You'll also find extensive liquors and a well-stocked bar, with occasional live music on weekends. (Open Su-Th 11:30am-11pm, Sa-Su 11:30am-1am.) **Robert Harris Coffee Shop,** 104 Russell St. South (tel. 878 2931), is in town center. Though part of a larger coffee shop chain that reckons itself the Starbucks of New Zealand, this cafe offers fresh sandwiches (under $4) and baked goods that reveal tender, loving, care. (Open M-F 8am-5pm and Sa 8-2pm.) **Countdown Foods** (tel. 878 5091) is your supermarket on Queen St. N. (open M-F 8am-9pm, Sa-Su 8am-8pm). Nightlife in Hastings, more often than not, includes a pint of Steinlager's or cider at the down-home English pub, the **Cat and Fiddle Ale House,** 502 Karamu Rd. (tel. 878 4111). Known for good eats (burgers under $8) as well as quality brews (more than ten on tap), it's crowded with locals, and has monthly Monday night "Live Poets' Society" readings (open Su-W 10:30am-11pm, Th-Sa 10:30am-2am). **Friends Bar and Cafe** (tel. 878 6701), sits by the Cobb and Co. in town center. If only all friends were this generous, with free $50 bar tabs for groups of six or more on Thursdays, free barbecue on Sundays, and a daily happy hour (7pm-9pm; open daily 11am-3am). In the upscale hamlet of **Havelock North** (7km east), several good pubs rock the night away.

SIGHTS AND ACTIVITIES Hastings shares many of its most compelling draws with Napier, such as area wineries, Cape Kidnappers, and killer surfing beaches like **Ocean Beach** on the south side of the Cape and **Waimarama** farther south. The **Hawke's Bay Exhibition Centre,** 201 Eastbourne St. East (tel./fax 876 2077), is a companion to the museum in Napier with showings of local and national art and scientific displays. *(Open M-F 10am-4:30pm, Sa-Su noon-3pm. Free.)* The town's gardens are celebrated in mid-September with live acts and a grand parade during the **Blossom Festival.** Sample over 85 different varieties of pip and stone fruits (in season) at **Pernel Fruitworld** (tel. 878 3383) on Pakowhai Rd., with hourly tours from 9am to 4pm.

As you walk down Heretaunga St., you may notice a large green lump welling up in from the otherwise pancake-flat landscape surrounding the city. That's **Te Mata Peak,** the sleeping giant rising abruptly from sea level to 399m, and the highest point in Hawke's Bay. As Maori legend has it, the peak is the prostate body of chief Te Mata, a giant man who choked to death while eating a hill in an attempt to woo his beloved. From certain angles, the fatal chomp is clear just above the head of Te Mata. Stand atop his protruded belly for impressive views of Hawke's Bay and the Tukituki Valley below (those white blobs are sheep). The lights of the twin cities sparkle in the evening on the plains below.

Te Mata requires a two hour round trip hike to the peak. You could cut your time in half by arranging for an exhilarating **tandem paraglide** off the skimpy ramps at the top into the valley beyond (done mostly in summer when the winds are right). Contact Tim Whittaker (tel. (025) 480 480) or Shaun Gilbert (021 645 643) for a 15-minute, $90 glide ($70 per person for 3 or more).

Wellington and the South

Unlike the thrill-seeking epicenters in much of the rest of New Zealand, Wellington and the south is more of a region for catching your breath than for losing it. Captain Cook sailed by several times through his eponymous strait, but never managed to enter the harbor. That honor fell to a colony of settlers unceremoniously plunked down and left behind on an empty beach. Despite its inauspicious start, Wellington celebrates the event as a regional holiday every January 22. Today, the capital engages with eye-catching museums and original theater, catering to the worldly wise with a thriving cafe culture and urban nightlife. Upbeat bedroom-beach 'burbs light up the westerly Kapiti Coast, while the easterly Wairarapa region is a vineyard-dotted escape for Wellington's restless and well-to-do. The pastoral university town of Palmerston North in the Manawatu keeps the crowds cheering its two great loves: movies and rugby. Whether you surge with the mob through nightclubs in Wellington or tramp through Wairarapa's Tararua Forest Park, you won't miss the region's trademark style and sass.

✋ WELLINGTON AND THE SOUTH HIGHLIGHTS

- The spectacular Te Papa Museum (see p. 230) is Wellington's pride and joy.
- Fine wines can be tasted at the vineyards of the Wairarapa (see p. 234).
- National affairs are hashed out on the floors of Parliament (see p. 230).

◼ Wellington

Lying directly on a major earthquake fault, teetering at the edge of the ocean, and jostled on all sides by steep green hills, the compact capital city of Wellington is a topographical microcosm of New Zealand. Sitting in a gorgeous hook of harbor near the North Island's southern tip, New Zealand's second-largest city and major cultural center is also a crossroads and important shipping port. Here in the throbbing heart of the country, you'll find a blossoming bouquet of cultural options including an impressive series of festivals and events, as well as New Zealand's strongest set of theater and dance options. The enormous, $300 million **Museum of New Zealand Te Papa Tongarewa** opened its doors in February 1998, becoming the gem in Wellington's cultural crown. Raise your freak flag high on youthful **Cuba Street,** join the buzz from the **Beehive,** sophisticate over a flat white at one of scores of cafes, catch that new modernist play, or savor the harbor view from **Mt. Victoria.** Before you head back out into adventure wonderland, take a dip into the worldly savoir-faire of New Zealand's cosmopolitan capital.

GETTING THERE

By Plane

The **Wellington International Airport** stretches across the narrowest portion of the Miramar Peninsula in the city's southeastern suburbs. (Luggage storage $2 per 6hr.) Largely a domestic hub, the only international flights here are those from Sydney, Brisbane, or Melbourne, Australia, on **Qantas** or **Air New Zealand. ANZ Link** (tel. 388 9737, arrival and departure info tel. 388 9900) has an office at the corner of Lambton Quay and Panama St. (tel. 471 1616). **Ansett** (tel. 471 1146 or (0800) ANSETT/287 388), is at Shop 10, Harbour City Centre on Panama St. Both fly to Auckland (1hr., 1-2 per hr., $290) and Christchurch (45min., about 1 per hr., $216). With an **International Student Identification Card** or advance booking, fares can drop dramatically. **Soundsair** (tel. 388 2594 or (0800) 505 005) flies daily to Picton (25min., 6-8 per day, $45) and on request to tiny airstrips throughout the Marlborough Sounds. **Super Shuttle** (tel. 387 8787) runs between the airport and railway station ($5), as does **Capitol Shuttles** (tel. 570 0003; $8, additional person $2).

Wellington and the South

By Train

The **railway station,** on Bunny St. at Waterloo/Customhouse Quay, houses the train and bus depots. **TranzScenic** (0800 802 802) provides daily service to Napier (5hr., 8am, $70) via Palmerston North (2hr., $30); to Auckland (11hr., 8:45am, $135) via Palmerston North or Hamilton (9hr., $108); and an overnight train to Auckland (7:50pm, $120). **The Travel Centre** (tel. 498 2058) handles bookings for Tranzscenic, InterCity, Newmans, domestic air, tours, accommodations, and rental cars.

By Bus

Most buses depart from the railway station; **Mt. Cook** leaves from the Saatchi and Saatchi Building on Courtenay Pl. at Taranaki St. **InterCity** (tel. 472 5111), **Newmans** (tel. 499 3261), and **Mount Cook Landlines** (tel. 382 2154) go daily to Palmerston North (2hr., 1-4 per day, $25-30); Rotorua (7½hr., 1-3 per day, $40-75) via Taupo (6hr., $55-65); and Auckland (11hr., 1-3 per day, $96) via Hamilton (9hr., $72-79). InterCity and

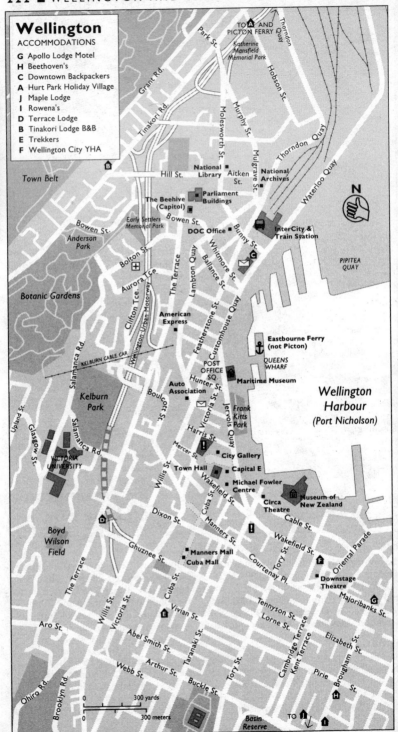

Wellington
ACCOMMODATIONS

G Apollo Lodge Motel
H Beethoven's
C Downtown Backpackers
A Hutt Park Holiday Village
J Maple Lodge
I Rowena's
D Terrace Lodge
B Tinakori Lodge B&B
E Trekkers
F Wellington City YHA

Town Belt

TO A AND
PICTON FERRY

Katherine
Mansfield
Memorial Park

Park St.

Thorndon Quay

Grant Rd.

Tinakori Rd.

Murphy St.

Molesworth St.

Mulgrave St.

Hobson St.

Hill St.

National
Library

Aitken St.

National
Archives

Waterloo Quay

Thorndon Quay

N

Bowen St.

The Beehive
(Capitol)

Parliament
Buildings

PIPITEA
QUAY

Bowen St.

Early Settlers
Memorial Park

DOC Office

Bunny St.

InterCity &
Train Station

Anderson
Park

Bolton St.

Whitmore St.

Ballance St.

C

Botanic Gardens

Aurora Tce.

Clifton Tce.

The Terrace

Lambton Quay

Featherstone St.

Customhouse Quay

American
Express

Eastbourne Ferry
(not Picton)

QUEENS
WHARF

KELBURN CABLE CAR

POST
OFFICE
SQ.

Maritime Museum

Kelburn
Park

Boulcott St.

Auto
Association

Hunter St.

Victoria St.

Jervois Quay

Frank
Kitts Park

Wellington
Harbour
(Port Nicholson)

Upland St.

Salamanca Rd.

Glasgow St.

VICTORIA
UNIVERSITY

Salamanca Rd.

Harris St.

Mercer St.

City Gallery

Willis St.

Town Hall

Capital E

Wakefield St.

Michael Fowler
Centre

Cuba St.

Circa
Theatre

Museum of
New Zealand

Boyd
Wilson
Field

D

Dixon St.

Manners St.

Cable St.

Wakefield St.

Ghuznee St.

The Terrace

Manners Mall

Cuba Mall

Courtenay Pl.

Tory St.

F

Oriental Parade

Aro St.

Willis St.

Victoria St.

Cuba St.

Vivian St.

E

Downstage
Theatre

Majoribanks St.

Tennyson St.

Lorne St.

Cambridge Terrace

Kent Terrace

Elizabeth St.

G

Abel Smith St.

Taranaki St.

Tory St.

Pirie

Brougham St.

Ohiro Rd.

Brooklyn Rd.

Webb St.

Arthur St.

Buckle St.

Basin
Reserve

TO

H

0   300 yards
0   300 meters

Newmans also go to Tauranga (8-8½hr., 3 per day, $86-89); New Plymouth (6hr., 2-3 per day, $59) via Wanganui (4hr., $34); and Napier (5hr., 2-3 per day, $58). **Tranzit Coachlines** (tel. 387 2018) goes to Masterton (1½hr., 9:15am, $13).

By Ferry

The ferry terminal is inconveniently located on **Aotea Quay,** north of town on SH1. There's a free shuttle from Platform 9 of the railway station 35 minutes before each scheduled departure, and back to the station upon ferry arrival. The **Interislander** (tel. (0800) 802 802; fax (0800) 101 525) runs daily to Picton on the South Island (3hr., 4-5 per day, $46). Bookings are essential, especially during the summer. (Small car transport $165; large sports equipment and dogs $10). Ask about one-day and four-day excursion fares.

By Thumb

Hitchhikers report that riding from Wellington is sometimes difficult, but the old main road (where SH1 and SH2 branch a couple kilometers north of the ferry station on Hutt Rd.) is a good spot with its heavy traffic flow and stoplight. This branchpoint is a long walk, so some hitchhikers try their luck where the cars roll right off the boat at the ferry terminal, or at the railway station. Some believe it's best to train it out to Paraparaumu (45km north on SH1) or Masterton (on SH2) and catch a ride there.

Wellington's Wind

Q: "Do you know why ropes were installed on Lambton Quay?"
A: "To hold on for dear life!"

Jokes such as this and cunning truisms like "You can spot a Wellingtonian any-where—they walk with a stoop from the wind" point to a fundamental character-istic of New Zealand's capital city. When you ask how long it takes to walk somewhere, the answer depends on whether you're walking upwind or down-wind. The worst winds are the Southerlies, bringing their Antarctic chill across the Cook Strait (effectively a massive wind tunnel between the Tasman Sea and the Pacific Ocean). Wellington's reputation was sealed in 1968 when gusts recorded at 167 mph caused the inter-island ferry Wahine to founder as it tried to enter the harbor, drowning 51 people. Most locals respond to derogatory com-ments about the weather with zen-like responses such as "If you want the views and sun, you're going to get wind." In recent years, the city has tried to embrace its reputation with events like the kite, plane, and flag-filled Wind Festival held for nine days every March. Despite such reconciliations, however, the spring and autumn winds all too often rage with a bluster that surpass even those gusts of hot air inside the Parliament buildings (see p. 231).

ORIENTATION

Central Wellington is remarkably compact, though its suburbs stretch up around the harbor into nearby valleys and out onto the **Miramar Peninsula.** Its main downtown zone (most of the city's flat land) sits between the **Railway Station** and **Cambridge/ Kent Terraces** at the base of **Mt. Victoria,** and can be explored in the course of a day. The main artery snaking through the business area is **Lambton Quay.** At the **Cuba** and **Vivian Street** intersection is the "red light district," as the locals say. **Courtenay Place,** between Cambridge Terrace and **Taranaki Street,** hops with nightlife on the weekends. Cuba Street between **Abel Smith** and **Manners Street** maintains a more bohemian air, providing the haunts of students and twentysomethings. The **Civic Centre** is both a conceptual and spatial bridge between downtown and the harbor, leading to the harborfront with its public parks, **Queen's Wharf,** the colossal new **National Museum,** and **Oriental Bay's** flashy shops, cafes, and beach. Government buildings, such as the **Beehive** of Parliament, stand near the **railway station.** At the southern edge of downtown are the little wooden houses and quieter streets of the Mt. Victoria area, where many budget accommodations lie.

GETTING AROUND

Ridewell Service Centre (tel. 801 7000 or (0800) 801 700) can answer any and all questions about fares, routes, and timetables for buses, trains, or the cable car (phones answered M-Sa 7:30am-8:30pm, Su 9am-3pm).

By Train

The **Tranz Metro** (tel. 498 3000), a regional commuter line, leaves from the Railway Station. There are four regular lines with many stops on the way: to Johnsonville (20min., M-Sa, full peak fare $2.50), Upper Hutt (50min., 1 per day, $5.50), Paraparaumu (1hr., 1 per day, $7.50), and Melling in Lower Hutt (M-F peak morning and afternoon hours only, $3). Ten-trip, monthly or day-rover tickets (unlimited travel, $10) are available. Limited service to Palmerston North is offered by the **Capital Connection** (2hr., M-F 5:17pm, $18), as are trips to Masterton on the **Wairarapa Connection** (1½hr., 2-4 per day, $11.50; same-day round-trip $15).

By Bus

Stagecoach (tel. 387 8700) services the main city and all but its northern suburbs (which are served by Newlands Coach Service). Main line buses run from 5am to 11pm daily, while some of the peripheral lines run approximately 7 to 9am and 3 to 6pm. Frequent buses run between the main stops at the Railway Station and the Cambridge Terr. end of Courtenay Pl. The fare in this stretch is $1; beyond it rises by distance. (The #1 and #2 run between these points for $1 every 10-15min. during the day, and every 30min. during evenings and weekends.) Buy tickets from the driver. A **Daytripper ticket** ($5) is valid for an unlimited day of travel on bus and cable car (includes two children; fares valid only after 9am). The **City Circular** (tel. 801 7000) runs every 10 minutes from all the top inner-city locations (single ride fare $1; all day $5). **Cityline Hutt Valley** runs the #81 and #83 buses between Courtenay Pl. and the railway station and around the bay to Petone and Eastbourne hourly during the day (more during peak, fewer on weekend evenings).

By Car

Budget, Hertz, and **Avis** are at the airport. All visitors center branches have complete listings and will book cars. You can often arrange to meet your car at the ferry terminal. **Omega Rentals,** 3 Vivian St. (tel. (0800) 667 722), has free pick-ups and 24-hour AA breakdown assistance. Four days of unlimited mileage for a budget car is $39 per day, an economy car is $49 per day, while a touring car is $59 per day (min. bond $750). **AA,** 342-352 Lambton Quay by Willis St. (tel. 470 9999) has a **Travel Centre** and shop.

By Taxi

Taxis line the streets of **Lambton Quay, Courtney Place,** and many other drags. If you need to call one, try **Wellington Combined Taxis** (tel. 384 4444) or **Safeway** (tel. 802 5111). A taxi between the railway station and downtown costs about $6.

By Bike, In-line Skate, Ski, and Surfboard

Penny Farthing Cycles, 89 Courtenay Pl. (tel. 385 2279), isn't as cheap as its name implies, but it has a good selection of rental bikes from September to April with racks, tools, helmets, and locks included ($25 per day); longer term rentals are $75 per week with some equipment. On weekends, **Cheap Skates** (tel. 499 0455) and the **Rollerblade Van** (025 540 747) park by the wharf opposite New World grocery store at Cambridge Terr. ($10 per hr.). **Mainly Tramping,** 39 Mercer St. (tel. 473 5353), has a full stock of outdoors and camping equipment.

PRACTICAL INFORMATION

Tourist and Financial Services

Visitors Center: The Wellington Information Centre, 101 Wakefield St. (tel. 802 4800; fax 802 4803), is at the Civic Centre. Reduced price rush tickets to theater shows. Day luggage storage $2. Open M and W-F 8:30am-5:30pm, Tu 8:30am-5pm, Sa-Su 9:30am-4:30pm. Airport branches (tel. 385 5123) meet most incoming flights.

DOC: In the Old Government Building across Lambton Quay from the Beehive (tel. 472 7356; fax 471 2075). Wellington area activities info is limited, but they sell Backcountry hut passes, Great Walk passes for the Kahurangi's Heaphy Track and Abel Tasman's namesake track, as well as permits for Kapiti Island.

Budget Travel: Wellington has almost as many travel shops as cafes. **STA Travel,** 37 Willis St. (tel. 472 8510), is near the Lambton Quay end. Open M-F 9am-5:30pm, Sa 10am-1:30pm. **Budget Travel,** 100 Victoria St. (tel. 473 1230), is a block up from the visitors center. Open M-F 8:30am-5:30pm, Sa 9am-1pm.

Embassies and Consulates: Australia, 72 Hobson St., Thorndon (tel. 473 6411; fax 498 7103), north of the railway station. **U.K.,** 44 Hill St. (tel. 472 6049; fax 471 1974). **Canada,** 61 Molesworth St. (tel. 473 9577; fax 471 2082). **Germany,** 90 Hobson St, Thorndon (tel. 473 6063). **Japan,** corner of Victoria and Hunter St. (tel. 473 1540; fax 471 2951), off Lambton Quay in the Norwich Insurance House. **U.S.,** 29 Fitzherbert Terr., Thorndon (tel. 303 2724; fax 472 3537).

Currency Exchange: In the main downtown areas you're never more than a mad dash from an ATM or bank. **BNZ,** 100 Lambton Quay (tel. 472 2560) and 38-44 Courtenay Pl. (tel. 801 2663). Open M-F 9am-4:30pm. **Thomas Cook,** 358 Lambton Quay (tel. 472 2848), near Willis St. Open M-F 9am-5:30pm, Sa 9am-1pm.

American Express: 280-292 Lambton Quay, P.O. Box 10182 (tel. (0800) 801 122 or 473 7766), in the Cable Car Complex. They hold mail—no parcels—for members for up to 30 days. Open M-F 9am-5pm.

Local Services

Bookstores: Lambton Quay has most of the big chain stores. Cuba St. is littered with small second-hand shops or stores specializing in New Age. Specialty shops include **Unity Books** (tel. 385 6110; fax 385 4957), at the corner of Willis and Manners St. Open M-Th 9am-6pm, F 9am-8pm, Sa 10am-3pm, Su 11am-3pm. **The Map Shop** (tel. 385 1462), at Vivian and Victoria St., rocks your tramping world with a complete set of New Zealand park, city, and topographical maps. Open M-F 8am-5:30pm, Sa 9am-noon. **Out! Bookshop,** 15 Tory St. (tel. 385 4400), has a wide array of gay-oriented magazines and other items. Open M-Sa noon-11pm.

Library: The Wellington Public Library (tel. 801 4040) is a stylish space with free **Internet access.** Open M-Th 9:30am-8:30pm, F 9:30am-9pm, Sa 9:30am-5pm, Su 1-4pm.

Bi-Gay-Lesbian Organizations: Gay Switchboard (tel. 385 0674) runs daily 7:30-10pm and provides support and info on the Wellington scene. It's also a contact point for other area groups like **Icebreakers,** a young gay/bi social group. Call the **Lesbian Line** (tel. 389 8082) on Tu, Th, or Sa 7:30-10pm. The well-distributed fortnightly **Express** paper has info on Wellington options.

Emergency and Communications

Emergency: Dial III.

Police: Corner of Victoria St. and Harris St. (tel. 472 3000).

Hotlines: AIDS hotline (24hr. tel. (0800) 802 437). **Rape and Sexual Abuse Support Hotline** (24hr. tel. 801 8178), run by the Help Foundation.

Medical Services: The David Donald Pharmacy (tel. 499 1466), at the corner of Cuba and Manners St. Open M-Th 8:30am-6pm, F 8:30am-9pm, Sa 9:30am-6pm, Su 10am-6pm. **Wellington Accident and Urgent Medical Center,** 17 Adelaide Rd. (tel. 384 4944), by the Basin Reserve, has a doctor on duty 24hr., and a pharmacy next door (tel. 385 8810; open M-F 5-11pm, Sa-Su 9am-11pm). The **hospital** (tel. 385 5999) is in southern Wellington on Riddiford St.

Post Office: Scattered throughout the city. Only the main office across from the railway station (tel. 496 4068) holds *Poste Restante* in the Post Shop (tel. 496 4951). Open M-F 7am-5:30pm and Sa 9am-12:30pm.

Internet Access: Net Arena Computers, 110 Cuba St. (tel. 385 2240), $1.50 per 5min.; **Wellington City YHA,** $2 per 5min.; and the **library** (see above).

Telephone Code: 04.

ACCOMMODATIONS

Wellington has a range of good backpackers, all of which lie within walking distance of the city, though the **Broughman Street** offerings are a bit farther. From the Railway Station, the #1 bus (among others) goes to the end of Courtenay Pl.; from there, cross Cambridge and Kent Terr. and walk up the hill about a block to Brougham St. Or take the #2, which goes all the way to Brougham St. Even cheaper accommodations can be found among the old wooden hill houses of the **Mt. Victoria** area in the quieter south end (15min. walk from Lambton Quay/Civic Centre area, 5min. from Courtenay Pl.). Call ahead at all times of the year.

Wellington City YHA (tel. 801 7280; fax 801 7278; email yhawgtn@yha.org.nz), at the corner of Cambridge Terr. and Wakefield St. A 15min. walk from the railway station. Capital Shuttle stops here on its way to the ferry ($5) and the airport ($8). In a hard-to-miss, hulking six-story former hotel, the hostel is well located near Courtenay Place nightlife. The outstanding organization, conveniences, and harbor vistas compensate for the lack of atmosphere. Helpful young staff, supermarket across the street, internet access ($2 per 5min.) and **YHA Travel Agency** (tel. 801 7238). 4-bed bunks $19; 6-bed dorms $17. Doubles with a view $46; family rooms $58. $4 extra for non-members. Book ahead.

Rowena's (VIP), 115 Brougham St. (tel. 385 7872 or (0800) 801 414; email rowenas@extra.co.nz). This bright and jazzy house on the hill has great balcony views. Staff has plenty of daytrip ideas, and you can hire a motor scooter ($20 per day). Giant kiwi statue in the front garden; TV lounge, smoky pool room, and piano inside. Free shuttle service to ferry, buses, trains, and hitching points. Long-term locked storage; off-street parking. Dorms $16; singles $23, weekly $105; double with sheets $40. Tent sites $10. Breakfast $5. Key deposit $10. Book ahead.

Trekkers (VIP), 213 Cuba St. (tel. 385 2153; fax 385 8873; email info@trekkers.co.nz). The views of fire escapes and the street are less than inspiring, but this warren of long, branching hallways and bare-walled bunkrooms is wonderfully central. Communal space and kitchen facilities may be lacking, but most everyone congregates in the popular cafe or bar downstairs (Th-F 7-8pm $2 handles). Backpacker travel center **The Hub** (tel. 385 3580), is in the lobby. Master agent for Kiwi Experience. Bunks $19, twins $21. Hotel rooms have bath and TV (singles $59, twins $79), while motel rooms in a separate building come with bath, cooking facilities, TV, and separate bedrooms (3 beds $89, 4 beds $99). 24hr. reception.

Maple Lodge, 52 Ellice St. (tel. 385 3771). Just around the corner from Brougham St. Another of Mt. Victoria's small and old wooden houses, the quietly informal Maple Lodge is off the typical tourist loop but features a homey atmosphere and affable manager. Decent kitchen, TV lounge, dinette, book swap, and wood-fired stove. Weekly long-term storage. Dorms $16; singles $18; twins $34; doubles $36. Reception 8:30am-noon and after 5pm.

Beethoven's, 89 Brougham St. (tel. 384 2226). If the no-smoking signs posted everywhere or the complicated entry don't warn you that this place isn't for everyone, then the owner likely will himself. Once you've been accepted into this cluttered turn-of-the century house, you may be in for an unforgettable experience. Drag yourself downstairs at 8am for the superb complimentary breakfast in the garden patio and a "good morning" to your fellow guests, enforced by Beethoven's ebullient owner. Alas, one of New Zealand's oldest hostels may soon shut down—get there while you can. Dorms $16-17. Doubles $40. Long-term rates "for nice people," says the owner; others stay on the varying daily rate. Cash only.

Tinakori Lodge B&B, 182 Tinakori Rd. (tel. 473 3478; fax 472 5554; email 100035.3214@compuserve.com), in Thorndon. From the railway station, turn right on Bunny St., follow it through Molesworth St., and turn left on Hawkestone; the lodge is at the top of the street. With leaded glass windows, a gracious courtyard, a solarium, and airy white rooms, the Tinakori is the home you wish were yours. Breakfast is an extravaganza of fruit, cereals, cheese, fresh bread, and a daily hot dish. Singles $70, with bath $85; doubles or twins $95, with bath $120.

The Terrace Lodge, 291 The Terrace (tel. 382 9506; fax 475 3719), at Ghuznee St. This well-kept turn-of-the-century cottage appears to be sliding slowly down the hill. Pale pink rooms all differ slightly in size and set-up (with any or all of the following: desk, TV, sink, springy mattress). All have heating panels. Free tea, coffee, and morning papers in the sunny front lounge. Cooking facilities. Communal bathrooms. Dorms $16; singles $40; doubles and twin $40; long-term rates negotiable.

Apollo Lodge Motel, 49 Majoribanks St. (tel./fax 385 1849), at the end of Brougham St. Big, new, and slightly pricey motel rooms with separate bedrooms, TV, phone, fridge, microwave, and tea and coffee. The typical cinderblock-and-sliding-glass-doors rooms are routine; brightly painted "pink block" rooms have a fresher feel and benchtop cooking facilities. A third option is the classy colonial-style house rooms with wooden banisters, fireplaces, and wall windows. Off-street parking, breakfast available. Twins and doubles $100; family rooms (sleep 4-5) $140.

Downtown Backpackers (VIP), 1 Bunny St. (tel. 473 8482; fax 471 1073), across from the Railway Station. While it's close to transport terminals, Downtown is on the other side of town from many of Wellington's choice bars and restaurants. Formerly the grand Waterloo Hotel and one-time choice of the Queen, most of the elegance has faded away, leaving traces in finely papered hallways and dark wood. Most rooms with bath. Free pickups. Mega kitchen facilities, cafe, lounges, and inhouse bar (open from 5pm; Wednesday night pool competitions). Bunks $18; twin bunks $20. Singles $32, and doubles $40. Linen provided on request. Internet access in the lobby. 24hr. reception. Free blankets on request.

Hutt Park Holiday Village, 95 Hutt Park Rd. (tel. 568 5913; fax 568 5914), in Lower Hutt some 13km from Wellington. By far the closest motorcamp, it's mostly a pass-through stay for ferry-catchers. Kitchen, TVs, trampolines, and playground. Pohutukawa-lined tent sites $18 for 2; caravans $20; small, basic cinderblock cabin units $32 for 2. Nicer tourist cabins with kitchen $42 (extra person $8-11).

FOOD

Wellington boasts a global menu with a preponderance of Chinese, Malaysian, Thai, and Indian food. **Lambton Quay** and **Willis Street** are full of lunch spots, but are rather dead at night. The fashionable length of **Courtenay Place** is where Lambton Quay's young and well-salaried migrate on evenings and weekends, while **Cuba Street** is riddled with smaller, cheaper, ethnic restaurants and cafes. You'll find groceries at **New World** supermarket on Wakefield St., at the corner with Cambridge Terr. (open daily 8am-10pm). **Cuba Fruit Mart,** 168 Cuba St. (tel. 385 0634), is a fruit and veggie wholesaler (open M-F 7am-6pm, Sa-Su 8am-1:30pm).

Cafes

Cafes are designated as such because they sell espresso, but you'll also find good food within their walls, or on their patios.

The Krazy Lounge (tel. 801 6652), at the corner of Cuba and Dixon St. Bizarre decor and techno soundtrack, with prices that reflect the privilege of being served by hip staff in tight T-shirts while sitting in leather booths under large, bisected, life-size papier-mache cow installations. The $3 muffins are loaded with goodies and are too big to finish. Both the delicious salads ($8-10) and hot breakfasts (up to $10) are huge. The espresso drinks rock your world at any hour ($2.50). Open M-F 7:30am-late, Sa-Su 9am-late.

Tree House Cafe, 123 Cuba St. (tel. 385 0887), upstairs above Narnia. Escape into the comfortable loft space that you dreamed of building as a kid. The vegetarian-friendly food (around $5) and quality coffee ($2.50) are almost superfluous as you retreat for the day with your book, or enjoy the nightly activity of music, poetry or film. Open M-F 9am-late, Sa-Su 10am-late.

Espressoholic, 128 Courtenay Pl. (tel. 384 7799), by Taranaki St. Ponder the graffiti of the chic subway station interior over your tall morning black ($2.50). As in its subterranean inspiration, it's often rush hour here; office crowds line the wall booths during the day, chowing $9 burgers or jump-starting their veins with $3.50 lattes. At night, an eclectic crowd of locals, students, artsy twentysomethings, and bar-hoppers soak up terrific espresso and chatter away to the techno beat. Open Su-M 7:30am-midnight, Tu-Th 7:30am-1am, F-Sa 7:30am-3am.

Midnight Espresso, 178 Cuba (tel. 384 7014), by the corner of Cuba St. and Vivian St. You can ash on the well-worn floors and not worry if anyone saw you. Time stands still in this cafe, fixed by the constant presence of good music and laid-back students. Open daily until 3am.

The Lido, (tel. 499 6666), corner of Wakefield St. and Victoria St., near the Civic Centre. Slightly upscale and patronized primarily by suits, the Lido has table service, outdoor seating and excellent jazz on Sunday nights. Open M-F 7:30am-1am, Sa 9:30am-1am, Su 10am-1am.

Restaurants and Takeaways

Ali Baba, 203 Cuba St. (tel. 384 3014). The pin-marked map inside asks, "Where have you been in Turkey?" Ali Baba, with its gorgeous rugs and soothing Turkish rhythms, is so authentic that they might as well put it on the map. Not even the most skillful 40 thieves could steal away your kebab once you've had a bite. Doners come in 3 bulging sizes ($5, $7-8, $10). Take your little gold-rimmed basket and hunker down on a low cushion seat in your own cozy rug den. Open M-Th 11am-11pm, F-Sa 11am-midnight, Su noon-9pm.

Kopi Malaysian Restaurant, 103 Willis St. (tel. 499 5570). Manager James has built a strong local following of people who obviously know good food when they eat it, or savor it, as you will when you try the lamb korma ($13.50) or Nasi Paging ($14.50). Get there early or be prepared for a wait. Open daily 10am till late.

One Red Dog, 9-11 Blair St. (tel. 384 9777), off Courtenay Place. The menu ambitiously lists locations in Paris and London, but judging from the crowds, it's not just wishful thinking. There's never a dull bite with these thick pies bolstered by intriguing toppings (medium $12, large $15). Call ahead or expect a wait at dinner. Open daily from 10am.

Sahara Cafe, 39 Courtenay Pl. (tel. 385 6362). Sahara's speedy service will ease your anguish with deliciously filling lamb ($5), chicken ($7), and falafel ($5) doners. Open M-Tu 10am-midnight, W-Th 10am-2am, F-Sa 24hr.

Uncle Chang's Restaurant, 72 Courtney Place (tel. 801 9568). The banal name and decor belie the original and flavorful dishes, especially the Sichuan specialties ($14.50). At lunch, you can select from a feast of carefully prepared entrees from spring rolls to beef rolls ($3-$4). Open for lunch and dinner daily.

Catch Sushi, 48 Courtenay Pl. (tel. 801 9352). A sharp young crowd of suits crams the long table at lunch to snag salmon and yellow tail rolls off the belt. The belt dinners add up quickly if you're not counting; try the $12 sashimi set with miso soup, rice, and a selection of fish to build your own pieces. Takeaway available: an $8 set has 8 pieces of varying size. Open M-F for lunch 11:30am-2:30pm and dinner from 5pm, Sa for dinner from 6pm.

Wellington Fish Supply, 40 Molesworth St. (tel. 472 4059), just across from Parliament. Lurking in an ancient red building is a city institution, a 100-year-plus tradition of ruling-class fish 'n' chips. Lick your fingers knowing the Parliament's bills are stained with the same grease. Takeaways have been so popular with politicians over the years that a group of Labor MPs in the 1980s were known as the "Fish 'n' Chips" brigade. A sizeable, fresh fish 'n' chips is $3. Open M-Th 9am-7:30pm, F 9am-9pm, Sa 9am-7:30pm.

Bandong Country Food, 134 Cuba St. (tel. 384 5489). There's not much delicacy here, but it's still one of the better values around; nothing on the menu is over $9. The $5 "special meal," roti canai, is the ultimate bargain, with heaps of flat roti bread and a bowl of your choice of curry (slightly soupy, but flavorful and excellent for soaking bread). Open for lunch M-F 11am-2:30pm, Sa noon-2:30pm; for dinner M-Tu 5-10pm, W-Sa 5-10:30pm, Su 5-9:30pm.

BARS AND NIGHTLIFE

The cosmopolitan nightlife of Wellington sustains a noticeable split between business chic and skater cool. The **Courtenay Place** stretch is clogged with stylishly slick bars frequented by suits; most are indistinguishable from one another. For those who can't take the rock remixes any longer, the pubs on **Cuba Street** and the nearby blocks tend to be just as crowded but more relaxed. While Wellington party life mainly centers around bars and pubs, the weekend rush to the late-night clubs begins at 3am (when all the pubs close) and lasts until 5 or 6am. For all the latest happenings, grab the free weekly *City Voice* from newsstands or check cafes for fliers.

Bar Bodega (tel. 384 8212), at the corner of Willis and Abel Smith St. There are few lounge chairs and back tables in this small space, but come for some of the best live music in town. Bodega features local or touring bands Tu-Sa nights, and an eclectic but leaning-toward-alternative crowd fills the house most nights. Cover charge up to $5 on weekends. $2.50 champagne 9-11pm on Tuesdays. Handles $4. Bar snacks available. Open daily 4pm-3am.

Molly Malones (tel. 384 2896), on the corner of Courtenay Pl. and Taranaki St. Every hour is happy hour at this popular pub with live Irish and cover bands every night at no door charge. There's a Whiskey Bar upstairs offering 87 different reasons to give yourself a kick in the pants. Tidy but casual dress. Open daily 11am-1am.

Valve, on Vivian St. by Cuba St. Entrance to this windowless little joint is, as advertised, through a knocked-out hole in the brick. Decidedly anti-cosmopolitan, inside are the strutting grounds for the young, pierced, and studiously cool members of Wellington's alternative scene. Rock and dance music usually reigns, with occasional live bands and Thursday night garage band jams. Tuesday's $2 handles pack the house. Open Tu-Th and Sa 8pm-3am, F 6pm-3am.

The Grand, 69-71 Courtenay Pl. (tel. 801 7800). Like Las Vegas casinos, the bars of Courtenay Pl. compete for attention with imperious names and displays of glamour. This 4-floor giant is the current multi-media King of the Boulevard, though the question remains: is it all a mirage? Tidy dress with shoes. Open Tu-Su from 11am.

Tatou, 22 Cambridge Terr. (tel. 384 3112), by the corner of Courtenay Place and Cambridge Terr. This leading wee-hours option holds Wellington's latest liquor license. Throbbing techno and strobe lights sustain many until sunrise. There's a big rush when the bars close at 3am. Tidy dress. $3 cover. Open Th-Sa 9pm-8am.

THEATER AND CINEMA

Downstage (tel. 801 6946), at the corner of Courtenay Pl. and Cambridge Terr. by the YHA. Wide range of productions from classic and modern drama to cabaret and comedy. $27, students $20, gallery seats $15.

Circa (tel. 801 7992), at the end of Taranaki St. next to the Museum of New Zealand. Mainstage plays and a studio with smaller, more experimental shows and cheaper prices. $25, students $19. Ticket office open M-Sa 10am-4pm, or from 4pm until the hour before the show.

Bats, 1 Kent Terr. (tel. 802 4175), is the most experimental, on-the-fringe venue, putting on exclusively New Zealand artists—you won't stumble into any of the classics here ($15-18, students or unwaged $10-12).

The St. James Theatre, 75 Courtenay Place (tel. 802 4060). Recently restored, and home to the Royal New Zealand Ballet as well as opera and orchestra performances. Show prices vary.

Wellington Festival and Convention Centre (tel. 801 4242), stages mostly lectures and classical and chamber music concerts at the Michael Fowler Centre and other venues ($6 service charge for phone bookings). Also book through MFC Ticketing, 111 Wakefield St. (tel. 801 4263).

Cinemas: Paramount, 25 Courtenay Pl. (tel. 384 4488), dishes out arthouse cinema fare, while **Embassy** (tel. 384 7657), at the far end of Courtenay Pl., shows commercial cinema flicks. **Hoyt 5** (tel. 472 5182) is located at Manners Mall.

SIGHTS AND ACTIVITIES

Ever since the national government was moved from Auckland in 1865, Wellington has fancied itself the country's trend-setter. With a recent spate of massive construction and improvement projects, the capital today is a lavish mix of architecture, urbanized hills and valleys, and renewed harborfront. Pick up a *Museums, Archives, and Galleries* brochure for details on many Wellington sights.

Civic Centre

With an impressive collection of public buildings, Wellington's **Civic Centre** clusters around a bricked space that makes for fine people-watching on sunny weekends. At one side sits the elegant **City Gallery** (tel. 801 3021), which uses its terrific space for well-curated, contemporary exhibitions featuring both national and international artists of top caliber. *(Open daily 11am-5pm. Admission by donation, except for some of the biggest name exhibitions.)* In the far corner of the Civic Centre reposes the huge, circular **Michael Fowler Centre,** an events and conference center. Take a quick look inside at the two towering modern Maori pillars, *Te Pou O Wi Tako.*

Just under the base of the bridge sits **Capital E** (tel. 384 8502), a new children's center with constantly changing Events, Exhibitions, and Experiences for *les Enfants. (Open daily 10am-5pm. Admission varies with events.)* Cross the bridge to the harborfront and the green public space of **Frank Kitts Park.** To the left up Jervois Quay sits the **Wellington Maritime Museum** (tel. 472 8904), constructed in 1891. Stalwart ship-lovers will be captivated by its extensive and somewhat disturbing ship models. *(Open M-F 9:30am-4pm, Sa-Su 1-4:30pm. Admission by donation.)*

Te Papa

The massive hangar-like structure on the harborfront at the end of Taranaki St. is the incredible new **Museum of New Zealand Te Papa Tongarewa** (tel. 381 7000). *(Museum open daily 10am-6pm, Th until 9pm. Admission free.)* Te Papa, as it's affectionately called, is Wellington's pride and joy, and an ambitious attempt to both celebrate and reconcile the country's identity while still packing in the crowds. Te Papa opened its doors in February 1998 and reached its first anniversary goal of 700,000 visitors in only four months. **Free admission** may be Te Papa's first appeal, but enjoyable exhibits on New Zealand's land, history, culture, and art are the real attractions. For slightly stiffer fees, try the interactive exhibits: a virtual earthquake, a virtual reality swim with whales, virtual sheep-shearing (complete with virtual blood if you do a bad job), a virtual bungy jump, and the virtual "Time Warp" that takes you through prehistoric, moa-laden New Zealand and ends by shooting you up out of a volcano.

Parliament

Another of Wellington's visual attractions (or distractions, as the case may be) is the government building known as the **Beehive,** home to the offices of the Prime Minister and other bigwigs. *(Open M-F 9am-5pm, Sa 10am-4pm, Su 1-4pm.)* The building is somewhat of an embarrassment to many Wellingtonians who have since renounced the architecture of the 70s, and may actually be moved a few hundred yards to extend and complete the missing wing of the Edwardian Neoclassical **Parliament House.** At any time of year, the **visitors center** (tel. 471 9999) on the ground floor offers free hourly tours of the grounds and buildings that would otherwise be off-limits. See sights like the carefully designed Maori Affairs Select Committee Room and the huge art installation representing New Zealand's cultural traditions. The gorgeously ornate **Victorian Gothic Parliamentary Library,** restored from a 1992 fire, is part of the tour as well. You can even send a letter postmarked "Parliament" from here. Call 471 9999 or look for the flag flying over the entrance to find out when you can watch the House in action.

Point of Order

The Labour Party leader is loudly denouncing a bill. The Prime Minister is tossing a grin to his Deputy Prime Minister. Mr. Speaker, in a powdered wig, is checking his notes. Alliance Greenies in the corner are murmuring over the morning paper. An MP two rows back is sleeping. Welcome to the **New Zealand Parliament House** (open to the public Tu 2-6pm, W 2-10pm, Th 10am-6pm). The best time to watch is the hour-long "Questions for Oral Answer" session (around 2pm), when MPs get to bicker, interrupt, point fingers, laugh contemptuously, and generally carry on like national leaders should. Come early, as a line can form for this popular session. The visitors sitting obediently in the balconies above the chamber are much better-behaved: they've been told not to place their hands on the balustrade, much less talk, laugh, or throw things (especially since all their bags, jackets, phones, pagers, and writing utensils were taken upon entrance). Cameras are emphatically not allowed, lest you escape with a snapshot of a sleeping Member of Parliament.

Libraries and Cathedrals

Across Molesworth St. and up a bit is the **National Library** (tel. 474 3000). Sleep easy knowing it houses over 1.8 million books, including the **Cartoon Archives,** the **Gay and Lesbian Archives** (curator tel. 474 3000; open M-F 9am-5pm), and the **Alexander Turnbull Library** with its collection of early printed materials, extensive photographic archives, and occasional exhibitions in the gallery. *(Open M-F 9am-5pm, Sa 9am-1pm for research and gallery only.)* Around the corner are the **National Archives,** 10 Mulgrave St. (tel. 499 5595), and the dimly lit, thick-walled, guarded vault in which the original copy of the 1840 Treaty of Waitangi is kept. *(Open M-F 9am-5pm, Sa 9am-1pm.)* A short walk away is the 1866 **Old St. Paul's Cathedral** (tel. 473 6722), Wellington's old colonial church with superb stained glass. Although the church was built in Gothic style, the medium of choice is native New Zealand timber instead of stone.

Museums

Literary history buffs can head up Molesworth St. to the painstakingly restored **Katherine Mansfield Birthplace,** 25 Tinakori Rd. (tel./fax 473 7268), where New Zealand's beloved short story writer spent her first six years. An elaborate doll house based entirely on one of her story's descriptions has been carefully constructed; strong debate apparently raged over what shade "oily spinach green" should be. *(Open daily 10am-4pm. Admission $4, children $1, student discounts and guided tours available.)* **The Colonial Cottage Museum,** 68 Nairn St. (tel. 384 9122), dates from 1858, 30 years prior to the Mansfield Birthplace and not long after Wellington was settled by Europeans. *(Open M-F 10am-4pm and Sa-Su 1pm-4pm. Admission $3.)* Catch the Eastbourne bus to Queensgate from Courtenay Pl. to get to **Lower Hutt's Dowse Art Museum,** 16 Laings Rd. (tel. 570 6500), with one of the country's best collections of craftwork. *(Open M-F 10am-4pm, Sa-Su 11am-5pm. Free.)* If you miss the thwack of the national past-time, the **Cricket Museum** (tel. 385 6602 or 384 3171), in the Basin Reserve grandstand, offers a historical perspective and lots of old bats. *(Open in summer daily 10am-3:30pm; in winter M-F 10am-3:30pm; all day during matches. Admission $3, children $1.)* To see bats of a different sort, take bus #10 to Newtown Park to the **Wellington Zoo** (tel. 389 8130), with its tuatara, weta, and kiwi exhibits. *(Open daily 9:30am-5pm. Admission $9, children $4.50.)*

Gardens and Tours

Similarities between Wellington and San Francisco may come to mind when you ride the **Wellington Kelburn Cable Car,** 610m up to the Kelburn Terminal. *(Departs every 10min. from Cable Car Ln. on Lambton Quay. M-F 7am-10pm, Sa-Su 9am-10pm. $1.50 one-way, students $1, children 70¢.)* Disembark atop the city's impressive 26-hectare public **Botanic Gardens**. The Gardens are always open, though some special spots, like the excessively gorgeous **Lady Norwood Rose Garden,** have special hours (open 10am-4pm). Walk down the lush length of the gardens and follow Bolton St. out to the terrace and downtown. Anyone with a botanical bent should also check out the **Otari Native Botanic Garden** (tel. 475 3245), the largest collection of native New Zealand plants anywhere (take the #14 Wilton bus).

In addition to the Botanic Gardens, killer views are to be had from atop **Mt. Victoria,** rising from the city's south end. You can drive, take bus #20 (runs M-F), or hike it up (30min.). Some locals assert that the view from the **ECNZ wind turbine** is even better. Take bus #7 from the Railway Station or Willis St. up to the shops on Brooklyn St.; there are signposts from there. It's a steep climb. Guided city **tours** cater to those with more money and less time (the visitors center has a full list of operators).

Turn the scenic views around by taking the **WestpacTrust Ferry** (tel. 499 1273), a cheap and excellent way to get out onto the harbor. Full of Wellingtonians escaping the city, it leaves from Queens Wharf (M-F 8 per day, Sa-Su 5 per day) and crosses to the little cafe-and-antique-shop community of **Day's Bay** ($7 one-way) with its small but popular swimming beach. A bit farther down is the village of **Eastbourne,** similarly bedecked with cafes, little blue penguins, and a pebbly and rather narrow beach good for a wander. The ferry also stops at **Somes Island** (M-F noon, Sa-Su 3 per day). A former quarantine island with historical significance, the smallpox and rats have now been eradicated, and DOC is developing the island's potential as a wildlife sanctuary. It's a good three-hour getaway; there's not much to do but picnic, wander the re-vegetating bush, and admire a 360° panorama of Wellington and surrounds.

OUTDOORS

Although Wellington is better known for its cultural options, this being New Zealand, there are plenty of outdoor opportunities. The **Northern, Southern,** and **Eastern Walkways,** laid out in leaflets from the tourist or DOC office, are tame and accessible walks through the city's greenbelt and coastline. The **Red Rocks Coastal Walk** is a terrific 8km round-trip along the jagged southern coastline, taking you past the pillow lava formation of Red Rocks. The walk then heads out to the crashing surf of **Sinclair Head,** where in winter a colony of fat fur seals is sure to be lazing around.

Oriental Beach, though popular with city dwellers, is less a beach than a grassy strip of peopled promenade overlooked by trendy cafes. Better beaches can be found on the east side of **Miramar Peninsula.** In the **Seatown** area Scorching Bay is reputed to be a good one; **Lyall Bay** has a patrolled main swimming stretch and relatively consistent surfing breaks at the airport end. Seatown beaches are within walking distance of the #2 Miramar bus. Along the southern coastline the bays are rockier and rougher: **Island Bay,** and particularly **Houghton Bay** and **Owhiro Bay** are better for surfing and scuba diving than for safe swimming. Wellington surfing is rather wind-dependent: winter southerlies make for stronger waves, but breaks are more consistent east of the Wairarapa towns of Martinborough and Masterton. Get a list of outdoor outfitters from the visitors center, but be aware that most true adventure destinations are a fair distance from the city.

FESTIVALS

January looked at July: "Whatcha got?" March upped the ante. And then November held firm. The annual competition between the months for best festival is always intense, and the cards for the 1999 pot are on the table. January and February have combined their forces for the **Summer City Festival,** a brilliant parade of concerts, celebrations, and events like Sunday night jazz in the Botanic Gardens, mass walks up Mt. Victoria, and a Pacific Island festival. March's ace is the **Fringe Festival,** an annual theatrical event that celebrates alternative and experimental artistic offerings. April plays the joker with the ASB Bank **Laugh! Festival,** showcasing comedians from inside and outside New Zealand. Just when it looks the game is up, July presents the **Kings and Queens of the Silver Screen** in the annual **Wellington Film Festival.** And, last but hardly least, November's week-long **Devotion Festival,** a celebration of Wellington's gay and lesbian community, may make you flush, if not straight.

Terra Firma in Transit

Forget the wind—residents know that Wellington's real attention-grabber is the ground beneath their feet, which contains a massive fault line. Few buildings in town are brick; the newly renovated Parliament buildings and the Museum of New Zealand are both equipped with state-of-the-art "base isolators" and "seismic gaps" that allow the buildings to move over 30cm without structural damage. An 1855 earthquake that rocked the city at 8.0 on the Richter scale raised the foreshore over two feet. The potential damage such a quake could do today makes the wind look veritably charming—over eight billion dollars is one estimate. A spate of small tremors shook the city in 1997, prompting hopes that the stress is being alleviated, as well as darker forecasts that "the big one" is coming.

■ Near Wellington: Kapiti Coast

Arcing up the west coast for 32km, and a 40-minute drive from the city, the Kapiti Coast is Wellington's scenic bedroom. The one-stop towns and mildly hokey tourist attractions sit among small wildlife sanctuaries, stretches of beach, and the centerpiece of wild, bird-filled Kapiti Island. Easily accessible by Wellington train or national buses, the coast makes for a good daytrip or a quiet weekend away from the city.

Several Wellington tour operators "do" Kapiti, but the truth is that you're not going to get much out of the coast if you're tied to a van. There's a fair amount of regional traffic all the way from Otaki to Paekakariki, and some hitchers try to bum rides. Others take the train to Paraparaumu from Wellington rather than hitchhike out of the big city.

KAPITI ISLAND Unfortunately, a three-month advance booking requirement makes Kapiti Island accessible only to locals or the insanely organized traveler. You must book a landing permit from the Wellington DOC office ($8, children $4), and indicate which day you plan to go. The DOC keeps human influence to a relative minimum by only letting 50 people visit per day. These lucky visitors can enjoy a re-vegetating nature reserve with dramatic green slopes (lacking the introduced mammals that have decimated mainland avian populations) teeming with bird life. Spotted kiwi and other endangered native species make their home here. The waters between the island and the mainland are a marine reserve, but scuba diving, boating, and any other water activity besides fishing is allowed; the western side and northern end are reportedly the best for scuba diving.

PAEKAKARIKI At the southern point of the Kapiti Coast, Paekakariki is somewhat less flashy than its name, "resting place of the green parrot," might suggest. The town's main street is shorter than its name, but residential areas string out along its long golden strip of shell-filled beach. **Tranz Metro** (tel. 498 3000) trains from Wellington stop here frequently (30min., $6), as do **Newmans** and **InterCity** buses on request ($14). One of the best things about Paekakariki is getting there: if you have your own transportation, take **Paekakariki Hill Road,** which branches off SH1, to climb the hill as it winds up through a blindingly green valley before turning the corner to a drop-dead view of the Tasman Sea and the entire curve of Kapiti Coast. **Kapiti Island** and the **Marlborough Sounds** float in the distance. A newer craze in Paekakariki (near the BP station) is yet another invention in the country's endless search for an adrenaline rush: the **Fly By Wire** (tel. (025) 300 366), a world-wide patented thrill ride in an open-air rocket-like contraption (7min. ride $99; includes video).

PARAPARAUMU The main town of the Kapiti and full of retired folks, Paraparaumu is home to the illustrious **Coastlands Shopperworld,** overlooked by the gleaming white **Our Lady of Lourdes statue** on the hill above town. The town also has a beachfront extension (the town of Paraparaumu Beach), with a developed shorefront complex. While its narrow beach has rockin' views, it's better suited to water activities than to lounging in the sand. The **Kapiti Information Centre** (tel. 298 8195) is an island in the Coastlands shopping complex (open M-Sa 9am-4pm, Su 10am-3pm). **Tranz Metro** runs daily from Wellington as far as Paraparaumu every hour and more frequently at peak times (45min., $7.50). **TranzScenic** stops at Paraparaumu on its way north, as do **InterCity, Newmans,** and **Mt. Cook** ($14). Paraparaumu has a ridiculously complex local bus service: **Mana Coach** (tel. (0800) 801 700) runs to Paraparaumu Beach and Waikanae (M-Sa); try to catch the faster bus #2 or 3 ($1.60) from **Coastlands** (which also happens to have the post office and pharmacy).

Motels stretch all along Kapiti Rd. and down the beachfront, but **Barnacles Seaside Inn,** 3 Marine Parade (tel. 298 4856; fax 298 7142), is cheap, ivy-covered, and beautifully seaside. Rooms are well kept and private, with heaters, electric blankets, original wood furnishings from the 20s, and shared baths. (Dorms $15; singles $20; twins and doubles $35. Linen $5.) North of Paraparaumu, **Waikanae Beach** is the region's finest, with a long stretch of often uncrowded white sand. Waikanae's **DOC office** (tel. 293 2191) is on Parata Rd. (open M-F 8am-4:30pm). The #5 **Mana Coach** runs from the railway station at Paraparaumu to Waikanae (M-Sa, hourly, $2). It also makes stops at two worthy attractions. The **Southward Car Museum** (tel. 297 1221) has an impressive collection of vintage autos and motorcycles, and the **Lindale Centre** (tel. 297 0916), a country farm complex, will put a cherry on top of your day with outstanding homemade ice cream. There's also a cheese factory, barnyard, and motor camp with tourist flats. (Open daily 9am-5pm.)

■ Near Wellington: The Wairarapa

In summer the Wairarapa coast buzzes with Wellingtonian daytrippers and weekenders. While gardens brighten almost every town, the **wineries** centered around **Martinborough** are the most celebrated attraction. Divers, surfers, and other wild-at-heart funsters all flock to the cold water coast (though south of Riversdale to Tora is off-limits for surfing). Those with a taste for aesthetics tend to devote a day or few to exploring the area's natural offerings, such as the high and mighty **Castle Rock** (east of Masterton on Castlepoint Road), **Palliser Bay,** with its fur seal colony and majestic **Putangirua Pinnacles, Mt. Bruce National Wildlife Centre,** and **Tararua Forest Park.** Transport is a little pricey, since cars or tour buses are needed to access the coast, but once there, the attractions are easy on the wallet.

■ Masterton

The main transportation hub and tourist information mecca of the Wairarapa, Masterton (pop. 19,800) has grown out of its agricultural roots but still hosts the fantastically popular annual **Golden Shears** sheep-shearing competition (March 4-7, 1999). **Queen Street** and **Chapel Street (SH2)** are home to most of Masterton's cafes, stores, and restaurants.

PRACTICAL INFORMATION Tranz Metro (Masterton tel. (04) 498 3000 ext. 44933) runs to Wellington more frequently than the bus (1½hr., 1-3 per day, $11.50). **Tranzit Coachlines** (tel. 377 1227) depart from the Queen St. Terminal for Palmerston North (2hr., 1-2 per day, $15) via Mt. Bruce Wildlife Centre (25min., $6); and daily for Wellington (2½hr., 4:40pm, $13) via Carterton (15min., $2.20), Greytown (25min., $2.60), and Featherston (40min., $3). **Tranzit** also heads directly to these small Wairarapa towns (M-F 4 per day). **Car rentals** are available at **Graeme Jones,** 88 Dixon St. (tel. 378 6667). The **Tourism Wairarapa Head Office,** 5 Dixon St. (tel. 378 7373; fax 378 7042), sits at the corner of Queen St. and Lincoln Rd. and sells hut tickets and fishing licenses (open M-F 9-5pm, Sa-Su 10am-4pm). Pick up a free guide to the Wairarapa region. The **DOC office** (tel. 378 2061) is on South Rd. (open M-F 8:30am-4:30pm). Get quick cash at **ANZ** on Queen St. (open M-F 9am-4:30pm), or at **National Bank** on Lincoln Rd. (open M-F 9am-4:30pm). In an **emergency,** dial **111.** The **post office** is on Queen St. (open M-F 9am-5pm). The **telephone code** is **06.**

ACCOMMODATIONS AND FOOD Those limited by transportation can stay at the spacious and comfortably lived-in **Masterton Backpackers (YHA)**, 22 Victoria St. (tel. 377 2228). Friendly manager Lynette offers encyclopedic knowledge of the area. Free pickup and dropoff from the bus or train; once there, use one of their free bicycles to get around (dorms $14; doubles $16). **The Empire Lodge,** 94 Queen St. (tel. 377 1902; fax 377 2298), is a centrally located hotel above O'Toole's Slug and Lettuce Pub. Slightly dim rooms come with bath, and have bathtubs and coffee- and tea-making facilities ($45). **O'Toole's Slug and Lettuce Pub,** 94 Queen St. (tel. 377 3087), offers hearty helpings of good food, including the tender Slug Sandwich ($10). Small tables make friends of strangers. (Cash only; open daily from 11am.) More formal and expensive, with incredibly fresh food and a tasteful, candle-lit atmosphere is **Bloomfields Restaurant** (tel. 377 4305), on the corner of Chapel St. and Lincoln Rd. Dip into the bowl of spicy sauteed vegetables topped with dried figs and cashews ($12.50), or the kumara, pumpkin, and walnut pie and salad ($12.50; open for lunch W-F from noon, for dinner M-Sa from 6pm). Your markets are **Write Price** (tel. 378 7592) on the corner of Queen St. and Bruce St. or **New World** on Church St.

SIGHTS AND ACTIVITIES Masterton's 32-hectare **Queen Elizabeth Park** on Dixon St., with its suspension bridge, rose gardens, small aquarium, pedal-boat pond, and miniature railway, is perfect for a picnic. (Railway runs in summer Sa-Su 1-4pm.) The last Sunday in February, the park is transformed by the **Masterton Wine and Food Festival,** spawned by the growing fame of the area's vineyards and wineries. Along with Wellington tour operators, several Masterton-based operators conduct tours of the Wairarapa's hotspots. **Wairarapa Sightseeing Tours** (run by Tranzit Coachlines, tel. 377 1227) tours Mt. Bruce (daily 11:40am, $18), Cape Palliser and Martinborough (M, W, and Sa 9:30am, $50), and farms in the region (Tu, Th, and Su 11:30am, $44, YHA and family discounts). Located 30km north of Masterton on SH2, the **Mt. Bruce National Wildlife Centre** (tel./fax 375 8004) is your chance to see both a kiwi and a tuatara in the same day. (Open daily 9:30am-4pm. Admission $6, children $1.50, families $12.) Now boasting 15 different aviaries and outdoor reserves, Mt. Bruce bursts with pride over its many successful captive breeding programs. The wildlife center has numerous displays on the management regimes for rearing threatened native birds.

Say it Ten Times Fast

In a forgotten corner east of Palmerston North and north of the Wairarapa (40.35°S, 176.53°E, to be precise), within 10km of the hamlet of Kaitoke, just east of SH2, but close to nothing in particular, sits the renowned, unassuming hill of **Taumatawhakatangihangakoauauotamateapokaiwhenuakitanatahu.** The name recounts a Maori legend of Tamatea's lamentation for his beloved, and the extended version of the moniker is the world's longest place name. It also involves a little-known ongoing feud with Australia to claim the place with the longest name in the world. In 1991, the NZ Parliament added the suffix 'kitanatahu" to the end of the name in order to displace then Aussie title holder **"selenmorgideselianjenruledaplanetanbymorletsgogidespoly."**

■ Martinborough

The major wine village of the Wairarapa, Martinborough (some 40km east of Masterton) pays homage to its British roots with streets laid out in the pattern of the Union Jack. High sunshine and low autumnal rainfall make for choice vintages (such as the famed Pinot Noir) from the 20 wineries in the area. Their close proximity makes tours unnecessary. Some of those open year-round are the **Palliser Estate** (tel. 306 9019) on Kitchener St., **Martinborough Vineyard** (tel. 306 9955) on Princes St. (tours M-F), and **Te Kairanga Vineyard** (tel. 306 9122; tours Sa-Su 2pm), on Martin Rd. Most other vineyards are clustered west and south of town. Find guidance for your winery addiction at the **Martinborough Information Centre** (tel. 306 9043), on Kitchener St., or at the **Tourism Wairarapa Head Office** in Masterton. Victorian trinkets, moa bones, and Maori artifacts are all on display at the **Colonial Museum** (open Sa, Su, public holidays, and school holidays 2-4pm). The **Martinborough Country Fair** takes place the first Saturday of February and March, revealing the region's rural splendor, while the **November Wine, Food and Music Festival** gives you the opportunity you've been waiting for to sample the region's best.

Follow the signposted road from Featherston and Martinborough to the beguiling, inviting **Cape Palliser.** The drive alone is attraction enough, as tidal pools along the coast become impromptu venues for the slapstick antics of resident seals. The notice-board at the carpark by the lighthouse describes numerous nearby walks. From the carpark, it's only a 30-minute walk to **Putangirua Pinnacles,** "echo of the bird-calling flute." Sculpted by hundreds of years of rain, these mighty rock formations give breathtaking testament to the will of the elements. Hardy hikers can take the two- to three-hour walk up to the spine-tingling view at the lookout. Two kilometers away, a towering sandstone bluff keeps archaeology buffs happy with its precious, detailed fossils. Four kilometers past Ngawi Village, the ponderously heavy **Kupe's Sail** serves as a natural sandstone monument to the legendary Maori explorer. Cape Palliser is also home to New Zealand's largest fur seal breeding colony, off the main road east of Ngawi Village (breeding time is Nov.-Jan.). For both their safety and yours, look but don't touch the ear-wiggling, flipper-waving marvels.

■ Tararua Forest Park

The **Tararua Forest Park** offers some great hikes off the tourist map, though the weather can be harsh. Covering 117,225 hectares and 75% of the Tararua Range, it was the first forest park established in New Zealand. Marked tracks range through beech forests, alpine grasslands, and even leatherwood shrublands. Severe wind and mist have made this region famous for its capricious weather. Get **hut tickets** from the **DOC office** in Masterton (tel. 378 2061 or Holdsworth DOC ranger tel. 377 0022), local visitors centers, and various hunting and fishing sports shops. The popular **Mt. Holdsworth Circuit** (20km, 2-3 days) begins at **Mt. Holdsworth Lodge,** 20 minutes west of Masterton, and climbs through bush to the mountain before winding its way back to the lodge (huts $4-8). The 15,000-year-old Grade 2 **Waiohine River** runs through the Waiohine Gorge in the southeastern part of the Tararuas. A large swing bridge crosses the river by the carpark for the popular camping and recreation areas nearby, surrounded by rimu, beech, rata, and kahikatea trees. The **Loop Track** (1½hr.) leaves from here to cross through regenerating bush, while the **Cone Hut Track** (6hr. round-trip) climbs to a terrace of the **Tauherenikau River.**

■ Palmerston North

How Palmerston North expects to woo tourists with its nickname of "Knowledge City" is somewhat mysterious, but this city of 72,500 deserves the title. Home to **Massey University,** New Zealand's second-largest university, and a host of other schools, some 40% of the local population is involved with higher education in one way or another. More of a transportation hub than a top destination, the center of the pastoral Manawatu region has the highest movie-going population in the country. Still, "Palmy," as Kiwis call it, can easily occupy you during a day's stopover with its adequate, if not abundant, commercial and dining options.

ORIENTATION AND PRACTICAL INFORMATION

All roads lead to **The Square,** Palmerston North's well-kept central green space. **Rangitikei Street** heads north, while **Fitzherbert Avenue** leads south toward the Manawatu River. **Main Street** heads east and west from the Square. **George Street** is short but offers character rather than commercial buzz.

Trains: TranzScenic (tel. (0800) 802 802) leaves from the Railway Station off Tremaine Ave. Trains leave daily for Auckland (8½hr., 10:55am and nightly except Sa

10pm, $108 day/$97 night) via Ohakune, National Park, and Hamilton; for Wellington (2hr., daily 5:10pm and nightly except Sa 5:25am, $30/28); for Napier (3hr., 10:14am, $44). **Tranz Metro** runs to Wellington via the Kapiti Coast M-F ($18).

Buses: Simply put, Palmerston North is a transportation hub. **InterCity/Newmans** leave from Travel Centre at Pitt and Main St. (tel. 355 5633), and **White Star** (tel. (0800) 800 287) from the courthouse on Main St., both going daily to Wellington (2hr., 1-5 per day, $20-30). InterCity/Newmans also head daily to Auckland (8-10hr., 1-2 per day, $70-85) and Rotorua (5hr., 2-5 per day, $45-55) via Taupo (4hr., $45-60). InterCity/Newmans and White Star go daily to New Plymouth (4hr., 1-2 per day, $30-40) via Wanganui (1½hr., $10-15). InterCity/Newmans and **On Ground Airlines** (tel. (0800) 755 575) head daily to Napier (2¾hr., 2 per day, $35-40). **Tranzit Coachlines** heads to Masterton (1¾hr., 1-2 per day, $15).

Taxis: Palmerston North Taxis (24hr. tel. 357 6076). To railway station $7-8.

Hitchhiking: Thumbers report luck in getting rides out along any of the main roads: Rangitikei St. joins SH1 at Bulls, heading toward the volcanic heartland and Auckland. Napier Rd. (Main St. E.) heads to Napier. Main St. W. and Fitzherbert St. both head to Wellington.

Visitors Center: The Palmerston North Information Centre (tel. 358 5003; fax 356 9841), in the Civic Centre on the Square. Open M-F 8:30am-5pm, Sa-Su 9am-5pm.

DOC: 717 Tremaine Ave. (tel. 358 9004), a good kilometer along from Rangitikei. They're most helpful if you're planning on tackling large undertakings like the Tararuas or Ruahines; they also sell hut passes. Open M-F 9am-4:30pm.

Currency Exchange: BNZ (tel. 358 4149; fax 354 9783), at the corner of the Square and Rangitikei St. Open M-F 9am-4:30pm. **Thomas Cook** (tel. 356 2962), at the corner of Broadway and Princess St., is open M-F 9am-5:30pm.

Library: Knowledge City has just spent $13 million building a wonderful new library on The Square—help 'em recoup by checking out the cafe. The library also has extensive **Internet access** ($5 per 30min.) Open M, Tu, Th 10am-6pm; W, F 10am-8pm; Sa 10am-4pm; Su 1-4pm.

Emergency: Dial 111.

Medical Services: City Health, 22 Victoria Ave. (24hr. tel. 355 3300; pharmacy tel. 355 5287). Open daily 8am-10pm. Palmerston North Hospital, 50 Ruahine St. (tel. 356 9169).

Police: On Church St., off the McDonald's corner of the Square (tel. 357 9999).

Post Office: Several around town, but get your *Poste Restante* at 338 Church St. (tel. 358 5188; fax 356 7111). Open M-F 8am-5:30pm.

Internet Access: At the public library (see above).

Telephone Code: 06.

ACCOMMODATIONS

Not part of the standard backpackers' circuit, Palmerston North is relatively lacking in appealing budget accommodation. More expensive motels are on Fitzherbert Ave.

Peppertree Hostel (YHA), 121 Grey St. (tel. 355 4054), at the intersection of Princess St. and Grey St. Host Cherie runs a tight ship, and the best and busiest budget option in town. TV/VCR lounge, good kitchen, and sheltered deck where smokers are adamantly sent to keep things friendly in the rest of the house. Swarming co-ed bathroom. Off-street parking and bike shed. Linen $2. Small, adequate rooms. Bunks $15 (weekly $85); singles $25; doubles or twins $35; tents $7.50.

Palmerston North Holiday Park, 133 Dittmer Dr. (tel. 358 0349). From Fitzherbert Ave., turn on Park Rd. towards the Esplanade, turn left on Ruha St., and descend into the park. Suitably park-like, with large trees and a riverside spot. Adequate kitchen, sterile TV lounge, trampoline. Tent sites $8.50, powered sites $20 for 2 people. Cabins $28-55 for 2 people, but bring your own blankets.

Grey's Inn, 123 Grey St. (tel. 358 6928; fax 355 0291), next door to the YHA. A small, trim home offering bed and breakfast. Airy rooms with bath have inviting comforters, TVs, and tea and coffee facilities. Continental or cooked breakfast included, as are the attentions of a golden lab and two cats with three eyes and seven legs between 'em. Singles $58; doubles $90; families $120.

The Green Scheme

Soon, there may be more than 500 of them, each a hideous Kermit green, roaming the streets, leaning on storefronts, scattered through yards, even sneaking into homes. You may have looked away at the sight of one, pointed, even laughed. "They should be under lock and chain," you say. But no! They are free, and we are all the better for it. In February 98, Palmy was hit by the **Green Bike Scheme,** a brilliant community initiative based on a similar idea implemented in Amsterdam. More than 500 bicycles have been donated for uninhibited community use. While you ride the hand-painted green bike, you own it. But dart into the dairy to check your lotto ticket, and that may be the last you'll see of "your" bike—finders keepers, losers weepers. Lock it up or remove a pedal, and face the shaming glare of the town. Steal one of the bright yellow companion helmets, and you may find yourself on the cover of *The Daily Standard.* The project promotes noble causes, as its main objective is the development of employment opportunities and skills for disadvantaged persons through the maintenance, painting, and dismantling of the bicycles. Other objectives include the promotion of environmental awareness about recycling and pollution, the creation of low-cost transportation, and the liberation of inanimate objects.

FOOD

Knowledge City needs food for thought and food it has. Anchored by its student population, Palmy has the usual array of takeaways and chain fast food. **George Street** contains more original flavor. **The Square** and its side streets are the main culinary loci.

George Street Deli (tel. 357 6663), corner of George St. and Main St. If the rarity of delis in New Zealand is not reason enough to go here, then the stuffed potatoes ($4) and chorizo rolls ($2) should be. Sandwiches ($5-8) and shakes ($4). Open daily 7:30am-5pm.

Pizza Piazza 16 The Square (tel. 358 7424), by the library. This 19-year-old dive serves thick-crust, gourmet pies from small ($13.50 basic) up to giant ($29.50 gourmet). The $5 6-incher lunch special with soda is a satisfying fill. The other big attraction is their banana SupaShake, a thick blend of mushed fruit, egg, cinnamon and cream ($3.50). Open M-W 11am-9pm, Th 11am-10pm, F-Sa 11am-3am, Su 11am-10pm.

Markets: Truelife Bakery and Lunchbar, 47 The Square (tel. 358 3630). Health food fanatics will find their mini-mecca at this religiously wholefood store. It even smells healthy. Open M-Th 9am-6pm, F 9am-4pm. **Countdown Foods** (tel. 357 3645), at Cuba and George St., is huge. Open M-W 8:30am-8pm, Th-F 8:30am-9pm, Sa-Su 8:30am-7pm. There is a **Flea Market,** Albert St. and Church St., every Saturday from 6am-10am.

Tierra Latina, 133 Broadway St. (tel. 356 5990), does nachos, quesadillas ($5-8) and heaping enchiladas ($15) nicely in its colorful and warm restaurant and bar. Sombreros, candles, and a chicken coop in the rafters provide unusual ambience, sometimes enhanced by a live Latin band. Open daily 11am-2pm and 6-10:30pm, often later on weekends. Occasionally closed Mondays.

NIGHTLIFE

Palmerston North can get lively during the school year—on Saturday rugby days, drinking starts at 3pm. In the Old Post Office building, **Highflyers** (tel. 357 5155), at the corner of Main St. and The Square, delivers frenzied weekend dancing, as well as a cafe and restaurant with an open four-sided fireplace and brick walls (open daily from 11am). **The Celtic Inn** (tel. 357 5571), off Broadway opposite the Downtown Cinema, is an Irish pub with all the trimmings: friendly atmosphere, $5 Guinness, festive music on weekends, and diverse crowd (open M-Sa 11am-1am, and Su 4pm-11pm). Things can get raucous at the **Old Railway Hotel** (tel. 354 9862), at David St.

and Main St. West, what with the big screen TV and the barmaids who have been known to dance on the tables. **The Cobb** (tel. 357 8002), in the Empire Hotel at the corner of Princess and Main St. East, fills its big dance floor on weekends, though the DJ refuses to pick a genre (open nightly). There's more than drinking going on: when in Rome… join the crowds at the hot **Downtown Cinema 8** above a food court (tel. 355 5655; admission W-Su $9.50, M-Tu $7).

SIGHTS AND ACTIVITIES

The west side of downtown, beginning with the snazzy new library and cafe at **the Square,** is touted as the cultural center. Don't be intimidated by the oversized bronze beetles creeping over the roof of the **Manawatu Art Gallery,** 398 Main St. W. (tel. 358 6282), which showcases contemporary works of New Zealand artists. *(Open daily 10am-5pm. Admission by donation.)* Next door is the **Science Centre & Manawatu Museum** (tel. 355 5000). *(Open daily 10am-5pm. Museum free; Science Centre $6, children $4, families $15.)* The museum has good regional cultural history displays, while the Science Centre is full of interactive exhibits. The pinnacle of culture, one block north and several west of The Square, is the **New Zealand Rugby Museum,** 87 Cuba St. (tel. 358 6947). *(Open M-Sa 10am-noon and 1:30-4pm, Su 1:30-4pm. Admission $3, children $1.)* Quite the shrine for die-hard fanatics of The Game, this two-room gallery is cluttered with uniform displays, trophies, and memorabilia. From the world's oldest remaining jersey (tattered 1904 British Isles) to the intricate "All Black Stars" quilt made by an enthusiastic fan to commemorate the team's 1995 World Cup run, the museum has it all—there's even a reference library of famous international games. On Saturdays in winter, go outside to watch the real thing in the **Showgrounds** next door.

SOUTH ISLAND

CANTERBURY

Stretching from the mountainous backbone in the west to the coast of the Pacific Ocean, Canterbury steps gracefully from ambling farmlands and little agricultural burgs to abruptly rising majestic alps. Skiers flock to the treeless heights of the slopes near Christchurch, the country's second-largest city, while summer visitors fall willing victim to the charms of the Banks Peninsula and nearby beaches. Christchurch itself offers the best of Kiwi culture and ethnic dining under the Gothic guise of its British heritage. Extending in orderly blocks from its central cathedral, Christchurch gradually gives way to orchards and vineyards. Farther from the city, green sweeps of the sheep covered Canterbury plains charm visitors on their way down south. Canterbury draws equally from its cosmopolitanism and provincialism—you're apt to find the best of gourmet cafes as well as farmstays here in the agricultural center of the South Island.

> ### ⊛ CANTERBURY HIGHLIGHTS
>
> - Christchurch's vibrant cultural scene (p. 251) features thriving artisans, traditional architecture, and copious festivals.
> - The skiing in Southern Canterbury (see p. 253) is some of the nation's finest.

■ Christchurch

The Garden City remains closely bound to its English roots, but has a flamboyant tilt that could only be Kiwi. The massive bell-tower of its Anglican cathedral casts a conservative shadow over the colorful nightclubs and artsy shops that pepper the city. Named after Oxford's Christ Church College, the city is full of gray and white stone Gothic Revival churches and meeting houses that front the grassy, willowed banks of the Avon River. Christchurch maintains a vibrant community of artists and artisans who instill a proud cultural spirit into the city's 300,000-some inhabitants. Foreigners flock to Christchurch's innumerable seasonal festivals, when street entertainers, flowers, and ethnic food stalls clog Cathedral Square and the nearby Arts Centre. The assortment of museums provides a vivid historical backdrop, outlining the interplay between Maori and European cultures that gave birth to what today is distinctly New Zealand. As the South Island's ruling city, Christchurch sits at the head of the Canterbury Plains against the impressive backdrop of the rounded Port Hills and the more distant spine of the Southern Alps. Although it's the gateway to the more remote promontories of the Banks Peninsula and the prelude to the majesty of the country's best scenery, Christchurch and its many museums and gardens merit a lingering visit.

GETTING THERE

By Plane

The Christchurch airport is about 9km from the city on Memorial Ave., and is served by Air New Zealand, Ansett, United, and a number of Asian and South Pacific carriers. Call for **international** (tel. 374 7100) and **domestic** (tel. 353 7774) flight info. Flights go direct daily to Auckland (1½hr., 1 per hr., $176-388) and Wellington (45min., 1 per hr., $99-219) along with most other domestic destinations. The **Airport "A" bus** ($2.70) leaves from Gloucester St. near Colombo St. and the airport every 30 minutes on weekdays, and hourly on weekends. **Super Shuttles** (tel. 365 5655) costs about $10; a **taxi** to the airport is $20-25. **Ansett** (tel. 371 1185; fax 379 1147) also has an

South Island

Cape Farewell

ABEL TASMAN NATIONAL PARK

Marlborough Sounds

Cook Strait

Tasman Bay

KAHURANGI NATIONAL PARK

Motueka

Nelson

Picton

Blenheim

Karamea

Karamea Bight

Lake Rotoroa

Lake Rotoiti

NELSON LAKES NATIONAL PARK

Westport

Kaikoura

TASMAN SEA

Reefton

PAPAROA NATIONAL PARK

Punakaiki

Hanmer Springs

Greymouth

Lake Sumner

ARTHUR'S PASS NATIONAL PARK

Pegasus Bay

Hokitika

Arthur's Pass

CRAIGIEBURN FOREST PARK

Christchurch

Banks Peninsula

Lake Coleridge

Mount Hutt

Akaroa

Franz Josef Glacier

MOUNT COOK NATIONAL PARK

Methven

Fox Glacier

WESTLAND NATIONAL PARK

Ashburton

Lake Tekapo

Canterbury Bight

Haast

Lake Pukaki

MOUNT ASPIRING NATIONAL PARK

Lake Ohau

Twizel

Lake Benmore

Timaru

Milford Sound

Lake Wanaka

Lake Hawea

Wanaka

Oamaru

Queenstown

Lake Wakatipu

Alexandra

Lake Te Anau

FIORDLAND NATIONAL PARK

Te Anau

Dunedin

Manapouri

Lake Manapouri

Gore

Balclutha

CATLINS FOREST PARK

PACIFIC OCEAN

Invercargill

Bluff

Foveaux Strait

Stewart Island

Halfmoon Bay (Oban)

N

0   50 miles

0   50 kilometers

office on Worcester St. near the visitors center (open M-F 8:30am-5pm). **Air New Zealand** is at 702 Colombo St. (tel. 353 2800; open M-W, F 8:30am-5pm, Th 9am-5pm, Sa 9:30am-2pm). As with every form of transportation in the country, great discounts can be procured simply by booking ahead (see p. 28 for more details).

By Train

To reach the station (tel. (0800) 802 802), located about 3km from Cathedral Sq., head away from town on Riccarton Ave., turn left on Deans Ave., right onto Blenheim Rd. at the roundabout, and finally left on Clarence St. Several hostels offer a free shuttle from the station (6:30-7am), or you can take the $25 Templeton bus (be ready for a 1km walk). Taxis to town cost $10. **TranzScenic** runs daily to Picton (3¼hr., 7:30am, $72) via Kaikoura (2½hr., $41); Invercargill (8¾hr., 8:30am, $117) via Dunedin (5½hr., $74); and Greymouth (4½hr., 9am, $76). TranzScenic has a designated **backpackers car** and offers substantial discounts (30% or more) to students and those who book in advance (see p. 29).

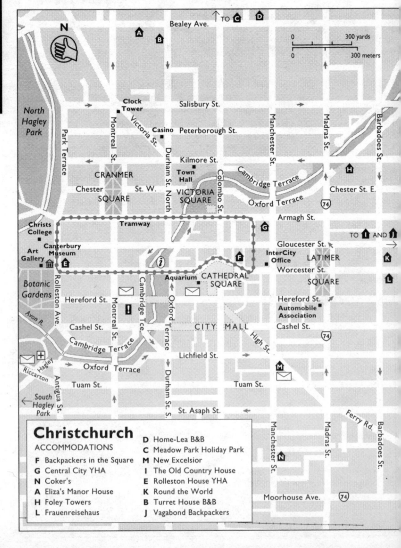

Christchurch

ACCOMMODATIONS

F Backpackers in the Square
G Central City YHA
N Coker's
A Eliza's Manor House
H Foley Towers
L Frauenreisehaus
D Home-Lea B&B
C Meadow Park Holiday Park
M New Excelsior
I The Old Country House
E Rolleston House YHA
K Round the World
B Turret House B&B
J Vagabond Backpackers

By Bus

InterCity, 123 Worcester St. (tel. (0800) 731 711 or 379 9020) and **Mt. Cook Landline,** 47 Riccarton Ave. (tel. (0800) 800 287 or 348 2099) both run daily to Queenstown (10¾hr., 1-2 per day, $85-95) via Dunedin (6hr., $55); Wanaka (9½hr., transfer in Tarras, $82); or Mt. Cook (5hr., $55). InterCity also runs direct to Dunedin (6½ hr., 3 per day, $55); Nelson (7¾hr., 7:30am, $66) via Kaikoura (2¾hr., $27); and Greymouth (4½hr., 9am, $74). Substantial discounts are available (30% and up) for students and advance bookings. A range of **shuttle** options also serves the same cities with prices that are often much cheaper. Call one of the following companies for current routes and prices: **Atomic Shuttles** (tel. 322 8883), **Southern Link Shuttle** (tel. 358 8355), **South Island Connections** (tel. 351 6726), **East Coast Express** (tel. (0508) 830 900), **KO-OP Shuttles** (tel. 366 6633), **Coast-to-Coast** (tel. (0800) 800 847), or **Akaroa Shuttle** (tel. (0800) 500 929). The visitors center has info and does bookings.

CANTERBURY

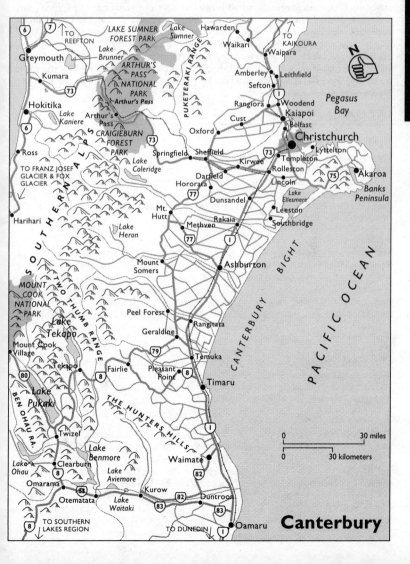

Canterbury

By Thumb

Thumbers report success from the city outskirts, where there's steady traffic from the city. Those heading north toward Kaikoura often take the Belfast bus ($2.70) and ask the driver to be dropped off, while those heading south take the #8 Hornby bus ($1.80) and do the same. West toward Arthur's Pass is still a reasonable prospect; hitchhikers report taking the #8 Russley bus ($1.80) to the Yaldhurst Roundabout.

ORIENTATION

Christchurch's flat grid of streets stretches on indefinitely in every direction from **Cathedral Square,** at the city's heart, where food stalls and artisans congregate beneath the bell-tower of **Christchurch Cathedral.** Facing away from the cathedral, cobblestoned **Worcester Boulevard** stretches east through **Latimer Square,** and west past the visitors center, over the river, and up to the Gothic **Arts Centre** buildings, **Canterbury Museum,** and the extensive **botanic gardens.** The city's main thoroughfare, **Colombo Street,** lined with wool and jewelry souvenir shops, runs north and south through the square. Arcades and plazas extend out from the **City Mall,** the pedestrian walkway a block south from the Cathedral where Cashel St. would be. North of the Cathedral, **Victoria Square** fronts both the town hall and the domineering Park Royal hotel. The shallow **Avon River** runs through the square along **Oxford** and **Cambridge Terrace.** Central Christchurch is bordered to the west by the gigantic **Hagley Park,** to the north and east by residential suburbs, and to the south by **Moorhouse Avenue,** the boundary of the industrial area.

GETTING AROUND

By Bus

The bus info kiosk (Infoline tel. 366 8855) is at Cathedral Sq. (open M-F 7:30am-5pm, Sa-Su 9am-3:30pm). Most buses depart from here roughly every 30 minutes from 6am to 10:50pm. Fares are by zone; most are $1.80 within the city and allow for four hours of transfers on the same line; purchase tickets on board. Buy a **Big Red Bus Pass** ($5) for a full day of travel on all city buses if you're going to more than one sight (available at the visitors center or on-board).

By Car

The major car rental companies are all in town, but for cheaper deals, try **Atomic Rentals** (tel. 322 8883), which begins at $27-30 per day with unlimited distance; the $750 credit bond is standard. **Pegasus,** 127 Peterborough St. (tel. 365 1100 or (0800) 803 580), and **Rent-a-Dent,** 132 Kilmore St. (tel. 365 2509 or (0800) 736 823), are both available 24 hours and do inter-city transfers. The **AA office,** 210 Hereford St. (tel. 379 1280), sells excellent road maps and offers sound traveling advice (open M-F 8:30am-5:30pm). For more on driving in New Zealand, see p. 30.

By Taxi

Christchurch has 24-hour metro area service. A trip to the train station costs $9-10; a ride to the airport runs $20-25. Discount cards are available from the visitors center, restaurants, or the taxi driver. **First Direct** (tel. 377 5555), **Gold Band** (tel. 379 5795), and **Blue Star** (tel. 379 9799) are your options.

By Bike, Surfboard, and Skis

Trailblazers (tel. 366 6033), on Worcester Blvd. between Cathedral Sq. and the visitors center, has standard mountain bikes for $5 per hour or $20 per day. **Cyclone Cycles,** 245 Colombo St. (tel. 332 9588), has mountain bikes with suspension for $30 per day. **Ski Windsurf City,** 64 Manchester St. (tel. 366 6516), rents surfboards ($30 per day), boogie boards ($15 per day), and wetsuits ($15 per day). The store also has ski rental packages (from $15) and snowboard rental (from $35). Free **bicycle storage** is available behind the Lichfield St. carpark (M-Th 7:30am-7:15pm, F 7:30am-11:45pm, Sa 9am-11:45pm).

PRACTICAL INFORMATION

Visitors Center: The **Christchurch Visitor Centre** (tel. 379 9629; fax 377 2424), at the corner of Worcester Blvd. and Oxford Terr. Well staffed, with German, French, Spanish, and Japanese spoken. Open in summer M-F 8:30am-6pm, Sa-Su 8:30am-5pm; in winter M-F 8:30am-5pm, Sa-Su 8:30am-4pm. Another office in the domestic terminal of the airport (tel. 353 7774).

DOC: 133 Victoria St. (tel. 379 9758). Canterbury and all of South Island hiking info and maps. Open M-F 8:30am-4:30pm.

Budget Travel: STA Travel, 90 Cashel St. in City Mall (tel. 379 9098). Full-service worldwide student travel. Open M-F 9am-5:30pm, Sa 10am-3pm. **YHA Travel** (tel. 379,8046), 158 Cashel St., is there for train, plane, and automobile bookings. Open M-F 9am-5:30pm, Sa 10am-1pm. **Budget Travel,** 683A Colombo St. (tel. 366 6032), is a general travel agency. Open M-F 8:30am-5:30pm, Sa 9am-1pm.

Currency Exchange: BNZ (tel. 353 2532), in the glass and steel building in Cathedral Sq., does cash advances from Visa and Mastercard only (M-F 9am-4:30pm) and exchanges money (M-F 9am-6pm, Sa 10am-1pm). **ANZ** (tel. 371 4714), across the street, exchanges money M-F 9am-4:30pm. Branches are widespread around the city center, and most work without commission.

American Express: 773 Colombo St., P.O. Box 2160 (tel. (0800) 801 122 or 365 7366). Mail held for 30 days for card members and AmEx traveler's check holders. No commission; good exchange rates. Open M-F 9am-5pm.

Bookstores: Scorpio Books, 79 Hereford St. (tel. 379 2882), has a wide selection of everything, especially science fiction and New Zealand literature. Open M-Th 8:30am-5:30pm, F 8:30am-9pm, Sa 9:30am-4pm, Su noon-4pm. **Smith's Bookshop,** 133 Manchester St. (tel. 379 7976), boasts three rambling levels of stocked wooden bookshelves and second-hand treasures. Open M-Th 10:15am-5:30pm, F 10:15am-8pm, Sa 10:30am-1pm.

Library: A busy 3-story place (tel. 379 6914), at the corner of Gloucester St. and Oxford Terr. Open M-F 10am-9pm, Sa 10am-4pm, Su 1-4pm.

Bi-Gay-Lesbian Organizations: Gay Information Line (24hr. tel. 379 3990); **Gay Information Collective** (tel./fax 379 9493; email df@burnside.school.nz). **Lamda Walking Group** (366 0962 or 332 8724).

Emergency: Dial **111. Deaf Emergency** (tel. (0800) 161 616).

Police: Cathedral Sq. Kiosk (tel. 379 0123). Open Su-W 8am-11pm, Th-Sa 8am-2am. Main branch (tel. 379 3999), at the corner of Hereford St. and Cambridge Terr.

Hotlines: Lifeline, 24hr. counseling (tel. 366 6743); **Rape and Incest Survivors Support Group** (tel. 364 7324); **Victim Support** (tel. 379 6767); **AIDS Hotline** (tel. (0800) 802 437); **New Zealand Aids Foundation** (tel. 379 1953); **Disability Info,** 314 Worcester St. (tel. 366 6189), open M-F 9am-4:30pm.

Medical Services: Bealey Avenue After Hours Surgery, 931 Colombo St. (tel. 365 7777). Open M-F 5pm-8am, Sa-Su 24hr. The **Late-Night Pharmacy,** 931 Colombo St. (24hr. tel. 366 4439), is open M-Th 6-11pm, F 9-11pm, Sa 1-11pm, Su 9am-11pm. **Christchurch Public Hospital** (tel. 364 0640), is at the corner of Oxford Terr. and Riccarton Ave.

Post Office: The Cathedral Sq. branch (tel. 353 1899) has *Poste Restante*. Open M-Tu 8:30am-10pm, W-Th 8:30am-11pm, F-Sa 9am-2am, Su 9am-10pm.

Internet Access: There are places all over the city. **Molten Media Trust** (tel. 377 1154), 148 Lichfield St. just west of Manchester St., may be in a dingy building, but at $6 per hr., it's the cheapest place in town. (Open M-F 10am-8pm, Sa noon-4pm.) **E-Caf** (tel. 372 9436), 28 Worcester St. in the Arts Centre, offers special deals with the coffee shop downstairs ($2.50 per 15min., $10 per hr.). Open daily 8am-midnight. Some larger backpackers have connections; call to reserve time.

Telephone Code: Throughout the South Island, the telephone code is **03.**

ACCOMMODATIONS

Christchurch has a solid selection of hostels, but few of the charmingly quirky gems that are found in the smaller towns of the South Island. Nonetheless, there are plenty of stately Victorian houses throughout the city that have been converted into a range of hostels, B&Bs, and hotels. In summer, many places fill to capacity (especially near the Cathedral), so book ahead. **Summer/winter rates** listed, where applicable.

Foley Towers, 208 Kilmore St. (tel. 366 9720; fax 379 3014). Take Worcester to Madras St., take a left, and then right on Kilmore St. Spacious villa with back patio, gardens, and lawn surrounded by rooms. Vine-covered trellis and tiled drive give a Mediterranean feel. Poster board with daily Christchurch events. Dorms \$15/\$13 (no linen); doubles or twins \$35/\$32. Reception 9am-9:30pm. Check-out 10am.

Frauenreisehaus: The Homestead, 272 Barbadoes St. (tel. 366 2585; fax 366 2589). Past the Cathedral on Worcester Blvd., hang a right on Barbadoes St. Women are fortunate to have this **female-only** homestead to themselves. The owners go to great lengths to make living easy, with free laundry and a Japanese room with floor mattresses. The big brick house features comfortable bedding in sun-drenched rooms and a formal common area; multiple lounges. Dorms \$15/\$13; singles \$20; twins \$34/\$30. Reception 8:30am-10:30pm. Book ahead.

Vagabond Backpackers, 232 Worcester St. (tel. 379 9677). About 5 blocks east of the Cathedral. An extremely popular pink and green house with skylights and bright, white-washed upstairs rooms. 21 beds that fill up quickly. Quiet location close to the city. Dorms \$16/\$14; singles \$23; doubles or twins \$35. Linen \$1 per stay. Check-out 10am. Book at least a week ahead.

Central City YHA, 273 Manchester St. near Armagh St. (tel. 379 9535; fax 379 9537; email yhachch@yha.org.nz). Central, modern, ultra-clean, and centrally heated with tremendously helpful staff. Bright, open dining area and kitchen with cappuccino machine. Snug though bare rooms, new bathrooms—has that YHA manufactured feel. Be prepared for a 10pm lockout. Dorms \$18; doubles \$42; twins \$40/\$36, with bath \$50. Reception 8am-10pm. Check-out 10am.

Turret House B&B, 435 Durham St., right near the intersection with Bealey St. (tel. (0800) 488 773 or 365 3900; fax 365 5601; email turretb.bchch@xtra.co.nz). A cozy Victorian homestead with wall-to-wall oriental carpeting, quilts, wooden chess set, and lots of New Zealand books. Everything has a luxurious feel. Fresh-baked bread for breakfast; free sherry in evenings. Singles \$65/\$55; doubles \$95/\$85; twins \$85/\$75; family suite \$120/\$110. 10% off for *Let's Go* users. Bikes \$10 per day. All rooms with bath. Check-out 10am. Free pickup from town.

New Excelsior Backpackers, (tel. 366 7570; fax 366 7629; email newexcel@ihug.co.nz), at the corner of High and Manchester St. A large, brand-new hostel boasts sinks in most of the rooms, cushion-filled TV lounge with a large stereo, and a big, wooden deck outside amid the rooftops. Internet access for a startlingly cheap \$5 per hr. Dorms \$17/\$15; singles \$32; doubles \$45, with bath \$55; twins \$38. Linen \$2. Towels \$1.

Coker's (VIP), 52 Manchester St. (tel. 379 8580; fax 379 8585). This once posh hotel retains the regal red chairs and ornately carved painted wooden ceilings from 1875, if not the luster. A tropical garden ushers guests into the foyer. Beyond lies the clash of Baroque elegance with modern dinge in the TV lounge, enormous kitchen, and dining room. Rooms have ancient 1920s heaters. Vintage video games and full bar. Dorms \$16; doubles or twins \$44. No linen. Check-out 10am.

Home-Lea B&B, 195 Bealey Ave. (tel./fax 379 9977). Past the Cathedral heading east, turn left on Manchester St. and walk about 1km to Bealey St.; it's on the corner. Floral bedcovers and thick carpeting, and an exceptionally sunny single with windows on 3 sides. Singles \$50; doubles or twins \$80, with bath \$85-95; triples \$110; quads with bath and fireplace \$120. Check-out 10am.

Rolleston House YHA (tel. 366 6564; fax 365 5589), at the corner of Worcester Blvd. and Rolleston Ave., across from the Arts Centre. With a great location in the city's cultural heart, the beautiful old Rolleston has spacious (but basic) rooms with sliding windows and a pool table. Dorms \$15-17; twins \$38. Reception 8-10am and 3:30-10pm. Check-out 10am.

The Old Country House, 437 Gloucester St. (tel. 381 5504), 2km up Gloucester St. to the east. An earthy, quiet place with lemon and plum trees. Undergoing intense renovations; the newer rooms are colorful and attractive. Free pickup from Cathedral Sq. Dorms \$12-14; doubles and twins \$32; quads \$50. Check-out 10am.

(social studies)

Use **AT&T Direct**[SM] Service
when you're out exploring the world.

It's all within **AT&T** your reach.

 On your next journey bring along an

AT&T Direct^{SM} Service wallet guide. It's a list of

access numbers you need to call home fast and clear

from around the world, using an AT&T Calling Card or credit card.

What an amazing culture we live in.

For a list of **AT&T Access Numbers,**
take the attached wallet guide.

For your calling convenience tear off and take with you!

 AT&T

 AT&T Direct℠ Service

WALLET GUIDE

Inside you'll find simple instructions on how to use AT&T Direct Service to place calling card or collect calls from outside the U.S.

All you need are the AT&T Access Numbers when you travel outside the U.S., because you can access us quickly and easily from virtually anywhere in the world. And if you need any further help, there's always an AT&T English-speaking Operator available to assist you.

www.att.com/traveler

Calling From Specially Marked Telephones

Throughout the world, there are specially marked phones that connect you to AT&T Direct℠ Service. Simply look for the AT&T logo. In the following countries, access to these phones is *only* available from these phones: Ethiopia, Mongolia, Nigeria, Seychelles Islands.

Public phones in Europe displaying the red 3C symbol also give you quick and easy access to AT&T Direct Service. Just lift the handset and dial ✱60 (in France dial M60) and you'll be connected to AT&T.

Pay phones in the United Kingdom displaying the New World symbol provide easy access to AT&T. Simply lift the handset and press the pre-programmed button marked AT&T.

NEW WORLD PAYPHONE

Customer Care

If you have any questions, call 800 331-1140, Ext. 707.

When outside the U.S., dial the AT&T Access Number for the country *you are in* and ask the AT&T Operator for Customer Care.

108-25   © AT&T 6/98

Printed in the U.S.A.
on recycled paper.

To Call the U.S. and Other Countries Using Your AT&T Calling Card* or credit card^∞, Follow These Steps:

1. Make sure you have an outside line. (From a hotel room, follow the hotel's instructions to get an outside line, as if you were placing a local call.)

2. If you want to call a country other than the U.S., make sure the country *you are in* is highlighted in blue on the chart like this:

3. Enter the AT&T Access Number listed in the chart for the country *you are in.*

4. When prompted, enter the telephone number you are calling as follows:
   - For calls to the U.S., dial the Area Code (no need to dial 1 before the Area Code) + 7-digit number.
   - For calls to other countries,† enter 01+ the Country Code, City Code, and Local Number.

5. After the tone, enter your AT&T Calling Card* or credit card number (not the international number). If you need help or wish to call the U.S. collect, hold for an AT&T Operator.

* You may also use your AT&T Corporate Card, AT&T Universal Card, or most U.S. local phone company cards.
† The cost of calls to countries other than the U.S. consists of basic connection rates plus an additional charge based on the country you are calling.
^∞ Credit card billing subject to availability.

AT&T

Special Features

Just dial the AT&T Access Number for the country *you are in* and follow the instructions listed below.

- To call U.S. 800 numbers: Enter the 800 number *you are* calling. (Note: Based upon the 800 number dialed, calls may be toll-free or AT&T Direct℠ Service charges may apply for the duration of the call; some numbers may be restricted.)

- To set up conference calls: Dial AT&T TeleConference Services at 800 232-1234. (Note: One conferee must be in the U.S.)

- To access language interpreters: Dial AT&T Language Line® Services at 408 648-5871.

- To record and deliver messages: Dial #123 if you get a busy signal or no answer; or dial AT&T True Messages® Service at 800 562-6275.

Here's a time-saving tip for placing additional calls: When you finish your conversation, or if there is a busy signal or no answer, don't hang up – press # and wait for the voice prompt or an AT&T Operator.

AT&T Access Numbers

(Refer to footnotes before dialing.) From the countries highlighted in blue below, like this [____], you can make calls to virtually any location in the world; and from *all* the countries listed, you can make calls to the U.S.

AT&T

It's all within your reach.

Country	Number	Country	Number	Country	Number	Country	Number
Albania ●	00-800-0010	Bosnia ▲	00-800-0010	Dom. Rep. ★, □		Guam	1 800 CALL ATT
American Samoa	633 2-USA	Brazil	000-8010		1-800-872-2881	Guantanamo Bay ↑(Cuba)	935
Anguilla	0199	British V.I. ✦	1-800-872-2881	Ecuador ▲	999-119	Guantanamo Bay ↑(Cuba)	935
Anguilla ✦	1-800-872-2881	Brunei ●	800-1111	(Outside Quito)	8●27007007	Guatemala ○, ☀	99-99-190
Antigua ✦	1-800-872-2881	Bulgaria ■, ▲	00-800-0010	Egypt● (Cairo)	510-0200	Guyana ★	165
(Public Card Phones)	#	Cambodia ✱	1-800-881-001	(Outside Cairo)	02-510-0200	Haiti	183
Argentina ●	0-800-54-288	Canada	1 800 CALL ATT	El Salvador ○	800-1785	Honduras	800-0-123
Armenia ◆, ▲	8●0111	Cape Verde Islands	112	Estonia	800-12001	Hong Kong	800-96-1111
Aruba	800-8000	Cayman Islands ✦		Fiji	004-890-1001	Hungary●	00●800-01111
Australia	1-800-881-011		1-800-872-2881	Finland●	9800-100-10	Iceland	800 9001
Austria ○	022-903-011	Chile	or 800-800-311	France●	0800 99 00 11	India ★, ✓	000-117
Bahamas	1-800-872-2881		800-800-288	French Antilles	0800 99 00 11	Indonesia→	001-801-10
Bahrain	800-001	China, PRC ▲	10811	French Guiana	0800 99 00 11	Ireland✓	1-800-550-000
Bahrain ✦	800-000	Colombia	980-11-0010	Gabon●	00●001	Israel	1-800-94-94-949
Barbados ✦	1-800-872-2881	Cook Island	09-111	Gambia●	00111	Italy●	172-1011
Belarus ✱, —	8●800101	Costa Rica	0-800-0-114-114	Georgia ▲	8●0288	Ivory Coast●	00-111-11
Belgium●	0-800-100-10	Croatia ▲	99-385-0111	Germany	0130-0010	Jamaica ○	1-800-872-2881
Belize ●	811	Cyprus●	080-90010	Ghana	0191	Jamaica □	872
(from Hotels Only)	555	Czech Rep. ●	00-42-000-101	Gibraltar	8800	Japan KDD●	005-39-111
Benin●	102	Denmark	8001-0010	Greece●	00-800-1311	Japan IDC▲, ▲	0066-55-111
Bermuda ✦	1-800-872-2881	Dominica ✦	1-800-872-2881	Grenada✦	1-800-872-2881	Kazakhstan	8●001-21-4321
Bolivia ✦	0-800-1112			Guadeloupe ✦, ☀		Korea●	00729-911 or 0030-911
				(Marie Galante)	0800 99 00 11	Korea →	550-HOME or 550-2USA

Country	Number	Country	Number	Country	Number
Kuwait	800-288	Netherlands ●	0800-022-9111	Russia ●, ▲, ▲	
Latvia (Riga)	7007007	New Zealand	000-911	(St. Petersburg)	325-5042
(Outside Riga)	8●27007007	Nicaragua	174	(Outside St. Petersburg)	8-812-325-5042
Lebanon●(Beirut)	426-801	Norway	800-190-11	Saipan ▲	1-800-872-2881
(Outside Beirut)	01-426-801	Pakistan ▲	00-800-01001	St. Kitts/Nevis & St. Lucia ✦	1-800-872-2881
Liechtenstein ●	0-800-89-0011	Palau	02288	St. Pierre & Miquelon	0800 99 00 11
Lithuania ★, —	8●196	Panama	109	St. Vincent △	1-800-872-2881
Luxembourg†	0-800-0111	(Canal Zone)	281-0109	Saudi Arabia ◇	1-800-10
Macao	0800-111	Papua New Guinea	0507-12680	Senegal	3072
Macedonia, F.Y.R. of ●	99-800-4288	Paraguay ▲, ▲		Sierra Leone	1100
Malaysia ○	1800-80-0011	Peru ▲	0-800-50000	Singapore ■	800-0111-111
Malta ●	0800-890-110	Philippines●	105-11	Slovakia ▲, ▲	00-42-100-101
Marshall Isl.	1 800 CALL ATT	Poland	0●0-800-111-1111	Solomon Isl.	0811
Mauritius	73120	Portugal ▲	05017-1-288	So. Africa	0-800-99-0123
Mexico∇, ¹	01-800-288-2872	Qatar	0800-011-77	Spain	900-99-00-11
Micronesia	288	Reunion Isl.	0800 99 0011	Sri Lanka ■	430-430
Monaco●	800-90-288	Romania●	01-800-4288	Sudan	800-001
Montserrat	1-800-872-2881	Romania →	01-801-0151	Suriname △	156
Morocco	002-11-0011	Russia ●, ▲, ▲		Sweden	020-795-611
Netherlands Antilles ✦	001-800-872-2881	(Moscow)	755-5042	Switzerland ●	0-800-890011
		(Outside Moscow)	8-095-755-5042	Syria	0080-10288-0
				Taiwan	0080-10288-0
				Thailand✓	001-999-111-11
				Trinidad/Tob.	1-800-872-2881
				Turkey●	00-800-12277
				Turks & Caicos ✦	
					01-800-872-2881
				Uganda	800-001
				Ukraine ▲	8●100-11
				U.A. Emirates ●	800-121
				U.K. ▲, ✦	0800-89-0011
					or 0500-89-0011
				U.S. ▼	1 800 CALL ATT
				Uruguay ■	000-410
				Uzbekistan 8 ◆	641-744-0010
				Venezuela	800-11-120
				Vietnam●	1-201-0288
				Yemen	00 800 101
				Zambia	00-899
				Zimbabwe ▲	110-98990

● Public phones require coin or card deposit. ✱Press red button. ✡ Additional charges apply when calling outside of Moscow. ■ AT&T Direct™ calls cannot be placed to this country from outside the U.S. ✦ Available from pay phones. ✱ Not available from public phones. ✦ From Phnom Penh and Siem Reap only. ★ Not available from public phones. ✦ From St. Maarten or phones at Bobby's Marina, use 1-800-872-2881.

◇ From this country, **AT&T Direct™** calls terminate to designated countries only. ✡ From U.S. Military Bases only. ▲ May not be available from every phone/public phone. ☀ Available from phones with international calling capabilities or from most Public Calling Centers. ✓ From Northern Ireland use U.K. access code.

★ Collect calling only. ○ Public phones require local coin payment through the call duration. ▼ Await second dial tone. ∇ When calling from public phones, use phones marked ▲ Ladatel. ¹ If call does not complete, use 001-800-462-4240. △ Available from public phones only. ● Public phones use phones marked ✦ When calling from public phones use phones marked Lenso.

□ Calling Card calls available from select hotels. ▲ Use phones allowing international access. ▼ including Puerto Rico and the U.S. Virgin Islands. ✦ **AT&T Direct™** Service only from telephone calling centers in Hanoi and post offices in Da Nang, Ho Chi Minh City and Quang Ninh. ✤ If call does not complete, use 0800-013-0011.

Meadow Park Holiday Park, 39 Meadow St. (tel. 352 9176; fax 352 1272). 10min. drive from the Cathedral north on Colombo St. (which becomes Cranford St.). Sprawling complex with waterslides and playground. Cabins for 2 $33 (extra person $10); doubles $57 (extra person $15). Tent sites $10 per person; powered $15-20. Linen $4. Reception 8am-10pm. Check-in 2pm. check-out 10am.

FOOD

From sashimi to panini, Christchurch's ethnic offerings will make everybody happy. Varied cuisines are concentrated on **Colombo Street** north of Kilmore St., and on **Manchester Street,** south of Gloucester St. Cafes are often the best bet for hearty breakfasts and lunches (generally with lower prices), and there's always pub food to be found. Vendors in Cathedral Sq. sell a range of kebabs and stir-frys around lunchtime; on weekends they take over a corner of the Arts Centre.

Worcester Street and South

Ⓜ**Il Felice,** 56 Lichfield St. (tel. 366 7535). Hugely popular upscale authentic Italian in an often boisterous and close-knit environment where frescoes and a Pavarotti portrait deck the walls. Fresh-made pastas ($15) and mains ($20-25) are worth the splurge, as the portions make up for the price. BYO. Open M-Sa from 6pm.

Ⓜ**Blue Jean Cuisine** (tel. 365 4130), at the corner of Manchester and Hereford St. Big steaks and fish dishes among license plates, chalk-written song lyrics, and Americana. The noise level reflects the popularity. You won't leave hungry. Lunch $8-11, light meals $10-13, dinners $18-19. Open M-F from 11am, Sa-Su from 5:30am.

Alva Rados (tel. 365 1644), at the corner of Worcester and Manchester St. Pitchers of margaritas and mega nachos amid Mexican pottery, hangings, and cacti everywhere make this Tex-Mex popular with groups and a younger crowd. Light meals from $9, mains $16-18. Open Tu-Su from 6pm.

Dux de Lux, 41 Hereford St. (tel. 366 6919), at the Arts Centre. The Dux serves only vegetarian and seafood, in a variety of forms from pizzas to tapas ($9-17). Popular with students, the enormous place is a great hangout in summer when the patio, surrounded by the neo-Gothic masonry of the Arts Centre, is in full swing. Seven homebrews, too. Open daily 10am-midnight.

Pyramids of the Sahara, 105 Manchester St. (tel. 379 7565). New Zealand's only little Egypt, with belly-dancing Friday and Saturday, painted camels under pontooned ceilings, and soup made from specially imported Egyptian vegetables—they're only missing the sand. Dine among the Pharaohs on medams, a hummus-like dip, or whole grilled fish. Dinners $11-18. Open daily from 5pm.

Panini Bar (tel. 377 5570), at the corner of Lichfield and High St. An intimate little place redolent with Italian specialties. The big gilt mirror and shadowy fan add true atmosphere, and the food is divine. Lunch paninis (toasted sandwiches on delicious homemade bread) are a steal at $5-7; dinners $13-18. A number of tasty pasta dishes on the dinner menu; grab a $2 beer during happy hour, 5-7pm. Treat yourself to a Cuban cigarillo ($4). Open Su-Th 9am-midnight, F-Sa 9am-2am.

Phu Thai, 176 Manchester St. (tel. 366 9006). A tiny lamplit Southeast Asian place with just 5 marble tables, but excellent Tom Yum soups served in big crock pots ($7). Quintessential Thai meals $7-12. Open M-Sa 11am-10pm, Su 11:30am-9:30pm.

Topkapi Turkish Kebab House, 185a Manchester St. (tel. 379 4447). In this tiny piece of Turkey, sit on low benches or pillows amid oriental wall hangings, posters of the Middle East, and copper coffee vessels while kebabs and falafels are prepared windowside (small $5, large $7.50). Open M-Tu 11:30am-10pm, W-Th 11:30am-10:30pm, F 11:30am-11pm, Sa 3-11pm.

North of Worcester Street

Ⓜ**South of the Border,** 834 Colombo St. (tel. 379 7808). Delicious Mexican food in a festive place complete with a revolving parrot, bright colored napkins, and several imported habanero sauces to complement your burritos and salsa (dinners from $11-16). BYO. Open daily from 6pm.

Sala Thai (tel. 365 5447), at the corner of Colombo and Kilmore St. Huge range of Thai and Lao dishes. Pad thai ($13) is an eternal favorite, but there's chili and curry, too. Posters of Thai fruit and a shimmering wall hanging of elephants contribute to the unpretentious atmosphere. Mains $12-18. Open daily noon-9:30pm.

Death by Chocolate, 209 Cambridge Terr. (tel. 365 7323). Head north on Colombo St. and turn right Cambridge Terr. As the name implies, you may have to be carried out—the namesake dessert alone ($15) could do in a couple, and the "Multitude of Sins" ($24 for 2 people) is enough to inspire a gastronomic orgy. Open Tu-Su from noon, M from 6pm.

The Tin Goose (tel. 365 2866), at the corner of Victoria and Salisbury St. Chrome and glass usher passengers through the portal into this homage to flight. The dinner ($10-19) is fortunately much better than one you'd get on an airplane. Vibrant airplane posters complement the futuristic decor. Open M-F from 7am, Sa-Su from 8am; in winter M-F from 8am, Th-F from 7am, Sa-Su from 8:30am.

Oxford on Avon (tel. 379 7148), at the corner of Colombo St. and Oxford Terr. The pinnacle of New Zealand pub food: carved meats, bowls of veggies, and creamy cakes served cafeteria-style. Daily specials from $8-15, and a riverside garden bar. Open daily 6:30am-midnight. Also check out the smorgasbord restaurant upstairs. Lunch ($12) from 11am-2pm and dinner ($16) from 5:30-9:30pm.

Spagalimi's Pizza, 155 Victoria St. (tel. 379 7469). A Christchurch institution with celebrity caricatures lining the walls, Spag's serves great, cheap pizzas. A medium pie is $9-10, and the thin-cut pizza is the best value around. Open Su-Th 11am-11pm, F-Sa 11am-midnight.

Joji's Sushi Bar, 186 Manchester St. (tel. 365 0500). Incredibly fresh sushi and sashimi form a beautifully prepared lunch ($8) or dinner ($14-24). A tidy little place out of the way of the tourist hordes. Open M-Sa noon-2:30pm and 6-10pm.

Santerini Greek Ouzeri (tel. 379 6975), at the corner of Gloucester and Cambridge Terr. When the Bouzouki Band gets going, patrons are encouraged to dance on wine casks; the conga lines have been known to invade the kitchen. A fun-loving family place with big Greek dinners ($19-21). Open Tu-Sa from 6pm.

Markets

Closer to town, several butchers and produce stores clog the corners of Armagh and Manchester St.

Pak'N Save, at the corner of Moorhouse Ave. and Manchester St., is the cheapest supermarket around. Open M-W 8:30am-9pm, Th-F 8:30am-10pm, Sa-Su 8:30am-7pm. The megamarkets in general are all stuck together a few blocks from Cathedral Sq.

Big Fresh, one block east, has the freshest produce and is a little more upmarket—it's even themed as a pioneer town. Open Sa-W 8:30am-9pm, Th-F 8:30am-10pm.

Countdown Foods, on Colombo St. in the south City Mall, has great discount seafood and an adjacent butcher. Open M-Tu 8:30am-6pm, W-F 8:30am-9pm, Sa 8:30am-7pm, Su 9am-6pm.

CAFES

Fly in the face of tradition in Christchurch (spiritual home to the custom of tea) by going for an alternative caffeine kick. Generally consistent, reasonably priced, and with outstanding food, Christchurch's cafes are always a good breakfast or lunching option (even without the actual coffee).

⊛Caffe Roma (tel. 379 3879), on Oxford Terr. near Gloucester St. An elegant brunch place with windows overlooking the Avon and fireside couches. Excellent muffins ($1.50) and breakfasts ($8-15). Open daily 7am-4pm.

The Coffee House, 290 Montreal St. near the Arts Centre (tel. 365 6066). Not for the indecisive; shelves of tea tins house an enormous selection of teas ($3-3.50) and coffees ($2.50-4.50). The mosaic-bordered convex mirrors on the wall give a warped reflection of the attractive little cafe where full meals are served all day, and all week. Open M-Th 7:30am-11pm, F-Sa 7:30am-midnight, Su 7:30am-6pm.

Java Cafe, at the corner of High St. and Lichfield St. (tel. 366 0195). An alternative corner stronghold with two levels of empty olive oil cans, pop art, and plants. Iced

The Joy of Yeast

What little joy our lives would have without yeast! No bread, wine, beer—or, for that matter, brewer's by-products. And without the by-products, to the shock and horror of millions, that would mean no **Marmite,** the salty, yeasty brown paste with the look, consistency, and taste of spreadable bullion. The staple and ambrosia of New Zealand (and British) breakfast tables is a bit of an acquired taste. But, contrary to popular belief, you don't need to have been weaned on the stuff to truly enjoy it. The trick is to remember: 1) it's not sweet, and 2) it's *not* meant to be slathered across the bread. Scores of tourists every year make the mistake of smearing it on like so much peanut butter, a move that sends them spitting and cursing to the nearest sink. To look local, not yokel, scrape just the tiniest bit across hot buttery toast, or grate some cheese on top and broil to make "Mousetraps." A "100% vegetarian" delight brought to you by the Seventh Day Adventist Church-run Sanitarium Foods Co., Marmite is good for your body and redeeming for your soul. In contrast to Vegemite, the Aussie version of the sassy spread, Marmite is slightly sweeter. It's even rumored to prevent hangovers (due to the high content of B vitamins). In the end, though, it's really all about nationalism—true Kiwis eat Marmite.

mochas served in jam jars ($4), a variety of bagels, and the massive vegetarian planet burger ($10) are among the all-day dining options. Open daily from 7:30am.

Coffee D'Fafo, 137 Hereford St. (tel. 366 6083). "For serious coffee drinkers," D'Fafo boasts modern art and a svelte newspaper bar in an unhurried environment. Le French toast ($11.50), lunch ($10-12). Open M-F 7am-6pm, Sa-Su 9am-3pm.

Main Street Cafe (tel. 365 0421), at Colombo and Salisbury St. Hippyish bar/cafe/restaurant with a yellow brick floor that'll lead you to loads of vegetarian and dairy-free options. Specializing in lentil dishes and hearty salads. Quiet and mellow, the courtyard fills up in summer. Dinners from $13-15. Saturday night acoustic music in the bar. Open daily from 10am. Bar, with excellent Guinness, open from 5pm.

Vivace (tel. 365 8248), on Hereford St. Bean roasters for much of the city, Vivace's small, artsy, tile-floored cafe offers citrus- and mint-water and Botticelli frescoes. Loud and pleasantly fragrant when the coffee's roasting. Open M-Th 7am-5pm, F 7am-9pm, Sa-Su 8am-3pm.

Le Cafe (tel. 366 7722), on Worcester Blvd. in the Arts Centre. Among several cafes secreted in medieval crannies, Le Cafe is always busy, always lively, and almost always open. Dine on the patio or up the tiny stairs that pass by geometric stained glass windows. Dinners from $10, breakfast from $6.50. Open Su-Th 7am-midnight, F-Sa 24hr.

Yum Yum Cafe (tel. 365 5557), on New Regent St. by the tram route. Arched windows and fresh flowers make for a quaint rendezvous spot at this undiscovered locale. The Swiss owner prides himself on his cured meats. The pretty view, cheap lunches ($2.50-5), and pastas ($9) are a great value. Open daily 8am-6pm.

Venus Coffee, on Lichfield St. across from Cashel Plaza. Described as a "Brady Bunch Lounge," a communal, gay-friendly gathering place for faux-fur lovers. Pieced together with knick-knacks and paraphernalia, it borders on the indescribable. Open Su-Th 8am-11pm, F-Sa 11am-1am; in winter Su-Th 8am-7pm, F-Sa 11am-1am.

NIGHTLIFE AND ENTERTAINMENT

Rugby pubs and boutique bars dominate Christchurch's somewhat uninspired dancing and drinking establishments, although nightclubs and breweries have eked out a permanent niche among the locals. Cruise the **City Mall** by the Avon and the action-packed corner of **Manchester** and **Cashel Streets** for after-dark hotspots.

Loaded Hog (tel. 366 6674), on Manchester at Cashel St. Filled with business suits it may be, but they still pour an excellent lager from this homebrew chain. Posters near the entrance depict famous beer drinkers. Solid snack food ($6-11) as well. Open Su-W 11am-midnight, Th 11am-1am, F-Sa 11am-3am.

UBQ (tel. 379 2910), on Lichfield St. across from Cashel Plaza. Wild gay club with spinning light ball, frescoed walls, TVs everywhere, and even cage dancing. The bar is streaked with psychedelic colors. The best-equipped Christchurch nightclub with frequent outside entertainers. Open daily from 7pm.

Coyote Bar (tel. 366 6055), at the corner of City Mall and Oxford Terr. "Jack lives here" (Mr. Daniels, that is) beneath the metallic cactus terra cotta walls and the high-raftered ceiling. Packed most nights with well-dressed twenty-something tap hounds; dancing Th-Sa. Open daily 10am-3am.

Platinum (tel. 377 7891), Lichfield St. across from Cashel Plaza. The bar in this downstairs club is bathed in an eerie, fluorescent blue light, with artsy metallic lamps dangling from above and dropping circles of light onto the drinkers below. A second bar in the back serves wine and cocktails to a more upscale clientele. Dance floor holds a gyrating posse of locals, drag shows, comedy acts, live DJs and even a pool table. Open M-W from 4:30pm, Th-Su from 7pm.

Dux de Lux, 41 Hereford St., by the Arts Centre (tel. 366 6919). An enormous old house with free local bands Wednesday through Saturday, jazz Tuesdays, and two separate bars. Seven fresh-brewed beers attract a student crowd most nights; in summer the outside patio overflows with easygoing pint-in-hand crowds. Open daily 11am-midnight.

Sullivan's, 150 Manchester St., near Cashel St. (tel. 379 7790). This spacious pub is adorned with vintage Irish photos (including one of a lamb drinking Guinness straight from the bottle) and a large map of the homeland. Acoustic jam session Wednesday, Irish dancing Thursday, live bands F-Sa. Open M-Sa from 4pm.

Sneakers Sports Bar (tel. 379 9368), at the corner of Cashel and Manchester St. Sports mavens from any culture will appreciate the rugby, hockey, and even snowboarding paraphernalia around the enormous television; note the hockey goalie above the bar. Monday through Thursday, 2-for-1 meals. TVs even in the bathroom. The menu includes the "superbowl of the day" (soup) and "fowl play," among other ill-wrought sports puns. Open daily from 11am.

Bailie's (tel. 366 5159), behind the Cathedral. The original Christchurch Guinness pub, Bailie's now has 9 U.K. brews on tap, Irish bands Fridays and Saturdays, and backpackers specials with the hostel next door. The quieter back bar has a great stained-glass ceiling (from its former hotel days) above the beer and rugby posters plastered to the walls. Rarely closed.

Bar Particular (tel. 365 0781), at the corner of Colombo and Lichfield Sts. This happening gay bar has a big dance floor and a DJ on Friday and Saturday nights, plus occasional drag shows. Open W 8:30pm-1:30am, Th 8:30pm-2am, F 9pm-4am, Sa 9pm-4:30am.

The Jolly Poacher (tel. 379 5635), on Victoria St. opposite the Casino near Durham St. Neon rabbit over the doorway sets the stage for the trophy heads, mounted fish, and even the stuffed weasel that provide the company in this English-style pub. Locals flock here for the ancient wood paneling, loud jukebox, and pool table of this homage to taxidermy. Open 24 hr.

Christchurch has several excellent art cinemas and a professional theater company at the Court Theatre; check the back page of *The Press* for a full current listing. The **Court Theatre** (tel. 366 6992) at the Arts Centre, has two theaters running some of New Zealand's best professional repertory productions (tickets generally $20-25). The **Theatre Royal,** 145 Gloucester St. (tel. 366 6326), is a forum for touring musicals and ballet companies. The **Repertory Theatre,** 146 Kilmore St. (tel. 379 8866), is a community theater running five plays a year (tickets about $15).

Gamblers can try their luck at the **Christchurch Casino,** at Victoria and Durham St. While it may resemble an overgrown parking garage from the outside, the gaming room and cafes feature tasteful balconies and chandeliers. Slots, $2 blackjack tables, and a dozen roulette wheels fill the gaming floor. Giveaways and cash contests take place nightly (no jeans, shorts, or sneakers allowed; must be 20 to gamble). There is even a free pickup and drop-off (tel. 365 999) to and from all local accommodations. (Pickup offered nightly from 6pm to 2am. Casino open daily 24hr.)

SIGHTS

Christchurch is oriented around the Gothic revival 1865 **Christchurch Cathedral,** built both from Canterbury quarried stones and root from native matai and totara. *(Free tours M-F 11am and 2pm, Su 11:30am; in winter Sa 11am.)* Ornate stained-glass windows imported from England contrast with the Maori *kai kai* (flax) weavings and the modern windows at the altar end of the church. The ornate font commemorates Captain Owen Stanley's landing at Akaroa just before the French reached the shore in 1840. You can even climb the cathedral's **tower.** *($4, children $1.50.)*

Walk down Worcester Blvd. west toward the visitors center and you'll pass over the **Avon River,** meandering away through the city under willows and arched bridges. Seeing Christchurch by boat can be an enchanting experience, as you punt past historic buildings and the statues on the Avon. Tours depart from Worcester Blvd. frequently, including **Punting on the Avon** (tel. 379 9629) and **Punting in the Park** (tel. 366 0337; both about $12 per person per 30min.). You can also tour the expansive **Botanic Gardens** on your own, which feature one of the country's best arrays of grand trees and indigenous plant life tucked away between the curving pathways. Even in winter, the gardens are immaculately maintained, and the indoor cactus house and rainforest rooms shouldn't be missed. **Hagley Park,** with its jogging tracks and rugby fields, surrounds the Gardens on three sides.

Wizardism

King of Christchurch's motley array of eccentrics, **The Wizard** makes his presence known around noon in Cathedral Square during the summer. Dubbed the official wizard of Christchurch by the local government, the outspoken linguistic Merlin will do everything in his power to rile up the crowd. Don't expect liberal views on politics or gender issues; you may flee disgusted, which means that the pointed cap and cape-bearing wizard has won the day. Still, he's a strikingly intelligent orator and entertainer, and has created his trademark upside-down maps proclaiming an enlightened understanding of the world. The wizard even flees the country during census time to escape political oppression from the forces of government. In- and out-of-season you can find The Wizard on the Web (http://www.chch.planet.org.nz/wizard/).

Arts, Museums, Aquarium

The impressive **Arts Centre** borders the gardens on the east, and stretches over an entire block back toward the city. *(Guided tours given by the town crier depart from the Arts Centre Information Centre near the end of Worcester Blvd. M-F 11am and 2pm. $5.)* A former university, the Gothic revival complex now houses cafes, art studios, shops, the Court Theatre, and two cinemas. On weekends, craftsmen and clothiers sell goods in the outdoor market, and ethnic food stalls crowd the back courtyard.

Beyond the Arts Centre, the **Canterbury Museum** (tel. 366 5000) houses one of the best regional museums in the country, home to several enormous panoramas of the moa, a Maori artifact room, and excellent natural history exhibits. *(Open daily 9am-5pm. Free.)* Around the other side of the museum rests Canterbury's premier art salon, the **Robert McDougall Art Gallery** (tel. 365 0915), specializing in New Zealand and British painting. Beyond its columned foyer are several galleries of permanent and temporary exhibitions ranging from local works to traveling collections. The **Arts Annex**, in the Arts Centre, exhibits contemporary sculpture and multimedia works. *(Both free and open daily 10am-4:30pm.)* The **Center of Contemporary Art (CoCA)** (tel. 366 7261), on Gloucester St. a block from the Arts Centre, is an independently supported gallery of innovative modern works. *(Open Tu-F 11am-5pm, Sa-Su noon-4pm; free.)* Check out the giant cow made of tomato cans.

Right in Cathedral Sq., **Aquarium of Discovery** (tel. 377 3474) is a brand-new addition to Christchurch's cultural gems. *(Open daily 9am-9pm, in winter 10am-6pm. Admission $12.50.)* On display are fish and other sea creatures exclusively from the South Island, including several pools of crayfish and tanks of fish so well camouflaged you may not be able to spot them. The eels are fed at 11am (twice a day in summer) while the marine tank, complete with deep sea bass and two large sharks, is fed daily at 3pm (twice a day in summer). Excellent short films on South Island wildlife run continuously in the theater.

Just down the road, **Science Alive** (tel. 365 5199), on Moorhouse Ave. near Manchester St., is a hands-on science experience geared toward children, which generally surprises and enlightens adults as well. *(Open daily 9am-5pm. Admission $6.50, students $5.50, children $5.)* A vertical slide, wind tunnel, and various engineering challenges provide innumerable mind-twisters. Classic cars and other motorized masterpieces are exhibited at **Yaldhurst Museum of Transport** (tel. 342 7914), 1km west of the city on Yaldhurst Rd. *(Open daily 10am-5pm. Admission $6.50.)*

Architecture and Tours

Art for art's sake represents only a fraction of Christchurch's artistic heritage. Alongside its gallery pieces, the city is full of architectural marvels. Benjamin Mountfort conceived many of the Gothic Revival stone and brick structures in the 1860s and 1870s that today provide the city with its distinctive architectural character. Pick up a copy of the *Christchurch Central City Walks* pamphlet, which details three walks past churches, government houses, and statuary along the banks of the Avon. The brightly painted, arched wooden ceiling, magnificent secular stained glass windows, and long neo-Gothic hallways of the impressive **Provincial Council Buildings,** at Gloucester St. and Cambridge Terr., have yet to be discovered even by many locals. *(Open M-Sa 10:30am-3:30pm, Oct.-May also Su 2-4pm.)* For more comprehensive commentary, contact the **Personal Guiding Service** through the visitors center (tours $8). **Private Garden Tours** also runs tours from the visitors center. *(Mid-Sept. to Dec. Tu-Sa 9:30am; Jan.-Mar. daily 9:30am; $20.)* **Scenic Tours** (tel. 366 7898 or (0800) 922 299), in the Cathedral Sq. kiosk, does a wide range of bookings for sights and activities. *(Open M-F 8:30am-5:30pm, Sa-Su 9am-3pm.)*

Outlying Sights

Nga Hau E Wha National Marae, 250 Pages Rd. (tel. (0800) 456 898), east of Christchurch and the country's largest Maori fort, provides an excellent window into Maori culture and history. The *marae* represents the body of an clever ancestor who fished the North Island out of the sea using his grandmother's jawbone; it's this hook that is symbolized by the popular jade or bone hook carvings. The flax ornamentation and painted carvings of ancestors are each uniquely symbolic, with a range of fascinating myths associated with them. A guided tour plus an evening concert is available ($25; call to book in advance), as is a complete *hangi* (meal), tour, and concert ($55). Take bus #5 ($1.80) from Cathedral Sq.

Museums and attractions ring Christchurch city, and most are accessible by a short bus ride from the city center. The **Top Attractions Voucher Booklet** gives discounts at most museums (sometimes available at the visitors center). The **City Circuit Bus** (tel. 332 6012) runs two loops around outlying sights. The **International Antarctic Center** (tel. 358 9896) brings you as close as you'd like to get to the coldest, driest, windiest continent on earth. *(Open daily in summer 9am-8pm, in winter 9am-5:30pm. Admission $12, YHA $10.80, families $28. Take the A bus for $2.70 or drive out to the airport; head north around Hagley Park and follow the signs.)* Interactive exhibits go so far as to include the "snow and ice experience" room, kept at Antarctic temperatures and stocked with real snow.

Two nearby wildlife reserves north of the city off Johns Rd. house native and exotic wildlife. **Willowbank** (tel. 359 6226) operates extensive walk-through aviaries and a nocturnal kiwi house. *(Open daily 10am-10pm. Admission $11, students $9, children $5. Accessible by car, or with the City Circuit Bus.)* The exceptionally rare and exceptionally ugly *kune kune* pig roams freely, forcing inquisitive peacocks into fence-jumping routines. **Orana Park** (tel. 359 7109), 18km from the city, is a complete African Plains park with lions, zebras, rhinos, a variety of savannah animals, native birds (including the rare mountain blue duck), and the ageless tuatara. *(Open daily 10am-4:30pm. Admis-*

sion $12, children $6. Inquire at the visitors center regarding the $14 shuttle.) Beyond Hagley Park to the west, the **Mona Vale Homestead** (tel. 348 9659) sits amid rose gardens and rhododendrons on the banks of the Avon River, totally secluded from the city. Morning or afternoon tea on the patio is a relaxing indulgence on a sunny day.

ACTIVITIES AND FESTIVALS

Christchurch is the gateway to the serene, albeit mostly agricultural, outdoors of Canterbury. If the weather's good, take the free bus out to **Port Hills** and the **Mt. Cavendish Gondola** (tel. 384 0700), departing from the visitors center every two hours starting at 10am. *(More frequently in summer; the #28 Lyttelton bus also runs out here regularly for $1.80.)* Numerous **walking tracks** leave from the top of the hills; it's also a popular mountain biking area. **The Mountain Bike Adventure Company** (tel. (025) 336 333) will bring you and a rented bike up the gondola so you can cruise down for about $38-49; book at the visitors center. Take the gondola ($12 round-trip, students $9, children $6) or walk up the steep bridle path (about 1hr.) to the top for a view encompassing Christchurch, the distant Southern Alps, and, on the Banks Peninsula side, Lyttelton Harbour. If you've got a car or bike, continue along the summit road to **Godley Head,** a rugged promontory of grassy paths and sheer cliffs overlooking the austere Pacific, with superb stargazing at night. In the other direction along Summit Rd., down Dyers Pass Rd., is the **Sign of the Takahe** (tel. 332 4052), one of three Gothic mansions built as a stopping point for travelers decades ago. If you've got a car and a fair night, the Takahe offers a magnificent view of the lights of Christchurch and the Canterbury Plains. *(During the day, the #2 Cashmere bus runs up to the hills.)*

Hot-air balloon enthusiasts flock to the vast flatness of the Canterbury plains. Join either **Up Up and Away** (tel. 358 9859) or **Aoraki Balloon Safaris** (tel. 0800 256 837) for a leisurely float ($220). Skydiving with **Jump in the Park** (tel. (025) 321 135) lands you a half km from Cathedral Sq., after a harrowing free fall (with guide; $245). Or, paraglide from the Gondola down to Sumner with **Phoenix Paragliding** (tel. 326 7634), an exhilarating descent of near weightlessness (to match the state of your wallet afterward; glides start from $80). Equestrians have a range of options for exploring the Canterbury countryside: some of the best short trips are run by **Longspur Lodge** (tel. 329 0005), on the road to Akaroa. A one-hour trip by the edge of Lake Ellesmere is $25. *(2hr. $40; transport to and from Christchurch $25.)*

Christchurch also hosts an amazing number of **festivals** for a city its size. In November, **Showtime Canterbury** hits the city with its concerts, fireworks, and parades. After the New Year, the **International Buskers Festival** brings crazy, nutty street entertainers from around the world to the city in one of the wackiest outdoor festivals in the world. The Festival **of Flowers** blooms every February, bedecking Cathedral Sq. with a floral carpet. It includes garden competitions, street decorations, and visits to private gardens. Summer is also the season for outdoor opera and rock concerts, a wine and food festival in February, and **Adventure Canterbury** in April, which celebrates Canterbury's adrenaline activities for two weeks. The **Christchurch Arts Festival** runs at the end of July in odd years, with multimedia performing arts and exhibitions, and every August a **winter festival** celebrates the ski season, with imported snow (part of Cathedral Sq. is even covered with make-shift drifts and huge snow sculptures).

■ Canterbury Skiing

The skifields in Canterbury's Southern Alps heat up in winter, with ski fever hitting full speed around May and June. Many fields are only a short distance from Christchurch or **Methven** (see below), and offer most of the same activities with less glitz and cheaper rates than the tourist-heavy locales in the southern lakes. For detailed information on skifields, pick up the complementary *Brown Bear* guide, or check out their website (http://www.brownbear.co.nz).

Porter Heights (tel. 379 7087) is the closest field to Christchurch, and boasts the country's longest vertical drop and Monday two-for-one deals (lift passes $44, student $34). With the longest season in New Zealand (May-Oct.), **Mt. Hutt** (tel. 308 5074) attracts crowds of skiers who base themselves at Methven. The 2075m summit boasts 365 hectares of beautiful powder and 42 hectares of snow-making, as well as fabulous views into the heart of the Southern Alps. Challenging terrain suitable for all skiing abilities and a new half-pipe more than justifies the $53 lift pass (students $45; children $26). In addition to the commercial skifields, several club fields open their slopes to the public—at a much cheaper price. Be prepared for T-bars and rope tows. Arthur's Pass is the base for skiing at **Temple Basin** (tel. 377 7788), which has some of the best snowboard terrain in New Zealand. Night skiing is included in the price of a day pass ($30; 45min. walk to the skifield). Other skifields include **Mt. Olympus, Mt. Lyford, Mt. Cheesman, Amori Skifield** near Hammer Springs, and **Craigieburn Valley Ski Field** (see p. 259). Several companies provide transport from Christchurch. **Snowline Tours** (tel. (0800) 275 4669) runs door-to-door service to Mt. Hutt, Porter Heights, Mt. Cheeseman, Mt. Olympus, and Craigieburn Valley ($35 return; students $30). The **Ski Shuttle** (tel. 324 3641) is cheaper, but runs only to Mt. Hutt ($32; students $28) and Porter Heights ($26; students $24).

METHVEN Every winter the tiny community of Methven (pop. 1000) swells with skiers and snowboarders eager to take on the slopes of nearby **Mt. Hutt**. A sleepy town of residential cottages and gardens surrounded by patchwork farmland with the Rakaia and Rangitata Rivers on either side, Methven's proximity to the Southern Alps has earned it the title **Mt. Hutt Village**.

Restaurants and ski shops line **SH77** (also known as Main St.) and accommodations are scattered within a 5-minute walk. The **Visitors Information Center** (tel./fax 302 8955) on Main St. has maps, accommodation, and transport info (open in winter daily 8am-5:30pm; in summer M-F 9am-noon and 1-5pm, Sa-Su 9am-noon and 2-5pm). To get anywhere from Methven, you're better off heading to Christchurch and leaving from there. **InterCity** (tel. 379 9020) runs from the visitors center to Christchurch (1hr., 4:55pm, $14) and Queenstown (9hr., 9:35am, $78). **Methven Travel** (tel. (0800) 764 444) goes to the Christchurch airport (3-4 daily, $20) and Christchurch (2 daily, $20, $35 return). Numerous shuttles run to Mt. Hutt for around $18 return; your best option is to go to the visitors center and take the next departure. **BNZ** is on Main St. (open M-F 9am-4:30pm). The **post office** (tel. 302 8463) is in Gifts Galore on Main St. (open M-F 8am-6pm, Sa-Su 9:30am-12:30pm and 3:30-6pm). In an **emergency,** dial **111** or try the **local police** (tel. 302 8200). The **telephone code** is **03.**

Methven boasts a remarkable number of hotels and lodges catering to the crowds of skiiers. **Agnes Rose Lodge** (tel. 302 8556) is a mint green cottage on McKenew St. (3 blocks from the visitors center). Stained glass windows, bean bag chairs, and an endearing potbelly stove grace the spacious lounge and kitchen. Well-heated dorms are $15. Turn onto Bank St. (next to the visitors center) and left on McMillan to reach **Snowline Lodge** (tel./fax 302 8883). Two fires burn in the kitchen and lounge, and the intimate dorms have solid wood frame bunks with ladders. (Dorms $15, $100 per week; check-out 10am.)Unless you're a connoisseur of pub meals and takeaways, cheap food options are hard to come by in Methven. With salmon walls and spare decor, **Cafe 131** (tel. 302 9131) on Main St. has $6 snack and drink après-ski specials daily from 4-6pm, but the meal options are more expensive ($15-23). After a hard day on the slopes, skiers and snowboarders pack into the **Blue Pub** (tel. 302 8046). You can't miss the blueberry-colored building illuminated by Christmas lights on Main St. Decent pub meals hover around $8. **4 Square Supermarket** (tel. 302 8114) on McMillan St. has fresh produce (open daily 7am-8pm).

Methven is primarily a stop en route to the **Mt. Hutt** (see p. 253). Several ski and board shops have rental deals a bit cheaper than on the mountain. **Big Al's** (tel. 302 8003) in the Square rents skis ($21) and boards ($35) in addition to clothing and mountain bikes ($25 per day). **Wombat's Ski Shop** (tel. 302 8084) has similar prices (open in winter 7:30am-6:30pm).

■ Near Christchurch: Lyttelton and Sumner

Christchurch's port and beach suburbs make for convenient and pleasant daytrips from the city. **Lyttelton** slopes down the far side of the port hills to the industrialized harbor. Fifteen minutes from the city via the tunnel road (bus #28, $1.80), the port is home to a compelling mix of far-flung sailors and bohemian locals. Little Edwardian cottages line the steep streets, and several oddball curiosity shops and cafes dot the town. The **Volcano Café and Lava Bar** (tel. 328 7077), on London St. at Canterbury St., erupts with barbed wire art and stucco walls that vaguely resemble cooling lava. Carved wooden benches and hanging plants adorn the back garden. Big portions of food and excellent coffee are draws themselves; most dinners range from $15 to $23 (open daily from 5pm). Right next to the supermarket on London St, a neon sign announces **Wunderbar** (tel. 328 8818). Follow the signs down the stairs, through the parking lot, and up the ramp—it's worth the walk. Illuminated mannequins in silk shirts and a lamp made of dolls' heads cast light on the velvet seats and tribal masks along the bar. In the **Backroom Bar,** a shimmering cabaret stage complete with a Saturn-shaped disco ball opens Thursdays through Saturdays for dancing, live music, and cabaret shows. Despite over-the-top trappings, the mood remains entirely relaxed. (Open M-F 5pm-3am, Sa-Su 3pm-3am.)

The **visitors center** (tel. 328 9093) on London St. at Oxford St. has self-guided walking tours ($1.50) of this historic port, while the exhibits of the **Lyttelton Museum** ($1-2) will answer the pressing question: Where did Scott and Shackleton train their teams for their Antarctic expeditions? (Museum open Tu, Th, Sa-Su 2-4pm in summer). The **Lyttelton Timeball Station** (tel. 328 7311) once communicated Greenwich Mean Time to the boats in the harbor so they could accurately gauge their longitude. One of five remaining in the world, the station is a curiosity befitting this somewhat anachronistic maritime town ($2.50, children $1; usually open daily 10am-5pm). Summer Sundays at 2pm, the 90-year-old **Tug Lyttelton** (tel. 322 8911) sets out on a 1½ hour historical cruise of the harbor ($12). **Lyttelton Harbor Cruises** (tel. 328 8368) has a half-hour tour every day at 2:45pm ($8, children $4).

Surfers and sun-worshippers flock to the little stretch of beach at **Sumner** (accessible by bus #3, $1.80), Christchurch's summer beach resort town. **Cave Rock,** near town, is a natural grotto accessible at low tide; beware of sudden surges if you choose to venture inside. After a beachside stroll, enjoy a coffee drink at **Coffee Culture** (tel. 326 5900), along the main street. Plan your next world sojourn with the inlaid coffee-bean world maps on the tables as you sip a chocolate latte ($3.20; open M-F from 7:30am, Sa-Su from 9am). Spend the evening at the **Ruptured Duck** (tel. 326 5488) next door, which serves an enormous array of gourmet pizzas (medium $14). The big window has a great vista of the sea, and the occasional wine tastings and comedy nights in the bar downstairs may quack you up (restaurant open daily from noon; bar open nightly from 5pm).

■ Akaroa and the Banks Peninsula

Pale green hills dotted with dark pines slope down toward the amazingly blue bays of the **Banks Peninsula.** From Lyttelton Harbour in the west to the rugged Pacific shore, the bare rolling hillsides and bracing air are a refreshing change from the eternal flatness of the Canterbury Plains. First sighted by Captain Cook in 1770, the area's safe harbors attracted the attention of French whalers, who purchased the land from the Maori in 1838. It wasn't until colonist **Charles Lavaud** had completed the harrowing voyage from France that he learned of the Treaty of Waitangi and British sovereignty (see p. 55). The French may have been forced to sell their land claims to the British, but they left their cultural mark on **Akaroa,** the area's chief city.

Magical and anachronistic, Akaroa's French-named streets and *maisons,* little fishing harbor, and many herb gardens seem worlds away from urban Christchurch, despite the mere 82km that separate them. Cyclists, hikers, and equestrians who have discovered Akaroa's small-town friendliness all head for the provincial charm of its misty hills come summer. As proud of their history as they are of their way of life, Akaroans are quick to tell a tale or two. Although there's not a French speaker to be found on the peninsula, the cheese factory and winery retain whispers of the area's cultural legacy. When you're ready to escape the city, don't miss spending a quiet night beneath the peninsula's mystical stars.

ORIENTATION AND PRACTICAL INFORMATION   Running past the varied avifauna of shallow **Lake Ellesmere** and through several tiny towns, **SH75** finally winds down to the harbor of Akaroa, some 1¼ hours southeast of Christchurch. The town itself lies along **Rue Lavaud** and **Beach Rd.** along the water. Akaroa's **visitors center,** 80 Rue Lavaud (tel. 304 8600), has info on local accommodations and walking tracks (open daily 9am-5pm). The **post office** (tel. 304 7701) is right next door (open M-F 8:30am-5pm). **BNZ** (tel. 304 7050), in the artful pink- and blue-trimmed house across the street, distributes money and postcards of itself (open M-F 9am-4:30pm). In an **emergency,** dial **111,** or contact the **police** (tel. 304 7030) or the **local hospital** (tel. 304 7023).

The **Akaroa Shuttle** (tel. (0800) 500 929) leaves from the Akaroa visitors center for Christchurch daily (1-3 per day; $15, round-trip $25). The **French Connection** (tel. 377 0951) includes commentary and stops at the cheese factory; it departs from the Christchurch visitors center, returning the same day at 3:30pm from Akaroa's main wharf (daily in summer 8:45am; in winter M, W, Sa 9:30am; $19, round-trip $38, backpackers $26). **Hitchhiking** is also possible to and from Christchurch, as most traffic goes all the way to Akaroa; most thumbers first take the #7 Halswell bus from Cathedral Sq. **Renting a car** is a good idea for exploring the Banks Peninsula (see p. 244 for Christchurch rental options). Otherwise, you can hop on the **mail run** (tel. 304 7207) to see the remotest reaches of the peninsula (8:20am and 2pm, $20). The **telephone code** is **03.**

ACCOMMODATIONS   Loaded with character, Akaroa's accommodations will entice you to stay longer than you might plan at first—even if you can't move in for good. **Chez La Mer Backpackers,** on Rue Lavaud (tel. 304 7024), built by a Spaniard from Madeira in 1871, still exudes Old World charm with its herb garden, gazebo, endearingly uneven floors, and free muesli and spices. Incredibly cozy little rooms above the rose trellis overlook the hills. The owner will even take guests on his yacht for a few hours ($15). Check-out is at 10am, but the house is available all day. Towels and linen are $3 (dorms $15; singles $25; doubles or twins $36; one double with bath $40). Mountain bikes are free for guests. An excellent bargain in the B&B department is **Lavaud House** (tel./fax 304 7121), next door to the BNZ on gardened grounds. View the bay from the sitting room in the historic house filled with antique tables and dressers. Check-out is at 10am (singles $60; twins and doubles $80; with bath add $10). More remote is **Mount Vernon Lodge** (tel. 304 7180), 2km up Rue Grehan off Rue Lavaud; phone and they'll pick you up. The rustic lodge runs a stable and encourages a rural experience through the raftered, two-level rooms with ladders leading to upstairs beds. The sunken wood stove in the dining area is more than comfortable; it may addict you. Horse treks are $30 per hour. (Dorms in summer $18, $20 with bedding; in winter $20 for 2 nights; cabins $70 for 2, additional bed $10. Reception open daily in summer 8am-6pm, in winter 9am-5pm. Check-out 10am.)

FOOD   Don't miss having tea or coffee at **Tree Crop Farm** (tel. 304 7158), up Rue Grehan half an hour by foot from the town center, where the blueberry-colored dwelling is more mythical myopia than conventional cafe. Relax on lambskins and chairs crafted of gnarled branches while coffee is served on wooden flower-strewn trays presented with fruit and nut brownies ($5). A stream runs past the gnome-ish huts and weathered white house, down the valley toward the triple hills beyond Akaroa Harbour. The place exudes magic; go at dusk to be transported to another time and place. When you return to town, walk around and check out menus before settling on a bite to eat. Several Akaroa eateries gain inspiration from the French, and unless you adore pub food and pies, they're worth the extra dollars. **Bully Hayes** (tel. 304 7533), on the waterfront, has gourmet lunches for around $10 to $14, while evening cuisine runs around $19. Windows surround the diners, and a fish-shaped lemon wedge is included in your water. (Open W-Th and Su-M 10am-3pm and 5-8pm, F-Sa 10am-3pm and 5-9:30pm.) For those with empty stomachs and empty wallets, the **Akaroa Bakery,** next to Bully Hayes, has fresh baked bread ($2 per loaf) and home-made sandwiches ($2.50; open daily 7:30am-4pm). The **Four Square** supermarket, on Rue Lavaud across from the museum, fills your grocery needs (open daily 9am-6pm).

SIGHTS AND OUTDOORS The **Akaroa Museum** (tel. 304 7614) encompasses four buildings, including the **Langlois-Eteveneaux Cottage,** which was partially prefabricated in France before being brought over in the 1830s. *(Open daily in summer 10:30am-4:30pm; daily in winter 10:30am-4pm; $3, children $1.)* Well-conceived exhibits include everything from traditional Maori clothing to a 1910 gig complete with nearly 2m high wheels.)

Many of Akaroa's activities are centered around its beautiful bay and varied marine life. **Akaroa Harbour Cruises** (tel. 304 7641; fax 304 7643), on the main wharf, operates the Canterbury Cat (2hr.; $27), which visits much of the harbor, including the seal and cormorant colonies. You can also swim with the rare Hector's dolphins that frequent the sheltered bay. *(Call ahead for times and to book. $65, children $45; spectators $29.)* Independent cruising may be the best way to experience the placid bay; **Banks Peninsula Sea Kayaks** (tel. 304 8776) hires kayaks ($45 per day) and runs guided tours ($48-95). Go paddleboating ($12 per hr.) or boating in an aluminum motor boat ($30 per hr.) through **Akaroa Boat Hire** (tel. 304 8758), by the wharf. Numerous tracks depart from Akaroa; ask at the visitor's center for details.

■ Arthur's Pass National Park

Nested amongst the towering peaks of the Southern Alps, the tiny village of **Arthur's Pass** serves double duty as a crucial pass through the mountains and a jumping off point for skiers and hikers. The building of a viaduct just down the road (due for completion in November of 1999) may have boosted the town's population from 50 to a whopping 120, but don't expect to find more than the basic amenities. Straddling the Main Divide of the Southern Alps, the village is dramatically perched between two tectonic plates and two natural habitats, as the beech forest of Canterbury meet the rain forests of the West Coast. During winter it's not uncommon to find the road through the pass, **SH73,** closed due to snow (something that outsiders are frequently aware of even before villagers). The railroad, completed in 1923, has always managed to plow its way through snowdrift and avalanche, however. The journey up to Arthur's Pass provides endless breathtaking views of the plunging valleys and soaring mountains of the surrounding 250,000-acre **Arthur's Pass National Park**.

PRACTICAL INFORMATION The **Arthur's Pass Visitor Information Centre** and **DOC office** (tel. 318 9211; fax 318 9271) is on the left as you walk towards the village from the train station (open daily in summer 8am-5pm, in winter 9am-4pm). **TranzScenic** (tel. (0800) 802 802) crosses through the heart of the South Island to explore gorges, river valleys, and alpine fields not visible from SH73. It runs daily to **Christchurch** (4:30pm, 2hr., $54, with return $76) and **Greymouth** (11:20am, 2hr., $34). As for shuttles, **Coast-to-Coast** (tel. (0800) 800 847) and **Alpine Coach and Courier** (tel. (0800) 274 888) both run daily to **Christchurch** (1 per day, 2hr., $18-25); **Greymouth** (1 per day, 1½hr., $12-15); **Hokitika** (1 per day, 2-3hr., $13-15). **KO-OP Shuttles** (tel. 366 6633) runs only to **Christchurch** and **Greymouth**. Contact **police** (tel. 318 9212) in an emergency. The **telephone code** is 03.

ACCOMMODATIONS AND FOOD Backpackers relax in the coal stove lounge presided over by a Maori statue at the **Sir Arthur Dudley Dobson Memorial YHA** (tel. 318 9230). The mural in the lounge illustrates the life of Sir Arthur Dudley Dobson, the first man to survey Arthur's Pass in 1864. The owner can give plenty of advice on

The Mysterious Moa

Have moas really been extinct for about 500 years, or are they still roaming deep in the New Zealand bush? Occasional reports have trickled in from time to time from deep in the mountain country of Fiordland. The debate rekindled to full fury in January 1993 after three hikers reported seeing a live moa in the Craigieburn Range. A blurry photograph accompanied the story and thrust the travelers out of the bush and into front-page headlines for over a week. While there were some believers, others saw it as just a publicity stunt. Follow-up letters and articles recalled past moa sightings and speculated on what other animal the hikers might have seen: an emu, red deer, goose, or ostrich were some suggestions. A pair of German backpackers in the Craigieburn Range had written in the Bealey Hut intentions book the year before that they had seen two moa in the Harper Valley (authorities were unable to track down the Germans to question them). Following the more recent 1993 account and attendant publicity and interest, the DOC almost went ahead with a field search. Don't expect to bring home any moa trophies, however: regardless of whether they exist, moas are reputed to be protected species under the Wildlife Act (just in case). The only way to shoot a moa, if you're lucky enough to see one, is with your camera. If you go tramping around Lagoon Saddle in the Craigieburn Range, don't forget your camera—and most importantly, don't forget to focus.

hunting in the region. Storage available. (Reception open daily 8-10am and 5-10pm; when closed, a board on the office door indicates where there is room in the hostel.) Check-out is at 10am. Bunks $15, doubles $36 (non-YHA $4 more). **Mountain House Backpackers** (tel. 318 9258), located across from the YHA, twinkles with its periwinkle kitchen, spiral staircase, and glass-house room (a veritable sauna during the day and an ice-house at night). One owner works at the visitors center and knows plenty about the area. Rent ice-axes, crampons, sleeping mats, and more. Bunks are $16, or camp on the gounds and use the facilities for $9. From May to September, take advantage of the winter special: stay 2 nights and get the third free. A self-booking system is available; check-out at 10am. (Reception open daily in summer from 10am-noon and 5:30-7:30pm; in winter from 9:30-11am and from 5:30-7pm.) There is a **DOC campsite** with a shelter across the street from the visitors center for those looking to rough it while in town, complete with toilets and water in the summer ($3 per person). **Klondyke Corner,** which is 8km up the road towards Christchurch, provides free roadside camping with pit toilets (water must be fetched from the river).

Chalet's Restaurant and Bar, (tel. 318 9236), in town a few minutes walk past the hostels to the right, infuses a glint of glamour into this homey town. Between walls peppered with serene artwork matching the slopes outside, the hungry traveler can snag a sandwich ($2.20) for lunch of spaghetti ($9.50) for dinner. Just be sure to sit in the laid-back dining room, not the fancy one (yes, there are two) as the menu in the latter is limited to more costly items (open 11am-2pm, 5:30pm-8:30pm; closes an hour early in winter). For an exotic twist, try **Oscar's Haus Cafe** (tel. 318 9234), right next to the YHA hostel. Mediterranean and vegetarian dishes grace a friendly vibe. But for the truly economical, **Arthur's Pass Tearooms** (tel. 318 9235) is a cheap and speedy alternative. Wash down a chicken or mince pie ($2) with one of many beverage choices.

OUTDOORS With spectacular mountain terrain, gorges, rivers, waterfalls, alpine meadows, and glaciers, **Arthur's Pass National Park** has something for everybody, but especially pleases the seasoned veteran. Always be aware that the extreme weather can be dangerous, and check with the **DOC** before heading out. Shuttles run sporadically from Arthur's Pass village to a range of **ski clubs,** including the popular **Temple Basin Skifield,** which was recently voted the country's best snowboarding area. Although the majority of the ski clubs are private, they can be joined and enjoyed inexpensively. Most slopes require a high level of proficiency. For the scoop on skiing, pick up the free *Brown Bear Guide* or ask at the visitors center. There is a great range of hikes available, including some which are suitable for all levels. The **Devil's Punchbowl Waterfall** (1 hr. round trip) trail begins several hundred meters down the road from the visitors center and leads trampers to an arrestingly gorgeous view of the falls. The **Cass-Lagoon Saddle,** a popular summertime tramp (beware avalanches in winter) is one of the easier overnight hikes (arrange in advance with DOC for Arthur's Pass hut tickets, ranging in price from free to $8).

Craigieburn Forest Park, just south of Arthur's Pass, extends from Highway 73 in the east almost as far as the Mian Divide in the west. Sprawled between the Waimakariri and Wilberforce Rivers, the park delights botanists with its eastern mountain beech forest and mixed podocarp, treefern, and moss-covered forest. Although small, the park is a haven experienced outdoor enthusiasts. The best day hikes are clustered around the **Park Headquarters** (2km off of SH73, about a half hour drive east of Arthur's Pass village), where travelers can also find information, picnic sites, camping sites, and a shelter. There is a smattering of huts and shelters throughout the park, but most are on multi-day hikes and are accessible only to the experienced tramper. **Skiing** dominates the chillier months with very limited slopes for beginners but plenty of options for advanced skiers. Fly down **Mt. Olympus** ($30, $20 for students) or pay a visit to either of the area's small clubs, **Broken River** ($30, $20 for students) and **Craigeburn Valley** ($28, $25 students on weekdays, $35 weekends). Both clubs offer accommodations, packages, lessons, and reduced rates for members, but you'll have to bring your own equipment. If you've got a little extra time, the huge limestone formations of **Castle Hill** (off of 73 about a 45 minute drive east of Arthur's Pass, 7km past the turn-off to the Craigeburn headquarters) are a smashing place for a picnic when the weather is decent. Castle Hill is most easily reached by travelers with their own transportation, as shuttles run very infrequently.

SOUTHERN CANTERBURY

Sheep. New Zealand is known for them in the millions, and much of Canterbury south and west of Christchurch is full of them. Speckled with small agricultural outposts, the unending Canterbury plains slowly blend into the coastal climes of Timaru. Heading inland from Timaru, the plains give way to the mountain passes leading to an area known as the Mackenzie Country. It gained its name when over a thousand sheep were discovered missing one day in 1843, and James Mackenzie, a Scotsman, was caught, tried, and imprisoned. He allegedly escaped from jail three times and quickly became New Zealand's most famous outlaw. This area has seen little development in the years since Mackenzie's escapades, remaining an agricultural region whose serene beauty provides welcome relief from the bustle of cities to the north and south. The mighty Mt. Cook reposes at the northern end of Lake Pukaki, and in the heart of the Southern Alps mountains everywhere are reflected in the basin's most famous lake, Tekapo. Covered with tussock grassland and sheep paddocks, and dotted with brilliant lakes against a backdrop of incomparable mountain scenery, southern Canterbury is quiet and ruggedly pastoral.

▓ Timaru

Gateway to the Mackenzie Country and situated on the rolling hills above the sandy crescent of Caroline Bay, Timaru has yet to trade in its honest charm for tourist dollars. First named Te Maru, meaning "place of shelter," Timaru once provided water and rest for traveling Maori hunters. The British found Timaru less welcoming, managing to accidentally sink two of their own ships on a single day in 1882. The whaling industry flourished here in the early 1840s, leaving washed-up rubbish and whale bits all over the beaches. Luckily for surfers and beachgoers, Caroline Bay has fully recovered from the trauma. However, Timaru remains a port town. Today, an artificial harbor begun in 1877 protects the international fishing fleet and rigs full of live sheep bound for Asia. Taking its maritime history in stride, the city has renovated many of the Victorian buildings that catered to overseas travelers throughout the last century. While the verdant parks and ocean vistas of Timaru persevere, hints of cosmopolitanism are emerging in this town of 27,000.

CANTERBURY

ORIENTATION AND PRACTICAL INFORMATION Midway between Christchurch and Dunedin, Timaru is poised on the foothills of the Central Alps, just south of the road to Mt. Cook. From the train station, head left across **George St.** to the visitors center, where you'll find free maps, local bus schedules, self-guided walking tours, and information on regional events. **Stafford St.,** the main drag, is just outside and to the left; tranquil **Caroline Bay** is a 15-minute walk uphill through the business district. The **Visitor Information Centre** (tel. 688 6163; fax 688 6162) is located at 14 George St. (open M-F 8:30am-5pm, Sa-Su 10am-3pm). You can change money at **BNZ,** near the visitors center (open M-F 9am-4:30pm). **TranzScenic** (tel. 688 3597) leaves daily for **Christchurch** (2hr., 3:10pm., $36), and **Invercargill** (7hr., 10:35am, $85) via **Dunedin** (3½hr., $41). Inquire about advance bookings with 20% to 50% discounts at the train station. The **telephone code** is **03.**

Buses run by **InterCity** and **Ritchie Transport** (tel. 684 7195) leave from the train station for Christchurch (2¼hr., 3-4 per day, $26) via Ashburton (1¾hr., $14), and to Dunedin (3½hr., 2-3 per day, $30) via Oamaru (1¼hr., $14). Various **shuttle** services ($15-25 to Christchurch) are also available; check with the visitors center for more info. **Hitchhikers** heading north report that the base of the highway up to Mt. Cook is a good place to catch a ride to the mountains. Otherwise, SH1 north or south of town (before cars speed up into the countryside) is considered the easiest place to grab a ride. The **hospital** is on High and Queen St. (tel. 684 3089). The **police** (tel. 688 4199) are at North and Barnard St., while the **post office** (tel. 688 5518) is on Sophia St., off King George Place (open M-F 8:30am-5:30pm, Sa 9:30am-12:30pm).

ACCOMMODATIONS Spacious, well-equipped triples in a three-bedroom home with a cheery fireplace are the norm at **Timaru Backpackers (YHA),** 42 Evans St. (tel. 684 5067). The lounge area boasts a TV, a kitchen, and a wee little potbelly stove. Phone and the owner will pick you up. All rooms with heating units and shared shower/bath are $17. A poorly marked entrance on the corner of Stafford St. and Church St. leads to **Old Bank Backpackers** (tel. 684 4392), a bare-bones accommodation run by the Old Bank Cafe. Spare but clean dorms have metal frame bunks and wall heaters (dorm $14, twin $32, linen at additional cost). The **Timaru Selwyn Holiday Park** (tel. 684 7690), an extensive camp facility 2km outside of town on Selwyn St., has 100 powered sites sitting by a swift creek as well as a pinball machine, TV lounge, and immaculate shower blocks. (Tent sites $8; self-contained tourist flats $52 for 2, extra person $11.)

FOOD "Man cannot discover new oceans... until he has courage to lose sight of the shore," opines a scrawled aphorism on the wall of **Cafe Cino's** (tel. 688 9439), on Stafford St. between Church and Canon St. Lose sight of your hunger with the famous Dunheath House custard squares ($2), fruit smoothies ($3.50), or the meatless options like the scrumptious veggie filo ($2.50). (Open M-F 9:30am-4:30 pm, Sa 10am-2pm.) **The Loaded Hog** (tel. 684 9999), in the Landing Service Building by the information center, is a trendy microbrew chain that serves as the late-night hot spot for the younger crowd. Affectionately called "the Pissed Pig" by the locals, agricultural tools adorn the walls of a vast, restored bluestone building dating back to the 1870s. Bite into the $5 lunch specials such as Malaysian chicken on foccacia and wash it down with a $4 pint of Hog's Head Dark. (Open daily 11am 'til late.) Close to the backpackers and campground, ukulele- and sombrero-bedecked walls comprise the entirety of Timaru's Little Mexico at **South of the Border,** 88 Evans St. (tel. 688 5189), 1km north of town. Amid the Corona signs, you'll find wooden tables, beer, port, sherry, and extravagant servings. The $7 lunch special is siesta-inducing. (Open M 5:30-8:30pm, Tu-Su 11am-8:30pm.) Head over the hill via Stafford St. and you'll hit the cozy wine bar of **Boudicca's,** 64 Bay Hill (tel. 688 8550). Besides a large wine selection, the all-day menu includes Middle Eastern falafel-stuffed pitas (small $5, large $8; open M 5-9pm, W-Sa 11am-10pm, Su and Tu 11am-9pm).

SIGHTS AND ACTIVITIES While Timaru serves as a base for cyclists, boaters, fishers, and skiers hankering for a bit of fresh air, its local charms are not to be missed. Walk up the Benvenue Cliffs on the far side of the beach for a view of the harbor. Today, memorial plaques nailed to the post commemorate lost ships. **Caroline Bay** and its shallow sweep of sand bustle in the summer months—the reclaimed park contains an **aviary** with bevies of technicolor parakeets, an open stage, miniature golf during the summer, and a host of other activities. From Boxing Day (Dec. 26) until mid-January, the bay area hosts a grand **Christmas/New Year Carnival** that draws crowds to concerts and contests.

Built in 1908, the Edwardian mammoth of the **Aigantighe Art Gallery** (tel. 688 4424) has manicured grounds and a sculpture garden overlooking Timaru's rooftops. *(Aigantighe Art Gallery open Tu-F 11am-4:30pm, Sa-Su 2-4:30pm; free.).* Gaelic for "at the house," the Aigantighe (EGG-and-tie) houses mainly early colonial New Zealand paintings, but includes rotating exhibitions in a modern room with ethereal landscapes. Glance into the **Mooseum** to see a room devoted entirely to paintings of...you guessed it, cows. On Perth St. near the post office, the **South Canterbury Museum,** an antique collection-cum-natural history gallery of mostly regional interest, features an odd assortment of artifacts, including drawers of Victorian clothing and a (sadly nonfunctional) kiss-o-meter. *(Open Tu-F 10am-4:30pm, Sa-Su 1:30-4:30pm; free.)*

Re-Wrighting the History of Flight

Though his neighbors believed the inventions of "Mad Pearse" were the work of the devil, by contemporary standards Richard Pearse's efforts were closer to miraculous. Pearse built a powered plane in 1903 and made several shaky flights some nine months before the Kittyhawk flight of the Wright brothers. Although Pearse didn't consider his achievement to have been true "flight," his plane stayed aloft longer and was technologically superior to the Wright brothers' device. A tattered replica on display at the South Canterbury Museum is the only remainder of his aerial ingenuity. Since officials were later unable to verify the exact flight date, Pearse gave up striving for fame after learning of the exploits of the Wright brothers. Forever the tinkerer, Pearse also produced many inventions with fewer consequences for the modern world, including a needle threading device and a potato planter.

The **Timaru Botanic Gardens,** a 15-minute walk south along Stafford St. (which becomes King St.), includes lush walkways, ponds, and even a fernery. Beer, a major fixture of the South Islander's diet, is produced in massive fermentation vessels at **DB Brewery** (tel. 688 2059). *(Free tours M-Th at 10:30am; machinery running W-Th. Enclosed footwear required.)* If you can, get a ride to Sheffield St. and sample just one of the 55 million liters produced here. On Wednesdays, watch endless columns of bottles move through the factory. You'll leave happy—maybe a little too happy.

■ Tekapo

Encircled by the majestic peaks of the Southern Alps, the milky blue waters of Lake Tekapo lap gently against smooth pebble beaches. The tiny stone church perched on the edge of the lake (see cover) makes for a mesmerizing view, enhanced by the pure air brought down from the mountains by the relentless wind. With a moon bright enough to cast spooky shadows off the pines, and a great swath of stars arcing across the horizon, Tekapo's nights complement the serenity of the day.

Tekapo is centered along **SH8,** which crosses the dam controlling the Tekapo River. The hide shop functions as the **visitors center** (tel./fax 680 6721) and has information on several homestays (open daily in summer 9am-8pm, in winter 9am-6pm). Book your **bus,** stock up on **groceries,** and mail letters from the **Shell Station** (tel. 680 6809), which also functions as the **post office** (open M-Sa 7:30am-7pm, Su 8am-7pm). **InterCity, Mt. Cook Landline, Southern Link Shuttles,** and **Atomic Shuttles** (tel. 322 8883) all run daily to Christchurch (4hr., 1 per day, $20-42) and Queenstown (5½hr., 1 per day, $25-55). Book InterCity at **High Country Crafts** (tel. 680 6895), Mt. Cook and Southern Link at **Alpine Adventures** (tel. 860 6858), and Atomic Shuttles at the YHA. The local **police** are at 680 6855.

The **Tekapo YHA** (tel. 680 6857) is on Simpson Ln., past the pub on the west side of town and through the little gate. The common room has massive windows, a soulful view of the lake, board games, and a blue upright piano. Stoveside couches are outside the intimate dorms. (Dorms $15; twins $36; tent sites $9; non-YHA members $4 extra. Reception 8am-10am, 5-6:30pm and 8-10pm; check-out 9:30am.) Up Aorangi Crescent across from the tavern is **Tailor-made Tekapo Backpackers** (tel. 688 6700), with three spacious buildings on gardened grounds. The yellow kitchen is graced with a wooden chess board and an edible mushroom poster (sampling not recommended); some bathrooms have glowingly mint-green walls. (Dorms $15; doubles or twins $34. Linen $1.)

Restaurants and takeaways dot SH8. **Kohan Restaurant** (tel. 680 6688) in the Alpine Inn complex has a generous array of sushi ($16), and their seared salmon steaks are widely renowned. After being greeted in Japanese and receiving a hot towel, nibble on a vegetable appetizer while you peruse the menu. Dinners start at $10 (open daily 11:30am-2pm and 6-9pm). **Reflections** (tel. 680 6808), by the pub, has won cuisine awards for its meat dishes; if you're game, there's beef, lamb, venison ($18.50-21.50), and a warm fire. Lunches cost around $10, while dinners start at $12.50. (Open daily 11am-8pm; later in summer.)

Stroll across the bridge and down to the **Church of the Good Shepherd,** a tiny interdenominational church of wood and stone constructed in 1935 (see cover). Another kind of good shepherd is immortalized just down the shore in the form of a proud bronze sheep dog, silhouetted against the sky (the statue commemorates the dog's years of faithful service). Walks in the area include the popular 2½-hour circuit up **Mt. John** and back, through pine forest and up to the observatory (it begins past the motor park, near the ice skating rink along the lake's western side). A circuit track to **Cowan's Lookout** leaves from the far side of the bridge, offering comparable views of Mt. John (in about 1hr. less), but the track can be difficult to follow—watch for the red and white markers. In summer, you can rent all sorts of items from the **Alpine Inn** (tel. 680 6848), including mountain bikes ($30 per day) and kayaks ($10 first hr., $5 each additional hr.); they run **High Country Horse Trekking** ($45 for 2hr.), boat fishing ($65 for 2hr.), and water skiing ($100 per hr.). **Alpine Adventures** runs boat trips ($70 for 2hr.), and rents fishing gear (rods $15 per day, day license $12). For quite a bit of money, they can also arrange just about any activity with the prefix "heli."

■ Mt. Cook National Park

With one-third of its 70,000 hectares permanently snow-covered, Mt. Cook National Park's jagged peaks present an austere and forbidding profile; notoriously capricious weather and frequent avalanches make it one of the most dangerous regions in New Zealand. Dark lateral moraines and milky blue glaciers give an inhuman aspect to the desolate landscape, mitigated only by the screeching calls of the world's only mountain parrot, the kea (see p. 293). With 19 peaks over 3000m and a few hundred over 2000m, Mt. Cook National Park is near the top of the bottom of the world.

MT. COOK VILLAGE At the end of SH80, about an hour away from Twizel, tiny Mt. Cook (pop. 300 in summer) nestles in the heart of Mt. Cook National Park. The dominant feature of town (aside from the mountains) is an upscale hotel known as the **Hermitage.** The **Mt. Cook Visitor Centre** and the **DOC office** (tel. 435 1818; fax 435 1080), near the Hermitage, are the check-in and check-out points for all hikers and mountaineers planning trips in the park (open daily in summer 8:30am-6pm; in winter 8:30am-5pm). Call ahead for **InterCity** (tel. (0800) 686 862); the schedule is flexible, with buses usually departing from the Hermitage and the YHA for Christchurch (5hr., 1pm, $59; YHA members $41) and Queenstown (4hr., 2:45pm, $57; YHA members $40) via Twizel. Head to the **Hermitage** (tel. 435 1809) for the **post office, petrol station** (credit cards only), **grocery store,** and **currency exchange** for those in dire need. Consider bringing enough food and cash to avoid the high prices in Mt. Cook. With pine panelling and plenty of heaters, the **YHA Mt. Cook** (tel. 435 1820) is remarkably well equipped. The drying room and free sauna (open 7-9pm) keep both you and your clothes warm. Some groceries, free movies, and lockers ($2) are available. (Dorms $20; twins $23; doubles $26; non-members $4 more. Reception in summer 8-10:30am, noon-3pm, 5:30-9:30pm; in winter 8-10am, 5-6:30pm, 8-9pm.)

IN THE PARK The peaks, glaciers, and ice cliffs of Mt. Cook National Park draw visitors from all over the world. Those more used to traveling on a shoestring than a belay rope can get a taste of glacial terrain with the many short day walks in the area. The strenuous climb up to **Red Tarns** (2hr. return) rewards exertion with unbelievable views down into the Hooker Valley and up into the cloud-piercing Alps. If you're not up to an hour of steady uphill climbing, the **Kea Point Mountainview Walk** (2hr. return) leads through scraggly gorse to a lookout over the Mueller glacier, with Mt. Sefton's azure ice falls in the background. The only feasible overnight tramping option is the three-to-four-hour route to **Mueller Hut** ($18). The rest of the huts in the park ($8-18) are accessible to experienced climbers and mountaineers, and serves as bases for technical ascents. Always check in with the DOC if you are planning a trip. The Hermitage and the YHA have information on (and serve as booking centers for) several tours.

In the summer, **Glacier Explorers** (tel. 435 1809) runs a boat tour of the Tasman Glacier that glides past the icy blue cliffs jutting out over the lake (2½hr., $60, children $30, YHA $55). **Alan's 4WD Tours** (tel. 435 1809) drives to the Tasman Glacier ($60, children $30). Guided flights are expensive but breathtaking: soar over the highest mountains in Australasia past seas of snow and ice with jagged outcrops of dark rock creating stark outlines against the sky. A variety of flight-seeing operations take off from Mt. Cook airport. **The Helicopter Line** (tel. 435 1801 or (0800) 650 651) has a 20-minute flight with a snow landing for $125 and **Air Safaris** (tel. (0800) 806 880) flies the "Grand Traverse" of Mt. Cook (45min., $160, children $110).

Marlborough and Nelson

Stretching from the tip of Farewell Spit to the tranquil Marlborough Sounds, and from the marine paradise of Kaikoura to the lesser known Nelson Lakes, the "top of the south" provides an incredible variety of natural gems and endless ways to appreciate them. Whether it's skiing down the alpine slopes, tasting award-winning wine, swimming with pods of playful dolphins, or hiking through fern-filled forests with the surf pounding in the distance, Marlborough is unlikely to bore even the shortest attention spans. The wine valleys of Nelson and the hippie, greenie outposts of Golden Bay are all within sight of three national parks. Take advantage of the well-developed tourism infrastructure, or escape it all in the majestic seclusion of the Sounds.

While a few of the area's more isolated towns may be accessible only by mail truck, numerous buses and shuttles connect virtually all of the region. Travelers too impatient to wait try their luck at hitching (though traffic can be light in the winter). With the panoramic views of oceanside snowcapped peaks and winding roads that pass by stands selling crisp, sweet apples, Marlborough *is* the good life.

🖐 MARLBOROUGH AND NELSON HIGHLIGHTS

- In Kaikoura (p. 267), visitors can swim with dolphins, frolic with seals, and search for surfacing whales.
- The Abel Tasman coastal walk (see p. 282), with terrain ranging from verdant rainforest to golden beaches, is the most popular in the country.
- The fresh, relaxed attitude of Nelson (see p. 275) is endlessly welcoming.
- Days drift lazily by in the small towns of Golden Bay (see p. 280).

MARLBOROUGH

▨ Picton

The **Interislander** ferry maneuvers daily across the thin strait that divides New Zealand in two, connecting Picton to Wellington on the island above. Far from being a mere ferry terminal, Picton awes and waylays passers-by with the tranquil beauty of its many surrounding coves and inlets. The region's geological eye candy has resulted in an overwhelming array of tourist-oriented adventures; you can tour everything from vineyards to seal colonies. Picton played a major part in shaping the culture, politics, and economy of New Zealand as we know it today. It was here that the first European child was born and the first sheep stepped onto New Zealand soil, creating the dynamic of mutton, wool, and Pakeha that has shaped the island ever since.

ORIENTATION AND PRACTICAL INFORMATION

Home to the ferry terminal and other crucial transportation links, the whole area lining the harbor is known as Picton's **"Foreshore." Auckland Street** is the hub of transportation activity in Picton, while **High Street** is home to many of the town's shops and cafes. Residential neighborhoods stretch up into the hills. **Waikawa Bay** lies down Dublin St. and left onto Waikawa Rd.

The **Picton Visitor Information Centre** (tel. 573 7477; fax 573 5021) on Auckland St. near London Quay on the same side as the water, has information and bookings for the ferry, shuttles, and the maze of water operators. (Open daily Dec.-Mar. 8:30am-8pm, Apr.-May and Sept.-Nov. 8:30am-6pm, June-Aug. 8:30am-5pm.) The **domestic travel center** (tel. 573 8857), just across the street at the railway station, offers a similar range of bookings (open daily 9am-5 or 6pm). The **DOC office** (tel. 520 3007) is located at the official visitors center. Come here for info, bookings, and

Marlborough and Nelson

permits of all kinds (open M-F 8:30am-4:30pm). Change money at **BNZ,** at the corner of High St. and Waikawa Rd. (open M-F 9am-4:30pm) or at **TrustBank,** at Mariners Mall on High St. (open M-F 9am-4:30pm, except W 9:30am-4:30pm). **U-Square** supermarket (tel. 573 6443), 49 High St., will change money after hours.

The Picton area uses the **Koromiko airstrip,** about 9km away, for its flights. **Sounds Air** (tel. 573 6184 or (0800) 505 005) has daily flights to Wellington (25min., 6-8 per day, $47; $2 off for YHA, VIP, or student) and a free shuttle bus in Picton. **TranzScenic** (tel. (0800) 802 802 or 573 8857) offers daily train service from Auckland St. to Christchurch (5½hr., 1:40pm, $76) via Kaikoura (2½hr., $39; cheaper backpacker rates available). **InterCity** leaves for Christchurch (1:15pm, $57) via Kaikoura ($33) and Blenheim (25min., $8); and for Nelson (2¼hr., 1-2 per day, $27). All prices are significantly lower if you book through the visitors center. At least nine other shuttle services run to the same destinations with a wide range of departure times and competitive pricing; again, see the visitors center for details. The most famous of Picton transportation options, the **Interislander Ferry** (overseas bookings tel. (04) 498 3301; in country tel. (0800) 802 802) leaves from the Foreshore daily for Wellington. (3-3¼hr., 4-5 per day, 5:30am-9:30pm, $23-46). If you're traveling in the summer, the speedy **Lynx** (also run by Interislander) cuts the travel time in half (3 per day, $30-59). **Cook Straight Sea Cat Ferries** (tel. (0800) 732 228) runs daily from Picton to Mana (just north of Wellington) with available dropoffs in the Bay of Many Coves (in the Sounds) and shuttle service on North or South Island, both for an additional cost (1¾hr., 1-2 daily, basic crossing $45). To get a ride in town, call **Blenheim Taxi** (tel. 578 0225) or rent your own car from any of the companies lined up by the ferry terminal. **Internet access** is available at the Queen Charlotte Pharmacy in Mariners Mall ($3 first 5min., 20¢ each additional minute; open M-F 9am-6pm, Sa-Su 9am-5pm; in the winter M-F 9am-5:30pm, Sa 9am-2pm). In case of an **emergency,** dial 111 or head to the **Rob Roy Pharmacy,** 6 High St. (tel. 573 6420), or the **Picton Medical Center,** 71 High St. (tel. 573 6092). The **police** (tel. 573 6439) are located at 36 Broadway St., and the **post office** is at Mariners Mall on High St. (open M-F 9am-5pm). The **telephone code** is 03.

ACCOMMODATIONS AND FOOD

Picton is well equipped to house the swarms of sightseekers. Hotels and motels are on the main streets, while the quiet side streets are home to many B&Bs.

The Villa Backpackers Lodge, 34 Auckland St. (tel/fax. 573 6598), near the intersection with Dublin St. A charmingly restored villa with brass double beds and vases of flowers, it is the unexpected bonuses that take the Villa from standard to stellar. Free breakfast, free apple crisp with ice cream every night, free bicycles and fishing gear, free pickup, and $2 each night for all-you-can-eat vegetable soup—all this adds up to a unique backpacking experience. The helpful staff will plan trips on the Queen Charlotte Track, and Internet access is available ($3 per 15min; $10 per hr.). Be sure to book ahead as it fills up year-round. Dorms $16; doubles or twins $42 (with made-up bed). Spa $2 per 30min. Linen $1 per sheet; towels 50¢. $20 min. for Visa or MasterCard.

The Juggler's Rest Backpackers, 8 Canterbury St. (tel. 573 5570). Call for pickup or directions. The red train mailbox next to the almost-hidden wooden door foreshadows a place that's more circus than backpackers. The owners (3 professional jugglers) give free workshops daily. Aside from the 1½m high unicycle and the swimming pool for the bumblingly inept, you can shower in the celestial bathroom or have a candle-lit bath surrounded by plants. With the right weather conditions, fire-eating lessons are even offered. Dorms $15, $14 in winter (bring a sleeping bag); doubles or twins with linen $32. Juggle 5 balls and get a $1 discount, or 10 for a free night and dinner with the owners. Otherwise, cash only.

Picton Backpackers on the Square, 3A Nelson Square (tel./fax 573 8399, or tel. (0800) 222 257; email drkett@voyager.co.nz). This comfortable eye-catching hostel has recently been refurbished and beautified, and includes free homemade bread and soup in the winter, as well as free linen, free pickup, and outdoor gas-heated baths. Dorms $15, doubles and twins with bathroom $40.

Baden's Picton Lodge, 9 Auckland St. (tel. 573 7788; fax 573 8418), the closest accommodation to the ferry. The rooms may be barren, but the walls are insulated and the stove keeps the whole place warm throughout the winter. Mountain bikes are available for free, as well as ferry drop off and pickup. The owner is also an experienced tramper and can offer advice and bookings for the Queen Charlotte Track. Dorms $15-16; doubles and twins $38; front double with bed-turning $44; $1 discount for YHA, VIP, or student.

The Wedgewood House (YHA Associate), 10 Dublin St. (tel. 573 7797; fax 573 6426), white with blue trim, has a large wooden porch, a minuscule kitchen, and a smoking room out back. Cute on the outside, but not particularly remarkable on the inside. Free lockers in the rooms, as well as longer term storage out back (50¢). Free duvets and blankets as well. Dorms $15; twins $34. Reception 8-10am, 1-2pm, 5-6:30pm, and 8-10pm.

Alexanders Holiday Park (tel./fax 573 6378), at the end of Canterbury St. Stay in a converted 1906 railway carriage (now a cabin) and store your gear overhead in the luggage racks. It all has an in-the-bush feel to it. Converted army bunkers are cheaper than the standard cabins. Standard cabin with electric jug and toaster (no linen) $30 for 2; caravan and tent sites $16 for 2. Waitohi Stream swimming hole. Book ahead in summer for all but the tent sites. No dogs permitted.

High St. is home to a variety of restaurants and cafes. **Le Cafe,** 33 High St. (tel. 573 5588), is a good place to sit, drink tea, and read. A pot of tea and a muffin runs about $3 (open daily in summer 8am-10:30 or 11pm, in winter 10am-8pm; closed July-Aug.). You'll catch on fast to the theme of **The Dog and Frog Cafe,** 22 High St. (tel. 573 5650), with its scattering of amphibious statues and pictures. An all-day breakfast of sausage and eggs runs $8.50, while fish and chips are $10 (open daily in summer 7am-9pm; winter hours vary). Down on Auckland St. near the visitors center, **Toot 'n' Whistle** (tel. 573 6086) has a friendly, laid-back atmosphere and a broad menu. Meals start at $5.50; the steak open sandwich ($9.50) is a special favorite (open daily from 7am; in winter 9am-11pm). The **Picton Fruit and Vege Mart,** 20 High St. (tel. 573 6456), has deliciously crisp apples and ripe kiwifruit (open M-F 8am-6pm, Sa 9am-3pm). **Supervalue** (tel. 573 0463) is waiting in Mariner's Mall, chock-full of groceries for your cooking pleasure (open M-W 8am-6pm, Th 8am-7:30pm, F 8am-8:30pm, Sa 8am-7pm, Su 9am-5pm).

SIGHTS AND ACTIVITIES

Picton, which was almost made the capital of New Zealand in the 1850s, retains vestiges of its dignified history all about town. One of the first things to confront you on the Foreshore is the **Edwin Fox,** a restored ship floating in Picton Harbour. Built in 1853 in Calcutta, the *Edwin Fox* carried tea from Calcutta to London, British immigrants to Australia and New Zealand, convicts to Australia, and troops in the Crimean War. The ship is scheduled to go on display in a newly constructed drydock in January 1999. Until then, visitors can see a detailed display of the ship and learn about the many roles it has played at the **Edwin Fox Maritime Centre** (tel. 573 6868), on the Waterfront. *(Open daily in summer 8:30am-6pm; in winter 8:30am-5pm. Admission $4, under 16 $1, families $9.)* The **Picton Museum** (tel. 573 8283) on London Quay has a renowned exhibit on the local whaling industry, a giant collection of seashells, and a *very* old-fashioned bicycle. *(Open daily 10am-4pm. Admission $3, children 50¢.)* Although the prime natural attractions near Picton are the Marlborough Sounds, the visitors center has brochures and maps for a number of local walks.

■ Marlborough Sounds

Many travelers use Picton simply as a jumping-off point to the North Island, but the path out to sea glides past a world of natural beauty and that warrants a closer look. The intricate web of waterways at the South Island's northeastern extremity is the **Marlborough Sounds,** a haven for penguins, seals, dolphins, and a serene getaway for people. The most popular and easiest way to explore the Sounds is on the **Queen Charlotte Track** (3-4 days), 67km of exquisite tramping from **Anakiwa** out to **Ship Cove.** Hikers of varying physical ability can enjoy the thrill of walking the tracks' ridges with Queen Charlotte Sound on one side and Kenepuru Sound on the other. Numerous hostels, lodges, and campgrounds are spaced along the trail, and the various water taxi services mean that less ambitious trampers can hike for just a day or two, getting dropped of and picked up at whichever stopping points they choose. The self-registration **DOC campgrounds** along the way cost $3 per night and are at Resolution Bay, Camp Bay, Bay of Many Coves Shelter, Cowshed Bay, Misteltoe Bay, and Umungata (Davies) Bay.

The **Picton Visitor Center** has information on the multitude of water taxi services. **Cougar Line** (tel. 573 7925) services the area between Torea Bay (30min., 2-4 per day, $12) and Ship Cove ($35) and can take you to the Lazy Fish (see below). **Endeav-**

our **Express** (tel. 579 8465) heads twice daily to Ship Cove ($25; packs often carried free). **Arrow Water Taxis** (tel. 573 8229), also serves the Queen Charlotte Track on demand. To get to **Anakiwa** from Picton, you can take the **Sounds Connection** (tel. 573 7125 or (0800) 456 900), which leaves twice daily (30min., $10).

In addition to the Queen Charlotte Track, the Sounds are full of activities and adventures for the visitor of brave heart (and stout wallet). Renting a **sea kayak** will give you the freedom to explore the curving coastlines, tranquil inlets, and hidden accommodations of the Sounds. **Marlborough Sounds Adventure Company** (tel. 573 6078), located on the waterfront on London Quay, has single and double kayaks for hire ($40 per day per person, $35 per day per person after 3 days); they do not hire to solo paddlers. Those who want a guided trip can choose among evening and overnight trips (includes a barbecue and accommodation; $55-700, depending on length of trip). In addition to kayaks, rent your own boat or yacht for fishing and diving from the **Portage Bay Shop** (tel. 573 4445). **Sea Kayaking Adventure Tours** (tel. 574 2765) offers guided day trips ($60), as well as kayaks ($40 per day) and mountain bikes ($25 per day). **Dolphin Watch Marlborough** (tel. 573 8040), located next to the railway station, offers ecotours to the **Motuara Island Bird Sanctuary** and **Ship Cove,** (3½-4hr., 2 per day, $55), returning in time for the ferry. Track walkers can take the tour and then be dropped off at Ship Cove to begin tramping, or conversely can be picked up at Ship Cove at the end of their walk and enjoy the tour on the way back to Picton. To enjoy the Sounds from the road, those driving to Havelock or Nelson can wind along the scenic (and sealed) **Queen Charlotte Drive,** connecting Picton with Havelock. Another way to see the Sounds is to ride along the **mail runs** on the Queen Charlotte Sound ($54) or the Pelorus Sound ($66; departs M-F mid-morning and returns mid- to late-afternoon; no food provided). Contact **Beachcomber Cruises** (tel. 573 6175), on the Foreshore, for details.

But perhaps the most peaceful way to absorb the Marlborough Sounds is to spend a few days relaxing at the water's edge. Accommodations are scattered throughout the Sounds, but two in particular combine a laid-back and uncommercial aura with a load of free activities and a low price. Both are accessible only by water taxi; call ahead to arrange transport, or try the Cougar Line (see above). The aptly named **Lazy Fish** (tel. 579 9049; fax 579 9089; email lazyfish@voyager.co.nz) embodies relaxation. From the picnic table and telephone booth at the end of the wharf to the free spa beneath the stars, there are hundreds of ways to be lazy here. Free canoe, rowboat, fishing gear, windsurfer, towels, and snorkeling gear are included. Remember to bring a good stock of groceries, though a stocked cupboard dubbed "The Shop" sells basic food items. (Dorms $20; doubles $45; book well ahead in summer. Call to arrange water transport, $25 return.) A little closer to Picton, the recently expanded **Lochmara Lodge** (tel./fax 573 4554; email lochmaralodge@xtra.co.nz) includes over 10 acres of native bush, scattered throughout with trails, benches, hammocks, and tree carvings. Lying just 40 minutes off the Queen Charlotte track, the lodge also has an array of extras, such as a spa, sea kayak, rowboat, fishing and snorkeling gear, a rope swing over the water, and resident glow-worms. Seal and shag colonies are within kayaking distance. Choose between a dorm in the main lodge ($20) or a completely self-contained cabin unit, including your own deck with a view over the water ($80 for 2 people; $12 each additional person; call ahead to arrange water transport, $20 return).

■ Blenheim

In addition to being the largest town in Marlborough, Blenheim is famous for its prime vineyards; tourists flock to the area, eager for a swig of the award-winning wines of the region. Many wineries are open to the public and offer tastings in addition to their exquisite restaurants. More thrifty travelers in need of work often head to the vineyards seeking vines in need of pruning and grapes in need of plucking. Blenheim also hosts crops of cherries, apples, peaches, apricots, and even garlic—so there is plenty of work to go around. Besides its top-notch harvests, Blenheim provides easy access to the recreational activities of nearby Picton (29km) and the Marlborough Sounds.

PRACTICAL INFORMATION The **Blenheim Information Centre** (tel. 578 9904; fax 578 6084; email blm_info@clear.net.nz), on the corner of High and Queen St. (open daily 8:30am-6:30pm; in winter M-F 8:30am-5:30pm; Sa-Su 9am-5:30pm), is for those already licking their parched lips for a map of the Marlborough wine region. Travelers in search of employment in Blenheim's busy fruit industry can talk to hostel owners or look in local newspapers. The **DOC field center** (tel. 572 9100) is on Gee St. but information on local walks is offered at the information center. The open, bricked area lined with shops behind the visitors center is known as the **Forum.** The **railway station** (tel. 577 2835), which also serves as a bus station, is located across the river at the end of Alfred St. If you fancy the train, **TranzScenic** (tel. (0800) 802 802) goes to Picton (30min., 12:20pm, $19) and to Christchurch (5hr., 2:10pm, $66). **InterCity** (tel. (0800) 731 711) heads daily to Picton (30min., 2 per day, $7) and Nelson (1¾hr., 1-3 per day, $22). InterCity goes daily to Christchurch (4½hr., 1:45pm, $55), via Kaikoura (1¾hr., $30). **Sounds-to-Coast** (tel. (0800) 802 225) goes to Greymouth (4½hr., 2-3 per week, $44) and daily to Picton (30min., 5:45pm, $5). **Kiwilink** (tel. (0800) 802 300) and **Knightline** (tel. 547 4733) go to Nelson (1¾hr., 4 per day, $17), as well as Picton (30min., 3 per day, $6). To call a taxi, contact **Blenheim Taxis** (tel. (0800) 802 225 or 578 0225). In an **emergency,** dial 111. Call the **medical center** (tel. 578 2174), 24 George St. (open 7 days a week) or the **police** (tel. 578 5279), 8 Main St. **Internet access** is available at the **information center** ($2/15min.) or at **Internet Direct** (tel. 578 1100), on the 4th floor of the post office building ($2.50/15min; open M-F 8:30am-5:15pm, in summer open Sa 9:30am-1pm). The **post office** is down Market St. on the left. The **telephone code** is **03.**

ACCOMMODATIONS Despite Blenheim's high-falutin' wine-culture scene, budget places are not hard to find. Play billiards in the kitchen of **Koanui Backpackers,** 33 Main St. (tel./fax 578 7487), toward the railroad pass, a carpeted, colorful backpackers with sinks in each room. They also offer free bicycle use and free pickup. Get a key if you go out at night (dorms $15; twins $18; singles $23; doubles $36; reception open 7am-10pm). Follow Main St. past the Pizza Hut and take a left onto Park Terrace to get to **Blenheim Backpackers,** 29 Park Terrace (tel. 578 6062). Tall triple bunkbeds reach up to the high ceilings in this 110-year-old, comfortably creaking and groaning maternity-home-turned-backpackers. Feel the zinc-plated walls in the double at the front of the house, paddle the free canoes in the adjacent river, or ride a free bicycle. Free pickup and laundry are available (dorms $14; doubles or twins $32-36). **Grove Bridge Holiday Park** (tel./fax 578 3667), 78 Grove Rd., has a range of choices for all inclinations and budgets, from completely self-contained tourists flats ($60-68 for 2 people), tourist cabins ($50 for 2, no bathroom), and standard cabins with communal facilities ($25, in winter $20; doubles $40; tent sites $9, powered $10).

The concentration of restaurants and cafes is greatest near the center of town. The modernist stools and sharp decor at **Tuscany's** (tel. 577 5050) 36 Scott St., accompany a varied menu. Don't miss an unbeatable array of gourmet burgers ($9.50), including beef, chicken, fish, and even lamb varieties (open daily from 10am, meals 'till 10pm, bar open later.) **Litchfield's** (tel. 578 4369) 2 Wynen St., serves a range of light meals, soups, and desserts. Seafood lovers can down the Marlborough Mussels ($8), or leave it up to the chef with the $5.50 soup of the day (open M-Tu 11am-7:30pm, W-Sa 11am-late). Get your groceries at **New World,** next to the McDonald's on Main St. (open M-Tu 8am-7pm, W-F 8am-8:30pm, Sa-Su 8am-6pm).

OUTDOORS Visit a **vineyard** by bike, car, or taxi and see row after row of vines, learn about winemaking, and take part in savoring Marlborough's red, white, and rosé treasures. Different wineries offer different tour and tastings options, so plan ahead and peruse the literature at the visitors center first. For an organized packaged trip, contact **DeLuxe Travel Line** (tel. (0800) 500 511) to wander the Marlborough region by coach. Day-long tours depart from Blenheim daily from December to March ($36; Sat. from Apr.-Nov. for $38); the coach drives along scenic Queen Charlotte Dr. from August to April. A number of smaller personalized minivan wine tour operators are listed at the information center.

The 25-acre **Brayshaw Museum Park** is about 3km out of the center of town off Maxwell Rd. Take a look at the Blenheim of 100 years ago in **Beavertown**, a replica of area shops and buildings from around the turn of the century. The **Riverside Railway** is an old-fashioned train running from Brayshay Museum Park into Blenheim and back ($3, children $1, leaving the park 2pm, 3pm, and 4pm; every Su in summer, first Su of the month in winter). For a collection of artifacts and historical treasures from the entire Marlborough area, visit the main museum in the park, the Marlborough Historical Society and Archives (tel. 578 1712; $2, children 50¢; open Tu-F 1-4pm, Sa 10am-4pm, Su 1-4pm). Just a little further down Maxwell Rd., **Wither Hills Walkway** provides a pleasant assortment of quick jaunts and good views of the countryside.

▨ Kaikoura

Surrounded by a brilliant blue bay and the snowcapped peaks of the Kaikoura Range, Kaikoura attracts both marine life and ecotourists by the drove. Lazy seals stretch out along the rocky coast as hungry albatrosses and sea gulls soar overhead, and acrobatic dolphins dance in the swelling waves. The waters just off the coast of Kaikoura balance an immense and elaborate food chain, supported at the bottom by the nutrient-rich ocean itself. The abundant wildlife is matched only by the abundant land, sea, and air activities that give visitors a variety of perspectives (literally and figuratively) on the unique ecology. The various tours and accommodations in this town of 3000 fill up early during the summer, while the winter scene is more hushed. Kaikoura means "meal of crayfish," and a multitude of the crunchy crustaceans can be found paddling beneath the waves. Grouper, blue cod, and terakihi fishing have taken the place of earlier whaling and sealing expeditions. All in all, Kaikoura is the perfect place to get in touch with Mother Nature.

ORIENTATION AND PRACTICAL INFORMATION

Midway between Picton (154km away) and Christchurch (183km away), **SH1** becomes, at various points, **Churchill Street, Beach Road,** and **Athelney Road,** but always remains the main road through town. Most shops and accommodations are along the beach on the **Westend,** which turns into the **Esplanade** about a kilometer south. The **Kaikoura Visitor Information Centre** (tel. 319 5641; fax 319 6819), located on the Westend, will store luggage ($1 per day) and changes money on the weekends (open daily Sept.-May 8am-6:30pm; May-Sept. 8:30am-5pm). The **DOC office** (tel. 319 5714) on Ludstone Rd. has the usual assortment of crucial tramping information. There are intentions books here and at the visitors center. Near the center of town are the **BNZ,** 42 Westend, and **Trustbank,** 34 Westend. **TranzScenic** (tel. (0800) 802 802) has daily train service to Christchurch (3hr., 4pm, $41) and to Picton (2½hr., 10:20am, $39). In addition to **InterCity** (tel. (0800) 731 711) at least 7 other bus and shuttle companies run daily to Christchurch (2½hr., $15-30) and Picton (2hr., $15-35). Book at the visitors center. **Hanmer Connection** (tel. (0800) 377 378) also heads to Hanmer Springs (2hr., 3 per week, $25). For a **taxi,** call 319 6214. **Internet access** is available at the **public library** (tel. 319 6280) across from the visitors center (sign up in advance; $2.50 per 15min.; open M-Th 9:30am-5pm, F 9:30am-7pm, Sa 10am-1pm). The **post office** is at 41 Westend (open M-F 8:30am-5pm, Sa 9am-noon). In an **emergency,** dial **111,** call the **police** (tel. 319 5038) or call the **hospital** (tel. 319 5027). The **telephone code** is **03.**

ACCOMMODATIONS

Many accommodations line **Westend** and the **Esplanade** along the beach, while a few others are on the hill overlooking the bay, a short, steep walk from town center.

⊛**Dusky Lodge,** 67 Beach Rd. (tel. 319 5959; fax 319 6929; email dusky.lodge@xtra.co.nz). This spunky new backpackers shows just what you can do with a lot of space and creative planning. The rooms are named after birds, the enormous lounge and dining area sport attractive, hewn wooden furniture, and a ping-pong table in the entrance area awaits challengers. Free pickup, free breakfast in the winter, and even a couple of gym machines outside. Dorms $16; doubles or twins with linen $40; 2hr. summer fishing trips $30.

Topspot Backpackers, 22 Deal St. (tel. 319 5540; fax 319 6587). From the visitors center, walk across the street and uphill on the Lydia Washington Walkway onto Deal St. Loud music and busloads of backpacker tours will let you know you've found this lively hotspot. Shore-based seal swims ($35) can be arranged in summer, and the garden fruit is free for the picking. Internet access. Gray tubing bunks $16; doubles with bath $40. Linen $1. Check-out 10am.

Cray Cottage, 190 the Esplanade, (tel. 319 5152). A stay at the Cray gets you more than just a bed; the owners offer free sunset tours of Kaikoura, 4-wheel-drive trips, and even fishing trips (off boat or shore) in the summer. Stays of 3 nights or longer include linen; otherwise $2 for made beds your entire visit. Dorms $16; one twin $36; closed June and July.

Maui YHA, 270 the Esplanade (tel. 319 5931; fax 319 6921). No pickup; from the train or bus stations figure on a $6 taxi ride. The magnificent view afforded by this beachfront backpackers is coupled with clean, modern rooms and free linen. Dorms $16; doubles or twins $38; ages 5-17 $11, under 5 $8. Check-out 10am.

Dolphin Lodge, 15 Deal St. (tel. 319 6048). A lodge with a quiet and peaceful air, the Dolphin prides itself on not having a TV. Pay extra for the double room's great mountain and sea view, or recline on the window seats lining the kitchen and lounge area. Dine on the deck while drinking in the luscious scents wafting from the garden. Bright red metal bunks $16; doubles $40. Closed in the winter.

Moby Dix, 65 Beach Rd. (tel./fax 319 6699). Settle any dinnertime disputes with fellow backpackers at the pool table nested in the middle of the dining area. The gorgeous ocean murals and low lights by the TV make it an underwater scene. Dorms $15.50; twins $33; double with linen $37; VIP, YHA, or student $1 off. Linen $1.

Adelphi Lodge (tel. 319 5141 or (0800) 423 574; fax 319 6786), on Westend. Right smack in the middle of town, the lodge's budget accommodations are a little bare but nonetheless comfortable. Free canoes are available for braving the stream out back. Dorms (some with private bathroom) $16; doubles and twins with linen $40.

A1 Kaikoura Motels and Holiday Park, 11-15 Beach Rd. (tel./fax 319 5999 or (0800) 605 999). Follow Beach Rd. away from the town center and cross under the railway overpass. Dorms $15. Standard cabins: singles $24; doubles $30. Deluxe cabins: $30; $37. Tourist cabins: doubles $41 (extra person $12). Tent sites $17 for 2 (extra person $8.50), powered $20 for 2 (extra person $10).

FOOD

No self-respecting world traveler should pass through Kaikoura without at least tasting the town's eponymous crayfish. Lobster fans may be initially disappointed with these small-clawed crustaceans, but their flavor tops off any day in Kaikoura just right.

A blue Matisse woman, hanging spider plants, Pink Floyd, and comfy couches greet those who enter the **Kebab Cafe** (tel. 319 7070), on Westend. Delight in the chicken, beef, lamb, or falafel souvlakis (wrapped in pita bread) for $6-7, while sitting in one of the spinning metal seats taken from several brands of tractors. The passionfruit smoothie ($3.50) is brilliant, as are the extra-large cookies for $2 (open in summer daily 11:30am-9pm; in winter W-Su noon-7pm; cash only). The cozy, candlelit **Act One Pizza Cafe and Bar** (tel. 319 6760), 25 Beach Rd., offers an array of gourmet pizzas in creative varieties for all tastes and appetites ($6.50-$27; open daily 5pm-midnight). The **Craypot Cafe and Bar,** 70 Westend (tel. 319 6027), located across from the ocean, is the place to go for a fine meal with soft music and even softer lighting. A scattering of fishy art and artsy fish overlook diners seated in wooden furniture appropriate for the beach. The freshly caught crayfish ($28) and other delicious seafood fill empty stomachs, while mussel lovers crave the big New Zealand green-lipped mussels in tomato sauce ($16.50). Fish phobes, don't despair—T-Bone steaks are $18.50 (open from 7:30am, in winter from 9:30am).

One For You, One For Me...

Children for centuries have been trying to solve the "giant cookie" problem: how to get a fair split. Solutions include bully takes all, "you split I choose," and the patented resort-to-mother strategy. But for Kiwi paleontologists, fate made things a little easier as far as the proverbial big cookie goes. Last year, a giant rock in the Amuri Bluffs (near Kaikoura) came loose, plummeted to the ground, and split in half, revealing a plesiosaur fossil inside. Both the Kaikoura Museum and the Auckland War Memorial Museum were interested in the specimen—but who had the better claim? Fortunately, both ended up satisfied. The skeleton had split along with the rock, so half of the giant dino went to each museum. Plesiosaurs include a number of marine dinosaur species from the mid to late Mesozoic, and it is suspected that there are other such fossils in the Bluffs awaiting discovery—or uncovering, as the case may be.

SIGHTS AND ACTIVITIES

There are several options for those wishing to experience the sea first-hand. **Dolphin Encounter** (tel. (0800) 733 365) gets you into a wetsuit and transports you right to the edge of a pod of **dusky dolphins,** a small, friendly, and playful species found year-round off the Kaikoura shore. *(From Oct. to May, tours leave daily at 6am, 9am, and 1pm (book well in advance); from June to Sept. tours leave daily at 9am and 1pm. $80, under 15 $65; spectators $48, under 15 $38.)* The water can be chilly and the frolics exhausting, but the thrill of being circled and assessed by a posse of sleek dolphins is unmatched. The **Kaikoura Wildlife Centre** (tel. 319 6622) offers a variety of ecotours ranging from diving with dolphins from Sept. to May (daily 8am, 12:30pm; $80, under 15 $60), to snorkeling with seals ($45, under 15 $30, under 7 free but may view only), to scuba diving ($90 for 1 dive, all equipment supplied). **Graeme's Seal Swim** (tel. 319 6182) operates land-based seal snorkeling from Nov. to Apr. (2hr.; $35, ages 5-12 $25). If all of that sounds like sissy stuff, let **Kaikoura Shark Meet** drop you among a swarm of sharks inside a special bite-proof cage. *(3hr. trip; 20 min. in cage, $85, all equipment provided, operates Nov. to May.)*

But you don't have to actually be in the ocean to appreciate it. The Ngai Tahu Maori-affiliated **Whale Watch Kaikoura** (tel. 319 6767 or (0800) 655 121), located at the old railway station, conducts information-packed three-hour tours of waters filled with whales, seals, royal albatrosses, and gulls (anti-seasickness wristbands that work by utilizing pressure points are provided). *(Weather-dependent; book 1-2 weeks ahead in summer, 3-4 days in winter. $95, ages 5-15 $60.)* They even offer a guaranteed 80% refund if no whales are seen during the trip. Crowd around the windows and viewing decks to see the juvenile male whales with their overactive hormones (banished from the pod by the dominant female) spouting and diving, tails flipping out of the water on their way down. In June and July, keep an eye out for **humpback whales;** in summer, look for **orca,** instead. **Hector's dolphins** and **dusky dolphins** are occasionally seen as well. **Ocean Wings** (tel. 319 6777 or (0800) 733 365), run by Dolpin Encounters, is a two-to three-hour boat trip to view Kaikoura's pelagic (ocean-going) bird life. *($60, children $35.)* Using pieces of fish liver, the knowledgeable skipper draws huge crowds of birds, many of them very rare. Kaikoura also hosts a slew of fishing and crayfishing charters; see the visitors center for details. **Wings Over Whales** (tel. 319 6580 or (0800) 226 629) operates year-round aerial whale-watching tours. *(Half-hour flights; $85, children $50, $5 transportation to airfield.)* Circle above a surfacing whale as it gathers oxygen and then dramatically dives under. The flight also provides a beautiful view of the entire coast and mountains. At the old railway station you'll find **Kaikoura Helicopters** (tel. 319 6609), another aerial/marine adventure operating year-round (20-40min. flights; $125-230). You can even pilot yourself over the beautiful terrain and ocean with **Pilot a Plane** (tel./fax 319 6579), including pre-flight instruction and a 30-minute flight ($59; 3-flight package $159).

If you're after something more solid than air or sea, Kaikoura can still deliver for you. Take a guided motorbike ride through bush and hill with **Four Wheeler Safaris.** (tel. 319 6424 or (025) 362 120). *($85 per 3hr., $100 per half-day, $140 per full day.)* Hop on your personal Black Beauty for a two-hour guided journey ($35) with **Fyffe View Horsetrek** (tel. 319 5069) or **Ludley Horse Treks** (tel. 319 5925 or 319 5978). **Kaikoura Scenic Tours** (tel. 319 6214) runs on-demand land tours that include the seal colony, overlooks, and historical features (1½hr., $12) as well as custom tours.

Of course you can always fend for yourself and save some cash in the process. Be careful of stepping on **seals** on the **Peninsula Walkway** (3hr.) that follows the shoreline starting 45 minutes down the Esplanade from the visitors center; check the tide schedule first at the visitors center. The **Dempsey's Track** (30min. one-way) leads to a panoramic view of the town, the bay, and the ocean. The **Hinau Track** (45min. return, starts 15km out of town) and **Fyffe-Palmer Track** (1½hr. return, starts 6km out of town) are steep but manageable mountain trails where you might run across the **Kaikoura black-eyed gecko** or one of the three endangered species of the world's heaviest insect, the giant **weta.** As both trails start well out of town, would-be hikers without a car may wish to rent a bike from **West End Motors** (tel. 319 5065), 48-52 Westend ($3.50 per hr., $10 for half-day, $18 full day). Check out the stalactites and stalagmites at the two-million-year-old **Maori Leap Cave** (tel. 319 5023), a young sea-formed limestone creation full of the bones of unlucky penguin and seals. *(40min. guided tours 10:30am-3:30pm, 6 per day, $8.50, children $3.50.)*

For ski addicts, **Mt. Lyford** (tel. 315 6178) is a mere 60km from Kaikoura (day pass $35, students $30; ski rental $15-25, snowboard rental $40). The **Kaikoura Museum** has exhibits on the Maori, whaling, and current social history of the area. *(Open in summer daily 2-4pm; in winter M-F 2-4pm. Small suggested donation.)* Celebrate Kaikoura's claim to fame at the **Pacifica Kaikoura Seafest** on the first Saturday of October in Takahanga Domain, a giant sea festival with plenty of food, entertainment, beer, and Marlborough wine. Just 24km north of Kaikoura off the main highway lies **Ohau Point,** where the DOC has kindly set up a public viewing platform overlooking the scores of seals that gather here.

■ Hanmer Springs

The rare combination of converging faultlines and connected underground fractures brings Hanmer Springs to geothermal life. Years and frown-lines melt away in the thermal springs at the center of this small resort town (about 10km off SH7 and 136km north of Christchurch), where shivering skiers from the nearby slopes and bone-weary jetboaters flock to unwind in the steaming waters. After drying off, the relaxation therapy can continue with soothing walks through the gentle surrounding hills and shadowy peaks. The region was used as an experimental planting zone around the turn of the century; keep an eye out for the great variety of exotic flora.

PRACTICAL INFORMATION The **Hurunui Visitor Information Centre/DOC office** (tel./fax 315 7128), on the corner of Amuri and Jackson Pass Rd., sits to the side of the thermal pools (open daily 10am-5pm). **BNZ** (tel. 315 7220) is located in the shopping center on Conical Hill Rd. (no ATM; open M, W, F 10am-2pm). The **Four Square** supermarket (tel. 315 7190), on Conical Hill Rd., has a small **post office** (open M-F 8:30am-5:30pm, Sa 9am-4pm, Su 10am-2pm). Coming by bus from the West Coast via Lewis Pass, you will probably be dropped off at Hanmer Corner, unless the driver has time to run you into town, which may cost a few extra dollars. Otherwise (if you don't feel like walking the 10km into the village), arrange for a pickup from **Hanmer Connection** (tel. (0800) 377 378 or 315 7575) for $5. They also run to Christchurch (2hr., 1-2 per day, $22) and Kaikoura (2hr., 3 per week, $25). **White Star** (tel. (0800) 829 982) and the less frequent **Lazerline** (tel. (0800) 220 001) head daily to Nelson (5hr., 1 per day, $44) and Christchurch (1 per day, $20). Again, you may need to arrange transport to Hammer Corner. To trek all the way to Westport, take White Star west to Spring's Junction and transfer buses. The **telephone code** is **03.**

ACCOMMODATIONS Only a couple of budget accommodations are within walking distance of the pools. The small wooden lodge of **Amuri Backpackers,** 41 Conical Hill Rd. (tel. 315 7196), a five-minute walk past the thermal reserve on the right, houses guests in a loft and in a shed out back. Two friendly canines battle it out for the guests' attention. There is laundry, but no dryer. (Dorms $15; linen $3.) **Mountain View Holiday Park** (tel. 315 7113; fax 315 7118) is the most convenient motor camp to town, on the corner of Bath St. and Hanmer Springs Rd. just a short walk out of town. The cheapest options are the standard cabins with communal kitchen ($35 for 2, extra person $10) or the tourist cabins with kitchens ($45 for 2, extra person $10). Powered sites are $20 for two (extra person $9.50); unpowered sites are $18 for two (extra person $8.50).

OUTDOORS The main attraction is never hard to find, and if the smell of sulfur isn't enough, follow the plumes of steam to the **Hanmer Springs Thermal Reserve** (tel. 315 7511), on Amuri Ave. Roast in the 40°C pool if you want to prove you're superhuman, or pull a Goldilocks and try each of the nine different public pools until you find one that's "just right" (open daily 10am-9pm; $7, ages 5-15 $3; day pass $9, ages 5-15 $4).

Once your skin is suitably shriveled, the great outdoors awaits. **Rollesby Experience** (tel. 315 7146 or (025) 442 550) leads guided trips across farmland and hills for both novice and experienced horseback riders (book through Hanmer Connection for free pickup; 1hr. $25; 2hr. $45). The more domestic at heart can watch sheep being shorn or herded on the farm tour ($12, children $6). **Rainbow Horse Trekking** (tel. 315 7444) offers guided horseback tours (30min. $15; 1hr. $25; half day $50; full day including lunch $110). **Argo Trips and Tours** (tel. (0800) 733 426 or (025) 228 4338) runs all-terrain 8-wheel drive trips (1½hr., $60). Or cut the wheels in half with a 4-wheel motor bike safari from **Backtrax** (tel. 315 7684; 2hr. $69; 4hr. $105). **Dust-n-Dirt,** 20 Conical Hill Rd. (tel./fax 315 7233), hires mountain bikes and offers trail maps (1hr. $9; 2hr. $12; 4hr. $16; full day $25). Contact **Rainbow Adventures** (tel. 315 7444 or 315 7401) for a slew of adventure options. You can slide down waterfalls on Rainbow's canyoning trips (daily 10am and 1pm, $39 per person, min. 2 people), go on a raucous rafting trip (half-day $58, full day with lunch $85), or even try your hand at paragliding ($100 or $185 depending on trip, includes helicopter flight). At **Thrillseekers Adventure Centre** (tel. 315 7046), you can hurl yourself off a bridge above the Waiau River for $89 (min. age 13), ride on a jetboat down the steep-sided gorge (20min. $40; 30min. $55, children $25) or raft down the steep-sided gorge of the Grade 2-3 Waiau River ($55; book through Hanmer Connection for free pickup).

In winter, hit the slopes at the **Amuri Ski Field** (tel. (025) 341 806) a mere 45-minute drive from Hanmer Springs (tow fees $35, students $30). Known as "the friendly field," some runs are groomed for easy going while others are left untouched for more experienced skiers. Call **Amuri Skifield Transport** (tel. 315 7401 or (025) 578 578) if you don't have a car. For a bit more skiing variety, **Mt. Lyford Ski Field** (tel. 315 6178) is just 1¼hr. away, with identical tow fees to Amuri. The field is more developed with many tourist services and is especially good for novice snowboarders. Catch the shuttle daily at the information center (1½hr., 7:30am, $20 return). Short walks, day hikes, and serious tramps run directly out of or near Hanmer Springs. The visitors center is stocked with maps, brochures, and advice to point you in the right direction.

■ Maruia Springs

Minuscule and remote, Maruia Springs provides a serene, sulfuric getaway from anything resembling civilization. One hour's drive west of big brother Hanmer Springs on SH7, the facilities consist entirely of three outdoor thermal pools, a traditional Japanese bathhouse complete with jacuzzi, a bar and restaurant, and varying levels of accommodations. Encapsulated under the umbrella of **Maruia Springs Thermal Resort** (tel. 523 8840), this Japanese-owned complex strives to combine both Kiwi and Japanese cultural flavors. The pools are as much a place to socialize as to soak, and fellow guests are happy to share a schmooze—all good clean fun, as the bathhouse is sex-segregated. While Hanmer Springs may have more pools to choose from, Maruia manages to escape the crowds and offers a greater sense of tranquility; the outdoor pools are surrounded by mountains and open 24 hours a day. If you're passing by, take a day to soak, even if it means a slight detour from your path. The price of all lodgings include 24 hour access to outdoor pools and 9am-11pm access to the Japanese bathhouse (dorms $20; hotel units $95-140; tent sites $5 per site plus $6 per person; checkout 10am). Non-guest access to outdoor pools and bathhouse costs $6.50 (9am-9pm).

NELSON AND ENVIRONS

■ Nelson

Home to the country's first game of rugby, the first eight-hour working day in the world, and the oldest New Zealand railway, the small city of Nelson (pop. 43,000) is the geographic center of the country and a popular domestic holiday destination. In addition to being New Zealand's biggest fishing port, Nelson is surprisingly on top of modern social trends for a city its size, with an artsy movie theater, snazzy coffee houses, and a wide range of dining and shopping options. Boasting a high percentage of sunny days, New Zealand's second city (originally Whakatu, established 1842) also attracts visitors to its wineries, orchards, and artists' studios. The clay in the area is particularly suited for pottery (it is exported throughout the South Pacific), making Nelson a haven for sculptors. The deep shelter of **Tasman Bay** keeps the weather clear and seafood lovers well fed. Meanwhile, the nearby hiking paradises of **Abel Tasman** (see p. 281), **Kahurangi** (see p. 285), and **Nelson Lakes National Parks** (see p. 279) ensure a steady flow of rough and ready backpackers to mingle with those more concerned with finding peak vintages than mountain peaks. Nelson's art scene reaches its zenith with the **Wearable Art Awards** (see p. 279) every September, but the scores of artisan dens and studios maintain a bohemian spirit year-round.

ORIENTATION AND PRACTICAL INFORMATION

The Nelson metropolis is rather spread-out with suburbs sprawling up into the hills on all sides, but the central part of the city is all within walking distance. **Christ Church Cathedral,** on Trafalgar St., dominates central Nelson and stands tall above its surrounding gardens. **Trafalgar, Bridge,** and **Hardy Streets** comprise the main shopping district with a plethora of shops, accommodations, and restaurants. From the bus depot, take a left on Bridge St. and you'll hit Trafalgar St.

Airport: Located past the Tahunanui Beach area. **Air New Zealand Link** (tel. (0800) 767 767) and **Ansett** (tel. (0800) 267 388) fly regularly to Wellington (30min., 1-2 per hr., $164) and Christchurch (45min., 4-5 per day, $214). Book well in advance for considerably lower prices.

Buses: All buses leave from the visitors center at the corner of Trafalgar and Halifax St. **InterCity** (tel. (0800) 731 711) heads daily to Fox Glacier (11hr., 7:30am, $91) via Westport (3½hr., $44) and to Picton (2hr., 10am, $27) via Blenheim (1½hr., $22). You can also take the bus to Blenheim and transfer to Christchurch (8½hr., $66). **Lazerline** (tel. (0800) 220 001) and **White Star** (tel. 546 8687) go daily to Christchurch (7½hr., $40-55) via Springs Junction (3½hr., $25-30). White Star also has a transfer at Springs Junction to Westport (6hr., $27), providing a cheaper, yet less direct option than InterCity. Call **Wadsworth Motors** (tel. 548 3277) or **Nelson Lakes Transport** (tel. 548 6858) to go to St. Arnaud. To get to Abel Tasman National Park, call **Abel Tasman Coachlines** (tel. 548 0285) or **Kahurangi Bus Service** (tel. 525 9434).

Taxis: Nelson City Taxis (24hr. tel. 548 8225 or (0800) 108 855). **Sun City Taxis** (24hr. tel. 548 2666 or (0800) 422 666).

Car Rental: In addition to international chains, try **Pegasus Rental Cars Nelson,** 83 Haven Rd. (24hr. tel. (0800) 803 580 or 548 0884) or **NZ Rent a Car,** at the intersection of Collingwood and Halifax St. (tel. (0800) 800 956 or 546 9172). Get advice and car help at the **AA,** 45 Halifax St. (tel. 548 8399).

Bicycle Rental: Stewarts Cycle City, 114 Hardy St. (tel. 548 1666).

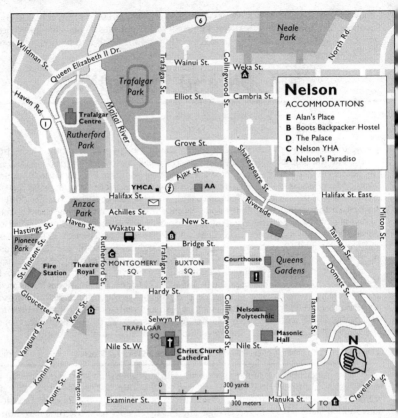

Nelson

ACCOMMODATIONS

E Alan's Place
B Boots Backpacker Hostel
D The Palace
C Nelson YHA
A Nelson's Paradiso

Visitors Center: Nelson Visitor Centre, at the corner of Trafalgar and Halifax St. (tel. 548 2304; fax 546 7393; email nsnvin@nzhost.co.nz). It's about a 10min. walk on Trafalgar St. from the cathedral steps. Those traveling by car may want to pick up the *The Coastal Way on Tasman Bay* brochure detailing the attractions of SH60, which runs along the Waimea Inlet and Ruby Bay coasts. Open M-F 8:30am-5:30pm, Sa 9am-5:30pm, Su 9am-5pm.

DOC: 186 Bridge St. (tel. 546 9335), in the Monro State Building, has the scoop on Abel Tasman, Kahurangi, and Nelson Lakes national parks. In the summer, the DOC provides information at the visitors center. Open M-F 8am-4:30pm.

Currency Exchange: BNZ, 226 Trafalgar St., **National Bank,** 248 Trafalgar St., **ANZ,** 265 Trafalgar St., at the corner of Trafalgar and Hardy St., and **ASB,** at the same intersection, are all open M-F 9am-4:30pm.

American Express: There is no office in town, but there is a travel service representative (tel. 548 9079) on Rutherford St.

Emergency: Dial III.

Police: On St. John St. (tel. 548 8309) in central Nelson.

Medical Services: Prices Pharmacy, 296 Hardy St. (tel. 548 3897), at Collingwood St. Open M-F 8:30am-8pm, Sa-Su 9am-8pm. **Nelson Hospital** (tel. 546 1800), on Waimea Rd. Emergency doctor, ambulance, and emergency dentist. **City Care,** 202 Rutherford St. (tel. 546 8881) has an on-duty doctor 24hr.

Post Office: 86 Trafalgar St. (tel. 546 7818). Open M-F 8am-5pm, Sa 9:30am-12:30pm.

Internet Access: Mandy Computing Limited (tel. 546 8045), 23 Alma Lane in the corner of Buxton Sq., has a quick connection for $10 per hr., $2.50 for first 15min. (open M-F 8:30am-5pm, Sa 9:30am-12pm). **Boots Off** (tel. 546 8981), 53 Bridge St. near the bus terminal, has a slew of terminals ($10 per hr., $6 per 30min., $4 per 15min.; open M-F 10am-10pm, Sa 10am-7pm, Su 3-9pm; in winter M-F 10am-6pm, Sa 10am-3pm, Su 4-7pm). **Telephone Code:** 03.

ACCOMMODATIONS

Nelson is crowded with as many places to crash as paintbrushes and palettes. Booking ahead in summer is a must.

◉**The Palace,** 114 Rutherford St. (tel./fax 548 4691). A magnificent, hilltop historic home whose spacious balcony and gardens overlook the city. Rooms have high ceilings, huge windows, and carved wooden fireplaces. Blankets and heaters provided. Free use of bicycles, free pickup, and on-site Internet access ($12 per hr.). Dorms $16; doubles $19. Reception 8am-9pm. No credit cards accepted.

◉**Nelson's Paradiso,** 42 Weka St. (tel. 546 6703; fax 546 7533). If a sauna, spa, swimming pool, and volleyball court sound like a smashing recipe for a good time, call the Paradiso for a free pickup and check it out. Free vegetable soup is served through the winter in the huge kitchen, and a giant, green tour bus named Bessie parked out back has been converted to a lounge. Dorms $16; 4-person rooms $68; doubles and twins $38.

Alan's Place (VIP), 42 Westbrook Terr. (tel./fax 548 4854). A small, friendly place located away from the center of town (call for transport). Free scones and tea upon arrival. Ask the very helpful and enthusiastic staff about area activities. Tramping gear available for borrowing and stoves for hire. Free towels and blankets as well as bicycle usage ($10 deposit). Dorm bathrooms located outside. Dorms $16; twins $32; doubles $36. Reception 8am-5:30pm and 7:30-9:30pm. Check-out 10am. YHA/VIP/student $1 discount.

Nelson YHA, 59 Rutherford St. (tel. 545 9988; fax 545 9989) Photos and paintings on the walls conspire with the pianos and guitar in the large TV lounge to lessen the rigid, manufactured feel of this immense hostel. The staff can help make tour arrangements. Get the combination before you go out at night. Blankets, sheets, and duvets provided, though the rooms come with heaters that automatically turn off after 30min. Dorms $18; singles $28; doubles and twins $40; doubles with bath $56. Non-YHA $4 more. Reception 8-10am and 3-10pm. Check-out 10am.

Boots Backpacker Hostel (VIP), (tel./fax 548 9001) is centrally located at the corner of Trafalgar and Bridge St. The rooms are on the barren side, but the cartoon characters on the hallway doors add color. Get the door combination before you go out at night. Bunks $15-16; singles $21; doubles or twins $34-36. VIP $1 discount. Key deposit $10. Reception 7am-9pm (from 8:30am in the winter).

Tahuna Beach Holiday Park, 70 Beach Rd., Tahunanui (tel. (0800) 500 501 or 548 5159; fax 548 5294). A huge, 54-acre facility with hundreds of tent and powered sites ($16-18) and an incredible variety of cabins and motels with seasonal rates from $26-80; $20-60 in winter. Reception 8am-9:30pm. No pickup offered.

FOOD

Many of Nelson's restaurants, cafes, and takeaways are located on Trafalgar, Bridge, and Hardy St., though several seafood restaurants along the oceanfront, on Wakefield Quay, can be reached by taxi ($5), bus ($2), or car. The numerous ethnic restaurants in town will satisfy diverse tastes. Home-cookers can collect supplies at **New World** supermarket, Montgomery Sq. (tel. 548 9111; open M-F 8am-9pm, Sa-Su 9am-7pm) or **Supervalue Supermarket,** 69 Collingwood St. (tel. 548 0191; open M-F 8am-10pm, Sa-Su 8am-9pm; in winter M-F 8am-9pm, Sa-Su 9am-8pm).

Zippy's, 276 Hardy St. (tel. 546 6348), between Hope and Collingwood St. Ponytailed Zippy laughs in his corner as alternative types drink coffee with soy milk and feast on vegetarian delights. Big, steaming pumpkin samosas ($4) with spirulina fruit smoothies ($4). Bagels from plain and buttered ($2) to avocado and tomato-topped ($3.50). Artwork on the walls provides the backdrop to postings of current musical events, festivals, and art shows. BYO. Open Su-W 9am-10pm, Th-Sa 9am-noon; in winter Su-M 9am-6pm, Tu-W 9am-10pm, Th-Sa 9am-midnight. Cash only.

Chez Eelco Coffee House, 296 Trafalgar St. (tel. 548 7595). Facing the cathedral, the cafe is on your right. Bright red doors and checkered tablecloths welcome you into Nelson's famed coffee house. Order off the lampshade menu as giant copper cockroaches and a rose-carrying grasshopper on the wall look on. Or sit outside for the view of the cathedral and the gardens. Internet access is available ($2 per 8min.), but be sure to stock up on $1 and $2 coins first. Muesli with fruit $7.50; delicious, creamy mussel chowder $7; vegetable bean-topped nachos $8.50. 10% student discount with ID. Open M-F from 6am, Sa-Su from 7am.

Land of Pharaohs, 270 Hardy St. (tel. 548 8404), between Morrison and Hope St. Tapestries and photographs of Egyptian monuments fill this tiny, red-lit restaurant. Vegetarians can choose from falafel, hummus, or feta cheese kebabs (small $4, large $6), while carnivores may prefer beef, lamb, or pork kebabs ($4-7.50). Top it all off with baklava ($2.50). Outdoor dining. BYO. Open in summer daily 10:30am-1 or 2am; in winter M-Sa 11:30am-9 or 10pm.

Akbabas Turkish Kebab House, 130 Bridge St. (tel. 548 8825). A small restaurant and takeaway whose low table is surrounded by floor pillows, with rugs and garlic hanging on the walls and Turkish music filling the room. Spicy chicken kebab in a pita (small $6, large $8). Falafels are $4 (large $5.50). Experience Turkish Delight for $2. Open daily 11am-8:30pm; closed Su in winter. Cash only.

Victorian Rose, 281 Trafalgar St. (tel. 548 7631). An elegant, traditional pub where pictures of roses and images of Victorian women dominate. Beer-drinkers can relax outside in the courtyard to enjoy one of 16 beers on tap. Rosie's jumbo burgers should fill you up ($9.95), but the truly ravenous can take on the Victorian Rose Challenge for $25 and join the few who have been able to finish the huge steak (free beer included). The Sunday roast ($10) is an all-you-can-eat ordeal that comes with a free dessert (from 5:30pm). Open daily from 11am.

Boat Shed Cafe and Restaurant, 350 Wakefield Quay (tel. 546 9783), on the oceanfront (a taxi ride away), is highly recommended by locals. In an old, converted boat shed practically sitting on the ocean, it's known for fresh seafood with a great view. The Tasman Bay Chowder ($9) or Marlborough Sounds mussels ($12) are both outstanding selections. For a candlelight dinner, you can begin with the delicious Japanese style Sashimi platter ($13.50), before feasting on the fish of the day ($23). Open daily from 11:30am; lunch served until 2:30pm, dinner from 6pm.

SIGHTS AND ACTIVITIES

A leisurely stroll through the downtown area provides a good introduction to Nelson's offerings. A mixture of industrial and Gothic architecture, **Christ Church Cathedral** sits atop Church Hill on Trafalgar St. Preceded by a tent church and various wooden churches, money for a permanent Gothic-style church was finally raised to begin the project—but not enough to complete it. Plans were withdrawn, and the result was left standing. Images of what-might-have-been can be found inside.

The best way to groove with the artistic side of Nelson is to take part in it yourself. Construct your own bead masterpiece or buy somebody else's at the **Bead Gallery,** 18 Parere St. (tel. 546 7807; open M-F 9am-5pm, Sa 9am-4:30pm). If you're tempted to picnic, head to **Anzac Memorial Park** (off Rutherford St.) or **Miyazu Japanese Garden** (on Atawhai Dr.) to escape the large flocks of hungry-eyed fowl in the Victorian **Queens Gardens,** with entrances on Hardy St. and Bridge St. The latter is next to the **Suter Art Gallery** (tel. 548 4699), on Bridge St., a public art museum housing both a permanent art collection and changing exhibits, as well as a craft shop, cinema theater, and restaurant (open daily 10:30am-4:30pm; $2, students and under 16 50¢). On a rainy day, head inside and curl up with your favorite tome from **Page and Blackmore's Booksellers,** 254 Trafalgar St. (tel. 548 9992).

Those in search of Nelson's natural history will find a number of nearby walks (a 50¢ brochure is available at the visitors center). The **Centre of New Zealand Walk** will get you close to, if not exactly to, the center of New Zealand (40min. round-trip), while the **Maitai River Walkway** (4hr. return) will take you along the river past homes and a wishing well out to sheep-grazed countryside. The fine sands of **Tahunanui Beach** ("shifting sands") make it a popular holiday destination; it's accessible by bike down Wakefield Quay, which turns into Rocks Rd. (20-30min.). Before heading off to one of the three national parks nearby, stop in and stock up at **Rollo's BBQ and Camping Centre,** 12 Bridge St. (tel. 548 1975).

Several adventure options give a look at Nelson's wild side. **Stonehurst Farm Horse Treks** (tel. 542 4121) offers a variety of one-to four-hour adventures, including the Rambler Trail through scenic farmland (1hr., $30) and the longer RiverRide, which includes a snack (3½hr., $65). Drive around on your own four-wheel motorbike with **Happy Valley 4x4 Motorbike Adventures** (tel. 545 0304), with rides such as the Farm Funride (1hr., $35), or the BayView Tour (2½hr., $65). Let **Sail Tasman** (tel. 547 2754) treat you to a day-long trip in the Nelson Harbour area (8hr., $80), a half-day version (3-4hr., $35-40), or a two-day, two-night extravaganza ($295). "Adrenaline dealers" **Natural High** (tel. 546 6936) hire out mountain bikes (full day $35, half day $25) and offer guided biking tours (2hr., $33). They also offer kayaking, wakeboarding, and waterskiing (2hr., $29-35, instruction available). Or if none of these options sounds heart-pumping enough, hop out of an airplane with a professional lashed to your back (from 3000m $195; 4000m $240).

To see the behind-the-scenes aspects of Nelson, head out of town by car or tour (walking isn't really feasible). **JJ's Wine Tours** (tel. 544 7081) offer tours of several local wineries (half-day, $45). **Nelson Day Tours** (tel. 548 4224) offer a range of tours to local highlights, including the city district (3-4hr., $25) and several wineries and craft centers (3-4hrs., $30). Stop by **McCashin's Brewery** (tel. 547 5357), 660 Main Rd. in Stoke, to see some of the bottling operations and check out the retail shops. **Mac's Beer** is a local favorite, made at the brewery without chemicals or preservatives but with a distinctive bottle and cap. Continuing on SH6 (but before Richmond, with Champion Rd. on your left), you'll find **Craft Habitat** (tel./fax 544 7481). Watch the artisans at work, as some weave lanolin-rich wool while others strive for perfection in their pieces of jewelry or pottery. Turning right on Queen St. in Richmond, and left on Lansdowne Rd. will bring you to the **Högland Art Glassblowing Studio** (tel. 544 6500), where two galleries display glass of every color and shape. Watch the glass-blowers at work (a particularly good idea on a chilly winter morning) daily from 9am to 5pm.

The fantastical becomes routine in Nelson every September as the **New Zealand Wearable Art Awards** come to the Trafalgar Centre in town. Everything from wispy, gauze dragonfly beauties and surreal spiked cyberpunks to people dressed up as jellyfish and mimes swathed in gyrating color takes center stage for the judging. Tickets can be sold out as early as six months in advance. Call **Everyman Records** (tel. 548 3083), 249 Hardy St., to reserve yourself a slot. For more info, contact the committee at P.O. Box 5140, Port Nelson (tel./fax 548 9299; email wearable@wearableart.co.nz). You can see some of the creations on the several web pages devoted to the event (such as http://www.wearableart.co.nz). For other transcendent experiences, the **Taste Nelson Festival,** usually held on the first Sunday of February at Founder's Park, celebrates Nelson's fine food and local vintages.

■ Nelson Lakes National Park

The main attractions of Nelson Lakes National Park are living on borrowed time. The harsh elements in the area are eroding the mountains and depositing the sediment into the lakes, dooming the region to one day be a vast flatland. But don't let this deter you from a visit, as it won't be happening for thousands of years. The park and its centerpieces of **Lake Rotoiti** and **Lake Rotoroa** today draw hikers eager to explore the unspoiled and uncrowded tracks that pass through evergreen beech forests, mountains, and tussock grasslands. In the winter, the slopes become a haven for skiers. The gateway to the park is the tiny, lakeshore village of **St. Arnaud,** which sits on the moraine of the glacier that originally formed Lake Rotoiti.

PRACTICAL INFORMATION AND ACCOMMODATIONS The **DOC headquarters** in **St. Arnaud,** on View Rd. off SH63, also serves as the **Nelson Lakes National Park Visitors Centre** (tel. 521 1806; fax 521 1896; open daily 8am-4:30pm). The after-hours intentions box is located in the foyer. **Sounds-to-Coast Shuttle** (tel. (0800)

802 225) and the **Nelson Lakes Shuttle** (tel. 521 1887; summer only) leave for **Picton** (2hr., 2-3 per week, $15-25) via Blenheim (1¼hr., $10-20). Sounds-to-Coast also goes daily to Greymouth (3½hr., 8:35am, $30). Booking ahead is essential for **Nelson Lakes Transport** (tel. 547 5912), which goes to Nelson (1½hr., M-Sa 5pm, $18). **Kiwilink** (tel. (0800) 802 300, or 577 8332 in Blenheim) runs daily to Picton (1¾hr., 4:30pm, $15) via Blenheim (1¼hr., $10) and to Greymouth (3½hr., 8:35am, $30). The **petrol station, post office,** and **general store** are in the **Nelson Lakes Village Centre** (tel. 521 1854; open daily 7:30am-6:30 or 7pm).

Sleeping options are slim pickings in St. Arnaud. The extremely bright **Yellow House (YHA Associate)** (tel. 521 1887) was just expanded, and the personable staff are great resources for park info. Camping gear is available for purchase or rental. Blankets are provided for the dorms ($18), as well as for doubles and twins ($42; reception 8am-6pm and 7:30-9pm). The **Alpine Chalet (VIP)** (tel./fax 521 1869, reservations (0800) 367 777), part of the swank Alpine Lodge, has budget accommodations for $16 ($15 VIP). The two **DOC campgrounds** at Lake Rotoiti, **Kerr Bay,** and **West Bay,** have tent sites ($7, powered $8). West Bay is closed in winter.

OUTDOORS The most well known of Nelson Lakes' untrampled trails is the **Travers-Sabine Circuit,** a strenuous, four- to seven-day hike that crosses over the 1787m Travers Saddle. The huts in the Travers Valley are first-come, first-served, and often fill in summer. One of the track's daytrips, the **Lake Rotoiti Circuit** (6-9hr.), also begins at Kerr Bay and circles the lake. **St. Arnaud Guiding Services** (tel. 521 1028) leads on- and off-track walking trips into the park, ranging from general nature tours to gold prospecting. The **Rotoiti Outdoor Education Centre** (tel. 521 1820) hires hiking gear year-round (including ice-axes, a must in winter, for $5 per day). Alternatives to hiking include **Action Rafting Tours** (tel. 523 9581 or (0800) 100 582), with half-day whitewater rafting tours down the Grade 2-4 Owen and Buller Rivers ($60-65 per person; pickup available). **Rainy River Rides** (tel. 522 4346) offers horse trekking ($25 per person per hr.).

The glaciers that carved out the Travers Valley were also responsible for creating **Lake Rotoiti,** 8km long, 80m at its deepest point, and jumping with brown trout. You can fish, canoe, jetboat, or waterski on the lake where Maori once fished for eels and mussels. **Rotoiti Water Taxis** (tel. 521 1894) can take you to the head of the lake (10min.; $40 for 4, extra person $10) among other spots. They also hire kayaks and canoes. Lake Rotoiti's big sister, **Lake Rotoroa** (off SH6), was carved out by the two glaciers that formed the Sabine and D'Urville Valleys (jetboating and waterskiing prohibited). Fisherfolk and birdwatchers can contact **Rotoroa Water Taxi** (tel. 523 9199) for a ride to the lakehead (1-3 passengers $60 one way, over 3 people $20 per person one way).

Wintertime revelers use St. Arnaud as a skiing and snowboarding base. The 350-hectare **Rainbow Ski Area** (tel. 521 1861) offers slopes for all levels of ability. Day lift passes are $44 (students under 23 $32), while afternoon passes are $33 ($22). Skis, boots, and poles rent for $30 per day ($24); snowboard and boots are $42 per day. **Mt. Robert Ski Club** (tel. 547 7563) is a private club, but non-members are still welcome (pass $20); call for transportation information. **Nelson Lakes Transport** (tel. 547 5912; fax 547 5914) and **JJ Ski Transport** (tel. 544 7081) offer daily transport to Rainbow Ski Area and Nelson; book ahead. Stop by the **St. Arnaud Snow and Information Center** (tel. 521 1850) for ice-skating rentals ($12) and information.

GOLDEN BAY

The stretch of SH60 north of Nelson leads into ever more remote backcountry, as well as the beauty of **Abel Tasman National Park,** the tranquility of **Golden Bay,** and the majesty of **Kahurangi National Park.** The road borders the bay for a while and then turns inland to wind and climb over Takaka Hill—all in all, a stunning strip of scenery. The first town of note as you head out SH60 from Nelson is groovy **Motueka,** the main jumping-off point for Abel Tasman National Park, with access to the more northerly towns of Kaiteriteri and Marahau, which are off the highway. Farther north along the limestone vistas of SH60 lies the artistic hideaway of **Takaka,** where pottery and wood carvings clutter every nook and cranny. Takaka sits at the bottom of Golden Bay and provides access to **Wainui and Totaranui,** which lie at the northern end of Abel Tasman. The highway dead-ends in distant **Collingwood,** though smaller roads continue north to Kahurangi National Park's **Heaphy Track** and the northernmost extremity of the South Island, **Farewell Spit.** Transportation in the region is not the easiest; having your own car makes things noticeably easier. A few buses service the region, but call ahead, as schedules vary. Traffic can be sparse for **hitchhiking,** but hitchers say locals are often willing to give a lift.

■ Abel Tasman National Park

With subtropical weather, turquoise waters, calm inlets, and golden sands, New Zealand's smallest national park (22,350 hectares) draws far-from-small crowds of hikers eager to attack the famous 51km **Coast Track.** Abel Tasman is a unique mix of endlessly curving beaches, native vegetation, and rocky outcroppings. Keep in mind, however, that you're likely to share the sea air and enchanting gold-and-blue views with plenty of other trampers. The track is the most popular Great Walk by far; more than 100,000 people access some sector of it annually, with 25,000 of these visitors spending at least one night in the huts and campgrounds. Solitary sojourners will be far from overjoyed, but those looking for superb scenery and a relatively easy walk will leave the park thoroughly rejuvenated.

Within Abel Tasman the two main tracks are the **Coast Track** and the **Inland Track** (both 3-5 days). Visitors in search of a less intense trip should consider using the various shuttle and water taxi services to walk a smaller piece of either of these tracks. In addition, the **Harwood's Hole** trail (1½hr.) lies 11km off SH60 and leads to a 178m deep hole in the marble ground. Eager hikers should keep in mind that it is not safe to get too near the giant abyss.

PRACTICAL INFORMATION

Maps and information about the park are available at DOC offices and visitors centers in Nelson, Takaka, and Motueka. **Marahau** (along with **Kaiteriteri**), about 30 minutes north of Motueka off SH60, is the main water transport base for the park and the main point of land access from the south. **Buses** to Abel Tasman from Motueka drop off in front of the information kiosk in Marahau (complete with intentions book and transportation schedules). They also run to the major access points in the northern end of the park, from the road leading east out of Takaka toward Wainui (21km from Takaka) and Totaranui (32km). **Abel Tasman Coachlines** (tel. 548 0285) heads daily from Nelson to Motueka (1hr., 2-3 per day, $8), continuing on to Marahau (1½hr., $11), and also has routes to Wainui carpark or Totaranui (3½-4hr., 1 per day, $24-26). For those blessed with their own wheels, there is plenty of parking in Marahau and Totaranui, with a secured parking lot in Marahau ($3 per day). Hitchhikers report there is usually plenty of traffic. From Marahau, no fewer than four water taxis operate up the coast, including the **Abel Tasman Seafaris Aqua Taxi** (tel. (0800) 278 282), **Abel Tasman Water Taxis** (tel. 528 7497), **Abel Tasman National Park Enterprises** (tel. 528 7801), and **Marahau Beach Camp** (tel. (0800) 808 018). The different companies' fares are all within a few dollars of each other, ranging from $15-30 depending on the distance. All also offer special tours and package deals for one-day hikes and same-day returns, and run all day. All transportation services are greatly reduced during the winter months.

Four **huts** with bunks (20-28 bunks per hut, with toilets, water, and heaters; no stove) and 21 **campgrounds** of varying quality are strewn along the Coast Track. Buy a **Great Walks Pass** from the DOC or a local visitors center before beginning the track (huts $12 in summer, $6 in winter; camping $6 year-round). Back Country hut tickets and Annual Passes are not valid for the Coast Track. It's wise to carry a tent in summer anyway, as the huts are often full. Definitely bring your **bug repellent** in the summer and autumn months when the sandflies and wasps can be fierce. The best map is not the DOC-produced pamphlet, but the glossy **free** map that advertises Marahau's services and is available at the information centers. Special hiking equipment is not necessary as the weather is relatively mild; however, **waterproof sandals** or similar footwear will come in handy for the many water crossings. A gas cooker is a must because none of the huts have cooking facilities. Giardia has been found in the park, so bring a filter, iodine, or enough gas and patience to purify all of your water. Camping supplies can be rented from the White Elephant in Motueka (see p. 284). Stock up on food in Motueka or Nelson at the supermarket, for supplies are extremely limited and expensive at both Marahau and Totaranui.

COAST TRACK

Most of Abel Tasman's visitors walk the Coast Track, the more famous of the park's two major tracks. Considered to be an easier hike on well-maintained and well-marked trails, the track follows the coast for the most part, along beaches and through subtropical forest, with climbs along beech-covered ridges. Avoid the track during holiday season, if possible; the beaches are mobbed, the ocean is a flotilla of speedboats and sea kayaks, and many campgrounds resemble tent ghettos. Luckily the track is easily done year-round, and winter affords more seclusion to trampers. Average wintertime highs are a comfortable 18°C, although the nights can drop down to freezing. The entire track can be done in three days, although four days allows for beach relaxation and side trips.

The track can be walked in either direction, from Marahau to Totaranui or Wainui, or vice versa (3-5 days). The only factor affecting choice of direction is that the **Awaroa Inlet** can only be crossed within two hours on either side of low tide—be sure to check the tide tables posted at information centers and in the huts beforehand (Barks Bay and Torrent Bay have high tide routes). There are four huts and 21 designated campsites on the track, all with toilet facilities and non-potable water. A few of the campsites are only accessible by sea.

Beginning at the southern end of the park, the track is entirely flat, and traverses the hill 10-20 meters above the ocean. A notable campground near this end of the track is **Akersten Bay,** which offers five secluded sites among trees next to a small beach. From here the track rises to a ridge, giving a good view of **Anchorage Hut and Campground.** Avoid the crowds there and take a side trip down the other side of the ridge to the ten excellent sites of **Watering Cove Campground,** located right on the beach with views of Adele Island.

The **Torrent Bay Estuary** can be crossed at low tide, or take the alternate high tide route. By all means continue past the **Torrent Estuary** and **Torrent Bay** campsites—you can do better. There is a public telephone in the Torrent Bay Township. The track descends in its steepest incline to Falls River; the beaches of this section can be seen but not accessed from the track. Nearby **Medland Camp** tends to get crowded, but has an appealing beach. Far worse during holiday is **Bark Bay Camp,** but it does offer a beachside location and free firewood. Close by, **Bark Bay Hut** is modern and spacious, with a welcome freshwater shower outside. Few people notice (or can fit into) the five sites at **Bark Bay Hut Campground,** but grab a spot there if you can. The track winds along for 4km before hitting **Tonga Quarry Camp,** an excellent place to call it a day, with well-spaced tent sites, a stream, and a nearby beach. If you're taking a water taxi, ask to be dropped at **Onetahuti Camp,** where there is free firewood and a beach long enough to allow escape from the crowds any time of year.

The track runs the length of the beach and crosses a river at the northern end before heading inland again. This river crossing is difficult for two hours on either side of high tide, when the water can be chest deep. There is no alternate route, but at low tide it is less than ankle deep. If you feel like a break from unspoiled nature, follow the detour marked by yellow wooden sunflowers to **Awaroa Lodge and Cafe** (tel. 528 8758), which offers an excellent **backpackers** accommodation with a nice open-air kitchen, comfortable beds, and a large grassy field ideal for frisbee and other non-beach activities ($20; open year-round, call ahead for winter discounts). The abutting luxury resort has a pricey cafe and some enjoyable lounge areas.

Back on the main track, the **Awaroa inlet** lies ahead—pay attention to tide times. Stay at the **Awaroa Hut and Camp** only if the tides prevent you from moving on; the hut is spacious but set amid mudflats, and the campground is on hard-packed dirt. A brief inland stretch gives way to an extended string of beaches on the way to **Totaranui.** It is probably best to pass by the **Waiharakeke Camp,** since it is quite popular with local wasps and other stinging insects. The beach at **Gant Bay** is long and wonderfully uncrowded even in peak times, but the Totaranui **caravan park** requires reservations and is extremely crowded in peak times. In summer, a **visitors center** offers potable water, limited food supplies, and listings for upcoming bus and taxi departures.

Resist the urge to end your hike here, because the last 10km after Totaranui are arguably the best section of the track, lined with majestic beaches and excellent overnight accommodations. This section makes an excellent two-day, one-night tramp. One hour from Totaranui, **Anapai Bay Camp** (10 sites) is on a beach fringed by towering rock faces and has secluded sites among dense trees. This outstanding location is matched by the **Mattan Cove Camp** (20 sites), an hour farther on. From here, the track turns west, travels along a road, and then descends gradually to **Whariwharangi Hut and Camp.** The hut is an old two-story farmhouse with a quiet bunkroom upstairs and a 20-site campground in an adjacent grassy field. Near a rugged beach, Whariwharangi is tranquil and isolated. From then on, the track has some good views of **Wainui Bay.** At the end, hitchers tend to cross the bay at low tide in order to reach the main road to Takaka. The track continues on to Wainui carpark.

INLAND TRACK

The less-traversed **Inland Track** also connects Marahau and Wainui, and is considerably more challenging than the Coast Track. Not as well-maintained as the Coast Track, the three- to five-day Inland Track has three huts (plus a small one, Wainui Hut, on a side track). Back Country Hut tickets or Annual Passes are valid for the Inland Track. The track can also be accessed at its midpoint (2hr. from the Wainui or Moa Park Huts) via the 11km **Canaan Rd.** near Takaka Hill, midway between Takaka and Motueka off SH60. Added to the park in the 70s, this section is a bumpy karst landscape where you're guaranteed to see lots of marble.

OTHER ATTRACTIONS

Tonga Island is home to colonies of seals, dolphins and even penguins, not to mention the spectacular underwater world of the **Tonga Island Marine Reserve. Abel Tasman Seal Swim and Water Taxi** (tel. 527 8136 or (0800) 527 8136) brings you even closer to the slippery suckers ($65, children $40); they also run a summer water taxi service out of Marahau (call for details). A **kayaking** explosion has hit Abel Tasman, as more visitors itch to paddle through the Tonga Reserve, near the Island, and through the calm inlets and bays in the park. Both **Abel Tasman Kayaks** (Motueka tel. 527 8022; Nelson tel. 546 7711) and **Ocean River Sea Kayaking** (tel. (0800) 503 003 and 527 8266) are based in Marahau and offer guided trips ($90-500) and kayaks for hire (from $95 for 2 days, $175 for 4 or 5). **Abel Tasman National Park Enterprises** (tel. 528 7801 or (0800) 223 582), based in Motueka, runs sea-kayaking trips in and around the park, guided walks, and cruises departing from Kaiteriteri ($34-50) and Marahau ($32-48). **The Sea Kayaking Company,** 54 Arapiki Rd. (tel. (508) CKAYAK/252 925 or 547 9436), in Nelson, is the only outfitter that runs continually through the winter ($60 for 1 day, $90 for 2 days). **Planet Earth Adventures** (tel. 525 9095) rents kayaks to anyone with some experience ($40-45), and offers guided tours ($45 half-day, $75 full day). In addition to offering accommodations, the **Marahau Beach Camp** (tel. (0800) 808 018) also rents out sea kayaks ($40 per day) and offers several water taxi services.

■ Motueka

Off-beat, muesli-crunching Motueka (pop. 5500) sits at the mouth of the Motueka River on SH60. The entire area was once under water, and today the land is unusually fertile, making it a choice location for fruit growing (the apple, pear and kiwifruit orchards attract legions of fruit pickers each summer). Motueka is also a base for hikers, due to its proximity to two national parks. **Marahau,** an important endpoint to Abel Tasman National Park, lies just 30 minutes away, while an uphill coastal drive brings visitors to Kahurangi National Park (2hr. return hike).

Most commercial buildings in Motueka are on **High Street.** Buses drop off at the **Motueka Visitor Centre** on Wallace St. (tel./fax 528 6543; open daily 8am-7pm; winter hours vary). The **DOC office** (tel. 528 9117) is on the corner of High and King Edward St. about 1km toward Nelson on High St. **BNZ** (tel. 528 7060), **ANZ** (tel. 528 6620), and **Trust Bank** (tel. 528 9710) are all on High St. **Abel Tasman Coachlines** goes to nearby Marahau (30 min., $6) or to the northern ends of the park (the Wainui carpark or Totaranui, $20) as well as to Nelson (1 hr., $8). **Kahurangi Bus Service** (tel. 525 9434) runs to Marahau (30 min., $8) and Nelson (1hr., $9). **Internet access** is available at **Cyberworld** (tel. 528 0072), 15 Wallace St., for 20¢ per minute (open daily 8am-10pm; winter hours vary). In **emergencies,** call 111 or contact the **Motueka Emergency Duty Doctor Number** (tel. 528 8770). The **police** are at 68 High St. (tel. 528 8800). The **post office** is on 123 High St. (tel. 528 6600; open M-F 8:30am-5:30pm, Sa 9:30am-12:30pm). The **telephone code is 03.**

The beautiful **White Elephant,** 55 Whakarea St. (tel. 528 6208; fax 528 0110), is a bright backpackers strewn with elephant miniatures and *Far Side* elephant cartoons. Camping equipment is available for hire, including sleeping bags, stoves, pots, and more. In the summer, a free shuttle runs to Marahau. (Bunks $15; doubles in summer $20, in winter $17.) Budget accommodations at the **Abel Tasman Motel and Lodge** (tel./fax 528 6688), 45 High St., are simple and well kept with a TV lounge and kitchen (dorms $15, doubles and twins with TV $35-40, with bath $55). **Twin Oaks Cottage** (tel. 528 7882), 25 Parkeu St., is fronted by a delightful garden. The 1km separation from town provides a peaceful solitude, and is easily bridged with a free pickup and drop off. There are a limited number of dorm beds, but free use of bikes. (Dorms $15, doubles and twins $40.) A central location near the visitors center on High St. makes **Motueka Backpackers** (tel. 528 7581) a low-hassle option. (Dorms $15, doubles $30; tent sites $9. Free laundry and bikes.) An astronomical ceiling is upheld by walls painted with brightly colored murals at **Hot Mama's Cafe,** 105 High St. (tel. 528 7039). Kites hang overhead as guests lounge in the wicker furniture or sit at tables of multiple hues as music fills the air. A bowl of muesli, fruit, and yogurt is $5; bacon and eggs cost $8. (Open daily from 8:30am.) The **Supervalue** supermarket (tel. 528 7180) is at 108 High St. (open M-W 8am-7pm, Th-F 8am-8:30pm, Sa 9am-7pm, Su 9am-6pm).

Kaiteriteri Beach is just a 15-minute drive away (13km), while the popular **Source of the Riwaka River Walk** (30min. return) is a half-hour drive on SH60 toward Takaka. At 140 High St. near the visitors center, the **Motueka District Museum** (tel. 528 7660) provides a chronological walk through the history of the area, including an assortment of Maori artifacts and an exhibit on the recently squashed tobacco industry. The moa bones of the **Ngarua Caves,** 29 Wilkie St. (tel. 528 8093), are only 20km away. Guided tours leave on the hour every hour (Sept.-start of June daily 10am- 4pm and during the winter holidays, $10).

■ Takaka

Artsy, hippie, dredlocked types inhale deep in Takaka, the main town of Golden Bay. Located 107km from Nelson, Takaka (pop. 1100) makes a convenient access point to both Abel Tasman and Kahurangi National Parks. It boasts its own attractions as well, including the famously clear **Pupu Springs,** the tame (and hungry) **Anatoki eels,** nearby golden beaches, and various limestone formations, including **Rawhiti Cave.** Hiring a bike is one good way to see the nearby sights if you don't want to take advantage of the many area tours that run out of Takaka.

Almost everything of import in Takaka is located on **Commercial St.** An exception is the **Takaka Visitor Centre** (tel. 525 9136), on Willow St. (open daily in summer 9am-5pm, in winter 10am-4pm). Some buses drop off here. The **DOC office** (tel. 525 8026) is across the carpark on Commercial St. (open M-F 8am-4:30pm). **Tickets and**

Trips, 49 Commercial St. (tel. 525 9864), is a great source for info about the entire Golden Bay area; they'll also make bookings for you (open in summer daily 8:30am-5:30pm, in winter M-F 8am-5pm). **Trust Bank,** 64 Commercial St. (tel. 525 8094), is home to one of the area's rare **ATMs** (Cirrus, MasterCard). **BNZ** is on Commercial St. **Internet access** is available at **Baylink Communications,** on Commercial St. near Motupipi St. ($3 first 5min., $1 each additional min.; open M-Th 8:30am-5pm, F 8:30am-5:30pm, Sa 10am-noon). The **Golden Bay Pharmacy** (tel. 525 9490; fax 525 8356) is on Commercial St., as is the **post office** (tel. 525 9916; open M-F 9am-5pm). **Abel Tasman Coachlines** (tel. 528 8850 in Motueka) goes daily to Nelson (2½hr., $20) via Motueka ($14) and to the Wainui carpark and Totaranui ($10). **Bickley Motors** (tel. 525 8352) runs in the summer to Collingwood (30min., 10:30am, $12) and the Heaphy Track (1½hr., $20). Call **Collingwood Bus Services** (tel. 524 8188) to arrange to go along with the mail run (30min., M-F. 9am, $8). **Kahurangi Bus Service** (tel. 525 9434) is another way to get to Nelson (2hr., 7:15am and 12:50pm, $20). In an **emergency,** dial 111. Or, contact the **police** (tel. 525 9211) or the **Golden Bay Medical Centre** (tel. 525 9911).

On the left on Motupipi Rd. as you walk away from Commercial St., **Annie's Backpackers** (tel. 525 8766) provides soft beds and free duvets, plus a clean and attractive kitchen and lounge (dorms $15; doubles $20). **The River Inn** (tel. 525 9425) may be 3km out of town, but it offers free on-demand pickup from the visitors center and free use of bikes to explore the area. The rooms are a bit bare, but they offer comfort and privacy. ($18 per person.) **The Junction Hotel** (tel. 525 9207), with its row of electronic gambling machines in the hallway, is an old country-style hotel with roaming chickens out back and $20 backpacker beds (singles or twins $32; doubles $40, with bath $50). **The Wholemeal Cafe** (tel. 525 9426) on Commercial St., combines a keen aesthetic with a deliciously varied menu. The choices rotate nightly, including curries, fresh pastas, and a range of Creole dishes (from $16; open daily from 8:30am). For some perilous pizzas, head farther down Commercial St. toward the visitors center to the **Dangerous Kitchen** (tel. 525 8686). Gourmet combinations like "the Godfather" and "Henny Penny" (small pizza $9, medium $15, large $22) will leave you wishing for just a little more danger (open daily 8am-midnight; in winter M-Th 8:30am-6pm, F-Su 8:30am-8pm). **Takaka Takeaways** (tel. 525 8225), also on Commercial St., is a less costly option, offering Chinese takeout ($7-9) and other fried goodies to the cholesterol-carefree (open daily 4:30-8pm). **Supervalue** supermarket (tel. 525 9383) is on Commercial St., like everything else (open M-F 8am-6 to 6:30pm, Sa 9:30am-12:30pm). The **telephone code** is **03**.

The **Quiet Revolution Cycle Shop,** 7 Commercial St. (tel./fax. 525 9555), rents mountain bikes ($35 per day, $15 per half day; less in winter) and offers a variety of guided trips to **Harwood's Hole, Pupu Springs** ($30 per person for 4-5 people), and other local destinations. Join in on a unique brand of Southern Hemisphere spirit with **Golden Bay Llama Safaris** (tel. 525 8406). Rather than carry your pack, hire a llama to do it for you while you explore the Golden Bay region during a one- to five-day trip. At the **Bencarri Farm Park** (tel. 525 8261), on McCallum's Rd. south of Takaka, you can court the risk of eel electrocution and feed the world's first tamed eels. (Open daily 10am-5pm in summer, by appointment in winter; admission $5.) The bubbling **Te Waikoropupu Springs** (referred to by most as "Pupu Springs"), 6km from Takaka, are New Zealand's largest freshwater springs system. Believed to be the clearest in the world, the crystalline depths have a horizontal visibility of over 70m. Ages ago, underground water carved out chambers and passages in the marble, which eventually filled with the rushing waters of an underground river. Northeast of Takaka, toward Totaranui, is the privately owned **Rawhiti Cave** (tel. 525 9061), a one-million-year-old hole filled with stalactites and boasting a huge, 50m-wide entrance (bookings essential; guided tours $14).

■ Kahurangi National Park

The vast untamed wilderness dominating the northwest corner of the South Island is contained in the 451,494-hectare **Kahurangi National Park.** The newest national park in the country and the second largest, Kahurangi ("blue skies" or "treasured possession") was formed in 1996 from the former North-West Nelson Forest Park. Snow-capped peaks, rolling landscapes, verdant valleys, and palm-lined coasts are all part of the richly diverse park. Over half of New Zealand's native plant species are found here; 67 species are found only within the park and nowhere else in the world. Kahurangi has some pretty cool endangered carnivorous land snails, too. Adventurous kayakers brave the thrilling Grade 5 **Karamea River** (see p. 293), as it slices down from the highlands to the sea. Kahurangi, which stretches west to east from the mouth of the Heaphy to Tapawera, and north to south from the base of Farewell Spit to Murchison, is accessible through challenging, well-maintained, and well-benched tracks scattered with huts. The best known tramp is the **Heaphy Track,** one of New Zealand's **Great Walks,** but there are myriad opportunities for hikers of every level.

OUTDOOR OPPORTUNITIES

The **Whangapeka Track** (3-5 days) is the most popular tramp in the southern half of the park. Leaving from the Waimea basin in the east (62km from Nelson), the trail surges above 1000 meters twice on its way to the west coast near Karamea, crossing through lush, beech-forested valleys. Although there are huts along the trail, the last hut on the western side was recently washed away, so trampers should either bring tents or be prepared to wrap up their treks with a grueling, ten hour day. The park is laced with many other tramps and day hikes; details are available from the visitors centers and DOC offices in Nelson, Motueka, Takaka, and Karamea. **Cobb Valley** (4-5hr. one-way) is an easygoing, subalpine walk along the Cobb River valley. **Parapara Peak** (4½hr. one-way), beginning just 2km off SH60 between Takaka and Collingwood, is a steep and narrow track that leads to an incredible viewpoint. On a clear day, everything from the mountains in the east to Golden Bay and peaks on the North Island are visible.

HEAPHY TRACK

Three unique environments are encountered on the 82km Heaphy Track. Rated as moderately difficult, the track passes through a mountainous beech forest, through flat and open expanses of alpine meadows (or downs, as they're called in New Zealand), and through the thickly vegetated primeval forest of the western coast that borders thundering surf and wild beaches. The track can easily be completed in four days (4-6hr. of walking per day) or can be stretched out to a more leisurely five or six days. The tramp can be done year-round, although the majority of the 5000 people who annually complete it do so between December and February. March and April are among the best months to hike, with mild and settled weather conditions. In winter, snow can occasionally cover the track.

The two endpoints of the Heaphy Track are **Brown Hut,** 25km east of **Collingwood** and **Kohaihai,** 15km north of **Karamea** on the west coast. Most people begin the track at Brown Hut, placing the bulk of climbing in the first three hours out and leaving the climactic coastal section for the last day. Hikers who are only on the track for one day usually walk the more beautiful sections that begin at Kohaihai.

Practical Information

Getting to and from the trailheads is a bit of a logistical challenge as each lie at the ends of a gravel road, but two companies run regularly to the eastern end of the track. Both depart from Nelson in the morning. **The Rose Express** (tel. 548 2206) stops at numerous hostels in the area and arrives at the Brown Hut end of the Heaphy Track at 1:30pm. (Departs Nelson 8:30am. From Collingwood $10; Motueka $30; Nelson $40; Takaka $20.) It heads back from the trailhead at 2:15pm. **Abel Tasman Coachlines** (tel. 548 0285 in Nelson, 528 8850 in Motueka) departs daily mid-October to April from Nelson at 7:20am, passes through Motueka and Takaka before arriving at the Brown Hut at noon, and returns at 12:15pm. In Takaka, check in with **Tickets and Trips** (tel. 525 9864), 49 Commercial St., which acts as a ticketing agent for all bus services in the area (open in summer daily 8am-6pm, in winter M-F 9am-5pm). Other options include **Bayway Travel** (tel. 525 9864), which runs to Brown Hut by arrangement only. To travel from Westport to Karamea, try **Cunningham's Coaches** (tel. 789 7177), which head north to Karamea from Westport (2½hr., M-F at 3pm, $15; from Karamea to Westport M-F at 8am). **The Last Resort** (tel. 782 6617) can then connect you from Karamea to Kohaihai during the summer (departs 1pm from Karamea, returning at 2pm; $5. Taxi service also available, $25). **Hitching** to either trailhead is difficult, as there is no through traffic, but patient hitchers report success. Extra luggage and gear can be sent by bus between Westport and Takaka ($6) or Westport and Motueka ($10) and held at the visitors centers; book at the Westport or Motueka visitors centers or through **Tickets and Trips** (tel. 525 9864) in Takaka (additional storage fee).

Information on the Heaphy Track can be obtained from the **Takaka DOC Center** (tel. 525 8026) at the southern end of Commercial St. (open M-F 8am-5pm, in winter 8am-4pm), and the **Karamea Information and Resource Centre and DOC office** (tel./fax 782 6652), on Market Cross (open 9am-5pm daily, winter M-F 9am-5pm, Sa 9am-1pm). Virtually all area information centers also have current track information.

Seven **huts** are spaced along the track, each with a designated **campsite** nearby. In addition, there are three other designated places for tenting. You may only camp in these areas. You must purchase a **Great Walks pass** to use the hut or camping facilities (huts $12 per night, camping $6 per night). Passes are available at all DOC centers in Nelson and Marlborough, at most visitors centers, and in many of the backpackers and campgrounds in Karamea, Collingwood, and Takaka. Those who get nabbed without passes on the track by a warden must pay a 25% surcharge. Wardens can also upgrade your camping pass into a hut pass for $6. The standard information brochure with an adequate basic map is available at DOC centers and information centers for $1; a detailed topographic map of the track area for those cartographically inclined is available at DOC centers for $11.

Equipment

The forest shields the Heaphy tramper from many of the elements, but the open and exposed 27km along Gouland and Mackay Downs necessitate being adequately prepared for **wet and windy conditions.** This section catches a lot of wind funneled between the east and west coasts, and the clouds often dump incredible amounts of rain upon the track. Be ready with waterproof clothes (for you and your backpack— a pack liner is a good idea), or be prepared to wait for good weather for crossing the downs. Another essential for this track is **insect repellent,** as scads of sandflies along the coastal section can make for a less than pleasant tramp.

Carry a tent if you want to save a bit of cash, but bear in mind that many of the campsites, especially on the Gouland and Mackay Downs, are soggy, damp, and exposed, and there is almost always space in the huts. Carrying a tent allows you to stay in one of the three campsites not located by huts, several of which are very nicely situated. With the exception of Brown Hut and Gouland Downs Hut, all huts have gas stoves for culinary masterpieces. These huts also have pots, but bring your own silverware and cups. Campers will have to bring all of their own cooking equipment. There is no convenient place to rent gear for the tramp, though it is possible to rent gear in Motueka (see p. 283). The supermarkets in Takaka and Westport are the best places to purchase tramp food; stocking up in Karamea or Collingwood will be significantly more expensive.

The Track

The eastern starting point of the track, **Brown Hut,** is right by the carpark. The hut has 20 bunks, a large fireplace, a phone, and an adjoining grassy area for tents. There are no cooking facilities. The **Aorere River** runs nearby for angling. From here the track follows a broad path, climbing steadily up both sides of a ridge on the western side of the **Aorere Valley** through dense beech forest. Although it is a steady uphill climb, it is not very steep and has a couple of long, gently sloping switchbacks. There is an occasional break in the trees but this is the least scenic section of the Heaphy Track. After three hours, you reach the **Aorere Shelter** and most of the climbing is done. The hut is a basic shelter with three walls, a covered deck area, and a wooden shelf inside that will sleep four people (a sleeping pad is essential). It has water, toilets, and a flat grassy area for tenting.

Shortly after this shelter, the highest point on the track is reached at **Flanagan's Corner** (915m). A short five-minute side trip takes you to a sweeping panorama of the entire upper Aorere Valley and the mountains that surround it. **Perry Saddle Hut,** can be seen from this point as well. About an hour from Aorere Shelter, this hut sits right on the edge of the valley with good views. It has a coal stove for warming up (coal provided), stoves, pots and pans, and very exposed tent sites on boggy ground.

From Perry Saddle, the trail gradually leaves behind the patches of beech and opens out into the **Gouland Downs,** the beginning of the exposed section of track. Some of the best vistas are in this area, but when it rains the trail can become extremely muddy. **Gouland Downs Hut** is the smallest on the track (10 bunks) but has a massive fireplace. The tent sites are unremarkable, but are the best you'll find between Aorere Shelter and Lewis Hut. The biggest draw of the Gouland Downs Hut is the opportunity to explore the eerie and mystical forest a few hundred meters further down the trail. Perched on a limestone outcrop, the Tolkienesque forest is full of bizarre rock formations, caves, arches, moss-shrouded rocks and trees, and several beautiful streams that wind around and through the rocks. From here, the track traverses the western end of Gouland Downs, and gradually re-enters areas of beech trees; **Saxon Hut** is a short hour-and-a-half farther on, offering 16 bunks, gas stoves, and a coal stove in addition to boggy tent sites.

The last uphill section comes shortly after Saxon Hut, as the track gradually winds up to **Mackay Downs.** This area can flood quite severely in rainy conditions; keep an eye on the weather. In general, the Mackay Downs are not nearly as open or expansive as the Gouland Downs and are considerably more boggy. **Mackay Hut** is three hours past Saxon Hut and has excellent views down the Heaphy River Valley to the ocean. The hut is quite spacious overall and boasts flush toilets (!) and 26 bunks in two separate rooms away from the communal lounge area. Unfortunately, the tent sites here are the worst on the track.

From here, it's all downhill to the sea. Although the track does not have any views as it winds through the forest, the forest itself is fascinating as it slowly changes due to the decreasing elevation and larger amounts of rainfall. By the time **Lewis Hut** is reached (three hours past Mackay Hut) the forest has thickened and diversified; the beautiful nikau palm begins to appear, huge treeferns loom overhead, and pohutukawa trees (in full flower during the summer) lace the hillsides with red. Lewis Hut is situated at the junction of the Heaphy and Lewis Rivers with excellent views across the Heaphy River to the hillside beyond. Lewis boasts 20 bunks in a spacious hut, and grassy and sheltered campsites. **Sandflies** begin to appear here: be ready.

Immediately after Lewis Hut, the intrepid tramper receives an introduction to the series of several **swing bridges** found on the last stretch of track. Spidery, narrow structures of wire, they bob up and down and swing from side to side. The longest bridge is the one across the **Heaphy River.** Its length allows optimum bob and twist and the howling wind creates additional lateral sway. Hang on!

For the next two hours, the track winds past moss-and-fern-encrusted rock faces, plants sprouting from soil embedded in twisted and gnarled overhanging branches, and plenty of elegant nikau palms. **Heaphy Hut** is by the mouth of the Heaphy River, yet protected from the hammering sea wind. New, spacious, and yellow, it is the nicest hut on the track, with a large fireplace, three separate gas stoves, flush toilets, and a view of the Heaphy River mouth from the window. A big grassy field is just out front and leads to the neighboring camp site, which is also excellent. The river mouth is quite wild; a final arc of the river has produced a massive stretch of beach littered with driftwood, and at high tide the ocean sends surges of waves a good distance up the river.

The final 16km flat stretch of the track runs entirely along the coast, is almost entirely flat, and allows access to numerous beaches. The surf is ferocious and rip-currents make the water too dangerous for swimming. The hills cascade steeply down to the beach and it is possible (unfortunately) to see the havoc the possums have wreaked on the forest in the form of plentiful brown and denuded dead and dying trees. Aside from this unfortunate sight, the entire final stretch is excellent. Two hours out of Heaphy Hut is **Katipo shelter,** another basic shack with a wooden shelf for four sleepers, a small number of tent sites, and no water. Shortly after the shelter is **Crayfish Point,** which can only be crossed three to four hours on either side of low tide. A high tide chart is provided; tide tables can also be found at Kohaihai and Heaphy huts. The final and longest beach before Kohaihai is **Scotts Beach.** Those on a short excursion from Kohaihai only need to visit here to have the full coastal experience. There is an excellent campsite here, ringed by Nikau palms with a water supply gushing out of a rock. After this, the track does its only real climbing along the coast as it skirts around **Kohaiai Bluff** before reaching Kohaihai itself. At Kohaihai there is a shelter, a phone for ringing a ride, and a very nice campground that is not part of the Great Walk system ($4; has water, toilets, and a great view of Kohaiai Bluff).

■ Collingwood

Collingwood's dreams of being a major shipping port (and possibly even the nation's capital) were brought to a bitter end by better roads, which made export to Takaka more efficient by land than by sea. Nevertheless, the seaside hamlet lives on today, having survived destruction by fire three times and a dramatic decrease in population (from nearly 4000 in the 1850s to 150 today). Collingwood sits north of the vast Kahurangi National Park and to the west of Abel Tasman National Park. The town is also close to **Farewell Spit,** the country's longest sandspit (35km) and a wetland of international importance. Full of huge sand dunes, swamp, scrub, and mudflats, it's also the northernmost point of the South Island, and the last point of land that Captain Cook saw on his first visit before sailing off to Australia. Flocks of migratory wading birds from far-flung locations appear on the peninsula from September to mid-March, and whales trapped and confused by the nearly-enclosed Golden Bay have been sighted from near the base of the Spit, and are sometimes found beached on the sandy shore.

Located at the far northern end of Golden Bay, Collingwood lies at the terminus of **SH60.** The **Farewell Spit Visitor Centre** (tel. 524 8454; open daily in summer 8am-6pm; winter hours vary) is at the base of Farewell Spit and a short distance above Puponga (23km north of Collingwood). Riding along with the mail run, **Colllingwood Bus Services,** is one of the few ways to get to Takaka and the only reliable way in winter. Make arrangements at the **post office** (tel. 524 8188; open M-F 8:30am-5:30pm) the day before and meet 10 minutes early beside the post office (30min., M-F 8:15am departure, $8). **Abel Tasman Coachlines** also departs daily in the summer for the Heaphy Track (50min., 11:10am) and for Nelson (4hr., 1:10pm) via Takaka (20min.) and Motueka (3hr.). The **telephone code** is **03.**

The **Collingwood Motor Camp** (tel. 524 8149), next to the beach at the terminus of SH60, offers cabins with windows overlooking the water (with communal kitchen and toilet facilities), as well as canoe hire ($5 per half day). Bunks are $16 in summer, $15 in winter (under 15 $5), while cabins are $50 for two people (extra person $10). Powered tent sites are $9. The proprietor of **Pioneer Motels** (tel. 524 8109), right next door on Tasman St., offers tales of the old days as well as attractive twins ($58) and motel units, complete with bathroom and kitchen facilities ($70 for 2 people, $63 in winter, $10 per additional person). Stock up on supplies at the **Collingwood General Store** (tel. 524 8221; open daily 8am-5:30 or 6pm).

The **Original Farewell Spit Safari** (tel. (0800) 808 257 or 524 8257) run by **Collingwood Safari Tours** offers four-wheel-drive tours to the Cape Farewell Lighthouse year-round (5½hr.; $52, under 15 $30). They also tour a gannet colony (6½hr.; $65, under 15 $35) and go "wader watching" on the inner beach (3-4hr., $40), depending on the season and the tides; call in advance. **Farewell Spit Nature Tours** (tel. 524 8188), run by **Collingwood Bus Services,** runs a guided trip to the spit, covering Cape Farewell, the **Pillar Point Lighthouse,** and to the **Farewell Spit Lighthouse** (daily from the post office, tide dependent; $60 with lunch). The same outfit operates the **Scenic Mail Run,** a 5½-hour trip through off-the-beaten track countryside with local commentary (M-F 9:30am; book in advance). Check at the post office for rides to the base of the spit; from there, many kilometers of sand await the eager walker. **Cape Farewell Horse Treks** (tel. 524 8031) offers a variety of horseback adventures, including one to the Pillar Point Lighthouse, where a seal colony sometimes gathers. Those with cars can head to the magnificent natural rock sculptures of **Wharariki Beach** or serene **Paturau Beach,** both on the west coast. From the carpark 29km north of Collingwood, walk 20 minutes from the east coast to the west coast along a track to Wharariki Beach, where large jutting cliffs, big sand dunes, and arches create a solitary atmosphere appropriate for surfing or relaxing. The Kaituna Track (7 hr. one-way), accessible by a drive from Collingwood, is one of the more serious hikes in the area. The **Collingwood Museum** (suggested donation $2) is small, but houses a variety of interesting historical objects.

Westland

However you get there, be it rail, air, or road, you'll notice the change as soon as you enter Westland. The towering Southern Alps shoot upward, bounding the region to the east and making a geological wall a mere 40 to 50 kilometers from the Tasman Sea and the fiery weather patterns that whirl above it. This unique combination produces the torrential rain (ranging from one meter in Greymouth to an astounding eight meters in Haast) that has earned Westland the nickname "Wetland" and created lush tropical rainforests throughout the region. The juxtaposition of snow-capped peaks, endless green forests, and pounding waves is candy for the eyes and grist for the mighty tourism mill that grinds throughout Westland. Gold rushes in the late 1800s first seduced outsiders to the west coast, but modern visitors are drawn to attractions like Fox Glacier, Franz Josef Glacier, and the jade shops of Hokitika, just as legions of sandflies are in turn drawn to them. Itchy bites notwithstanding, Westland is a powerful example of a land where humanity dwells at the fringes, and a visit to the west coast may feel more like a visit to the past. With all its sublime beauty, it's no wonder that over 80% of Westland is set aside in various national parks, forest parks, and scenic reserves, including the gigantic **Te Wahipounamu South West New Zealand World Heritage Area.**

While gold mining operations are still underway in parts of Westland, the distinct **lack of banks** for the long stretch from Hokitika to Wanaka in the southern lakes region means that you should carry a sufficient stash of your own gold coins. **Hitchhiking** through Westland can be a difficult undertaking in winter when the traffic disappears, and a miserable endeavor in summer, with hours spent waiting in pouring rain while swatting sandflies. Thankfully, daily **buses** provide a dependable way to travel.

WESTLAND HIGHLIGHTS

- A hike up the Franz Josef or Fox Glacier (see p. 300) is guaranteed to satisfy adventurous spirits.
- The beachside towns of the West Coast (see p. 290) are a relaxing place to unwind for a few days.
- The rugged terrain around remote Haast (see p. 305) is replete with wild, natural beauty.

Westport

Home to the Buller, bullion, and black lung, the three inseparable threads of Westport's existence are its river, its gold, and its coal. A gold rush town established in the mid 1800s, the original Westport was washed away by a flood in 1872. The town quickly bounced back to its boomtown size of 5000 even as the gold-fever subsided, due to the coal mining, shipping, and fishing that all rushed to take its place. The past continues to thrive in present-day mines such as **Coaltown,** and huge mounds of coal are visible during the drive up SH6. Westport has also learned to tame and utilize its two flanking beaches and the tempestuous Buller, providing for springtime whitebait fishing and thrilling rafting. **Cape Foulwind** and the **Tauranga Bay seal colony** are close by, while Karamea and **Kahurangi National Park** lie only 98km to the north. Westport perks up the second Saturday in February for the **Buller Half/Full Marathon,** which runs through Buller Gorge (near Murchison) to Victoria Sq., as part of the February **Seafest West** festival with live entertainment and seafood.

PRACTICAL INFORMATION Palmerston St. is Westport's main street, running parallel to and just north of the Buller River. Buses cut through Westport on their way around the region. **InterCity** (tel. (0800) 731 711) heads daily to Nelson (3½hr., 4pm, $44) and Greymouth (11:20am, $24) via Paparoa (1hr., $13). Pickup is at **Craddock's Service Station,** on Palmerston St. near Rintowl St. **Cunningham's Coaches** (tel. 789 7177) provides a bumpy ride to Karamea (2½hr., M-F 3pm, $15), acting as combina-

Westland

TO KARAMEA
Westport
Cape Foulwind
Buller R.
Inangahua Junction
67A
Charleston
67
6
69
Reefton
VICTORIA FOREST PARK
65
NELSON LAKES NATIONAL PARK
HANMER FOREST PARK
Hanmer Springs
7A
Lewis Pass
Maruia Springs
Springs Junction
7
TO CHRISTCHURCH

PAPAROA NATIONAL PARK
Punakaiki
Barrytown
6
7
LAKE SUMNER FOREST PARK
Lake Sumner
PUKETERAKI RANGE

TASMAN SEA

Greymouth
Lake Brunner
Shantytown
Kumara
73
ARTHUR'S PASS NATIONAL PARK

Arthur's Pass
CRAIGIEBURN FOREST PARK
73
TO CHRISTCHURCH

Hokitika
Lake Kaniere
SOUTHERN ALPS
Lake Coleridge
77

Ross
6

Pukekura
Lake Heron
Mount Hutt

Harihari

TWO THUMB RANGE

Abut Head
Okarito Lagoon
Okarito
Whataroa

Franz Josef Glacier
Mt. Tasman
MOUNT COOK NATIONAL PARK
Lake Tekapo
79
Fox Glacier
Mt. Cook
Lake Tekapo
Fairlie
WESTLAND NATIONAL PARK
6
Mount Cook Village
Tekapo

Heretaniwha Point
BEN OHAU RANGE
Lake Pukaki
80

Lake Paringa
Paringa
Twizel
Lake Benmore
Clearburn
Lake Moeraki
Lake Ohau
8
Omarama
Otematata
83
TO OAMARU

0   20 miles
0   20 kilometers
N
6
Haast
MOUNT ASPIRING NATIONAL PARK
6
Haast Pass
TO WANAKA & SOUTHERN LAKES REGION

WESTLAND

tion transport service and mailrun. **Karaka Tours** (tel. 789 5080) provides on-demand service to Karamea ($60 for 2 people) and to the Heaphy Track ($100 for 2). **White Star Passenger and Freight Service** (tel. 789 6200) heads daily to Springs Junction (2hr., 10:05am, $12), where you can continue to Christchurch (6hr., $33) or Nelson (6hr., $27).

The **Westport Visitor Information Centre and DOC office,** 1 Brougham St. (tel. 789 6658; fax 789 6668), is the place to get your questions answered (open daily 9am-7pm; in winter M-F 9am-5pm, Sa-Su 9am-3pm). The **House of Travel** (tel. 789 7209), on the corner of Palmerston and Wakefield St., serves your transport needs (open M-F 8:30am-5pm). Take your money matters to one of the several **banks** lining Palmerston St. (generally open M-F 9am-4:30pm). To rent bikes, head to **Beckers Sportsworld** (tel. 789 8787), across from the post office on Palmerton St.

In an **emergency,** dial 111. For medical attention, try the **Buller Medical Centre,** 45 Derby St. (tel. 789 7309; open M-F 8:30am-5pm, also Tu 6-8pm). **Ell's Pharmacy** (tel. 789 8466, after hours 789 8379) is on Palmerston St. right across from the visitors center (open M-Th 8:30am-5:30pm, F 8:30am-6:30pm, Sa 10am-12:30pm). **Internet access** is available at the **public library** (tel. 789 7239) across from the visitors center on Brougham St. ($2 per 15min.; open M-F 9am-5pm, Sa 10am-1pm). The **post office** is at the corner of Palmerston St. and Brougham St. (open M-F 9am-5pm, Sa 10am-12:30pm). The **telephone code** is **03.**

ACCOMMODATIONS AND FOOD   Old hotels line Palmerston St., but the back-packers may be a comfier option. The soft beds and toasty lounge at **Bazil's Hostel,** 54 Russell St. (tel. 789 6410; fax 789 6240), create an aura so friendly you'll feel like you've come home. If you're really lucky, you may bump into Bazil himself, a large, friendly guard dog who likes to howl with the fire sirens. (Dorms $16; doubles or twins $36; camping in back $9.) **Marg's Associate Hostel (YHA Associate),** 56 Russell St. (tel. (0800) 737 863 or 789 8627; fax 789 8396), is right next door to Bazil's. The rooms are spic and span and the bunks even have TVs. Some rooms also have kitchens or second-story lofts. (Bunks $17; doubles or twins $45; powered sites $18 for 2 people; credit card min. $45. Free duvets.) From Brougham St., take a right onto Queen St. to get to the **TripInn,** 72 Queen St. (tel. (0800) 874 7466; tel./fax 789 7367; http://home.clear.net.nz/pages/tripinn). A beautiful wooden staircase leads to plain but comfortable rooms in an older house. Free barbecue grilles and bikes for hire ($5) liven up your stay; area tours are available. (Dorms $15; doubles or twins $34; tent sites $9. Linen $2.) The closest motorcamp to the town center is the **Westport Holiday Park,** 31-37 Domett St. (tel. 789 7043; fax 789 7199). From Palmerston St., turn right at the post office onto Brougham St., then walk several blocks before taking a left on Domett St. Oscar the Australian cockateel greets guests to the few A-frame cabins (some with tiny bathrooms) and a single room filled with matzah-thin dorm beds. (Dorms $12; cabins $27, with bath $37; tent sites $8, powered $9.)

Most of Westport's dining choices line Palmerston St. and its side streets. One of the town's sweet spots is **Mandala's Coffee House,** 110 Palmerston St. (tel. 789 7931), where beautifully drawn blackboard menus display an extensive list of tasty food. Try the six-inch tall "giant burger" ($9). Vegetarians might find quiche, open sandwiches, and veggie burgers filled with sprouts, beets, eggs, and lettuce more to their liking ($10.50). Top it all off with a large dessert. (Open daily in summer from 7am, in winter from 8am.) Otherwise, make your own concoctions after you've shopped at **New World,** on Palmerston St. (open M-Tu 8:30am-6pm;W-F 8:30am-7pm, Sa 9:30am-4:30pm). There is also a **Supervalue** on Fonblanque St. between Russel St. and Queen St. (open M-T 8am-6pm, W-F 8am-7pm, Sa 9am-7pm, Su 9am-5pm).

SIGHTS AND ACTIVITIES   Float on an inner tube down a Styxian river alongside stalactites and stalagmites through Westport's underground **Metro Cave** system. A headlamp helps hundreds of glow-worms light your way in the **Glow-worm Grotto.** After floating out of the caves and **Ananui Creek,** the **Waitakere River** rapids await; then end up on your feet at the **Nile River** Canyon for a 20-minute walk. **Norwest Adventures** (tel. 789 6686; bookings tel. (0800) 116 686) offers a variety of trips to examine the famed West Coast limestone cave formations. The "Underworld Rafting" trip goes out twice daily year-round. *(8:30am and 1pm. 4-5hr. $90; all equipment provided. Participants must be at least age 10.)* The "Metro Cave" trip is a walk through cave landscapes and out into the surrounding rainforest. *(3hr. $45; family of 4 $120.)* The more adventurous can squeeze through narrow passages like the "Worm" with their slimmed wallet and abseil down the 120-foot hole. The "Adventure Caving: Te Tahi" trip also runs daily. *(4hr. $150. Equipment provided. Min. age 16.)*

The Buller River area (with the 5th-largest catchment in the country) provides plenty of above-ground rafting excitement, from calm scenic trips to raging whitewater expeditions. **Buller Adventure Tours** (tel. 789 7286 or (0800) 697 286; fax 789 8104) operates half to full-day tours on rougher waters (Grade 4-5); the Grade 4 Buller River trip is a serious whitewater rafting adventure for the brave of heart (half-day, $75), while the Grade 5 Karamea River trip is a heli-raft combination, including a "gourmet luncheon" on the river bank. *(Full day. $195. Min. age 15.)* They also offer jet-boating (1½ hr., $49), horse trekking (2hr., $35), and a safari in an amphibious all-terrain vehicle (30min., $15). **White Water Action** (tel. (0800) 100 582) also offers rafting trips, ranging from Grades 2 to 4. *($65-110.)* **Burning Mine Adventures** (tel. 789 7277) offers scenic tours on mountain bikes (4hr., $45, min. 2 people) as well as a tour of the Stockton Opencast Mine (4hr., $45, child $30). They also have white water kayaking for beginners in the Mokihinni river ($75).

If you'd rather use your own legs to propel you into bliss, try the nearby beaches with swimming areas: **Carters Beach,** which stretches from Cape Foulwind to the mouth of the Buller River, and the driftwood-covered **North Beach,** which stretches along Craddock Dr. to the north end of the river. To stay dry altogether, try your luck fishing for whitebait (a West Coast delicacy) around the Buller River in spring (Sep. 1-Nov. 15). The **Cape Foulwind Walk** (1½hr. one-way) is a short drive southwest of the town; a great coastal hike with beautiful views, it provides a splendid opportunity to see the seal colony. **Charming Creek** (3hr. one-way) lives up to its name north of Westport, winding through the rainforest along a river gorge and past two waterfalls. For a good introduction to the coal-bearing past of Westport, head to **Coaltown** (tel. 789 8204), south on Queen St. across the railway tracks. Experience coal mining both visually and aurally in the simulated mine. *(Open daily 8:30am-4:30pm.)* A drive along the 120km **Buller Coalfield Heritage Trail** hits the highlights of Westport's coal mining history. Flex your biceps taking a swig of beer made from a 16th-century recipe at **Miner's Brewery** (tel. 789 6201) on Lyndhurst St. for a more intrepid sort of recreation. *(Tours M-Sa 11:30am and 1:30pm; brewery open M-Sa 10am-5:30pm.)*

To Peck and Destroy

Mother Nature's saboteurs, the sharp-beaked **kea** is one of New Zealand's native birds, and a bloody nuisance at that. Among their notorious hobbies, keas are known to wait in carparks and nearby shrubs while searching for an unsuspecting bike seat left behind without an owner (or with an owner, for that matter). In addition to stealing food, untying shoelaces, and generally terrorizing tourists and locals alike, the cheeky birds also like to rip windshield wipers to shreds and have been known to feast on unattended camping and skiing equipment.

■ Near Westport: Karamea

The northernmost town of Westland, Karamea lies at the end of SH67, near the end-point of Kahurangi National Park's **Heaphy Track** (see p. 286). Famous for the nearby huge **limestone arches** and the delicate **Honeycomb Cave system** (complete with bones of extinct birds, including the moa), the **Oparara Basin** attracts most of Karamea's visitors.

The **Karamea Information and Resource Centre and DOC office** (tel./fax 782 6652), on Bridge St., has information on the park and sells hut tickets and passes for the Heaphy, Wangapeka, and Leslie Tracks. **Cunningham's Coaches** (tel. 789 7177) offers a jostling mail/passenger run to Westport (M-F 8:30am, $15). Karamea is home to a **grocery store** (tel. 782 6701) and **postal agency** at the Hardware Store (tel. 782 6700), as well as an end-of-the-road **petrol station,** all clustered around the information center. In an emergency, dial 111. The **police** (tel. 782 6801) and **doctor** (tel. 782 6737) are also available.

Contact the **Last Resort** (tel. (0800) 505 042 or 782 6617; fax 782 6820; email last.resort@xtra.co.nz) for a choice of comfortable accommodations (dorms $15; twins and doubles with linen $50, extra person $15; doubles with baths $75, extra person $15). The Last Resort also runs tours to **Honeycomb Cave,** which includes a tour of the **Box Canyon** and **Limestone Arch** (5½hr.; $60, under 14 $30; min. 4 people), and guided **cave trips** leaving from the Oparara carpark ($30, under 14 $15). If you want to explore the Oparara Basin area's spectacular limestone arches on your own, The Last Resort offers transport to the basin ($20 per person). Family rafting tours down the Karamea's rapids run $22 per person (under 14 $15, 2½hr., min. 6 people) and canoeing is available in the same place (2hr., $30 per person, $50 for a double canoe). Most of Karamea's trails require a short drive. Hitchhikers say locals are receptive to an outstretched thumb. Head north of Karamea following the signs to the Oparara Basin. Turning inland for 16km will lead you to a carpark on Oparara Rd., where you can take one of two trails. The **Oparara Arch trail** (20min.), in better condition, leads to the 43m high, 219m long Oparara Arch, while the **Moria Gate** trail (30min.) heads to the Little Arch. The **Fenian Track** (1½hr. return) is a picturesque hike through the rainforest; check at the resource center for directions, and to see if it is open. The **Nikau Grove** (20min. return), **Zig Zag Track** (30min. return), and **Scott's Beach** trail (1½hr. return) all begin at the start of the **Heaphy Track** (9-10km north of Karamea).

■ Paparoa National Park

Waves crash with thunderous claps against the layered rocks, drenching the sightseers clustered expectantly in their bright, crayon-colored raincoats. At last the waves strike just right, the blowholes spray high into the air, and the cameras click away in a fury of photographic zeal. Sharing gleeful smiles, the tourists congratulate each other on capturing that once-in-a-lifetime (or at least once-in-an-hour) shot of utterly unique **Punakaiki.** Located midway between Greymouth and Westport on SH6, the incredibly popular "pancake rocks" and blowholes are merely the highlights of the water-carved limestone landscape of Paparoa National Park. A 30,000-hectare park created to protect lowland forests from logging, it includes dense lowland rain forest, streams, waterfalls, twisting branches of beech forests, complex cave systems, and the dominating Paparoa Range. The nikau palm, the southernmost palm in the world, stands tall amid the flax, as the abundant rainwater works its magic on the surrounding landscape. The water drips through organic matter and eats away at the limestone beneath the thick tangle of forest. Paparoa, which entranced explorers like Heaphy, Brunner, and von Haast in the late 1800s, still knows how to seduce visitors today.

Punakaiki is the main town of the Paparoa region. **InterCity** passes through Punakaiki daily en route to Greymouth (40min., 12:50pm, $9) and to Nelson (4½hr., 3pm, $56) via Westport (1hr., $18). Buses stop near the **Punakaiki Visitor Centre** (tel. 731 1895; fax 731 1896), on SH6 across from the blowholes (open daily in winter 9am-4pm; extended hours in the summer). The **DOC** office (tel. 731 1893; fax 731 1888) is 1km north (open M-F 8am-4:30pm). If you have your own car, keep in mind that the nearest **petrol** stations are 35-60km away. In an emergency, dial 111, contact the **ambulance** (tel. 768 0499), or call the **police** (tel. 768 1600). The **post office box** is in front of the visitors center. The **telephone code** is 03.

While its limited services are clustered together, Punakaiki's accommodations are scattered along SH6. If coming by bus, ask the driver to drop you off at your destination, unless you're in the mood for a bracing walk. The **Punakaiki Beach Hostel** (tel. 731 1852; fax 731 1152), on the corner of Webb St. and Dickenson Parade, is about a 15-minute walk from the visitors center with the ocean on your left; otherwise, call for a free pickup. Driftwood adorns the lawn and balcony of the yellow and green house, and the nearby ocean lulls guests to sleep at night (dorms $15-16; twins and doubles $37). The **Te Nikau Retreat** (tel. 731 1111) is located even farther down SH6; call for a free pickup. The unusual setup consists of several separate buildings connected by narrow paths through the rainforest. So while there may be a bush walk to the kitchen or showers, the place has a unique aura of peace and isolation—not to mention a vast range of room options (dorms $16; doubles and twins $36, with bath $40; 2-person jungle huts $26; motel units with linen $55; reduced rates on multi-night stays in winter). Off SH6 near the Punakaiki Beach Hotel, the **Punakaiki Motor Camp** (tel. 731 1894; fax 731 1888) has a range of cabin choices ($26-33 for 2 people), as well as tent sites ($8.50-10) and motor vehicle sites. For groceries and takeaway stop by **The Pancake Tearooms** (tel. 731 1873), clustered right near the visitors center. Stamps and phonecards are also available. (Open daily 8:30am-8pm; closes at 5pm in the winter.)

To get to the area's main attraction, the Punakaiki blowholes and pancake rocks, take the **Dolomite Point Walk** (20min. round-trip) through flax and nikau palms (wheelchair-accessible with assistance). The blowholes are most spectacular at high tide when the waves have a good swell from the west. The **Trumans Track** (15min.) heads off SH6, about two to three kilometers north of the visitors center and out to a dramatic viewpoint at the ocean's edge. Or you can grab a flashlight and explore the **Punakaiki Cavern,** just 500m north of Punakaiki, to the right of SH6. The **Punakaiki Pororari Loop** (3hr. round-trip) is a longer walk through the stretch of rainforest from the Punakaiki River to the Pororari River (check before you go to see if the river crossing is possible). More rugged trekkers can explore the **Inland Pack Track** (27km, 2-3 days), which began as a safe alternative to the pitfalls of coastal travel during the 1860s gold rushes. Check with DOC before you go, and stay on the track as there are numerous sinkholes and other potentially dangerous formations (there are no huts on track).

Punakaiki Canoe Hire (tel. 731 1870) rents canoes for paddling in the Pororari Gorge ($10-40). They also rent bicycles (half day $10, full day $15). **Paparoa Nature Tours** (tel./fax 731 1826) can take you bird watching to see the only burrowing black petrel breeding colony in the world. (Tours run late Mar. to mid-Dec. at sunset and 2hr. before sunrise; 1½hr.; $25, families $50, children $10; min. $50.) You can watch their prenuptial antics (Mar.-May), followed by patient egg-sitting (June), chick-hatching (July-Aug.), and the exciting moment when the chicks finally learn to spread their wings (Nov.-Dec.; no flash photography is allowed). **Paparoa Nature Tours** leads daily, three-hour cave tours from the visitors center (10am, 2 and 8pm; $25, ages 4-14 $15; min. $75). They also give full-day guided canoe tours and half-day or full-day guided walks. Call **Paparoa Horse Treks** (tel. 731 1839) to view the pancake rocks from the back of a horse on the beach below the cliffs (1hr. $30), or take a longer trip through the Punakaiki River Valley (2hr., $50). **Kiwa Sea Adventures** (tel. 731 1813) offers "eco/nature" water tours to see dolphins, seals, petrels, and spotted shags (Oct. 1-Apr. 1;1hr., $50). You can swim with the dolphins if observation isn't hands-on enough (2hr.; $85); book at least a day ahead.

■ Greymouth

After the raucous gold-rush party of the late 1800s ended, Greymouth was forced to rally its timber, coal, and fishing resources to survive, eventually becoming the biggest town in Westland. It may strike you a bit differently on a gloomy, rainy day as you stroll along the gray gravel walkway and encounter the gray statue down by the Grey River (the town's namesake). For what it's worth, Greymouth's smattering of pubs and bars sees the most action on the coast. The city also serves up a potpourri of exotic adventures (it is one of only three places in New Zealand to offer blackwater rafting through underground caves).

ORIENTATION AND PRACTICAL INFORMATION

From the **Greymouth Railway Station** on Mackay St., you can walk straight to get to the Grey River and the "Great Wall" that runs along Mawhera Quay (the wall was built by the townspeople in 1988 to hold back the flooding Grey River). Greymouth's shopping area centers on **Mackay** and **Guinness St.**

WESTLAND

Trains: TranzScenic (tel. (0800) 802 802) leaves daily for Christchurch (4hr., 2:25pm, $76) via Arthur's Pass (2hr., $34).
Buses: InterCity (tel. (0800) 731 711 or 768 7080) heads daily to Franz Josef (4hr., 1:50pm, $41) and Fox Glacier via Hokitika (40min., $12); and Nelson (6hr., 1:50pm, $61) via Westport (2hr., $20) and Punakaiki (40min., $9). **Atomic Shuttles** (tel. 768 5101) runs south every day to Queenstown (10½hr., 7:30am, $75) via Hokitika (30min, $10), Franz Josef Glacier (2½ hr., $25), and Fox Glacier (3½ hr., $25). **KO-OP Shuttle** (tel. 366 6633) and **Coast-to-Coast** (tel. (0800) 800 847) run to Christchurch (4-5hr., 1 per day, $30-35) via Arthur's Pass (1½hr., $10-15). **Sounds-to-Coast** (tel. (0800) 802 225) leaves for Picton (6hr., 2-3 per week, $49) via St. Arnaud (3½hr., $30). **Alpine Coaches** (tel. 762 5081) goes to Christchurch (4hr., 8:30am, $35) via Moana (25 min., $14) and Arthur's Pass (1½hr., $18).
Taxis: Greymouth Taxis (tel. 768 7078).
Car Rental: West Coast Motors (tel. 768 5333), on Whall St., is open daily 24hr. **Value Rentals** (tel. 762 7503, fax 762 7500) offers free pickup and return.
Bike Rental: Mann Security and Cycles, 25 Mackay St. (tel. 768 0255).
Visitor Center: Greymouth Information Centre (tel. 768 5101; fax 768 0317), on the corner of Herbert and Mackay St. Open daily in summer 9am-5:30pm; in winter M-F 9am-5:30pm, Sa-Su10am-4pm.
Currency Exchange: ANZ, 36-40 Tainui St. (tel. 768 4529); **Westpac,** 89 Mackay St. (tel. 768 5125), at the corner of Tainui St.; and **ASB,** 44 Mackay St. (tel. 768 4458), or on High St. (tel. 768 4558).
Emergency: Dial **111.**
Police: On the corner of Guinness and Tarapuhi St. (tel. 768 1600).
Medical Services: Check with the pharmacies in town to get the number of the on-duty doctor. **Olsen's Pharmacy,** 50 Albert Mall (tel. 768 4075). **Mason's Pharmacy,** 34 Tainui St. (tel. 768 7470; fax 768 9993). Open M-Th 8:30am-5pm, F 8:30am-6pm. **Greymouth Hospital,** on High St. (tel. 768 0499; fax 768 2790).
Internet Access: Available at the library, which is on MacKay St. at Albert Mall (open M-F 8:30am-5pm). Check visitors center for other possibilities.
Post Office: On Tainui St. (tel. 768 0123; fax 768 7615). Open M-F 8:30am-5pm, except W 9am-5pm, Sa 10am-12pm.
Phone Code: 03.

ACCOMMODATIONS AND FOOD

You won't go begging for a comfy bed, given Greymouth's range of choices. Head north on Tainui St. and turn right after the KFC to reach **Noah's Ark Backpackers (VIP),** 16 Chapel St. (tel. (0800) 662 472; tel./fax 768 4868). This 104-year-old former monastery lives up to its name; every bedroom has a specific animal theme. As you're bedding down in the zebra room (with the striped sheets, artful murals and figurines on the mantle), don't forget to take advantage of the free breakfast, warm lounge, and shuttle pickup from the railway station (dorms $15; twins and doubles $35; singles $25). The cheerful yellow and green **Kainge-ra YHA Hostel,** 15 Alexander St. (tel./fax 768 4951) lives up to its optimistic name, "sunny home." On a clear winter evening you can see the sun set from the fire-warmed lounge, which is equipped with a guitar and piano for the musically inclined. **The Railway Hotel** (tel. 768 7023) offers private twins and singles ($20 per person) with TVs, heaters, and electric blankets in every room. Bathrooms are communal, but the wide-screen TV and pool table in the lounge/bar downstairs make some amends (reception at bar). If you're looking for holier water, head away from the center of town to the peaceful and mysteriously named **Living Streams Parkside Hostel,** 42-54 Cowper St. (tel./fax 768 7272). Walk down Tainui St. away from the river, bear right onto High St., take a right down Franklin St. and then a left on Cowper St. Breakfast is included, as are shuttle pickup from the railway station, kayaks, and bikes. Guided kayak and fishing trips are available with prior notice. The dorm mattresses vary in softness, but the lounge and management are friendly. (Dorms $15; doubles or twins $35.) Head down High St. away from town, make a right onto Chesterfield Rd., and arrive at **Greymouth Seaside Holiday Park** (tel. (0800) 867 104 or 768 6618; fax 768 5873). The kitchens are unequipped (reception may have a few pots to borrow), and the bunk beds are firmer than Arnold Schwarzenegger's abs, but the beach is well within reach and there is a free pickup from town. (Bunks $12; 2-person cabins $32-40, 2-person flats $59. Campsites $18, powered $20.) The reception is open daily in the summer 8am-10pm, but closes at 8pm in winter.

Eat, drink, and be merry in the town's assortment of quality cafes and restaurants. The stark decor, silver-gray walls, and cement floor of the **Smelting House Cafe,** 102 Mackay St. (tel. 768 0012) belie the colorful cuisine, but the new-age metal tables give a dash of pizzaz. Creative, mouth-watering sandwiches (including the chicken, apricot, and cream cheese, or the pesto, tomato, and cottage cheese) are a steal at $2.30, as are the $7 eggplant calzones. (Open daily 7:30am-4:30pm.) For a little slice of Italy, try the **Bonzai Pizzeria,** 31 Mackay St. (tel. 768 4170), where newspaper-covered walls surround the booths of pizza-munching patrons. Small pies run from $10-14 (larges $16-20), while alternatives like vegetarian nachos are $6.50. There is also a full *à la carte* menu and a bar for more ambitious patrons. (Open M-Sa 7am-10pm, Su 5-10pm.) **Maribel's Asian Restaurant and Takeaways,** 84 Tainui St. (tel. 768 9889), serves up mammoth portions of beef, chicken, and vegetarian noodles ($9-12; open M-F 10am-10pm, Sa-Su noon-11pm). Those watching their wallets should try the $3 all-you-can-eat barbecue at **The Railway Hotel,** including sausages, salads, and fried onions (offered daily in summer; M, W, F, Sa in winter). Strike out on your own at **Supervalue** supermarket (tel. 768 7545), on the corner of Guinness and Herbert St.

SIGHTS AND ACTIVITIES

Most of Greymouth's choice activities take you out of town, although it's worth a moment's pause to absorb a bit of West Coast settler history. The **History House Museum** (tel. 768 4028), near the visitors center on Gresson St., houses models of ships, railways, and photographs documenting the Grey River's many floodings. *(Open M-F 10am-4pm; $3, children $1.)* The **Jade Boulder Gallery** (tel./fax 768 0700), on the corner of Guinness and Tainui St., illustrates the intense hunger for jade that drew Maori and European settlers to the West Coast. *(Open in summer daily 8:30am-9pm; in winter M-F 8:30am-5pm, Sa 9am-5pm.)* Surround yourself with cases of intricately carved greenstone jewelry and sculptures of all colors, from the common opaque green to the dark, cloudy bluish hues. Witness jade in its raw form (giant nephrite boulders), or watch it being subjected to diamond-tipped carving tools. Envelop yourself in the area's past at **Shantytown** (tel./fax 762 6634), 11km south of Greymouth on SH6 (open daily from 8:30am). To get to Shantytown, you can take either **Greymouth Taxis** (tel. 768 7078; 3 per day, $21) or **Kea West Coast Tours** (tel. 768 9292 or (0800) 532 868; 10am and 2:15pm daily, $25 round-trip). Kea also runs a tour to **Punakaiki** daily (2 per day, $35 round-trip). Learn what a mash tun and a wortboiler do at **Monteith's Brewing Company,** on the corner of Turumaha and Herbert St. *(Open M-Th 10:30am, 1:30pm; free.)* Book at the visitors center for the chance to brush up on obscure beer terminology.

Outdoor adventurers will not go begging in Greymouth, as the rivers draining westward to the Tasman Sea offer ample opportunities for rafting and jetboating. **Dragons Cave Rafting,** run by **Wild West Adventures** (tel. (0800) 223 456 or 768 6649), runs an adventure caving trip through the **Taniwha Caves** and their underground world of lakes, streams, waterfalls, glow-worms, and even a love tunnel. The half-day excursion ends with an adrenaline-pumping ride on a slick natural water slide (free pickup and drop-off; $89; all equipment provided). If you're into the whole jump-out-of-a-moving-airplane-and-plummet-toward-the-ground thing, **Tandem Skydive** (tel./fax 468 4777) gives you the chance to do so from 12,000 ft. with a guide strapped to your back ($245). **Dolphin Watch,** run by **Scenicland Ocean Jets** (tel. 768 9770 or (0800) 929 991), brings you to the Hector's dolphin areas and shag nesting sites off the coast of **Point Elizabeth** (1½hr., $65). The nikau palms and podocarp on the coast can also be seen on foot along the **Point Elizabeth Walkway** (4km, 1½hr. one-way), although travelers without a car will need to take a taxi or catch a ride out. The same is true for **Lake Brunner,** about 30 minutes east of Greymouth (although Alpine

Coaches stops at Moana, which is right at the edge of the lake). Swim, kayak, or canoe among the white herons *(kotuku)* on the lake, bedding down at the campground at the Moana end of the lake. The **Moana Kiwi House and Conservation Park** (tel. 738 0009; fax 738 0007) displays two kiwis, among other birds, wallabies, and monkeys ($8, children $3).

■ Hokitika

Once the largest port in New Zealand, Hokitika (pop. 4000) is no longer the bustling center of activity it once was—and this may be its biggest selling point. New Zealanders and foreigners spend their holidays in this serene town to enjoy the natural beauty of the bay where the Hokitika river flows into the Tasman Sea, as well as the abundant crafts which make Hokitika famous. Virtually all of New Zealand's jade is quarried within a 20km radius of the city, and greenstone, wood, and blown glass stores line its wide streets. In addition to its shops, tourism and dairy farming keep Hokitika's economy flowing. The clock tower at the center of town (Weld St. and Sewell St.) makes a good starting point for exploration. But don't be surprised if you find yourself mysteriously drawn back to the exquisite panorama of the Tasman Sea—especially at dusk, when the sky flames around the setting sun.

PRACTICAL INFORMATION Nothing is too far to reach by foot in Hokitika. The **Westland Visitor Information Centre** (tel. 756 8088) is in the Carnegie Building on the corner of Tancred St. and Hamilton St. (open Nov-Apr. daily 8:30am-6pm, May-Oct. M-F 8:30am-5pm, Sa 10am-3pm), while **DOC** is on Sewell St. near the river (open M-F 8am-4:30pm). Change currency at **BNZ**, 9 Weld St.; **ANZ**, 14 Weld St.; or **ASB**, 99 Revell St. **Internet access** is available at the visitors center and the library on Weld. St. (Open M-F 10am-5pm, Sa 9am-noon.) In an emergency, dial **111**, call for **medical services** (tel. 755 8180) or call the **police** (tel. 755 8088). The **post office** (tel. 755 8659) is on Revell St. (open M-F 9am-5pm, Sa 9am-12:15pm). **InterCity** (tel. 0800 731 711) drops off in front of **Hokitika Travel Centre** (tel. 755 8557), on Tancred St., which runs parallel to the Tasman Sea two streets over. InterCity heads daily to Nelson (7hr., 12:45pm, $68) via Greymouth (45min., $12), and Westport (3hr., $30); and to Fox Glacier (3½hr., 2:50pm, $38) via Franz Josef (3hr., $35). There is a 20% student discount. **Coast-to-Coast** (tel. 0800 800 847) heads to Christchurch (4½hr., 1 per day, $35) via Arthur's Pass (2hr., $15). **Atomic Shuttles** (tel. 768 5101) has daily service to Queenstown (10hr., 8am, $65) via Franz Josef (2hr., $20), Fox (3hr., $25) and Haast (6hr., $45), and to Greymouth (1hr., 5pm, $10). The **telephone code** is **03**.

ACCOMMODATIONS AND FOOD Most shops, accommodations, and restaurants are clustered around the clock tower, down Weld St. towards the sea, and down Tancred and Revell St. Diagonally across from the visitors center, **Mountain Jade Backpackers,** 41 Weld St. (tel. 0800 838 301 or 755 8007; fax 755 7804) is as much an exhibit as a place to rest your head. From the mermaid peeking into the showers ("oh behave!") to the series of old photos depicting Hokitika as a port in its prime, the place is soaked with style. The tidy lounge has a TV and a stereo, and giant glass windows look over the adjoining jade store; a fully equipped kitchen and laundromat are also available for the hungry or dirty traveler. (Single-sex dorms $16; doubles $40. Reception 8am-10pm in the summer, 8am-8pm in the winter.) Located about 5km out of Hokitika central, the **Blue Spur Lodge** (tel./fax 755 8445) includes a free shuttle service from the visitors center and a host of other bonuses. Overlooking Mt. Cook and the Southern alps, the 100-acre property offers a one-hour bushwalk and an open gold mine tunnel where guests can pan for aural treasures using the lodge's free equipment. Canoes ($60 per day) and kayaks ($35 per day) are also available, with free transportation to and from Lakes Kaniere and Mahinapua. (Dorms $15, doubles $36). A short walk from the center of town, **Beach House Backpackers (VIP),** 137 Revell St. (tel. 755 6859), has a prime beach front location. The upstairs lounge and kitchen area may be worn and frigid in the winter, but the place is still tidy and the folks are friendly. The extras are nice, too (like free use of bicycles, gold panning equipment, fishing lines, and tennis rackets), and you can take an outdoor bushbath if you're feeling adventurous. (Dorms $15 in winter, $16 in summer, towel $1 extra; twins $35 in winter, $38 in summer, towel included; laundry facilities available to hostel guests and the public.) Lake Kaniere, 18km from town, has **DOC campground** facilities with water and toilets. There's another **DOC campground** 10km south of town at Lake Mahinapua with water, toilets, and fireplaces. Pay at the honesty box in both campgrounds.

The **Souvlaki Bar,** 89 Revell St. (tel. 755 8336), has tasty pita-wrapped meats ($5.90, double for $8.10) and falafel. If you overdo it on the hot sauce, cool your taste-buds down with some ice cream. (Open in summer Su-Th 10:30am-10pm, F-Sa 9am-8pm; winter Su-Th 11am-8pm, F-Sa 10:30am-10:30pm.) Travelers watching their wallet should snag one of the cheaply and deeply fried goodies at **Porky's Takeaways** (tel. 755 8029), a local favorite on Weld St. just a block from the clock tower. More originality can be found dining among teapots shaped like cows, fish, and shells at **PR's Coffee Shop and Bistro** (tel. 755 8379) on Tancred St. near Weld (open daily 8am-late). Or try **Cafe de Paris** (tel. 755 8933) a few doors down. The spiffy decor and enticing menu may make you expect a view of the Eiffel Tower instead of the Southern Alps. Choose from a large selection of wines and coffees. (Open daily 7:30am-11pm; breakfast served until 11am, lunch 11am-2pm (winter) and 11am-3pm (summer), dinner from 6pm.) If you need a quick bite to eat early in the morning, try a muffin or meat pie at **Prestons Bakery** (tel. 755 8412), on Revell St. (open M-F 6am-6pm, Sa-Su 9am-4pm). Fulfill your own dining expectations after grocery shopping at **New World,** 116 Revell St. (Open M-W and Sa 8:30am-6:30pm, Th-F 8:30am-8:30pm, Su 9am-6pm; winter hours flexible.)

SIGHTS AND ACTIVITIES

Hokitika is renowned for the expertise of its green-stone, woodworking, and glass-blowing artisans. **Westland Greenstone** (tel./fax 755 8713), on Tancred St., has plenty of jade pendants, pins, and paperweights (open daily 8am-5pm). **Quades House of Wood** (tel. 755 6061), located across the street, has palm trunk vases with incredible designs, a wide variety of wooden bowls, and a large, expensive wooden turtle with a removable shell (open daily 9am-5pm). The **Hokitika Glass Studio** (tel. 755 7775) exhibits glass artistry ranging from whimsical penguins and elephants to dainty flowers (open daily 7am-5pm). All three shops allow visitors to view the artisans at work. If you're around on the second Saturday in March, don't miss the chance to sample possum, whitebait, snail, venison, and even kangaroo at the **Wild Foods Festival.** The event quadruples Hokitika's population for a day, drawing visitors from around the world.

History buffs can walk the self-guided **Hokitika Heritage Trail** (1hr.) to learn about the significance of various sites and statues about town. Or, pick up a **Hokitika Attraction Pass** (tel. (0800) 242 324) for sweet deals on a paddleboat ride (tel. 755 7239), and a visit to Westland's Water World. The pass ($28) also covers the **West Coast Historical Museum** (tel./fax 755 6898) where you can imagine panning for gold after seeing a presentation on the growth of Hokitika. *(Open daily 9:30am-5pm, in winter Sa-Su 10am-4pm$3, children $1.)* Even without the pass, you can fish to your heart's content daily from 9am to 4:30pm at the indoor fishing lake of **Westland's Water World** (tel. (0800) 242 324 or 755 5251; fax 755 5451). Watch divers feed the largest freshwater eels in the world at 10am and 3pm, and the sharks daily at noon. ($10, students $8.) Head to **Phelps' Goldmine** (tel. 755 7766) for a current-day exposition of gold-mining technology. *(Open 8am-3:30pm, later in summer; $5.)*

Skydiving is available through **Skydive New Zealand** (tel. 755 7575 or (025) 359 123), or you can rush through the wilderness in a white-water blur with **Alpine Rafts** (tel. 755 8156 or 762 6152). Rafting costs $125 for a half-day, including a 4WD ride, and $195-$245 for a full day, which includes a helicopter ride. *(Weekends only from Apr.-Dec.)* For more sedate adventure, the **Glow-worm Dell,** on SH6, a 20-minute walk north of Hokitika on the right side of the road, is home to a host of glow-worms, best seen after dark (free). **Lake Mahinapua** is surrounded by walks and picnic areas, and

---

A Jaded Perspective

Green as the Westland rainforest and hard as the mountains to the east, **greenstone** (*pounamu*, or **jade**) has long been considered a precious mineral. Created millions of years of ago at the same time the Southern Alps were rising from their fault, greenstone is found primarily in Westland and around Lake Wakatipu. Greenstone factories in Westland today excavate, chip, and carve the opaque emerald stone for everything from touristy trinkets to flowing works of art. In ancient times (and even up to the present), the Maori used greenstone for tools and *tikis*, as well as for battle weapons and religious purposes. Famed worldwide for its wide range of coloration, *pounamu* was renowned among the Maori (who knew it by over a dozen different names) for its tremendous **spiritual value**—it was believed to retain and even magnify a person's *mana*, or spiritual power.

Lake Kaniere draws nature-lovers to its stands of rimu, tussock grassland, and subalpine scrub (walks vary from 10min. to 7hr.). There is no public transportation from Hokitika to the lake, but several hostels lend out bicycles for free. Rental is available from **Hokitika Cycles and Sports,** 33 Tancred St. (tel. 755 8662), for $20 a day.

■ Westland National Park:
Fox and Franz Josef Glaciers

Finding yourself face to face with several billion cubic meters of solid blue ice moving up to several meters a day is *de rigeur* when visiting the **Fox** and **Franz Josef Glaciers.** These twins are extraordinary not only because of their speed (they are two of the quickest glaciers on the planet), but also because they are located in such a temperate region. The warm climate at the glaciers' bases combined with heavy snowfall on top accounts for their rapid movement, and makes the surrounding towns more hospitable than one might anticipate. Rocky outcrops on the adjoining mountain walls forge deep crevasses in the ice, and the continual interaction between glaciers and mountains on either side shapes the sculptured streaks of blue and white that draw visitors year-round.

Fox and Franz Josef Glaciers are a part of the 117,547-hectare **Westland National Park** (recently made a World Heritage Area along with the rest of the Southern West Coast), which contains a feast of hikes and bushwalks. The glaciers are certainly the most touristed features of the park. Pressed for time, the hurried and harried traveler often comes down to choosing between Fox and Franz Josef Glaciers, and no small rivalry has developed between the two towns as a result. Fox offers a less-touristed atmosphere, the serene quicksilver reflections of nearby **Lake Matheson,** and rainforest hikes that conclude by stepping out of the bush onto the glacier itself. Franz Josef is a slightly smaller glacier but with large **Lake Mapourika,** more outfitters, and more choices for lodging, it's the destination of most tour groups. Both glaciers, however, offer a tremendous range of options for exploration, including helicopter rides, hikes directly on the glaciers, and ice climbing and skiing for true daredevils. Which glacier is the more spectacular? Hope for a clear couple of days, visit them both, and decide for yourself.

ORIENTATION AND PRACTICAL INFORMATION

Lying 27km apart on SH6, Fox and Franz Josef Glacier are both diminutive villages near massive glaciers. Running through the center of both towns, **SH6** is known in both as Main Rd. In Fox it heads north over three hills (cyclists beware) to Franz Josef, or south to one entrance of the **Copland Track,** and farther, to **Haast** (121 km). In Franz Josef, SH6 heads south to Fox, and north to **Hokitika** (140km). Away from both towns, peaceful rainforest walks twist and turn through the thick tropical bush.

FOX GLACIER The **Fox Glacier Visitor Information Centre** and **DOC office** (tel. 751 0807; fax 751 0858; open M-F 8:30am-noon and 1-6pm. closes at 5pm in winter) is located right on SH6 (known as Main Rd. in town), and has info on **Westland National Park,** the various walks around the Fox Glacier area, and the **Copland Track.** The famous reflecting **Lake Matheson** (6km) and the seal-colonized **Gillespies Beach** (20km) are located down Lake Matheson Rd., which is off Cook Flat Rd. **Inter-City** (tel. (0800) 731 711) heads daily to Nelson (11hr., 8:45am, $91) via Franz Josef (45min., $8), Hokitika (3½hr., $39), Greymouth (4½hr., $45), and Westport (7hr., $60). Going southward, InterCity heads daily to Queenstown (8:45am, 7hr., $88) via the Copland Track (20min., $13) and Wanaka (5hr., $64). Atomic Shuttles (tel. 768 5101) runs daily to Greymouth (4hr., 2pm, $15) via Franz Josef (1hr., $10) and Hokitika (3hr., $25). Southbound, Atomic goes to Queenstown (7hr.,11am, $50) via Haast (3hr., $25) and Wanaka (5hr., $35). The pickup point for both is outside **Alpine Guides** (tel. 751 0825; fax 751 0857), on Main Rd. Alpine Guides also serves as a **post office** and **currency exchange** (open daily in summer 7am-8pm; in winter 8am-6pm). **Internet access** can be found at the **Fox Glacier Hotel** (tel. 751 0839; fax 751 0868) for a pricey $5 per 15 minutes.

FRANZ JOSEF GLACIER The **Franz Josef Visitor Information Centre** and **DOC office** (tel. 752 0796; fax 752 0797), on SH6 just outside of town, has various displays on glacial formation and the ecological devastation wreaked by possums (see **Possum Problems,** p. 49), as well as information on walks in the area (open daily in winter 8am-6pm; extended hours in summer). There are **no banks or ATMs** in town, but **Glacier Motors** will cash your traveler's checks (open daily in summer 7:15am-10:15pm; in winter 8am-6pm). **Fern Grove Souvenirs** (tel. 752 0731; fax 752 0789) on Main Rd. in the center of town will do the same, provided they have enough cash available. **Internet access** is available on a first-come, first-serve basis at the **Punga Grove Motor Lodge** (tel. 752 0001) for $5 per half-hour (open daily 8am-10pm). **InterCity** (tel. (0800) 731 711) catches Franz Josef on the same routes as those listed for Fox above (leaving north at 9am and south at 8am; prices differ by $1-5). The routes are also the same as Fox for **Atomic Shuttles** (tel. 768 5101; leaving north at 3pm and south at 10am; prices may differ by $5 or less). The pickup for both shuttle companies is at the coach stop on Main Rd. The **post office** is located at **DA's Cafe** in the center of town on SH6 (open daily 9am-5pm).

ACCOMMODATIONS AND FOOD

Accommodation possibilities at both of the glaciers range from resorts to bottom-budget backpackers, but Franz Josef tends to have more options.

FOX GLACIER The decor may be sparse, but for $20 the budget rooms at the **Fox Glacier Hotel** (tel. 751 0839; fax 751 0868; email resort@minidata.co.nz) are really a steal. The hotel is on Cook Flat Rd. just off Main Rd. There are no kitchen facilities, but guests get a private room with free soap and a towel, a personal bathroom in some cases, and a bed that's softer than pudding. (Reception open 7am-10:30pm, closes at 8:30 pm in the winter.) Take a soak in the spa or just chill out on the porch with other backpackers at **Ivory Towers** (tel./fax 751 0838) on Sullivans Rd. If you're feeling immobile, rent a bicycle for $3 an hour ($15 per day) or take the $5 shuttle down to Lake Matheson. (Bunks $16; doubles and twins $40. Duvets are free, towels available for $1. Reception open 8am-8:30pm; check-out 10am.) If you're after a more personal touch, check in at the small and cozy **Roaring Billy Lodge** (tel./fax 751 0815, email billy@xtra.co.nz), diagonally across from the visitors center. A home-cooked breakfast is included, and you can relax afterward with the old gray cat. The 360 degrees of mountain views are stunning (singles $60; doubles and twins $75). The **Rainforest Motel** (tel. 751 0140 or (0800) 520 000; fax 751 0141), is about 100m down Cook Flat Rd. on the left. Treat yourself to incredibly luxurious, quiet, and fully self-contained units (including kitchen) with views of the mountain and surrounding pastures ($65-85).

WESTLAND

The **Cook Saddle Cafe and Saloon** (tel. 751 0700) will carry you away from Fox Glacier and drop you off in the American wild west. Try one of the salads (a little-known western favorite; around $10) or a tasty burger ($7.50) for lunch. The ribs ($18) are a local dinner favorite, and the spicy wedges ($5.50) are wicked tasty (open 10am-1:30am, from 11am in the winter; breakfast and lunch served until 4pm, dinner served after 6pm; bar open all day). On Main Rd. in the same building as Alpine Guides is a simpler dining option, **The Hobnail Cafe** (tel. 751 0005). Pick up a packed lunch before your trip to the glacier, or enjoy one of the light dishes after you get back (open daily 7am-5pm, in winter 8am-4pm). Groceries and gasoline can be picked up at **Fox Glaciers Motors** (tel. 751 0823), on Main Rd. next to Alpine Guides.

FRANZ JOSEF GLACIER Look for the two mountaineers climbing on the roof to find your way to the attractive **Franz Josef Glacier Chateau Franz (VIP)**, 8 Cron St. (tel./fax 752 0738). Grab a quick round of pool (50¢) or relax in your sunflower-sheeted bed (duvets $1). (Dorms $16; twins $17.50; doubles $20. Reception open 7am-9pm.) Join the bus-tour crowd and fellow backpackers at the **Black Sheep Lodge** (tel. 752 0007; fax 752 0023). It's got a large kitchen and a big, friendly TV lounge with a collection of Hollywood's finest to pop into the VCR. Duvets and towels are $1 each. They'll book helicopter flights and guided walks. (Dorms $16 and $14, doubles $35, reception closes at 8pm.) Across from the Chateau Franz, check out the dirt cheap dorms at **Montrose** (tel. 752 0188). If you're impatient to get out and about, hit the town on one of their rental scooters. (Dorms $15.50 in summer, $12.50 in winter; doubles and twins $40. Reception open in summer 8am-noon, 3-7pm; in winter 9am-noon and 3-6pm.) The bland but comfortable **Franz Josef YHA** (tel. 752 0754) is also on Cron St. Rejuvenate with some homemade yogurt ($2), conversation in the lounge, or a game at the pool table. They'll also store your bicycle and run a shuttle to the glacier carpark ($5 per person, min. 2). Rooms are replete with heaters and duvets. (Bunks $16; non-members $20. Reception open from 8-10am, 4:30 to 6:30pm, and 8 to 9:30pm. Check-out 10am.) Facing the glacier, the **Franz Josef Holiday Park** (tel. 752 0766 or (0800) 863 726) is to the right past the bridge in part of what is called Waiho Motel. Fully self-contained double motel units run $69-89, and 2-bedroom tourist flats (fully self-contained except for sheets and towels) are $49-59. Two-person cottages with kitchens but no baths are $40-49; squeeze in additional people for $14 per head. Tent sites are $9, while powered sites are $9.50.

For a tasty, all-purpose restaurant, stop by **DA's Restaurant** (tel. 752 0721) in the center of town. Light and more hearty meals are available, as well as special deals for groups (open 7am-10pm). **The Cheeky Kea Cafe** (tel. 752 0139) is right next door, and they carry a range of drinks and sandwiches ($2.40). Try the cheese scones ($1) if you're just a might peckish. Groceries are sold at the **Fern Grove Food Centre** (tel. 752 0731) if you prefer to exercise your own culinary skills.

GLACIAL ACTIVITIES AND THE GREAT OUTDOORS

Although there are kilometers of **hikes** and **nature walks** for those interested in exploring the biota of Westland, most travelers come for the glaciers—and, though their wallets may be a tad lighter after the fact, they seldom leave disappointed. There are many ways to explore the glacier, but two are the most popular. To feel the frigid and slippery ice first-hand and to gain a different perspective on what glacial immensity is all about, go for a **hike on the glacier.** To get a better sense of the scale and macroscopic patterns of the glaciers' tumble to the sea, consider a **helicopter tour.**

There are three different helicopter companies, none of which run on days with questionable weather. They all offer similar prices (and essentially the same tried-and-true routes), and the fluctuation is due mostly to demand and to the size of the helicopter (book ahead by 3 days or so Jan.-Mar.). Tours are offered from both Fox and Franz Josef, and most include snow landings. Book at Alpine Guides for **Fox and Franz Josef Heliservices** (in Fox tel. 751 0866; in Franz Josef tel. 752 0764), or consider **Glacier Helicopters** (tel. (0800) 800 732; in Fox tel. 751 0803; in Franz Josef tel. 752 0755), or the **Helicopter Line** (tel. (0800) 807 767; in Fox tel. 751 0767; in Franz

Josef tel. 752 0767). Prices to tour the local glacier (20min.) run about $100 per person; to visit both glaciers (30min.) costs about $150 per person; to see Fox Glacier and Mt. Cook (30min.) takes about $160 per person; and to take in Fox, Franz Josef, Mt. Cook, and the Tasman Glacier (40min.) sets you back about $240 per person (roughly 30% discount for children). **Air Safaris** (tel. 752 0716; fax 752 0701) offers a "Grand Traverse" airplane tour that, while it does not include a snow landing, covers a greater area than the helicopter flights ($160, children $110). More active visitors can combine a helicopter tour with a hike on the glacier in a "helihike" with **Alpine Guides** ($170, 3hr., min. group of 3). Air Safaris departs from Franz Josef, and Alpine Guides helihike departs from Fox.

FOX GLACIER For those who want to touch the glacier itself, **Alpine Guides** (tel. 751 0825; fax 751 0857) leads daily **guided walks** (with a min. party size). The half-day walk heads toward the glacier across the valley, with glacier-scraped rock walls on either side. After a steep ascent through the rainforest, you finally step out onto the top of the glacier to see the mountains that, according to the guide, are growing at the same speed as your fingernails (the glacier itself has been steadily advancing since 1987). If a morning walk isn't offered due to party size, an afternoon one will be. Full-day six-hour guided walks leave at 9:30am ($60 per person, min. 3); half-day 3½-hour guided walks leave at 9:30am and 2pm ($39 per person, min. 2). They'll also arrange **skiing** (call well in advance for booking) on Fox Glacier, or **ice-climbing** (group of 4, $135 each).

In addition to the actual glacier, paths and trails to explore writhe throughout the area. The **Minnehaha Walk** (20min.) gives a great sampling of Westland's rainforest as it wanders across bridges, over small trickling creeks, and through tall moss-covered trees laden with epiphytes and surrounded by huge ferns and other primitive plants. The **Ngai Tahu Track** (1¼hr.) follows part of the Minnehaha walk but veers off to the left into a glacial terrace and peat swamp. The trail itself can become swampy after wet weather. The **Chalet Lookout Walk** (1¼hr.) yields a fantastic peek of the town's namesake, while the **Fox Glacier Valley Walk** (1hr.) leads directly to the glacier itself. Wet weather may make this trail impassable. Travelers willing to traverse the 21km to **Gillespies Beach** can take the **Gillespies Track** (2hr.) when they get there to walk along the shore of the Tasman; the **Seal Colony Walk** (3hr.), also at the beach, leads to an endearing seal colony at Waikowhai Bluff. However, it must be undertaken at low tide, so visitors should check tides at the visitors center. The **Copland Track,** connecting Westland National Park to Mt. Cook National Park, has one trailhead 26km south of Fox Glacier (InterCity makes stops daily at 9am). This 17km tramp takes eight hours each way and should only be attempted by experienced and prepared hikers. Those who do undertake the Copland should expect to spend the night in a hut at the **Flat Hut Pools.** Six kilometers out of town down Cook Flat Rd., the **Lake Matheson Walk** (1½hr.) offers unequaled reflections of Mt. Cook and Mt. Tasman. Views are best in the morning and evening, when the water is undisturbed by wind. After dark, check out the **glow-worms** ($2 in honesty box) at the corner of Sullivans Rd. and Main Rd., next to the Glow Worm Forest Lodge. The luminescent little critters are not nearly so impressive as the incredible display in Hokitika, but you can get much closer to these. A flashlight is helpful.

FRANZ JOSEF GLACIER Gear up for your glacial experience at the **Alpine Adventure Center** (tel. 752 0793) with **Flowing West,** a movie of fast-moving scenes across glacial rivers, through tangled rainforest, over mountains, and onto glaciers. It's a heck of a lot cheaper than a helicopter flight, and well worth the price ($10, children $5; 4-7 per day; min. number required). Afterward, head outside and experience the real thing with **Franz Josef Glacier Guides** (tel. 752 0763; fax 752 0102), and their half-day (3½hr., daily at 9:15am and 2pm, $37) and full-day walks on the glacier (7-8hr., daily at 9:15am, $74). The guides chip steps into the glacial ice with an ice-axe to lead brave and sure-footed hikers up an astounding 300m (on the full-day walk). You'll be damp and chilly by the time you return to the glacier's base, but the experience is well worth it (boots, socks, crampons, and poles for ice-walking are supplied). **Kamahi Tours** (tel. 752 0795) also offers guided walks around the Franz Josef area (1hr. walk $12.50 per person; 2-2½hr. walk to the terminal face of the glacier $20 per person). Or head to **Gold 'N' Trees** (tel. 752 0145 or (0800) 752 111) to go prospecting near a historic gold mine ($25, children $10).

A pleasant walk heads down SH6 to **St. James Anglican Church** (turn onto the path at the right before the bridge; the church is through the bush at the end of the path). The church was built with a glacial view in mind, and a peace stamp with a picture of the view from the window was issued in 1946 to celebrate the end of World War II. The **Terrace Walk** (25min.) is particularly notable for its nighttime glowworm extravaganza; take a friend and a flashlight. On a clear day the **Alex Knob Walk** (8hr.), accessible when it's not snowed under, has breathtaking views from the ridge.

Consider renting a scooter from **Glacier Scooter Safaris** (tel. 752 0164) to get to some of the many trailheads in the area, Lake Mapourika, or the small settlement of **Okarito** ($10 for 30 min., $30 for 2hr., $50 for 4hr). The **White Heron Sanctuary Tour** (tel. (0800) 523 456) lets a limited number of visitors observe breeding pairs of White Herons. Considered sacred birds by the Maori, they are known to breed only in New Zealand. (Tours Nov.-Feb.; 9:30 and 11am, 12:30 and 2pm; $75). Nearby **Lake Mapourika** is stocked with brown trout and Quinnat salmon, and the surrounding bush is rife with chamois and possums; fishermen and hunters should get the appropriate licenses from DOC.

■ Near the Glaciers: Okarito

About 10km north of Franz Josef Glacier on SH6 lies the cutoff to the tiny seaside community of Okarito (pop. 20). Sitting on the edge of the enormous, 3240 hectare Okarito Lagoon, the town is known for its vast diversity of bird species and the fact that author Keri Hulme *(The Bone People)* lives and writes here—although eager visitors should not expect to meet the solitary Hulme without a personal invitation. Travelers often use Okarito as a jumping-off point to visit the glaciers, but the town has a charm that transcends logistical convenience. The rich green of the surrounding Kahikatea and Rimn rain forests, the snow-capped Southern Alps behind (Mt. Cook and Mt. Tasman are both visible), and the lapping waves of the Tasman Sea make Okarito a picturesque spot to relax for a few days... or weeks.

To cover the 8km between the SH6 cutoff and the town (if you don't have a car), call **Okarito Nature Tours** (tel./fax 753 4014) for a $15 shuttle. **The Royal Hostel** (dorms $15) and **Royal Motel** (tel. for both 753 4080; doubles $40; extra person $10) will pick visitors up for free if they are staying at either accommodation for two nights or more. A cheaper sleeping option is **The Okarito YHA Hostel** (dorms $10), a non-profit backpackers run by the town itself. Pay for your stay at the warden's house, across the street and several buildings down. Although the two-room building is quaint and conducive to meeting other travelers, there are no showers, so you'll have to resort to those at the **Okarito Campground** ($5 per person). The site is non-powered, but provides good shelter and free toilets. If you're part of a group, cottages that sleep four to eight people are available ($40-60; call Suzie Clapperton for details at 753 4124). Just remember to bring three things on your visit to Okarito: **food,** as there is **no shop** in town; **insect repellent,** for the hordes of **sandflies** that buzz and bite any flesh they can find; and **sunglasses** to protect you from the glaring light that bathes Okarito on a clear day.

The highlight of Okarito is the lagoon and the wildlife that goes with it, and the only way to really experience those treasures is by getting out on the water. **Okarito Nature Tours** rents kayaks and canoes for one or two people ($25 per 2hr.; $30 per half-day; $35 per day; all prices per person). Guided trips are also available on demand. Okarito has several beautiful hikes, including the **Okarito Trig Trail** (1hr. return), which leads you uphill through the bush to a breathtaking view overlooking the town, the lagoon, and the sea. Also try the **Coastal Walk** (3hr.), a wandering path along the rainforest above the shoreline. If you wish to return by walking on the actual beach, be sure to check the tides (schedules available in the hostels) as it can only be done within an hour of low tide.

Good as Gold

In Ross, just 28km south of Hokitika, the hum and clank of present-day mining operations belie the great discovery made there in 1909: the largest gold nugget ever to be found in New Zealand. Weighing in at 3.1kg, it was nicknamed **"the Honourable Roddy"** and was raffled off shortly thereafter to raise funds for the Ross Hospital. By 1911, poor Roddy had been transmuted into a gold tea set for King George V. A chunky replica of the famed nugget now hangs in the 1885 **Miner's Cottage,** luring tourists in search of their own Honourable lode. And that lode might be closer than you think—recent newspaper stories have reported that the town of Ross may be situated directly over some $700,000,000 worth of gold. For further details, check in with the **Ross Visitor Information Centre** (tel. 755 4077), located in the historic 1870 Bank of New South Wales on Aylmer St. (open about 9am-4 or 5pm). Both the visitors center and Miner's Cottage supply pans, shovels ($5), and prospectors' gravel to those willing to try their hand at sifting for a few hours. One lucky couple panned for three-and-a-half days, finding enough gold to make their own 18-carat wedding rings!

■ Haast

Unreachable by road until the 1960s, Haast is one of the last and largest refuges of rain forests and wetlands in New Zealand. Untouched acres of the giant, graceful kahikatea trees provide a towering symbol of a natural world with man dwelling unobtrusively at the fringes. Try one of the gorgeous inland hikes—or follow the coastal route south along the Tasman to the beautiful, rugged Jackson Bay, 54km away. From July to November, the Fiordland crested penguin (the world's rarest), can be seen on Monro Beach (40km north). During the spring, whitebaiters come to try their luck in catching the great delicacy in the coastal rivers.

ORIENTATION AND PRACTICAL INFORMATION Those in the know refer to the whole area as **"The Haast,"** and indeed there really is no specific site to pin down as the real Haast. The concentration of accommodations and eateries on **SH6** is known as **Haast Township,** while the intersection of SH6 with **Jackson Bay Rd.** 3km north (where the visitors center is located) is called **Haast Junction.** The area down by the beach (4km down Jackson Bay Rd. SH6) is **Haast Beach.** While a bike is adequate for reaching these three areas and some of the closer walks, a car is necessary to really explore Haast and see all that it has to offer.

InterCity (tel. (0800) 731 711) drops off at Fantail Restaurant and Tearooms in Haast on Panareka Rd., as it heads to Franz Josef Glacier (2½hr., 1:25pm, $32) via Fox Glacier (2hr., $32) or Queenstown (4½hr., 11:15am, $61) via Wanaka (3hr., $38). **Atomic Shuttles,** leaving from the same place, also runs north to Greymouth (6½hr., 11:30am, $60) via Fox Glacier (2½hr., $25) and Franz Josef Glacier (3½hr., $30). **Mini-bus Service** (tel. 750 0825), operated from the Haast General Store at Haast Beach, is a 24-hour on-demand taxi ($1 per km). It also makes a round trip each Sunday to Wanaka (departing at 7am, leaving Wanaka to return at 10am) for $25 each way. The entire West Coast is reportedly hellish for **hitchiking,** especially in southern areas like Haast. In winter, the situation is said to go from hellish to outlandishly hellish as passing cars are few and far between. **Rent a bicycle** from Wilderness Backpackers (see below) for $2 per hour, or $20 per day if you are a guest there. The wonderful **South Westland World Heritage Visitor Centre** and **DOC office** (tel. 750 0809; fax 750 0832) is right at the junction of SH6 and Jackson Bay Rd., 3km from Wilderness Backpackers. (Open daily early Nov. to mid-April 9am-6pm; mid-April to early Nov. 9am-4:30pm.) The 20-minute film "Edge of Wilderness" captures what makes Haast special ($2.50; children free). Come here for advice on tracks and updates on **weather conditions. Internet access** is available for a steep $10 per 30 minutes at the **World Heritage Hotel** (tel. 750 0828) at Haast Junction. There is **no currency exchange** in "The Haast." Dial **111,** contact the **police** (tel. 750 0850), or call for **medical assistance** (tel. 750 0800) in an emergency. The **post**

office is located in the **Haast Beach Service Centre,** on Jackson Bay Rd. in Haast Beach (open daily 8am-6pm). The **telephone code** is **03.**

ACCOMMODATIONS AND FOOD If you're willing to forego cooking your own meals for a day or two, check into one of the backpackers or budget rooms at the **World Heritage Hotel** (tel. (0800) 502 444 or 750 0828; fax 750 0827; email w-h-haast.hotel@clear.net.nz). With a TV and bathroom in every room and soft, comfortable beds, you'll be dreaming of home before you even close your eyes. (Rooms start at $15, prices vary according to season and availability. Check in daily 7am-10:30pm.) For a more traditional hostel setup, **Wilderness Backpackers** (tel. (0800) 750 029), located on Panareka Rd. in Haast Township, is just 3km from the visitors center. Some of the dorms are a little crowded, but there is a warm and attractive courtyard. (Dorms $15; doubles $34. Linen $2, towels 75¢. Reception open 8am-8:30pm in winter, extended hours in summer.) The **Haast Highway Accommodation (YHA)** (tel. 750 0703) is located nearby on Mark's Road, close to the grocery store and tavern. Bleak but spacious, the gargantuan lounge and kitchen area are clean and well-kept. (Dorms $15; doubles $36; motel units $75-90. Sheets $1, duvets $2.) A double/twin cabin (rather far from the bathrooms) is $36, while powered sites are $10 ($18 for 2 people). The **Haast Food Centre** is the local grocery store (usually open M-Sa 8:30am-7pm, Su 9am-6:30pm; winter hours vary). The **Haast Motor Camp** (tel./fax 750 0860) is 15km from the visitors center on Jackson Bay Rd. More convenient for those with a car, it's the perfect base for in fishing in the nearby rivers. The owners offer free pick-up if you arrive by bus. (Bunks $12, cabins $28-38. 2 person motel units $65; tent sites $8, 2 person powered sites $17.

The **World Heritage Hotel** at Haast Junction has two completely separate dining halls to choose from. The informal dining room features SkyTV and a monthly live band and serves a variety of soups, main courses, and desserts at reasonable prices. There is an adjoining bar and bottle store (open from 7am; bar opens at 11am). The main dining hall (closed during the winter) offers cafeteria-style lunches and a more formal (and costly) dinner menu (open until 10:30pm). Back in Haast Township, the **Fantail Restaurant and Tearooms** (tel./fax 750 0055) has both a backpackers' dinner menu ($6-10) and a more posh range of dishes ($20-25; open 7:30am-9pm; closes at 7:30pm in the winter; dinner served from 5pm). Or try **Smithy's Tavern,** also in Haast Township, where meat and seafood dinners ($16-17) are served from 5pm until 10pm. The bar opens at 11am (2pm in winter). Find excellent prices just next door at the **Haast Food Centre,** the local grocery store. (Cash only. Open M-Sa 9am-7pm, Su 9am-6:30pm; in winter M-Sa 9am-6pm, Su 10am-5pm.)

OUTDOOR ACTIVITIES There are many exciting ways to explore Haast's natural splendors. Check with the **DOC** office for details, and head down the **Monro Beach Walk** (40min. one-way) for a chance to glimpse the rare Fiordland crested penguin between July and December. Guided walks are available from **Wilderness Lodge Lake Moeraki** (tel. 750 0881); call in advance to make sure there is space available (guests of the lodge have priority). Guided **canoeing** is available from August to May ($48). Canoes are also available for guests to hire if not in use ($3 per hour) at the **Haast Motor Camp** (tel. 750 0860). Fishing opportunities are plentiful in the nearby lakes and in the Tasman Sea—contact Maurice Nolan of **Wilderness Tours** (tel. 750 0824; fax 750 0827) to arrange a fishing expedition in his jetboat ($50 per person; several tours per day) or for any of a number of other tours to see spotted cormorants, Fiordland crested penguins, and terns. You can see seals (often with their pups from Jan.-Mar.) in the distance from **Knight's Point** (30km north on SH6), but the only way to get up close is with **Maurice's Boat Tour** ($50 per person). His other tours head up to a reflecting lake or into the heart of the Southern Alps (prices vary). Scenic helicopter flights are easily arranged: call **Heliventures** (tel. 750 0866) year-round to schedule flights to see Mt. Aspiring, Mt. Cook, or Milford Sound. Ask at the visitors center for information about deep sea fishing, diving, or jet boat rides.

The Southern Lakes

The southern lakes region sounds its clarion call through lonesome fiords, deep expanses of bush, and lakes bearing the clear marks of glacial history. From the plummeting majesty of Milford Sound in Fiordland to the soaring peaks of Mt. Aspiring National Park, the peerless landscape entices visitors back again and again to some of the most famous walks in the world. Those seeking thrills rather than quiet meditation will rejoice in the riotous explosions of Queenstown, the heart of the region. Shock yourself awake with a shot of adventure by schussing down slopes, rafting through canyons, or bungying off perilous heights for an instant of eternity. A land of contrasts and superlatives, where every lake revels in its distinct character and every valley is more breathtaking than the last, the southern lakes never fail to inspire.

💧 SOUTHERN LAKES HIGHLIGHTS

- The striking beauty of Milford Sound (see p. 330) is incomparable, and can be explored by boat, kayak, or plane.
- The Milford Track (see p. 322) is regarded as the country's best tramp.
- In Queenstown (see p. 307), the adventurous ski, bungy, skydive, paraglide, rock climb, snowboard, and bike—along with whatever else gets their adrenaline flowing.
- Several of New Zealand's most spectacular walks are in this region, including the Rees-Dart (see p. 321), the Greenstone and the Caples (see p. 321), the Routeburn (see p. 325), and the Kepler (see p. 326).

■ Queenstown

Although the gold rush days are over, Queenstown has yet to lose its glitter. Where precious nuggets once sparkled in stony river beds, street lamps twinkle along the lake as adrenaline addicts worn from a day of thrills begin a night of hard partying. Drawn by whizzing jetboat rides and bungy jumps, international visitors of every wallet size flock to Queenstown's souvenir shops and jewelry boutiques. Despite its commercial glitz and glamour, this town's spot on **Lake Wakatipu** beneath the sun-drenched spine of the **Remarkables** mountain range still inspires awe, and remote wilderness lies only footsteps from busy streets. The quips of other Kiwis about Queenstown's loss of character are tinged with equal doses of truth and jealousy, but Queenstown still has small-town charm—and its raw beauty is indisputable.

ORIENTATION AND PRACTICAL INFORMATION

Queenstown's smaller satellite towns include **Glenorchy** (47km to the west, on the lake), and **Arrowtown** and **Wanaka** (to the north). From the Mt. Cook Bus Terminal on Church St., **Camp St.** is the first thoroughfare as you walk away from the water. Booking agencies and most bars are off **Shotover St.,** three blocks to the left, while shopping is centered around the **pedestrian mall.** Accommodations ring the town center, while the spine of the Remarkables mountain range runs south down the east side of the lake.

Airport: 6km east of town. **Air New Zealand** (tel. 0800 737 000), **Ansett** (tel. 442 6161 or (0800) 800 146), and **Mt. Cook** serve Queenstown, each with many daily flights to Christchurch (30min., $304) and Auckland (1hr., $602) and several to Milford (45min., $160, $90 standby) and other cities. To the airport, take the shuttle from the McDonald's on Camp St., leaving every hr. from 7:15am ($5), or phone **Super Shuttle** (tel. 442 3639 or 0800 727 747) for pickup ($5). Airport taxi $14.

Buses: InterCity (tel. 442 8238), departing from Camp St., and the less expensive options **Atomic Shuttles** (tel. 442 8178) and **Southern Link** (tel. 358 8355), all head daily to Christchurch (7-11hr., 1-2 per day, $40-95) and Dunedin (4hr., 1-2 per

Southern Lakes

TASMAN SEA

Lake Paringa

TO FRANZ JOSEF GLACIER AND FOX GLACIER

Haast

Jackson Head Jackson Bay

Haast Pass

30 miles

30 kilometers

N

MOUNT ASPIRING NATIONAL PARK

Big Bay

Makarora

Lake Hawea

TO SOUTHERN CANTERBURY **Lindis Pass**

▲ Mt. Aspiring

Lake Wanaka

Lake McKerrow

Milford Sound

Hollyford Paradise

Wanaka

Hawea Flat

Milford Sound

Glenorchy

Kinloch

8A

Tarras

6 8

Arrowtown

Lake Dunstan

FIORDLAND NATIONAL PARK

Queenstown Frankton

Cromwell

85

Lake Wakatipu

Clyde

Alexandra

Lake Te Anau

Kingston

Lake Manapouri Te Anau

6

Roxburgh

Manapouri

95

The Key

TO DUNEDIN

Mossburn

Lumsden

TO GORE

Raes Junction

TO INVERCARGILL

6 94

Riversdale

Heriot

Kelso

90

day, \$25-53). InterCity and **Topline Tours** (tel. 442 8178) head daily to Te Anau (2hr., 1-3 per day, \$35). InterCity heads daily to Invercargill (2¾hr., 8:15am, \$25-36). Southern Link and **Wanaka Connexion** (tel. (0800) 879 926) head daily to Wanaka (1¾hr., 1-2 per day, \$20-22).

Local Buses: The **Shopper Bus** (tel. 442 6647) runs between most accommodations and the town center (\$2) every hour, and to Frankton (\$3) and the airport (\$5) three times a day. Schedule at visitors center.

Taxis: AA Taxis (tel. 441 8222), **Alpine Taxis** (tel. 442 6666), and **Queenstown Taxis** (tel. 442 7788) serve all night. A ride to the airport runs around \$13.

Car Rental: The cheapest deals for local touring (from \$35 per day) are probably at **Network Car Rentals,** 34 Shotover St. (tel. 442 7055). Open daily 8:30am-6pm. Otherwise try **Pegasus Rental Cars** (tel. 442 7176), which includes insurance and unlimited distance for \$39 per day of a 4-day rental.

Bicycle/Moped Rental: Outside Sports (tel. 442 8883), at the top of the Mall, has mountain bikes with full suspension and equipment (\$40-70 per day). Mopeds \$25 per 2hr., \$45 per 8hr. **Reg's Rentals** (tel. 442 6039), on Beach St., is cheaper;

mountain bikes $24 per day, $8 per hr.; tandems $26 per day; scooters $45 per day. Open daily in summer 9am-7pm, in winter 8am-6pm.

Hitchhiking: Thumbers report that getting to Glenorchy requires walking along the lake beyond the rotary at One Mile Creek. Hitching to Milford is an unlikely prospect, involving taking the Shopper Bus to Frankton and walking past the airport along the road to Te Anau.

Visitors Centers: Numerous sources of info occupy three corners of the intersection of Shotover and Camp St. The official one is the **Queenstown Visitor Centre** (tel. 442 4100; fax 442 8907). Open daily in summer 7am-7pm, in winter 7am-6pm.

DOC: On Shotover St. (tel. 442 7935), below the Information and Track Centre. Pamphlets on local walks; get hut tickets here for the Routeburn and other area tracks. Open Dec.-Mar. daily 8am-7pm; Apr.-Nov. M-F 9am-5pm, Sa 9am-1pm.

Currency Exchange: BNZ (tel. 442 5820), on Rees St., has good exchange rates. Bureau de Change open daily 9am-8pm. **ANZ Postbank** (tel. 442 7170), on Beach St. near the waterfront, has similar rates, an **ATM,** and cash advances. Open M-F 9am-4:30pm. Otherwise, try the no-commission exchange in the station.

Ski/Snowboard Rental: Queenstown has the most per capita snowboard shops in the solar system. **Outside Sports** has a rental outlet (tel. 442 8870) in the Arcade behind Chico's that offers the best selection. Skis, boots, poles $28; board and boots $32. Open daily 7am-10pm. **Browns** (tel. 442 4003), the original at Rees and Shotover St., has the same ski prices and $40 snowboard packages. Open daily in winter 7:30am-10pm. **The Backpacking Specialists** (tel. 442 8172), 35 Shotover St., has **luggage storage** ($2) and occasional rental deals. **Kiwi Discovery** (tel. 442 7340), on Camp St., has similarly priced gear. Open daily in winter 7am-10pm.

Emergency: dial 111.

Police: 11 Camp St. (tel. 442 7900).

Medical Services: Wilkinson's Pharmacy (tel. 442 7313), on the Mall at Rees St. Open daily 8:30am-10pm. The **Lakes District Hospital** (tel. 442 3053), is in Frankton (the nearest major center is in Invercargill).

Post Office: At Camp and Ballarat St. (tel. 442 7670). Open M-F 8:30am-5:30pm, Sa 9am-5pm.

Internet Access: The cheapest connection is at **Abbey Road** ($2 for 15min.), lower Shotover St. (see p. 312).

Telephone Code: 03.

ACCOMMODATIONS

Catering to Gucci and LandRover junkies and broke ski bums alike, Queenstown has a staggering variety of places to stay, with B&Bs springing up endlessly like mushrooms after rain. Booking agencies, especially **The Sightseeing Shop** (tel. 442 7640), at the corner of Camp St. and the Mall, facilitate finding the ideal B&B, with photo guides of the 70 or so choices in town. Book far ahead in summer and ski season.

Bumbles Hostel, 2 Brunswick St. (tel. 442 6298). Walk left down Shotover St. and along the Lake Esplanade away from town. Palms and ferns abound in this beautiful hostel, which prides itself on providing a private and comfortable stay. Bumbles' 4-person dorms have wood-framed bunks and comfortable mattresses, while curtained windows in the bathroom add a touch of home. The newly renovated kitchen and lounge offer great views of the lake, although they are only open limited hours. Dorms $17; twin bunks $38; twins and doubles $45 (with linen). Reception 7:30am-7:30pm, check-out 10am. Duvet $1 per stay.

The Last Resort (tel. 442 4320; fax 442 4330), on Man St. Head up Camp St., take a right on Man St., and cross the stream over the Japanese footbridge. Drop the attitude at the door and prepare to chill in the rustic, wood-scented, wood-floored, and wood-stoved joint well within stumbling distance (if you can manage the creek) of the bars. The smallish two-leveled red and black *maison* is as unobtrusive as they get. Quads $18 per person (with linen and blankets). Reception is open whenever the staff is inclined to sit at the desk. Check-out 10am.

Pinewood Lodge, 48 Hamilton Rd. (tel. 442 8273; fax 442 9470; http://www.pinewood.co.nz). Somewhat far from town—starting at the visitors center, head up Camp St. to Robins Rd.; Hamilton is on the left. Relaxed seclusion in modern cherry-red cabins with cushy mattresses and ingenious personal food cabinets.

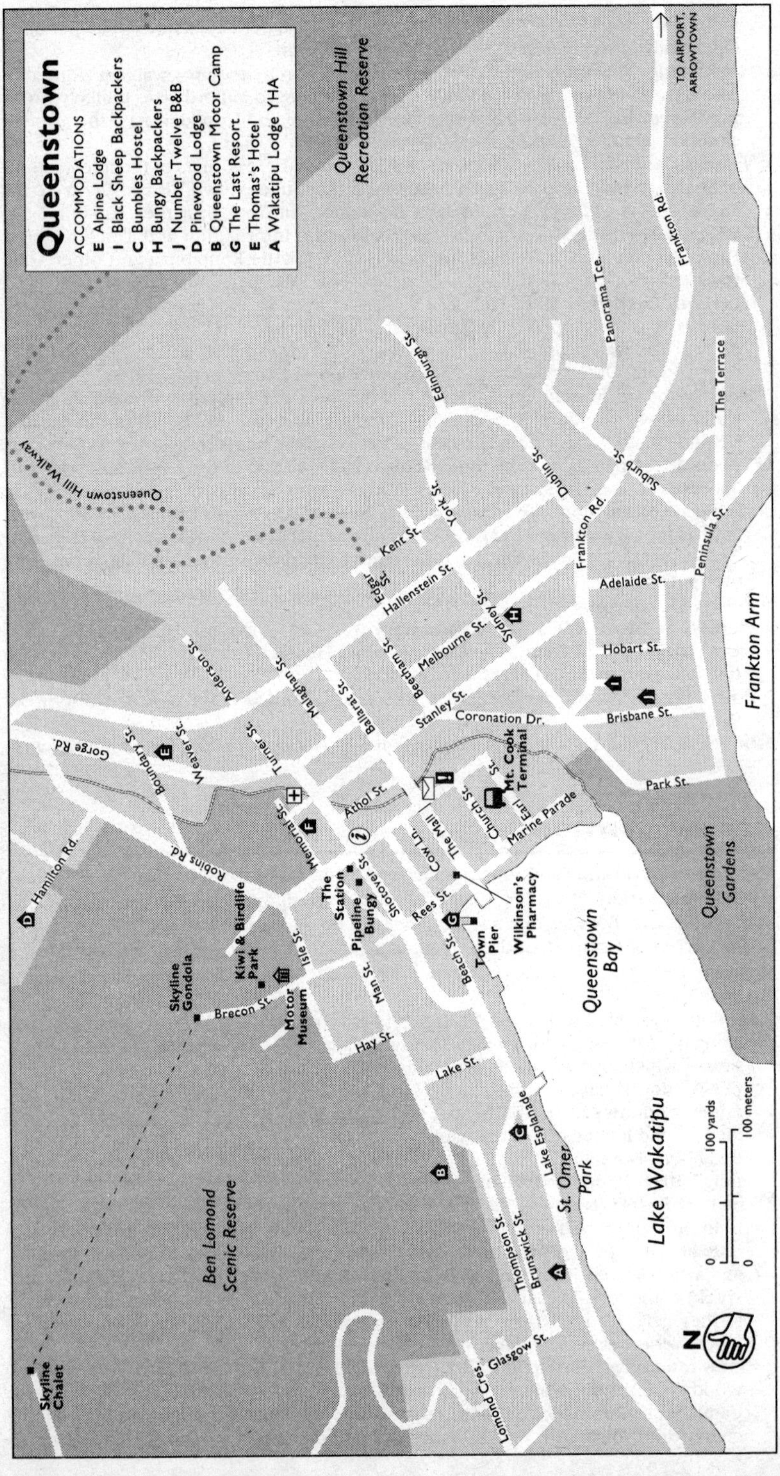

Queenstown
ACCOMMODATIONS
E Alpine Lodge
I Black Sheep Backpackers
C Bumbles Hostel
H Bungy Backpackers
J Number Twelve B&B
D Pinewood Lodge
B Queenstown Motor Camp
G The Last Resort
E Thomas's Hotel
A Wakatipu Lodge YHA
Queenstown Hill Recreation Reserve
Queenstown Hill Walkway
TO AIRPORT, ARROWTOWN
Frankton Rd.
Panorama Tce.
Edinburgh St.
The Terrace
Suburb St.
Dublin St.
York St.
Kent St.
Edgar St.
Hallenstein St.
Sydney St.
Adelaide St.
Peninsula St.
Melbourne St.
Beetham St.
Hobart St.
Frankton Arm
Anderson St.
Malaghan St.
Ballarat St.
Stanley St.
Coronation Dr.
Brisbane St.
Turner St.
Gorge Rd.
Boundary St.
Weaver St.
Athol St.
Mt. Cook Terminal
Earl St.
Church St.
The Mall
Cow Ln.
Marine Parade
Park St.
Queenstown Gardens
Memorial St.
Hamilton Rd.
Robins Rd.
The Station
Pipeline Bungy
Shotover St.
Rees St.
Wilkinson's Pharmacy
Town Pier
Beach St.
Queenstown Bay
Kiwi & Birdlife Park
Skyline Gondola
Isle St.
Brecon St.
Motor Museum
Man St.
Hay St.
Lake St.
Lake Esplanade
St. Omer Park
Lake Wakatipu
Ben Lomond Scenic Reserve
Thompson St.
Brunswick St.
Glasgow St.
Lomond Cres.
Skyline Chalet
0
100 yards
0
100 meters
N

Skip the bustle and star-gaze in the massaging jacuzzi ($5 per 30min. for up to 5 people), or rack some 8-ball in the vast semi-cylindrical rec room. Dorms $17; singles $25; twins and doubles $40; tent sites $10. Reception in summer 7:30am-10pm, in winter 8am-9pm. Check-out 10am. Linen $1 per item.

Wakatipu Lodge YHA, 88-90 Lake Esplanade (tel. 442 8413; fax 442 6561). Left down Shotover St., and 5min. along the lakefront away from town. A giant communal place, with gregarious staff. The pink and green dorms are warm but have thin walls. Dorms $18; doubles or twins $42; non-YHA $4 extra. Email $4 per 15min. Reception 6:30am-10:30pm. Check-out 10am. Book ahead in summer.

Black Sheep Backpackers (VIP), 13 Frankton Rd. (tel. 442 7289; fax 442 7361). Take a right up Shotover St. to Camp St.; turn right and go several blocks, head up the short trail in the park, and cross over to Frankton St. An old stone building with contemporary perks, such as a video library, jacuzzi, and big mountain views. Some genius marketer created an 18-hole frisbee golf course that runs through the adjacent park; ask for a free map and disk. You'll want the logo t-shirt when you're done here. Dorms $18, with VIP pass $17; doubles $44 (fully made up). Reception open 7:30am-9pm. Check-out 10am. Duvet $1.50, $20 deposit. Key deposit $10.

Bungy Backpackers (VIP) (tel./fax 442 8725 or tel. (0800) 7282 8644), at the corner of Melbourne and Sydney St. From the visitors center, take a right up Shotover St., a right on Stanley St., then a left up Sydney St. A very social hostel enclosed by freakish yellow-green walls. Massive video library, free jacuzzi, and dining room. Basic bunk rooms are a fab value at $12 per person; dorms $16; singles $25; doubles $35. Reception 8am-8pm. Check-out 10am. Key deposit $5.

Alpine Lodge (tel. 442 7220; fax 442 7038). Follow Shotover St. to Gorge Rd.; the lodge will be a block down on your right. Jules and George the cat keep a hot fire burning in the hearth. The loft rooms offer a cozy bed under the eaves, while the eight-bed upstairs unit has its own TV lounge and kitchen. Dorms $16; 2-person loft rooms $32; twins and doubles $40. Duvets $2. Reception 8am-8:30pm.

Thomas's Hotel, 50 Beach St. (tel. 442 7180; fax 441 8417; http://nz.com/Queenstown/Thomas's). Left down Shotover St., take the first left on Rees St., then the first right. A gluttonous tabby, the hotel's namesake, runs the waterfront hotel, tidying the private bathrooms, fiddling with the reception of the in-room TVs, and running the cafe. The portly feline watches over the kitchen and is an Internet guru (incoming mail $1.50). Dorms $17-19 (with linen $1 more). Hotel singles $70; doubles or twins $55-$84; triples $93. Duvet deposit $5, key deposit $10. Kayaks $75 per day. Breakfast $9.50. Reception 7am-8:30 or 9pm. Check-out 10am.

Queenstown Motor Camp (tel. 442 7252; fax 442 7253; http://webnz.co.nz/motorpark/), on Man St. Walk up Camp St. to the left, and take a left with the hill to the end of Man St. Green roofs match the pine-covered hillside behind the enormous park above town. More pavement than necessary, but more privacy as well. Cabins for 2 $38, extra person $14. Double tourist flats $68, extra person $14. Tent sites, powered sites $11. Linen $2.50 per stay. Email $4 per 15min. Reception in summer 8am-10pm, in winter 8am-9pm. Check-out 10am.

Number Twelve B&B, 12 Brisbane St. (tel. 442 9511; fax 442 9755). Follow Camp St. to the right up the paved pathway at the end, take a right on Brisbane St.; Number Twelve will be on the left. Ubiquitous bookshelves encourage reading by the solar-heated pool in summer or relaxing in the formal sitting room decorated with Asian antiques; contemplate the 12-layer Chinese ivory ball. Floral scents pervade the enormous double and rose-infused twin with private entrance. Singles $60; doubles or twins $100. Continental breakfast. Dinner $30. Check-out 10am.

FOOD

Chic eateries and sushi bars serve enlightened gourmet to the après-ski crowd; persevere to scavenge a cheap dinner. Many bars have reasonable meals at decent prices; the myriad cafes are ideal for sweet or savory snacks and innovative repasts. **Alpine Food Center** (tel. 442 8961), on upper Shotover St., is the largest and busiest of the supermarkets (open M-F 8am-8pm, Sa-Su 9am-8pm), but for fresh produce head to **Simply Fresh** (tel. 442 9636) on Camp St. near Shotover St. (open daily 8am-8pm).

⊛**Habebes Lebanese** (tel. 442 9861), on the Rees St. Arcade. A minuscule piece of the Middle East with a tiny counter and star-studded aqua blue decor. Add your choice of tabouleh and salads to the scrumptious lamb pita ($7) for a messy delight. Open daily 11am-7pm.

Wholefoods Cafe (tel. 442 8991), on the Trust Bank Arcade between Shotover and Beach St. "Mainly vegetarian, almost healthy" is their motto, but who cares when you're indulging on soup and homemade bread ($6), a giant chocolate-raspberry muffin ($2.50), or a fresh smoothie ($3.50)? Creeping tree branches decorate the ceiling. Open daily 8am-5pm.

Happy Wok (tel. 442 4415), in the parking lot next to Alpine Foods. Even the space-age chairs, Christmas lights, shimmering Siamese embroidery, and alien head bedecked restroom can't distract you from the authentic Thai food served here ($7.50-13). Lunch specials ($6.50) are a great bargain. Open daily from 11:30am.

The World (tel. 442 5714), on upper Shotover St. If you don't mind the blaring music and dim lighting in this enormous bar, you can get a cheap feed. The chicken *tikka masala* ($9.50) and the vegetarian meals ($9) are particularly good. The games of "Twister" and "Operation" are available as you eat and drink. Happy hour 5-8pm. Come back for the nightlife (see p. 312). Open daily 4pm-2:30am.

Surreal (tel. 441 8492), on Rees St. Wavy red benches, abstract ceiling art and subtly weird background music entertain both you and the fish swimming in the tank behind the bar. Asian inspired meals ($11-15) are a good deal, but tackle the chef's dessert special ($7.50) if you're feeling adventurous. Frequent DJs from 10pm. Open daily 5pm-2:30pm.

The Cow (tel. 442 8588), at the end of Cow St. A Queenstown institution, this former cowshed (dating from 1864) prides itself on excellent pizza and inefficient service. The Queen of England herself, whose jowly gaze greets diners from the mantle, can't stop the staff from ejecting you when you're finished eating. Nonetheless, Her Majesty's Pleasure, a fully decked-out pizza (large $25), is an indulgence that will feed two, and the bread ($3) is divine. Open daily noon-11pm.

Lone Star, 14 Brecon St. (tel. 442 9995). Started by a country-western music fanatic, this Texas-sized chain's carefully crafted ambience is achieved through boothside saddles (which people ride when it gets rowdy), stucco walls, and shadowy candles. Enormous portions of ginger-sesame ribs ($22) and cervena (farm-raised venison; $27). Not for the shy. Open daily from 5pm.

Little India, 11 Shotover St. (tel. 442 5335). Indian chants now resound in this former church, and three cross-legged carved musicians hold sway over the taps. *Naan* bread at lunch $2.50; dinners, including loads of vegetarian options, from $12. Minimum charge $10. Filling *samosas* $5. Open daily from noon.

Ken's Noodle House (tel. 442 8628), on Camp St. near Shotover St. Ken serves up bowls of authentic Japanese noodles ($5 and up) from the open kitchen. The twisted gaze of a Picasso presides over guests slurping up the satisfying noodles and tempura ($6.50). The six-piece sushi ($5) will satisfy any craving. Open M-Sa 11:30am-2:30pm and 5-8:30pm. Cash only.

Naff Caff (tel. 442 8211), on lower Shotover St. Although new owners have removed the famed espresso machine, the delectable muffins ($2.50) and hot soup ($5.50) remain a good value. Sip a strong flat white ($2.75) as you ponder the fishing equipment inexplicably hanging from the walls. Open daily 8am-6pm.

NIGHTLIFE

Queenstown's night rocks with a heady mix of well-off tourists and the requisite good-looking sporty locals. Although **movies** are shown at the Mall (movie-line tel. 442 9990) in the tiny single theater for $10 (students/YHA $7), the more adventurous cruise **Shotover St.,** search for inconspicuous **Cow St.** doors, visit the **Lone Star's** next door bar, and relieve the munchies late into the night at the **Jazz Bar,** a Camp St. cafe that occasionally turns into a street party.

Winnie Bagoes (tel. 442 8635), at the bottom of the Mall. Start your night here, where the party often spills over onto the deck overlooking the mall. Clever, boldly colored posters advertise safe sex and pizza flavors, while the scent of gourmet pizza wafts above dimly lit wooden bars and dance floor. Open M-F 5pm-2:30am, Sa-Su 11:30am-2am.

Abbey Road (tel. 442 8290), lower Shotover St. With pinball befitting of The Who and Beatles record jackets hanging about, Abbey Road draws mellower minglers and those on a quest for $6 pizza and upstairs pool. Laid-back couches inspire "Golden Slumbers" of your own, while the intimate pool hall brings you closer to your mates. Frequent beer specials. Open daily from 7am.

The World (tel. 442 5714), on Shotover St. Colored lights flash over the orange striped walls of the dance floor, where a younger crowd takes in the vibes of DJs and bands. Games downstairs entertain when the cheap drinks don't. Drink specials 10:30-11:30pm. Pool $2 per game. Open daily 4pm-2:30am.

Casbah (tel. 442 7853), upstairs on Shotover St. Microphoned security guards eye the adolescents gyrating beneath the multicolored dance floor lights at Queenstown's only true dance club. Casbah serves as an experiment for promotions and theme nights—you could win a free bungy and end up topless simultaneously. $1 drinks 10:30-11pm. Open daily 10pm-2:30am.

Chico's (tel. 442 8439), at the bottom of the Mall. A more traditional joint, frequented by a somewhat older crowd. Chico's starts hopping late, when the other places close down and well-lacquered partners are primed to dance on the tables and otherwise inspire mayhem. The pool/bar hybrid features local bands many weekends. Happy hour 10-11pm. Open daily 4pm-2:30am.

Red Rock (tel. 442 6850), on Camp St. Red Rock's black-lit Smirnoff collection casts an eerie light over the dark corners of this multi-leveled bar. Open Su-F 3:30pm-3am, Sa noon-3am.

ACTIVITIES AND OUTDOORS

Queenstown is known for its heart-stopping thrills and breathtaking scenery; if you want to ride, jump, walk, or glide through spectacular wilderness, this is the place to do it. The sheer number of booking offices is daunting—you could probably book a bungy-jump in the public restroom—but fear not. Give this town a week, and like Odysseus after a year of trials you'll be drained and grinning.

The Station (tel. 442 5252), at Shotover and Camp St., is gigantic; many activities depart from there (open daily 8am-8 or 9pm). **Backpacker Specialists** (tel. 442 8178) 35 Shotover St., pride themselves on finding cheap deals from flights to ski rentals. *(Open daily in summer 8am-8pm, in winter 9am-6pm.)* **The Information and Track Centre** (tel. 442 9708), a few doors down, is informed about hiking transportation and outfitting. *(Open M, W, F 7am-8pm; Tu, Th, Sa-Su 8am-8pm.)*

Shotover Jet (tel. 442 8570) balances thrills and scenery in a wild half-hour ride through **Shotover Canyon**. Skimming impossibly close to the jagged rock walls, the speedboats swivel and twist at 70 kph, even spinning 360°—but it's fit for anyone. Pickups are from The Station every half-hour; otherwise, drive 10 minutes up the road toward Arrowtown to the Shotover Canyon. *($69, children $30, 10% YHA and family discounts available.)* The **Skippers Canyon Jet** (tel./fax 442 9434 or tel (0800) 226 966) speeds 16km beneath the precipitous walls of the historical gold-mining canyon, under suspension bridges, and past abandoned pioneer settlements. *($69, with transport from the Pipeline Bungy office on Stover St. several times daily. Includes a guided tour of the museum and gold panning.)* **Dart River Jet Safaris** offers more remote trips (see p. 317). **The Kawarau Jet** (tel. 442 6142) leaves regularly from the lakefront, and gets you on both the Kawarau and Shotover Rivers in an hour for only $55.

Queenstown is the world's **bungy-jumping mecca.** Existential enlightenment is unlikely, but something will probably go to your head (be it adrenaline or all your bodily fluids). **Pipeline Bungy,** 27 Shotover St. (tel. 442 5455; http://www.bungy.co.nz/), offers the highest jumps in Queenstown, arranging a 340-foot plummet from a suspension bridge into Skippers' Canyon. *($135, with four-wheel-drive transport along the crazy road to the bridge, including humorous commentary, 4-5 times per day.)* In the station, **AJ Hackett** (tel. 442 7100), named in honor of the inventor of the bungy jump, runs no fewer than three jumps daily. **The Ledge** above Queenstown at the top of the Gondola may be the most challenging jump. *($89, includes gondola ride.)* Or request submersion at the 143-foot **Kawarau Bridge**, the world's first bungy bridge. *($99 with T-shirt and transport.)* Skipper's Canyon has another jump that includes a heart-stopping drive for $120 (a mere 75m).

From June to September, **skiing** and **snowboarding** take over Queenstown as downhillers flock to **Coronet Peak** and **The Remarkables.** Coronet is bigger, has a longer season, and offers night skiing and two half pipes. The Remarkables has a wider beginner slope and gets more sun. *(Coronet $59, students $53, children $29; Remarkables $57, students $53, children $27.)* Lift passes and transportation are cheaper in town, particularly when part of a package. The roads up to the mountains usually require chains; shuttles are a safer option. **Mt. Cook** (tel. 442 4630) runs to either mountain every hour or so in the morning. *($21, children $15; with ski pass combo $75, students $65, children $40.)* **Kiwi Discovery** (tel. 442 7340) also runs to the mountains several times in the morning. *($21, children $14.)*

For those who look down on skiers, Queenstown is one of the best places in the world—for skydiving, that is. **Skydive Tandem** (tel. 021 325 961) will pick you up, fly you up to 3100m, drop you and an instructor until you reach your terminal velocity, and then let you float down between Lake Wakatipu and the Remarkables ($245). The Ultimate Jump is the ultimate rush when bungying becomes routine. Other aeronautics include **paragliding** from above Skyline over Queenstown, a relaxing but exhilarating tandem ride. Call **Queenstown Tandems** (tel. 442 7319) or one of several operators; they all charge roughly $120. A faster, wilder ride can be had with **Sky Trek Tandem Hang Gliding** (tel. 442 6311), taking off from Coronet Peak or the Remarkables ($135). Try **Air Wakatipu** (tel. 442 3148), where 20-minute scenic flights are $48. **The Helicopter Line** (tel. 442 3034) has 20-minute Remarkables trips (including a snow landing for $125). The newest adrenaline rush to hit Queenstown is **Fly by Wire** (tel. 442 2116), a contraption that allows you to fly a personal craft up to 120kph. *(Costs around $115; ride lasts 6 minutes.)*

The **Shotover** and **Kawarau Rivers** also provide for various innovative whitewater adventures. The Shotover has more consistent Grade 4 rapids, but the Kawarau has a few wild sections (including the Chinese Dog Leg, New Zealand's longest commercial whitewater segment). **Queenstown Rafting** (tel. 442 9792; fax 442 4609) and **Challenge Rafting** (tel. 442 7318) run half-day trips on the Shotover ($99-109) and Kawarau ($89) mornings and afternoons. For uniquely self-controlled action during summer, try **Serious Fun River Surfing** (tel. 442 5262), a three-hour 7km Kawarau boogie board experience involving four rapids, standing waves, and mandatory adrenaline. *(4hr., training included, $95.)* **River Bugs** (tel. 442 9792) offers a similar experience in a polka-dotted personal craft akin to an arm chair. Flippers on your hands and feet let you control the buoyant raft. *(Trips run 8:30am-3pm; $140.)*

Mountain Works (tel. 442 7329), on Camp St., runs introductory rock climbing day courses from $85 in the summer and beginning ice-climbing from $185 in the winter, along with multi-day guided ascents for the hard-core. For an equally harrowing experience, the walls and precipitous road through **Skippers' Canyon,** constructed during the gold-rush days, now attracts four-wheel-drive tours that give the fantastic drive a historical perspective. **Outback Tours** (tel. 442 7386) and **Nomad Safaris** (tel. 442 6699) have morning and afternoon tours for $55. **Gravity Action** (tel. 442 8178) runs summer half-day **mountain biking trips** to the canyon morning and afternoon; for $55, they drive you up Coronet Peak and let you coast down through creeks and over gravel. To explore on your own bike, pick up a Red Trail map from any booking office. Wild, off-road two- and four-wheel biking treks through the canyon and other lands ($150 for 2½hr.) can be experienced with **Offroad Adventures** (tel. 442 7858).

Queenstown's attractions aren't solely for adrenaline addicts. Take the **Skyline Gondola** (tel. 442 7860) up to the restaurant and bar at sunset for panoramic views down the lake, including Coronet Peak ($6 each way), or better yet, walk up the **One Mile Creek Trail** (1hr. uphill), which starts along the lakefront toward Glenorchy, past the YHA, and passes through a canyon and pine forest to Skyline (where you can catch the gondola down). At the top, for your viewing pleasure, you can watch **Kiwi Magic,** a half-hour surround-sound visual experience about a bumbling American exploring New Zealand with a happy-go-lucky tour guide ($7, students $5, children

$3). **Skyline Luge** (tel. 442 7860) lets you hurtle down an 800m track in a steerable plastic cart for $4.50. *(5 rides $16.)* Back at the base of the gondola, check out the **Kiwi and Birdlife Park** (tel. 442 8059), which includes a nocturnal kiwi house, a range of native parakeets and ducks, and the head-bobbing **black stilt** *(kaki)*, the world's rarest wading bird (numbering around 70 in the wild). Proceeds support captive breeding programs. *(Admission $9.50, children $3.50; open in summer daily from 9am, in winter 9am-5pm.)* The **Queenstown Museum** (tel. 442 8775), down the street, houses the world's first skiplane, a missile-equipped Russian MiG-21, and loads of vintage cars, including a '39 Bentley. *(Open daily in summer 9:30am-5:30pm, in winter 10am-4pm, but call ahead to check. Admission $7, YHA $6, children $3.)*

For decades, steamships were the only form of transport across the lake, to Glenorchy and to the area's various sheep stations. Today, only the revamped **T.S.S. Earnslaw** (tel. 442 7500 or 0800 656 503) remains, once licensed to carry 1035 people (or 1500 sheep). While the comfortable cruising vessel has since become a Queenstown icon, the engine room remains unchanged since 1912 and burns a ton of coal per hour. You can walk in among the steamy pistons for a close-up view, or stay on deck and sing along with the piano. Several trips run daily in summer. *($43, children $10; less frequently in winter.)* The highlights, however, are the noon and 2pm farm cruises to **Walter Peak,** where you can watch sheep shearing and ride Robbie the Highland Bull, or undertake a horse trek. *(Cruises 3½ hr., $45, children $10; with horse trek $70, children $51.)* The dinner cruise involves a traditional lamb and pavlova dinner, and a rollicking farm show following the meal. *(4hr.; 5:30pm; $70, children half-price; departs from the summer wharf at the end of Shotover St.)*

Exploring the Queenstown area on foot (or hoof) is another attractive option. One of the most difficult and most rewarding is the climb to the top of **Ben Lomond.** Mt. Aspiring and an entire panorama of peaks can be seen from the steep summit on a clear day. Shorter tracks on the way to Glenorchy offer less-trodden native forest experiences (some are suitable for mountain biking or trail running). A number of stables operate up toward Arthur's Point in the valley, and include trips through farmland, foothills, and saddle tracks. Both **Moonlight Stables** (tel. 442 9792) and **Shotover Stables** (tel. 442 7486) provide transport. *(1½ hr., about $45.)*

Other random activities in and around Queenstown include ice skating at the **Fun Centre** (tel. 441 8000). *($9, children $7; 2hr. sessions. Friday night disco. Skate hire $3.)* You can tour art galleries if you have a car (pick up the **Arts Trail** brochure at a visitors center), or attend a Maori concert. *(Concerts $20, $45 with a traditional meal; call 442 8878 to reserve.)* The **Queenstown Gardens** at the end of the boardwalk offer secluded views of the lake. The **Kingston Flyer** (tel. 442 4600) is a vintage steam train that chugs from Kingston, at the lake's south end, on a 1½-hour trip twice daily; it's a relaxing journey if you're headed that direction ($25 round-trip). The lake comes alive in summer with **waterskiing, jetboating, water taxis** to secluded picnic spots, and **fishing** trips—just ask at any booking office.

■ Near Queenstown: Arrowtown

William Fox and a small band of miners pulled some 230 pounds of gold from the Arrow River in 1862, precipitating the formation of Arrowtown and its satellite towns throughout the rivers and canyon of the valley. Century-old frontage runs down the town's main street alongside equally old oaks and sycamores. Poems at the excellent regional **Lakes District Museum** (tel. 442 1824) pay homage to **Arawata Bill,** a legendary loner of a prospector who was still panning into the 1940s (admission $4, children 50¢; open daily 9am-5pm). The museum also serves as a **visitors center** of sorts.

Pick up the key ($5 deposit) at the museum and ramble down the **Avenue of Trees** to the old jail. At the other end of Buckingham St. is the historic **Chinese Settlement,** a series of mud-walled houses; Ah Lum's home also served as a store and opium den (the low ceiling prevented people from getting too high). You can duck (literally) into the reconstructed miners' huts, with flagstone floors and tiny proportions that bring to life the hard lot of the miners. One of the few remaining **Post and Telegraph** shops (tel. 442 1885) runs mail much faster than a century ago (open daily 9am-12:30pm and 1:30-3:45pm). If you're feeling lucky, rent a gold pan from **Arrowtown**

Stores and hit the streams (open M-Sa 8am-7pm, Su 9am-7pm; gold pans $3 per day, plus $20 deposit). The **Arrow Express** (tel. 442 1900) runs to **Queenstown** from outside the library (3-4 per day, $5). **The Double Decker Bus** (tel. 442 6067) also runs three-hour sightseeing trips from Queenstown to Arrowtown (10am and 2pm; $27). If you've got a car, continue to **Gibbston Valley Vineyard** (tel. 442 6910), where you can sample four vintages for $4. The **cave tour** is pricey ($8.50), but still includes wine tastings and the restaurant is an idyllic lunch stop when the sun is shining. Along the way to Gibbston, heading out of Arrowtown toward Arrow Junction, stop at the **Kawarau River bridge** to watch plummeting bungy jumpers regurgitated from the gorge. Or, stop in Cromwell to see the towering "statue of four fruits" that honors the town's designation as the "Fruit Bowl of the South."

■ Near Queenstown: Glenorchy

Surrounded by myriad frosty peaks reflected in Lake Wakatipu's azure waters, the "gateway to Paradise" has a magical setting. Closely tied to its Scottish roots, Glenorchy sits 47km north of Queenstown at the head of Lake Wakatipu, where **Fiordland National Park** (see p. 322) and **Mt. Aspiring National Park** (see p. 321) meet head-on. The tiny pastoral community of 120 is fueled by sheep stations and summer hikers eager to undertake the **Routeburn Track** (see p. 325) or other celebrated valley walks. Queenstown's hype seems decades away from the diminutive hamlet, which has the dubious honor of being home to **New Zealand's smallest library** (2-person capacity). The slow pace and quiet lifestyle of Glenorchy's 200 inhabitants demonstrate that the Queenstown region harbors more than transient pleasures.

ORIENTATION AND PRACTICAL INFORMATION The main road passes the stables and motorcamp before branching toward the lake and town on the left, and the road to **Paradise** and **Routeburn**, 26km away. **Backpacker Express** (tel. 442 9939) has shuttles to and from Queenstown every couple of hours in summer ($10). In winter, you might be able to get a ride with **Dart River Jet Safaris** if there's room in the bus ($10, leaves in late afternoon). The motor camp **store** (tel. 442 9939) functions as the **visitors center** as well as providing camping supplies and groceries (open in summer daily 7:30am-10pm; in winter open M-F 10am-5pm, Sa 10am-4pm, Su 10am-3pm). The **post office** (tel. 442 9913) is in the Mobil station at the end of town (open in summer daily 8am-6pm, in winter M-Sa 8am-4:30pm). Get the usual tramping paperwork at the **DOC office** (tel. 442 9937) at the end of Main Rd. (open M-F 8:30am-4:30pm).

ACCOMMODATIONS The old-fashioned **Glenorchy Hotel** (tel. 442 9902; fax 442 9912) is run by a motley crew of happy heartlanders. The little bunkhouse with an Oregon woodstove and a canary-yellow kitchen charges $14 per night; the more comfortable hotel rooms have wooden-headboard beds. (Singles, doubles, or triples $55; with bath $75; duvet $2.50. Try to book ahead in summer.) For supreme quiet, stay at **Little Paradise Lodge** (tel./fax 442 6196), 28km along the road to Glenorchy. The old homestead lives up to its name and offers peaceful views toward the lake, home-grown fruits and veggies when they're in season, and ample singles ($30-45), doubles ($65-80), and triples with private bath ($90). Kayaks and a canoe ($10) are offered at this complete escape. Ask the bus or shuttle to drop you off. The **Glenorchy Holiday Park** (tel. 442 9939; fax 442 9940) has bunks ($13) and basic units painted in every color located next to the stables ($15; tent sites $8, powered $9; check-out 10am).

Bobby, the chef extraordinaire at the **Glenorchy Hotel,** once served up *gateaux* on one of Her Majesty's royal ships; now he whips up culinary novelties including the not-so-novel beefy burgers (from $8.50). Save room for the artful desserts. The bar-restaurant is bedecked with ancient beer bottles, the brands of the 13 local sheep stations, and an enormous wall map of the region, not to mention Mac's microbrews on tap. (Restaurant open daily from 7:30am, bar open daily from 11am.) For fresh carrot cake or bagel sandwiches, head up the street to the **Glenorchy Cafe** (tel. 442 9958), a former post office now filled with dried flowers. Homemade jams and rye bread are available for tramping (open daily in summer 7:30am-late, in winter 9am-5pm).

OUTDOORS Dart River Jet Safaris (tel. 442 9992) is a fast-paced foray up the Dart River, past Mt. Earnslaw, and into the unreachable heart of Mt. Aspiring National Park. Uniquely designed to travel in just four inches of water, the jets ferociously spin and fly up the pebbled braids of the Dart River, stopping at the scenic **Routeburn Valley.** A unique combination of speed and scenery, the 2½-hour excursion is truly exceptional and worth the price ($119, children $55, $10 extra from Queenstown)—after all, the 350-horsepower boats consume a liter of gas per minute. (Runs in summer daily at 9am, noon, and 3pm; in winter at noon only; leaves an hour earlier from Queenstown.) **Fun Yaks** (tel. 442 7374) mixes tranquil inflatable canoe rides downstream with jetboating upstream (7hr. total). Wetsuits are included, and the personal crafts allow rowers to explore otherwise remote canyons without the drone of engines, while letting the river do most of the work. (Departs in summer 9am and noon from Glenorchy; $149, children half-price; $10 Queenstown transfers with pickup an hour prior to trip.) **High Country Horses** (tel. 442 9915) and **Dart Stables** (tel. 442 5688), on the road next to the motor park, offer guided and unguided tours from casual saunters to gallops through the breathtaking valleys. (High Country: $35 for 1hr. guided, $30 unguided; $60 all-day unguided; $20 transfer from Queenstown. Dart: 2hr. trek $50, with transport from Queenstown $70.)

Glenorchy is the gateway to several notable walks with stunning scenery. The **Routeburn Track,** 26km from town (see p. 325), crosses over to the road to Milford. Pickup or drop-off can be arranged through **Backpacker Express** (tel. 442 9939) for $10. The **Greenstone** and **Caples Tracks** form a loop from the far side of Lake Wakatipu, accessible by car or boat (see p. 321). **Backpacker Express** (tel. 442 9939) has boat service from the Glenorchy Holiday Park to the track (4 per day in summer; $10; pickup available). **Kiwi Discovery** returns from The Divide ($45). Other hikes abound in nearby **Mt. Aspiring National Park** (see p. 321).

■ Wanaka

Wanaka staunchly resists the pressures that would mold it into a second Queenstown. The alpine skiing, summer watersports, and velocity-driven ventures remain pleasantly inconspicuous. With the distant majesty of **Mt. Aspiring National Park** toward the north (see p. 321) and an expansive agricultural valley to the south, the town slopes gently along two main streets to the rubbly shores of its pristine lake, with little vacation homes dotting the lakeside.

ORIENTATION AND PRACTICAL INFORMATION

Looking toward town from **Lakeland Adventures** on the wharf, restaurants and shops are centered along **Ardmore Street,** which runs parallel to the lakefront and curves up the hill; accommodations are scattered about town.

Buses: InterCity and **Mt. Cook Landline** (tel. (0800) 800 287) run a shuttle to nearby Tarras (30min., 8:40am, $20), with connections to Christchurch (6-9hr., 1-2 per day, $90-95) via Mt. Cook (2½hr., $55-57). **Southern Link** (tel. 443 0804) goes daily to Christchurch (6½hr., 11:35am, $40). **Catch-a-bus** (tel. (0800) 287 800) runs to Invercargill (4½hr., around 1pm, $46). InterCity, Southern Link and **Wanaka Connection** (tel. (0800) 879 926) run daily to Queenstown (1¾hr., 1-2 per day, $15-26). InterCity runs to Franz Josef (10:15am, $68), and **Atomic Shuttle** (tel. 443 7885) goes to Greymouth ($65). Book InterCity, Atomic Shuttle, and Catch-a-Bus at the YHA or **Paper Place,** 84 Ardmore St. (tel. 443 7885; open daily 7:30am-6 or 7pm, Sa-Su 7:30-4pm). Many routes have significant YHA discounts.

Car Rental: Aspiring Car Rentals (tel./fax 443 7883), at Wanaka Motor Camp on Upton St. Cars from $85 per day. **Apex Car Rentals** (tel. (0800) 531 111) has cars from $49 per day all-inclusive (min. 4 days).

Taxis: Wanaka Taxis (tel. 443 7999) operates late most nights. Airport $20.

Hitchhiking: Most hitchhikers head out on Ardmore St. past the DOC office. Rides to Queenstown and toward Christchurch are reportedly feasible for the patient, though getting to the west coast is a more dubious prospect.

Visitors Center: Visitor Information (tel. 443 1233), on Ardmore St. before you reach the lake. Open in winter M-F 8am-5pm, Sa-Su 10am-2pm; in summer M-F 8am-5pm, Sa-Su 9am-4pm. The **Adventure Center,** 99 Ardmore St. (tel. 443 7414), books summer activities and even winter heliskiing. Open M-F 8:30am-5:30pm, Sa-Su 8:30am-noon.

DOC: Runs out of the same office as the visitor information center (tel. 443 8777; fax 443 8776). Come here for info on Mt. Aspiring National Park. Open in summer M-F 8am-5pm, Sa-Su 9am-4pm; in winter M-F 8am-5pm, Sa-Su 10am-2pm.

Currency Exchange: BNZ (tel. 443 8226), on lower Ardmore St., exchanges money and gives cash advances. 24hr. **ATM** available. Open M-F 9am-4:30pm.

Sports Rentals: Good Sports (tel. 443 7966), on Dunmore St., has mountain bikes for $25 per day or $15 per half-day; kayaks for $30 per day. **Racer's Edge Ski Shop,** 99 Ardmore St. (tel. 443 7882), has skis, boats, and poles for $26 (students $21), and snowboards for $35.

Emergency: Dial 111.

Medical Services: Aspiring Medical Center, 29 Dungarron St. (24hr. tel. 443 1226).

Police: 28 Helwick St. (tel. 443 7272).

Post Office: (tel./fax 443 8211), on Upper Ardmore St. Open M-F 8:30am-5:30pm, Sa 9am-noon.

Internet Access: Lakeland Adventures (tel. 443 7495), on the lake. $4 per 15min.

Telephone Code: 03.

ACCOMMODATIONS

Motels with names promoting their views or lake frontage fill the town along with resorts, motor parks, and an ever-increasing supply of hostels. Book ahead in winter.

Wanaka Bakpaka, 117 Lakeside Rd. (tel./fax 443 7837). Walk 5min. along Lakeside Rd. An odd sense of luxury pervades the spacious cherry-red carpeted common area and eating room with hanging ferns, and views to the town and mountains. Trees bear fruit behind the rustic cabins (unless the cat gets to them first). Cabins $14; dorms $16; singles $16; twins $36; doubles with bath $40. Reception in summer 8:30am-8:30pm, in winter 8am-8pm. Check-out 10am. Linen $3. Sea kayaks $18 per day, double canoes $24 per day, mountain bikes $15 per half-day.

Matterhorn South Backpackers (tel. 443 1119; fax 443 8379), on Brownston St. Walk up Helwick St. from the water, turn left, and it's on the right (poorly marked). Giant pillows and mattress allow for relaxation next to the two woodstoves and the curved stained-glass bay window. The few rooms are a *tour de force* in pine; motel units are next door. Dorms $15; twins and doubles $35, with bath $55. Reception in summer 8:30am-9pm, in winter 9am-9pm. Check-out 10am.

Holly's Hostel, 71 Upton St. (tel. 443 8187). With gorgeous bathrooms and several sunny lounge areas, Holly's offers a more home-style stay with two well-heated levels of simple dorms ($15). Bikes $20 per day. Check-out 10am.

Temasek House, 7 Huchan Ln. (tel./fax 443 1288). Walk 2km along Ardmore St. to the west, take Sargood Dr. to the right, and Huchan Ln. is to the left. Meaning "Lion City" (the former name for Singapore), Temasek is appropriately filled with Asian antiques and art. Private balconies for summer sunbathing. Free pickup. Singles $55; doubles $80, with bath $90.

Altamont Lodge (tel. 443 8864), 2km west along Ardmore St. The serene moose head above the fireplace regards the ubiquitous pine paneling with mild amusement. The ski-lodge atmosphere is enhanced by the spa, dining room, and ski tuning room (available in season). Singles $30; doubles $48; extra person $11. Linen $5 per stay. Reception 8am-8pm.

Wanaka YHA, 181 Upton St. (tel./fax 443 7405). Walk the length of the green to the west, and head up McDougall St., then take Upton St. to the right. A quiet place with an ample, social common area, crowded kitchen, and mentally straining puzzles from Puzzling World. Reception, bunks, bathrooms, and kitchen all in separate buildings (helps to keep the noise down). Dorms in winter $16, in summer $15; doubles or twins in winter $18, in summer $17. Mountain bikes $15 per day. Reception daily 8-10am and 5-8:30pm. Check-out 10am.

Pleasant Lodge Holiday Park (tel. 443 7360; fax 443 7354), 3km west along Ardmore St., on Mt. Aspiring Rd. Secluded, with maintained gardens; nearly all the rooms and the jacuzzi look out toward Mt. Aspiring. Pool, waterslide, volleyball court, barbecue area. Cabins for 2 $30 (extra person $13); tourist flats for 2 $55 (extra person $14); spacious motel doubles $70. Tent sites $8.50; powered $9. Reception 8am-9:30pm. Check-out 10am. Linen $5 per stay.

FOOD

Kai WhakaPai (tel. 443 9220), behind the bakery on lower Ardmore St. Decadence is an understatement in this small, earthy gourmet bake shop and restaurant. The name alone brings a smile to those recommending it. Enormous apricot pie slices $3.50. Veggie pizza slices overflowing with bleu cheese, beans, and roasted peppers $2.50, and dinners (from $7). Open daily 8am-9pm.

Amigos Cafe (tel. 443 7872), on Upper Ardmore St. The owner fries his own tortillas, makes his own salsa, and keeps the margaritas potent and the prices low. Burritos $10. During happy hour (4:30-5:30pm), get a pitcher of frozen contentment for $14, and a giant plate of nachos for $9. Courtyard and balcony dining, or firelit sombrero decor inside. Open daily in summer from noon, in winter from 4pm.

Te Kano Cafe (tel. 443 1774), on Brownston St. behind the barber shop. Interesting dinners such as pumpkin lasagna ($18) served in front of the open fire. YHA 10% discount. Open daily from 6:30pm.

Relishes Cafe, 99 Ardmore St. (tel. 443 9018). Highly polished wood floors reflect heat from the massive stone hearth. The blackboard menu features burgers ($9.50) for lunch and dinners from $18, but save yourself for the intricate desserts. Open daily 9:30am-3pm, and from 6pm.

Markets: New World (tel. 443 7168), on Donmore St., has complimentary tea and coffee along with tremendous selection. Open daily 8am-8pm.

ACTIVITIES AND OUTDOORS

Wanaka's got nearly everything Queenstown offers with half the pace and hype. For the region's plentiful snow, skiers flock to **Cardrona** (tel. 443 7341; $57, students $47, children $28) and the more challenging **Treble Cone** (tel. 443 7443; $55, children $27; students $46). The **Waiorau Nordic Ski Area** (tel. 443 7541), 23km from Wanaka in the Cardrona Valley, offers 56km of groomed cross-country trails, as well as tubing and sledding (field passes $20, children $10; ski rental $20). The **Bus Company** (tel. 443 8775) runs to all three ski areas in the morning from Wanaka Travel, but individual pickup is also available (Treble Cone $18, Wai Orau and Cardrona $19, roundtrip). **Tandem Skydive Wanaka** (tel. 443 7207) operates from the airport; their motto, "You call, we fall" is an apt description, as you float down 3000-4000m among the mountains and watch vintage aircraft meandering along the runway beneath you ($230; YHA $195; 20min. scenic flight included). **Air Wanaka** (tel. 443 7900) does scenic flights (Milford flyby $190, Mt. Cook $215, Mt. Aspiring $110).

Puzzling World (tel. 443 7489), 3km out of town and opposite Mt. Iron, is a must-experience (open daily 8:30am-5:30pm). Puzzles to percolate distant recesses of the brain and an eccentric tilted house featuring M.C. Escher sketches that come to life can easily consume a day for the curious. Don't miss the ingenious and challenging walk-through two-story maze—only vaguely maddening to the truly impatient. Puzzles are free to attempt; admission to the tilted house and hologram hall is $3 (children $2; with maze $6, children $3.50). Mini-golf is $2.50 (children $1.50). In even-numbered years, the **"Warbirds Over Wanaka"** show attracts vintage planes from every corner of the globe on Easter weekend.

Many of Wanaka's adventure activities seem more genuine than some of the mass-market tours offered elsewhere. **Deep Canyon Experience** (tel. 443 7922) runs intense canyoning trips daily, which involve rappelling down waterfalls to natural rock waterslides as well as some basic climbing in a full day of vertigo (includes lunch, $145). **Alpine River Guides** (tel. 443 9422) runs white-water kayaking trips for both beginning and experienced paddlers on many rivers in the area (all gear provided; $91-96, 5% YHA discount). **Jet Boat Charters** (tel. 443 8408) shoots up the Matukituki (3½hr., $75) and Clutha (2½hr., $65) rivers through freakishly shallow rapids and deep pools; the six-person limit makes for an intimate tour (summer only). Climbers will thrill at the endless terrain around Wanaka. **Out on a Thread** (tel. 443

8277) runs to over 150 sites. Bring a lunch and a modicum of fearlessness and you'll return pleasantly exhausted ($125 per day, $85 per half-day, $170 2-day climb training). **Wanaka Rock** (tel. 443 8178) runs an intro climbing course for $85. If you'd rather soar off cliffs than cling to them, **Wanaka Paragliding** (tel. 443 9193) will teach you to solo paraglide ($140). After you've mastered the basics on the grassy slopes of Mt. Iron, you can fly from the top whenever you want to for $12 per flight.

Horse treks run daily through **New Zealand Backcountry Saddle Expeditions** (tel. 443 8151), where a two-hour tour costs $45 (children $30). **Mt. Iron Saddle Adventures** (tel. 443 7777) runs two-hour horse treks up Mt. Iron daily at 10am and 2pm ($45, children $40). **Alpine Mountain Biking** (tel. 443 8943) guides cyclists across the country's highest terrain (full day $89, includes bike). **Heli Adventures** (tel. 4431869) offers heli-hiking, heli-biking, and heli-paragliding excursions in the Mt. Alpha Range for $112-185. You can rent virtually any water vehicle imaginable at **Lakeland Adventures** (tel. 443 1323), on the wharf. (Waterskiing $30 per 15min., kayaks $8 per hr., canoes $16 per hr., fishing rods $12 per day, guided trout trips $200 with a "no-fish-no-pay" policy; most activities are seasonal.) Tramping opportunities abound around Lake Wanaka and in the surrounding mountains. The three-hour return **Diamond Lake Walk** is one of the prettiest short hikes in New Zealand, while the five-to-six hour return tramp up **Mt. Roy** delivers outstanding views of Mt. Aspiring National Park, including glimpses of the Southern Matterhorn itself. Both treks require transport; **Alpine Adventure Shuttles** (tel. 443 7966) runs in the morning (Diamond Lake $10, Mt. Roy $5). Closer to town (beginning 2km down Ardmore St.) the **Mt. Iron** loop track (1½hr.) is wide and muddy; nonetheless it offers beautiful views and a fabulous picnic spot for relatively little effort. Beginning along the south side of the bay, **Waterfall Creek Walk** (45min. one-way walking) is a perfect short trip for novice mountain bikers looking for quiet views of Lake Wanaka. As always, the DOC office has up-to-the-minute information on track conditions.

Not to be missed is Wanaka's one-of-a-kind **movie theater** in the town hall on Ardmore St. Arrive early to secure an easy chair and a few scoops of homemade ice cream. The movies change weekly and screen Fridays to Sundays; all are introduced with a brief humorous live commentary ($9, children $6). A slightly more cultured experience is available at **Rippon Vineyard** (tel. 443 8084), on Mt. Aspiring Rd. several kilometers outside of town, where the long rows of vines provide stark contrast to the rocky surrounding mountains, making for a gorgeous spot (tastings start at $3; open July-Apr. 11:30am-5pm). Other cultural experiences include a visit to any of the several art galleries in town—check at the visitors center to see what's open.

■ Near Wanaka: Makarora

Tiny Makarora, on **SH6,** links Haast and southern Westland with Wanaka and the tourism heartland of the southern lakes. Lying near the northern tip of Lake Wanaka and near the scenic Haast Pass, frosty Makarora is often considered a gateway to **Mt. Aspiring National Park** (see p. 321). Known as "the place of abundant food," Makarora was a stocking-up point for Maori trading missions before they headed across Haast Pass in search of precious greenstone. Today, with twenty-odd houses, eleven children enrolled in the local school, and boundless opportunities for summer fly-fishing and hunting, Makarora makes it easy to get away from it all.

A number of coaches run through Makarora. **InterCity** (tel. (0800) 731 711) leaves from the information center to go to Haast (1½hr., 11:45am, $27) and Wanaka (1hr., 1pm, $17). **Atomic Shuttles** runs to Wanaka (1hr., 3:15pm, $10). Stop in at the **Makarora Visitor Information Centre** and **DOC office** (tel. 443 8365; open in summer daily 8am-5pm; in winter M-F 8am-5pm), a museum in its own right, with displays on the history of Haast Pass, the difficulties of building SH6, the flax and timber industry, and the Te Wahipounamu South West New Zealand World Heritage Area. Next door, the **Makarora Tourist Centre** (tel. 443 8372) sells petrol and snacks, serves as a postal agency, and runs the motor camp (open daily in summer 8:30am-7pm; in winter 9am-5pm). Basic 10-person dorms are $17 per person, while the A-frame cabins ($40 for 2, extra person $12) have cooking facilities. Tent sites run $8 per person; linen is $2. The **Makarora Bush Trail** (15min.) begins near the DOC office, winding its way through the tenacious moss that hangs from above throughout the podocarp and silver beech forest. A car is need to access many other short walks along the Haast highway; pick up a DOC brochure ($1) for details. Longer tramps abound in nearby **Mt. Aspiring National Park** (see p. 321).

Wilkin River Jets (tel./fax 443 8351) runs jetboat trips along the braided rivers of the region. Their main tour, the **Wilkin River Excursion** (1hr.) runs daily on demand year-round ($45, under 13 $20). Across the street from the Makarora Tourist Centre lies the airstrip for **Southern Alps Air** (tel. 443 8372; fax 443 1082), which offers scenic flights to Mt. Aspiring ($110), Mt. Cook ($175), and Milford Sound ($195), as well as a combination flight to all three sights ($350). Flights pass over mountains, river valleys, rainforests, lakes, and glaciers (minimum numbers apply). They also offer the **Siberia Experience,** an adventurous three-part mish-mash of a 25-minute scenic flight, a three-hour hike through nearby **Siberia Valley,** and a 30-minute jetboat ride ($135, min. 3 people).

■ Mt. Aspiring National Park

With craggy, snow-covered peaks aspiring ever higher, the 355,543-hectare Mt. Aspiring National Park never ceases to impress. Some 140km long and 40km wide, the park is at the center of the Te Wahipounamu South West New Zealand World Heritage Area (see p. 45). Of the park's 100-odd glaciers and 13 peaks of over 2500m, Mt. Aspiring is the 3027m pinnacle. Frequented more as a sidetrip from other destinations than as destination in itself, the park is accessible from just about every angle. Most activities, hikes, and scenic flights are run out of the gateway towns of **Wanaka** (see p. 317), **Makarora, Glenorchy** (see p. 316), and **Queenstown** (see p. 307). Even far-off **Te Anau** takes part, as the starting point for Fiordland's and Mt. Aspiring's shared **Routeburn Track** (see p. 325). Many of these tracks require experience with alpine conditions and river crossings, so it is imperative that you visit the local DOC office to ensure you are adequately prepared.

REES-DART TRACK This four-day loop track starts 20km north of Glenorchy. Silver and mountain beech forests dominate the Rees River valley; the track crosses avalanche paths along steep slopes before reaching the **Dart Hut.** The azure **Dart Glacier, Whitbourn Glacier,** or the **Cascade Saddle** are worthwhile daytrips from there. Returning over Cattle Flats, the track runs along the braided **Dart River,** alternating between gravel river beds and red beech forest before returning to **Paradise,** about 20km from Glenorchy along a different road. Hut passes are $8 (camping is unrestricted). **Backpacker Express** (tel. 442 9939) will drop you off or deliver you from Paradise for $10. Sleeping bags ($25 per week), packs ($5 per day), and other equipment can be rented at **Kiwi Discovery** (tel. 442 7340), on Camp St. in Queenstown.

GREENSTONE AND CAPLES TRACKS Forming a loop on the far side of Lake Wakatipo and crossing over into Fiordland National Park, this four-to-five day track is accessible by car or boat from Glenorchy. The walk crosses two deeply cut gorges and several grassy clearings along the **Caples River,** then climbs into the subalpine tussocks of **McKellar Saddle.** From there, hikers can continue to **The Divide** on the Milford Road, or down the **Greenstone Valley** for another two days, meandering through lowland beech forest down the narrowing valley, and skirting a long gorge before rejoining the Caples Track near the carpark. Purchase hut tickets ($4-8) from the DOC office. **Backpacker Express** (tel. 442 9939) has boat service from the Glenorchy Holiday Park to the track for $10. **Kiwi Discovery** and most other Milford tour buses will pick up from the Divide ($45 to Queenstown).

THE MATUKITUKI VALLEY The east and west branches of the Matukituki offer the closest views of Mt. Aspiring itself. Fantails and tomtits abound in the Southern beech forests of the valleys, while tussock grasses, rocky bluffs, and alpine tarn reward those who venture farther ahead. The **Aspiring Hut** (2½hr. one way, $10) makes a good base for daytrips along the many tracks branching off into sub-alpine wilderness. With views of snowfields, glaciers, sheer rock cliffs, and waterfalls, the tramp up **Rob**

Roy Valley (1½hr.) is particularly rewarding, as is the spectacular outlook from **Cascade Saddle** (5hr. from Aspiring Hut). Hut passes for NZAC/DOC huts must be purchased in advance at the DOC office in Wanaka. **Mt. Aspiring Express** (tel. 443 8422) and **Alpine Adventure Shuttles** (tel. 443 7966) run from Wanaka to Raspberry Hut daily at 9:30am in summer ($25). **Good Sports** (tel. 443 7966) on Dunmore St. rents tramping gear (sleeping bag $7.50 per day, ice axe $5 per day).

■ Fiordland National Park

Like a fabulous postcard come alive, the grandeur of Fiordland is almost unreal. Exhibiting the catastrophic force and delicate balance of a wild expanse barely touched by human hands, the awful beauty of Fiordland National Park evokes terror, fascination, and wonder. Fuzzy, moss-draped rainforest yields to frothing cataracts leaping over sheer cliffs into a turquoise sea. Jagged snow-covered peaks surround limpid ponds where wood pigeons rustle through the giant ferns. Located at the southwesternmost corner of New Zealand, the park is criss-crossed by over 500km of trails, including three **Great Walks,** and is part of the renowned Te Wahipounamu World Heritage Area. The three walks listed here (the **Milford, Routeburn,** and **Kepler**) only scratch the surface of the park. Numerous other tracks weave throughout the huge expanse of Fiordland, including the **Hollyford,** the **Caples** and **Greenstone** (see p. 317), and the **Dusky,** to name a few. It often pays to discover less-traveled trails and untrammeled paths for their solitude and freshness. Even a simple stroll along one of Fiordland's many lakes may be enough to banish earthly concerns.

TRAMPING IN FIORDLAND

The **DOC office** in Te Anau is the center of all things tramping in Fiordland. Stop in to get track info, fill out an intentions form, and purchase hut passes and maps. **Book up to a year ahead** to do the Milford or Routeburn Track in summer, and be prepared for a hefty price tag. **Te Anau** (p. 327), on the lake of the same name, is the main access point for virtually all of the trails and other points of interest in Fiordland. February and March bring optimum weather conditions; March is the best month for both solitude and sunshine. In the off-season (May-Oct.), the Milford, Routeburn, and Kepler tracks lose their celebrated Great Walk status and welcome regular track and hut passes. However, winter conditions are treacherous and suited only to the experienced winter hiker.

Equipment

To enjoy the splendor of Fiordland, one must be prepared to battle against the dual tramping demons of torrential rain and sandflies (see below). It rains two out of three days in Fiordland; you will get wet, so be prepared. The DOC sells indispensable heavy-duty **plastic pack liners** that will help keep your gear dry. Plastic zip-lock bags are a good idea for smaller items, and a nylon pack cover will help protect your entire ensemble. A windproof rainjacket of some type is also necessary to protect yourself from hypothermia, and the DOC recommends overpants as well. In particularly wet weather some people hike in swimwear. Most hiking equipment can be rented from **Bev's Tramping Gear Hire,** 16 Homer St. in Te Anau (tel. 249 7389; open daily 9am-1pm and 5-7pm). The Great Walks package includes everything an entirely unprepared tramper could need ($60 for 4 days rental). **Te Anau Sports World** (tel. 249 8195), in the town center, has a more limited selection (open in summer daily 8:30am-9pm, in winter M-F 9am-6pm). The cheapest place for groceries is the **Supervalue** in the center of town (open M-F 8am-8pm, Sa 10am-7pm, Su 10am-6pm). Extra luggage can be left at the **Te Anau Motor Lodge** ($2 per large bag, $1 per small bag). DOC offers free long-term parking in a safe lot by the information center.

MILFORD TRACK

The Holy Grail of hiking, the 54km **Milford Track** is a lifelong dream for the over 10,000 people that hike it every year. Dubbed "the best walk in the world" in 1908,

Shoo Fly

Captain Cook called it "the most mischievous animal" his crew had ever encountered. Maori legend recounts that Hinenuitepo, Goddess of the Underworld, thought people might be tempted to stay forever in the beauty of Fiordland, and so created the sandfly to keep them away. Rumor has it that for every sandfly you kill, 1000 more are born. No matter what you believe, sandflies are a hard fact of life in Fiordland, and their **bite** is fierce. They breed in moving water and are numerous near streams and lakes, but can also be found above the tree line in the alpine meadows. At night, the price of camping in the resplendence of Fiordland is eternal vigilance against sandflies in your tent. The keys to survival and maintaining sanity are **insect repellent** and **protective clothing.** Make a preemptive strike against the bloodthirsty enemy by slathering on repellent with a high percentage of active ingredient, and be prepared for multiple applications. Unlike mosquitoes, sandflies cannot bite through clothing, so even very light layers are an effective deterrent. In areas heavy with sandflies, tuck your pants into your socks; trampers' legs and feet are especially attractive to the ground-hugging swarms.

the track hasn't lost any of its luster, and aside from the road connecting the track's far end, the valleys haven't changed much since the last glacier receded.

Practical Information

Unlike most other tracks in New Zealand, the Milford Track is entirely scripted: you must have a reservation, and you must stay in a designated hut on each of three nights. Many people hike the track in guided groups; prices start at $1489. (For information on this option, call 249 7411 or (0800) 659 255, or email mtinfo@milfordtrack.co.nz.) The DOC allows 40 unguided trampers on the track each night. Day hiking is permitted, but you will not be able to reach the best scenery in such a short time. The following descriptions of the track are provided for independent trampers.

Hiking the Milford Track, with transportation expenses and hut passes taken into account, runs about $180 (children are roughly half-price; 20% family discount). The accommodation pass is $90, while the remaining cost is for boat and bus transfers (which should be booked when you apply, or at least a day before you leave). Applications to walk the Milford are first come, first served, starting July 1 for the following summer. Contact the DOC Great Walks Booking Desk, P.O. Box 29, Te Anau (tel. 249 8514; fax 249 8515; email greatwalksbookings@doc.govt.nz) for a complete application. To book from overseas, fax the DOC your party size, at least three possible departure dates, credit card number, and contact information. To get on the **waiting list** do the same; couples and solo trampers have the best chances. Or, show up at 11am with all your gear at the **Te Anau information center,** when unclaimed passes become available. Don't try to sneak onto the track or to camp without a pass; fines run over $200.

Transportation costs for the track are so high because the Milford does not leave directly from any points of civilization, running instead between transfer points on Lake Te Anau and Lake Ada. You can fly, sail, bus, boat, or even kayak your way there, but most charters from Te Anau connect to Glade House, the starting point at the northern tip of Lake Te Anau. One of the cheaper ways to the trail is by taking the bus run by **Mt. Cook Landline** (tel. 249 7516) from Te Anau to the transfer point at Te Anau Downs (30min., 2 per day, $11, children $7) and connecting to the morning boat run by **Fiordland Travel** that heads to Glade House (10:15am, $28). The afternoon boat is more expensive (2pm, $41). Return on the boat (2pm and 3pm) from Sandfly Point to Milford launch terminal (20min.; $22, children $12.50), and then catch the 3pm or 5pm Mt. Cook bus to Te Anau (2hr.; $35). Park your car in the DOC lot by the Te Anau Downs backpackers. Hitchers try to catch a ride the day before they want to start hiking in order to make the early boat the following morning. An interesting sail-kayak-bus option is $99 through **Rosco's Sea Kayaks** (tel. 249 8840) and **Sinbad Cruises** (tel. 249 8293).

The Track

The Milford Track lives up to its reputation; once you begin, any hassles of advance planning will be forgotten. Dramatic U-shaped glacial valleys, lush beech forests, fragile flowering plants, and gushing waterfalls create an indescribable environment.

The dynamic between you and your fellow trampers is worth keeping in mind as you hike the track. Guided walkers stay at more posh huts located about an hour behind the independent huts; they reach the independent huts between 9 and 9:30am each morning. Try to leave before they arrive in order to stay ahead of the pack during the day. As all 40 independent walkers are on the same itinerary, you will have an excellent opportunity to get to know your fellow hikers.

Overall, the track is in good condition, though the section surrounding **MacKinnon Pass** is rough, so hiking boots are essential. The first day out is the shortest and easiest on the track, and **Clinton Hut,** the first night's resting place, is a scant 90 minutes from the wharf. For those on the morning boat, this means reaching the hut around 1pm; bring cards or another indoor diversion. The hut is brand-new and spacious, although sandflies pose a perpetual problem. Top bunks are slightly less susceptible to the pesky insects.

The second day involves about five hours of flat and slightly inclined trails as you head up the Clinton River Valley to just below **MacKinnon Pass.** After passing the old **Clinton Forks Hut** (about one hour past Clinton Hut), the track begins to wind through open stretches, giving views of massive cliff faces towering over both sides of the river valley. Thin ribbons of water course down the bare rock, forming countless cataracts and waterfalls that are hundreds of meters long. A new view of a waterfall, mountain top, snowfield or glacier waits around every corner of this stretch. Approaching the **Mintaro Hut,** the track begins to get much rougher and steeper. Two shelters along the way offer places to rest, but neither is in a prime location. **Hirere Shelter** is reserved for guided walkers; continue on to **Bus Stop Shelter,** a corrugated aluminum structure that can keep out the rain. Your second night's lodging, **Mintaro Hut,** has three separate bunkrooms. It is near the small and beautiful **Lake Mintaro,** ideal for a bracing swim. Window bunks have maximum light and privacy. Step out of the front door, and you could strain your neck looking up at the 800m sheer rock face that towers above the lake. Access to the lake is 100m past the hut turn-off on the main track.

Day three is the most taxing and also the most incredible; pray for good weather and a clear day. Immediately after departing Mintaro Hut, the track ascends MacKinnon Pass, where the spectacular scenery makes tired legs an afterthought. At the MacKinnon memorial watch out for pack-shredding keas. The **MacKinnon Pass Shelter** is a good place to rest in preparation for the descent ahead. The track winds beneath a cliff face topped by a substantial glacier that sends forth wispy waterfalls. These blow away into mist before reaching the ground, swirling in fantastic shapes and patterns in the air. The track enters the trees shortly after this and the magnificent mountain scenery is replaced by a powerful series of waterfalls and cataracts, as the **Arthur River** begins its journey to the sea. At Quinton Hut, the next guided walkers' hut, a short 20-minute side trip leads to the base of the 580m **Sutherland Falls,** the highest waterfall in New Zealand and the fifth highest in the world. At its base, the crash of water into water blows out a circle of mist that rapidly drenches anyone within 10m. **Dumpling Hut** (1hr. farther) has two separate buildings, both with bunks and one with a communal kitchen area (dumpling not included). At night, check out the glow-worms in the rocks by the boardwalk. Leave Dumpling Hut by 8am in order to catch the boats. It is an easy, flat hike that takes around five hours and is punctuated by two more waterfalls, **Mackay Falls** and **Great Gate Falls.** The shelter near Great Gate Falls makes a good lunch stop. From here, the track slowly broadens and smooths out as it nears **Sandfly Point.** An enclosed shelter protects you from the point's namesake as you wait for transport to Milford Sound.

ROUTEBURN TRACK

Lying half within Fiordland National Park and half within **Mt. Aspiring National Park** (see p. 321), the 32km **Routeburn Track** is the shortest of the Great Walks, but none-theless packs in plenty of stunning alpine scenery. While hiking the track does require advance preparation, it is generally easier to reserve a space on the Route-burn Track than the Milford Track.

Practical Information

The huts and campsites on the Routeburn Track require reservations (see info for Mil-ford Track above), but the system is more flexible than at the Milford Track. Camp-sites often have space available when huts are booked, and you may choose where you plan to stay. There are four huts on the track ($30) and two designated camp-grounds ($9). DOC holds hut and camp passes until 24hr. before departure in the event of severe weather. Gas in the huts is available only to those staying there. There are fines for staying on the track without a pass (hut fine $40, campsite fine $15).

The track's endpoints are 84km from Te Anau and 75km from Queenstown. Bus transport is the most feasible way to access the track. Try **Fiordland Track Net** (tel. 249 7777) in Te Anau, which leaves town at 7:30am, or **Kiwi Discovery Track Trans-port** (tel. 249 7505); both are $20. Kiwi Discovery also runs along between the end-point Routeburn Shelter to Queenstown for $20; otherwise try **Backpackers Express** (tel. 442 9939) for $20. If you want to lighten your hiking load and don't plan on looping back to your starting point, **Topline Tours** will transport packs from hostel to hostel between Te Anau (tel. 249 7505) and Queenstown (tel. 442 8178) for $3-5 (leaves Te Anau at 10am, Queenstown around noon); coordinate transport and times before setting out. Hitchers are said to meet with hard luck 'round these parts.

The Track

Most trampers opt for three days and two nights (3-4hr. hiking per day) and travel east to west, as described below. The track begins 100m from the **Routeburn Shel-ter,** a primitive shelter with toilets; camping and overnight stays are not permitted. The **Routeburn Flats Hut** is two hours farther; nearby is a campsite with tent sites that are well located but somewhat exposed. A small shelter for cooking, an out-house, and water are available. Within eyesight is the upper section of **Routeburn Falls,** an hour's hike away up the forested flanks of the valley's southern side. Just at the edge of the treeline is **Routeburn Falls Hut,** the nicest hut on the track, with a long deck, two-tiered communal area, and bunkroom.

From here, the track traverses the tree line in a spectacular 11km stretch. The track is initially very steep and strewn with large rocks, making for dubious footing (although many of the rocks are a psychedelic purple or pink, so watching where you put your feet isn't all boring). It takes about 90 minutes of strenuous climbing to reach the high point of the track, a ledge above **Lake Harris.** The lake fills a beautiful alpine basin surrounded on three sides with moss-encrusted mountains fed by two waterfalls. At **Harris Saddle Shelter** a very steep side trip leads to the top of **Conical Hill,** where on a clear day the 360° panoramic view, the best on the track, includes a glimpse of Martin's Bay and the Tasman Sea. The track then sidles along the moun-tainside above the **Hollyford Valley** and gradually descends. As it runs just above the tree line, the track offers excellent views of the barren rocky top and forested flanks of the Darren Mountain across the valley. After two hours of hiking **Lake MacKenzie** comes into sight and the trail drops steeply to **MacKenzie Hut** (53 bunks; spacious communal area and separate cooking area). The views up the lake to **Emily Peak** are outstanding. **MacKenzie Campground** is 100m farther along the trail with eight grav-elly sites in the trees (water; toilets; open-air cooking shelter).

On the way to **Lake Howden** the track weaves through **"the Orchard"** (a patch of ribbonwood trees) and passes the thundering 80m **Earland Falls.** Roomy **Lake Howden Hut** is on the shores of the lake and boasts 28 bunks; the junction for **Greenstone Track** and **Caples Hut** is right by the hut. A 20-minute hike along the Greenstone track brings you to 15 free, unserviced campsites with a toilet but no shelter or water. From here, the track ascends briefly to the turnoff for **Key Summit,** a 30-minute side trip and popular day hike. The track then drops steeply in numerous switchbacks for about 45 minutes before reaching the **Divide.**

KEPLER TRACK

Although it was initially opened in 1988 to relieve pressure on the Milford and Routeburn Tracks, the 67km moderately-ranked **Kepler Track** more than holds its own.

Practical Information

No reservations are accepted for the Kepler; buy your Great Walks Pass at the DOC office in Te Anau (huts $15; camping $6). The prevalence of sandflies makes the huts a more attractive option than camping for this track. The huts have gas burners but no pots, pans, or utensils. In the off-season, the trail should only be attempted by experienced and properly equipped parties (off-season huts $4; no gas).

The track can be accessed at three points: **Brod Bay,** the **control gates,** and **Rainbow Reach.** The cheapest and easiest method of access is to walk to the control gates from Te Anau (a lakeside track begins behind the DOC information center). Alternately, **Fiordland Tracknet** (tel. 249 7777) runs a shuttle from Te Anau to the control gates (10min.; departs daily from the motor camp 8:30, 9:30am, 2:45pm; $5) and to Rainbow Reach (9:30am, 2:45, 4:45pm; return at 10am, 3 and 5pm; $8). **Manaska** (tel. 249 7106 or 249 8900) runs boats at 9 and 10:30am from Te Anau to Brod Bay; **Lakeland Boat Hire** (tel. 249 8364) runs at 9:30 and 10am (both companies $15).

The Track

The track forms a loop, beginning and ending at the control gates at the far end of Lake Te Anau. Although it can be hiked in either direction, the vast majority hike it in a counter-clockwise direction. There is no real advantage to going either direction, although one should try to time the section of the track on the exposed mountaintop for good weather. Three days and two nights is the optimum duration for the trip. If you take the shuttle to and from Rainbow Reach, this makes for three six hour days of hiking. It is easy to stretch the track out to four days by staying an extra night at Lake Manapouri and hiking all the way back to Te Anau.

About two hours from the control gates lies the first designated campsite, **Brod Bay.** It has several well-sheltered tent sites, water, and an open-air shelter. The views from the beach are excellent but the sandflies are atrocious; it is a better idea to continue onto **Mt. Luxmore Hut** for the first night. Past Brod Bay, the track climbs past bluffs (remnants of an ancient sea floor), through beech forest to golden alpine tussocks, reaching Mt. Luxmore Hut in three to four hours. Perhaps the nicest hut in the entire Great Walks system, it is a massive mountain chalet with two balconies and great views. Hiking here and back makes a good overnight trip. In extreme weather, wait here before continuing on the track in the morning.

The section from Mt. Luxmore Hut to the next hut is the highlight of the track. The track ascends steeply for about an hour until a point immediately below the summit of **Mt. Luxmore** (1471m). A short 10-minute scramble brings you to the top for a 360° panoramic view of the region. Find water two hours farther at **Hanging Valley Shelter;** by then, most of the climbing is behind you. The most difficult part of the track is the steep, 40-switchback descent to **Iris Burn Hut.** The hut is somewhat cramped, with sandfly-ridden tent sites about 200m away. Nonetheless, it is the only practical place to spend the night. Campers are not allowed to use the hut facilities, but water and toilets are provided. From the hut a side trip leads to the 10m **Iris Burn Waterfall** (45min. return).

The next 17km is easy walking but somewhat monotonous. **Moturau Hut** has only 40 bunks, but is by the shores of Lake Manapouri with a large communal area. You can spend your last night here, or push on 90 minutes to **Rainbow Road** and the afternoon shuttles back to Te Anau. Twenty minutes past Moturau Hut is the decrepit **Shallow Bay Hut,** which is not part of the Great Walks system. You can stay here for $4, or camp nearby for free. From here, the trail winds through bogland, crosses the **Forest Burn River,** and then reaches the swing bridge that leads to Rainbow Beach.

▓ Te Anau

"Walking capital of the world," Te Anau ("tee-an-OW") is a compromise between the unpeopled expanse of Fiordland National Park (p. 322), and the commercial buzz of Queenstown (p. 307). Beyond the milling mallards on the rubbled shore of Lake Te Anau's southern arm, the Kepler mountains soar to alpine heights around the open valley. Predominantly of Scottish and Maori heritage, the local population of nearly 3000 cheerily greets the transient swarms of summer sightseers.

ORIENTATION AND PRACTICAL INFORMATION

The town center runs west toward the lake to **Lakefront Drive**. The **Southern Scenic Route** runs west beyond the DOC office toward **Manapouri** (20km), while **SH94** runs inland toward **Mossburn** and points east. The road to **Milford** heads through town and away from the lake to **Milford Sound** (120km). Shops tend to be concentrated in the town center, while booking agencies and tour operators are dispersed along Lakefront Dr.

Buses: InterCity (book with Air Fiordland tel. 249 7505), **Mt. Cook Landline** (tel. 249 7516), and **Topline Tours** (book with Air Fiordland) head daily to Queenstown (2hr., 1-2 per day, $35). **Spitfire Shuttle** (tel. 218 7381) goes daily to Invercargill (2½hr., 8:30am, $34, backpackers $29). InterCity goes daily to Christchurch (10¾hr., 8am, $116) via Dunedin (4hr., $58). **Catch-a-Bus** (tel. 453 1480) runs to Dunedin daily (1:45pm, $39).

Car Rental: Major chains book through local travel agencies. **Rent-a-Dent** (tel. 249 8363 or (0800) 736 822) on the road to Milford. Open M-F 8am-6pm (on-call Sa-Su).

Bicycle and Kayak Rental: Fiordland Bike Hire (tel. 249 7211) has bikes available at the mini-golf course on Mokonui St. near the town center. $10 per hr., $15 per half-day, $25 per full day; call ahead. The golf course is only open May-Sept., Sa-Su. **Fiordland Wilderness Experiences,** 66 Quintin Dr. (tel. 249 7700), has guided trips from $85 per day. Rentals on Lake Manapouri and Te Anau for more experienced paddlers are $40 per day, $150 per 5 days. **Lakeland Boat Hire** (tel. 249 8364) has kayaks, canoes, and dingys for rent by the hr. or day.

Hitchhiking: Traffic to Milford usually consists of sightseers who rarely pick up hitchers. Hitching is nearly impossible in winter, but those who try often head out early and walk to where the houses end on the road to Milford. Getting to Manapouri or Queenstown is reportedly much easier; most thumbers simply walk to where the roads begin south of town, or fish for rides at their hostels.

Visitors Center: Fiordland Travel (tel. 249 8900) has an office on the lake at the end of the town center with plenty of brochures, bookings, and information (open daily 8am-5pm.)

DOC: On the corner of Lakefront Dr. and the road to Manapouri (tel. 249 7924; fax 249 7613). Regional office for local Great Walks, tramping information, and the road to Milford. Open daily Dec. 26-Jan. 31 8am-8pm, Feb. 1-Apr. 23 8am-6pm, Apr.24-Oct. 25 9am-4:30pm, Oct. 26-Dec. 24 8am-6pm.

Travel Offices: Nonsensical as it seems, all the booking agencies do bookings for each other (though hostels and motels are generally the easier and most certain way to book). Try **Air Fiordland** (tel. 249 7505) in the town center. Open daily in summer 7:30am-8pm; in winter 8:30am-5:30pm. **Fiordland Travel** (tel. 249 7416), on the lake at the end of the town center. Open daily in summer 7:30am-9pm; in winter 8am-7:30pm. **Mt. Cook Travel** (tel. 249 7516), open daily in summer 9am-6pm; in winter M-F 8:30am-5:30pm, Sa-Su 9am-5:30pm.

Currency Exchange: Trust Bank (tel. 249 7824) boasts the only **24hr. ATM.** Bank open M-Tu and Th-F 9am-4:30pm, W 9:30am-4:30pm. **BNZ** (tel. 249 7826) also exchanges money and does cash advances. Open M-F 9am-4:30pm. **Air Fiordland** (tel. 249 7505) offers good rates if banks are closed.

Emergency: Dial 111.

Police: 196 Milford Rd. (tel. 249 7600).

Medical Services: 24hr. doctor (tel. 249 7007).

Post Office: At **Paper Plus** (tel. 249 7348) downtown. Open M-Th 8:30am-5:30pm, F 8:30am-6pm, Sa 9:30am-5:30pm.

Internet Access: Air Fiordland (tel. 249 7505) has email for $2 per 15min.
Telephone Code: 03.

ACCOMMODATIONS

Nondescript motels abound on **Lakefront Drive,** but virtually all of Te Anau's beds fill up in December and January; book ahead.

Te Anau Backpackers Lodge, 48 Lakefront Dr. (tel. 249 7713; fax 249 8319). A rambling backpackers and former motel now has several stereos, huge chocolate easy chairs, a communal atmosphere, and a wide variety of rooms (most with bath) named after the local tracks. Dorms $16; huge doubles $18-$20. Reception daily in summer 7am-9pm; in winter 8-10:30am and 4:30-7pm. Check-out 10:30am. Email $1 for 5min.

Lake Front Backpackers Lodge (tel. 249 7974), right next door. Furnished in the same style and run by the same owners as its next door cousin, this hostel's solid wood bunks and sparkling kitchen nonetheless cater to a slightly older crowd. Dorms $17; doubles $19-20. Linen $1, duvet deposit $10. Reception in summer 8am-8pm; in winter inquire next door.

Rosie's Backpackers, 23 Tom Plato Dr. (tel. 249 8431). Head up the road to Milford, turn left on Howden St., right on Tom Plato Dr., and it's the last house on the left. A secluded residential home bordering sheep paddocks, Rosie's is a real homestay; the barbecue and picnic table out back are great escapes from the summer crowds. You can play the piano or strum one of Rosie's guitars in the huge wood raftered lounge area. Bunks and doubles $15. Cash only. Reception after 3pm.

Te Anau YHA (tel. 249 7847; fax 249 7823), on the road to Milford 800m from town. Friendly, witty, and knowledgeable staff know Te Anau back and front. Along with the wafflemaker and free ground coffee, Washington the pet sheep bleats every time you head to your room to give this rather traditional YHA a little flair. Dorms $16; doubles or twins $38; campsites $10. Reception daily in summer 8-11am, 4-9pm; in winter 8:30-10:30am, 4-8pm. Check-out 10am.

Te Anau Mountain View Holiday Park (tel./fax 249 7462), on Te Anau Terr. From town, turn right along the waterfront. Clean as Fiordland mountain water and recently refurbished, Mountain View boasts an old coal range converted into an outdoor gas grill, wall-to-wall carpeting, and a seaworthy boat-like jungle gym. Standard cabins for 2 $39, with bath $60 (extra person $14); tent sites $10, powered $10.50. Linen $5. Reception 8am-8pm. Check-out 10am.

FOOD

La Toscana (tel. 249 7756), in town center. About as Italian as you can get in New Zealand, with hanging wine bottles, high wooden benches, and Mediterranean memorabilia. Cheesy thin-crust pizza ($11 and up) and red wine ($4.50). Open in summer daily 5:30-10pm, in winter Tu-Su 5:30-9pm.

Redcliffe Cafe (tel. 249 7431), on Mokonui St. Universally recommended by locals, offering chargrilled fresh veggies to accompany saucy, original main dishes ($14-21). Jazz and folk most weekends, plus $8 backpacker meals and filling bar food. Open Sept.-May daily 4pm-late (may be closed 1 night per week during Sept.).

The Ranch (tel. 249 8801), in the town center. A popular pub with a huge open fire, nifty loft with pool tables, garish iced beer lights, and portraits of American West outlaws along the walls. The $12.50 menu is a good feed, as are Sunday meat roasts ($10). Pick up a free drink voucher from your hostel. Bands on weekends. Open in summer daily 11am-1am; in winter M-F 3pm-1am, Sa-Su 11am-1am.

Ming Garden (249 7770), in the town center. Round windows and calligraphy scrolls give the restaurant a spare simplicity, but the best deals are takeaway meals and free delivery within Te Anau, from $7. Restaurant open daily from 5:30pm.

Market: Supervalue (tel. 249 7311), in the town center, has the best grocery selection. Open M-Th 8am-7pm, F 8am-8:30pm, Sa 8:30am-7pm.

ACTIVITIES AND OUTDOORS

As a starting point for three of New Zealand's **Great Walks,** Te Anau could entertain the outdoors enthusiast for months on end with everything from hour-long strolls to 10-day adventures. Walk along the shore (15min.) away from town to the **Wildlife Center,** where you can commune with some of the earth's rarest birds: native owls, parakeets, and kea reside in natural caged habitats. The takahe itself, which may well be extinct before you are, is a sobering sight. Continue around the lake about two-hours (or grab a shuttle; see p. 326) to reach the **Mt. Luxmore Track.** The eight-to-ten hour round-trip tramp along the **Kepler Track** offers fabulous views of the lake and surrounding mountains.

Te Anau got its name from the **Te Ana-Au Caves** (Maori for "the caves of rushing-water"). Sluiced limestone walls worn away by 15,000 years of acidic waters have formed impressive caverns housing a spectacular glow-worm grotto (see p. 128). As you meander by pontoon through the blackness of the watery grotto, it feels as if someone collapsed the galaxy and turned the stars green. Located across Lake Te Anau, cave tours are run several times daily by **Fiordland Travel** ($36; children $10). Or sail above ground on the largest body of freshwater in the South Island, **Lake Te Anau,** on the hand-crafted and crimson-sailed gaff ketch known as the **Manuska** (max. 12). Other lake tours also await: **Sinbad Discovery Cruise** (tel. 249 7106) runs from the main wharf (4½hr., 10:30am, $45); shorter evening cruises are offered in summer. Shop around for the best charter sightseeing tours; try **Lakeland Boat Hire** (tel. 249 8364), **Deepwater Cruises** (tel. 249 7737), or any booking agent to find something to fit both your whimsy and your budget. Most charters also run fishing trips, and plenty of locals lead guided excursions for **hunting** and **fishing. Rainbow Downs** (tel. 249 8006) runs **horse treks** through the rainforest for $22 per hour; the stables are between Te Anau and Manapouri.

From Te Anau you can fly just about anywhere by plane or helicopter. **Waterwings** (tel. 249 7405), on the waterfront, runs a variety of flights (one for 10min. $39, children $24). **Air Fiordland** (tel. 249 7505) has a fantastic Doubtful Sound excursion ($125), while **Southern Lakes Helicopters** (tel. 249 7167), also on the lakefront, has a range of trips, some of which include snow landings and hike-down options (start-ing at $90). Finally, Te Anau boasts an impressive number of well-known hikes in the surrounding Fiordland National Park (see p. 322).

■ Near Te Anau: Manapouri

Surrounded by lush rainforests and backed by rugged white-capped mountains, Lake Manapouri is possibly the most beautiful lake in New Zealand. On the beech-clad banks of the "lake of the sorrowing heart," the town of Manapouri is surrounded by the alpine majesty of the Hunter and Kepler mountain ranges, covered in fog one moment and shining clear the next. The glassy placidity of the lake in winter and the natural beauty encompassing the town is further enhanced by a relative lack of devel-opment. Although tourist ventures are beginning to take hold, Manapouri remains a pristine gateway to the remote **Doubtful Sound** and the magnificent **Kepler Track,** lying just west of the junction of the Southern Scenic Hwy. and SH94, and 20km south of Te Anau (see p. 326).

Those who hitch report that getting a ride to Te Anau is quite easy, though buses are a better bet than thumbing for getting out again. Stand-by bus tickets to Queens-town with **Fiordland Travel** (tel. in Te Anau 249 7416) when the tour returns from Doubtful Sound around 5:30pm are $40; the company also runs to Te Anau. **Spitfire Shuttle** (tel. 249 7505 or (025) 359 529) leaves daily for Invercargill (2¼hr., 8:45am, $29) via Tuatapere (1¼hr., $17) and Riverton (1¾hr., $29). Heading into town, **Super 7** (tel. 249 6619) has two aisles of basic items, and you'll find a lake view and tasty ice cream, among other options, at the bright **Cathedral Cafe** next door (mar-ket and cafe both open daily June-Aug. 7am-5:30pm; Sept.-May 7am-10pm).

Possum Lodge (tel. 249 6660) was among the top-rated hostels in the country last year, though it's only open September through May. Big brown floor pillows and forest green bedsheets create a lived-in feel, while the two outdoor double cabins provide a modicum of privacy for those who want it. Possum offers free transport from Te Anau and local tracks, and rents mountain bikes and kayaks. Bunks are $16; doubles and twins $36. Check-out is at 10am. Book a week ahead in summer. The **Manapouri Glade Motor Park** (tel. 249 6623) is the nicest of the three motor parks in town, though it may be closed in winter; turn right at the Mobil Station down the dirt road. Set on botanically landscaped grounds and surrounded by lakefront beech trees, the park has new wooden beds, tiled showers, and a free rowboat for track access across the river. (Double cabins $30, extra person $15; motel doubles $70, extra person $15; tent sites and powered sites $8.50. Linen $1. Reception 8am-8pm.) When other beds are full, consider a stay at **Lake View Motel** (tel. 249 6624), whose basic backpackers accommodations ($18) deliver the promised motel feel and superb view. Private bathrooms and electric blankets are included. Tent sites are available. **The Shaws,** 1 Home St. (tel./fax 249 6600), run a laid-back B&B. Their self contained flat has a bath, a kitchen, and an open fireplace ($70 for 2; extra person $10). Wander through the garden to reach the cottage double ($40) where sheepskin rugs, an impeccable bathroom, and even a teddy bear will make you feel right at home. Breakfast is included.

Captain Cook was doubtful there would be wind to return his ship to sea, so he passed by **Doubtful Sound** in 1770, leaving only the name. Rounded glacial hills mark the entrances to over 100km of waterways. Often compared to Milford Sound, the two are in fact rather different: Milford is a land of dramatic extremes, while remote Doubtful promises placid, yet stunning vistas. Inaccessible by road, Doubtful Sound leaves its silence and serenity to the pods of dolphins and Fiordland crested penguins that call it home. For the more active, **Adventure Charters** (tel./fax 249 6626), next to the Super 7, rents kayaks for $40 per day and runs a 12-hour **kayak tour** of Doubtful Sound ($159; also an overnight option; ask about YHA discounts), as well as a variety of scenic lake tours (beginners welcome). Free transport is available from Te Anau, but book ahead (open daily in summer 8am-6pm; in winter around 9am-4pm).

Fiordland Travel (tel. 249 6602 or (0800) 656 501), at the end of the road, offers extensive full-day trips of Doubtful Sound, including a tour of the **Manapouri Power Station.** Accessed by a rough-hewn **2km tunnel,** the turbines generate up to 585 megawatts of power. After an overland jaunt with humorously dramatic ecological commentary, the tour heads through 40km of Doubtful Sound to the Tasman Sea before returning to Manapouri. (Tours offered Oct.-Apr. 8:15am, 9:30am, and one later in the morning; May-Sept. 9:45am; $150, children $40. Bus or flight from Te Anau or Queenstown available.) Summer power station cruises are offered three times per day ($43). Bring your own lunch or pay the expensive consequences. If you've got time and money, invest in a remarkable, environmentally oriented tour with **Fiordland Ecology Holidays** (tel./fax 249 6600). Get a natural history education while immersed in the splendor of Fiordland for three or more days on a 20m yacht (trips start at $155 per day; max. 12; book well in advance). Trips also run to New Zealand's incredibly remote subantarctic islands.

A variety of one-to-three day tracks in the area offer inexpensive—and relatively uncrowded—immersion in the grandeur of Fiordland. The **Circle Track** (3hr.) promises excellent lookouts over the Hope Arm of the lake, Mt. Titiroa, Manapouri, and Te Anau. Two huts ($4) are also available for longer hikes; pick up a pamphlet from Adventure Charters or the DOC office in Te Anau. You'll need to rent a rowboat to cross the Waiau River from Pearl Harbor in Manapouri as all tracks begin on the far side; Adventure Charters will do it for $5 per person.

■ Near Te Anau: Milford Sound

Mystical and dramatic, **Milford Sound** waits patiently to fulfill the expectations of the summer throngs and to reinstill a little modesty into the teeming masses. In the middle of **Fiordland National Park** (see p. 322), the Sound radiates strength and instability: waterfalls cascade from dizzying heights, falling past sheer rock walls rising hundreds of meters from crystalline waters. Barely marred by a century of eager eyes and increased accessibility (guided walks were undertaken as early as the 1890s), Milford Sound retains its inscrutable majesty.

Rugged **Mitre Peak** is the photogenic focal point immediately evident as you come into view of the Sound, but the fiord is surrounded in every direction by sheer cliffs and snow-capped mountains. Carved by a receding glacier, Milford and the rest of the sounds are true fiords. Particularly strong granite holds up the 600m of vertical walls along part of the Sound, walls that plunge up to 265m below the surface of the water. The 146m **Stirling Falls** are among the more spectacular of the cataracts pouring into the Sound; all the waterfalls are better seen after heavy rain. You shouldn't have to wait long, for the region averages 6½m of rainfall annually, and is occasionally doused with up to 50cm a day. So much rain can fall that there's often a freshwater layer over the ocean water in the Sound. The Sound still brims with marine life, however, from the unique flora near the waterline to the bottlenose dolphins, fur seals, and occasional Fiordland crested penguins that seek refuge here. View black coral and smaller sea life thriving 8m below the surface at the new **underwater observatory,** accessible with certain boat tours. (For more on hiking to Milford, see p. 322.)

DRIVING Half the Milford experience is getting there. The 119km **Road to Milford** climbs through Fiordland National Park past staggeringly beautiful valleys, lakes, and creeks. If you have a car, stop at will (pick up a guide to sights for $1 at the DOC office; Fiordland Travel has a less extensive guide for free). In winter, definitely stop at the DOC office in Te Anau to see if the road is even passable, or if tire chains are required (chains can be rented locally for about $25; when required, vehicles without them are subject to fines). After all, the stretch of road near the **Homer Tunnel** is the most avalanche-prone piece of highway on earth—one avalanche per day in winter keeps a full-time clearing crew stationed near the tunnel. **Te Anau** provides the only services for Milford and the road, and has the best accommodations. If you do somehow become stuck in Milford, you could stay at the **Milford Sound Lodge** (tel. 249 8071)—but try staying in Te Anau first. Dorms at the lodge are $18, while twins and doubles are $20 (open Sept.-Apr.). Daytrippers to Milford should try to get an early start as it sometimes clouds over on summer afternoons, while the morning fog in winter usually burns off by late morning. There are many **DOC camping sites** along the route ($4).

From Te Anau, the Road to Milford runs alongside Lake Te Anau through sheep stations before entering the red and silver beech forest of Fiordland National Park. Traversing the classic glacial U-shaped **Eglinton Valley,** the road runs through expanses of golden grassland, and past rocky creeks, with the Earl and Livingstone Ranges providing impressive backdrops. Stop at **Mirror Lakes** to reflect on the tussocked swamp and teal ducks beyond the pools, or take a bathroom break in **Knob Flats** (where the toilet-to-inhabitant ratio is 35:1), with its displays on avalanches and New Zealand's native bat. **Lake Gunn,** farther down the road, offers a 45-minute walk through the moss-covered glory of the forest. Beaches and fishing spots abound, and you can often see the trout you're trying to catch relaxing out in the water.

If you have time, consider ascending **Key Summit** (3hr. round-trip) from **The Divide,** the start of the **Routeburn Track** (see p. 325). Alpine tarns and panoramic views toward the **Hollyford Valley** reward the intrepid. The road continues past a lookout and over **Falls Creek,** where **Christie Falls** is visible from the roadside. Turn right on **Lower Hollyford Road** to reach the three-hour return track to **Lake Marian,** which passes through lush rainforest and past waterfalls to an idyllic picnic spot. As you continue through the Hollyford Valley to **Homer Tunnel,** try to have someone in the passenger seat (or your back-seat driver) keep an eye out for the impending possibility of being buried by one of the frequent avalanches that keep things rolling in the valley. After maneuvering hairpin turns down Milford Valley, stop at **The Chasm,** where a 10-minute jaunt leads to walkways covering the sleek rocks over which the **Cleddau River** plummets to the gorge below. You may see the **kea,** a native large green parrot known for its tenacious curiosity and destructive powers (see p. 293). A few kilometers beyond The Chasm lies Milford Sound itself.

TOURING The variety of tour options to Milford is staggering—as many as 150 buses head to Milford daily in peak season—and only a few of the selections are listed here. They can all be booked in advance from Te Anau. For all tours, pack a lunch or endure high-priced mediocrity; most tours return around 5pm. If you are after a more personal experience than a luxury coach tour with 50 other photo-snapping foreigners can provide, **Trips 'n' Tramps** (tel. 249 7081) runs daily small (max. 12) group tours from Te Anau. Friendly, tongue-in-cheek local guides tell the history of the area from every angle, commenting on everything from possums to Australia. Frequent stops for tramps, photos, tea, or even the odd conversation with a kea highlight the spectacular drive into Milford. Including a cruise, it's worth the splurge (pickup 8:30am; $88). **Fiordland Travel** (tel. (0800) 656 501 or 249 7416) offers coach tours, including cruises (10am; $88, children $44). **InterCity's Milford Experience** (tel. 249 7559) also comes with a cruise (10:30am from Te Anau; $88).

Most Milford tours include pre-booked cruises, but there are plenty of other cruising options available. Avoid the crowds and head out on the more intimate catamaran of **Deepwater Cruises** (tel. 249 7737). A two-hour tour of the Sound or Sandfly Point, the end of the Milford Track, costs $45 (children $16). **Fiordland Travel** (tel. 249 8090) and **Red Boat Cruises** (tel. 249 7926) have several boats and run three mid-day tours per day in winter and up to 15 tours per day in summer. Fiordland Travel's 45-passenger *Friendship* offers the longest tour (2¾hr.) and dips its bow in the waterfalls. (Tours with either company $40, children $10; with underwater observatory $50/25.) The *Milford Wanderer,* a sleek sailing vessel, runs a 2½hr. tour for $50 (children $10, 10% YHA discount). It also offers overnight trips that include a hearty dinner, breakfast, and even sea kayaking. Sleeping on Milford Sound is dreamy. Daily trips run from October to April ($125, children $10, YHA/VIP 10% discount). Sea kayaking may be the only way to comprehend the truly vast scale of Milford Sound. **Rosco's Sea Kayaks** (tel. (0800) 476 726 or 249 7695) has guided tours of the Sound for $59, leaving from Milford at 11am (earlier in summer); if you're departing from Te Anau, **Fiordland Wilderness Experience** (tel./ fax 249 7700) offers the best price for coach-kayak-coach tours at $90 (not always available in winter). Diving in the saltwater Sound allows for first-hand experiences with black coral and even blacker bottomless depths: **Tawaki Dive** (tel. 249 7847) has personal excursions from Te Anau with belts and tanks ($170) or with all gear ($215).

Helicopter and **flightseeing** tours may be the most breathtaking Milford experiences available, but getting high is generally expensive. **Waterwing Airways** (tel. 249 7405), on the lakefront, has hour-long seaplane trips of Milford from Te Anau ($170). Te Anau's **Air Fiordland** (tel. 249 7505) and the pricier **Milford Sound Helicopters** (tel. 249 8384 or 749 7845) do flights from Milford. Plane flights start at $50 for 10 minutes, while the helicopter tours are roughly twice the price. The 25-minute **Glaciers Galore** helicopter tour ($150) includes a glacier landing. **Air Fiordland** also flies from Te Anau (1hr., $160; ask about 10% YHA discount).

Otago and Southland

With rugged coastlines bordering rural towns and farms, Otago and Southland hold on to their early pioneer spirit. Those with a soft spot for marine life are drawn to the Otago Peninsula, which teems with seals, sea lions, dolphins, and rare penguins. The isolated, soft sand beaches and soaring rock formations of the Catlins coast satisfy a more pensive mood, while Stewart Island beckons to the south with even more remote beauty. A rollicking Scottish temperament gives a different flavor altogether to the university pub town of Dunedin (Scottish for Edinburgh), where Guinness and rowdy camaraderie invigorate urban life.

👐 OTAGO AND SOUTHLAND HIGHLIGHTS

- The quiet, rugged beauty of the Catlins, "New Zealand's best-kept secret," is perfect for casual exploration.
- The Otago Peninsula (see p. 340) is an ecological wonderland, home to seals, penguins, and other wildlife.
- Stewart Island (see p. 352) is remote even by Southland standards.
- The Moeraki Boulders (see p. 344) sit mystically near Oamaru.
- Youthful Dunedin (see p. 333) has all the amenities of a quintessential college town.

OTAGO

▓ Dunedin

"The people here are Scots. They stopped here on their way home to heaven, thinking they had arrived."

—Mark Twain

Dunedin's thriving pub culture is a testament to the days of its original Scottish settlers, but there are more highbrow remnants as well. Statuesque whitestone buildings and Edwardian galleries preserve the European atmosphere of this once-glamorous harbor port where Maori and Scot descendants continue to co-exist in relative harmony. Where seal clubbers once wandered with wooden implements, eco-tours lead wide-eyed, camera-clicking wildlife enthusiasts across the rolling hills, and once-splendorous hotels now cater to backpackers instead of land-hardened prospectors. The city's precipitous hills (its Baldwin St. is the steepest street in the world) and magical harbor are deeply inscribed in Otago's historical and industrial heart, from the proud walls of wealthy estates to the shipping center of Port Chalmers in Otago Harbor. The South Island's second-largest city, Dunedin's population peaks at 113,000 when students are in residence. While the city's student sub-culture (in the form of tatter-clothed, nose-pierced cafes and kitschy commercialized bars) has become a dominant theme, you can still spend more than a few days delving into Dunedin's past before the historic port gives up all its ghosts.

ORIENTATION

Dunedin is easily navigable and centered around **The Octagon,** where a statue of Robert Burns holds sway in front of the gothic revival spires of St. Paul's. **George Street** extends roughly north toward the University of Otago and is Dunedin's main (and mediocre) commercial shopping thoroughfare; it becomes **Princes Street** south of The Octagon, as it nears most of the backpackers. Pubs are scattered below George St. between The Octagon and the university, beyond which lie the Botanic

Otago and Southland

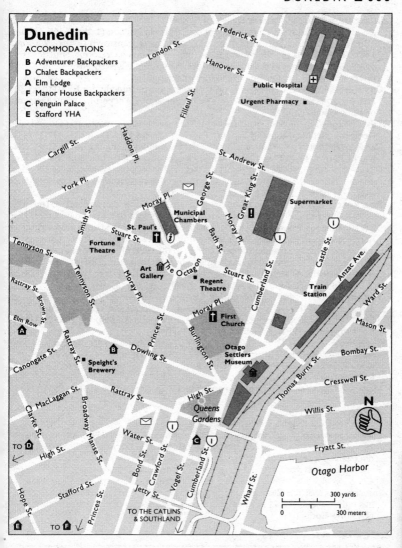

Dunedin
ACCOMMODATIONS

B Adventurer Backpackers
D Chalet Backpackers
A Elm Lodge
F Manor House Backpackers
C Penguin Palace
E Stafford YHA

Gardens. **Stuart Street** heads down the hill directly toward the train station and Otago Harbour. Otago Peninsula extends from the southeastern part of the city.

PRACTICAL INFORMATION

Airport: 45min. south of the city. **Ansett** (tel. 477 4146), at the George St. side of The Octagon. **Air New Zealand** (tel. 479 6594), on the Princes St. side of The Octagon. Both fly to Auckland (2¾hr., $452) and to Wellington (2hr., $313), often via Christchurch (45min., $101); or to Invercargill (M-F 3 per day, $89), going on to Stewart Island. Taxis to the city center start at $10.

Trains: Station located at the bottom of Stuart St. (tel. 477 4449; fax 477 4953). Open M-F 8am-5:30pm, Sa-Su 9am-2pm. **TranzScenic** goes daily to Invercargill (3¼hr., $51) or to Christchurch (5½hr., $74) via Oamaru (2½hr., $28), and Timaru (3½hr., $41). An unusual way to get to Queenstown is to make a bus connection after taking the popular **Taieri Gorge Train** ($99, children $50).

Buses: InterCity, 599 Princes St. (tel. 477 8860). Runs to Invercargill (3hr., 1 per day, $23); to Christchurch (6hr., 2 per day, $31) via Oamaru (1½hr., $11), Timaru (3hr., $17), and Ashburton (4½hr., $24); zand to Queenstown (4¼hr., 2:45pm, $30). Shuttles also ply the same routes (more in summer); **Atomic Shuttles** (tel. 322 8880) is cheap and reliable. All prices listed require a 3-day advance booking; prices may be higher (as much as $20) with less notice.

City Buses: 5 different companies provide transport in Dunedin for $1.10 to $3.70. Pick up a bus schedule in the visitors center; most buses depart from The Octagon or along Cumberland St.

Taxis: Stands on High St. off Princes St., and on St. Andrew and Hanover St. off George St., feature **Dunedin Taxis** (tel. 477 7777) and **City Taxis** (tel. 477 1771).

Car Rental: Large chains and smaller companies abound, including **Inner City Rentals,** 14 Harrow St. (477 3017), which hires cars from $28 per day and 28¢ per km. **Zoom,** 152 High St. below Princes St. (tel. 477 4938), is a fairly new service that doesn't rent cars but instead matches prospective drivers and travelers together, especially between cities. $2 success charge. Open M-F 9am-4pm.

Bike Rental: Cycle Surgery, 67 Stuart St. at the corner of Cumberland St. (tel. 477 7473), has a range of bikes with helmet and lock. $10-25 per day. Open M-F 8:30am-6pm, Sa 9:30am-3:30pm, Su 10:30am-3:30pm. A bike path follows Thomas Burns St. toward the Otago Peninsula—look for blue and white signs. Joggers can access the path by crossing the foot bridge to the right of the train station.

Hitchhiking: Hitchhikers often take a bus from The Octagon and ask the driver to let them off at the best spot. Those heading north usually take the Pine Hill bus ($1.50), while those heading south take the Mosgiel bus ($3.10).

Visitors Center: Visitor's Information Centre, 48 The Octagon (tel. 474 3300; fax 474 3311). To the right of the soaring clock tower of the limestone Municipal Chambers building. This should be your starting point for maps, advice, and boating tours. Open M-F 8:30am-5pm, Sa-Su 9am-5pm.

Currency Exchange: Thomas Cook (tel. 477 7204), on the corner of George St. and St. Andrews St. Open M-F 8:30am-5pm, Sa 10am-12:30pm. Other banks are located along George St. and Princes St. The visitors center can exchange money outside these hours.

Hotlines: Gay/Lesbian Support Group (tel. 477 2077) Tu 5:30-7:30pm for women, W 5:30-7:30pm and F 7:30-10pm for men.

Emergency: Dial 111.

Police: 25 Great King St. (tel. 477 6011).

Medical Services: The **pharmacy** is at 95 Hanover St. (tel. 477 6344). Open M-F 6am-10pm, Sa-Su 10am-10pm. **After-Hour Doctors** is next door (tel. 479 2900). **Dunedin Public Hospital** is at 201 Great King Rd. (tel. 474 0999).

Post Offices: Get your *Poste Restante* at the corner of Princes and Rattray St. (tel. 479 6458; fax 479 6419). Open M-F 8:30am-5pm, W 9am-5pm, Sa 8:30am-noon.

Internet Access: The **Dunedin Library,** on Moray Place behind the visitors center, has public access for $2 per 24min. Open M-F 9am-8:30pm, Sa-Su 10am-4pm.

Telephone Code: 03.

ACCOMMODATIONS

Edwardian hotels, former churches, and rambling homes converted into hostels provide Dunedin with an impressive array of budget accommodation. Most are found up the hill above Princes St., but all lie within a few blocks of The Octagon.

Adventurer Backpackers, 37 Dowling St. (tel./fax 477 7367). Down Princes St. 2 blocks, and then up Dowling. Situated on 2 levels around an open, 3-story great hall with the ceiling painted in sky and clouds. The skylit rooms in this brand new place are individually decorated; the corner music room, for example, has note and stanza wallpaper. Email/Internet access ($2 per 15min.), foosball, and even a breadmaking machine add to the communal ski lodge atmosphere. Dorms $14; twins $32; doubles $36; triples $45. Cash only. Reception 8am-9pm.

Chalet Backpackers, 296 High St. (tel. 479 2075). A spacious, exceedingly comfy hostel, with giant windows that offer a great view of Otago Harbour. You can't tell it was once a hospital, but you can stay in the operating room without the anesthesia—heck, you're already "down under." Free plush towels and blankets add to the hominess, as do the pool table and Zak the orange cat. Dorms $15; singles $25; doubles $35. Key deposit $10. Cash only. Free pickup. Check-out 10am. Reception open 8am-10pm in summer, 9am-9pm in winter. Bikes free; $30 deposit.

Elm Lodge, 74 Elm Row (tel. 474 1872). Head up Rattray St. to Brown St., then uphill to Elm Row; the backpackers is a few yards to your right. The hostel is smaller than most and an uphill battle from town, but the wood stove in the dining room and social atmosphere make it a standout nonetheless. Space is exchanged for intimacy, but it's got an excellent vantage point above the city. Dorms $13.50–$14.50; doubles $34. Free pickup. Reception open 8am-10pm. Check-out 10am.

Manor House Backpackers, 28 Manor Pl. (tel. 477 0484; fax 477 8145). 6 blocks down Princes St. An ancient Singer sewing machine and a 1930s radio give this hostel its own character. A cheery fire warms the TV lounge overlooking the harbor. New kitchen and dining area. Dorms $14-15; doubles $36. Reception open 8:30am-8pm, 8:30am-9pm in summer. Free pickup.

Penguin Palace (VIP), 1 Vogel St. (tel. 479 2175). Take Princes St. to Rattray St.; it's on the left, down the hill. This aptly named hostel's pastel panache lies in the garish color cartoons adorning every wall. Located on Queens Park, with new mountain bikes for hire (half-day $10, full day $15). Dorms $15-16; singles $25; doubles $34. Linen $3. Reception open 8am-8pm. Check-out 10am.

Stafford Gables (YHA), 71 Stafford St. (tel. 474 1919). Take Princes St. up several blocks to Stafford St.; Stafford Gables is on your left. This rambling old jaunt is supposedly haunted, although the school groups that frequent it are very much alive. Wide hallways, generous rooms. Dorms $16; singles $25; doubles $38. Book in advance for summer. Reception in winter 8-10am, 5-7pm, and 7:30-10pm; in summer 8am-noon, 1:30-3:30pm, and 5-10pm. Check-out 10am.

Castlewood B&B, 240 York Pl. (tel./fax 477 0526). Take Stuart St. to York Pl., then up the hill. A wood-paneled, sunny old Tudor residence with the host's watercolors on the walls. Excellent escape from the backpackers scene, with incomparable harbor views. Singles $60; twins $80; doubles $95, suite $120. Check-out 10am.

Leith Valley Touring Park, 103 Malvern St. (tel. 467 9936). A small, secluded park on Leith Stream, 2km from the city. Take George St., then turn left on Duke St. and continue up to Malvern St. Tourist flats $55 (single or double); caravan singles $22, doubles $30. Caravan and tent sites $9. Linen $2.50. Reception 9am-9pm.

FOOD

Ethnic places compete with the usual mince pie and Chinese takeout joints, making for some fine eating in this almost-Scottish city. **Markets** are **Countdown Foods** at Cumberland St. and St. Andrew St. (Open M-F 8:30am-10pm, Sa-Su 9am-7pm.) and **Taste Nature,** 59 Moray Pl. (tel. 474 0219), above Princes St., a small organic food co-op and bakery. (Open M-Th 9am-6pm, F 9am-6:30pm, Sa 10am-3:30pm.)

⊗Tull (tel. 477 5331), on Bath St. off Lower Stuart St. Dunedin's dessert mecca, this hippie ode to Jethro Tull rates its 17 sinful triumphs according to decadence. 1 star equals "strokes with a feather," 2 stars "a full body massage," and 3 "a chorus of angels" (desserts $7.50-$15). Bottomless homemade soups ($5) are a fabulous deal, and the distinctive freshly made French bread sandwiches (with tandoori beans $8) are as novel as the electric flute. Open M-F 11:30am-11pm, Sa from 5:30pm.

Aspara, 380 George St. (tel. 477 4499), opposite Albert Arms. The big Cambodian noodle soups ($5) warm you from the inside out and the curry veggies with coconut milk on rice ($5) revitalize the taste buds. Cash only. Open daily 11:30am-9pm.

Poppa's Pizza (tel. 477 0598) on Albany St., opposite the university campus. Friendly student pizza joint with an array of reasonable Italian pies. Small pizzas from $8, larges from $13. The seafood pizza is a yummy novelty (small $11). Delivery fee $3. Open M-Th 11am-2pm and 4-11pm, F-Sa 11am-1am, Su 11am-11pm.

Fuji (tel. 474 0323), in a red and white house just past Union St. on George St. Sit on solid wood chairs under paper lanterns and enjoy bargain lunch specials (sushi $6). Open M-Sa noon-2pm, 6-9pm.

Palms Cafe (tel. 477 6534), on Dowling at High St. on Queens Gardens. Earthy, eccentric gourmet place with garden views, portraits of Dunedin's ancestors, and indeed, palms. They cater to special diet concerns. The $15 soup and main course (served M-F 5-6:30pm) is a great splurge, and the yeasty honey-molasses bread and licorice ice cream are divine. An upscale eatery, but a great bargain for high-quality food. Open M-F from 5pm, Sa-Su from 6pm.

Little India (tel. 477 6559), St. Andrew St. below George St. Comprising the entire Indian quarter of Dunedin, this dimly lit authentic place has an extensive menu and large following. Fluffy naan bread $2.50-4, pungent curry dishes $15.50. Min. charge $15. Large vegetarian selection. Open daily from 5pm.

Potpourri (tel. 477 9983), lower Stuart St. below Moray Pl. The $10 3-course evening meal is a must for vegetarians or health-food fans. Salads, frozen yogurt, even a tiny private table for a vegan romance. Open M-F 9am-8pm, Sa 11am-8pm.

CAFES

Stewart's Coffee was the only choice until the recent influx of trendy little mocha and latte joints. In today's lively scene, lucky is the cafe that lasts more than a few months.

Percolater (tel. 477 5462), Stuart St. just below The Octagon. A spunky cafe with gaping vegetarian calzones ($4) and focaccia sandwiches $4.50. Try the delectable berry, banana, and chocolate muffins ($3). They brew enough hand-warming bowls of coffee to steam the windows over on cold nights. Open daily 9am-11pm.

Croque-o-dile (tel. 477 5455), at the corner of Princes St. and Dowling St. Crocodile chairs make the decor; there's even the tail of a crocodile protruding from the wall, adorning the only crêperie on the South Island. *Croque monsieur* $5.50, honey and almond crêpe $3. Open M-F 7am-4pm.

Cafe Zambezi, 480 Moray Pl. (tel. 477 1107), below Princes St. With vegan specialties and changing amateur art exhibitions, Zambezi is legitimately alternative and on the scene. Food is pricey, but email/Internet access ($6 per hr.) makes it noteworthy. Open M-Sa 10am-9pm.

Capers, 412 George St (tel. 477 7769), serves up great brunch foods in a comfortable setting that's less trendy than most. The gourmet pancakes with fresh fruit, cream and syrup ($7) deserve a try. Open M-F 7:15am-3:30pm, Sa-Su 7:45am-3pm.

Tangenté (tel. 477 0232), upper Moray Pl. off Stuart St. A New Age bastion of baking with light meals ranging from gourmet to just plain complicated. The avocado-parsley-pesto-cheese pastry ($3.20) and hot ginger-lemon-honey drink ($3.50) make excellent complements. Suck on the ginger ice cubes for a new sensation. Open W, Sa, Su 8am-3:30pm, Th-F 8am-11pm.

PUBS AND NIGHTLIFE

For those who want a change of pace from dance clubs and pubs, Dunedin sports a variety of theaters and performance venues. **The Fortune Theatre Company** (tel. 477 8323), on upper Stuart St. and Moray Pl., puts on a number of professional shows throughout the year. (Box office open M-F 10:30am-5pm, longer during shows. Admission $22.50, students $13.) The palatial **Regent** hosts an International Film Festival in June and July ($9.50, students $7.50) and provides space for traveling shows. The **Metropolis** (tel. 474 0800) shows foreign and independent films at two locations, behind the Municipal Chambers on Moray St. and a block down George St. ($9, students $7.50; Tu $7; matinees before 6pm $6.) Check the *Otago Daily Times* for screenings, or pick up a copy of *Fink* at most cafes for weekly entertainment listings.

As a university town, Dunedin has its fair share of standard student hangouts, and in recent years the variety of dance venues, counterculture clubs, and Irish pubs has multiplied considerably.

Captain Cook (tel. 474 1935), at the corner of Albany and Great King St. Even North Islanders have stories about this quintessential varsity pub and zenith of the university scene. A street level bar with pool and other games plus a throbbing dance floor upstairs provide 2 levels of debauchery. Meal deals $3, and drink specials Th-Sa. Open daily 11am-3am.

Bath St., 1 Bath St. (tel. 477 6750). Alternative types radiate to the lime-green leather couches and laser-lit dance floor. Candles and techno provide an atmosphere more suited to lounging than dancing—come here to look cool, or at least try. DJs Wednesdays through Saturdays, occasional fetish parties. Open Tu-Sa from 10pm.

The Woolshed, 318 Moray Pl. (tel. 477 3246). An eclectic Irish pub steadfastly popular with locals. Relax by the massive hearth or join the Wednesday evening jam session for free beer and barbecue. Live music nightly. Open daily from 11:30am.

The Statesman, 91 St. Andrews St. (tel. 477 8411). Lured by a big screen TV, dance floor, and games room, a mixed crowd turns out for rugby and beer. Live music most weekends. Open from 11am.

Divà, 101 Great King St. (tel. 477 1918). You'll pay a pretty penny for "toad sloth juice" or a "vasectomy" in this massive stucco Mediterranean-style dance bar with DJ. Swing your thing with the diverse crowd on the back-lit dance floor. A big screen TV and copper-walled games room. Open daily from 11am.

The Albert Arms (tel. 477 8035), at the corner of George and London St. Fairly quiet except for Mondays, when much of the city turns out for Gaelic good times and jigs to the cantankerous beats of a great Irish band. The "yummy doorstep" toasted sandwiches are celebrated, and even the floor fabric is tartan. Open M-Tu 11am-12:30am, W-Th 11am-11pm, F-Sa 11am-midnight, Su 11:30am-7:30pm.

Bowler (tel. 477 5272), on Cumberland St. just off Frederick St. A standard student hangout, the large screen TV and glass-walled, strobe-lit dance floor draw huge crowds, as do the 2-for-1 drinks every Friday and Saturday from 7:30-10pm.

SIGHTS AND ACTIVITIES

Dunedin's reputation as a university town and wildlife capital should not eclipse its architectural and historical attractions. The Scottish Edwardian architecture of Dunedin's **train station** is spectacular on a sunny day, and is rivaled only by the black and white facade of the **University of Otago's** main hall down David St. The gothic revival churches established by the early Scottish residents are worth a look, especially the **First Church of Otago** down Moray Pl. from Princes St., with its rose window and wood-ceiling sanctuary. **St. Paul's** in The Octagon has the only **stone-vaulted ceiling** in New Zealand, as well as a carved alabaster pulpit. Its flying buttresses are the most impressive in the city. For those who can't get enough stone churches, **St. Jospeh's Cathedral** (2 blocks up Rattray St.) and **Knox Church** (at the corner of George and Pitt St.) are also worthwhile visits. **Olveston,** 42 Royal Terr. (tel. 477 3320), is a perfectly preserved historic home built in 1904 that still feels lived-in. *(Tours are offered every 1¼ hr. from 9:30am-4:30pm. Adults $11, students $10, under 15 $3.)* Take George St. to Pitt St., then follow Royal Terr. until you see it on the right. All the clocks in this Edwardian mansion run, and even the 1926 Frigidaire still works. The benefactor's will ensured that anyone could tickle the ivories of the 1906 Steinway grand piano.

The enormous **Otago Museum** (tel. 477 2372), down the hill on Great King and Albany St., takes an in-depth look at the material culture and natural history of Otago, including a full-size Maori war canoe and a room full of Chinese clothing. *(Open M-F 10am-5pm, Sa-Su noon-5pm. Admission free.)* The museum's **Discovery World** has hands-on science exhibits that will enthrall children. *(Same hours. Admission $6, M-F students $4, children $3.)* Less extensive but more eclectic, the **Otago Settlers Museum,** 31 Queens Garden (tel. 477 5052), down Dowling St., is worth a look. You can ride an old pennyfarthing (turn-of-the-century bicycle) in the Art Deco former bus station or peruse the early portraits in the gallery. *(Open M-F 10am-5pm, Sa-Su 1-5pm. Admission $4, students and YHA/VIP members $3.)*

The **Dunedin Public Art Gallery** (tel. 477 4000), in The Octagon, has a surprising Renaissance collection with several good pre-Raphaelite works, along with modern New Zealand exhibitions. The spare foyer in The Octagon is impressive in itself, with the iron spiral staircase of the original building hanging two stories down. *(Open M-F 10am-5pm, Sa-Su 11am-5pm. Admission $4, children $2, residents free.)* Established in 1863,

OTAGO & SOUTHLAND

On A First Name Basis

Beer, a staple of the New Zealand diet, is a matter of pride for most Kiwis. The most popular drinks are Steinlager, DB Draught, and Export Gold (as well as the inevitable Guinness). Tui is also a good choice. It also pays to know that the big breweries generally have nicknames. A Steinlager is a Steiny, for example, and a Canterbury Draft is simply a CD. Be on the lookout for local brews and micro-brews; Mac's West Coast beers are exceptional and widely available. Just don't be surprised if the classics go by unfamiliar names.

Double: to Brits and Americans, a standard shot; always ask for one (often its just assumed that's what you want).

7oz. A denomination to avoid, unless the bartender is your best friend. 7oz. in a glorified shot glass.

12oz. Commonly called a "thirteen," nearly 13oz. of frosty brew in a tapering glass. A bar standard.

Handle Also called a pint, though it's not quite 16oz. For the thirsty.

Jug The American "pitcher," about 2½pt.

Schooner A rare promotional monster in a 1½L glass. Jump at the opportunity.

Dunedin's **Botanic Gardens** are perhaps the best in the country. The **Rhododendron Festival** in the third week of October is world-renowned in botanic circles, as is the large aviary with several native birds, including the kea. Take any city bus from The Octagon down George St. ($1.10).

You'll truly empathize with beer after experiencing the mashing, fermentation, and barreling processes at **Speights Brewery** (tel. 477 9480). Take Princes St., then turn right on Rattray St. and you can't miss the protruding barrel. Form your own impressions of the free samples of the "Pride of the South." *(Bookings required; tours M-Th 10:30am. $5, under 15 free.)* For teetotalers, Speights provides well water through a tap on the side of the building. Stand in line with the locals to fill up your water bottle. *(Open M-F 6am-6pm. Free.)* **Wilson's Whiskey Distillery,** on Willowbank St. off Great King St., is the only whiskey distillery in the country, featuring ancient copper four-story stills. *(Tours run M-F at 2:45pm in the summer. Admission $5, under 12 free.)*

If you're tired of being on your feet, take the **Taieri Gorge Railway** (tel. 477 4449) from the train station through the hinterlands of Dunedin's pioneer history. *(Departs Sept.-Apr. 2:30pm, May–Aug. 12:30pm. Tickets $49, students $39.)* Inaccessible to cars, the railway winds precariously through tunnels and over viaducts. The journey to Pukerangi on the tablelands of Otago passes over spectacular gorges and through native forests and sheep stations with commentary about the track's difficult construction.

Tunnel Beach is among the best of local walks: take the Corstophine bus from The Octagon to Stenhope Crescent, then walk down Blackhead Rd. Hike through a century-old tunnel onto a cliff-backed beach with sea caves carved into the walls. *(1hr. round-trip; closed Sept.-Oct.)* **Mt. Cargill** is a 4km track (3½hr. round-trip) through a former tree planting scheme; you'll be rewarded with a panoramic view of the harbor. Another hour's tramp will take you to the volcanic spires of the **Organ Pipes.** Take the Normanby bus to the start of Norwood St.; walk up to Bethunes Gully. If you have a car at your disposal, admire the stars above and the twinkling lights of the city below from **Signal Hill.** You can re-enact *Ben-Hur* with some excellent **horseback riding,** especially to the north on the beaches at Karitane. **Trojan Riding** (465 7013) offers half-day ($35), full-day ($75) and twilight ($25) treks at 434 Coast Rd. (pickup available for groups of 4 and over). Ben-Hur never went rafting on the Taieri, but you can: **Taieri River Trips** (489 6167) will take you on Grade 3 water for 4-6 hours. *($60, students $50, children $39.)*

■ Near Dunedin: Otago Peninsula

Serene Otago Peninsula is as popular an attraction for its penguin and albatross colonies as Dunedin is for its museums and pubs. Stretching nearly 20km from the city, the peninsula offers incomparable ecological opportunities. Yellow-eyed penguins, fur seals, and royal albatrosses lay claim to the peninsula's many weather-worn inlets, beaches, and promontories. Dramatic **Taiaroa Head,** a veritable avian Eden, drops off onto seal-encrusted crags and great swaths of billowing kelp, and the beach views from many of Otago Peninsula's bluffs are enough to inspire, if not endow, flight.

The best way to experience the peninsula is to rent or share a car. **Portobello Road,** the sinuous coastal route along the bay, is full of treacherous curves; aggressive drivers often end up like the seals, belly-up on a bed of seaweed. **Back to Nature Tours** (tel. 477 0484) does in-depth walking wildlife excursions (5hr., 2pm daily, $43, pickup from accommodations). Inquire about rentals and bookings at the visitors center. **Newton Tours** (tel. 477 5577) offers an array of packages ($35-90) out to the sights, as do many other carriers in the summer. Many buses and shuttles only run services around the peninsula in the summer. The **telephone code** is **03.**

Homestays are one possibility to aid exploration of the Otago Peninsula. Most run about $50 per night per person; the visitors center will provide brochures, recommendations, and bookings. If you're up to feeling like equine royalty, spend the night at the **Larnach Stables** (tel. 476 1616), at Larnach Castle, in stables that have been converted to a backpackers. Comfortable beds under the floating eaves are a true novelty and allow you to explore the grounds as if they were your own. (Doubles $55 for 1 or 2, extra person $17.50, children $12.50. Continental breakfast $10. No kitchen.) **Penguin Palace** (tel. 478 0286), right next to the Yellow-eyed Penguin Reserve, has sparsely furnished rooms with terrific views of the bay. ($15 per person. Linen $5. Free laundry. Book ahead.). **Portobello Village Tourist Park** (tel./fax 478 0359) in Portobello is a verdant place on 50 acres, featuring pink and purple bathrooms and a full-sized trampoline. (Bunk rooms and on-site caravans are $30 for 2, extra person $5; tent sites $8.50, powered sites $9.50. Linen $4.)

Otago Peninsula's best sights begin where it ends, and one easy way to do it all is to book activities in advance at the visitors center. At the **Taiaroa Royal Albatross Colony** (tel. 478 0499) you'll learn that these massive birds, immortalized by Coleridge, are not merely seagulls with pituitary problems. Taiaroa is unique as the only mainland colony on earth; these majestic wanderers fledge and rear their young here, then circumnavigate the globe without visiting land until they return. Entrance to the **Albatross Centre** (which houses extensive displays and live TV coverage of the birds' activities) is free, but the educational tour and observatory distance viewing is a rather steep $22 (children $7.50). For the chance to look down the 5m barrel of a 1886 breach loaded gun, you can combine the albatross tour with a visit to a fort established to ward off attacks from Tsarist Russia (combined ticket $27, children $11). **Monarch Wildlife Cruises** (tel. 477 4276) runs a jolly skiff from Wellers Rock near the head, 45 minutes from Dunedin ($22.50, children $12; 2 tours per day). Their tours are the best way to view the massive chimney roosts and rare species of cormorants coexisting there.

Not being able to fly is no albatross to the rare yellow-eyed penguins (*hoiho*) that have, with a little human assistance, recolonized Penguin Beach just beyond Tairoa Head. Speed through a maniacal camouflaged trench system at the **Yellow-eyed Penguin Conservation Reserve** (tel. 478 0286), some 50 minutes from Dunedin and two minutes from the Albatross Centre, to view these sleek divers from just a few meters away while they preen, yelp, and mate. Not priding themselves on privacy, they're more faithful than humans, though their monogamous devotion only goes so far (see below). Their mating habits are like a soap opera, and the penguins are even named to help you follow the drama. (Tours run every 30min. on the quarter hr.; Oct.-Apr. all day; May-Sept. 3pm until dark. $23, children $12, book ahead in summer.) Those with slim wallets and big binoculars may appreciate penguin viewing at **Southlight Beach** (tel. 478 0287), a few minutes down the road (adults $7.50, family pass $15, best in late afternoon). For hard-core enthusiasts, **Twilight Tour** leaves from Dunedin and does a six- to seven-hour tour of the seal, shag, and penguin reserves ($49, backpackers $43, children $38; albatross colony tours extra). To get up close and personal with Otago's rocky coastline, try **sea kayaking** (tel. 478 0820) from **Wellers Rock** ($10 per hr., $25 half-day, $35 full-day; no solo unguided trips; guide free for groups of 2 or more).

For the historically inclined, **Larnach Castle** (tel. 476 1574) is a 43-room architectural marvel, halfway down the peninsula and 3km up the winding Castlewood Road (admission $10, children $3.50). The aptly named **High Cliff Road** offers an alternate route with spectacular views of the south side of the peninsula. Indefatigable Mr. Larnach had six children by his first wife alone. Continuing on this prolific strain, he eventually married his third wife in his mid-50s (she was 17). When she ran off with his second son, however, he committed suicide in the Parliament building in Wellington. Take a self-guided tour through the inlaid mahogany, teak, and kauri foyer up the only hanging Georgian staircase in the Southern hemisphere. A sympathetic moment should be paid to the 12 men it took to carry the one-tonne marble Herculean bath to the third floor. The view of Dunedin and the entire peninsula from the battlements is incomparable. The Cheshire cat from *Alice in Wonderland* (in the form of a stone carving) is secreted among the lush 35-acre formal grounds on the purportedly haunted estate (garden access $5, children $1). Take the Otago Road Services city bus from Stand 5 outside New World on Cumberland St. to the Company Bay Stop ($2.50) and consider walking up the hill; or catch the noon tour from the visitosr center ($30, children $15). A mode of transport more befitting a stately visit, **Castle Discovery Horse Treks** (tel. 478 0592) embark on a three-hour trip to Larnach Castle daily at 9:30am and 1:15pm (based in Broad Bay; adults $35, ages 14-17 $27.50, under 14 $20.50; castle entrance fee included).

Penguins of Puzzling Persuasions

Once decimated by egg- and chick-eating ferrets, feral cats, and other introduced exotics, as well as by extensive clearing of native coastal habitat, numbers of yellow-eyed penguins (*hoiho*) are increasing today though it's hard to know where to assign the credit. Pairs often remain monogamous, but infidelity is common, and it seems that some of the waddling wonders may actually be bisexual—a Ben occasionally paddles away with a Sven as eagerly as he might with a Monica. Of course, distinguishing the sexes in these, the world's rarest penguins, is a bit difficult as neither leaves anything hanging out as a clue. Researchers originally thought that the male stayed on top during coupling, but who's to really say? Perhaps the penguins have as tough a time telling as we do. Maybe it's just free love. But if any love is good love for these feathery bundles of boundless libido, they may have a tougher time "getting their numbers up." Either way, you can watch the unabashed avians in action when they mate in the spring.

■ Oamaru

As pacific as its ocean, Oamaru has long been known for its limestone facades and Antarctic waterfowl. Soft whitestone was the favored building material and defining characteristic of many of the now-preserved town offices and commercial buildings of the historic harbor district. Endangered yellow-eyed penguins and blue penguins, Oamaru's second trademark, have long sought refuge from the deep Pacific on Oamaru's rocky coast. The penguins used to frighten horses into pulling U-turns on the main street; today they are more adept at attracting tourists than at inspiring equine terror. Add a splash of local color, a precipitous gravel coastal track, and the nearby boulders at Moeraki to the mix, and you'll find Oamaru a convenient and pleasant stop along the Otago coast.

ORIENTATION AND PRACTICAL INFORMATION A block up from the train station, **Thames Street** is Oamaru's very own Champs-Elysées. Although the main street is so long that it may look like a bowling alley for some celestial deity, the sights are thankfully concentrated at its southern end. Walk up one block from the train station, turn left onto Thames St., and walk 10 minutes to the **Visitor Information Centre**, 1 Thames St. (tel. 434 1656; fax 434 1657), the source of DOC info as well (open M-F 9am-5pm, Sa-Su 10am-4pm). Continue left into the historic district to get to the **pen-**

guin colony on the bluff. **TranzScenic** leaves daily from the station by the water on Humber St. for Christchurch (3hr., 2:10pm, $51) and Invercargill (6hr., 11:30am, $75) via Dunedin (3hr., $28). Buses leave from the station at Eden and Thames St. (tel. 434 8716). **InterCity** heads to Christchurch (4½hr., 3-4 per day, $37) and to Dunedin (2¼hr., 3-4 per day, $19). The **Oamaru Mini-Shuttle** (tel. 439 4765) leaves for Dunedin (M-F 7:50am, $20, door-to-door service). The **Atomic Shuttle** goes to Christchurch for $20. **Hitchhikers** report heading up Severn St. to the edge of town to catch a lift south. The upper end of Thames St. is reportedly the best place for a ride, but it's a hard walk with a backpack. In an **emergency**, dial 111. The **police** (tel. 434 5198) are located off Severn St. past the **post office** (tel./fax 434 7884), which is at Severn and Thames St. (post office open M-F 9am-5pm). Change money at the **BNZ** (tel. 434 8610) at 153 Thames St. (open M-F 9am-4:30pm). The **telephone code** is **03.**

ACCOMMODATIONS Small, recently renovated, and with the look of an American Wild West hotel, **Swaggers Backpackers,** 25 Wansbeck St. (tel. 434 9999) offers wheelchair-accessible accommodations with a distinctive character. Don't be fooled by the peeling paint outside—the generously furnished rooms retain the warmth of this 80-year-old home. Stay with the polka-dotted orange snake and stuffed penguin in the Gypsy Lee Shack for a sunrise view over the ocean. (Dorms $15; twins $17; cash only; reservations ideal in summer. Reception open 8-10:30am and 5:30-10pm; self-check chalkboard during the day.) The **Red Kettle Hostel (YHA)** (tel. 434 5008), distinguished by, yep, a red kettle on the corner of Cross and Reed St., is a sparse, spotless, seasonal hostel with a large common area. Even the resident cat recycles, keeping it "clean and green." (2 single-sex dorms and a co-ed dorm $14, non-YHA $16; double or twin $32, non-YHA $36. Reception open daily 8-10am and 5:30-10pm. Open Oct. 1- May 31.) Up Chelmer St., the **Oamaru Gardens Holiday Park** (tel. 434 7666) has an ideal location with a bridge to the botanic gardens next door. It's great for tent sites, but the cabins are a bit sparse. You can expect a concrete block-style kitchen, toilets, and showers. (Tent sites $9 per person. Cabins $28-50. Linen $3 per bed. Reception open 8am-10pm in summer, 8am-8pm in winter.)

FOOD Those determined to find culinary delight should be able to find a small treasure here and there. **Emma's Cafe** (tel. 434 1165) and its next-door neighbor **Bridge Cafe** (tel. 434 8827) share lunch-time crowds. Emma's filled rolls ($3) will leave you as content as the small green frog residing between the cases of pastries. (Open Tu-F 9am-6pm, Sa 9am-4pm, Su 10am-4pm.) Named after the Thames St. Bridge that once spanned Oamaru Creek, the Bridge Cafe offers up rollicking cheese puffs and muffins ($1.30; open M-Th 7am-5:30pm, F 7am-6pm, Sa 7am-2pm). If you're on the hunt for a pianola (hint: it's not edible), or if you just want a giant banana split ($7), stop by the **Star and Garter** (tel. 434 5246) across Itchen St. from the visitors center. Soup ($4) could be a meal on its own, and main courses run $15-23. A block down Thames St. from the visitors center, **Annie Flannagan's** (tel. 434 8828), a traditional Irish bar, serves up typical bar food (a lunchtime roast is $6) from noon to 2pm and 5:30 to 9pm. Check out live music—mostly Irish, rock, and blues on Friday and Saturday nights. Pints are $3.40, but try one of Annie's intricate cocktails ($5.50) for a more outrageous experience. (Open M-Th 11:30am-10pm, F-Sa 11:30-12:30am, Su noon-10pm.) The **T-Bar** in the Brydone Hotel (tel. 434 9892), at Thames and Wear St., has artistic pizzas with tandoori chicken and yogurt ($14.50), along with an impressive bar selection (shooters 6 for $18; pints $3; open daily from 11am; food served until 10pm). **Woolworths,** across from the BNZ, fills all your grocery needs.

SIGHTS Oamaru's attractions center around its penguins, but there's more than enough to fill a day here. The Historic Precinct surrounds Harbour and Tyne St. Some renovation has begun, but the many derelict whitestone buildings conjure an image of the old frenzied shipping port in the long-gone days when brothels outnumbered the pubs. Now the area boasts upscale antique shops and a small arts collection. Take the **historic tour** from the visitors center for a look inside some of the imposing structures. (*$5, students $3, under 17 free.*) Charming and well kept, the **North Otago**

A Bit of Boulder Bumblery

Prehistoric plesiosaurus droppings? Burgeoning sea creatures frozen in time and waiting for re-awakening? The lost marbles of some now insane colossus? Whatever they are, the Moeraki Boulders have always invited and inspired imagination and creative invention. Maori legend explains that the boulders (*Te Kai Hinaki*) are the food baskets and water gourds from the wreck of the *Arai-te-uru* canoe that broke apart 1000 years ago. Early European sea-goers nicknamed them the Ninepins, as though Hamden Beach were an ancient lawn bowling green and the boulders a forgotten game. One of the more creative tongue-in-cheek theories held that the boulders were plastic creations added to the beach in the 1950s by the local tourist board.

Museum and the **Forester Gallery** make worthwhile rainy day activities. *(Museum open M-F 1-4:30pm. Gallery open M-F 10:30am-4:30pm, Sa 10:30am-1pm, Su 1-4:30pm.)* The **Oamaru Gardens** on Severn St. feature secret clearings, feisty ducks, a redolent greenhouse, and a new Chinese water garden with a full-size mountable elephant.

Take the cliffside **Graves Walkway** as it winds steeply above a tiny sand beach, up through a rare patch of coastal shrubland to a spectacular lookout. On the shore below the lighthouse look at low tide for the 40 million-year-old "pillow lava." Continue on for a half-hour to Bushy Beach to see the rare yellow-eyed penguins (*hoiho*). Only 400 breeding pairs remain on the mainland (they are also found at Katiki Point near Palmerston, and near Dunedin and Balclutha). Heading out at dawn to fish and returning at dusk every day, they can sometimes swim up to 40km in a day. To find the **Oamaru Blue Penguin Colony** (tel. 434 1718), head south to Waterfront Rd. along the water; come at dusk to watch the timid waddling lilliputians come into shore. *(Viewing $8, students $6, under age 15 free.)* Flash cameras are not permitted, and you may want to bring warm clothes and a pair of binoculars. Seals and seabirds can also be spotted near Oamaru.

■ Near Oamaru: Moeraki Boulders

The small hamlet of **Moeraki** and the nearby 60-million-year-old **Moeraki Boulders** lie some 40km south of Oamaru. Like gargantuan stone turtles, the Moeraki Boulders remain patiently half-buried, unyielding to the battering sea. Early European arrivals snatched up the smaller boulders for themselves; only one- to two-meter high giants remain. Scientifically known as **septarian concretions,** the 50-odd stones started out as little bits of animal or plant matter on which successive layers of calcite grew, forming the 4-ton boulders in much the way a pearl develops. While the Moeraki Boulders are not the only such concretions, they are the largest, most spherical, and most densely concentrated in the world. The boulders, the largest of which took four million years to develop, are best viewed at low tide.

Moeraki is a sleepy fishing village just south of the boulders. It is most easily accessible by car; Oamaru mini-coaches and InterCity buses will take you near Moeraki, but they leave you with a 2km walk to get to town. **Natures Shuttle** (tel. 434 7027) runs both evening trips to the boulders (2½hr., departs from Oamaru, $15) and daytime boulder and wildlife excursions (4-5hr., leaves from Oamaru at 11am, $35). Consider a stay at **Lighthouse Backpackers** (tel. 439 4834 or (025) 376 729), which has basic dorms ($15), a kitchen, and a hot tub just a short walk from rare yellow-eyed penguins, seals, and other wildlife. Call and the owner will pick you up from Moeraki, Oamaru, or even Dunedin. Nearby, take a five-minute walk on the trail at the **Moeraki Esplanade Reserve** to a wide, secluded swath of beach. If you're driving, follow signs to the lighthouse for a true piece of the rugged, untouched (except by the sheep) Waitaki region. Look all you want, but don't disturb the penguins and fur seals that inhabit the small reserve on the point.

THE CATLINS

An oasis of untouched beaches, rugged promontories, and ancient forests amid a desert of sheep paddocks, the region of the Catlins lives up to its glorious reputation as the best kept secret in New Zealand. Cliffs dotted with native bush drop into swirling Antarctic waters while rare penguins waddle awkwardly across white sand beaches. With a bit of exploring, you can discover a private inlet shared only with your fellow sea lions. Its remoteness tempered by cordial coastal villages, there are few places in New Zealand where civilization can be so close and yet seem so distant.

The **Southern Scenic Route (SH92),** runs 172km over pavement and gravel through the Catlins from Balclutha to Invercargill. A car or mountain bike (and strong lungs) is the best way to appreciate the coast at your own pace, although several tours run through the area. **Kiwi Experience's Bottom Bus** (tel. 442 9708) departs from Dunedin on a 10-hour backpacker-oriented tour. Unfortunately, with ever-changing tides, it's rare to make it by bus at the right time to **Cathedral Caves** (see p. 346; the bus runs daily in summer time; M, W, F in winter; departs at 7:30am; $75; free pickup). **Catlins Coastal Link** (tel. 474 3300) runs similar trips from Invercargill to Dunedin (Tu, Th, Sa, Su; 8am; $75). As the name suggests, **Catlins Flexi Tours** (tel. (0800) 353 941) gives you more input into your itinerary ($85 between Dunedin and Invercargill). More comprehensive overnight tours are available through Catlins **Wildlife Trackers** (tel. 415 8613), which runs from Balclutha ($200; M, Th, and Sa, 10:30am; reservation required). **Hitchhiking** through the Catlins is said to be feasible in summer, but is an unlikely prospect in winter. There are **no banks** between Balclutha and Invercargill, so be sure you have enough cash when you set out. The nearest northern access point for the Catlins is **Balclutha,** where SH1 bends north to Dunedin or west to Invercargill. The Catlins abound with secluded camping sites; it has excellent, albeit limited, accommodations options (booking ahead is vital during the summer). With so many hidden waterfalls, inlets, beaches, and mystical tracts of forest, budget at least twice as much time as you think you'll need in New Zealand's forgotten corner—the best part of the Catlins is the freedom to explore it.

OWAKA The major town of the Catlins with a population of 400, Owaka lies only 25km south of Balclutha. The large **visitors center** (tel. 415 8371) at the **Catlins Diner** offers area maps, accommodation listings, and $2 access to the DOC displays (open M-F 6:30am-8:30pm, Sa 8am-8:30pm, Su 9am-8:30pm). **Helen's Dairy** (tel. 415 8304) operates a **post office** (open M-F 6:40am-8:30pm, Sa 8:30am-8:30pm, Su 9am-8:30pm), while **Niles Four Square** (tel. 415 8304) has provisions (open M-Th 8:30am-5:30pm, F 8:30am-7:30pm; Sa 9am-noon in winter, and 9am-5pm in summer). The gas station (tel. 415 8179) is also an **AA service station** (open M-Th 7:30am-6pm, F 7:30am-7pm, Sa 9am-1pm). The local **museum** is there for a rainy day ($1).

Catlins Backpackers (tel. 415 8392), at the diner, has simple bunks and doubles ($14) with home-made curtains and a hot fire in winter. Kitchen, laundry facilities, and TV are available; bikes $20 per day (tent sites $5, reception open whenever the diner is, check-out 10:30am). The huge kitchen and sunny lounge at **Highview Backpackers** (tel. 415 8686) somewhat mitigate the unfinished floors and ripped wallpaper in some of the dorms (dorms $12; double $15; tents $8; caravan $10). **Pounawea Motor Camp** (tel. 415 8483) has up-to-date cabins ($15) and backpackers ($10) by Owaka Lake. Caravan sites ($7) and tent sites ($6) abut a scenic nature reserve (cash only). Boats and canoes are available. For a cold brew by a toasty fire, mosey on into the incongruously modern **Lumberjack Bar and Cafe** (tel. 415 8747). Sally up to the enormous macrocarpa bar (which 10 men had to carry in) and feel like you've hewn Burnham wood with the best of them. A half kilo rump steak is $18; the blackboard menu features entrees for $7 (open W-F from 3pm, Sa-Su from 2pm in winter; open daily from noon during Christmas holidays). Toss back a few cold ones with the old-timers at **Catlins Inn** (tel. 415 8350). An inveterate standby, this pub has happy hours Monday through Friday from 5 to 7pm (open daily from 11am).

KAKA POINT The coastline is rife with fine sand beaches and jutting headlands. Start exploring at Kaka Point, some 12km north of Owaka on a well-marked road off the southern scenic route. The sandy swath at Kaka arcs toward Nugget Point, 8km south down a bumpy gravel road, where you can empathize with the windblown shrubs on a blustery day. The view from the little lighthouse is worth the 10-minute jaunt above the blue-green waters. Fur and elephant seals frolic on the waterlogged crags of what appear to be the bows of great sinking ships stretching toward the horizon. Just past Nugget Point, **Roaring Bay** is home to several yellow-eyed penguins, who can be seen hopping up the cliffs before sunset. A sign for **Tunnel Hill** on the main road leads to a short walk (5min.) through an abandoned railway tunnel. Turn off your flashlight for a spooky experience (the track is quite flat and smooth). Clamber up the path through lush native bush to reach tiny **Fernlea Backpackers** (tel. 412 8834). Overlooking Molyneaux Bay, the lounge and the double room share fabulous views. (Bunks $15; doubles $30. Linen $2. Cash only.) Relish the two simple cabins at **Kaka Point Camping Ground** (tel. 412 8800), although you'll miss the ocean views (singles $14; doubles $25; extra person $8). Caravan sites are $10 and tent sites are $8 ($11 for 2; cash only).

CANNIBAL BAY **Seals** and **sea lions** congregate on the expanse of beach at Cannibal Bay; in winter, clamber over the dunes to **Surat Bay** to see the animals. Human bones were once discovered here, but it's more likely that the unlucky chap was killed in a Maori battle than eaten by cannibals. The road continues back toward Owaka, where you can continue down the coast or up the Owaka Valley through unfelled forests along the **Catlins River gorge.** Get a ride to the top of the **Catlins River Track**, a rare and well-maintained tramp through unspoiled beech forest and over three soaring suspension bridges (5hr. one-way). When the trout are biting, this is where to catch them. The **DOC campsite** at the top of the track has no facilities; the **Tawanui campsite** ($4 per person) at the base has bathrooms. For a less strenuous escapade, follow the road to **Ratanui** (5km south of Owaka) and the signs to **Jack's Blowhole.** More aptly named a slurp hole, the deep depression is connected by caves to the ocean 200m away (walk the easy 30min. paddock track to reach it).

PURAKAUNUI BAY AND FALLS Local beach cows munch kelp on the sand of **Purakaunui Bay** (a surfing beach for the brave-hearted). The mist from crashing waves lends a magical effervescence to the view down the coast at the popular **DOC campsite** ($4; has bathrooms). To reach it, take the rough road south of Ratanui. A few km farther south on the scenic route is the turnoff to **Purakaunui Falls** (follow the signs toward Maclennan). The walk beneath the soaring canopy of ancient trees on the way to the falls is as spectacular as the multi-tiered cascades themselves (which are best appreciated in heavy rain; it's only 10min. from the car park). A little luxury is available at **Greenwood Farmstay** (tel. 415 8259), a warm, sophisticated B&B with meticulously gardened grounds. A massive deer head beneath the burnished wood ceiling gives the place the feel of a hunting lodge. (Singles $45; queen with day room and a suite $60. Dinner $25. Cash only).

PAPATOWAI Gigantic bull kelp litters the beach and estuary here, which flows among dune forest into the frigid waters. The **Papatowai Trading Post** (tel. 415 8147) has gas and groceries. (In summer open daily 8:30am-8pm; in winter Su-Th 9am-6pm, F-Sa 9am-6:30pm.) The amazing **Hilltop Backpackers** (tel. 415 8028), 1km above the bay, is the be-all and end-all of backpackers and a true budget paradise. The Oriental rugs, Russian water kettle, glowing wood stove, lavish modern kitchen, and bathrooms with tub all invoke instant relaxation. Canoes, boogie boards, and wetsuits are available for free. Bunks are $20, or get the double ($25) for an incomparable beach view and thick bed covers (cash only). The **Papatowai Motor Park** (tel. 415 8500; fax 415 8503), behind the trading post, has adequate dorms ($12), doubles ($15), caravan sites ($7), and tent sites ($6). (Cash only.)

Don't miss the **Cathedral Caves** turn-off, 16km from Tautuku. Unequivocally the highlight of the Catlins, the sand-tongued gaping maw of the sea-hewn caverns make

Chartres look like a local monument. The caves are only accessible at low tide; check a tide table before making the half-hour trek down under dripping tree ferns and tortured kamahi trees to **Waipati Beach** and the caves. South of Papatowai, the gravel road winds to **Florence Lookout** and its spectacular view of perfectly curving **Tautuku Beach.** Backed by the olive and rusty hues of the native forest, Tautuku may be the best of the Catlins's remarkable beaches. Turn off for **Lake Wilkie** and its 20-minute boardwalk a bit farther down the hill. A few km back towards Owaka is the marked turnoff for Catlins's **Woodstock,** a festival held in the middle of January.

PORPOISE BAY Continue on to **Invercargill** via **Tokanui** on the main road, or turn back onto gravel toward **Waikawa** some 20km beyond the Cathedral Caves. **Curio Bay Campground,** a long, sheltered stretch of sand home to a few stout-hearted swimmers, has somewhat exposed tent sites ($6 for 2; extra person $1), powered sites ($10 for 2), and non-powered sites ($7.50 for 2). The **Dolphin Information Centre** in Waikawa (tel. 246 8444) has displays on the mammals that inhabit the bay (open daily Oct.-Apr.). **Koramika Charters** runs a unique Hector's dolphin tour (the smallest and rarest in the world), from Porpoise Bay between October and April. (4 tours per day; $45-65; reserve at the Dolphin Centre.)

Just beyond the beach lies **Curio Bay,** undoubtedly named for the 180-million-year-old **petrified forest** visible on the rocky coast at low tide. Among pools of bead-like seaweed and unhinged bull kelp are the mineralized trunks of several tall trees; more interesting are the umber bumps of former stumps in which you can still count the rings of ancient species. Massive surf and white breakers smash against the tidal outcrops. Continuing from Porpoise Bay toward **Haldane** (the road occasionally floods at peak tide along the estuary), you'll pass the road leading to a sheep farm and hostel known as **Pope's Place** (tel. 246 8420). The **email access** in the simply furnished kitchen and common room seems anachronistic, but it's quite real ($1.50 first email, 50¢ each subsequent). Deeply cushioned beds are $14 (doubles $30) in a house surrounded by flax plants. There's even a jacuzzi next door ($5 per 30min.). The toilets are a short walk from the dorms. Across from the Dolphin Centre, **Waikawa Lodge** (tel. 246 8552) boasts spare, immaculate rooms with metal frame bunks (dorms $15; twins $17). **Waipapa Point,** 20km from Pope's Place on the way past **Otara** toward **Invercargill,** is worth a stop (if only to be thrown down by the battering southern wind at the foot of the lonely lighthouse). If the apocalypse came while you were here, you'd already be at the end of the world.

SOUTHLAND

■ Invercargill

Flat and uneventful, Invercargill remains little more than a transfer point to Stewart Island or onto Fiordland, unless sheep are your chosen idol. Dated cafes, trinket stores, and car service centers line the main streets of town, which become quite deserted after dinnertime. Despite its population of 53,000, Invercargill retains a small-town feel. Linger longer than a day and you'll likely end up at the movie theater for lack of better in-town options.

ORIENTATION AND PRACTICAL INFORMATION From the train and bus station, cross **Leven Street** and pass under the **clock tower. Dee Street,** Invercargill's diesel-fumed main thoroughfare, runs to the right toward Bluff and the Catlins, and to the left toward Queens Park and Queenstown. North of the city, it becomes **North Road.** Across from the clock tower, **Esk Street** is the main shopping thoroughfare. SH1 from Dunedin cuts through the city via **Tay Street** and ends up on Dee St. The length of blocks in Invercargill is enormous; it will take you twice as long as you may think to get from one place to another on foot.

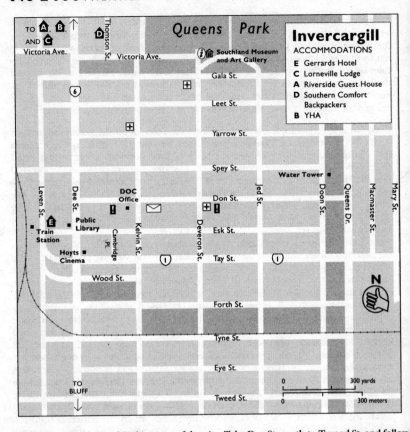

The **airport** is located 2½km west of the city. Take Dee St. south to Tweed St. and follow the signs. **Air New Zealand** and **Ansett New Zealand** fly frequently to Auckland ($483, thrifty fare $339) and Christchurch ($254, thrifty fare $179). Get picked up by **Spitfire Shuttle** (tel. 214 1851) for $5 (extra person $3); a taxi to the airport costs $8. Trains cruise in and out of the station on Leven St. behind the clock tower (tel. 214 0599). **TranzScenic** goes daily to Christchurch (9hr., 8:25am, $117) via Dunedin (3hr., $51). **InterCity** buses (tel. 214 0599) leave from the train station daily for Christchurch (9hr., 9am, $85). **Inter City** and **Catch-a-Bus** (tel. 218 9000 or 217 4040) head to Dunedin (3hr., 1 per day, $35-40). **Spitfire Shuttle** (tel. 214 1851) runs to Te Anau (2½-3hr., 1pm, $30). **Catch-a-Bus** and **Southern Air Land Travel** head daily to Queenstown (2hr., 1 per day, $35). Call for bookings and pickup. **City Buses** (tel. 218 7108) serve the suburbs (departs M-F every hr., $1.20). Most depart from the library on Dee St. or across the street; the visitors center has schedules. **Blue Star** (tel. 218 6079) and **Taxi Co.** (tel. 214 4478) are 24hr. taxis. Among other smaller operations, **Pegasus,** 18 Teviot St. (24hr. tel. (0800) 803 580 or 214 3210) has cheap rental cars from $35 per day, plus negotiable long-term rates. Mountain bikes are available from **Wensley's Cycle Centre,** 53 Tay St. (tel. 218 6206). **Hitchhikers** heading toward Queenstown are said to take the Waikiwi bus from the library up North Rd. as far as possible and then walk to the city limits. For Dunedin, hitchhikers take the Hawthornedale bus (departing from 14 Tay St.) as far as it goes.

The **Invercargill Information Centre** (tel. 214 6243) is on Gala St. inside the massive white pyramid. Go left up Dee St., then take a right at McDonald's onto Gala St. (Open M-F 9am-5pm, Sa-Su 10am-5pm.) Although you won't see a sign, rest assured that the **DOC** is on the 7th floor of the State Insurance building, on Don St. (tel. 214 4589; open M-

8am-5pm). Change money at the **BNZ** (tel. 218 9179) at the corner of Esk and Kelvin St. (Open M-F 9am-4:30pm.) Other banks dot the city center. **Internet access** for $2 per 15 minutes is available at the **public library** (tel. 218 7025) on Dee St. (open M-F 9am-8:30pm, Sa 10am-1pm). In an **emergency, dial 111** or call the **police** (tel. 214 4039). For medical help, try **Urgent Doctor** (tel. 218 8821; available M-F 5-10pm, Sa-Su 8am-10pm). **Urgent Pharmacy** is at 90 Kelvin St. (tel. 218 4893; open M-W 7-10pm, Sa 2-4:30pm and 7-10pm, Su 10am-noon, 2-4:30pm, and 7-10pm). The **Southland Hospital** (tel. 214 5735) is on Kew Rd. The **post office** is at 51 Don St. (tel. 214 7700; open M-F 8:30am-5pm, W 9am-5pm, Sa 10am-1:30pm).

ACCOMMODATIONS Most hostels lie along and beyond Queens Park; the following represent the cream of the crop. To reach the incomparable **Southern Comfort Backpackers,** 30 Thomson St. (tel. 218 3838), from the visitors center, turn right down Victoria Ave., then take a right on Thomson St. An airy blue-white ultra-modern kitchen with a bay window and matching china leads into the dining room, with 4m floral curtains rising to the ornate ceiling of this former villa. This is one of those rare places where you'll probably think you're someone's houseguest. (Dorms $16; doubles $18. Linen $3. Reception until 10pm. Reserve a week ahead in summer. Cash only. Free bikes.) **Gerrards Hotel,** 3 Leven St. (tel. 218 3406; fax 218 3003), is located opposite the train station. In this European-style hotel with a large set of antlers in the foyer, the rooms are simple but attractively decorated with antique oriental greens or understated rose hues. (Singles $25; doubles $50. Flexible prices. Check-out 10am.) **Lorneville Lodge,** Lorne-dacre Rd. (tel. 235 8031), is a sunny caravan park on a small farm 10km from town on SH6 toward Queenstown. (Cabins $15 per person; standard cabin singles $20; doubles $29. On-site caravans $13, extra person $8.50. Tent sites, powered sites $8.50 per person. Linen $3.)

FOOD AND NIGHTLIFE Fast food and cheese rolls dominate Invercargill's eateries (and arteries), with precious few alternatives to deep-fried madness. Most restaurants are scattered about the city center. The **Zookeepers Cafe,** 50 Tay St. (tel. 218 3373), is reminiscent of the singles deck on Noah's Ark. Sip a bottomless coffee ($2.50) amid ferns and palms while animal illustrations peer at you from the walls. A half order of nachos is big enough for a meal (open daily from 10am). **The Cod Pot,** 136 Dee St. (tel. 218 2354), has four booths for in-house fish feeds, Bluff oysters (dozen $11), or $2 fresh breaded blue cod (open M-Th 9am-8:30pm, F-Sa 9am-10pm, Su 10am-9pm). At **Tillerman's Cafe,** 16 Don St. (tel. 218 9240), lunch is an affordable indulgence—the baked potato and salad option is only $6—and the intimate wine bar in back has deep red armchairs and a hot fire for a night away from the elements. The cafe features a wide range of bands upstairs on Friday and Saturday nights. (Open M-F 11:30am-2pm, and 6:30-10pm, Sa-Su 6:30-10pm. Bar open daily from 6:30pm.) The **Pak 'N Save** market is at 95 Tay St. (tel. 214 4864; open M-Tu 9am-7pm, W-F 9am-9pm, Sa 9am-7pm, Su 9am-6pm). Aside from the **Hoyts 5** movie theater, 29 Dee St. (tel. 214 1110), or the bars at **Zookeepers, Lone Star,** or **Tillerman's,** there just ain't much local entertainment here. **Players,** 25 Tay St. (tel. 218 1857), has 20 pool tables ($10 per hr., students $8) and email ($2 per 15min.) in a wide-open room with overhanging table lights (open M-W noon-11pm, Th-Sa noon-1am). The **Frog 'n' Firkin,** 31 Dee St. (tel. 214 4001), has cheap bar food (bread and soup $6) and a livelier crowd (open M-F from 11:30am, Sa from 2pm).

SIGHTS AND ACTIVITIES Invercargill's attractions can be covered in a day. The **Southland Museum and Art Gallery** (tel. 218 9753), at the city end of **Queen's Park,** is conveniently located in the same gleaming white pyramid as the visitors center. *(Open M-F 9am-5pm, Sa-Su 10am-5pm. Museum is free. Slideshow $2, children 50¢; 2-5 shows per day, more on weekends.)* The highlight of it all is the **tuatarium,** a live exhibit of the nocturnal reptiles that once roamed all of New Zealand. Walk through the rata forest into the Roaring 40s gallery upstairs to discover New Zealand's subantarctic islands and the megaherbs that thrive there, supremely adapted to the severe conditions. The dynamic slide show includes strobe lightning and may be as close as you can get to the restricted-access isles. Take a stroll through the formal English rose garden or the veritable forest of rhododendrons near the pyramid. The long lines of closely planted trees are reminiscent of ancient chateau grounds, stretching away out of the dew. On a clear night, view the stars at the **Observatory** next to the visitors center. *(Open W 7pm-9pm. 50¢ admission includes slideshow.)*

■ Near Invercargill: Bluff

Calling itself "the oldest European town in New Zealand, having been settled continuously since 1824," seaside Bluff (Invercargill's peninsular port town) lies at the tip of a long spit of land 27km south of the city. Though fishing and shipping industries dominate the port, it's still worth looking around here en route to Stewart Island. As the departure point for the ferry to Stewart Island (see below), Bluff also marks the beginning (or end) of **SH1.** The frequently photographed signpost at **Stirling Point,** just beyond town, marks the occasion with distances to far-flung cities. Bluff's **visitors center** (tel. 212 8305) is on Gore St., inside **Foveau Souvenirs and Antiques,** where Dawn will answer your queries and match your bluff. (Open daily in summer 9am-5pm, in winter 10am-4pm.) **Trust Bank** (tel. 212 8689) is the only gig in town for currency exchange (open M-Tu and Th-F 9am-4:30pm). The **Campbelltown Passenger Service** (tel. 212 7404) runs to and from Bluff and Invercargill (M-F 5 per day; $6; bookings required), with pickup from near the city center ($1-2). Invercargill's **Spitfire Shuttle** (tel. 214 1851) will run to Bluff ($6.50) to make the ferry to Stewart Island; book the day before for pickup. Provision yourself for the *terra australis* at the Four Square Market (tel. 212 8170; open M-W 8am-6pm, Th-Sa 8am-7pm, Su 9am-6pm). The **post office** (tel. 212 8759) is a few doors down (open M-F 8:45am-5pm, Sa 10am-7pm). In an **emergency,** dial **111.**

Flynn Club's Hotel (tel. 212 8124), on Gore St., gives you that Arthurian feeling, with regal red bedspreads, a medieval court painting, and dark foyer. Head down the long jointed corridor of this historic, 140-year-old building to travel back in time. (Dorms $15, spacious doubles $30. Check-out 10am.) Up Gregory St. you'll find **Bluff Camping Ground** (tel. 212 8774), with two tiny unadorned cabins ($8 per stay; max. one week), caravan sites ($6), and tent sites ($5). Use of the concrete showers and kitchen both cost $2 (honor system payment). Nondescript fish 'n' chips shops dot Gore St., offering artery-clogging versions of their town's namesake oysters.

■ Invercargill to Tuatapere

If you're heading to or from Te Anau and Invercargill (and have a choice about the route), take the **Southern Scenic Route.** While the inland route passes through the service towns of Lumsden and Mossburn, the Southern Scenic Route takes an alternate but equally efficient path, sidling the coast and affording both ocean vistas and mountain panoramas before heading inland and upland to Te Anau. **Kiwi Experience** (tel. 442 9709) runs from Invercargill to Te Anau (daily in summer, M, W, F in winter; overnight in Riverton; departs Invercargill 6pm), while **Spitfire Shuttles** (tel. 214 1851) runs daily in both directions (departs Te Anau 7:45am, departs Invercargill 1pm; $29). **Hitchhiking** along this stretch of the Southern Scenic Route is reportedly a good summer prospect. Dotted with small towns and innumerable bays and inlets, the stretch from Riverton to Tuatapere is a solid slice of small-town Southland.

RIVERTON One of New Zealand's oldest towns, **Riverton** (pop. 1850) is a quiet seaside retreat, its sand flats stretching toward the ocean and high-bowed trawlers bobbing at the pier hearkening back to more carefree days. **Riverton Rocks,** over the bridge and a few kilometers along the coast, is a popular sheltered swimming beach and picnicking area with views toward Invercargill and Stewart Island. Numerous short tracks start at the **Aparima River Road** bridge, leading through native bush to beaches or unusual rock formations such as the precarious balancing rock. The visitors center is located at the marvelous new and modern **Riverton Rock Backpackers** (tel. (0800) 248 886 or 234 8886; fax 234 8816). All the doors upstairs are identical, but eventually you'll find the wood-stove-heated TV lounge with its free tea and coffee (bunks $19, in winter $17; linen $3). Intimately furnished doubles are also available: the deep green and red Fireside Forest double is $78. (Reception open 9am-noon, 4-7pm. **The Riverton Supervalue** across the street and down a bit, is the place for groceries; it also houses the **post office** (both open M-Th 7:45am-6:30pm, F 7:45am-8pm, Sa 9am-4:30pm).

OREPUKI From Riverton, the Southern Scenic Route traverses open country past the Longwood Range and on to Tuatapere. **Colac Bay,** 10km beyond Riverton, is a former Maori settlement and popular surfing beach. **Te Waewae Bay,** which appears suddenly over the hill 15km on, is often battered with the full force of the southern ocean. Through the mist in summer you can sometimes see Hector's dolphins or the occasional right whale spouting off. Look out for windblown macrocarpas (the trees are reminiscent of Medusa on a bad hair day) as you pass through **Orepuki** (pop. 150). Originally situated on Omnekey Island, this gold-mining town was relocated three times to satisfy prospectors. Nearby at Orepuki Beach, you can find tiny, low-grade gemstones amid the grains of sand, though the gold is long gone.

TUATAPERE A little logging town (pop. 700) situated at the base of southern Fiordland halfway between Invercargill and Te Anau, **Tuatapere** (Tua-TAP-pery) smells of freshly cut and burning wood. Though Tuatapere means "the hole in the bush," the only native grove you'll see today is in the town domain—two logging companies employing most of the populace have hewn much of the area's timber. As an attractive and undiscovered base for the many tramps and wilderness activities in the area, only provincial pride could cause the town to seek fame in other quarters (billing itself as New Zealand's "sausage capital"). Tuatapere is also home to the annual **Wild Challenge** (tel. 226 6568), a 35km whitewater canoe, 30km run, and 32km bike race held in early January. If you're only a minor masochist, the **Waiau Grunt** (13km canoe, 8km run, 20km bike) might be more appealing.

Tuatapere's **visitors center** (tel. 226 6399), south of the bridge over the **Waiau River,** shares its space with a craft center and **logging museum** (open in summer daily 9am-5pm; not attended in winter). Get your area **hut passes** at the **DOC office** (tel. 226 6607) down the street. The **Spitfire Shuttle** (tel. 226 6399) runs in the afternoon to Te Anau and in the morning to Invercargill; book ahead for pickup. **Fraser's Pharmacy** (tel. 226 6999), across the way from the DOC office, doubles as the **post office** (open M-Th 9am-5:30pm, F 9am-8pm, Sa 11am-noon). **Dowling's Pricecutter** (tel. 226 6250), around the corner, may have the better selection (open daily 8am-8:30pm), but **Western Foodmarket** (tel. 226 6292), north of the river, is cheaper (open M-Th 7am-7pm, F 7am-8:30pm, Sa 7am-5pm, Su 9am-4pm).

The **Waiau Hotel** (tel. 226 6409), south of the town center, has airy, modern rooms with burgundy carpets and hand basins (in addition to pink bathtubs in some of the rooms). Enjoy a beer from the pub in the spacious TV room (singles $25, with bath $30; doubles $50, with bath $60). More budget-oriented and far less glamorous lodging can be found at **Five Mountains Holiday Park** (tel. 226 6418), north of the bridge. Cookware, a stove, and a sink all come with the small, mustard-curtained rooms, as does free laundry (no dryer). (All beds $15; linen and blanket $5; tent sites $8; powered caravan sites $15. Check-out 10am). Better camping sites can be found down by the river past the Domain, though the cabins there are starkly basic. A few standard restaurants grace Tuatapere's streets.

Several tours and guides operate out of Tuatapere. Some of the most exciting are on the jetboats that fly over **Lake Hauroko** and down the rock-strewn rapids of the **Wairaurahiri River.** The most untamed of the jetboat tour lot, **Wairaurahiri Wilderness Jet** (tel. 225 8174) and **Wairaurahiri Jet** (tel. 225 8318 or 236 1137) both run full-day trips (around $100; book ahead). The visitors center has details on guided walks, helicopter tours, and other services in remote southern Southland.

The **Tuatapere Scenic Reserve** is home to the towering beeches and ancient tuataras that once dominated the region; grab an informative pamphlet from the visitors center and follow signs for the Domain to begin the **Tuatapere Walkway.** Also popular is **mountain biking** along the gravel former logging roads. Rides to Lake Hauroko and down winding Borland Rd. to **Lake Monowai** are most popular. Endpoint for the

---

Paua Power

Of the 144 types of abalone (shellfish) found around the world, the New Zealand paua boasts the most brilliant peacock shades and the greatest variety of shapes, as well as a hefty price tag. On the South Island there is a strict harvest quota of 400 tons; a one-ton permit costs $100,000. Harvested by fishermen who free dive up to 10m to pry the crustaceans from rocks, paua can live up to 100 years and grow up to 220cm in size. Paua meat, at $95 per kilo, is an expensive and acquired taste. Much of New Zealand's catch ends up in Asia among the festivities for Chinese New Year. Should you chance upon an extra $100, the best way to cook fresh paua is to boil it whole before removing the shell. But don't throw out that exoskeleton; New Zealanders decorate just about anything with paua—including chairs, surfboards, and even entire rooms. Like a fingerprint, each shell is unique. Ground, polished, and lacquered paua run $10-20, a small price for a shell that took 20-50 years to create.

---

rugged **Dusky Track,** Tuatapere also serves as a departure point for the spectacular wooden 36m **Percy Burn Viaduct** and the **South Coast Track,** which follows a former logging tramway. The latter requires two nights at Port Craig Hut, a former schoolhouse, to reach the viaducts that were once constructed for timber transport. The track begins 28km from Tuatapere at **Bluecliffs Beach,** at the signposted road on the north side of town. The **Dusky Track** is a rough trail for the experienced only and requires at least a week.

CLIFDEN North of Tuatapere 17km along the road to Te Anau, the hamlet of Clifden is notable for its limestone caves, located 1km up the road after the lime works on the route toward Winton. Prospective spelunkers should pick up a map in Tuatapere and bring a flashlight; the caves are extensive, cramped, and sometimes flooded. Also take a moment to walk the suspension bridge at Clifden, completed in 1902. Downstream, the protruding cliff face is the profile of a legendary Maori maiden thwarted in love who leapt off the precipice. From Clifden, the road heads through the Waiau River valley as the inaccessible Takitimu mountains to the east and the distant heights of Fiordland to the west are occasionally visible over the foothills.

■ Stewart Island

Aptly named Rakiura ("the place of glowing skies") by the Maori, Stewart Island's summer days are finished off by fiery red sunsets that stretch across the horizon. Muddy trails and untracked beaches retain the wild flavor of a land belonging not to humans but to the kiwis, kakas, seals, and penguins that make their home here. Indeed, most of the island, lying 47° below the equator, is without both trails and people. The 350 or so local fisherfolk are mostly concentrated near **Halfmoon Bay,** and their Zen-like attitude is infectious. Despite the temperate climate, the weather is hardly predictable—you're likely to see all four seasons within an hour here, and it often rains more than 200 days per year.

ORIENTATION AND PRACTICAL INFORMATION Bring waterproof gear and solid boots if you plan on spending any time outside on the island. Since there's no bank, having extra cash on hand is essential, as many lodgings don't take credit cards. Food is expensive on the island, and Eftpos is not widespread; your best bet is to visit a supermarket before the 32km crossing. **Oban,** Stewart Island's township, is centered around three streets at **Halfmoon Bay;** services and most of the accommodations lie here, and the remainder are scattered on the surrounding hills and inlets.

The **visitors center** (tel. 219 1218) is on Main Rd. in the same office as the **DOC** office (tel. 219 1130; both open Dec. 26-Mar. 31 M-F 8am-7pm, Sa-Su 9am-7pm; Apr. 1-Dec. 24 M-F 8am-5pm, Sa-Su 10am-noon). Head here to book accommodations. Pick up a town map or track info, or watch a range of free nature videos in the display area on a rainy day (small lockers $2.50, large $5). You can change New Zealand travelers' checks at **Southern Air** (tel. 219 1090) on Elgin Terr. (see post office, below), but there are **no banks or ATMs.** Southern Air (tel. 218 9129 or (0800) 658 876) flies in a cozy nine-seat prop plane to and from Invercargill (3 per day, $65 one-way; YHA/ student stand-by $40, round-trip $75; sign-up 1st thing in the morning) and runs a free airport shuttle to Halfmoon Bay. A 15kg luggage limit applies for full flights. From Invercargill, there is standard stand-by to Dunedin (M-F 2 per day, $45 one-way). Once on the mainland, **Spitfire Shuttle** (tel. 214 1851) runs to Invercargill (2 per day, $5, extra person $3; call ahead).

The **Foveaux Express** (tel. 212 7660) runs a catamaran (1hr., 2 per day, $37 one-way) to and from Bluff and Halfmoon Bay, though the trip is not for those with sensitive stomachs. Reservations are suggested. Alternatively, the record for swimming the Strait is 9 hours and 41 minutes (don't even think about it). **Oban Taxis** (tel. 219 1456) runs daily 7am to 7pm, and also rents **mopeds,** as does Stewart Island Travel (tel. 219 1269; $16 per hr., $45 per half-day; driver's license required).

In an **emergency,** dial **111.** The **police** (tel. 219 1020) are on Golden Bay Rd. The **district nurse** (tel. 219 1098), can be found on Argyle St. You can find a **post office** at Southern Air (tel. 219 1090), on Elgin Terr. (Open in summer M-F 7:30am-6pm, Sa-Su 9:30am-5pm; in winter M-F 8:30am-5pm, Sa-Su 9:30am-5pm.)

ACCOMMODATIONS AND FOOD The island's range of rustic accommodations is impressive, though many hostels work on a first-come basis. The visitors center has a complete accommodations listing with photos; they'll help you find your niche. Reserve well in advance in summer. **Jo and Andy's B&B** (tel./fax 219 1230), on Main Rd., is a tiny homestay with a warm, dimly lit family room loaded with bookshelves and plastered with world maps. (Rooms $16 per person. Linen $3. Check-out 10:30am. Mountain bikes $10 per day. Email $2.50 per 15min.) Near the wharf and down the hill over Mill Creek lies the rambling old house of **Ann's Place** (tel. 219 1065), up Horseshoe Bay Rd. The uneven floors accent the "no frills" accommodation, though the bellbirds and tui that flock to the fuchsia grove behind the house in summer are enchanting. (Beds $10. Cash only. Kitchen available. No linen, but blankets are free.) **The View** (tel. 219 1328), up steep Nichol Rd. past the Southern Air office, is a three-level affair. The modern open lodge has fantastic harbor views, a huge deck, an organ, and a pool table. Rooms are decidedly pink. (Doubles $20; cash only. Linen $5.) Private, motel-style accommodation surrounded by moss and ferns can be found at **Shearwater Inn** (tel. 219 1114), on Ayr St. with a big TV lounge and a new outdoor barbecue for muttonbird roasts. (Dorms $14; backpacker doubles $30; singles $36; doubles or twins $60. Reception open summer 8am-7pm; winter M-Sa 7:30am-7pm, Sa-Su 9am-7pm. Check-out 10am.) **The Ferndale Campsite** (tel. 219 1176), on Horseshoe Bay Rd. has $2 showers and grassy tent sites for $5 with new pine bathrooms. Newly manicured grounds have terrific views of the bay. Just across from the wharf, also on Horseshoe Bay Rd., **Dave's Place** is airy and has a large sunny lounge with a superb view of the bay. Watch the birds that flock to the feeder on the deck, or head inside and enjoy a rare massage shower. (Dorms $15, no linen.)

Muttonbird Steaks

Named for its fragrant and intensely gamey flavor, **muttonbird** (*titi*) is a delicacy enjoyed both on Stewart Island and in Invercargill. Today it can only be harvested by the Rakiura Maori, who move onto the muttonbird islands for the annual catch. These hunts date back hundreds of years to when the ancient Maori harvested juvenile muttonbird from the islets near Stewart Island, dipping the birds in wax to ease feather removal before storing them in rubbery bull kelp. Adult muttonbirds would fly to Siberia for the summer, leaving their young behind in deep burrows. By day, Maori harvesters pushed sticks down these burrows and scooped the baby birds out. By night, they hunted with torchlights, capturing the babies as they emerged from the holes. Immediately killed by a bite to the back of the neck, the *titi* was either stored or grilled on the spot.

Although fish is readily available in Halfmoon Bay, getting someone to cook it for you is a bit more difficult. Bring your own food and plan on whipping up some self-made masterpieces. Brass plates adorn the walls of the comfortable **South Sea Hotel Restaurant and Pub** (tel. 219 1059), where locals mingle in the pub. Muttonbird meals run $12, and green-lipped mussels are $8. Get camping supplies (and expensive food) at **Ship to Shore** (tel. 219 1069), on Elgin Terr. (Open in summer M-F 8am-6:30pm, Sa-Su 10am-4pm; in winter M-F 8:30am-5:30pm, Sa-Su 10am-4pm.) Check with locals if you want to buy seafood.

OUTDOORS Renowned for its tracks, Stewart Island doesn't disappoint. The **Rakiura Track,** (see below) one of New Zealand's **Great Walks,** is a three-day trek over muddy, boardwalked paths through lush rimu and kamahi forests. The 10-12 day **North West Circuit** is for experienced trampers only. **Observation Rock** (15min. from town) is the place to see sunsets, while **Horseshoe Point** (4hr. from town) offers views over Halfmoon Bay. Take the opportunity to spot nocturnally foraging kiwis in their natural habitat with **Bravo Adventure Tours** (tel. 219 1144), the only tour with the right to run on conservation land ($55; book ahead; max. 15 people). Throngs of sonorous native birds flock to **Ulva Island** in summer; **Seaview Tours** (tel. 219 1014) and **Stewart Island Watertaxi** (tel. 219 1394) run tours ($20 round-trip, $16 with 2 or more; prior booking essential). Fishing trips, salmon farm tours, diving boats, and twilight cruises are also available; check with the travel center across from the DOC. **Oban Taxis and Tours** (tel./fax 219 1456) incorporates local history, short walks, and wildlife viewing in scenic bus tours ($15; 2 per day). **Sea kayak tours** are a great way to explore hidden inlets and wild corners.

THE RAKIURA TRACK The least crowded of New Zealand's Great Walks, the Rakiura Track is an extensively boardwalked moderate 36km walk. The trail plunges down steep slopes to abandoned beaches, passes through former Maori habitations, over a swing bridge, and up to a lookout tower on the second day. Almost entirely within the trees, it lacks the spectacular vistas of the other Great Walks. Don't expect to see a kiwi either, as the canines of Halfmoon Bay have decimated much of the population. As always, check in with the DOC; you must fill out an intentions form for all overnight hikes. A **Great Walks pass,** available only at the DOC in Halfmoon Bay or Invercargill, is necessary to access the track (huts $8; camping $6). Essential gear for the tramp includes boots, raingear, toilet paper, and a portable stove. It rains on 270 days of the year on Stewart Island; you will get wet. Due to the mud, footwear should reach at least to the ankle. The **general store** in Halfmoon Bay has plenty of tramping food at inflated prices; try stores in Ivercargill instead.

The two ends of the track are at **Lee Bay,** 5km north of town, and at **Kaipipi Road,** about 1km west of town. It is an easy walk to both ends, or get the **Oban Tours** (tel. 219 1456) shuttle (on demand only; $14, min. 6 people). Another option is an on-demand **water taxi** (tel. 219 1078; $30, min. 2, max. 6).

The track can be done year-round, though the island's southern location means limited daylight hours during the winter. Walking four hours a day, the track can be completed in a leisurely three days. If it's a nice day, begin counter-clockwise to hit the northern shore beaches in good weather; otherwise, start the opposite way and hope the weather turns by the time you reach the beaches. The DOC estimated walking times tend to be overstated for those of average fitness. The following description is of the track running in the counter-clockwise direction.

As you face the harbor in Halfmoon Bay, the road to **Lee Bay** heads off to the left. Follow the signs to Horseshoe Bay; at the bay's northern end, the turn-off for Lee Bay is 1km along a gravel road. This is the official starting point of track. Skirting the coastline, the track reaches **Little River** after about 20 minutes; if it isn't high tide, cross the sandy estuary to connect with the trail, as the alternate high tide route is rather treacherous. **Maori Beach,** one of the sweet spots of the track, makes an excellent day trip. The campsite here has a few grassy spots, a basic shelter, water, and an outhouse. At its western end, a swingbridge crosses a wide tidal estuary before climbing steeply to the top of a ridge. Take the right fork or travel via **Magnetic Beach** to the basic **Port William Hut** (20 bunks). Spook legions of small flounder by wading in the water of the nearby beach. Five minutes before the hut along the track just prior to the wharf is the junction for the **North West Circuit.**

At the fork on the ridge, the main track heads left, ascends steeply, and after about three hours reaches the 300m **Lookout Tower,** the last panoramic viewpoint on the track. Forty-five minutes on, **North Arm Hut** has another 20 bunks, a communal area, and a deck for lounging; no camping is permitted. One hour farther is **Sawdust Bay;** though sheltered amid trees, it is quite muddy. The track skirts **Kaipipi Bay** before joining **Kaipipi Road** and continuing back to civilization.

Appendix

■ Holidays and Festivals

Cities and towns across New Zealand hold countless festivals and craft fairs throughout the year. Most take place from December to February; ask the local tourist office for information. If you're anywhere near a festival of whatever stripe, it pays to alter your plans to attend; most are ebullient explosions that draw Kiwis from the surrounding area. A few popular ones are listed below; for more, see p. 232 and p. 253.

1999 Date	Festival	Town
January-February	Summer City Festival	Wellington
February	Festival of Flowers	Christchurch
February 4-20	HERO Gay and Lesbian Festival	Auckland
May 1	Wearable Art Awards	Christchurch
June 16-19	National Fieldays	Hamilton/Cambridge
July	International Film Festival	Auckland
August	Winter Festival	Christchurch
October (third week)	Rhododendron Festival	Dunedin

Holidays can put a less pleasant crimp in your plans. During the days listed below, banks, restaurants, stores, and museums may all close, and public transportation may be considerably more difficult to use. During the summer holidays (roughly Christmas to Waitangi Day) finding a place to stay in the country's major vacation destinations can be harder than spotting a kiwi in the bush; book ahead whenever possible.

1999 Date	Holiday Name
January 1-2	New Year
February 6	Waitangi Day
April 2	Good Friday
April 4	Easter
April 25	Anzac Day
June 7	Queen's Birthday
October 25	Labour Day
December 25	Christmas
December 26	Boxing Day

■ Time Zones

New Zealand has one time zone, 12 hours ahead of Greenwich Mean Time (GMT). If the world ran only on standard time, New Zealand would be two hours ahead of **Sydney,** twelve hours ahead of **London,** seventeen hours ahead of **New York** and **Toronto,** and twenty hours ahead of **California** and **Vancouver.** But due to Daylight Savings Time, calculations can easily be confused. In New Zealand, Daylight Savings Time runs from the first Sunday in October, when the clocks are sprung ahead one hour, until the last Sunday in March.

■ Telephone Codes

Auckland	09	South Island	03
Bay of Plenty	07	Taranaki	06
Coromandel Peninsula	07	Taupo	07
Eastland & Hawke's Bay	06	Waikato	07
Northland	09	Wanganui	06
Palmerston North	06	Wellington	04

■ Glossary of Kiwi English

abseil: rappel

Aotearoa: "land of the long white cloud," the Maori name for New Zealand

Anzac: Australia New Zealand Army Corps (p. 57). Anzac Day is a national holiday (April 25th).

All Blacks: The national rugby team

Aussie ("Ozzies"): Australian

B&B: bed and breakfast

bach ("batch"): Small, often beachside holiday house; known as a "crib" on the South Island

backpackers: hostel

basin: bathroom sink; geological feature, a depression

bathroom: room with a bath; not necessarily a toilet

belt bag, bum bag: hip pack, fanny pack ("fanny," should not be used in New Zealand; it's a slang word referring to female genitalia)

bikkies: cookies, crackers

biscuit: cookie

bloke: man

bloody: all purpose curse

boot: trunk of a car

brasserie: trendy cafe

brekkie: breakfast

bugger all: very little

bum: one's rear-end; also arse

bush: forest; wilderness

BYO: bring-your-own wine (or more generally, bring your own anything)

camper: motorhome

capsicum: green peppers

caravan: trailer, mobile home

cashpoint: ATM, automated teller machine

chat up: to hit on (eg. "I'm going to chat up that girl")

cheeky: rude, impertinent

cheers: goodbye

chemist: drugstore, pharmacist

chillie bin: portable cooler

chips: french fries

chocka, chock-a-block: packed, crowded, very busy, full

choice: awesome, good, proper, sweet, fresh, live

coach: bus that travels for long distances; not a local bus

college: secondary school

crib: South Island version of "bach," beachside vacation home

crisps: potato chips

cuppa: cup of tea or coffee

dairy: convenience store

dear: expensive

Devonshire tea: afternoon tea and scones, often with whipped cream; p. 52

DOC ("dock"): Department of Conservation (see p. 34)

dodgy: sketchy, something's fishy

domain: public park

doughnut: cream- and jam-filled sweet dough roll (not an American-style doughnut)

duvet: comforter, inch-thick feather blanket

entree: appetizer

Enzed: New Zealand (from "NZ")

fair go: gave me an opportunity

filled roll: sub sandwich

filter coffee: filtered, drip coffee

flash: snazzy, upscale, smart, trendy, glam

flat: apartment

flat white: coffee: a long black with a dollop of milk

footie: soccer

footpath: sidewalk

for donkey's years: for a long time

fortnight: two weeks

get on the piss: get drunk

Godzone: New Zealand (from "God's own")

g'day: hello

good as gold: fine, sure, great

good on ya: good for you, good job

gridiron: American football

grotty, scungy: dirty, run-down

ground floor: an American first floor (and first floor is second floor, etc.)

gumboots: rubber boots

hard case: difficult to get to know

heaps: lots

hire: rent

hockey: field hockey

hoe: to eat quickly

holiday: vacation

hoover: to vaccuum, or eat quickly

hottie: hot water bottle

howzit: how's it going

ice block: popsicle, frozen liquid treat

jandals: sandals, flip-flops

jersey, jumper: sweater

judder bar: speed bump

keen, keen on: psyched, ready; to fancy or be interested in

Kiwi: New Zealander; of or relating to New Zealand

kiwi: small flightless bird; the national symbol (never short for kiwifruit)

kiwifruit: a furry greenish-brown fruit (formerly known as the Chinese gooseberry, *Actinidia chinensis*).

knickers: underwear

kumara: sweet potato, *Ipomoea batatas;* a Maori food staple

lemonade: lemon-flavored carbonated soft drink; e.g., Sprite, 7-Up

licensed: legally allowed to sell alcohol

lift: elevator

local rag: local newspaper

long black: espresso with hot water

long-distance call: toll call

long drop: outhouse

loo: toilet

main: the main course of a meal

mainland: South Island

Maori: the indigenous Polynesian peoples of New Zealand

Marmite: New Zealand yeast spread (see p. 249)

mate: friend, buddy, pal

metal road: gravel road

milk bar: convenience store

nappy: diaper

not a problem: you're welcome;

that's okay: don't worry about it

note: currency bill

no worries: sure, fine

Oz, "Ozzie": technically "Aussie"; Australia, Australian

packed: well fed, full

paddock: sheep pasture

Pakeha: person of European descent; foreigner

petrol: gas

paua: shellfish

pavlova: a creamy, fruity meringue dessert

pie: flaky pastry shell with a variety of fillings, usually with meat (mince)

pipi: clam-like shellfish

pissed: drunk

pissed off: angry

pissing down: raining hard

Pom: Englishman (sometimes derogatory)

to post: to mail

powerpoints: electrical hook-ups for tents or caravans

prawns: jumbo shrimp

+pudding: dessert

push bike: bicycle

queue: "Q"; a line (typically of people)

rag: local newspaper

rap-jumping: face-first abseiling down the side of a building

reckon: to think

return: round-trip

ring: call

rubbish: garbage, trash

sealed road: paved road

see ya: farewell

serviette: napkin

shagging: having sex

shares: shared rooms at an accommodation, smaller than "dorms"

short black: coffee, flat white without the milk; between an espresso and a long black

shout: to buy (eg. "I'll shout you a drink")

skivvies: turtle-neck sweater

skull: to swallow rapidly (usually beer); to chug

SkyTV: satellite television

snog: kiss or make out

strewth!: an exclamation; truly (from "God's truth")

stubby: small bottle of beer

sultanas: raisins

suss out: to figure out

swimming togs: swimming suit

ta: thanks

TAB: shop to place bets without actually going to the tracks

takeaway: food to go, or a place that offers such

tariff: price

that's all right, that's okay: you're welcome (said in response to "thank you")

tomato sauce: ketchup; sold in small packets at restaurants

torch: flashlight

toll call: long-distance telephone call

track pants, tracksuit: sweat pants, sweats

take the piss: to poke fun at someone

take the mickey out of: to ridicule

trainers: sneakers

tramp: hike

tyre: tire

uni: university

ute: pick-up truck ("utility vehicle")

varsity: university

Vegemite: Australian yeast spread (see Marmite)

wanker: jerk

wedges: large, thick slices of deep-fried potato; often served with sour cream

wellies: rubber boots

wicked:

woolies: winter clothes; long underwear

Xena: "Xena, Warrior Princess" a TV show filmed in Northland (see p. 52)

yonks: forever

zed: the letter "z"

ao: cloud

Aotearoa: land of the long white cloud

atua: gods or spirits

awa: river, valley

e noho ra: goodbye (said by the person leaving)

haere mai: welcome

haere ra: goodbye, farewell (said by the person staying)

haka: intensely fierce war dance

hangi: underground Maori oven

hau: wind

Hawaiki: mythical (?) ancient homeland of the Maori

hoa: friend

hongi: Maori welcome expressed by the touching together of noses once or twice (depending on the tribe); literally, the "sharing of breath"

hui: meeting

ika: fish

iti: small

iwi: tribe, people, nation

kai: food

kainga: village, town

ka pai: thank you, good, excellent

■ Maori-English Dictionary

For more background information and details on pronunciation, see Language, p. 41.

karakia: chants, prayer
kei te pehea koe/korua/ koutou: how are you? (one/two/three or more people)
kia ora: hello, health, luck
koe: you (singular)
koutou: you (plural)
kumara: sweet potato, Ipomoea batatas; a Maori food staple
mana: prestige, power
manga: river, stream
manuhiri: guest
Maoritanga: Maori culture
marae: a meeting place, sacred ground, often with a whare
maunga: mountain
mere: greenstone warclub
moana: sea, lake
moko: traditional Maori facial tattoo
motu: island
namu: sandfly
nui: big, large
ngai, ngati: prefix indicating tribe, people, or clan
ngaru: wave
o: of
ora: life, alive, healthy, safe
pa: fortified Maori village, often on a hilltop

Pakeha: person of European descent; foreigner
po: night
pohatu: stone, rock
poi: a dance involving twirling balls on the ends of strings
pounamu: greenstone
powhiri: formal welcome ceremony
puke: hill
puna: spring (water)
rangi: the sky, the heavens
roa: long
roto: lake
rua: two
takiwai: translucent greenstone
tane: man
tangata: humans, people
tangata whenua: local Maori people; "people of the land"
taniwha: water spirit, demon, monster
tapu: taboo, holy, sacrosanct
te: the
teka: peace offering
tenakoe/korua/koutou: hello (to one/two/three or more people)

tiki: small carved figurine of a human in wood, stone, or greenstone; when hung around the neck, a heitiki
tino rangatiratanga: sovereignty, self-determination
tohunga: priest or specially learned men
tomo: shaft
tukutuku: woven, decorated reed panels frequently found in marae
umu: underground oven
wahine: woman
wai: water
waiata: traditional song, often of mourning or unrequited love; see p. 47
waka: canoe
wai: water
wero: challenge
whanga: bay, body of water
whanau: family
whare: house
whenua: ground, land

Index

Researcher-Writers

Lily Childress   *Canterbury, Southern Lakes, Otago and Southland*
Intimidating us with research that was more exacting and accurate than we thought possible, Lily blazed through the South Island at an astonishing pace. Subsisting for days on bread and jam even as she embarked upon grueling multiple-hour runs through the misty mountains, Lily thrilled to the incredible scenery she passed through. Her no-nonsense approach to budget travel and her glowing descriptions of New Zealand's beauty reminded us that the best things in life (and traveling) can't be bought.

Nick Grossman   *Bay of Plenty, Eastland and Hawke's Bay,*
Taupo, Wellington, Coromandel
Nick G. hit the spot with cyber-copy that made us swoon like any love-lorn Kiwi waitress. Hobnobbing with Oscar-winners, NZ politicos, and rugby stars, Nick kept his eyes on the prize and proffered endless incisive commentary about the overarching issues of the summer. He flung himself fearlessly from flying planes (taking notes all the while), and also managed to amass a prize-worthy anthology of sheep jokes. We feared by the end of the summer he'd consummate his love of all things Kiwi, and trade in his U.S. citizenship for good.

Matt Heid   *East Cape, Great Walks, National Parks*
Braving battalions of bloodthirsty sandflies, slogging through pits of sucking mud, fearlessly crossing optimally bobbing wire bridges, and resolutely tramping through wind and drenching rain, our intrepid winter researcher gave us the skinny on all nine of New Zealand's Great Walks and assorted adventure centers. The chillest of the chill, Matt managed to catch some transcendent moments along the way as he transmogrified the book into a powerhouse guide to the outdoors.

Ron Rosenman   *Auckland, Northland, Waikato, Taranaki*
Researching the meaning of life along with the sunset side of the North Island, our electric R-W sent back copy that lifted us to a higher plane. Rhyme-master Ron got it on; armed with the power of electronica, he broke down cultural barriers on the dance floors of Auckland and beyond. Ron gathered a posse within days of arrival and enjoyed the company of farmer, backpacker, and complimentary automobile alike. Eliminating all atmosphere-deficient establishments, he brought the beat down under up above, and gave our guide a thorough upgrade.

Nick Weiss   *Christchurch, Westland, Marlborough and Nelson*
Cruising through the most remote parts of the South Island in various states of dress and mind, secret agent Chief Five-Star General Pimp Dog came through when we needed him the most. Entire cities and massive typographical errors fell quivering beneath his penetrating researcher gaze, and even the darkest, kebab-ridden corners of Christchurch were no match for his *chutzpah*. Infiltrating sketchy hostels and airlines alike, Nick came through his identity crises no sweat, because he knew we knew he was *the man*.

Acknowledgments

The R-Ws blew our minds with stories, words, and personalities second to none. Good thing it's hard to be jealous of people you like. The other people who made the job worth it were back in Cambridge—especially podmates Sonja, Kristin, Monica, and Heath. After all, you can't dance the Macarena alone. Allison was the best ME any bookteam could ask for, going above and beyond the call of duty as she guided us through our ignorance. Producers Dan, Maryanthe, and Heath were always a bridge over troubled waters. We remain awed by Luis and Monica's Herculean achievement.

Thanks to my family, especially my parents for putting up with their busy daughter (and sending me to NZ in the first place), my sister for her support and friendship, my newest brother for being so darn cool, and everyone else for enthusiasm and interest. To the Cabotians in my life: Susannah for advice, gossip, and tenant resistance; mechanic Jeff for 3am Oxford St. chats; John for distributing my card to the greater Grand Rapids area. And of course thanks to Ben—you'll always be the flaming chinchilla of *my* solar plexus. Only super cool people could have made the office tolerable for 18hr. stretches, especially Eli, my better half—I only wish I could have had all of you. To the pod (Biosphere III) we are eternally bound together by the bloodstains of countless plants. My erstwhile blockmate Alex brought both continuity and Celeste pizza-for-one. And to the artist formerly known as Prince for making it all happen.—**JLB**

First and foremost, thanks to my family, especially Mom, Dad, Mark, Beth, Susan, Bernard, and both pairs of grandparents, for never expecting me to be anything more than myself. Thanks to Jen, for working like it was your job, and playing like you were getting paid for it; Allison, whose incisive knowledge made it all possible and sense of humor made it all bearable. To T.J., for so avidly pursuing the good life, and Mateo, for selfless involvement in all those pieces of my existence, from the sublime to the mundane. Finally, to Gundersen, who was and is the ideal traveling companion—the finest thing a person can have on any journey. —**Eli**

Editor	Jennifer L. Burns
Associate Editor	Eli Ceryak
Managing Editor	Allison Arwady
Publishing Director	Caroline R. Sherman
Publishing Director	Anna C. Portnoy
Production Manager	Dan Visel
Associate Production Manager	Maryanthe Malliaris
Cartography Manager	Derek McKee
Design Manager	Bentsion Harder
Editorial Manager	M. Allison Arwady
Editorial Manager	Lisa M. Nosal
Financial Manager	Monica Eileen Eav
Personnel Manager	Nicolas R. Rapold
Publicity Manager	Alexander Z. Speier
New Media Manager	Måns O. Larsson
Map Editors	Matthew R. Daniels, Dan Luskin
Production Associate	Heath Ritchie
Office Coordinators	Tom Moore, Eliza Harrington, Jodie Kirschner
Director of Advertising Sales	Gene Plotkin
Associate Sales Executives	Colleen Gaard, Mateo Jaramillo, Alexandra Price
President	Catherine J. Turco
General Manager	Richard Olken
Assistant General Manager	Anne E. Chisholm

Thanks to Our Readers...

Mano Aaron, CA; Jean-Marc Abela, CAN; George Adams, NH; Bob & Susan Adams, GA; Deborah Adeyanju, NY; Rita Alexander, MI; Shani Amory-Claxton, NY; Kate Anderson, AUS; Lindsey Anderson, ENG; Viki Anderson, NY; Ray Andrews, JPN; Robin J. Andrus, NJ; L. Asurmendi, CA; Anthony Atkinson, ENG; Deborah Bacek, GA; Jeffrey Bagdade, MI; Mark Baker, UK; Mary Baker, TN; Jeff Barkoff, PA; Regina Barsanti, NY; Ethan Beeler, MA; Damao Bell, CA; Rya Ben-Shir, IL; Susan Bennerstrom, WA; Marla Benton, CAN; Matthew Berenson, OR; Walter Bergstrom, OR; Caryl Bird, ENG; Charlotte Blanc, NY; Jeremy Boley, EL SAL; Oliver Bradley, GER; A.Braurstein, CO; Philip R. Brazil, WA; Henrik Brockdorff, DMK; Tony Bronco, NJ; Eileen Brouillard, SC; Mary Brown, ENG; Tom Brown, CA; Elizabeth Buckius, CO; Sue Buckley, UK; Christine Burer, SWITZ; Norman Butler, MO; Brett Carroll, WA; Susan Caswell, ISR; Carlos Cersosimo, ITA; Barbara Crary Chase, WA; Stella Cherry Carbost, SCOT; Oi Ling Cheung, HK; Simon Chinn, ENG; Charles Cho, AUS; Carolyn R. Christie, AUS; Emma Church, ENG; Kelley Coblentz, IN; Cathy Cohan, PA; Phyllis Cole, TX; Karina Collins, SWITZ; Michael Cox, CA; Mike Craig, MD; Rene Crusto, LA; Claudine D'Anjou, CAN; Lizz Daniels, CAN; Simon Davies, SCOT; Samantha Davis, AUS; Leah Davis, TX; Stephanie Dickman, MN; Matthew Dittrich,GER; Tim Donovan, NH; Reed Drew, OR; Wendy Duncan, SCOT; Melissa Dunlap, VA; P.A. Emery, UK; GCL Emery, SAF; Louise Evans, AUS; Christine Farr, AUS; David Fattel, NJ; Vivian Feen, MD; David Ferraro, SPN; Sue Ferrick, CO; Philip Fielden, UK; Nancy Fintel, FL; Jody Finver, FL; D. Ross Fisher, CAN; Abigail Flack, IL; Elizabeth Foster, NY; Bonnie Fritz, CAN; J. Fuson, OR; Michael K. Gasuad, NV; Raad German, TX; Mark Gilbert, NY; Betsy Gilliland, CA; Ana Goshko, NY; Patrick Goyenneche, CAN; David Greene, NY; Jennifer Griffin, ENG; Janet & Jeremy Griffith, ENG; Nanci Guartofierro, NY; Denise Guillemette, MA; Ilona Haayer, HON; Joseph Habboushe, PA; John Haddon, CA; Ladislav Hanka, MI; Michael Hanke, CA; Avital Harari, TX; Channing Hardy, KY; Patrick Harris, CA; Denise Hasher, PA; Jackie Hattori, UK; Guthrie Hebenstreit, ROM; Therase Hill, AUS; Denise Hines, NJ; Cheryl Horne, ENG; Julie Howell, IL; Naomi Hsu, NJ; Mark Hudgkinson, ENG; Brenda Humphrey, NC; Kelly Hunt, NY; Daman Irby, AUT; Bill Irwin, NY; Andrea B. Jackson, PA; John Jacobsen, FL; Pat Johanson, MD; Russell Jones, FL; J. Jones, AUS; Sharon Jones, MI; Craig Jones, CA; Wayne Jones, ENG; Jamie Kagan, NJ; Mirko Kaiser, GER; Scott Kauffman, NY; John Keanie, NIRE; Barbara Keary, FL; Jamie Kehoe, AUS; Alistair Kernick, SAF; Daihi Kielle, SWITZ; John Knutsen, CA; Rebecca Koepke, NY; Jeannine Kolb, ME; Elze Kollen, NETH; Lorne Korman, CAN; Robin Kortright, CAN; Isel Krinsky, CAN; George Landers, ENG; Jodie Lanthois, AUS; Roger Latzgo, PA; A. Lavery, AZ; Joan Lea, ENG; Lorraine Lee, NY; Phoebe Leed, MA; Tammy Leeper, CA; Paul Lejeune, ENG; Yee-Leng Leong, CA; Sam Levene, CAN; Robin Levin, PA; Christianna Lewis, PA; Ernesto Licata, ITA; Wolfgang Lischtansky, AUT; Michelle Little, CAN; Dee Littrell, CA; Maria Lobosco, UK; Netii Ross, ITA; Didier Look, CAN; Alice Lorenzotti, MA; David Love, PA; Briege Mac Donagh, IRE; Brooke Madigan, NY; Helen Maltby, FL; Shyama Marchesi, ITA; Domenico Maria, ITA; Natasha Markovic, AUS; Edward Marshall, ECU; Rachel Marshall, TX; Kate Maynard, UK; Agnes McCann, IRE; Susan McGowan, NY; Brandi McGunigal, CAN; Neville McLean, NZ; Marty McLendon, MS; Matthew Melko, OH; Barry Mendelson, CA; Eric Middendorf, OH; Nancy Mike, AZ; Coren Milbury, NH; Margaret Mill, NY; David H. Miller, TX; Ralph Miller, NV; Susan Miller, CO; Larry Moeller, MI; Richard Moore, ENG; Anne & Andrea Mosher, MA; J. L. Mourne, TX; Athanassios Moustakas, GER; Laurel Naversen, ENG; Suzanne Neil, IA; Deborah Nickles, PA; Pieter & Agnes Noels, BEL; Werner Norr, GER; Ruth J. Nye, ENG; Heidi O'Brien, WA; Sherry O'Cain, SC; Aibhan O'Connor, IRE; Kevin O'Connor, CA; Margaret O'Rielly, IRE; Daniel O'Rourke, CA; Krissy Oechslin, OH; Johan Oelofse, SAF; Quinn Okamoto, CA; Juan Ramon Olaizola, SPN; Laura Onorato, NM; Bill Orkin, IL; K. Owusu-Agyenang, UK; Anne Paananen, SWD; Jenine Padget, AUS; Frank Pado, TX; G. Pajkich, Washington, DC; J. Parker, CA; Marian Parnat, AUS; Sandra Swift Parrino, NY; Iris Patten, NY; M. Pavini, CT; David Pawielski, MN; Jenny Pawson, ENG; Colin Peak, AUS; Marius Penderis, ENG; Jo-an Peters, AZ; Barbara Phillips, NY; Romain Picard, Washington, DC; Pati Pike, ENG; Mark Pollock, SWITZ; Minnie Adele Potter, FL; Martin Potter, ENG; Claudia Praetel, ENG; Bill Press, Washington, DC; David Prince, NC; Andrea Pronko, OH; C. Robert Pryor, OH; Phu Quy, VTNM; Adrian Rainbow, ENG; John Raven, AUS; Lynn Reddringer, VA; John Rennie, NZ; Ruth B.Robinson, FL; John & Adelaida Romagnoli, AZ; Eva Romano, FRA; Mark A. Roscoe, NETH; Yolanda & Jason Ross, CAN; Sharee Rowe, ENG; W. Suzanne Rowell, NY; Vic Roych, AZ; John Russell, ENG; Jennifer Ruth, OK; William Sabino, NJ; Hideki Saito, JPN; Frank Schaer, HUN; Jeff Schultz, WI; Floretta Seeland-Connally, IL; Colette Shoulders, FRA; Shireen Sills, ITA; Virginia Simon, AUS; Beth Simon, NY; Gary Simpson, AUS; Barbara & Allen Sisarsky, GA; Alon Siton, ISR; Kathy Skeie, CA; Robyn Skillecorn, AUS; Erik & Kathy Skon, MN; Stine Skorpen, NOR; Philip Smart, CAN; Colin Smit, ENG; Kenneth Smith, DE; Caleb Smith, TX; Geoffrey Smith, TX; John Snyder, NC; Kathrin Speidel, GER; Lani Steele, PHIL; Julie Stelbracht, PA; Margaret Stires, TN; Donald Stumpf, NY; Samuel Suffern, TN; Michael Swerdlow, ENG; Brian Talley, TX; Serene-Marie Terrell, NY; B. Larry Thilson, CAN; J. Pelham Thomas, NC; Wright Thompson, ITA; Christine Timm, NY; Melinda Tong, HK; M. Tritica, AUS; Melanie Tritz, CAN; Mark Trop, FL; Chris Troxel, AZ; Rozana Tsiknaki, GRC; Lois Turner, NZ; Nicole Virgil, IL; Blondie Vucich, CO; Wendy Wan, SAF; Carrie & Simon Wedgwood, ENG; Frederick Weibgen, NJ; Richard Weil, MN; Alan Weissberg, OH; Ryan Wells, OH; Jill Wester, GER; Clinton White, AL; Gael White, CAN; Melanie Whitfield, SCOT; Bryn Williams, CAN; Amanda Williams, CAN; Wendy Willis, CAN; Sasha Wilson, NY; Kendra Wilson, CA; Olivia Wiseman, ENG; Gerry Wood, ENG; Kelly Wooten, ENG; Robert Worsley, ENG; C.A.Wright, ENG; Caroline Wright, ENG; Mary H. Yuhasz, CO; Margaret Zimmerman, WA.

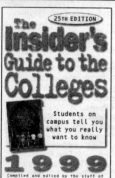

★Let's Go 1999 Reader Questionnaire★

Please fill this out and return it to **Let's Go, St. Martin's Press,** 175 Fifth Ave., New York, NY 10010-7848. All respondents will receive a free subscription to *The Yellowjacket,* the Let's Go Newsletter. You can find a more extensive version of this survey on the web at http://www.letsgo.com.

Name: _____

Address: _____

City: _____ **State:** _____ **Zip/Postal Code:** _____

Email: _____ **Which book(s) did you use?** _____

How old are you? under 19   19-24   25-34   35-44   45-54   55 or over

Are you (circle one)   in high school   in college   in graduate school
employed   retired   between jobs

Have you used Let's Go before? yes no   **Would you use it again?** yes no

How did you first hear about Let's Go? friend   store clerk   television
bookstore display   advertisement/promotion   review   other

Why did you choose Let's Go (circle up to two)? reputation budget focus
price   writing style   annual updating   other: _____

Which other guides have you used, if any? Fodor's   Footprint Handbooks
Frommer's $-a-day   Lonely Planet   Moon Guides   Rick Steve's
Rough Guides   UpClose   other: _____

Which guide do you prefer? _____

**Please rank each of the following parts of Let's Go 1 to 5 (1=needs
improvement, 5=perfect).** packaging/cover   practical information
accommodations   food   cultural introduction   sights
practical introduction ("Essentials")   directions   entertainment
gay/lesbian information   maps   other: _____

**How would you like to see the books improved? (continue on separate page,
if necessary)** _____

_____

How long was your trip?   one week   two weeks   three weeks
one month   two months or more

Which countries did you visit? _____

What was your average daily budget, not including flights? _____

Have you traveled extensively before? yes no

Do you buy a separate map when you visit a foreign city? yes   no

Have you used a Let's Go Map Guide? yes no

If you have, would you recommend them to others? yes   no

Have you visited Let's Go's website? yes no

What would you like to see included on Let's Go's website? _____

_____

What percentage of your trip planning did you do on the Web? _____

Would you use a Let's Go: recreational (e.g. skiing) guide gay/lesbian guide
adventure/trekking guide   phrasebook   general travel information guide

**Which of the following destinations do you hope to visit in the next three to
five years (circle one)?** Canada Argentina Perú Kenya Middle East
Caribbean   Scandinavia   other: _____

Where did you buy your guidebook?   Internet   independent bookstore
chain bookstore   college bookstore   travel store   other: _____